On Writing Qualitative I

'Our lives teach us who we are.' I have learned the hard way that when you permit anyone else's description of reality to supplant your own — and such descriptions have been raining down on me, from security advisors, governments, journalists, Archbishops, friends, enemies, mullahs — then you might as well be dead. Obviously, a rigid, blinkered absolutist world view is the easiest to keep hold of, whereas the fluid, uncertain, metamorphic picture I've always carried about is rather more vulnerable. Yet I must cling with all my might to my own soul; must hold on to its mischievous, iconoclastic, out-of-step clown-instincts, no matter how great the storm. And if that plunges me into contradiction and paradox, so be it; I've lived in that messy ocean all my life. I've fished in it for my art . . . It is the sea by which I was born, and which I carry within me wherever I go.

(Salman Rushdie, 1991)

On Writing Qualitative Research:
Living by Words

MARGOT ELY

RUTH VINZ

MARGARET ANZUL

MARYANN DOWNING

RoutledgeFalmer
Taylor & Francis Group
LONDON AND NEW YORK

UK	The Falmer Press, 11 New Fetter Lane, London EC4P 4EE
USA	RoutledgeFalmer, Taylor & Francis Inc., 325 Chestnut Street, 8th Floor, Philadelphia, PA 19106

First published in 1997 by Falmer Press
Reprinted 1999, 2004
Reprinted 2001 by RoutledgeFalmer

RoutledgeFalmer is an imprint of the Taylor & Francis Group

© M. Ely, R. Vinz, M. Anzul and M. Downing, 1997

A catalogue record for this book is available from the British Library

Library of Congress Cataloging-in-Publication Data are available on request

ISBN 0 7507 0602 3 cased
ISBN 0 7507 0603 1 paper

Jacket design by Caroline Archer

Typeset in 10/12pt Times by
Graphicraft Typesetters Ltd., Hong Kong

Printed in Great Britain by Biddles Ltd, King's Lynn, Norfolk, on paper which has a specified pH value on final paper manufacture of not less than 7.5 and is therefore 'acid free'.

Contents

Table of Contents — Version Two

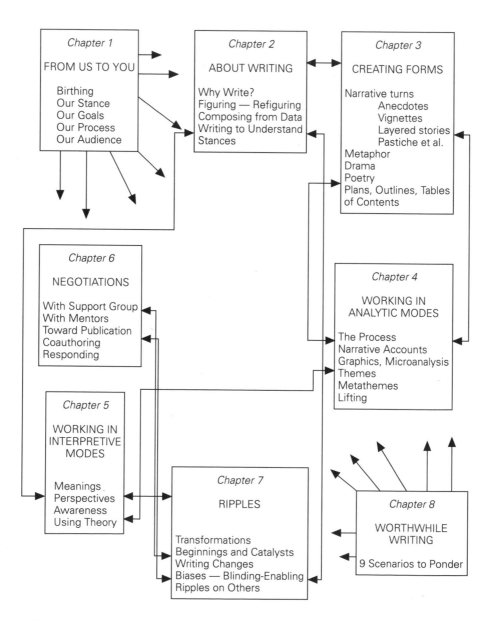

Acknowledgments

Acknowledgment is made for permission to quote from the following works:

'Rashomon' drawing by R. Chast; © 1993 by The New Yorker Magazine, Inc.

'Ficpro' drawing by R. Chast; © 1996 by The New Yorker Magazine, Inc.

Kevin Dwyer, *Moroccan Dialogues'* copyright © 1982, The Johns Hopkins University Press.

Ana Castillo, *So Far From God*, copyright © 1993, Penguin USA.

Wallace Stevens, 'The Man with the Blue Guitar,' from Collected Poems by Wallace Stevens. Copyright © 1936 by Wallace Stevens and renewed 1964 by Holly Stevens. Alfred A. Knopf Publisher.

Annie Dillard, *The Writing Life*, copyright © 1989, HarperCollins Publishers, Inc (U.S.), and Blanche C. Gregory, 2 Tudor Place, NY, NY 10027 (U.K. and British Commonwealth).

Peter Warshaw, 'Anaximenes,' copyright © 1996 by Commonweal.

Stephen Sondheim, 'Sunday' and 'Finishing the Hat', copyright 1984, 1987 by Rilting Music Inc. All rights administered by W. B. Music Corp. All rights reserved. Used by permission.

Chapter 1

To You From Us

This was not going to be our next book. Definitely. But then, we didn't know we were pregnant already.

Perhaps we should have had an inkling of what was in store when we received Dan Rose's reply to our bid to enlist him on our team in what we felt was a splendid concept for an ensuing writing project about qualitative researchers who were studying themselves. We were rather puzzled that Dan's long and detailed response scarcely mentioned our grand vision. He talked instead of the need for a book about and to people who write research — a book similar in spirit and tone and presentation to the one that two of us had just completed. So, we took Dan's response to be his more pressing musings as a researcher and teacher rather than as a direct message to us and called him to discuss our original idea. After all, there are so many books — interesting, useful books — about writing. Do we need another one? From this vantage point, we can now see how events already afoot and those soon to come would convince us unfalteringly that the book you are holding is the only one we cared to write. Our project with Dan will have to wait.

We write as a team and often think as a team. Nevertheless, each of us has a different life story and different professional concerns. As we each thought through the implications of this project, our starting stances emerged:

> The key for qualitative research writers is to breathe into our words the life we have experienced. How to communicate this fires my imagination and resolve. I want to help to produce a text about process, strategies and feelings that places writing in a broad humanistic context. (Margot)

> I have a growing appreciation that qualitative reports are inevitably ways of telling stories, and that the wealth of literature in narrative theory has much to say to writers of qualitative research. (Margaret)

> I have continuing professional concerns for the barriers and stumbling blocks we place in our own ways as writers, and a conviction that examining these might help us remove them from our own paths and the paths of others. (Maryann)

> We have something to say that will contribute to the growing literature on writing research, and this contribution derives largely from the impetus of our own need as writers to find ways to evoke the stories of others and to tell the stories of ourselves as researchers. (Ruth)

Margot and Margaret were two of five people who wrote *Doing Qualitative Research: Circles within Circles*, published by Falmer Press in 1991. In that book about the qualitative research process as a whole, the authors examine processes of 'research' not only through their eyes but also through the eyes of other researchers, both less and more experienced. Even as they were finishing that project, however, they were aware that there was much more to say about the writing and presentation of research narratives. Realizing the complexities of the process, Margot has expanded a Qualitative Research Methods course to two semesters to allow sufficient time for doctoral researchers to work through some of the issues surrounding writing during and toward the final phases of field study. Margaret has for some years been working as a research consultant, primarily with doctoral students who need specific help when writing their dissertations. Maryann has also been involved with this work as well as with the development of process writing curricula in classrooms. Ruth has been a researcher, a teacher, and a prolific author with a particular interest in writing. All four of us have our own writing and research agendas. Thus, our interest in the writing of research is powered by both theoretical and intensely practical considerations.

Our concern with writing parallels a surge of interest in writing seen throughout the entire qualitative community. Within the past few years, as we have been considering writing more deeply among ourselves and with our students, our own thinking has been extended and challenged by such works as Wolcott's *Writing Up Qualitative Research* (1990), Clifford and Marcus' *Writing Culture* (1986), and Atkinson's *The Ethnographic Imagination* (1990). Moreover, in our teaching and consulting we have found ourselves synthesizing and adapting insights from this rapidly growing body of literature. In this book we have, in short, followed a similar process to that used when writing *Doing Qualitative Research: Circles Within Circles* (Ely, Anzul, Friedman, Garner and Steinmetz, 1991). We want to challenge, model, question, illustrate and examine the processes as well as the rhetorical devices and other tools for writing qualitative research.

Our goals are very specific. This book is powered by the writing and reflections-on-writing of students of qualitative research as they emerge as researchers in the process. This is quite intentional. Perhaps because these people are new to this area we find their insights particularly vibrant and on-target. For those of us who may by now take much for granted about research writing, they allow us to see the essentials once again. Their writings provide a database which we have, in turn, presented in this book. To that base we have amalgamated accounts of our own experiences, those of our colleagues, and other published authors. All of these are woven into a framework that illuminates for us, and that we hope will illuminate for you, some of the ways in which writers work to evoke the complexity of the experiences within their studies.

Our intention is to write a book for qualitative researchers, at all stages of experience and sophistication, and for teachers of research methods, a text that encourages its readers to study, explore, create, and take some leaps of faith, all in the service of writing worthwhile research. We are writing to people who see themselves as ongoing learners of qualitative research, open to reviewing what they believe they know; to those who may just be starting to learn about qualitative research writing; and to those who have completed research pieces but who are still eager to continue questioning, honing skills, and deepening their grasp. We talk in this book about primary and natural human activities — thinking, analyzing, storying, lifting, interpreting — activities we often take for granted. What may be our particular twist is that on these pages we attempt to cast these human activities into sharp relief as we consider the whole business of research writing.

Our plan at the beginning was that each of the four of us would speak primarily in first person as we crafted what we then thought would be our individual chapters. However, as we met in our writing group in order to respond, discuss and produce ongoing text, our first drafts went through a metamorphosis of cohesion. We wrote to each other's work, added pieces or larger sections to all chapters, increasingly claimed an overarching stake in the entire presentation, committed to far greater revising than we had envisioned. In essence, our writing process was surfacing our stances about authorial ownership and responsibility as well as the sticky conundrum of how best to move toward an equitable sharing of power. Our writing was demanding more we-ness and less I-ness and we followed where we had led ourselves. Other research writers have also grappled with these issues:

> In collaborating on writing this book we searched for a single voice — a way of submerging our individual perspectives for the sake of a collective 'we.' Not that we denied our individual convictions or squelched our objections to one another's points of view — we argued, tried to persuade, even cried at times when we reached an impasse of understanding — but we learned to listen to each other, to build on each other's insights, and eventually to arrive at a way of communicating as a collective what we believe. (Belenky, Clinchy, Goldberger and Tarule, 1986, p. ix)

Throughout this book, then, there is a communal base. Our four voices do enter separately as we share individual accounts to highlight facets of each chapter, but overall this book comes to 'you' from 'us.'

In this book the quotations that we have blended in are essential to what we intend to communicate. Far from being embellishments, these quotations often carry primary meaning. To miss them would be to miss the heart of the matter. They should be read with that in mind. Our publisher has supported our vision by printing quotations so that they are clearly important and readable. Most of the quotations appear one time only. Some very few are repeated in different sections of the book. This is a conscious strategy. The same statement may and does take on different shades of meaning when it appears in different contexts. A quote may support or illuminate more than one idea. Then again, a statement may be so powerful, in our opinion, so essential, that its very repetition signals the reader to attend both to its message and ours.

In addition to repeating a small number of quotations for specific reasons, we also tackle a small number of topics in more than one chapter so as to view each from different angles. This happens, for example, when we discuss personal stance and writing community. Based on our attempts to interweave in these ways, you might now understand why we have a second Table of Contents, a Version Two.

We have asked those qualitative researchers who provide many of their writing pieces to mask identifiers in the material such as names, titles, places. This is to protect, as far as possible, the privacy of their participants. Our work presents you with examples and quotations from a great variety of fields since this book speaks to interdisciplinary interests and endeavors. In the long run, however, while this may add color and seasonings, it is not as important as our primary messages about research writing. These, we feel, pertain to all fields. In one sense, then, you can consider the examples and quotations as modules that you can slide out and replace with your own or others. Working in another way, you might track the stories of individual researchers that run through several chapters by using the name index. Actually, if you did enter into the conversation this way, we'd judge our book a success.

We would like to share with you some of the assumptions that undergird our work. The qualitative fold embraces such a range of philosophies, intellectual traditions, and points of view that it seems only fair to our readers that we try to explain where along that range we place ourselves. There have been many attempts to trace the development of various qualitative traditions — in anthropology, in sociology, in psychology, in the professions. We will look at some of the historical movements and theoretical perspectives in Chapter 5. All of them, however, represent steps away from the positivist position traditionally espoused by researchers who work within the quantitative paradigm. At the heart of the differences between the quantitative and qualitative paradigms are assumptions about how humans know, about what can be known, about what are suitable approaches to inquiry.

This writing team and most of our readers (we suppose) were educated within the positivist tradition so we grew up believing that knowledge was fixed and objective and that good students were expected to absorb it passively. Even when we read literature we knew that there was one 'right' interpretation and that our task was to 'learn' it. There was for each of us a point at which we stepped away from that position and moved toward an appreciation of knowing as an active process, with the knower at the heart of the construction of her or his knowledge. We recognize that our individual positions now fall along a continuum of qualitative theoretical constructs. These range somewhere between the 'posts' — postpositivist, constructivist, interpretive, critical, feminist, to poststructural. We all accept enough of these perspectives to work well together and at the same time we recognize that our differences at times vary as relativists, feminists, or postmodernists. We would like you, the reader, to know that we are no more interested in prescribing within these pages adherence to one or another of the possible qualitative positions for you than we are for one another.

Increasingly we found references in the literature to the eclectic nature of the qualitative enterprise. Further, each researcher is seen as structuring the research project by using to a large extent whatever is called for during the emergent processes of data collection, data analysis, and the construction of the final document. We are intrigued with the use of the term *'researcher-as-bricoleur'* when qualitative work is characterized (see for example, Denzin and Lincoln 1994, pp. 2–3). Each of us is highly aware of herself as the carpenter of her own personal, continually evolving theoretical constructs. Like the process of *bricoleurs*, our qualitative works, as well as our lives, are products that we ourselves build from materials that we find most appropriate to what we believe.

We are struck, in addition, by what we see as great chunks of overlap in many qualitative research positions that are posited to be distinct and unique. In our experience it is an unending task — an often maddening one — to tease out where the similarities and differences lie. When we set about constructing the theoretical or methodological framework for a study, or when we consider what our personal theoretical frames of reference are for our scholarly work as a whole, we tend to blend compatible positions, looking out all the while for consistency. This job is anything but haphazard or specious.

A perspective we've found useful, and probably ingrained as a result of our experience, is that of transaction as posited by John Dewey and Arthur F. Bentley (1949). In the light of transactional theory, all knowing is viewed as taking place in transaction between what's 'out there' and the 'self.' When Louise Rosenblatt (1978) delineated her transactional theory of the literary work, she argued that the transaction between reader and text produces the 'poem-as-event' (p. 17). Each of us must recognize that whatever any thing-in-itself may be 'out there,' it exists only as we know it. As will be seen in the pages that follow, this has implications for us as researcher/writers. We transact as observers, as writers, and as readers of our own logs; we transact again as we shape the findings in our logs into a more finished product, we transact as we write and our readers transact with what we have written. We hope.

Not that all four of us subscribe with equal enthusiasm to the entirety of transactional theory of literature or to its terminology. We do, however, as you will see in the chapters that follow, subscribe to the importance of the transactive, emotional, experiential, aesthetic aspects of writing. A theme that runs through each of the chapters of this book is that all of the powers of the mind are at work and play in every aspect of writing qualitative research. The living stuff of our research and our writing on it are presented mainly in a linear fashion in a book, however, and when we want to consider any one aspect of it in detail we must lift a thread out of the mesh of life and distort it somewhat by looking at it in isolation.

The universe of qualitative research and its writing is a rapidly expanding one. We have our own Big Bang! This makes it difficult, perhaps impossible, for mere mortals to keep up. We suppose, however, that the effort counts for something. Keeping that in mind, and remembering that some key characteristics of qualitative researchers reside in their flexibility and openness to well-reasoned change, we will at times share with you some changes in our own positions, our own points of view over the last ten years or so. Some of these changes, often so subtle that they are seen only in a shift of emphasis, center around our convictions about the substance and presentation of qualitative research writing, the sharing of self, the representation of others in our writing, what counts as credibility-acceptability, issues about our responsibility to and with participants, and to action in broader society.

Lest we leave you with the idea that we believe change is the only useful process to reach for, we add hastily that, to us, the steady enduring commitments, processes and insights are crucial — those that we test and affirm over time and experience. They demand attention and documentation. In essence, one way to conceptualize this book is to see it as a product of where we are at this moment.

This book asks much of you, our reader. To get full value, as they say, this is not an easy read to slide through in an hour on the beach. This book requests that you join into our thinking, consider a variety of lenses on research writing, ponder about where and how you stand, allow your emotions/mind full sway as you enter into the sometimes heart wrenching, sometimes humorous, and we hope always pertinent bits about other people's research, try some writing experiences, mesh a flow of ideas within and across the chapters, assess your place in qualitative research writing endeavors, create your own plans and solutions as you see fit, and take some chances.

It was our conscious intent in writing this book to reach out to you in this manner. Not as an exercise but because all of our experiences tell us that this is the only way to go. In a sense we four are talking to ourselves. We talk to those things we have learned over the years, to those things that devil us, puzzle us still, to those unfinished raw issues that get clearer as we write. We invite you into our continuing conversation. We hope you enter the dance. We sincerely invite you to share your experiences and thoughts with us as you work to shape your materials. We need to be part of the widening circle — from 'you' to 'us.' It is no accident that we have subtitled our book Living by Words.

Margot Ely
Ruth Vinz
Maryann Downing
Margaret Anzul
March, 1997

Chapter 2

What Is There about Writing?

Consciousness, I suggest, is in part defined by the way it always reaches beyond itself. (Maxine Greene, *Releasing the Imagination*)

This book is about creating research writing that is useful, believable, and interesting. Toward that end, we connect what we've learned through our own writing of research with the strivings of others, both experienced and novice, who are trying to understand how writing helps us compose and represent meaning from data. However, this book is not a treatise on theories and strategies about writing in general. Many others have produced these, and we'd only create detours and possibly some ennui and irritation were we to go down that path. Our aim in this book, our contract with you, our readers, is to highlight those aspects of writing that help us compose meaning from our research data and present it in meaningful ways for others.

We've had a very hard time coming to grips with what to exclude. We are, after all, academics! What to include? What to winnow? Here we attend to a very select number of issues about writing research and foreshadow some others to be developed later on. We focus on these issues precisely because we believe that they constitute the heart of the considerations that must be faced and internalized by writers of qualitative research. We discuss how the act of writing itself involves us in a quest. Writing helps us attend to the odd intersections or unexpected corridors of meaning and to the unexamined echoes and resonances that lead to sense-making as we write our way through various versions of understandings. Aware, then, of the importance of writing in composing and articulating meaning, we suggest ways in which the writing leads toward intensified discovery and representation.

Why Write?

While one premise of this book is that there are some ways and means that make writing more do-able and worthwhile, we cannot — we do not wish to — escape saying that writing demands commitment, serious intent, and hard work. It seems almost embarrassing to put these words on paper. However, we feel that in a society much given to offering painless ways to do hard things — lose 20 pounds in three weeks, do five minutes of these daily exercises for a wonderful body, use this cream and shed your wrinkles, read this book and rejuvenate your marriage — it is worth emphasizing that writing takes great dedication and effort. Out of the writing itself may come understandings that enhance our lives, insights that stun and energize, products that touch us and others deeply, and pleasure in the writing that is narcotic in its call to stay at it — but not without effort.

In our work with other qualitative researchers we've found this committed spirit present more often than not. Many of us burn to tell well-crafted stories, and we're aware of the price — perhaps more as we go along than at the beginning. This makes perfect sense. One novice researcher, Sally Smith, explained that through continuous writing she came to understand her data differently:

> Meta-thoughts about writing rarely occurred to me at first: Writing was transcribing. Looking more closely at the field logs, I began to pull out themes to analyze, to look at my own stance toward this new experience. At the end of this phase, I wrote an article — which required me to step back from the field — in it I explored an important metaphor — messiness, the often awkward, confusing untidiness of making one's way in qualitative research, the messy quality of knowledge/learning in general.
>
> After a time, I 'lifted' a little more, and composed poems, playlets, layered stories. I pushed and prodded to think about the various ways the writing could represent and reveal meanings.

Gayle Newshan, who was also a newcomer to qualitative research, recognized that the writing was a way to keep her focused on the data:

> Qualitative research writing is a process, a becoming. There is a discipline required in the going back, thinking, writing, rewriting. Zen Buddhists call the undisciplined mind the 'monkey mind' — our thoughts constantly flit from one thing to another, rarely dwelling for more than a few moments on any one thing. There is something to be said for the qualitative research writing in that it requires an almost Zen-like concentration and thoughtfulness. To stay with the process, to stay IN the process is to become a qualitative researcher/writer.

Staying 'IN' process requires a vigilance of sorts, Gayle suggests, an awareness that writing will help move understanding forward.

Michele Bellavita, a psychotherapist who was stepping into the unfamiliar terrain of writing up what she was learning from the field, found that with the guidance of her reading she could find ways to move her writing forward:

> Here come Lincoln and Guba again! Or was it Guba and Lincoln last time? After all the articles they've written I feel like they are my qualitative mother and father or my qualitative superego ... Dear Yvonna and Egon. I was moved by their discussion of Zeller's ideas about craftsmanship. What moved me was the desire to write the way they describe; to do justice to my participants with writing that is powerful, as elegant as I can be, creative, courageous, and egalitarian. Courage is, I believe, an important factor. I cannot be powerful and creative if I am not courageous in expressing my vision and able to take risks that allow my constructions and analyses to go beyond the safe and fairly obvious.

These researchers express what we've learned as a central tenet: trust the process of discovery. Tony Messina expressed the feeling this way:

I heard things I never heard before. I saw things I never saw before. I told stories I never told before. I saw meaning in mere movement. After stripping away the years of displeasing experiences with writing, I have finally found my voice.

Tony, Michele, and Gayle realized that the writing helped them to develop their ideas and to structure these as each draft involved them in circles of understanding that continually changed and shaped as the writing progressed.

As we face that blank paper or screen, most of us wrestle with moments of silence and with our inabilities to find the words powerful or honest enough to describe what we've seen, heard, or felt. Fear often overtakes us, carrying us down that path of insecurity where we question whether or not we really have the insight, knowledge, or skill to write up what we are beginning to understand. Getting through those moments isn't always easy as Iris Goldberg, another first-time researcher, confirms in the following reflection. To get beyond the preface of silence through the act of writing is an ongoing struggle:

Reflections of the Inner Struggle to Write

The End_____The Beginning

I'm sitting at the computer, waiting. The preface to my writing is silence. But the silence is usually brief. I listen. I tune in. I listen. I begin to hear my inner voice, my writer's voice. Through the silence, I call up thoughts and feelings. My writer's voice puts them into words. I listen inside and it sounds like me. Only I really know this voice as it sounds at this minute. The words are like a string wound round into a circle, like a familiar melody humming behind my breath inside my head. There is no beginning or ending — or only in the sense that the voice starts at a point when I call it up and stops when I am finished.
    I listen to it in its circle form. Then I pick a place in the circle
      and I begin
      to write . . .

We find it helpful to remind ourselves, before we become too confused, beleaguered, or weepy about writing and writing more, what Flannery O'Connor (1985) learned about the process of writing: 'I have to write to discover what I am doing. I don't know as well what I think until I see what I say; then I have to say it over again' (p. ix). Flannery O'Connor trusted that writing would lead her to the ideas that often lurk below the surface of conscious thought, and she understood that to 'say it over again' is essential to the quest for understanding. We take heart in her reflections. We believe that people like Flannery are 'practiced writers.' That doesn't mean they know more; it means they have practiced more and trust the process. It does give us the faith to just get on with the writing. Iris Goldberg likened the writing experience not only to circles of understanding but also to cooking. She reminds us of the importance of digging deep, feeling the work shaping, nearly tasting and smelling what we are creating:

I'm reminded of cooking lessons with my mother. Too young to reach the counter, I stood on a chair next to her, waiting for her to pass on the secret formula for all the great aromas and flavors that passed through her kitchen. 'You don't learn how to cook with recipes,' she said. 'Put your hands in it. Taste it. Feel it. Then you'll know it.'

Some fortunate people would no more consider the question 'why write?' than 'why breathe?' To them, the practice of writing is so integral to their process of making meaning, the uses for writing so essential, the art of writing so pleasurable that the question would not occur to them. For many of us, probably the great majority, the question 'why write?' needs to be tackled periodically, usually in the form of a reminder that what is already accepted, what we assumed to be finished thinking, is open yet to further clarification and exploration. We have come to recognize that we question most, no, let's be honest, we scream most about the need to write yet more and once again when we are over-committed, over-tired, filled to the ears with observation or interview data, or discouraged by what we see as the failure of the writing to convey the message that seems beyond our grasp in words. Actually this failure of words often results from our muddy thinking. When we reshape meaning through the writing, it helps us to clarify our understanding. Often but not always. For many of us, trying to answer the question 'why write' means reflecting on why we sometimes consider writing as onerous, boring, and someone else's talent.

Perhaps some of the hesitancy, maybe hatred, for writing has roots in our past experiences. Most of us can remember from our earliest schooling that the purpose of writing was to record in some succinct and correct way what we knew about a topic, or probably more to the point, what others thought they knew about it. And so, many of us transfer these feelings and beliefs from school to our attitudes and ways of writing up to this day. What many of us learned about writing can be likened to catching some kind of long-lasting disease, highly resistant to modern medication and easily triggered by the slightest reminder. This means that many of us aren't practiced at using writing to *learn* what we know rather than to *state* what we know. As Vivian Gussin Paley (1992) remarks, 'The natural connections between storytelling and learning are often obscured in school.' This same concern is voiced by many qualitative researchers.

Michele Bellavita tells about an experience when she was a student in an 8th grade literature class, an experience that shaped some of her beliefs about writing. She recalls earlier times when she was an avid writer:

> I was told that writing fanciful fiction stories, as I still loved to do at the time — unbelievable as this might sound — would get me nowhere, that only writing nonfiction reports would help me function in college. And in poetry I was taught to chop poems into little bits and look for the symbolic meaning of every discrete part, thereby destroying any possible beauty of the rhythm and any sensuous pleasure in the almost tactile feel of the sound of the words; and, of course, destroying any meaningful sense of what it was about.

Michele's story is not uncommon. Autobiography and fiction writing have an uneasy relationship with school writing. Michele also notes that analysis was the typical way of responding to literature which seems too often the message many of us may have taken away from our own school histories. In many ways Michele's early encounters with writing frame the way she approaches research. The mere fact that she recognizes these influences may help her get beyond them.

When Laurie Dieffenbach was a beginning qualitative researcher, she looked back and nicely summed up the old requirements of form and style:

> Most of us 'learned to write' in an academic setting, but there were only certain acceptable forms that one's writing could take in that setting . . . The only 'official' writing done during my school years was usually of the dead and lifeless variety . . . I think many of the qualitative researchers in our support group were frightened at first because they had become so used to the 'academic' style of writing . . . the cramped, uncomfortable style that was usually expected.

The lifeless, the cramped, the uncomfortable style of which Laurie speaks will produce research reports that exhibit the same qualities unless all of us can go beyond the boundaries of what we were taught and what we have experienced. The members of this team still fight that demon as we write, as we decide whether our reports are 'worthy' of the academic community, as we struggle with *how* to write differently from the forms and styles we learned through the lessons of school. We keep searching for and creating forms that will more richly depict the meanings that we are making from the data, and we'll share what we've learned about some ways of creating these throughout the book.

We think the writing can be alive. That's exactly what draws us to a book, isn't it? On vacation, and, yes, sometimes during the work year, Margot buries herself in mysteries and novels to the point that she hardly comes up for air. She says she can't leave the life she is living with, in, and through that book, and woe be to the intruder! This also happens when we read some non-fiction and particular qualitative research writing. We could liken this avid reading to our own writing as well. When we are as crazy about and as eager to stay with our own writing as we are to continue reading a good book, we know that we are on to something good. Actually, the deep conviction that good writing comes to life is what powered the writing of this work. Otherwise we might just as well have produced a lengthy bibliography. Many people are repelled by writing that dispenses with or makes short shrift of curiosity and messiness. In this book we're talking about writing that rebels against and distrusts easy conclusions and academic knowledge. We're thinking about writing that deliberately hums with reflections, that is crafted, not to harness, but to liberate discovery and learning. This is easier said than accomplished however.

Most of us haven't learned to be tolerant of the messy and chaotic work associated with generating and forming ideas into some coherent presentation. Somehow we were led to believe that writing was the fully formed presentation of knowledge. Jill Schehr, school psychologist, recalled having these fears in the late stages of drafting her report. After writing hundreds of pages of field logs, analytical memos, and reflective pieces, she still faced the demons of uncertainty and insecurity:

> Writing always seems 'so definitive' to me. This may be one reason why I've had such a difficult time writing up my experiences. However, in response to reading Wolcott (1990) and *Circles within Circles* (1991), I decided that perhaps I was

dawdling and creating excuses. I never do, after all, think I've gotten enough information about people ... life is so complex and reactions and feelings so diverse and fluid. I certainly did have some nascent understanding of the prison nursery community that I was part of, so why not begin to commit myself to paper? I forced myself to begin by giving myself permission this way: 'This is only an exercise. Write freely; this is just a rough draft.' In studying my prison nurseries, I observed, interviewed, analyzed, reflected ... and learned, only to find out what I didn't know. In similar ways, writing up this experience enabled me to further understand and question.

Some of us hesitate or get blocked because of our fear of failure. Valerie Martin, after writing piles of memos, making lists and charts, talking through the data with her support group, and presenting her work-in-progress at a national convention, froze when it was time to commit to writing what she believed would be the final draft. She suffered a not-so-unusual malady that afflicts writers when they come to the end of the process:

> Suddenly I felt like I didn't know anything. All my confidence withered. I became hyper-critical. For every sentence I wrote, I'd think of all the reasons someone would find fault with what I said. I felt that I was spreading myself across the pages and that with my words others could dissect me. After all, this was the time that the writing would be finalized and made public. I imagined someone pulling my dissertation from the library stacks. And, what if that someone found fault? I would be a failure.

Part of what Valerie discovered as she described her fears was the ever-present critic in herself. This seems common to many writers. Writers experience such moments of self-doubt, of feeling like an impostor, of knowing that the writing doesn't communicate the intricacy and complexity of the thoughts swirling through the mind that seem to turn lackluster when put as words on paper. It's easier to say 'Trust Yourself' than, in fact, to believe it.

In addition to, or perhaps along with uncertainty about writing, some of us get angry. This is an anger that sometimes creates a writing block. Sam Milburn directed his anger toward others:

> I've not had the help or support that I should in this writing. I don't get enough feedback. I get frustrated by that and can't write. The books on writing research don't help me with the problems that I'm facing. They are mostly off-the-target. I know I could do this if I had more help either in models of quality reporting or quality input from others.

Sometimes this anger at others gets downright personal. One of Margot's students — having a difficult time after it was suggested that she needed once again to edit and reshape pieces of her dissertation — stormed into the office yelling 'I HATE this! I HATE you! I HATE YOU!' At first Margot thought that the student, a close friend and colleague, did not mean it. But it did not take long for her to realize that, at this time, it was indeed true. That it was also temporary was a great relief in hindsight. Producing writing that is acceptable to ourselves and to others demands much rewriting. We anticipate it. We know it. Yet, there are times, such as the one described here, when one more rewrite seems just too much to bear.

Other people direct their felt anger toward themselves. Celia Thomas, who was close to finishing the last chapters of her study, found the writing was still difficult:

> It's like I've planted this seed and then I haven't watered it enough, or I haven't fertilized it, or I haven't moved it into a window that has the right combination of sun and shade. I 'haven't, haven't, haven't' constantly rings in my ears. It's like that with the writing. I get mad at myself for not spending every waking moment in front of the computer. I have these little punishments if I don't get a predetermined number of pages written in a day — I won't have a hot bath. I won't watch the news or read the newspaper. I won't take a walk.

Whether the anger is directed at others or at the self, we've found that it isn't productive when it shuts off thinking, feeling, creating. Period. Thank goodness most of us have our 'moments' and then go on to look deeper at what we are really saying, such as: 'I feel I'm not good enough.' 'I'm scared.' 'I'd rather be at the movies.' 'I'm tired.' 'I need help with this.' These insights usually help us to gird our loins once again and face the task with better spirits and better feelings about ourselves. Does that sound too treacly? Wait. There's even more. Often, getting on with the work provides an amazing lift in morale and energy. At other times, revising brings with it not only new ways of saying but also new discoveries or a renewed consciousness of possibilities. We've just experienced such feelings again while rewriting this very chapter for, well, maybe the twentieth time.

Of course we recognize that writing in itself is often wrenchingly difficult, lonely, and brutally upsetting. But it also holds the promise of a certain glory. It helps us to remind ourselves and others that even the most prolific and public writers struggle:

> Thus was born and baptized my first novel, *The House of Spirits*, and I was initiated into the ineradicable vice of telling stories. That book saved my life. Writing is a long process of introspection; it is a voyage towards the darkest caverns of consciousness, a long slow meditation. I write feeling my way into silence, and along the way discover particles of truth, small crystals that fit into the palm of one hand and justify my passage through the world. (Isabel Allende)

> I can't change the past, and I don't think I would. I don't expect to be understood. I like what I've written, the stories and the two novels. If I had to give up what I've written in order to be clear of this disease, I wouldn't do it. (Harold Brodkey, about two weeks before his death)

> I rewrite a great deal. The language is very important to me and it takes a long time to get the language right . . . Good work is always difficult. I try to create a place where the reader can walk around on a solid floor, where a reader can get the feeling that the writer has built a solid foundation . . . So your job as a writer is to do all that research to build a floor on which a reader can wander around, and then create an environment in which thinking and reaction and wonder and awe and speculation can take place. (Barry Lopez)

Well, it's definitely a journey, an odyssey. It's fun and it's edifying, and it's laboriously hard work and it's terrifying and it's very, very mysterious. The truth is, I don't know how to talk about writing . . . all I can think to say is that it's like a cross between flying to the moon and taking a shower in a motel. (Tom Robbins)

So all that I ask of my writing I ask of the rest of my life too. *Here, (I say) the words are too thin. I have heard this before, I say, and there is more to this than is being revealed.* And, so I mark out these old words and write again. I cross out all the words except those that affect me deeply, those for which I have some 'irrational' love. I keep those and build again. And again. All the while knowing that deeper meaning will rise to the surface like the form in a piece of stone, or the grain of a polished wood. If I keep working. (Susan Griffin, original emphasis)

On a good working day, working from nine o'clock in the morning to two or three in the afternoon, the most I can write is a short paragraph of four or five lines, which I usually tear up the next day. (Gabriel García Márquez)

There are three rules for writing the novel. Unfortunately no one knows what they are. (Somerset Maugham)

I still think, but because writing has become impossible for me the real activity of thought has in some way been repressed. (Sartre at 70 years old)

From the desk where I write today, I face a window three-quarter full of sky. At my left hand is a chip of copper ore that shows azurite. For no other reason than these, I see all at once that everything is possible. I have recovered my houses. Now I can bring back the rest, picnics and circuses, train rides and streamers, labels on trunks, and wreaths for the dead on front doors. I have everything I need. A square of sky, a piece of stone, a page, a pen, and memory raining down on me in sleeves. (Harriet Doerr)

We often marvel at how understanding is informed through writing. For us as researchers, writing is the mainstay of our research endeavors from the earliest halting scribbly steps before the field to the final draft for publication. We can't unbraid an exact process — there just isn't one process that works for everybody. Think of how monumental an effort writing is to some, and just how diligently and courageously they strive to write. But this makes the case for the importance of writing all the more clear.

We visualize Steven Hawkins with his mechanical contraptions which, while successful, must call on his tremendous will power and physical effort to coerce his thinking into writing. Or Christy Brown who valiantly broke through the walls of silence by teaching himself to write with his left foot. People who have suffered strokes use alphabet boards, typewriters, or computers, all to make communication possible. Famous or not, however prolific or productive, whatever their varying degrees of success, these people are making a vibrant statement about the importance of writing to extend meaning in our world — to communicate as fully and richly as possible. Perhaps the urge to communicate subsumes more than writing — the eye blink of a paralyzed person, the one word repeated over and over again by a child who has been labeled autistic, the simple gesture that signals peace —

but writing carries the complexity of each of these messages to fullness. While most of us will never struggle so completely as Hawkins, all of us have our struggles.

After all that has been said, we hope that you will clarify in your mind this question we posed: Why write? We, of course, have our answer: we write primarily because writing is at the heart of our endeavors to reflect, to be thoughtful, to tame and to shape the compost heap of data that is filled with disparate, confusing, and overwhelming raw impressions. Writing helps us to consider, reconsider, plan, replan, make order, check with ourselves and others, and to tell the story of the research in precisely the ways that we feel do justice to it. We hope and trust that you will make statements of your own in answer to 'Why Write?'

Writing the Field

The field:

'My field is physical therapy.'
'Nobody has studied the field I want to study.'
'I need to get a feel for the entire field before I narrow it down.'
'I am out in the field today.'
'I've changed my field.'
'I've left the field.'
'I'm not certain what to look for in the field.'
'I'm letting the field speak to me.'
> *The field: A specific area of academic study?*
> *The field: The site of one's study?*
> *The field: The human action and physical surroundings of the site for study?*

Field is indeed an ubiquitous term. And, it is used as if its meaning in qualitative research is straightforward and readily evident. Whatever meanings we attribute to 'field,' these will likely influence what we see and how we interpret in the place where research is conducted. As experienced researchers, Lincoln and Guba (1989) see the field of qualitative research as a muddy and swampy place, often obscure and always complex. However, soon-to-be-first-time researcher Sandra Nixon expected the field to be unproblematic and relatively straightforward:

> I expect to take a field log with me to the site of my study. I need to determine how to record everything I see and hear — maybe a dialectic journal with my impressions on the right side and literal translations on the left. Later I'll sift through everything and figure out how to categorize the findings and make sense of all I've observed.

Sorry. It doesn't work that way. Sandra discovered this at a later point. However, it may be precisely because of interpretations such as this or because the concept of the field has seemed straightforward in research literature that we need to consider it further.

Although 'the field' may be the locus of our research activities or it may be defined by the disciplines that undergird how, why, and where we study, there is more to it than that, and it can be rather slippery and complicated. This struggle to understand 'the field' is ongoing for the researcher. Barbara Ball, an art therapist, wrote:

> What was my purpose in this field? I would learn about methodology and about myself. But what about the FIELD? I had often and carefully thought about the purpose of my study in the therapeutic nursery. Before I got in I wasn't aware that I would be observing parent–child and teacher–child interactions. Now, these interests emerged 'surprisingly' out of the field.

In essence, 'the field' is always what each researcher understands it to be. The field is a series of internal constructs — perhaps shifting, extending, changing — but internal constructs nevertheless. 'So!' you might be saying, 'Am I being told that there is no such thing as the field I am studying? That the only reality is inside of me?' No. This is not what we mean. Knowing the field is always a transaction between what is out there, what is not out there, and the meaning we interpret from both.

What we are suggesting is that researchers have done themselves a disservice by overemphasizing the concept of field-as-external as opposed to the concept of field-as-internal. To us, this is a view that plays right into the either/or distinctions of an outside objective truth and an inner subjective truth. True, it may be far easier for some researchers to think of the field as essentially external. It may be less threatening to seek certainty outside of ourselves rather than to accept the sometimes awesome responsibility of trusting the subjective realities within. We have discovered through our own research that the transaction between what we're experiencing and how we feel about what we're experiencing deserves to be written about as part of our representation of the 'field.'

The inside/outside distinction just isn't that simple, and qualitative researchers must struggle to articulate this relationship for themselves over and over again. Iris Goldberg studied the culture of a ballet school. She created a metaphor of the mirror to illustrate how multiple reflections of truth may be captured in this complex environment:

> Here in this place of thought and feeling, I have faced the existential experience of a writer: standing outside of myself looking in — inside of myself, looking out. I look into the mirrors reflecting external realities and try to capture them in writing, only to see the reflection of my inner self set into the *real* scene, casting shadows of bias and memory. I write to merge these images into TRUTH. I turn to look into the mirror of my own writing — poetry, narrative, layered stories, playlets — ultimately seeing only the reflections of *my own truth* in multiple images.

What troubles us are too-easy answers to these representational dilemmas of objective/subjective or outside/inside. Representations of the field as orderly and coherent and possibly even 'hygienic,' couched in quasi-logical language, offer misleading versions of the ease with which the field can be defined, rendered, and known. Through the research experience itself and the attempts to write about what we have learned or are learning, we begin to understand the field as filled with complex and contradictory versions of meaning. And we are trusting this complexity as a resource to pose less monolithic views of a field. Every writer of research will struggle with this differently, but struggle we must. Michele Bellavita articulated the tensions of representation that resonate through the entire field:

> The search for meaning has always been one of the preoccupations of my life. For me, meaning has always implied a sense of wholeness. The whole may be, and usually is, made up of interconnected parts; but the whole is always greater than the sum of its parts. And meaning, for me, cannot be separated from context. Chopping reality — anyone's reality — into little bits and pieces does damage to meaning.

In this quote Michele sees her search for meaning as an intense, organic process, analytical to be sure, but always grounded in what she considers the 'whole' context. In a way, Michele's description of her approach to analysis shows one version of how a researcher takes both what is from 'the field' and what is from the 'self.' We remain alert to how other researchers describe their processes to keep ourselves open to multiple ways of understanding the field. For example, Atkinson (1992) shares his understanding of the field through various enactments:

> ... 'the field' of fieldwork is the outcome of a series of transactions. To begin with, the field is produced (not discovered) through the social transactions engaged in by the ethnographer. The boundaries of the field are not 'given.' They are the outcomes of what the ethnographer encompasses in his or her gaze; what he or she may negotiate with hosts and informants; and what the ethnographer omits or overlooks as much as what he or she observes. Secondly, 'the field' is constructed by what the ethnographer writes. In other words, our sense of 'the field' resides in what may be written and read. (p. 9)

Here Atkinson suggests that researchers figure the field through various actions — to transact, engage, encompass, negotiate, omit, overlook, observe, and, oh yes, to read and to write a particular version of the field.

Many researchers, and these include us in the past, have intoned the phrase 'your log is the data.' But, is it? We fear that it might be cavalier to gloss over this concept without further consideration. While the fieldnotes constitute the reservoir of 'facts' with which we make ongoing meaning, they are not impersonal descriptors. Instead, the fieldnotes are the written record of the data as shaped through the researcher's eyes, with all that this implies about the way individuals see the world, how they interpret what they see, both explicitly and implicitly, and why.

We shape rather than compile our fieldnotes, and we aren't apologizing any longer for that. But, we are trying to recognize, to value, and to explain how personal views direct our attention. For example, what causes us to focus on the boy in the back desk of a third grade classroom rather than the girl in the second row? On the quiet person who has sat waiting for a doctor for two hours in a hospital emergency room rather than on the person who has loudly demanded action from a nurse? Unfolding meanings that we make from the data requires that we reflect on the work in which we are engaged. Writing helps us to make explicit our interests and yearnings and curiosities. Judith Singer found that writing illuminated her under-standing and helped her make more complex versions of the data in her log:

> The most stimulating part of this experience was writing the log. The writing itself helped me reflect on the observation and allowed me to notice relationships that I hadn't consciously thought about while observing. Writing detailed descriptions definitely helped to clarify what may be considered relatively objective and what was totally interpretive on my part. The results were often sensitive, complex portraits of children who had originally been portrayed as one-dimensional.

As Judith indicates, the log helped her to locate and ground meaning. Writing the log, rather than solely collecting more information, helped her to reconceive and elaborate on what she was learning. It's often more frightening to write about 'data' than to collect more of them because of the all too common fear that we may miss something important. But, the log is a tool, a way 'in' to an ongoing exploration. From it we rethink, undo, and shape the ongoing research process and products.

From this earlier writing, we evoke the field in ways that invite readers to trans-act with our interpretations. In essential ways, the writing is a transaction between the data and ourselves and ourselves and our readers. Whether we highlight, add, minimize, or shape a version of the field, we are implicated in the final and deepest sense that 'the field' is within us. Our emotional, intellectual, and aesthetic involve-ments in the field inform the ways in which we write up our understandings of what we have learned. As researchers, we learn to trust the voices within and the ways in which we make those heard. Vincent Crapanzano (1992) likens the task to the one performed by Hermes, the messenger of the gods:

> I liken the anthropologist to him. All truly informative messages have a puckish dimension that jolts us from our ordinary expectations. The messenger has power only if he is heard. He cannot simply repeat the message he has heard ... When Hermes took the post of messenger of the gods, he promised Zeus not to lie. He did not promise to tell the whole truth. Zeus understood. The ethnographer has not. (pp. 2, 3, 4, 45)

Does this mean that many researcher-writers fear that their interpretations might be seen as invention? Our belief is that while the field is a construction, it isn't a lie.

Part of the ongoing process of coming to understand is refiguring the data — thinking about what they mean in particular contexts and testing out how our assumptions inform how we read meaning into them. As Susan Goetz Haver, who was studying life in a public library, discovered:

> An important, yet difficult, aspect of this year was learning to trust: trust that my beginning categories didn't fit, trust the observations that seemed compelling, trust my own perceptions as valid and useful, and trust that out of the burgeoning logs I could construct meaning, whether I could see it now or not. I realize now that I still held onto an old notion of meaning: that it was 'in there' somewhere, waiting to be discovered. Gradually I understood that making meaning was something I had to do by interacting with the log text, using a variety of approaches and lenses.

This is a little like navigating a House of Mirrors. I'm learning to move inside and outside of my text, reading and writing, creating and interpreting, responding and shaping, all at the same time.

So, the answer to whether we invent a field is 'no and yes.'

But, inventions need not be false. They can be stunningly true to our experience. We invent the field because the minute we begin thinking about the field, the second we put pen to paper for field log entries, we are already selecting, dropping, or figuring data from the far more complex real thing that we have witnessed in order to tell a credible story. How and what we categorize, order, or abstract is a refiguration. After all, putting words on two dimensional paper is not what happens in a three dimensional world.

As we've suggested, writing the report isn't where the work of writing the field begins. It starts in the field log with the tentative planning, reactions, lists, descriptions, or bits of overheard conversation. Out of the runes of unshaped interview transcripts, observation notes, or descriptions, we've created vignettes, elaborated descriptions, analytic memos, and poems. However, when we ask first-time researchers to begin writing out of their logs, some resist these tentative moves into interpretation, protesting that this 'alters the data too much.' Several found that it was difficult to braid their own voices into the discussion and that doing so seemed to distort the 'facts.' And while all of these people may now be amused by the memories of their first draft agonies, it was not amusing then, and it is not amusing now for people who are beginning the first rounds of writing. Accepting the fact that one is recreating and thus changing the raw data can be ultimately freeing. This highlights the fact that we must attend to ways of shaping the data.

Figuring and Refiguring Meaning

The questions for us as we begin to write out our data become: How do we animate that which we studied? How do we bring to life what was buried beneath the obvious and literal? In some ways it's like trying to figure the undercurrents beneath the surface of what we studied and then refiguring those through writing. As we've suggested before, often we need to explore the meaning for ourselves first, before we worry about communicating it to others. That's why we recommend getting to know the data and ourselves through a good bit of writing and rewriting in various forms, through feedback from support groups, and by discussing the data with participants in the study. In truth, we take a leap of faith as we begin slogging around in this messy and chaotic work. In what follows, we offer examples of how researchers create meaning out of their fieldnotes. There are no blueprints for starting this writing. But we've found that it's helpful to remember that lurking in the fieldnotes are reminders of a multitude of our untapped stories, only some of which we can and ought to release. We hope that the descriptions to come of other people's insights will help you to find or add more ways of helping yourself through this part of the process.

Composing Meaning from the Data

In order to figure and refigure our thinking about the data, we need to listen, attune, and grow familiar again with what brought us to our interest in the topic in the first place. So, very early in the process it is important to write, consider, talk, think, and write more. Revelations won't burst forth automatically from the data. Emphatically said, the rounds of writing, thinking, analyzing and forming will aid the search toward understanding. Our definition of how meaning is produced is essential here. Instead of an attempt to *find* or *see* meaning 'in the data' it is far more productive to *compose* meaning that the data may lead us to understand. In life, we create our own reality out of persons or situations; it isn't that the person or situation *is the reality*. This is an important distinction that researchers must recognize each time they work with their data. Rhonda Weller Moore recounted that her initial jottings were 'very literal and lacked creativity in the way I described what the data revealed.' She explained that her beliefs about research were challenged as she continued to engage in the process of learning from her data:

> I would have to say that one of the most surprising realizations for me has been the extent to which meaning is constructed. At times throughout the course of this process, I felt that I was escaping from a positivist paradigm having been quite unaware of being held captive there. The fieldnotes became sort of a map to get me into a richly detailed narrative.

As Rhonda struggled with what it means to construct meaning, we thought again how important Flannery O'Connor's understanding of writing is to all of us who participate in these struggles. O'Connor described how writing about the same subject, over and over again, leads to discoveries — new ways of seeing, saying, and thinking about what it is that the writer is trying to understand. And she said this as a seasoned writer, not a neophyte. A strong recommendation then: it is important to create versions of the data from early on. Such ongoing versions allow us to tease out assumptions, find more questions and gain insights about ourselves as researchers. They summon us to the task of acting on the data and become a launching place for reflection. And, indeed, various meanings accumulate through the writing. Finally, we have been delighted to discover that such writing comes to represent the footprints of our thoughts as they progress over time.

We can't stress enough that further clarification comes through exploration. The messages of any data are multiple and multi-layered and blurred at times. If it's possible to rebel against finding answers and, instead, to construct a momentary version of data, a writer might be liberated to move forward. Writing will keep the work dynamic; writing is a tool for sorting through and finding nuggets of ideas that trigger new ways of seeing and understanding.

Elizabeth Merrick, whose research was about pregnant teenage girls who chose to have their babies, struggled for at least one year to move beyond her transcript notes into interpretations of what her participants said. Notice, in the following excerpt from Elizabeth's log, her attempt to create a profile of Kim, a teenager who chose to bear and keep her child. The profile was intended to reveal something more about Kim than the transcript alone could do. However, Elizabeth summarizes what Kim had said to her rather than interpreting her meaning. Elizabeth hesitated on the brink of composing in this profile, not yet ready to step into the space where she could interpret something about who Kim was, how Kim was feeling about herself, or Kim's relationship with her family:

Kim's Transcript

K: My mother basically did every little thing for me. And whatever cause my mother's Asian first, she's Chinese. And they're very manipulative people, they really are. I mean they will choose out your path. You don't really have a real relationship with your parents. Basically they think that it's, you know, that 'We're just doing enough giving you a home you know and paying for this.' 'But, Mom, I need love.'

I: So love is a different thing than providing for school?

K: Right! Support ... exactly. But that's what she's doing to me now I mean. But anyway regardless.

I: Wait. What is she doing to you now?

K: Well, basically when I told her about this pregnancy she had a hard time. Calling me a disgrace and everything. And she doesn't let anyone know especially Chinese. And you know she's been giving me a lot of hard times. Um and I told her that you know it was my decision and I'm not asking you ... I mean, I'm not asking you to like it. I'm just asking you, 'just be there for me.' 'Coz she thinks I'm gonna have the child and just dump the child on her. But this is my responsibility and something I want to take care of.

Kim's Profile

My mother did everything for me and my life is supposed to go according to her direction. She raised me to believe that you go to school, you go to college, you get a job, you get married, and then you have children. And nothing can get in the way of that — you have to stay on that path.

My mother basically did everything for me because my mother's Asian, she's Chinese. Chinese are very manipulative people, they really are. I mean they will choose out your path, and they'll tell you what to do. You don't have a real relationship with your parents. They think that they're doing enough by giving you a home and paying for it. But that's not enough — I've always wanted more. I wanted love.

My mother thinks I'm gonna have the child and dump it on her. She says that I better not expect her to take care of it. I don't. This pregnancy isn't my mother's decision, this is my responsibility. I mean, I'm not asking her to like it, I'm just asking her to be there for me. This pregnancy is my responsibility and something I want to take care of.

Elizabeth did make the transition from summary to composing. This is shown clearly in Chapter 3, pp. 92–3 where you'll find the layered story that she writes about Marisol, a participant in another of her studies. To us, these snippets from Elizabeth's writing journey illustrate that through writing she did move ahead into places she once thought were not hers to reach. Here are some of Elizabeth's reflections about her writing at the end of her study:

> I found it difficult to let go of the idea of pursuing research as an impersonal, rational process. This may also have been influenced by my training as a psychologist. In some instances, this made me hesitant to speak with the voices of the participants when I wrote their narratives. In time, I realized that these fears were not realistic and that the research process was usually helped if I allowed myself to be more personally involved.

An important related issue is the difference in background and perspective between my participants and me. I think part of keeping myself out was related to my own negotiation of boundaries when I was challenged to consider these matters on a deep and personal level. At the start of this study, a fellow colleague who later became part of my support group asked me whether I thought there was any connection between what I was studying and my own childbearing. At the time, I dismissed it by saying, 'Of course not, I'm not a minority, nor an adolescent, and I'm not going to have children for a while anyway.' In hindsight, as I finish my writing with my daughter on my lap, I have a different perspective. When I began, I perceived a large gap between my participants and me. Now, I believe the distance between us is much less than one might like to think.

Rhonda Weller Moore explained that rereading and rewriting led her to richer and different understandings of her data:

> Looking at it now, it is as if reading the logs over and over again was like kneading a handful of potter's clay in order to make it pliable enough to work with. Reading and rereading is the way in which the author comes to know the data, making them pliable enough in his mind to work with. Coming to 'know' the data is the reading stage, and a very necessary component that precedes the ability to begin truly working the clay.
>
> Working it is the meaning-making stage which involves touching it by adding the self, blending data and author, potter and clay. Through the process of writing, the author is confronted with the self and meanings for her which emerge as a result of shaping. Shaping the data into written form from which both author and reader are able to derive meaning is somewhat like sculpting. The product initially is necessarily crude.

Rhonda's sense of the pliable nature of data helped her begin to shape her presentation. She reminds us that this process of figuring and refiguring takes the researcher back to the field to find more data, into the data yet once again, or through the researcher's current understandings of data to fill in and smooth gaps and to examine the emerging project as it begins to take form, as Rhonda said, through the 'sculpting fingers that are analogous to the process of qualitative research.'

Making choices is a part of the composing process. The entire business of writing out one's fieldnotes, of having the logs and reflections read by a support group and facilitator, and the habit of re-seeing the data in various ways can and does encourage us to rethink and wonder. Of course there are moments of frustration when the emerging understanding and form don't seem to be taking shape. But we keep shaping — deciding where and how ideas are juxtaposed, discovering how data relate one piece to another, making choices. Rhonda articulated many of these points when she said, 'As with the clay's potential to take on a myriad of shapes, there is a kaleidoscope of possible meanings which may emerge as the writing turns the data over and over.'

Certainly the work of shaping data takes time, and the initial struggles cannot be avoided. We think it is important here to document in some detail another first-time researcher's 'breakthrough,' in moments added one upon the other, as she shaped her work. Rosemarie Lewandowski, instructor of college English, conducted her qualitative study in a 1st grade classroom. As her log grew fat with descriptions

of interviews and observation data, she began the tricky process we have alluded
to here — composing:

First I wrote about any metaphors that I used to describe what was going on
between Joey [a first grader] and Mrs. Cato [Joey's teacher]. I had a strong sense
of metaphors around Mrs. Cato as those of the burden of her teaching, and of a
lab technician with the children as laboratory rats. Next, I wrote about this in a
vignette that also described some of Mrs. Cato's actions that supported these
metaphors. Then, the hard part. I took the profile for Mrs. Cato to read as part of
a participant check. Mrs. Cato and I faced each other across the large table in the
back of her classroom. Now, the room was empty of children, who would return
from music class in forty minutes. Like everything else in Mrs. Cato's school
setting, I thought, we are on a schedule, our motives confined within the timed
sequence of activities. I fidgeted as she read silently. 'All of this is taken from our
first interview last December,' I explained, 'except for these last two separated
paragraphs. They are what I imagined you would have said about Joey. This is
what I think you think of him,' I stammered.

'That's great. You got it right,' Mrs. Cato said. After reading the two paragraphs on Joey, as I had perceived him through her eyes, she said, 'Yeah, this is
it — the old broken record.' What a powerful feeling that she approved my profile
of her, even admired it. Then I shared with her a copy of a story that I wrote after
from my observations, 'The Kite Drawing Incident.' This is a layered story, from
both Joey's and Mrs. Cato's perspective about an interaction they had. Mrs. Cato's
attitude and demeanor completely changed during reading it. She relaxed. She
asked me questions about how I managed to remember the observations without
taking notes, what other researchers in the class had observed, what other types of
assignments I had done. She was curious and interested. I think she finally felt
included in what I had been doing. She opened up and discussed individual children and their families for the first time, showing me Joey's work. We went on to
discuss Joey's 'problems' with writing.

Mrs. Cato casually handed me Joey's journal, and I felt a moment of excitement as well as a deep connection with him. His journal spoke to me. As I turned
the pages, I saw that Joey had been physically struggling with paper and pencil.
There were torn pages, crumpled erasures, backwards letters. Joey had written, 'I
love school' on a page, then further on, 'I hate school.' Mrs. Cato dispassionately
spoke of his problems as 'trouble getting started,' 'getting it down,' 'the fine
motor,' 'he just can't get it together,' 'immature in drawing.' She showed me the
work of other children for comparison.

This discussion led me to consider the impact of beliefs about education in
Joey's case. Mrs. Cato seemed much more concerned with getting her students to
'fit into' the requirements of the institution. I begin to see an interesting parallel
between Joey's resistance to writing, and Mrs. Cato's resistance to 'the writing
process.' Just as Joey drags his feet when asked to write, pursuing other interests
and distractions, Mrs. Cato resists the notion of writing as the development of the
child's voice, of empowerment. She 'needs to get these children ready for second
grade.' I wrote a metatheme, 'Mrs. Cato sees first grade as a step on the ladder of
education.' Mrs. Cato is caught between two competing metaphors. I thought
about what Witherell and Noddings (1991) said, '. . . individuals who experience
little or no responsibility or authority in crisis situations are much more likely to

act in ways that are harmful to their fellow human beings than are individuals who assume responsibility or claim authority for their own actions' (p. 181).

How is Joey to develop as a learner, how will his experience influence his desire to write, his feelings as a learner in school? Mrs. Cato's eyes are focused on that ladder, while Joey, the individual in the process of growth and development, blurs and loses shape and voice before her eyes.

'What does that ladder look like?' someone in my group asked me. 'Where does it lead?' I thought of some multiple images. I drew a few. One is a Cubist rendering with overlapping planes, fragmented, disjointed, in dark pastel colors. Faces of children like Joey peer out from between the rungs on a huge, monolithic ladder. Or, I think of a cool, impersonal image of ladders connecting with multiple landings. The light is dim, the figures all look the same, with no distinguishing features, their clothing in muted tones. The walls are gray. Everything lacks color, except the yellow rungs of the ladders. At the bottom of the image a short ladder appears first. This is kindergarten. Joey huddles in the far left corner of a small landing floating in space above that kindergarten ladder. Behind him is a projected moving image: sometimes a wall, sometimes a frosted-glass window letting in cool, gray light. Through the window smokestacks are visible, suggesting the technology and precision of a factory. To the right of the landing, another ladder turns at right angles toward the second grade landing high above. Joey ignores it, looking through the frosted glass at the shadow of his kite floating in the sky. Then the wall and window disappear, and Joey is left clinging to the edge of the landing, with the abyss below. He watches Mrs. Cato move up the ladder to the right, taking some children by the hand. 'Come on, Joey, you can make it,' she calls to him across the distance. But now the landing changes shape to become a maze of paths across the void, ascending in a steep angle toward Mrs. Cato. Joey has no idea how to reach her. He turns his eyes to watch the window dissolve, then grasps onto the kite string, smiling to himself. Mrs. Cato calls again. He doesn't hear her. She turns away, leading the others, calling to Horace, 'Give me your hand,' pulling him so his feet can reach that first big step.

A careful reading of Rosemarie's dual-visioned writing — revealing her process as researcher and shaper of data into a powerful analysis of the situation — shows us some steps in her own ascent up the ladder of understanding. She seeks out metaphors that help her to make sense of her experiences with participants; she shares that profile with one participant and in doing so elicits more data that help her rethink the metathemes that were emerging for her; and she begins to imagine a new metaphor out of the old one that articulates her current understandings. And what will tomorrow bring for Rosemarie? New insights, we suspect, another layer of meaning that she will undoubtedly uncover as she continues to figure and refigure meaning. What Rosemarie accomplishes at this point in her work as a researcher echoes what her fellow researcher Sung-Goo Hur described as his trust in the process: 'I grew in the strength that I could find rich meaning from the ordinary.'

Data can be construed and reconstrued in many different ways. One effective strategy for many people is a double entry log — that is, writing a side column of comments or engaging in written 'dialogue' with the data in your log. In a way, it is like having a conversation with yourself except in this case you have a written record of it. As Rosemarie suggests:

I've tended to have conversations with others, bouncing ideas and observations about those ideas off others. I'm learning to bounce ideas off my writing with side comments. It's a way of standing inside and outside the text at the same time. The side comments add layers to my writing. Newer drafts emerged with new comments. The side comments kept the log episodes alive, ongoing, and developing.

We've begun to think, as Rosemarie said, that it is important to write both 'inside and outside the text.' Write about questions, uncertainties, or contradictions that lead you inside the literal data to grapple with meaning at particular moments. Buried in the notes that describe literal happenings, quote passages of dialogue, or catalogue events or actions, we find the subtle, blurred, and often important meanings that are the essence of the most obvious parts of the data to us. In some ways the process could be likened to the pearl encased in the meat and shell of an oyster — it's not so obvious at first.

Gayle Newshan found that her ideas about her research on the pain experienced by AIDS patients evolved as she worked with her support group. Out of this, she shaped new questions for herself:

Yesterday, at 12:15, Scott died of a pulmonary embolism. It was quite unexpected and sudden. His nurse practitioner, Frank, had told me that Scott was actually beginning to move his leg and the physical therapist was going to try standing exercises. He was so happy and even planning to return to his apartment. His mom was up from Louisiana. Then, he died. I was feeling overwhelmed and sad. I felt like the angel of death — now, 3 out of 5 persons I interviewed have died. And none of them or I expected it.

I talked about this with my support group and how I hadn't considered death part of my study. They said, 'What do you mean? Of, course it's your study.' I was thinking about how the focus of my study was pain. I suddenly saw and continue to see that Scott's death and the talk with my support group opened my eyes. I ask again, 'What am I studying?' Am I studying the experience of being an end-stage person with AIDS in the hospital? Pain is only part of that experience. I am studying people who are close to death. I was thinking these thoughts about dying were peripherally related to pain, if at all. Now, I need to rethink this. Is my focus pain? Or something else with pain a part of it? I rethink the questions: What is it like to have AIDS? What is the hospital experience like? What is it like to face death? I'm still interested in the experience of pain but excited with how the topic is opening up.

To look and relook at what motivates the study helps us to understand what we find along the way. We need to examine how writing reveals relevance in what we may not have noticed earlier. To take the opinions, theories, notions, and actions that call out to us and to make sense of them — that's the shaping process. Gayle's thinking and intuition served as complementary partners in opening the inquiry that took place as she wrote her way toward understanding.

As Barbara Ball learned to work as a qualitative research writer, she found that the relationship between thinking and intuition became clearer to her when she wrote several versions of the data. This tactic helped her to capture the rhythms and intonations of conversations, describe a particular scene in multiple ways, and create layered stories as Rosemarie did with Joey and Mrs Cato. For Barbara, this led to the realization that experimentation with language can aid the process of figuring and refiguring the data toward meaning:

> I suddenly realize that all my writing has already been analysis and interpretation. It began when I left the observation site and jotted down phrases on scrap paper that I had heard in the classroom and that seemed important. It continued when I sat at home writing my log, trying to express on paper the rhythms and melodies of the interactions that I had observed. Writing my weekly log was already shaping and creating a narrative, playing with words, making meaning, and forming gestalts. How much is said in the choice of words, in the intonation and the rhythms of speaking? How careful need I be in my choice of words? How different are the children's and the adults' language? How similar?

The flimsy first-words-put-on-paper become shaped and sharpened through the writing itself. The writing is a dialogue with the data, with you as the person making meaning from them.

We've found it helpful to encourage the researchers with whom we work to engage in braiding facts and analysis/interpretation as they lift data from the log. Barbara explained her process of braiding in this way:

> Three approaches seem possible to describe and analyze the classroom life: (1) I could tell the story from the point of view of a few children (Dustin, Annie, Moni). How do they relate to their parents or caregivers, to the teachers, to other children, to the materials and objects in the classroom? (2) I could focus on the interaction of the teachers with these three children. This has essentially been the focus of my last analytic memos with categories like parallel activities, timing (rhythms), initiative, response, mutuality, structure and direction, control, physical contact, comments. (3) A third approach would be to concentrate on the theme of control and to analyze the various aspects of control in the classroom life. For example, internal versus external control, rules, limit setting, decision-making, mastery, shared responsibilities, control in interaction with peers. For now, I will focus on the interaction of the teachers with Dustin, Annie, and Moni. This means that other data become background data. They may set the context, while the theme of control will be highlighted for now.

In this first paragraph, Barbara considers the *how* of her presentation — shaping how the presentation will unfold. What she says is replete with indications that she has been engaged in making meaning from her 'facts.' Her emerging insights, sometimes voiced as categories and themes, drive her plans for presentation and demonstrate her earliest attempts at analysis. That analysis continues as she chooses to focus on a select number of children instead of all, winnowing data at this earliest juncture in an attempt to define the parameters of her study.

However, in her final sentences of this paragraph the phrase 'for now' seems particularly worth noting. To us, Barbara indicated that she has shaped the data in a particular way for the moment and that she chose 'for now' to highlight the theme of control. This idea that the same data may be presented in multiple ways to support multiple purposes is important and often liberating:

So, the purpose of this study is to describe, analyze, and interpret the interaction between teachers and children in a pre-kindergarten classroom. I will do this by weaving the interactions of the teachers with Dustin, Annie, and Moni in narrative with analysis of these interactions. Another strand will be to use descriptions of setting to bring forward the context and atmosphere in the classroom and the unfolding life there. These layered descriptions will help me analyze the theme of control that I weave into this version of the data. Maybe my analysis will frame the stories, anecdotes, poems, or pieces of my log that I use as illustrations. Particularly poems might be helpful in illustrating the rhythm, timing, and sound of the interactions, so that the voices become audible and held for a moment so the reader can do some of the interpretation.

In this second paragraph, Barbara weaves a tighter fit between the purpose of her research and the forms of her presentation. She considers here how best to involve her readers in 'seeing' the classroom and in joining her in interpretive acts:

Here's an example of my attempt at doing this: Structure and direction are often given by the teachers, but the children also direct their own activities and they build structure. This is clearly evident in the woodblock area. Many tasks that the teachers offer are prestructured (e.g., making the Christmas decorations, providing outlines, stencils), they involve making order (e.g., sorting, finding corresponding shapes), forming categories. Sometimes they seem to be geared toward channeling children's behavior in more acceptable forms (e.g., transfer-exercise for Moni, offering Dustin an area where he can build with wood blocks). Is structure a 'scaffold,' helping the children grow and learn, or is structure a narrow 'outline'? Sometimes children paint over and grow out of the outlines that are given. It is important to distinguish between the control that the teachers have in the classroom and the control that the children have in their play. In giving directives, rules, and limits, the teachers exert control. This is particularly obvious in Clara's behavior and communicated directly. In part this might be her understanding of her responsibility as the headteacher.

In this third paragraph, Barbara digs in to what she had previously called 'the theme of control.' In doing so, it becomes clear that this control is a complex issue and that, as she considers the ideas more deeply, Barbara will need to provide a complex presentation of facts, analysis, and interpretation to offer a rich portrayal of the theme. What is more, Barbara strives to make both the teachers and children believable. That is, she works against a stereotypical picture of teachers' control as she identifies control as multifaceted, multifunctional, and context bound. Through writing, the focus and ideas are figured and refigured, and the writer's understanding of self in relation to the data is constantly re-forming as well. We get to know ourselves better as we wrestle with what the data come to mean for us.

Writing Our Way Toward Understanding

In many respects, writing our way toward understanding provides us researchers with a way to tap into the web of meanings that exist for us both within the field and in our relationship to it. We have teased out two labels for memos to distinguish different processes at work — *reflective* and *analytic*. *Reflective memos* help us to critique our own work and to develop insights or directions. Reflective memos help us move the writing out of the fieldnotes and into other forms. They are produced by rereading the fieldnotes and the writing around them in order, for example, to tease out assumptions, to find more questions, to gain insights about self as researcher, and to find the encouragement to keep the search going.

Writing in a reflective memo about the choices that she made about her research topic, Barbara Miller, high school teacher and department head, discovered that her primary interest in a classroom of five and six year olds related to her humane interest in how children's sense of self gets defined in schools. She describes her discovery in this way:

> I never would have guessed that I would end up this little project looking mainly at Morris' experience in Ms. Fowler's classroom. And yet, there it is. Somehow, Morris has crystallized for me all that I really care about in education: students as individuals, as individual learners, as individuals interacting with teachers and other adults. I thought that I would be drawn to other issues more strongly: the relative impact of direct or indirect instruction on young students, student-centered vs. teacher-centered instruction, ways in which gender affected learning or access to learning, the relationship of verbal (or logical-mathematical) ability to success in school. It's not that I found that I was uninterested in these areas and the questions which they raised. In fact, I found that much of my data recorded instances in which I observed these dynamics. But over and over, my log kept coming back to the marginalized student. Who was he (or she)? What had gotten him there? What behaviors — on his part, on the parts of the other students, of the teachers — kept him marginalized? What had to happen for him to have a successful academic experience? Was that likely to happen in this K/1 classroom? Why or why not? Where was I located in these questions, both as a participant observer and as a teacher?

Very neatly, Barbara underscores the fact that through the writing of reflective memos she is led to new questions about herself as a participant observer. Not a bad finding! We've discovered the move true of many qualitative researchers. One of our colleagues, Carolyn Arnason, sums it up nicely: 'Peering into the mirror of qualitative research gives back a reflection of me engaged in self-discovery.'

We like to think that reflective memos help researchers become conscious of how they construct their realities while living the research experience, how they grasp the appearance of things, or interrogate and acknowledge aspects within their field of study. Rita Kopf's memos offer a powerful example of reflective writing that opens such spaces where understanding can take shape. They demonstrate the moves from the particularities of initial reactions and documentation to fuller graspings. Rita returned to nursing on the wards after more than twenty years of doing other, more distanced jobs such as being an administrator of nurses at another hospital. Rita documented the experiences of her return and found that particularly through reflective memos she could explore how her extremely personal connection, developed through years of first-hand work in hospital environments, affected her motivation to conduct this study as well as how memory reshaped the data. Through the next several excerpts from Rita's reflective memos, we share her journey toward self-understanding:

> I believe in nursing and have always found deep personal meaning in my work as a nurse. I feel strongly that I am defined as a person by my work in nursing and that I have defined and given meaning to nursing through my work. My practice has been focused in the specialty of Maternal and Child Health, specifically, pediatrics, newborn intensive care, and high risk prenatal care. I have always relished the challenges and opportunities to grow, to learn, to interact, to excel and to feel that I made a difference for patients, for their families, and for my co-workers. Part of the reason for this study is to see in more detail what has drawn me to make it my life's work.
>
> When I assumed a position as Director of Nursing I was, in some ways, out of my element. I missed the direct participation in practice. I spent long periods immersed in paper and projects related to the predictable but difficult realities of working in a bureaucratic, intractable institution. It was during periods of frenetic paper processing that I fantasized most vividly about returning to the world of nursing. There I would be — knowledgeable, caring, and expert — making a measurable difference in people's lives. Like my colleagues, I would be a part of people's lives at very meaningful moments. Because administration wasn't satisfying, I found a way back to my 'home' through my motivation to research in the places I loved to work most.
>
> As a way of preparing for this study, I spent several weekends in limited observer-participant experience with staff nurses. I knew that staff nursing was not for the faint of spirit, mind or body. Staff nursing is tough on the heart, tough on the knees and tough on the back. Staff nursing can be boring, task oriented and repetitive. Then again, there is the opportunity for connectedness. It was a realization that occurred during one of those moments that I knew I wanted to study staff nursing. I remember how Nadine was working quickly — soaping up with one washcloth and rinsing with another. Face, neck, underarm, chest, groin, thighs — the front was 'done up.' As we turned the patient on his side to 'do up' his back, he had a large, loose, foul smelling bowel movement. He apologized. Nadine patted his shoulder gently. I got clean water, more washcloths and more towels. It's what we do I thought. We enter people's lives when they are most vulnerable. We are strangers and they expose themselves to us. How to do all this and do it with dignity so that we and they are more enabled, more ennobled? Each encounter is an opportunity for enrichment. My decision was made. I would attempt to go beyond my own current experience and tackle the job of staff nursing. I would collect the richest possible data by living the experience. I would immerse myself. Perhaps in this way, I would be able to serve my profession with a heightened understanding.

Rita takes us into the wards with her to feel the shocks, the frustrations, and the loneliness of what she lived, but she shapes and gives her reflections on those experiences — the noises, demands, smells, meticulous tasks — in the memos where she works at composing the human drama around her:

The nursing station was full of people. Edna, the unit secretary, was on the phone talking about 90 decibels to someone in the laboratory. 'We need it STAT,' she yelled and slammed down the phone. Terry was talking to one of the physicians about finding a nursing home for Mrs. Thomas. The discharge planning nurse had squeezed out a space for herself at the writing shelf behind Edna. Two physicians were writing in patient charts behind me and Terry. The phones were ringing; the patient call bells were buzzing; the elevator just outside the station went bing, bing.

The 'desk' was in a state of pandemonium. Ringing, buzzing, and dinging. I asked Edna, 'How can you work with all this racket?' 'I don't even hear it anymore,' Terry answered my question even though it wasn't directed at her. 'You get used to it.'

The emergency bell in a patient's bathroom was going off. It sounded as if a fire truck was driving through the unit. The nursing assistants were nowhere to be found. I ran to answer bells, responded to the emergency bell, got bedpans for patients, pulled one guy who was hanging through a side rail back onto the bed. Families stopped me to ask questions. I found myself irritated. I was behind with all the medications, and I was sure I was going to make an error. I find myself having difficulty 'keeping up.' I find myself assessing more than is required for my 'do patient care' role. I do neurochecks on P. J., a 17-year-old admitted over the weekend with multiple trauma. I check LMSTS and Homans sign on A. M. I search for evidence of petechiae and bleeding on M. C. and advise her to have her husband bring a softer toothbrush. I watch S. A. breathe and we discuss the pros and cons of the flu vaccine. Six of the patients are DNR, three are on oxygen, five have IVs, one has an N-G tube, one has a heparin infusion, one has a triple lumen subclavian catheter, three have foley catheters and eight require complete care. At 11:30 I'm still giving out my 10:00 medications. I stand at the medication cart with my palms sweaty and my heart racing. I can hear it thump, thump through my blouse.

Further, Rita used reflective memos as a place where she dealt with her bouts of anxiety bred by the conviction that people might question whether she could take the pressure as a 'returning newcomer nurse':

I couldn't keep up with the IVs, all the meds were late, I assessed patients without even knowing their diagnosis and I had no time to answer their questions or to comfort them. I hate this. As I said, I can't do this and I really don't know whether my view of things will be valued or if my opinions will be viewed as unrealistic because I don't 'have it' anymore.

These concerns culminated in a reaction that caused Rita temporarily to produce writing so dry and impersonal that at one stage of drafting the final version she abandoned it entirely. Finally, Rita's image of the ethos of nursing, as shaped by her past experiences, was recreated in writing, but the process was painful even if it was victorious.

We've found that reflective memos lead us to think about how we, as researchers, make sense of the data and what may influence our feelings or beliefs. Writing *analytic memos* helps us to examine from various vantage points the objects, articulations, events, and people within our research studies. They go hand-in-hand with the analytical processes to be described in Chapter 4, pp. 160–222. Analytic memos, then, become vehicles through which we shape the lived experience. Seeing the analytic memo as the process and product of a quest opens the possibility that we can also find other avenues and vistas opening that will lead us down other interpretive paths. We found a light-hearted but poignant example of this in one of Eileen McEvoy's memos:

> As I sat listening to Father Daniels [all names have been changed to protect the innocent] begin his homily it hit me. I had all my 'vegetables' (themes, metaphors, plays, poems) but I didn't do enough with them. You see, I never used my vegetables to make a 'garden' salad. So, the following are my thoughts about the salad.
>
> I began 'hunching' themes after my interview with Mrs. Sullivan. After reading and rereading the transcript I saw certain themes in Mrs. Sullivan's statement about her relationship with the children.
>
> • I care about these kids.
> • I know these kids.
> • I want these kids to learn.
>
> As I saw it, my next task was to see whether I could find more support for these themes. I did. However, when I tried to come up with metathemes, the result seemed forced and unnatural. It occurred to me that perhaps the problem was with my themes. So I returned once again to themes. I re-examined and refined:
>
> • I know others care about these kids.
> • I care about these kids.
> • I want these kids to care about each other.
>
> Rethinking and refining my themes helped me get a better grip on my metathemes. The main one was about the idea of caring relationships — a cycle of caring.

As Jane Martin worked through this reconstructing process she found that the data took her into a variety of paths:

> Last week I decided to write a poem based on a possible theme — The Right Man At The Wrong Time. I thought I was writing a poem based on this theme, but when I began writing and finished the poem, I'd written about 'What More Could I Want?' It was as if I was kidnapped by my data and was riding their wave. When searching through the transcript, it was my participant's words about wanting more for herself in a relationship and her expectation to feel a certain, passionate way with Mr. Right that surfaced from the transcript, thus freeing her words for me to shape. Now, another stepping back. What started with a theme about the right man at the wrong time evolved into a broader concept for Nancy [Jane's participant] about 'What More Could I Want' or something about wanting more.
>
> I feel as if I should make a sign to wear around my neck which says, 'At Work,' and I can sit at my computer just thinking, talking to myself on the screen. As I continued, the theme evolved into 'I Want More From A Relationship Than My Parents Had.' Perhaps this is a metatheme for Nancy at this moment but I suspect there are more. Or, 'I Thought There Should Be More In A Romantic Relationship.' Or, 'I Want More In A Relationship With A Man.' Or, 'When It Comes To Marrying Someone, I Don't Want Something To Be Missing.' My point is that this kind of research seems to be constantly evolving as I go through many levels of analysis. So, where am I with metathemes? Immersed in many possibilities.

We return to our data, add insights, collect more, then write more. We analyze again, then write. We read, then write. Parenthetically *final writing* begins the moment the first words appear on the clean, white paper in the log. It is through various kinds of refiguring of any type including these memos that we return to our data. Some research writers do not distinguish between reflective and analytic memos. They reason that any memo which helps them bring a sharper focus functions in similar ways. So they call them reflective memos, analytic memos, research memos, or just plain memos. We endorse that decision. We have made a rather fine distinction between the two, but certainly we agree that reflection is a product of analyzing and vice versa. What is important is to write memos and to use them in the service of the research.

Write memos about your data all the way through the research process. Consider multiple ways to give form and substance to your report. Do not wait until some arbitrary point where you believe you'll begin to draft a *final* analysis and the *final* writing. Do not allow yourself to escape the stress of actually writing by those two time-honored detours: freezing or reverting to a headlong flight into more data collection. There seems to be a persistent myth that the more data one collects, the more chance that one will have a meaningful and believable study. That myth doesn't hold. It is through the continuous, recursive process of thinking, collecting, writing, reading — the same process by which we create our ongoing research strategies — that our search to discover the essence of what we are studying must mesh with our search to communicate these essences in worthwhile ways. Our writing should reflect what we've heard or seen. How we punctuate or edit, and later what and how we select to quote, or how we write around what we quote, all these acts are interpretive and require that we examine seriously our relationship to the data that we are shaping into meaning.

Researchers' Stances

Wherever we locate ourselves — in the back row of a sixth grade classroom, in an observation booth overlooking an emergency operating room, in the underground tunnels to describe the living conditions of the homeless in New York City — those positions in the field influence what we see and the ways in which we see the substance and contexts of our studies. Stance means more, however, than the literal locations where we collect data. Stance is the various perspectives through which we frame the collection and interpretation of data, or, as we will suggest through the metaphor *angles of repose*, those that influence how and what we see and the interpretations in writing that arise from that seeing. Traditionally many researchers have written a theoretical framework statement to set the stage for their studies. Such theoretical frameworks carry with them the assumption that an already existing theory brings scholarly validation to the research study. However, researchers have not been as forthcoming in their explanations of how philosophical, ideological, and especially political or moral positions influence the ways in which they analyze and present data. The upfront theoretical framework is not what we have in mind when we talk about stance, and we'd like to take some time to develop our ideas of the importance, complexity, and promise of being more conscious about stance.

Harry Wolcott (1992) urges new qualitative researchers to take strategic positions 'vis a vis the many alternatives' available to them under the qualitative research umbrella. As is so often the case, Wolcott has done it again! We only wish that he had addressed this to all qualitative researchers, seasoned as well as new. Wolcott's statement rests on a belief that one's research stance, one's framework for thinking and doing in light of the spirit of a theoretical position, must be a conscious choice; at the same time, there is room here as one goes along to alter one's stance, to amalgamate it with others, to create one's own, to select another and begin all over again. Thus, symbolic interaction, critical ethnography, phenomenology, action research, hermeneutics, and case study, among others, become alternatives and possibilities rather than rigid corsets. To us, this is a liberating view.

Some researchers have immersed themselves in a particular theory and the practice of its methods. They have nourished themselves, breathed their own special air from a position that has become increasingly familiar and supportive, and one that allows them to contribute to its knowledge base. Even for those researchers who are driven by, passionate about, and internally knowledgeable about their research paradigm, we think that there is more than a theoretical position present in their work. We see a complex network of belief systems and positions embedding, superimposing, and undergirding any research project, and we are making a plea to be more aware of and more upfront about how these stances are accounted for in research writing.

Figure 2.1: RASHOMON

Drawing by R. Chast; @ 1993 The New Yorker Magazine, Inc.

Angles of Repose

Because self is somehow implicated in where we position ourselves, it is important to tackle the issue of how 'truth' can be found or how 'validity' and 'reliability' can be gleaned from one person's interpretations of qualitative data. We feel that a responsible research report is a report that can be believed. This is linked directly to how each researcher-writer shares the story of meaning making that underpins the writing. Read Rosemarie's piece again on pages 23–4 to see how she takes us, her readers, into her process. Is she believable? We think so. And even if we do not share her ladder metaphor and collage, she provides us with plenty of other data so that we can reach conclusions of our own.

Documentation of in-process stumblings, mis-steps, insights, and the various avenues we travel through data is essential as a record of how we shape the data. Additionally, it is through revelations of this type that we establish our trustworthiness as researchers. 'Truth' is always in flux. Too bad we had to mention such loaded terms as 'truth' and 'validity' anyway. But their specters must often be addressed by qualitative researchers — over and over again it seems. One beginning researcher, Rebecca Mlynarczyk found her way of making sense of the link between 'facts' and 'truth':

> It is important to be aware of the difference between 'facts' and 'truth.' The great masterpieces of literature, works like *Hamlet*, *Middlemarch*, or *Anna Karenina* are fictional but they are also true; they are true to the psychological processes of their characters and the societies in which these characters live. Their authors have captured the essence. In contrast, works of nonfiction are sometimes factually correct but not true in the sense of getting at the essence.
>
> I certainly don't wish to suggest that ethnographers are budding fiction writers, that they can blithely ignore the facts in trying to get at the truth. The ethnographer's job is to get at the essence of what is being studied through the most accurate observation and analysis possible.

Some, many quite experienced qualitative researchers, still feel that they need to defend the fact that they are not doing quantitative research. One way of shielding from that criticism is to use the language of quantitative research such as 'subjects' and 'sampling error' as if this would make qualitative approaches acceptable. Bluntly, it just doesn't work.

Qualitative researchers have need for congruent concepts and a living language to describe what it is that gives integrity to the work. Many people have provided a wonderful base for that. The list of names is long — Lincoln and Guba, Wolcott, Lofland and Lofland, Agar, and van Manen come to mind. But even here, the evolution of the language within qualitative methodology fascinates us. Take the case of the language and meaning of 'triangulation.'

Before 1985, but certainly with their classic *Naturalistic Research* (1985), Lincoln and Guba were among many who highlighted the process criterion of triangulation. This meant 'validating' findings by comparing data collected by a variety of methods, or from a variety of sources, or by a variety of researchers, or via the lenses of a variety of theoretical perspectives. In 1991, Ely, Anzul, Friedman, Garner, and Steinmetz added another spice to this brew by stating that one can also trian-gulate data by comparing those that were collected by the same person using the same method at various points over time (p. 97). In our experience, triangulation was eagerly, if not passionately, embraced as the banner of qualitative research respect-ability. If trustworthiness was written about at all in research, there was every chance that triangulation would get mentioned in an elaborated statement about how it was 'done.' However, for some, and this included us, the language didn't suit. It was mechanistic, positivistic — it represented data as a series of unchanging and fixed events, most of which could and should be corroborated. It promised far more than it could deliver. And what is more, with its message, 'triangulation' drew people away from the difficult but essential job of wrestling with complex ideas of multiple perspectives and meanings. By 1989, Guba and Lincoln pared down the scope of the concept by stating that '. . . triangulation should be thought of as referring [only] to cross-checking specific data items of factual nature' (p. 241). That seems reasonable.

Laurel Richardson (1994), in the *Handbook of Qualitative Research*, under-scored the need to move away from the language that conceptualized the practice of triangulation when she wrote that 'in postmodernist mixed-genre texts, we do not triangulate; we *crystallize*.' Recognizing that most often there is no fixed reality to triangulate, Richardson notes that there are more than 'three sides from which to approach the world.' For us, her metaphor of the crystal describes not only the habits of mind and ways of being that inform the researcher's gaze, but also how the writing is shaped. The written document reflects the complex, partial, and multi perspectives that refract meaning for and from the reader. The crystal, she tells us:

> . . . combines symmetry and substance with an infinite variety of shapes, sub-stances, transmutations, multidimensionalities, and angles of approach . . . Crystals are prisms that reflect externalities and refract within themselves, creating different colors, patterns, arrays, casting off in different directions. What we see depends upon our angle of repose. (Richardson, 1994, p. 522)

Richardson's reference to angles of repose helps to define the multiple positions from which writers present a variety of dimensions or points of view in the writ-ing. A concrete illustration of such angles is evident in the character Lyman Ward. Confined to a wheelchair, he chronicles his grandparents' story from letters, family anecdotes, and through his imaginative reconstruction of their history in Wallace Stegner's Pulitzer Prize-winning novel *Angles of Repose*. Lyman discovers that it is not so much what he sees as how he sees it that gives the external and internal worlds their truths. His journey through his grandparents' history led him to the many angles that revealed the 'truth' about his family:

> 'What do you mean, "Angles of Repose"?' she asked me when I dreamed we were talking about Grandmother's life, and I said it was the angle at which a man or woman finally lies down. I suppose it is; and yet it was not what I hoped to find when I began to pry around in Grandmother's life. I thought when I began, and still think, that there was another angle in all those years when she was growing old and older and very old, and Grandfather was matching her year for year, a

separate line that did not intersect with hers. They were vertical people, they lived
by pride, and it is only by the ocular illusion of perspective that they can be said
to have met. But he had not been dead two months when she lay down and died
too, and that may indicate that at that absolute vanishing point they did intersect.
(Stegner, 1971, p. 568)

As Lyman learned, the 'truth' is implicated in a series of shaping discoveries rather
than in a search for some elusive 'right' way of describing. Although particular
study designs and much of the language of reporting have been accepted as giving
data the garb of 'truth,' we are more cautious about the idea that facts can really
be constructed as truth — ever. Figuring and refiguring the report, a forthright
record of, a vigilance to tracing the relationship between fact, analysis, truth, and
opinion is obviously central.

Our own issues of how to document angles of repose through the writing are
reflected in current discussions on reporting in journalism as well. One of the best
treatises we've read on ways of understanding the presentation of data was written
by Max Frankel (1995) for *The New York Times Magazine*:

> Facts and analysis are the bricks and mortar of responsible reporting. To be sure,
> they are subject to news fashions: the age or ethnicity or childhood experiences of
> a person in the news may or may not be rated as significant at various times. But
> however detailed, facts and analysis lead only slowly and cumulatively to a per-
> ception of truth, a perception also colored by individual, value-laden opinion.
>
> Fact, analysis, opinion: they are neighbors, but well fenced. Any rendering of the
> words that [the] President . . . will utter to Congress in his State of the Union
> address next Tuesday will be factual. Why he says what he says will require ana-
> lysis. Whether what he says or advocates is good or bad will be opinion. (p. 18)

And, so for our qualitative data. In this process of figuring and refiguring we face
the uneasy responsibility of writing about how we see the relationships between
facts, truth, reporting, and opinion in the write up of our reports. First, qualitative
researchers, like all others, do report. Second, there are great similarities between
honest reporting and honest qualitative research writing. Notice please, the word
'honest.'

Because this business of reporting and analyzing 'facts' is of deep concern to
qualitative researchers, we cannot emphasize enough that writing about how a researcher sees the relationship is essential from the beginning. So, we take you back
to Max Frankel who helped us clarify possible approaches through his example of
reporting about a presidential speech:

1 [The] President called on Congress last night to enact his middle-class bill of rights.
2 Although [the] President's . . . tax cut proposal is an obvious political ploy to pre-
   empt the Republicans . . . and you know the rest.
3 Trying to pre-empt a Republican campaign pledge to reduce Federal taxes, [the]
   President . . . challenged Congress last night to enact his more modest mix of tax
   credits and education. (Frankel, 1995, p. 18)

Each of these three approaches, says Frankel, works the facts differently. Frankel sees (1) as 'objective misrepresentation.' The wording sounds factual and contains no errors, but 'offers not even a clue to the proposal's purpose and scope.' It pulls no punches about what side the reporter supports. Frankel interprets (2) as a piece of opinionated editorializing: 'It is partisan.' Frankel applauds (3) for its 'disinterested interpretation' (p. 18). That account provides readers with some political context, information about possible beneficiaries of the President's proposal and some estimate of its effects on the budget. All this suggests that it would be a distortion to consider interpretation as context free. Any time phenomena are explained, they are explained from the perspectives of those presenting them. Frankel reminds us:

- Beware of just the facts.
- Beware of unattributed declarations.
- Question aggressive interpretation by examining it for accuracy and fairness.

And, we suggest that it is important to be wary of researchers who don't deal with such issues in writing. Our individual modes of perceiving data and expressing their meanings in language, then, need to be interrogated and explained in our reports. It is certainly possible for qualitative researchers to learn the various skills of lifting from 'the facts' without losing their factual ground.

We ask over and over during the multiple drafts leading to final writing: What language will I use to communicate the experience? What forms will best do justice to the people who were my participants? What data will I include so that my readers have sufficient bases to understand how I came to my insights? How do I create a partnership with my readers? How do I keep the thinking open rather than neatly closing it off? From whose point of view will I present the narrative — or, better asked, how many points of view will communicate sufficiently the real complexity of what I studied and learned? How can I come across as a person and as a person who is a researcher? These are the questions that help us clarify our own angles of repose as we shape the field in the written report.

What we are really suggesting is that as researchers we need to be conscious of what causes us to be startled, provoked, angry, or challenged by the material and meaning of our studies. We need to record, name what is being recorded, and construct meaning from our explicit confrontations with the perspectival nature of the data and the knowledge that helps us produce analyses of it. After all, language helps us to construct and to represent. We're thinking that multiple perspective and multi-voice analyses of many types might bridge the network of meanings in written reports. We'll deal with this directly in the next chapter where we show ways that researchers are enlarging the possibilities of negotiating new discourse in multiple contexts; rotating the lenses of their stances to embrace the ambiguities and multiplicity of meaning.

By final writing time, we have in front of us the data from various levels of abstraction out of which we work to create another abstraction; hopefully a cohesive, interesting, useful, and trustworthy essence that we call a report, a book, an article, a dissertation. That this report represents only pieces of what actually happened, leaves out a great deal, presents a sequence that may be other than chronological, does not take away from what it comes to be — the ongoing, multifaceted, and often cacophonous stream of narratives shaped into the essence of experience. The big job for qualitative researchers is not to make a slick piece but to strive for writing a report that gets as close as possible to the essence — the whole business of what we studied, felt and tentatively made sense about in the field. This means that our reports may echo our doubts, discontinuities and various ways of understanding. Indeed, writing that communicates well may be lumpy and bumpy, but is always as true as possible to the important legs of the journey and, thus, always fascinating and worth reading. As Ronna Ziegel talked about her very new research study, she said, 'The title of my study is *Six Writers Writing*. I *should* have titled it *One Researcher Learning*.' Ultimately good qualitative research writing is the communication of how someone comes to understand various perspectives 'on the field,' 'that exist in the field,' and that 'exist within the self.' Writing begins to move us in this direction.

This search for multiple meanings is related to the idea of essence or what Tyler (1987) labeled 'evocation,' which highlights an important aim of qualitative research writing. As research writers, we strive to distill the heart of the matter, knowing all the while that creating exact copies of what we have studied is not only impossible but also undesirable. The crafting and recrafting of essence takes time. It also takes knowledge of rhetorical, structural, and narrative devices. Atkinson (1992) talks of writing for readability and representation. He says the ethnographer is undoubtedly an artisan who *crafts* narratives and representations. But it is an illicit sleight of hand to refer to these products as 'fictions' just because they are 'made' (p. 51). And the historian David McCullough (1992), in describing his aim for writing, quotes the French artist Delacroix who said, 'What I demand is accuracy for the sake of the imagination' (p. 1). The idea here seems to be similar.

We want to emphasize the point that as researchers our stances, our angles of repose, do affect what we are interested in, the questions we ask, the foci of our study, and the methods of collection as well as the substance of analysis. And the meanings we make from our research projects are filtered through our beliefs, attitudes, and previous experiences as well as through both the formal and informal theoretical positions we understand or believe in. As researchers we bring multiple stances to our studies — in degrees of conscious and subconscious awareness — as we choreograph, depict, and resculpt stories and meanings from what we are examining. In what ways, as researchers, should we take the opportunity to bring these stances explicitly to bear through the writing? These stances both express and shape our beliefs and positions as researchers. Now, mind you, we've come to be even more radical and suggest that it might be important to dabble with wearing multiple interpretive lenses that do not fit us comfortably. We are trying to grapple with how we might present competing and even contradictory viewpoints through the writing.

Take, for example, Christine Lewis who, in a research study for Ruth's class, examined how teachers of adolescent girls in juvenile detention classrooms managed the classroom and developed curriculum. Many of the teachers stated that physical punishment or confinement were proper disciplinary action for classroom disruptions. How was Christine to write about the teachers' perspectives? What value should she place on the moral or political implications as well as ideological positions that could be teased out of the teachers' beliefs? Should she grapple with the fact that more women teachers than their male counterparts believed in physical punishment? Would it be fair to suggest that a sampling of nine teachers was representative of the thousands throughout the nation involved in the education of females in juvenile facilities? She decided that through the writing she could present all of these facets in a multidimensional telling. As Christine struggled with the meaning of what she was learning, she asked:

> Isn't it important to tell the story of one juvenile detention facility and the lives of these particular girls and their teachers' beliefs as a way to begin or continue a discussion about education in juvenile facilities? Does the fact that these students are young women and that I am a woman researcher have a particular impact on my interpretation of the teachers' perspectives? How will these young women's experiences in these classrooms affect their future lives?

Obviously, Christine's questions offer an example of the multiple stances that will influence what and how she writes about her data. Moreover she applies three lenses to her data. The labor of presenting these multiple stances through the writing has the effect of challenging her readers to consider their own perspectives. Additionally, such writing requires her to grapple with the multidimensional meaning for herself.

Christine consistently monitored her beliefs and how those influenced what she was learning through the writing, but she did more. She positioned herself as much as possible into various stances as a way to examine her data. She found feminist perspectives gave her a lens for analyzing the reactions of male and female teachers to the girls' behavior and performance. What is more, this lens helped her to consider the girls' responses to the classroom situation as it affected their concept of self and more particularly their concept of themselves as female. Christine wrote:

> One of the pregnant seventeen-year-olds, Larissa, told me that she saw herself as baggage to her family and herself. Larissa said that, 'girls can't get anywhere, you know Christine. Anybody, any time can put you down if you be a woman. Here, these teachers treat us like we're of no use.' Larissa prays she'll have a son who can 'whip those who try to take advantage. Men is stronger, you know. We women don't have the strength.' Larissa associates physical strength and gender with the lack of freedom and absence of control she has over her life.

Additionally, Christine's working knowledge of critical theory guided her analysis of the power relations and the resulting marginalization and silencing that resulted from the young women's status as 'law-breakers.' Noting that these adolescents were learning particular representations of themselves from the ways in which they were treated, Christine suggested that:

They take away from this classroom environment a message that they have no self-determinism. They are not learning how to take control of their lives from the education they receive in these classrooms, but how to give up voice completely and be controlled by other's demands. They are appreciated most when they do not deviate from direct and simple answers to content questions. Their only pro-active moves in this environment are in defiance, that is, behavior which results in disciplinary action.

Christine didn't stop with the feminist and critical lenses. She chose to write about her data from constructivist principles as well. Christine asked: 'What do these young women learn about how to solve conflict from their experiences in these classrooms? What knowledge do they gain about literacy acts (i.e., writing, reading, talking) as a way toward self-expression or self-reflection?' Christine analyzed the curriculum and the ways of thinking and making knowledge that were being promoted through it. She suggested:

> If the purpose of education is to promote producers of knowledge, then acts of literacy would need to be learned as tools to express that knowledge. These young women do not write; they study grammar. They do not read literature; they read excerpts for comprehension tests. They do not talk to one another about what they are learning; they fill in sheets to demonstrate what they have learned. Their thinking and imagining and creating have no place in this classroom environment.

In some ways the conscious presentation of multiple theoretical perspectives (though each is not entirely separable one from the other) does have the power to focus attention on a specific facet as each contributes to the complexities of the fuller experience. We think of this layering of interpretation or experience as a concrete example of what Homi Bhabha (1990) described as hybridity — that is, two or more perspectives, themes, ideas brought together to produce a new variety. Bhabha (1990) suggests that hybridity affects developing knowledge:

> For me the importance of hybridity is not to be able to trace two original moments from which the third emerges, rather hybridity to me is the 'third space' which enables other positions to emerge. (p. 211)

Hybridity is seen when the act of writing engenders various contextualizations of the data in order to yield different avenues of insight with the purpose of challenging, mixing, testing, and ultimately transgressing what the researcher or the reader 'knows.' Hybridity underscores new articulations of perspective by delimiting and determining how any one position might fail to explain a 'reality,' and might more essentially contain conceptual prisms through which we attempt to see into new spaces or, as Bhabha suggests, emerge into a third space.

As qualitative researchers we feel obligated to inform our readers of the positions we have taken as we collect, interpret, and write up reports. If such stories of stance can be told, the reader has multiple ways of seeing and thinking about what is being researched and the researcher's journey toward understanding. All this gives particular credence to the notion of being explicit with ourselves and others about the stances we take as researchers and of promising ourselves to monitor and report our stances as we best understand them throughout the gathering, the figuring, and refiguring, and on to final publication. That is most directly done through deliberate writing about stance throughout the process. Following are two stance statements that were written at the planning stages of research. Sarie Teichman studied people diagnosed with fibromyalgia who met in a mutual support group:

My Stance as Researcher

My interest in the experiences of people with fibromyalgia stems from very personal issues and a growing social concern about the health care industry and practices from the patient's perspective.

In this study with people with FMS, I am in some ways close to this population of the group. I was diagnosed with FMS two years ago after being incorrectly diagnosed with a series of autoimmune diseases, including Lupus and Rheumatoid Arthritis. I am in the process of finding effective treatments and medical personnel, as well as struggling with the changes to my life.

My participant role in this study may indeed be an asset. In fact, one theme I teased out in my preliminary study of people with FMS is their frustration and reluctance to go for outside help — to a counselor or therapist, for example, unless the person has actual experience working with FMS patients, or has the diagnosis him or herself.

However, while I am a member of their community, my experience diverges from the group in some important ways. First, as I begin this study, I have less distance from my own initial experiences. Some members of the group have had their disease for years, allowing time for more adjustment, growth, and reflection. Second, I am not as physically challenged as some members of the group. Many have more severe symptoms and less mobility. Third, I do not experience the multiple disease patterns prevalent in the group, another finding in my preliminary study.

As I am human, there are parts of this study that I may find difficult. It is hard not to feel some of the pain, both physical and psychic, that gets expressed in the group meetings and interviews. It is hard at times to look at people more disabled than I am and wonder if I will get like them, wonder how and if I could handle it, even experience some 'survival guilt' because my illness is not as bad. It is hard to feel their anger and frustration at a medical system that really is not as patient-oriented as it professes to be, that forces them to take control of their own care just when they need to be 'taken care of.'

I will be careful to try to be aware of these feelings. I plan to keep a separate journal about these issues for myself, and to write pertinent observer comments in my logs and analytic memos.

I come into this study with other biases. I am concerned with the fair treatment of patients in our society, and with doctors who are becoming so specialized that they can't see the forest for the trees. I have some anger at the mostly male-dominated medical profession that does not take as seriously women's health issues, and that despite evidence to the contrary still labels as hysteria some very real physical complaints. I believe this whittles away at women's images of themselves, as well as keeps women from valuable diagnoses and treatment. I'm angry at the lack of money being spent on research for FMS and other diseases, and finally, I'm angry that I have a disease for which there is no cure, and frustrated about the paucity of information and educational materials available to patients.

Another issue I must grapple with is my view of the meaning of illness. I was brought up with a 'survival of the fittest' philosophy. Sickness was a form of weakness — equated to a 'bad trait' — lower on the human scale than wellness. I know that I am not alone in this. There is still a societal view of disability as some sort of personal defect. Intellectually I see the flaws in this argument, and personally I am learning to let myself feel pain and not be less of a person for it. But deep down this could affect my lens on the experiences of others. Again, I will try to keep this, and my other potential biases, in tow by dealing with these issues in my journals, logs, memos, and with my dissertation support group.

Finally, throughout this study I will be very careful and conscious to keep in focus that mine is just one experience of FMS, one view. It is not the same for everybody. While there may be some common themes, each person's experience is unique, whether in circumstances, degree, or intensity. So I will make a real effort to bracket where I'm coming from, and not just look through my own eyes. I am committed to letting the words of the participants do the talking.

Sarie's statement of stance establishes at the onset that she comes to her research as a person who is diagnosed with the same disease that affects the people she intends to study. Phillip Johnson also talks of his relationship to the people and focus of study. He weaves into his stance his history as a black male and as a black male student as he discusses how his beliefs may have an impact on his research about the experience of six black men at a predominantly white university:

Personal Stance

For qualitative researchers, topics for research typically mesh intimately with their deepest professional and social commitments. In this instance, it is the story of my own attempt to obtain a formal education that largely determines the theoretical and philosophical approach I adopt in this study. I am a black male who was reared in a lower socio-economic, southern, African-American family. Neither of my parents managed to complete their high school education. While gender, racial, ethnic, economic, and social factors partially explain the level of my academic achievement over the years, it would be inaccurate to suggest that they have been the sole determinants or even the most influential. This is so because throughout my educational history I have maneuvered situations as best I could to attain the goals that were most important to me at the time. My conceptualizations of educational situations and the actions that flowed from them have been equally important determinants of my level of academic achievement, if not more so. Several examples will serve to clarify this point.

Although I had a desire to and actually did excel academically during my first three years of school, I also adopted the belief that schools controlled by white people could not be trusted. It was during my third grade year that the city decided to close my school in an effort to integrate the public school system. On the last day at my old school my third grade teacher gathered us into the auditorium, and told us 'No matter what happens don't let those white teachers tell you that you are not smart.' She then accompanied us on the piano as we sang the school song and then the Negro National Anthem, and I cried. I sensed on a deep level that my education was somehow inextricably entwined with the liberation of black people. On an intuitive level I understood that education was political and though I could not articulate it, I certainly felt it. White people were our enemies, our oppressors, and had to be resisted everywhere; most of all they had to be resisted in the classroom.

The tension around academics that I experienced was further heightened when all of the black students from my old school were assessed intellectually in order to determine proper grade placement. Thus many of my friends were required to repeat the third grade, while I was permitted to enter the fourth grade. The initial feeling of relief that I experienced gave way to a feeling of superiority; I felt smarter than my friends who were forced to repeat the third grade. This created a dilemma for me, however: if I excelled academically it meant leaving my friends behind. My friends were from the same place, ethnically and racially; I could depend on them. The same could not be said for the white teachers and students.

Upon arriving at the newly integrated school I concluded that I was in one of the two dumbest fourth grade classes in the school because those classes had the most black students. The class made up entirely of white students had to be the 'smart' class because no black students were in it. I felt the teachers didn't like me, and I didn't like them too much either. It was during that fourth grade year that I adopted a strategy to resolve the inner tension that I experienced in academics. I did only enough in school to pass each year, the bare minimum. To an outside observer such a strategy might seem totally irrational and short sighted. Some persons might even say that I collaborated with my oppressors. However, for me the minimum effort approach was a way to resist my white teachers and advance to the next grade level each year without alienating or losing my friends. My fifth grade teacher's comments for the first and second report periods were 'Phillip can and should do better work — he needs to try harder.' 'Phil is working well, I hope he keeps on trying.' But I applied myself only when I was in danger of failing.

My combined SAT score was below 700 and my high school guidance counselor, who happened to be black, told me that she was surprised to learn that I had performed as well as I had. My class rank was 265 out of 270, and by the time I reached college I was totally unprepared even for an institution that had an unselective admissions policy. I was so unsophisticated that the first college term paper I ever wrote, I typed in red ink. I earned a 1.2 and 1.4 that first year and seriously considered quitting college because I wasn't quite smart enough to do college work.

Contemplating my situation over the summer I decided to give it one more shot: if I didn't earn better grades this time I would quit. I promised myself that when I returned to campus that fall I would apply myself. My desire to excel academically became more powerful. During my sophomore year I earned grade point averages of 2.7 and 3.0. It was the bit of evidence that I needed to allow myself to go forward. I made steady progress for the remainder of my undergraduate education.

My high school record, standardized test scores and first year's grades in college all indicated that I was a weak student at best, and that the army, which had been suggested, would be a more realistic career choice for me than college.

To an outside observer my decision to return to college after that first semester may have seemed unrealistic, immature even, given the 'objective' evidence. However I could not accept the evidence: deep down I knew I could do better. Rather than quit college I decided to remain, to prove to myself that I could do it.

Whether employing a strategy of minimal effort, applying myself to my studies or rejecting an indictment of my ability, I have played an active and central role in my own education. It is my contention that all black men play an active role in determining the course that their education will take.

Studying a population that is very close to me personally has advantages and disadvantages. Since my background will be similar to some of the men I will interview, I should bring a certain level of sensitivity and understanding to the interviews and analysis. On the other hand, my personal familiarity with the subject matter could make it more difficult for me to pursue beyond the obvious, 'facts' which I already 'know' and take for granted. My loyalty to the black community and its members could also give rise to an impulse or desire to highlight those images which are favorable to black men. Ultimately, if I am to construct a human portrait of black undergraduate males, it is essential that I try to convey them, not as I or others would have them be. My tendency to do otherwise will be guarded against by using the strategies outlined in the trustworthiness section of this proposal.

Both of these researchers' statements serve less to dramatize or emotionalize — although they are dramatic and do arouse our emotions — than to describe clearly the lenses that Sarie and Phillip bring to their studies. We are privy to their pertinent history as well as to some of the strategies that they will put into place in an effort to counter bias — to be fair.

Such statements of stance are a help in several ways. In writing them, researchers come to terms with how and why they approach their studies as well as what needs watching. This look is both backward and forward. For their readers, the statements serve to introduce the researchers as people, interesting, fallible people, who are sufficiently open to share those issues and concerns that can be applied later as criteria for assessing the believability of the studies. How did Sarie work to counter her preconceived conclusions about the medical profession? How did Phil give voice to his participants when they provided him with views that were not particularly complimentary to them?

Both Sarie's and Phillip's statements were placed near the beginning of their research reports. They came around to stance again at the end in the final reflection piece. They reflected on themselves as researchers and shared highlights about what they learned from the process. On pages 21–2 is an excerpt from Elizabeth Merrick's final reflections on stance. There she writes of how her stance has changed. By so doing, she is providing her readers with a way to understand the vision that undergirds much of her presentation.

We've tried to make it clear that researchers interpret meaning from the data through many layers of understanding. For now, we'll highlight a few obvious and not so obvious stances that we believe influence the shaping of data and ones that we'd like to see made more explicit in the written reports of qualitative researchers.

Most obvious are the 'isms' — those beliefs (feminism, postmodernism, progressivism, constructivism, to name a few) that in formal and informal ways influence where people locate themselves in their responses to and interpretations of various situations, people, or events. These 'isms' have embedded within them certain ways of attending to the world and certain habits of mind that guide how the world is interpreted. For example, it is sometimes obvious through a person's response to a situation what beliefs guide them. To make clear how 'isms' may be implicated in the ways we interpret data, Ruth asked four researchers to read a scenario she'd written of a class period in a high school English classroom and write about their interpretations of what took place there. For context, here is Ruth's narrative:

Joe's Class Session

As the bell rings, students lean across aisles chatting with friends. A few open their binders. Fewer still are reading the story assigned for today, John Cheever's 'Torch Song.' As Joe walks to his podium, the chatter subsides and these twelfth grade students reach for notebooks. Joe begins: 'Let's start with a quiz. I'll ask four questions, so one sheet of paper will do.' Noticeable groans, shoulders shrug, and Ray sighs before he buries his head in his arms on the desktop. Joe asks the following questions: What was Jack's attitude toward Joan at the end of the story? What was Joan's most common way of helping the men in her life? Why did Jack lose his job? Where did Joan and Jack meet?

After students hand in the quiz, Joe asks: 'What did you think about Joan?' 'She's weird,' Jeff answers. 'Well, the guy has an overactive imagination,' Rita retorts. 'This lady is seriously weird,' Jeff persists.

Joe asks again. 'What about the rest of you? Is Joan weird? What makes you think so?' Stephanie answers, 'I wouldn't say weird. I thought she was mysterious.'

'Okay,' Joe says. 'Let's take some time to figure her out. I'd like you to get together in groups of four or five and sort this out, talk about it and see if you can come to some agreement. Then, get some quotes to support this and narrow what you're thinking into a simple statement about Joan. Make that statement into a cinquain. Do you remember the form? I want you to give a concentrated portrait and the cinquain is a way to give impact to your impression of Joan. Anyway, get together and start. There's butcher paper on the wall for the quotes and cinquains. If you have questions let me know.'

Joe walks over to Ray. 'Hey, Ray, are you feeling okay?' Ray lifts his head momentarily. Then slumps back to the desk top. Joe persists, 'I know you worked late but you need to get the work done. Come on, at least listen to the group. Do a quick read while they get started.' Ray grudgingly gets to his feet, surveys the groups, and gets in with four other boys.

Soon, one group is writing quotes on the graffiti wall. Denise writes in large green letters, 'It troubled Jack to see in these straits a girl who reminded him of the trees and the lawns of his home town' (Cheever, 1980, p. 58).

Jason finishes in bold red calligraphy, 'Her voice was sweet, and reminded him of elms, of lawns, of those glass arrangements that used to be hung from porch ceilings to tinkle in the summer wind' (p. 59).

Audrey and Bob leaf through the pages for another quote. 'Oh, here it is. Let's put this up.'

Bob begins to write in purple, 'She stood by the hat rack, bathed in an intense pink light and the string music of heartbreak, swinging her mane of dark hair' (p. 57).

Scrawled in black above, 'He began to think of her as The Widow . . . She always wore black' (pp. 56–7).

Again, in black: 'He had the impression that there had been a death there recently' (p. 60). Kate and Elizabeth finish writing this cinquain above all their quotes:

Black Joan

dealing slow death

caught in her serene web

lured by her despairing 'Torch Song'

Jack's trapped

To the side of their work, Andrea and Sue are searching for a final word for their cinquain:

Sweet Joan

a trail of men

nursing them through sickness

drugs, meanness, selfishness, greed, spite

'I've got it!' Sue yells as she scrawls:

Victim

'Perfect,' Andrea steps back to admire the work.

Joe brings the class back together. [Approximately 30 minutes were devoted to the discussion, quotes, group cinquain.] 'Now then,' he surveys the graffiti wall. 'So, what have you learned about this character?'

Sue starts. 'Andrea and I discussed how Jack is confused about how he feels from the first. He sees her as black and associated with the undertaker from the beginning. She's also serene and oblivious to the faults of the losers she's with . . . I think there is an attraction.'

Tony interrupts, 'But death is everywhere and Jack finally catches on. It reminded me of the knitting women in *Heart of Darkness*. She's just fate that he doesn't want to meet. Joan is death and that's dark and serene too.'

Joe sits on a stool, the graffiti on Joan as a backdrop.

'It's a beautiful set-up job. Cheever lures us into the trap. I admit it. I thought Jack and Joan would get together . . . You know, the happily ever after story. Weird. I didn't expect it to turn out the way it did.' Randy looks around for a reaction to what he has said.

Trina chimes in, 'What do you mean how it ends? I don't know what is going to happen to Jack. Will he die? The story ends while he's trying to escape.'

'Yeah,' Randy is thinking about it. 'Well I just assumed because he packed up and was getting out that he might escape her.'

Kate adds, 'At the end he's flushing nail clippings . . . wasn't it Pythagoras who believed if you left hair or nail clippings exposed the evil spirits could enter? I mean, he gets rid of all the signs.'

Lillian adds, 'It's just too, I mean like we don't know about those powers.'

Morgan asks, 'What was that deal with Pythagoras?'

Kate clarifies, 'Well it's just about superstitions, like we just don't know.'

Cyndi says, 'Well that's just the point. We don't know and that's the way Cheever wanted it.'

Joe ends, 'Think about how Cheever can make us feel so many ways at the same time. You've shown that here.'

The bell rings.

In response to the narrative reconstruction, four researchers offered their initial interpretations.

Researcher 1: Joe gives contradictory messages to students. The reading quiz (and he doesn't seem to know anything about higher level thinking) usurps the students' power to construct text. He turns around and gives that back in the graffiti wall activity. I'd suggest Joe is a teacher caught between two worlds and with one foot in each camp he can't decide which way to go. I suspect he would have a hard time explaining the purpose of each part and where he believes that students have a sense of autonomy and power in the class. He seems to be toying with the idea that the classroom is a place for students to control their own learning, but he doesn't really give them those opportunities. It is his agenda, his choice of reading, and his structuring of the assignment and class sequence. The power is clearly in his hands.

Researcher 2: Joe is very conservative as evidenced by the reading quiz that doesn't encourage individual interpretation, connections with life or experience or attention to literary conventions. He encourages a literal reading of text. The graffiti wall doesn't fit with that. I suspect he has read about it somewhere and finds it a way to get students talking but may not understand why he does it. The practice should support the theory and I can't think that having two opposing practices could be seen as complementary under any circumstances. The actual activity has some threads of reader response theory within it, but Joe doesn't know what to do with the knowledge that the students are constructing from the story. They have a narrow conception of Joan as a character that comes from the text of the story but not from any of their life experiences with people who might have similar qualities. What do the students bring to the assignment other than the text?

Researcher 3: Joe encourages student responses to literature with the graffiti wall. He follows that up nicely by clarifying what it is they are trying to make of the characters. From this scenario I'd say Joe is reader response oriented and interested in students' interpretations. The quiz seems a way to get students to read. The quiz is a training mechanism if it is used regularly then students know that the homework must be done and the teacher doesn't need to deal with that each time. Joe gets the students involved in making their own sense of the character by manipulating her qualities through their own language, that is, through the cinquain. He structures the class carefully to give ample time for students to come up with their own interpretations. In fact the bulk of class time is given to their small group work and the development of their own interpretations of the character of Joan.

Researcher 4: The structure of the graffiti wall is much too narrow. Students are not empowered to determine what in the story is meaningful to them. The quiz is further support of this. This is the classical case of a very traditional teacher hiding behind a bag of tricks. Joe does not seem conscious of the power he wields and even while he stands back and does not direct the class overtly during most of the period, he is clearly directing. It is a teacher-centered class still and the students are mostly pawns although seemingly happy and productive ones on the surface of things. The assignment focuses too narrowly on one aspect of the story. I believe the students carry away the wrong message about the relationship of parts in the story. Context. Context. Context. I keep saying. Joan cannot be dealt with as a separate entity for she is only part of a larger context and exists only as a constellation within the many constellations of the story.

Four readers. Four interpretations. Four different portraits of Joe, each based on the readers' assumptions and values related to their beliefs about learning and teaching and much more. We can hear in the language and in the perspectives some strains from the discourses of constructivism, critical theory, reader response, and even a touch of behaviorism. Obviously these readings truncate the meaning inherent in this one classroom scenario and all that can be made of it. Each is intended to demonstrate how embedded our stances are in what we see and say. Research reporting should and can keep pushing at the boundaries and reframing our researcher interpretations as we examine and make explicit our stances, but we need to monitor this through the writing all the way along.

Of course, these 'isms' are not entirely straightforward and least of all clear. The best we can suggest is that terms often serve to narrow and codify what is complex. Researchers can use labels narrowly in carrying out their studies and defining their stance or they can use labels as springboards to possibilities. The characteristics we hope for that go beyond any theory or 'ism' are open, flexible, contextually based, constructed, and collegial stances. And because labels set people off to create stereotypes and schisms, labeling often leads to extremes. Thus, labels must be watched carefully. Possibly thinking of the use of stances as constructed knowing, similar to the 'constructed knowing,' as identified by Belenky and her colleagues (1986), might help us to think about how to write stance into research reports. They identified five perspectives of how 'women know and view the world.' The most integrated and powerful perspective is called *constructed knowing*. This is a 'position in which women view all knowledge as contextual, experience themselves as creators of knowledge and value both subjective and objective strategies for knowing' (p. 15). This perspective may give us potent parallels for research writers' stances if we substitute the word 'writers' and 'researchers' for 'women'. Our stance in this book is that if qualitative researchers' writing demonstrates constructed knowing, the reader will be invited into reflectivity — into the worlds of the study and the researcher's thinking and feeling.

It's not only the 'isms' perspectives that we must write about but also how close or distant we are to the events in time, place, or commitment. For example, memory makes it possible to experience an event over and over again, to discover meaning from the original moment at various distances from the happening. The immediacy of living a moment and responding to events as they unfold elicits an intensity that has different aspects and consequences from the remembering. Then, there are experiences we understand from abstract knowledge, and often, conversely, we try to make connections with something familiar and concrete in order to articulate the abstract. Additionally, our understanding of events, situations, or persons is structured in advance by our previous experiences and our beliefs, blurred by a proclivity to generalize or stereotype or judge.

Through the writing, we qualitative researchers work on the edge of awareness, looking both outside and inward for sources of potential translation of *event* into *meaning*. Each moment is a pulling into or a pushing back from what is being examined. Mary Catherine Bateson's (1994) exploration of perspectives in *Peripheral Visions* has been helpful to us in reconsidering the habits of perception and attention that inform the work of qualitative researchers. Bateson suggests:

> It is important not to reduce understanding to some narrow focus, sacrificing multiplicity to what might be called the rhetoric of merely: merely a dead sheep, only an atavistic ritual, nothing but a metaphor . . . Openness to peripheral vision depends on rejecting such reductionism and rejecting with it the belief that questions of meaning have unitary answers . . . The process of spiraling through memory to weave connection out of incident is basic to learning. (1994, p. 11)

These perceptions that result from multiple layers of distancing are not only the private processes of the researcher. The researcher's modes of perception and consciousness resonate throughout the interpretation of the study and how it is written. We are trying to discover the various forms, the 'process of spiraling' that Bateson suggests, that influence how interpretation takes shape and is organized.

Distancing may not always have positive consequences. One quite common form of distancing is 'not seeing,' or 'editing out' what we may not choose to see. For example, the members of one support group — Susan Schlechter, Lori Berman Wolf, and Li Shen — discovered that they 'edited out' aspects of their field experiences from their fieldnotes. They found that this occurred most often when they were puzzled or embarrassed by particular incidents or when they did not want to validate occurrences that went against their sensibilities. As they wrote about their stances in memos, the problem surfaced and they could talk it through and determine a course of action that might be more productive.

Lori, a reading specialist, described how she used distancing techniques to avoid becoming too close to the fifth grade children and teacher in a classroom where she was learning what it is like to be a student, labelled gifted, in a public school setting. This type of distancing, she admits, has inherent problems:

> Distance can be an obstacle to being a good researcher. Coffee drinking was only the first distancing mechanism that I recognized in my research. Another way I kept my distance was by unconsciously omitting what I considered inappropriate participant behaviors from my log. I realized after the fact that I have censored my logs so as not to deal with sensitive issues like Violet dressing like she is on her way to a disco instead of a classroom. I have prevented myself in some ways from being intimate with the data. I'm learning that these distancing mechanisms have prevented me from becoming a better researcher. If we undertake to study human lives, we have to be ready to face human feelings.

In the case of these researchers, they found it important to monitor what they were editing out of their fieldnotes by reflecting on this through their writing. As Li suggested, 'Sometimes I avoid noticing because of my own intolerance or sense of values. That brings issues of trustworthiness and ethics into my desire to create an honest representation.' What they gave themselves was a record that they could use at a later date when they were trying to account for their various stances in written reports of their studies.

Mark Lipton found via his reflection that his physical placement in the room made an impact on how he wrote his fieldnotes:

> I am so conscious of where and how I'm feeling and can't help believing that my personal state of mind affects what I am observing. Even my very position in the room can alter my experience. I was constantly questioning this. For example, I attempted to change the place I sit in the hope of seeing new and different things. Perhaps it would have been more beneficial to try to keep the same seat, so that I always had the same physical point of view. I still am not sure of an answer; this is what I mean, in part, when I say I still have many questions.

What Mark did do subsequently was to try to record, as best he understood it, what each location provided to him. Mark understands that something as seemingly subtle as his position in the room influences what he sees, what he writes down, and how he interprets what is going on. Another conundrum not voiced but implicit in this excerpt, at least by our reading of what Mark said, is that he struggles to get the entire picture — all of the data at all times.

Mark's desire was to create reality and it took him some time to understand that one reality just doesn't exist:

> I attempted to keep my log as simple and as clear as possible. I felt so restricted by language and was so keenly aware of the words I chose. For example, I could write she 'asked,' 'requested,' or 'demanded' all to mean the same thing but each illustrated my feeling of a given situation.

Mark seems to be saying that he was burdened by his awareness of the crucial aspect of language choices. We've found that such awareness can indeed prod, push, and worry. That is happening as we write this book! It can also move us forward to write in ways that come closest to our intended meanings at any particular time.

Priscilla Butler, in a reflective memo about her study of adult students in one English as a Second Language (ESL) classroom, brings up another issue related to stance. She describes how difficult it is to determine her role as researcher in the lives of others and to write about that effectively:

> Yes, sometimes I feel like a spy. In my second log (and in my third, fourth, fifth . . .), I write: 'Once again, as I sit in the class, I feel some pressure . . . I feel out of place, especially as more and more students enter and the room fills with conversation. I try to think about how I should act. I am divided between the roles of researcher (as I perceive it) and of stranger in a public place. I hate feeling like a snooper or eavesdropper.' These types of observations are interspersed throughout my log entries. When students were discussing their private lives or things that had happened to them outside of class, I felt very strange watching and listening to them from across the room. I felt so uncomfortable that I would shift my eyes

away if someone noticed me looking. I even deliberately tried not to hear on a couple of occasions. How do I write this up honestly in the reports?

As Priscilla continued to write, she began to describe the system of beliefs that informs her feelings in a personal narrative that she wrote about her early life experiences:

> In fact, it was drilled into me from the time I was a young child that it's impolite to listen and look when someone is not directly addressing me. Perhaps the experience which implanted this lesson most rigidly in my mind, though, occurred when I was about ten years old . . . I remember that this girl came along, and she and her friends were also relaxing in the shade of the trees, and I was looking at her. I remember that she wore brick-colored cotton pants and had long, black hair, and was very big. Then, she suddenly turned to me and said, 'What are you looking at?' I wasn't sure how to answer this question, and soon everyone else got involved. My brothers came to my defense and things got resolved without fighting, but I remember at the end, when the other people had left, we discussed what had happened. At first, my brothers were all on my side, but then when they asked me whether I had really been looking at her as she had accused, and I said that I thought so, my oldest brother said, 'Well, you shouldn't have been looking at her.' The first girl I had been staring at happened to be Mexican, and this probably made the situation more sensitive than it otherwise might have been. All I knew from this scene, though, was that it's dangerous to stare: that staring is like a challenge, a call to fight.

Many subtleties, then, affect our stances, from the ambiguous roles of the researcher as participant and observer to the tacit assumption that the researcher is able to study other cultures. Stances certainly complicate the relationships and blur the boundaries and assist us in accepting various organizing concepts and claims to authority. Sometimes we move the lens too slightly and focus too firmly, looking for the villains or the heroes in our data. Stances which are too narrow do not allow the research project to breathe. It is a matter, as Stegner's character Lyman found, of being able to articulate the angles of repose. Lyman becomes fully aware of his perspectives both intellectually and through sensation. Even from his wheelchair, he has the power to move himself into new perspectives:

> I pushed back from among the sun-dazzled papers and rotated my chair. Two years' practice has not fully accustomed me to the double sensation that accompanies wheelchair locomotion. Above, I am as rigid as a monument; below, smooth fluidity. I move like a piano on a dolly. Since I am battery-powered, there is no physical effort, and since I cannot move my head up, down, or to either side, objects appear to rotate around me, to slide across my vision from peripheral to full to opposite peripheral, rather than I to move among them. The walls revolve, bringing into view the casement windows, the window seat, the clusters of wisteria outside; then the next wall with photographs of Grandmother and Grandfather, their three children, a wash drawing of the youngest, Agnes, at the age of three . . . and then the spin slows and I am pointed toward the door with the sunlight stretching along the worn brown boards. (Stegner, 1971, p. 20)

We need to be vigilant about how the language and method of analysis situate our movement, our spins, our revolutions, and our peripheral visions as we collect and write up our studies. To look and to see, to see and to gaze — all the work of researchers. But, the stance in looking, seeing, and gazing must have in it some desire to faithfully represent through the writing what we think is happening while at the same time remaining open to other explanations. A difficult call all the way around.

Telling Moments

It does well for qualitative researchers to keep in mind some essential ideas. So far this chapter has been about those ideas. In this section we'll first touch on several key distillations. Next we'll consider some issues about getting started. As the book develops we will cycle back in several ways to all of these critical considerations.

Qualitative researchers are interested in telling, and are often consumed by the need to present their stories of research as an ongoing journey. Their writings must, therefore, reflect the process of research — the character and foundational beliefs of the original conceptual framework as well as the evolving one, considerations on the stumblings, in-progress victories, insights and puzzlements of the researcher as the research unfolds, disclosure of the researcher's stance and limitations as well as descriptions of the successes and failures of the ongoing stories of multiple meaning making. So, the process *is* the product.

In this sense, qualitative research reports are more analogous to movies than photographs. Part of the job of a qualitative researcher is to portray the dynamic and telling moments as fully and poignantly as possible. And just as movie makers leave most of the film takes on the editing room floor, so qualitative researchers have the often gut-wrenching job of selecting far fewer data pieces to write with, about and to than they leave behind — all this while simultaneously working to create a final report that communicates the wholeness of their vision.

The movie analogy seems apt in other ways. A good movie engages viewers, involves them in considering what the director has chosen to spotlight, leaves them open to create other plot possibilities, to wonder what was not shown, and to analyze the presentation. A good movie shows, not tells, and involves the viewer in living the emotional life, settings, and action. Just so, a 'good' qualitative research report draws the readers into the life events and the interpretation of what those may mean. What is more, a good movie is an experiment in forms and while it nests within a history of other cinematic forms, the director creates new ways of showing, of moving the plot ahead, of juxtaposing events, characters, and sequences. Some movies start in medias res; others are structured as a story within a story. Films rely on many of the traditional devices of narrative — flashback or flash forward, silence, pacing and momentum, a close focus on particular scenes. Possibly we've been thinking of qualitative research writing as still photography for too long. We anticipate that qualitative researchers will need to become skilled in the crafting of narrative and will need to develop a repertoire of strategies and forms for reporting research. You'll find an elaboration of these ideas in our next chapter.

Another characteristic of qualitative research writing is that it emphasizes subjectivities as an integral part of the research process. It follows that totally cool, distanced and distancing research writing would be alien to what qualitative research is all about. It is our task to write in order to communicate people's emotions, their life cycles, and how researchers face what they learn about themselves and others in the process of the research. This is not to say that qualitative research writing focuses solely on emotions. Indeed, useful products present data and interpretations through a variety of lenses — from the very intimate to the very abstract. It is the inclusion of the personal and emotional that is sometimes difficult in the world of academia where emotional and intuitional aspects of research have long been denied, suppressed, and considered suspect if not unworthy.

So! We are left with a situation that calls for particularly sensitive, personal and creative ways of writing by researchers who must take courageous leaps of daring and imagination. Sometimes this is coupled with less support than is needed or wanted. We have a hunch that the litmus test for qualitative researchers is their dedication, passion-seen-as-stubbornness, and grasp. Perhaps and as important, we'll need a litmus test of institutions and the understanding, intelligence, and support that the people therein can provide to qualitative researchers — fledgling and more seasoned. How fortunate to be in a situation where such understanding and support work in tandem with qualitative research stances, indeed with all research stances.

We have known many people who are deeply given to qualitative research and also deeply given to facing and overcoming their institutional odds so that they may do their research and present it 'how it should be.' In this, we are all pioneers. Being a pioneer can be hard, lonely, and frustrating but eventually more gratifying in spite of the minuses. If qualitative research is your fire and flame, you have no choice but to follow your lead. Thus, a dilemma. Recognizing that there are many ways to tell the story of research is one thing. Doing it effectively is quite another. The more we work with the writing of qualitative research from the first fledgling fieldnotes and attempts at making sense of the research, the more we are convinced that the entire endeavor often gets mired in our lack of trust for the process. Part of this probably results from the vestiges of doubt that remain from the positivist mentality that has been drummed into so many of our heads for so long. We can foreground the process and describe various crafting devices and strategies that can bring lifeless reports to life. What is infinitely harder is to help you trust that such writing is valuable and valued, both for you as a researcher and for those reading your reports.

And then, there is the business of getting started.

> Life is not fair. Here I sit after having written my fingers to the bone! Fieldnotes, marginalia, analytic memos, tentative categories, themes, letters, notes to my support group, interview transcripts. Name it. I've written it all. What do you mean that now it is time for me to write the final report? Aren't 678 log pages enough? (Belén Matías)

Ah! Haven't we all felt this way? Haven't we all planned a trip to Paris at this particular juncture? Anything but to face the pages yet once more. But it is precisely because we have 678 log pages — or 536 — or 2,241 for that matter — that we must now head into the final writing. 678 is not enough. It is too much. It is true that many of us find wondrous ways to avoid beginning. Priscilla Butler writes:

> In looking back at the past few weeks, I have to say that I've been in nothing less than an intense state of malaise about everything — especially writing about this research project. A major part of my malaise goes back to the uncertainty of my future — an uncertainty which drives me crazy at times while, at others, just makes me want to climb under a rock and wait out the waiting. In some ways, avoiding what needs to be done is like climbing under a rock. My evenings with the television and my sudden obsession with early birthday shopping for all family members seem to be ways of hiding. Ways that aren't always successful though.

Many of us fall into this particular pattern at times. Anne Lamott (1994) shares a pertinent anecdote about her father and brother as the boy sat paralyzed when attempting to write a report:

> Thirty years ago my older brother, who was ten years old at the time, was trying to get a report on birds written that he'd had three months to write, which was due the next day. We were out at our family cabin in Bolinas, and he was at the kitchen table close to tears, surrounded by binder paper and pencils and unopened books on birds, immobilized by the hugeness of the task ahead. Then my father sat down beside him, put his arm around my brother's shoulder, and said, 'Bird by bird, buddy. Just take it bird by bird.' (p. 19)

Lamott next describes how she approaches her own writing:

> Say to yourself in the kindest possible way, Look, honey, all we're going to do for now is to write a description of the river at sunrise, or the young child swimming in the pool at the club, or the first time the man sees the woman he will marry. That is all we are going to do for now. We are just going to take this bird by bird. (p. 20)

This quote struck a chord with us, because we too have found, and so have others, that we are not the secure, mature people we'd like to be. Here comes that baby again, mewling because she'd rather go out and play. Here come these doubts. Here come those fears. We've concluded that qualitative research writing brings out our most rocky characteristics as well as our most sturdy. This is certainly so for us at the final writing time. It is acceptable to meet one's less desirable selves in the act of writing. Often they can be understood better. Sometimes they can be reshaped. The more desirable selves are nice for balance, believe us.

Now, how to move on? The trick here seems to be to find something to write about and to do it quickly without too much agonizing. Harry Wolcott (1990) makes suggestions for some jump starts. As Rhonda Weller Moore pointed out: 'One of the most helpful things I read was Wolcott's recommendation to "just do it." Just getting something on paper made it so much easier to begin to work with the data.'

Other jump starts include beginning with an anecdote about a highlight of the work — any highlight — a la Max Van Manen's (1990) ideas. Here is one written by Laurie Holder in her study of a Board of Directors:

> I suddenly heard a loud thud and a gasp from someone in the audience. I look over to see Ken, pushing up from the floor, his somewhat bulky shape pushing himself up from behind the Board's table, looking far more embarrassed than injured. He righted his chair, reseated himself, and sat for a time with his elbows planted firmly on the table in front of him, playing with a pencil and staring straight ahead. Then he bowed his head, put a hand in front of his face, and stared down at the surface of the table. He alternated these actions for quite a while, as if embarrassed by his fall.

Or, write a poem. This one by Rhonda Weller Moore was crafted from an interview transcript with Mim who lived in an adult day care facility:

> You could be me you know
> with gnarled up legs that don't go
> and twisted fingers that can't walk
> anywhere let alone the Yellow Pages.
> I used to think a button, signing my name,
> feeding myself, pulling down my pants to
> pee was a piece of cake.
>
> You could be me you know
> but he didn't give it to YOU
> He gave it to me. Now my kisses
> are twisted and the legs I used to wrap
> around his on lazy mornings
> before are wrapped in bracing
> chains by him around mine. I used
> to wear pretty clothes, you know, not
> sweatpants and sneakers and a bib
> for every day of the week. Damn
> that the brain still works and the only
> thing worse than the pain your eyes
> won't see is the sadness in his
> I can't take away, I can't take away,
> You could be me,
> you know.

Or, write a poem about yourself such as the one created by Barbara Goddard in which she grapples with her view of writing:

> I
>
> Coals embered on a craggy rock ledge
>   whiten precariously near a chasm called Learning.
> Slowly, they smolder, relentless and reaching,
>   while stinging and sifting each truth over truth,
>   dusting them over, all ashened and grey.

II

Dark questioning eyes, unclear, water
  as fires, licking, shot up,
    transformations of thought
      deepened dreams and desire,
        lifting upward and inward,
          each, intense and aflame . . .

III

Though mind-blinded, but new-visioned,
  strange lenses appear; and beginning,
    they focus, refocus; and, then,
      squinting doubtfully at past
        and leering at present,
          they are caught, rapt, distracted,
by feet, tiny and thin,
  teetering out at the edges,
    so dangerously near,
      enticed by strange dancing
        and spiralling limits,
mental music and searching
  and searching and searching,
    both discovering and re-covering,
      re-constructing the 'self.'

IV

Advice to the initiate:
  Be careful where you step.
  The pit is deep.
  And one fire does, inevitably, fuel another.

Or, write a scene from or outline of a television episode that would dramatize part of what you have studied.

    Or, write a brief account in first person from the vantage point of one of your participants.

    Or, return to your log, reread a number of pages, and write about your thoughts and feelings. Throughout this book we'll describe additional ways of getting into final writing. For now, suffice it to say that the big idea is — get started.

    Or, select one of the many strategies suggested in the next chapter.

    Lest we leave you hanging at that imperative, let us share how we get started writing. This *circle diagram* (Figure 2.2) presupposes that we've done much writing, reflecting, analyzing, and rewriting from the time that the idea of the research first hit. Now, time in the field is ebbing while work away from field must swell. This diagram presupposes also that you may have a different way to begin. Fine. There are probably as many ways as there are writer's moods. Please write to us and share your ways.

Figure 2.2: *A way of starting*

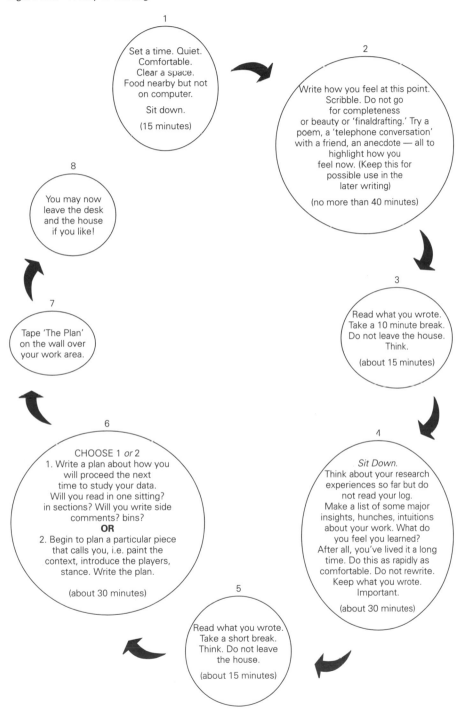

1
Set a time. Quiet.
Comfortable.
Clear a space.
Food nearby but not
on computer.

Sit down.

(15 minutes)

2
Write how you feel at this point.
Scribble. Do not go
for completeness
or beauty or 'finaldrafting.' Try a
poem, a 'telephone conversation'
with a friend, an anecdote — all to
highlight how you
feel now. (Keep this for
possible use in the
later writing)

(no more than 40 minutes)

8
You may now
leave the desk
and the house
if you like!

7
Tape 'The Plan'
on the wall over
your work area.

3
Read what you wrote.
Take a 10 minute break.
Do not leave the house.
Think.

(about 15 minutes)

6
CHOOSE 1 *or* 2
1. Write a plan about how you
will proceed the next
time to study your data.
Will you read in one sitting?
in sections? Will you write side
comments? bins?
OR
2. Begin to plan a particular piece
that calls you, i.e. paint the
context, introduce the players,
stance. Write the plan.

(about 30 minutes)

4
Sit Down.
Think about your research
experiences so far but do
not read your log.
Make a list of some major
insights, hunches, intuitions
about your work. What do
you feel you learned?
After all, you've lived it a long
time. Do this as rapidly as
comfortable. Do not rewrite.
Keep what you wrote.
Important.

(about 30 minutes)

5
Read what you wrote.
Take a short break.
Think. Do not leave
the house.

(about 15 minutes)

One student, it remains a mystery who she is but we do know it is a she, provided us with the following proverb that may be of consolation to us all. Our friend Zoraida Soliman-Cyr went to great lengths to hunt down its source, and as far as we can tell it is known as 'a popular Hebrew proverb' although also found in Italian Proverb books, Spanish usage, and the Oxford Dictionary of English Proverbs as far back as 1530 (see Figure 2.3). It certainly must speak to many people. It does to us:

Figure 2.3: 'A popular Hebrew proverb'

כל התחלות קשות

difficult (are) beginnings All

And while we agree that all beginnings are difficult, all of us can benefit from some of what others before us have learned. Start by reminding yourself of the power of selective attention. Trust that you have become purposeful and skillful during the proccss of making sense of what you've studied. Allow the tentative nature of initial drafts to guide you and know that with each retelling the terrain will shift and change as new insights surface and take shape. The ongoing, swampy and often shifting written narrative of the research is not reality, but a representation of that — a highly selective, virtually constructed understanding of what you have penetrated by being there and listening, writing, thinking, interpreting carefully and thoughtfully. Yes, take pains to present the experiences, but don't be afraid to create from your data. Yes, think about ways to bring out the life and drama in the data. Start with an incident you've been mulling over and talking to yourself about. Ask questions: What details condense, exemplify, or evoke the world of the research? As you read, be on the lookout for examples of qualitative research narrative that will illustrate the possibilities of carrying readers into the research.

Clifford Geertz (1988) suggests that we need to 'convince our readers that we have actually penetrated (or been penetrated by) another form of life, of having, one way or another truly "been there"' (pp. 4–5). We work to build our own sense and our readers' sense of awareness in a cumulative effect that develops through the texts patterns and devices. We work to create the movement of thought — the images, feelings, and associations stirred by the text as it unfolds.

Chapter 3

Creating Forms; Informing Understanding

White. A blank page or canvas.
The challenge: bring order to the whole.
Through design.
Composition.
Tension.
Balance.
Light.
And harmony.
(Sondheim and Lapine, 1991, pp. 17–18)

This chapter presents a closer look at the working parts; the forms, rhetorical and literary devices, and layouts, which can configure meaning in writing. We say working parts precisely because the forms we discuss here are integral rather than add-ons. They have purpose and provide the techniques through which writers describe, shape, and emphasize their meanings. So what we hope to demonstrate in this chapter are the relations between form and meaning, the agents of representation and evocation, and the various devices that guide the reader.

Forms shape the subject matter to enrich meaning and understanding. Form and function are connected, and the examples given throughout this chapter are intended to help you and us understand the nature of these connections more fully. Although we have started to struggle with how various written forms affect meaning, we've also come to recognize how difficult this is to explain. Traditional forms, as well as imaginative transformations and blurrings, guide textual production in ways that puzzle and exhilarate us at the same time. Indeed, we have received our share of bumps and bruises as we have tilted at these windmills. As we learned about the choices involved in giving form to subject, it became harder to divide form, function, meaning, and understanding. It has not been easy to select, define, and describe particular modes of representation that give shape to the experiences in the field.

What we say and suggest here is based in part on some of the ideas we presented in Chapter 2, 'What is There about Writing?' In Chapter 5, we delve more deeply than we do here into theorizing representation. However, we want to emphasize that what seems a simple act of choosing form is integral to analysis and interpretation. Form shapes meaning.

Please note that many of the forms we suggest are literary tools — genres, organizational structures, and rhetorical and narrative devices. Some have been with us since the first spoken and written words. Our upcoming sections on narrative, drama, metaphor, and poetry do not claim that these are new ways to represent meaning. Instead, we are suggesting a break from a tight definition of 'scholarly' presentation as many of us have come to know it. This seems particularly important for people who have not already been mentored by the many already existing texts that work against the linear and stultifying, as well as for people who feel painfully constricted by what they believe, mistakenly, is the 'only' way to write about research. They are not only students:

> ... the new ethnography and some feminist critical approaches pose similar challenges to positivism by unmasking modern, Western structures of knowledge and discourse and hegemonic modes of representation. Both seek to reveal the political foundations of knowledge, to shatter lines of authority in texts, and to create liberatory narrative forms. (Linden, 1993, p. 4)

When we talk of research writing, our position is broader than the two stances of new ethnography and critical feminism cited above. However, our views and suggestions about writing are firmly based on the following tenets that might also be acceptable to people from a wide variety of positions on the spectrum of qualitative research. Said one way:

1 There is no single way for us to come to know something.
2 There is no one way for us to report.
3 Our messages are not neutral.
4 Our language does not merely mirror reality.
5 The researcher is not separate from what and who is being studied. Research is not context-culture free.
6 Affect is not separate from cognition.
7 What we understand as social reality is not neat, linear and fixed.

Said better the other way around:

1 There are many ways to come to know something and even then such knowing is partial.
2 There are numerous ways for us to report.
3 All of our messages have agendas.
4 Our language creates reality.
5 The researcher is deeply interrelated with what and who is being studied. Research is context-culture bound.
6 Affect and cognition are inextricably united.
7 What we understand as social reality is multifaceted, sometimes clashing, and often in flux.

Atkinson (1992) sums up what we've tried to say here about research presentation when he talks of the crux of many contemporary research approaches:

> ... radical questioning of the certainty and authority of the scholarly text; a rejection of the search for 'truth' and reason as absolutes; a rejection of the moral and

intellectual distance between the academic and his or her human 'subjects'; a suspicion of the 'big' narratives of totalizing theory. (p. 38)

In one sense, when we open ourselves up to how these tenets actualize themselves in writing research there is often such relief at the sudden freedom, such surprise at the invitation to create, such grappling with the awesome responsibilities about self in the process, and such joy at finding one's resurrected passion, that the important point may be overshadowed. It must not be. Vehemently said: the shapes and content of research presentation must not be chosen primarily to amuse, shock, or entertain, although they often do. Certainly they must not be chosen to manipulate. The overriding aims must be to make ongoing meaning for ourselves and to communicate that meaning with people in order to involve them in thinking about and living our research experiences. That is the heart of this chapter.

Actually these aims are not unique to this or any other time in the development of rhetorical conventions. We do not intend to set up a dichotomy of 'conventional' versus 'unconventional' writing. Such dichotomies rarely work. Think of the time and energy so many of us have devoted to countering a popular but false dichotomy of qualitative versus quantitative research when we might have worked to clarify more productively their real distinctions and similarities. We know quite well that so-called 'conventional' research writing of every ilk runs the gamut from fascinating to deadly. And we know quite well the dangers — the beliefs and pressures — that prod qualitative research writing to gravitate toward the deadly side of that continuum. We present possibilities of form and function to remind ourselves and you that various forms allow very different meanings and emphases because of the different conventions each uses.

Authors from a number of disciplines — sociologists, anthropologists, archaeologists, literary theorists, playwrights, poets, screen and fiction writers — consider how to present their work through a variety of forms and by choosing carefully the rhetorical devices that best elicit their intended meaning. However, as is true of many advances, knowledge about or acceptance of changing conventions is uneven. There may be, and indeed there are, seasoned qualitative researchers, faculty, qualitative researchers-to-be, editors, publishing reviewers and readers to whom it is a new idea that research writing can be presented in a variety of forms.

In the context of this chapter, it was of great interest to us to find that Sigmund Freud grappled with the question of form over a hundred years ago:

I have not always been a psychotherapist. Like other neuropathologists, I was trained to employ local diagnoses and electro-prognosis, and it still strikes me as strange that the case histories I write should read like short stories, and that, as one might say, they lack the serious stamp of science. I must console myself with the reflection that the nature of the subject is evidently responsible for this, rather than any preference of my own. The fact is that local diagnosis and electrical reactions lead nowhere in the study of hysteria, whereas a detailed description of mental processes such as we are accustomed to find in the works of imaginative writers enables me, with the use of a few psychological formulas, to obtain at least some kind of insight into the course of that affection. Case histories of this kind are intended to be judged like psychiatric ones; they have, however, one advantage over the other, namely an intimate connection between the story of the patient's sufferings and the symptoms of his illness — a connection for which we still search in vain in the biographies of other psychoses. (1893–95, pp. 160–1)

While what Freud describes seems shot through with his reliance on 'a few psychological formulas' and an underlying message that one set of answers can be discovered, what he shares is wonderful for several reasons. It is courageous. It flies in the face of what then must have been even more fixed views of what is acceptable as scholarly writing. Freud followed where his intuition led him, where the 'nature of the subject' became more telling than any of his preferences. Or so he says. Our hunch is that he did not deny his preferences as much as he intimates. But then, who are we to analyze the father of psychoanalysis? In any case, our reading of his sentence is subjective and contextual. We see it in our time and with our experience. Probably most important, Freud highlights that writing in particular ways helps him to obtain insight about what he is studying. That, as we may have emphasized too often, is the purpose of much of writing.

Freud's thinking on the subject of writing-as-inquiry may place him ahead of what was conceived as the purpose of writing by the majority of the academic community of his time. Writers of literature, of course, have long trusted that through the 'telling' of story both teller and listener would learn. From the beginning of time both audience and the communal fire served as contexts for narrating the lives and ideas of possibility. But Freud is a different case. Imagine how he might have ventured forward in these hundred years from suggesting the importance of story in his 'case' to what he might have produced as story if he had lived and plied his profession to this point in time. For instance, Susanne Langer (1953) noted that in his preface to the third edition of *Traumdeutung* (1913), Freud observed that in the future the book should be revised 'to include selections from the rich material of poetry, myth, usage of language [idiom], and folklore' (p. 239). So by 1913, Freud had already greatly expanded his 1895 vision about presentation.

In this chapter we have selected to focus on a variety of writing forms as exemplars of what is available to qualitative research writers. The forms on our 'menu' have been especially helpful to a wide variety of qualitative researchers in illuminating aspects of their inquiry research process as well as in creating publishable writing. However, these forms do not constitute the entire group of possibilities. We choose to be more provocative than encyclopedic, more complex than superficial in how we describe and discuss these forms. While we urge you to try the forms suggested here, we trust that you will create your own or find others in the literature that will serve your research presentation. Sometimes the forms we describe stand alone. Sometimes they are woven into the larger text to illustrate, foreshadow, or contrast.

Today, as we write this book, we offer the view that research presentation can be multifaceted and multiformed. It can be composed of many examples of literary traditions and technical and rhetorical devices. It can be 'finished' or more 'open,' it can play, demand, question, and offer insights. But in all of this, it must be created with purpose and commitment to that purpose.

Narrative Turns

Ways of understanding are integrated works of art created by many minds, like cathedrals, as much masterpieces of the human spirit as the Greek tragedies or the paintings of the Renaissance. Human beings construct meaning as spiders make webs — or as appropriate enzymes make proteins. (Mary Catherine Bateson, 1994)

Often meaning is constructed through story. We can only speculate upon the rich ways of understanding, the infinite and curvilinear mindwork that cradled Mary Catherine, the child of Gregory Bateson and Margaret Mead, as she learned and imagined. 'Perception, attention, grace, all of these, varied or sustained, provide materials for constructing both self and world, and patterns for joining in the dance' (Bateson, 1995, p. 235). Bateson explains that as a child she was encouraged to tell stories that she dictated to her mother. In one of her narratives, 6-year-old Catherine composes an analogue of learning. The story goes like this:

Once upon a time there was a sad, dreary kingdom that had no colors . . . But after a while the king and queen of that kingdom had a baby girl, and she seemed different from all the other children of the kingdom . . . She went and sat in the queen's lap and said, 'Look into my eyes and tell me what you see.' 'Why, you have beautiful gray eyes,' said the queen, 'as pale gray as egg yolks or lettuce leaves.' 'No,' she said, 'look more deeply.' They sat for long minutes, and finally the queen said, 'I see something I have never seen before. And what I see is different from egg yolks or lettuce leaves.' So the princess said, 'What you see is called blue. If you look now at an egg yolk, you will see that it is yellow, and the lettuce leaves are green.' (pp. 46–7)

'Look more deeply,' the baby girl reminds us. Her narrative provides one story of the legacy of recognition. In seeking to comprehend blue, we are, of course, inevitably engaged in a circle of learning to 'read' yellow and green and whatever other circles of reappropriation come from deeper or peripheral looking. Through her narrative, the reader is invited to participate in the story of this recognition.

Whether we tell stories to each other of what happened, rehearse what will happen, or invent what we wish had happened, the pervasiveness of story emphasizes our need to tell 'Once upon a time' versions of experience. Story surrounds us. We hear stories through newscasts, read them in the newspaper — in the form sometimes of economic projects or stock market tables. A scientific equation tells a story. Most theorizing does. Albert Einstein reportedly storied himself travelling alongside a beam of light at 186,000 miles per second to reformulate the electromagnetic theory. Story is presented through visual representations of all types — film, television, cartoons, billboards, and advertisements. Speeches are often stories. Imagine having been in the audience when Abraham Lincoln began his 287 word story at Gettysburg: 'Fourscore and seven years ago . . .' — another version of 'Once Upon A Time' through which we are invited to live again the founding of a nation. Story can enable us to move through events leading up to World War II through the eyes of Trudi, a dwarf, in Ursula Hegi's novel *Stones from the River* (1994). In this stunning novel, we readers experience the beginning of Trudi Montag's desire not to

be different, the 'agony of being different, and the sin of ranting against an ineffective God' (p. 9). We are taken on a whirlwind journey through the times when
she will:

> ... pull her mother from the earth nest beneath the house; dismantle a section of
> the stone wall in the cellar and dig a secret dirt tunnel to the Blaus' house; stroke
> her lover's back with both hands, and feel the fine oval of hairs at the base of his
> spine as the night sky swirled around them; recoil from the heat of the flames that
> spurted from the broken windows of the synagogue and showered the school and
> the Theresienheim with sparks the color of the fabric star, *Judenstern*, that her
> friend, Eva Rosen, would have to wear on her coat. (p. 11)

It isn't only the story itself that makes this novel compelling. Rather, as various
reading theorists have pointed out (Iser, 1980 and Eco, 1979), story has power partially because of the rhetorical devices that writers use which allow their readers to
enter into a vicarious experience. That is, of course, what we hope to demonstrate
— how writers of research might construct stories in ways that bring readers into
the settings, characters, actions, dialogue and events of the research story using many
of the same devices that other writers of narrative employ. Given that the experience
and meaning we take from research projects are reconstructed into a text, the rear-
rangement of events — that is, the compressing, emphasizing, ignoring, and sequenc-
ing — and the narrative aspects of story help us as research writers to create
vicariously lived and realistically comprehended stories of what was researched.

'Stories' in the previous sentence is a carefully chosen word. We don't believe
stories are exclusively the stuff of imagined reality or the well-turned fabulistic
tale. Stories constitute lived stories, individual and collective, retold and reconstrued.
In this section of the chapter, you will read research stories and be encouraged to
write them. Various tools of narrative — characters, setting, sequences of events,
atmosphere, plot, theme, dialogue, motifs, figurative language, and many other
literary devices — render the stories complex and significant. Storytellers learned
long ago that such devices have the power to bring the reader along on a voyage
of sorts. As researchers we have something to learn from them: the means to let our
readers experience along with us the unfolding of the research story. Barbara Hardy
(1978) has said that narrative is:

> ... a primary act of the mind. [There is an] inner and outer storytelling that plays
> a major role in our sleeping and waking lives ... for we dream in narrative, day-
> dream in narrative, remember, anticipate, hope, despair, believe, doubt, plan, revise,
> criticize, construct, gossip, learn, hate, and love by narrative. In order really to live,
> we make up stories about ourselves and others, about the personal as well as the
> social past and future. (p. 12)

Narrative is a method of inquiry and a way of knowing — a discovery and
analysis — just as scientism and quantitative research have methods and ways. As
Clandinin and Connelly (1994) have pointed out, they '... use the reasonably
well-established device of calling the phenomenon *story* and the inquiry *narrative*.
Thus we say that people by nature lead storied lives and tell stories of those lives,

whereas narrative researchers describe such lives, collect and tell stories of them, and write narratives of experience' (p. 416). We might think of narrative as a bundle of elements useful in storying — structures, points of view, spatial and temporal devices, characters, plots, themes, and, of course, a narrator or narrators. The particular version of the story is located in some partial knowledge so we cannot say that narrative reflects *a reality* but we can say that, with the help of the reader, narrative produces meaning and *creates a version of reality*. The reader participates vicariously — living in the experience figured through narrative rather than standing on its periphery.

The use of various structures and devices of narration have helped us tell the stories of our research. While it is hard to put into words both the uses and effects of various forms, we hope to share some of these versions as a way to whet your imagination with what might be possible as you shape your own research projects into various texts, each of which might foreground differently the particular meanings you hope to share with your readers.

Anecdotes

An anecdote is a mysterious animal. A story but more. One writing experience that we recommend to people is to think back to their fieldwork and to tease from that an outstanding event that can be told as an anecdote. The event can be about something that happened to others, to the researcher or both, but the key is that it means something to you as the person writing it and that in the anecdote the nugget of meaning somehow gets put into writing. At this point, that 'nugget of meaning' may be more in the body than the mind — a faint hint or an urge that something within the incident is important. On the other hand, it may be adamant in its call to be heard.

Actually, Max Van Manen, in his *Researching Lived Experience* (1990), first brought this form to our attention in terms of qualitative research writing. 'Anecdote can be understood as a methodological device in human science that makes comprehensible some notion that easily eludes us' (p. 116). So, we'd like to share some of the anecdotes that qualitative researchers have written. We want to consider the function and effects of anecdote on the discovery of meaning for writers and how this form may influence the reader's construction of meaning.

Gayle Newshan's anecdote, written early in her research, helped her as she, along with her support group, began to reshape the questions of her study. For Gayle, the event that triggered her decision to write the following anecdote is described in its last two lines. The incident evoked in her a powerful need to make some sense out of the sequence of events that led up to the final moment she describes:

> I found a resident who was charting at the nurses' station and introduced myself and my task — to interview an AIDS patient who was experiencing pain. I asked if he knew any likely candidates. The resident barely looked up at me and shrugged. But a nurse overheard me and said, 'What about Jay?' The doctor said, 'Sure, you could see him, but he's not really in pain. He just wants drugs. You know, he's

a junkie.' I said, 'Well, let me talk to him anyway.' I got his full name and went to his room which was down the hall.

Jay shared a room with one other patient who was not in the room at the time. After hearing about my study, he agreed to be interviewed. Jay was black, about 5'10", slightly taller than me, of medium build. He was clean-shaven, with close-cropped hair. He wore hospital pajamas and his bedside table was bare — no flowers, no cards and no snacks piling up. He walked slightly bent over as he went to the bathroom before we began and eased himself gingerly into the bed. His face seemed somewhat older than his 32 years.

Jay told me he'd experienced severe abdominal pain for about a month. He had lost 20 pounds during that time and was feeling more and more fatigued. Although he had an alcohol and cocaine habit for ten years, he hadn't been using anything in the last two months because alcohol made him vomit. He spoke in a monotone, as if he had given up. 'No one will listen to me — they think I'm faking. But my belly hurts; something's wrong!' He spoke simply, as if it were matter of fact. When we were finished, he agreed I could come back. He said he was homeless and was waiting to be placed in a [single-room occupancy] hotel.

When I returned a week later, Jay's face was gray and his temples and cheeks looked sunken. He was too weak to talk much. Before I left, the intern stopped by and said to him, 'Jay, you could get up if you wanted. You gotta try.' Turning to me, he said, 'You know, there's nothing wrong with him!' I expressed my concern that he appeared to have deteriorated quite a bit since I last saw him but the intern shrugged and walked off.

I found out later that Jay died that week. An autopsy showed a large tumor occupying more than half of his liver.

In an important way, Gayle's anecdote became a metaphor of the human and ethical issues central to her research project. What is more, several questions surfaced immediately from this incident: Has Gayle given fair and accurate representation? If so, how can people be treated in this way? What pressures and experiences influence this intern's or any of the doctors' attitudes and actions? How many more patients are subject to less than caring interactions? What part does the specific disease play in this? Poverty? Race? What more needs to be known?

From this one anecdote, Gayle received a variety of possible directions for further analysis and for presentation. A piece such as this one can and did act as a header in her discussion of findings. Anecdote served as a structure through which to describe Jay's journey and became a focal point that held the possibility of becoming part of Gayle's final reflections about self-as-researcher and about the research process. Gayle understood how useful this anecdote might be to her concluding sections about the nursing profession and needed research. And, of course, she understood that the story of Jay might serve to illustrate a variety of meanings in any one of several sections. At this stage, Gayle knew the possibilities better than the actual placement or how she might finally write this up.

In our experience, anecdotes emerge easily. Different from other forms that depend on experience over time, anecdotes can be crafted at any stage because they can rest on a single incident. Further, each researcher has one story or even several that burn to be told. We know it when we live it, when we come home literally chomping at the bit to write it or to call a colleague and share the core of a story that keeps hounding at us to be told and told again. You know those anecdotes when they resonate for you: you're taken by it; you talk to yourself about it. Dream it. If it has happened to you, you'll know what we mean. This is why anecdote should be among the first narrative forms to write — a bellwether to reveal insight, something to hold onto and play out in many possible forms and venues.

Rhonda Weller Moore studied life in an adult day care center. Her anecdote highlights rather clearly that an anecdote need not be long:

> One day, as the staff finished their lunches in the day room, Mim wheeled her chair to the door of that room. She was greeted by Nancy's icy tone: 'You have to wait until we finish lunch.' Taken back myself, I wasn't surprised to hear Mim mutter angrily about this being 'unfair.' Her 'Why do THEY get to go in there?' was pouted out in a manner under her breath that suggested to me that she felt helpless to assert herself out loud.
>
> A short time later, Katherine asked Ruth to wheel her into the day room. As she wheeled by me, I moved to get Mim's chair out of her path. Katherine indicated her desire to sit in the large, soft chair, a request which to me, seemed reasonable. As we reached the table, I realized Mim and her chair were right behind us; apparently she had mustered courage again. Now Nancy's tone was disapproving, her voice too loud. 'WHOA! Where are you all going? We didn't say you could come in here. You NEED to go back there.'

An anecdote does need to tell a story, and in that Rhonda succeeds. From this beginning, Rhonda wrote the layered story that appears on p. 86 and a variety of reflective memos that provided her with directions for method and insights for analysis. Following is one piece that she wrote specifically about the anecdote we just quoted:

> This actual incident illustrated for me the sense I took away from the center, which generally was not very positive. I was left with very deep concerns for the dignity of the people being cared for in this setting, issues for me as a professional which I would share with other professionals in similar settings.
>
> Depersonalization was a theme running through the interactions of staff with clients. While most clients did not seem to react to this, it very definitely brought forth feelings in me. I responded also as a person in that I was able to empathize with Mim's railing against the injustice of not being allowed in the room. It was easy for me to put myself in her shoes because of the universality of the experience — an outrage at injustice. What I heard in her response was the unfairness at being treated as less than a person.
>
> This anecdote also reflects the tendency by staff to talk down to or to talk to clients as if they are bad children. Another aspect concerned the fact that often, as in this incident, comments were made with clients in very close proximity as if they were not present at all. This, too, tended to impress me with the air of dehumanization and detracting from the worth of clients.
>
> The incident illustrated the theme of control by demonstrating the staff's need to keep clients in line. It occurred to me that the control issues were perhaps derived from the staff's fears arising in response to continually being faced with people who are impaired either cognitively or physically.
>
> As a nurse, I felt betrayed by Nancy. Again, my professional values as a nurse

dictate that humans, regardless of cognitive or physical ability, deserve the same amount of respect. Frankly, I did not see respect coming through in these interactions. Part of me was feeling that, by association, I was siding with the enemy. I think that this anecdote taps the dimensions of my own vulnerability as well, particularly with the sense of being caught in the middle between being a professional and being a client. I had the feeling of being caught, and of breaking rules I had not known existed, and some sense of responding as I did as a child to unwritten rules. Something about this went very much to the core of me, and I have spent much time asking myself why Nancy was able to generate such intense feelings of guilt over a rather insignificant encounter. I think in terms of analysis that this, too, is something I would be interested in pursuing. Interestingly, I felt a fair amount of anger at being 'caught in the middle,' a sense of moral outrage that the staff's response was not a justified one. I have the sense or an awareness perhaps, because of this incident, that the more people are ingrained or embedded in a situation, the less able they are to see behaviors that are problematic.

Rhonda's two paragraph anecdote was only the beginning of the writing that she did as a result of working in more detail through the issues she introduces here. In addition, she learned that '. . . the other meaning-making features of the story . . . affect me and generate . . . feelings in me.' Confronting one's feelings as a qualitative researcher is essential. While this can occur in a variety of ways, for Rhonda it was spurred by writing an anecdote.

Magdalen Radovich was a participant observer of people's experiences in a soup kitchen. In her anecdote, she chooses to retain her third person stance, possibly because she feels that the story needs this distance. The anecdote was written for the category that Magdalen labeled 'Faces of the Hungry', subcategory, 'The Elderly:'

Social Security: 'A Tradition in Personal Savings'

Overwhelmed by the thick, rich smell of cooked meat and spices, Robin struggles to keep the trays of macaroni and beef sliding down the serving counter to the peaches and bread volunteer. She had chosen this position, this station, her back to the mass of what seem to her predominantly black and hispanic men who had crowded the staircases and sidewalk outside when she first arrived an hour ago. What would she say or could she say to any of them should their eyes meet hers, should they make the uneasy small talk she imagined must be mandatory?

She looks to Jack, a seasoned volunteer who she'd met earlier, for support, but he's busy supervising the crew dishing out the hot food on the other side of the counter. 'Just keep your pace sending these trays down,' she thinks, 'and you'll be fine.'

A soft, girlish voice, accompanied by a jangling sound, tugs at Robin's sleeve as she struggles to keep up with the increasing speed of the assembly line. 'Can you give me some extra slices of bread to take home?'

Robin turns jerkily, nearly colliding with an elderly woman in a heavy, oversized red wool coat and a little box hat perched upon long, wispy, white hair. 'Where is that jangling sound coming from?' Robin asks herself. 'Ah, yes,' she thinks, her gaze falling on the numerous strands of chains and faux pearls hanging around the woman's neck, for each time the woman shifts her weight from one foot to the other, the necklaces clatter together.

Robin hesitates. What is the policy on take home? The old woman's sagging, rouged cheeks rise and fall as she laughs soundlessly, waiting for Robin's response. Amidst the dense throng of men, the woman strikes Robin as a stereotypical bag lady.

Again Robin looks to Jack, catching his eye this time, and shrugs her shoulders. Deftly, he by-passes Robin, stretching across the distance to give the woman more white bread. 'How's it going, Lucy? Where are you off to?' Jack asks loudly.

'Home after I eat,' she smiles broadly.

Turning to Robin, she flashes her left hand in front of her face. 'Do you like my rings? They're marcasite. Real marcasite.'

'They're very nice,' Robin murmurs uneasily.

Lucy hobbles off on thick, swollen legs, further encumbered by several shopping bags hanging off of either wrist. Robin stares after her a moment. 'How sad,' she says aloud. 'That poor old woman!'

Another volunteer adds, 'You see a lot of them at this time of the month, right before their Social Security checks come in.'

Jack laughs. 'Don't let Lucy surprise you! A few weeks ago she had another woman down on the floor and she was all over her. She's also a kleptomaniac. If it's not nailed down, she'll take it!'

'How can that be?' she wonders silently, watching Lucy at the door now, preparing to leave, adjusting her shopping bags. Robin strains her eyes to read the logo on the fullest one. 'Federal Savings Bank: A Tradition in Personal Savings.'

While Magdalen achieved a sense of distance as researcher by using a third person point of view, for us she does make the scene of the anecdote as immediate as those in the two other examples because she used present tense while the others were written in past tense. It has been interesting for us to note how the use of various rhetorical devices indicate where the researcher places self as well as positions the reader. We believe these things are worthy of notice. Obviously in this book we cannot deal with each and every one, but by pointing out a few as we go along, we hope to increase your sensitivity to the resources available to you in shaping the subtleties that affect meaning as well as form.

We might measure the impact of the preceding three anecdotes by asking several questions engendered by the work of Harold Rosen (1986):

- Have the writers compelled our attention as readers?
- Have they led us to reflect on the significance of the events they describe?
- Have they touched, moved, and/or taught us?
- Have they helped us to see layers of meaning in the story?

Certainly, for us, all three anecdotes meet these criteria. We might add another question that you cannot answer for these researchers, but that you can ask yourself about your own work:

- Do the anecdotes that I write give me a clearer focus on the essential core of my research and help me see more clearly aspects of the work in which I am engaged?

Anecdotes, then, are intimately tied into the research presentation by how they function. By their very particularity, they help us to think more deeply; to move from one scene to a larger drama, and then, perhaps, back again to the scene that, because we have reflected on it, holds far greater meaning. This power to help us shift gears is a beautiful thing about anecdotes. Yet, anecdotes have not gotten good press from many, particularly academics. Some see anecdote as a lower level of discourse. A mere entertainment. This misses the point entirely. Certainly anecdotes are interesting. They enliven a text. They also help our readers to understand what we may have laboriously written thus far. How often have we sat in despair at the dryness and distance of what we are writing and said: 'Now, this needs a good story, a good anecdote!' Anecdotes are higher levels of discourse.

Vignettes

We thought at first that we would title this section Vignette/Constructs. It rang true. But on rethinking, it became clear to us that every piece of writing, from title to text to extended metaphor to bibliography is a construct, a construction of the writer. Bruner (1991) recognized the importance of the reciprocal interplays of form and process. He urges that we recognize that 'Eventually it becomes a vain enterprise to say which is the more basic — the mental process or the discourse form that expresses it — for, just as our experience of the natural world tends to imitate the categories of familiar science, so our experience of human affairs comes to take the form of the narratives we use in telling about them' (p. 5). Vignettes, much in the same way as anecdotes, are narrative investigations that carry within them an interpretation of the person, experience, or situation that the writer describes. Yet, we see an important difference in intent. While anecdotes tend to be a written representation of a meaningful event, a vignette restructures the complex dimensions of its subject for the purpose of capturing, in a brief portrayal, what has been learned over a period of time.

As we see them, vignettes are compact sketches that can be used to introduce characters, foreshadow events and analyses to come, highlight particular findings, or summarize a particular theme or issue in analysis and interpretation. Vignettes are composites that encapsulate what the researcher finds through the fieldwork. In every case, vignettes demand attention and represent a growing sense of understanding about the meaning of the research work.

Michelle Haddad studied a principal as he went about his daily work. Pieces from her vignette of Marty, the principal, include his own words which Michelle edited and wrote around to present a holistic 'portrait':

'I'm Not a Rebel, Just a Maverick'

It's been said that I don't care about the outside educational bureaucracy. That's not so. I don't consider people outside the school the enemy; they're just secondary. They are not bad people trying to destroy us. It's not a fight; it's just that, you know, they think they need something, and it's important to them.

Listen, I do what is my priority, which is the internal. I recognize responsibility for external authority as well because you can't just say, 'I'm not going to do anything they want or need.' They have their needs, too, and they have their purposes, but it's basically unimportant. And, of course, the other part of the responsibility that I have is I can't punish my children or my teachers by not doing what the outside authorities say they need to do in order to go on to high school. We do what the children need, and everyone else be damned. There are rules and regulations for everything, and those are sort of parameters. You try to the extent possible, and where it makes sense, to stay within them. But I break rules and regulations continuously.

I don't mean to say I'm always right, or that the system is always wrong, but sometimes the system makes mistakes. Take, for example, the Iraq war. We were mandated to have shelter drills. Now, we haven't had shelter drills since World War II. They said you should have the children duck under the desk. And I said no because the kids are scared as it is that some of these Scuds might be here. They don't understand a distance of 8,000 miles away. This is wrong. They said, 'Oh, no, no, you've got to have it.' The answer was, I never had the drills. I got back a note saying, 'You have to have shelter drills.' I just didn't respond to it. I just ignored it, that's all.

Most principals did it though. You know, it's easier not to disobey. It's easier just to do it. The answer is, you pick your battles. Let me put it this way: I'm really going around the side. I'm flanking them. Because, if you butt them, then they're going to fight you back. Then they have the authority to say, 'You're not meeting your mandated needs,' or whatever it is. So I say, 'Okay, I understand. Okay, I'll see you next year.'

Yeah, I love beating the system because the system stinks. It really does. And one other thing. It's lovely to have tenure.

From reading Michelle's vignette, you might get a feel for Marty as a person, as a principal, and as a member of the larger school community. You may be hypothesizing how Marty is viewed by administrators, parents, and children. You might go so far as to imagine what will happen if Marty is placed in an irreconcilable position where he must act as he has been instructed by higher authorities when his personal beliefs tell him that he should act in a different manner for the sake of the children. If these considerations strike you, then Michelle used characterization and foreshadowing successfully.

Researchers find that attempts like Michelle's to write 'for' another person fill them with some trepidation. Michelle recognized the difficulty in creating her vignette in Marty's voice. She feared that she might co-opt his voice and not accurately portray a living rather than a fictional person. She reflected on the problems inherent when taking on the voice and point of view of another:

Writing about Marty in the first person was and still is very difficult. I had a lot of trouble with even daring to attempt to write in first person, believing that to make a statement in Marty's voice would be presumptuous. What right did I have to assume that I could speak for Marty? On an intellectual level, I thoroughly agree that everything is subjective, relative to interpretation, and that writing in first person is no more presumptuous than writing in third person. But it still is hard.

Even though she had her doubts, Michelle found that she could tell Marty's story. She included this vignette in her dissertation and it was well received by others, not the least of whom was Marty. One workable solution to the fear of misrepresenting another person's thoughts or language is to take some writing to the research participants for their response.

If vignettes are taken seriously as a useful interpretive tool, you might find that writing them raises more questions than answers about how you are representing the participants of your study or how you might proceed with the report. Vignettes, then, help you tap into what you are learning as well as help you identify gaps, silences, and contradictions you might address. They offer an invitation for the reader to step into the space of vicarious experience, to assume a position in the world of the research — to live the lived experience along with the researcher.

In terms of narrative technique, the vignette sandwiches together the particulars of people, time, places, or events to reveal implicitly the significance of the story told. For example, the next vignette, written by Magdalen Radovich, introduces a participant and a particular event in her research of the soup kitchen, but it is meant to do more. See what you think:

Pete's Story

Can I have that marker for a minute? Don't worry. I'll give it back. I'm a main volunteer here. I'm THE Main Volunteer. Anyway, I just need it to write my combination on this piece of paper. Oh, yeah, they gave me a locker 'cause now I have more responsibility.

I've been doing this for six months already. I was recruited. Came in one day and Carole said, 'We need an extra hand. Get over here.' So I did. Been coming every Saturday since then. I open up the place, get the coffee going, open the cans up, all that stuff.

They helped me out too. I'll tell you, if it weren't for this place, I'd be upstate again. This time I told Carole what was happening, that it looked like I was going again. [Laughter]. She said, 'I don't want you to go to jail because I think it's a real hardening process. The people who come out are not as nice as they were when they went in.'

'Yeah, don't I know that,' I told her. 'I've been upstate for two years at a stretch so I don't think they can do anything more to me.' But she got Father Jim, that's the pastor here at St. Theodora's, to write a letter, and she wrote a letter. You know, she's the coordinator and all. I called them right after court. 'They threw it out, Carole!' I said. 'The judge threw it right out of court.'

The rest of the time? I don't do nothing. I walk the streets. Enjoy life. I'm an alcoholic. I think about one thing: 'Don't drink.'

Thanks for the marker. Gotta go get that coffee on.

'Pete's Story' introduces him, to be sure. It also foreshadows the consideration for social outreach in this center and how the goal is carried out by people who play central roles there. Further, it spotlights issues of trust, responsibility and empowerment. Meaning in the vignette, then, is partially generated by the linkages the writer makes between the stories of the research and the researcher's need to understand and possibly take action. Kierkegaard's famous transposition is appropriate here to the intent of vignettes: 'We live life forwards but understand it backwards.'

The authors of the previous vignettes, Michelle and Magdalen, depended on observations and interviews to construct the pieces through which they gave voice to their characters. Judy Walenta faced a unique challenge in doing hers. Judy struggled to determine just what was going on in Sonny's mind as she read some of his overt actions and responses in order to give voice to this person who was labeled autistic. How would empathy work as the experiential core in her attempts to create a portrait of Sonny? What aspects of her knowledge of autism could be brought to bear? What is, after all, happening in Sonny's mind with the inner processing of language if he produces so little external language? Here are Judy's speculations:

Sonny

My name is Sonny Carter. People say that I am autistic. They also say that I am retarded. My mom says I will always be this way. I don't know what autistic or retarded mean but I do know that I am different. People around me talk and say things. I understand a lot of what they say but usually I can't say anything back. Sometimes I try to say a word but only a little piece of it comes out. Then lots of times I say something and no one understands me.

Sometimes people ask me questions and I want to answer, in fact, I know the answer, but it won't go into words. I don't know how to make it come out. If it's an easy question, I can sometimes show the answer with my hands or even say one word that answers. Words are very hard for me! They are hard to control. They don't always come out the way I hear them in my head and some people ask me to repeat them over and over because they don't understand.

If things are very noisy and loud around me or if someone is yelling, it feels uncomfortable and makes me feel like I might disappear. I feel like I might explode. If I rock my body back and forth and hum a little, I feel better.

I like things around me to be neat and clean and to stay in their places. When I notice something out of place in a room, I like to put it back where it belongs. I get scared when things are out of place. I feel safer when things are the way they should be, the way they have always been.

Sometimes people can help. My teacher, Elizabeth, often seems to know what I need. If she is there, talking to me, explaining that everything will stay ok, it can feel all right for things to be different. My mom can do this, too. She explains that the changes are good and that I will like them and get used to them and that I don't have to be frightened. My mom gets frightened, too, though, and I can tell when she's frightened because her voice goes up and she gets a look on her face. My mom and my teacher understand me. Some people in the group home, like Wilma understand some too. But most of the time I feel that there is a part of me that nobody knows. Sometimes it feels like a big part. There are many things that I see and hear. But they just stay inside. It feels like I have a heavy weight inside of me. It feels very lonely, carrying this weight around. When I feel like this, if I look out the window and rock a little I feel better, and when I rock and hum or practice looking at the world through one eye or even pick off the hard skin on my fingers I feel better.

We're wondering how Judy's vignette might help her readers broaden an understanding of Sonny. Does it help you put Sonny's life experiences with autism into richer context? It seems important to mention that Judy wrote the vignette only after a long series of observations and discussions with people at the group home, many of whom had particular experiences with Sonny. Certainly, Judy's portrayal rests on the empathy that she has gained through long experiences with Sonny. While she does literally and metaphorically put words in his mouth and presupposes ways that he might think about himself and the larger world, Judy 'senses' an interpretation. Rather than providing her readers with a vicarious experience, she accomplishes what Heinz Kohut (1977) described as 'vicarious introspection' (p. 301).

Vignettes, then, are portraits created through condensing and compiling. These are described by our colleague Diane Garner in Ely *et al.* (1991) as presentation devices. So far, we've introduced vignettes of the type where the participants in research studies have been given voice. Additionally, a vignette may provide a contextualized single picture, a snapshot, intended to represent an entire issue, phenomenon, or case. *Snapshot vignettes* function toward the same ends as *synecdoche*, a figurative device using a part of something to represent the whole. Writers often use, for example, a wave to stand for the ocean or the North Star to stand for a galaxy. Consider the difference between Magdalen's anecdote in the soup kitchen, when she describes meeting Lucy, or the vignette where Pete relates his experiences at the kitchen with the following snapshot vignette from the same place:

Changing Fortunes

The soup kitchen is bustling with activity, infused by the energy of a visiting group of West Pointers. Carole, the coordinator, stands at the door with several men who are waiting to get on the serving line.

'Well,' says Carole, 'isn't it nice of these West Pointers to come down and help us?'

One man, a grizzled fellow in his fifties, steps back and raises an appraising eyebrow at the clean-shaven cadet. He passes an unconscious hand over his rough, stubbly chin, and blows a silent whistle laced with odor of stale tobacco and alcohol. 'I used to train you guys,' he says to the cadet as he passes through into the crowded basement.

Carole watches him shuffle away. Then, to the cadet, 'I think these guys weren't trained for anything except to carry guns. And, when they came back from Nam there were no jobs.'

While this example may strike you as very much like Magdalen's earlier soup kitchen scene, we feel that the intention is to encapsulate a particular theme that runs through her research — the idea that changing fortunes control life circumstances. While this snapshot omits many details and descriptions of other experiences being played out in the soup kitchen at this very time, it is a figurative representation of the life experiences of the people who come there. Magdalen uses this particular incident to stand for the whole of experience as she finds it in the kitchen — fortunes change and reverse. Magdalen gives us the essential details so that we may fill in a larger picture.

A *moving vignette* is characterized by a flow of events over time. A vignette that 'moves' is particularly useful for creating portraits of people in order to characterize an array of their evolving experience. Vignettes of this type may have multiple sections that are dispersed throughout the longer text of the report. In the paragraph that follows, Elizabeth Merrick gives her first impression of Marisol, a teenager in the group home which was the research site of one of Elizabeth's studies:

Marisol attracts attention. She is a big girl, with a loud voice and, usually, enormous gold earrings. Teasing playfully with other students and singing, she clearly stands out as a personality. At first glance, she struck me as an energetic, almost aggressive, 'streetwise kid in an alternative school.' However, as soon as the class assembled, she became a leader, encouraging others in the group to participate. As the weeks went on, I came to know something of her personal history and views.

Another part of this moving vignette was created to compress aspects of the first four years of Marisol's life:

You want to hear about my life? Well, I wasn't raised by my mom — my real mom. When I was little, I lived with my grandmother's friend. They took me in when I was young ... real young ... when I was born. My mother didn't want me. My grandmother couldn't take care of me because she was taking care of my other cousins, so my grandmother's friend took care of me. Understand?

I lived with them from then until I was about 4 and my mother came back to town. Who knows where she'd been. I always remember that day she came and got me. You gotta understand I was just 4 years old. The people I was living with never told me that they weren't my mother and father, so I always thought they were and their sons were my brothers. They never told me for fear it would hurt me. And when she came and got me, I was crying. I always remember that day because it was hard. This lady coming in and she was like 'I'm your mother' and all this foolishness. And I was screaming, 'NO! No, you're not!'

Much of what is encapsulated in this vignette is told throughout the presentation of Elizabeth's research. The tug between the many people moving Marisol around is told in various short vignettes, all of which make a larger, moving vignette that, in form and substance, portrays life as a series of moves for Marisol. The next part of the vignette described Marisol's life with her mother from age 4 until 11. Then because 'I knew how to ride the trains by myself' she ran away and ended up back with the people who raised her:

My mother used to come back and get me and I'd get beaten. I stayed with her one more year, then I went to live with my grandmother, my real grandmother. That was when I was 12, when my grandmother got custody of me. I lived there but it was too crowded. There were 5 of us living in a 2 bedroom apartment. My grandmother, my uncle, my cousin, her husband and my cousin's little sister. I had to sleep with my grandmother. And my cousin was pregnant.

So I was getting older and thought I wanted to leave. I was too old to be sleeping with my grandmother. I was 14. I wanted to live with the woman who raised me. But I knew I couldn't live with her for long. My mother and grandmother would let me go and they'd tell me, 'You can stay, live there, we don't care.' Then the next minute they'd take me back. You know they would always make it hard for me. So, I told them I wanted to go to a group home.

This moving vignette allows Elizabeth to weave the stories of Marisol's displacements, replicating the near volley rhythm of these significant moves which resulted in Marisol's current situation.

Grappling to create a rich characterization of the people in the soup kitchen, Magdalen found vignette to be a form that communicated in some detail the inherent positions of the people she met there. Because Magdalen wished to avoid portraying people as finished products, she described their passions, desires, ideas, and actions through vignettes. She portrayed them through various conversations that depict something of their interactions with others. In one example of a *portrait* or *characterization vignette*, Magdalen creates a portrait of Harold in which she brings something of his internal world forward and represents him in greater complexity as an inconsistent, relativistic, and unfolding 'character' whom she is getting to know:

Harold's Story

Bob, the meal ticket collector for the day, sets up his station at a small grey metal desk just inside the main entrance to the basement. He and Robin, one of the new volunteers, are going over procedures for preparing tickets and reasons for keeping an accurate count of the tickets for funding purposes when someone shouts from outside, 'Harold is back!'

Within moments, a large, bulky man with long unkempt strands of white hair lumbers through the door with a metal shopping wagon. His eyes are small, in scale with his face which is wide and square. A large, bumpy protrusion on the left side of his forehead calls immediate attention to the otherwise high, smooth forehead.

Bob, smiling, greets him as he approaches, 'Hi, Harold.' But Harold does not smile back. He stalks behind Bob to a dark corner where he rummages amongst cartons and other seeming debris.

'Are you staying?' Bob asks as Harold finally emerges from the shadows with an unwieldy black garbage bag.

The bag rattles as Harold stuffs it hastily into the rusted cart. 'You know I can't stay here! I was fired . . . sort of,' Harold admonishes, his thick white brow pinched into a tight scowl. Harold lumbers off through the doors with his wagon.

'What was that all about?' Robin asks.

'Oh, he used to sit at the door and if there was any trouble, he'd break it up. Then last week he had some words with someone back there,' Bob says, nodding towards the crew behind the cafeteria counter. 'They told him nicely that his services were no longer needed.'

Several weeks later, Robin returns and meets Harold up on the street outside the Church. 'Hi,' she says, surprised to see him back.

'Are you a volunteer?' Harold asks in a formal tone, his face set sternly.

'Yes,' she hesitates.

Suddenly Harold's face comes alive with a laughter that sets his shoulders shaking. 'I'm CIA! I stand at the door, sometimes outside too, when it's nice like today, and I watch people come in. If you're a volunteer, then it's okay for you to go in!'

Robin laughs too. 'I'm a writer, a researcher really. I'm writing about the soup kitchen and the people here.'

'Oh, yeah? Well, you can put this in your composition then. I used to do dishes, but it was a dirty job and I didn't like it. So now I have a good job. I stand at the door and watch people come in. I make sure people don't lock the door and don't cause trouble,' he laughs.

'Like a bouncer?' she asks.

'No,' he shakes his head, strands of hair falling into his face. 'No. More like a greeter.'

A *rerun vignette* presents a story of cycles, repeated over time. These cycles are characterized by specific patterns or phases that play themselves out and then begin again at a similar place. We've found rerun vignettes particularly useful in longitudinal studies as well as in all studies that present complex, widely disparate information. These vignettes serve as a cohesive element for a cacophony of data. They say, both to reader and writer, 'Look here! Here is one way to find a meaningful pattern in all of this.'

Our colleague Belén Matías studied the experience of a Board of Directors over one year. She writes of her insights about cycles in the following vignette:

> It did not take me long to determine that I could do well to continue to focus on some of the repetitions in group dynamics that I observed from the very beginning. They became very interesting to me because of the insight this 'cyclic dance' afforded me. Generally, here were the elements of the repetitive patterns: The Board met at a restaurant — a public versus private place — and away from the situation with which they were dealing. The setting provided enough seclusion so that they could talk, but at the same time this was not the place for loud blow ups. Two people inevitably arrived and sat together. The others straggled in, but also sat together. This arrival and seating arrangement foretold the existence of two camps with widely different opinions on the topics at hand. The first minutes were spent in social talk:
>
> 'Well, you look good!'
>
> 'How are your children?' 'Did your daughter finally make up her mind? Is she going to graduate school?' The main business of the meeting, on typed agendas, began just after people ordered food. There was a beginning period of seemingly harmonious exchange as the item under consideration was introduced by its originator. This gradually but inexorably evolved at particular points into visible differences of stance by the two camps which, to me, held together in an amazingly cohesive way. The points of difference had to do with money, future goals, and professional management. This pattern did not show itself when the group discussed other items such as social activities and calendar of events.
>
> For the items that brought forth intense disagreement, these would be characterized by sharp exchanges, clear non-verbal signals such as particular eye contact, touching and slight raising of voices. Inevitably, at a point that threatened major splits and disruptions, one person, always the same one, sent humor and light comments to people in both camps and through this the heat of the exchange was diffused.
>
> To me, this was an example of one large cycle, from meeting to meeting which held within it a number of sub-cycles.

In this writing Belén does more interplay within the text than did the preceding authors of vignettes who told the story and discussed it after and/or before. Belén might have done the same but she judged it stronger to weave together description and discussion. Reruns are helpful also in highlighting the cycles in the researcher's own developing story of understanding, as anchors in the final discussion, and in researcher's reflections toward the end of the document.

At the end of this section about vignettes it seems critical for us to emphasize that we use all of these types of vignettes as well as blend some to create others. We often juxtapose vignettes for an oppositional effect as in a series of portrait vignettes of several people who take a different read on a situation. At other times, we found that several snapshots and moving pictures placed together are far more effective when allowed to 'speak' to each other than if they were placed singly. This has worked particularly well for irony and satire where often the point is so strongly made in the presentation and blending of vignettes that there is far less need for discursive text than envisioned. We have at times witnessed also the use of juxtaposed vignettes to a sarcastic effect. Finally it's more important to use vignettes rather than to worry about naming them. Long ago, we figured out that the line between 'moving picture' and 'snapshot,' for example, is often blurry at best. We first placed 'Marisol' as an example of a snapshot vignette. Later we moved it to 'moving picture.' We provide such titles as food for thought and to extend the possible character and use of vignettes. The aim is to let vignettes work for you to support your intended meaning.

Behind all this work you may experience some uneasiness about what appears our glib way of recommending that researchers move into other's lives, experience those lives as best they can through their imaginations, and write those up as part of the reports on research. Jerome Bruner helped us sort through the issues surrounding such researcher moves. He points to the essential role of imagination and feeling in all disciplines and in all thinking that makes possible the construction of new knowledge. Bruner reflects that in narrative thinking a writer needs to attend to two landscapes simultaneously: the outer landscape of action and the inner landscape of consciousness. How might anecdote and vignette have unique qualities that help us reveal both of those landscapes? How do vignette and anecdote tend to structure the researcher's viewpoint on the topic of the study differently from more analytical writing? We've tried to demonstrate at least our responses to these questions in this section. For all narrative, the subject matter is brought to the reader through the filter of the narrator's consciousness, reminding us that the only realities of the moment come to us through the sway of the narrator's creation.

Layered Stories

In August of 1949, Norman MacLean arrived at his summer home in Seeley Lake, Montana only to hear that thirteen Forest Service Smokejumpers had burned to death a few days before. Most were college students who, less than two hours after their jump into Mann Gulch, had been consumed by a forest fire that was 'something like a hurricane to an ocean storm' (MacLean, 1992, p. 33). When MacLean's *Young Men and Fire* was published in 1992, shortly after his death, his need to understand what had happened in that brief period took shape as a layered story filled with emergent, relative, and changing perspectives.

During the last fourteen years of his life, MacLean wrote the story of his forty plus years of investigations into the event. In layer upon layer of narrative, he documented his search — the starts, dead-ends, speculations, and growing understanding of the Mann Gulch fire. On that first journey in 1949, a few days after the fire, he found:

... a world of still-warm ashes ... It was an amphitheater of the afterlife where passion had destroyed life ... A little farther into the fire a black pole would now and then explode and reproduce a progeny of flames. A cliff would tear loose a tree it had kept burning in a secret crevice and then toss the sacrifice upon the rocks below. (1992, pp. 11–12)

Nearly forty years later, in the 1980s, MacLean discovered yet another layer when he found that:

... small trees have just started to grow along the bottoms of dry finger gulches on the hillside in Mann Gulch, where moisture from rain and snow is retained underground. Since even now these little evergreens are only six or eight inches high, the grass has to be parted to find them, but I look for such things. I see better what happens in grass than on the horizon. Most of us do, and probably it is just as well, but what's found buried in grass doesn't tell us how to get out of the way. (1992, p. 196)

MacLean presents the findings of his research as a layered story containing fragments of information, splintered remembrances of many people, and ruptures of logic as various explanations are juxtaposed to suggest why the tragedy occurred. Through observing the tensions and flow in various aspects of his investigation, MacLean discovered the dynamic relations of one part to others:

... we do have to know in what odd places to look for missing parts of a story about a wildfire and of course have to know a story and a wildfire when we see one. So this story is a test of its own belief — that in this cockeyed world there are shapes and designs, if only we have some curiosity, training, and compassion and take care not to lie or be sentimental. It would be a start to a story if this catastrophe were found to have circled around out there somewhere until it could return to itself with explanations of its own mysteries and with the grief it left behind, not removed, because grief has its own place at or near the ends of things, but altered somewhat by the addition of something like wonder — wonder, for example, because now we can say that the fire whirl which destroyed was caused by three winds on a river. If we could say something like this and be speaking both accurately and somewhat like Shelley when he spoke of clouds and winds, then what we would be talking about would start to change from catastrophe without a filled-in story to what could be called the story of a tragedy, but tragedy would be only a part of it, as it is of life. (1992, pp. 37–8)

For MacLean, narrative layers became his way of looking and inquiring and finally knowing the story about a wildfire and catastrophe. So, in the writing of research stories, we find it a useful technique and, not incidentally, a special challenge to braid together the layers of story that reveal the larger narrative as we learn to write the 'clouds and winds.'

We don't know how the term 'layered stories' was coined. Someone somewhere probably did, given the huge panoply of literary possibilities, but we first put it together for use in 1985. To us, one sort of layered story arises from different players about the same event(s). This makes for a Rashomon-like rhetorical presentation that can function in very specific ways for writers and their readers. Second, some layered stories are structured as both spoken and internal speech. They demonstrate the more complex realities of the relationship between what is thought and what is, in fact, said. Juxtaposing the participants' stories with the researcher's account illustrates another example of the multivocality that any layered story has the potential to emphasize. Temporal considerations may also structure the layers. For example, bringing together a person's perspective of a personal past, present, and anticipated future can be useful in characterizing a life on an interpretive continuum over time. Thus, layered stories have the effect of showing the social construction of individual lives and perspectives, and they underscore each person's creative, active interpretation of experience.

Jill Schehr, in her study of a prison nursery,

> ... learned the value of 'layering' from another vantage point. For example, while describing the social context of the prison nursery, I can 'zoom' in on the individuals who comprise this community: inmate mothers and their babies. Closer still, I can write about a mother's experience, at times from her viewpoint, using knowledge gained from hours of observation and interview.

Jill reminds us that layering can show the dynamic relation of one person to another or offer different points of view from various perspectives. In these ways layered stories reflect the diverse ways through which experience is interpreted and constructed.

To begin, we will go back to the research study that Judy Walenta, a nurse, conducted in a group home. Earlier in this chapter we included her vignette about Sonny, the young adult labelled autistic. Judy's layered story 'One Day in the Park' runs to thirteen double-spaced pages. What follows are excerpts from four people's stories about how they organize and represent the events of the same incident:

Sonny
I am sitting on a bench in the park with some other people from the house where I live. It is hot. We are all just sitting on the bench. I am squinting my eyes at the trees as the leaves move and the light bounces off. It feels like the light could bounce so far it could come and hit me in the eye. That scares me a little but still it is fun to watch.

Suddenly, everything goes black and I feel like I am falling. When I open my eyes, I am lying on the ground with a lot of people looking down at me. My head hurts. Things look fuzzy. I close my eyes again. All those people staring at me and I feel so tired.

'He seems like he's awake, but he's not opening his eyes,' Sammy is saying. 'I hope Wilma comes back soon with the ambulance.'

Next I remember a lot of activity. I hear Wilma's voice saying, 'There he is, down there.' Someone is kneeling beside me, wrapping something around my arm and somebody else is trying to open my eyes with his fingers. That feels terrible and I pull away. 'What's his name?' Someone strange is asking.

'Sonny,' Wilma replies.

'Sonny, Sonny, wake up, open your eyes.' I don't want to open my eyes, especially with all of this commotion, but I decide to try, anyway, and maybe these people will be quiet and go away. 'Sonny, we're going to take you for a little ride.'

A ride, where? By now I've closed my eyes again. I just want to go home to bed but I don't have the words to say this. I open my eyes again and look at

Wilma. She says, 'Don't worry, Sonny, I'll stay with you. We're going to the hospital to make sure you're OK.'

No, not the hospital. I definitely don't want to go to the hospital, but I feel too weak and tired to resist. I mean, I feel safer with Wilma with me but what will they do to me in the hospital? All those people in white coats with needles and things.

At the hospital, Wilma says she is going to make a phone call. I am scared but I don't feel I can do anything to stop this. I just go away inside and let things happen. Wilma comes back and says she will not leave again. She says mom is coming. Nobody will do anything to me until she gets here. Wilma says this to the people in white.

Wilma stays beside me. Every once in a while someone comes over to make the thing on my arm tighter for a minute or to touch me somewhere or to try to look in my eyes. I feel very scared when this happens and just keep going inside. I don't even feel like moving my body back and forth which sometimes makes me feel better when I'm scared.

Mom comes in. She is very upset. She yells at Wilma. I wish she wouldn't yell. I feel bad when mom is upset, but I feel safer with her here. She will not let them do bad things to me.

Now the man in the white coat with the black tube around his neck comes back and Wilma asks him a question. Mom gets quiet when the man comes in but when Wilma speaks to him she yells at her again. Mom speaks to the man. He answers her and then he leaves. As soon as he leaves, mom tells Wilma to go away. Wilma says something back to her and leaves.

My mom does a lot for me. She knows my favorite foods and everything I like. I feel safer with her than I do with Wilma. But sometimes mom gets upset with other people around and, when we're home, she doesn't want to leave me alone. In the group home I get to do some things that I don't get to do at home. I carry out the garbage and bring in the groceries and set the table. I am almost never completely alone but often I am left to sit and be with myself. The people in the group home don't know what I want the way mom does most of the time but they do let me have time to be with myself and I get to eat things like ice cream that mom doesn't let me have.

Mom and Wilma and I get into a yellow car. Mom and Wilma fight all the way to the group home. Mom threatens to throw Wilma out. The fighting hurts my ears. I go back inside and try to shut out the noise. Mom's voice gets very high. I wish she didn't let other people upset her so much.

Wilma

I was busy with some of the other boys when Sonny went down. I saw it out of the corner of my eye. I also saw that Sammy and Luke were with him. I heard Sammy tell Sonny he was OK. I said, 'What's going on?' Sammy said Sonny had hit his head and seemed to be shaking. And he wasn't waking up right away. He said somebody better call for an ambulance.

'I'll go,' I heard myself saying. Now I was getting scared. What could be the matter with Sonny? Of all people. His mother would *kill* us if anything happened to him. I wasn't directly caring for him but just by my being here I was responsible. 'Luke, come here and watch these guys.'

I started to run out of the park. I'm pretty out of shape but the thought of what

Mrs. Carter's reaction would be kind of kept me going. We were close to a hospital so I figured it was faster just to run to the hospital and get an ambulance there. I ran as fast as I could until I ran out of breath and then I walked some and ran some more. I thought I would never get to the hospital fast enough. What if Sonny were seriously injured? I care about these kids as if they were my own, but I also worry about what Mrs. Carter might do to us.

What if we lost our jobs? I am the oldest person present and felt like the most responsible. I need my job because my husband is disabled and can't work. I have no other skills.

Finally, I reached the Emergency Entrance to the hospital and blurted out my story. Two paramedics were right there and we jumped into the ambulance and drove a few blocks to the park entrance and then right across the lawn.

I kept trying to reassure Sonny, telling him things would be okay. He didn't seem too scared. Maybe because he was still out of it. Sonny is one of our best residents. He's usually pretty cooperative, unless he gets into one of his ornery moods. He doesn't like noise and commotion, though, and he hates yelling. And, like most of the residents he's pretty scared of doctors.

Once Sonny was safely inside the examining room with nurses and doctors in attendance, I ran out to call the group home. John, the assistant manager, answered. I told him it seemed like Sonny passed out and fell off a bench and shook some but we had gotten an ambulance right away and he seemed Ok now. I thought maybe he had a seizure but I didn't know for sure and didn't want to say something that wasn't true. I figured that was for the doctors to determine. John didn't get upset but said that he would have to call Sonny's mother and that she would want to come to the hospital. I knew what that meant — I had expected it — and I steeled myself for it. John said, 'Don't let them stick him or do any procedures until she gets there.'

I waited with Sonny. He was awake but calm. Suddenly his mother burst in, bleached blonde hair flying. 'Sonny!' she screeched and ran over to him, her long fingernails curling like talons around his hand. Sonny immediately seemed to become slightly agitated as he often does when his mother is around. Now he was definitely awake.

Mrs. Carter asked what happened and I told her as best I could, being that I really didn't see it. I didn't say he had a seizure since I thought that was for the doctors to determine. I only reported what I saw and heard. Before I could finish, Mrs. Carter was yelling at me, saying, 'Why did they let him fall? Why did they let him fall? You know you never watch them closely enough!' Then, 'Oh, Sonny, are you all right'

A doctor came in and she was quiet suddenly. I asked him what else was being done for Sonny. He said there wasn't much more to do since his mother was refusing any tests. I said I wanted to make sure he was thoroughly examined before he went back to the group home. Then, right in front of the doctor Mrs. Carter started screaming at me to mind my business and let the doctor do his work. I was so embarrassed. I also felt terribly caught. As the representative of the group home, I had to make sure that Sonny was well cared for. I was still worried about what the agency would think about the incident and now Mrs. Carter was trying to prevent me from doing my job. When the doctor left, she yelled at me to leave the room. Her words rang through my head like sirens. Now, I was panicked. I could feel my mouth getting dry and my heart beating fast. I felt that I should stay with Sonny but I also felt like disappearing through a hole in the floor. I decided to leave because I didn't want to make a scene and I felt the hospital people would listen to her before they listened to me because she was his mother and white.

I left and called the group home to let them know what happened. I knew they didn't like Mrs. Carter. I only hoped they would listen to me. John answered again and was very understanding. I hoped the director would be understanding as well. John told me to go back to the examining room, that I had a right to be there. I went back to find that Sonny was being discharged. Mrs. Carter looked up and told me we would be taking a cab back to the group home. Once in the cab, Mrs. Carter started talking about taking Sonny home with her. I groaned inwardly, anticipating another struggle. I said I would have to notify the group home. She finally decided against it and I was relieved, but not for long as she soon started yelling at me again for interfering with Sonny's medical care and who did I think I was? I told her I was merely doing my job and she started threatening to have me put out of the cab. By now Sonny was seeming very agitated, rocking back and forth and picking at his fingers, but somehow we both made it back to the group home in one piece.

Mrs. Carter

When I got the call that Sonny had fallen in the park, I was scared out of my mind. How could they let that happen? How could they let him out of their sight? Ever since he went to live in the group home two years ago, I felt I had done the wrong thing. They just don't take care of him right. I come there and he's unshaven and his hair is messy. Sometimes he smells like he hasn't been washed — when he was at home he never had any body odor. I've even found him wearing other people's clothes! And now he's fallen in the park and hit his head. I know I should never have trusted those people. They leave him unsupervised all the time. They crowd them into elevators where they could hit or bite each other. They let him sit next to people he doesn't like. They don't listen to me! They just can't be trusted.

As soon as I heard about Sonny's accident, I jumped into a cab and rushed to the hospital. It seemed to take forever. I told them I didn't want any tests done until I got there. At the hospital, there was Wilma, ordering the doctors around and acting like she owned the place. I just can't stand her. She's always lying and making apologies for the agency. And she had no explanation for why Sonny fell. She just said that Sammy tried to stop him but couldn't and that he seemed to pass out and go stiff and then hit his head. Anyway, she was so rude to the doctor — *imagine, Wilma* ordering the *doctor* around — that I had to ask her to leave the room. Sonny was lying there on the stretcher looking very helpless. He was glad to see me, I could tell. He started to get more agitated and restless which he does often when he's happy. I told him that I wouldn't let them stick him with any needles. He had a terrible scrape over one eye and the area around his eye was swollen. I told him that I thought it was terrible that these people let him fall, but I didn't dwell on it too much. I didn't want to make him feel worse than he already did.

The doctor finally came back and told me that since I wasn't authorizing any tests, Sonny was cleared to leave. I was relieved that they couldn't find anything wrong with him. I didn't want them to draw blood because I knew it would be traumatic. What would it show anyway? They wanted to do an EEG but that scares me too, all those things that they stick to your head. I knew that would frighten Sonny.

Wilma came back. I hate the sight of her. I think she is a horrible, sick person who shouldn't be working in a position where she is responsible for other people. I tried to be polite to her for Sonny's sake. I got Sonny dressed and got him up. He seemed fully awake and able to walk with us outside to get a cab. I was trying to decide whether to take Sonny home with me when Wilma started going on and on about how she represented the agency and she was responsible for Sonny. I just got sick of it and asked her to get out of the cab. She refused and became very aggressive like she does, saying I can't talk to her like that and it's her job to stay with Sonny. I finally decided that it would be confusing for Sonny to come to my house now since the group home is where he lives and I just got tired of arguing with Wilma. Ever since Sonny moved into that place, it's like I'm really not his mother anymore, according to *them*. The worst part was having to ride all the way to the group home with *Wilma* in the cab, then having to leave Sonny there and go home.

Sammy

I was just sitting on the bench next to Sonny and Charles when all of a sudden, out of the corner of my eye, I saw Sonny start to fall forward. I turned around right away and tried to stop him, but it was too late: his head had already hit the ground by the time I grabbed him. His whole body seemed sort of stiff and his arms were jerking a little. I tried to get him comfortable on the ground. He was *out*, but it was hard at first because of the stiffness and jerking. Luke came over to help me and I called to Wilma to run for an ambulance. Wilma left and Luke went over to keep an eye on the other residents.

After a minute or so, Sonny's body stopped being stiff and then he was just lying there, unconscious. He had a scrape over one eye where he hit the ground. I knew his mom would have a shitfit when she found out. What made him fall like that? Was it a seizure? Did he hurt himself when he hit his head? After a *few* minutes he started moving around a little and tried to open his eyes. I breathed a sigh of relief. I really love these guys, you know? They're like family to me. I can't stand to think of anything happening to them.

I felt Sonny would be OK, but I hoped the ambulance would come soon. I felt bad that I hadn't been able to stop him from hitting his head, but it all happened so fast. I doubt that anyone else could have reacted quicker. Thank God the ambulance came quickly and Luke and me could get back to concentrating on everyone else. The other residents were a *lit*-tle freaked out by the commotion. And by the time he got on the ambulance, Sonny seemed almost back to normal. Just a little groggy, I guess. I knew he'd be OK, but he did have me a little worried there for a minute, you know?

To us, in its juxtapositions, Judy's layered story provides far more food for thought than would a single construct from the eyes of any one person. This 'forcing' oneself to see an event from a variety of viewpoints is particularly useful. It helps us, as researchers, to face and often open up our previous leanings and conclusions about a person. For example, Mrs. Carter who seemed to set so many people's teeth on edge — even perhaps Judy's — deserved her say. This layered story supports one tenet with which we introduced this chapter. There are many ways for us to come to know something and even then our knowledge is partial. How does Judy's vignette on p. 73 work in tandem with her layered story?

Judy reflected on her motivation for writing the layered story in her log:

The pieces which I wrote in 'One Day in the Park' are impressionistic. My pieces are 'impressions' of a scene, or, in the case of Sonny's story, a life seen through someone else's eyes, with the purpose of inviting the reader into another reality. The hope is that the reader will make her/his own observations about the scene and draw conclusions from that. I chose to present my layered story through the eyes of four people in order to help me get a better look at what might have happened on that day.

I had concluded earlier that Sonny had a seizure from the way the counselors told the story, but Sonny's mother disagreed and felt that the counselors were just covering up for negligent acts on their part. Sonny's story seemed important to present. He is the silent one who speaks for himself rarely, and then in one- or two-word messages. I needed to see it from Sonny's point of view, from his mom's, and from the perspective of two counselors, Wilma and Sammy. I did not write the story to entertain, but as an exercise in experiencing someone else's point of view.

Of course, layered stories depend on the information we have collected. In Judy's case, she was not present that day in the park. Her data sprang from interviews with, and observations of, Wilma, Sammy, and Mrs. Carter and from detailed, ongoing observations of and interactions with Sonny. After gathering this information, Judy writes her layered stories in first person. She says:

My writing concerning my fieldwork has primarily been done in the first person narrative style. For two pieces — the layered story 'One Day in the Park' and the construct told by Sonny himself — I switched to other voices but maintained the first person perspective. I feel comfortable with the first person narrative as it is closest to the way I would tell a story to a friend either verbally or in a letter. I feel that it lessens the distance between the writer and reader.

In our experience, many layered stories are written in first person. Certainly layered stories might be written in third person. This creates a more distanced presentation, on the one hand, but might serve other purposes as well. A third person narrator predominantly describes what is seen and heard, recording what is taking place outside of self more than the interior thinking or feeling that is often associated with first person. The third person narrator tends to stand back, to *observe* rather than to express *feelings*.

Sarie Teichman studied the experience of a self-help group for people who were labeled by themselves and others as anorexics/bulimics. Here is one of Sarie's major themes, in first person, about her participants:

My life is about my disease. It touches everything. I cannot separate this disease from any other aspect of my life. It always pulls at me, reminding me that I'm not worth much except when I can control it. It is overpowering. I'm in a lot of pain.

We've rewritten this theme in two ways, each with a change in voice. The third quote is a dictionary definition:

Anorexia/Bulimia is a complex disease that impacts on all facets of life of those so afflicted. It is overpowering and debilitating.

Anorexia/Bulimia is characterized by low self-concept, desire for control, compulsivity, displacement, dependency, fears, unresolved problems of affect.

Anorexia nervosa. The pathological loss of appetite occurring chiefly in young women that is thought to be psychological in origin. (*American Heritage Dictionary*, 1983)

Which of these four examples speak to you most powerfully? Why? For us, each provides its own information, focus, and its position in the continuum of 'feeling narrator' to 'telling narrator.' Indeed, we see one of these as a 'labeling narrator.' Perhaps two. However, the issue is a bit more complicated in its overtones.

The struggle for acceptance of first person voice in qualitative research writing has been long and difficult. It is by no means won, although most leading thinkers, researchers, practitioners, publishers, and professional organizations in the field find this issue long solved and in no need of further deliberation. See your own style guide. There is simply no case to be made *against* the use of first person writing in research that seeks to see life from the eyes of its participants, that rests on the assumption of multiple meanings, that shares with the readers the stance and process of the researcher, that is produced within an interactive vision of language. (We believe this is so for all research: but that is the stuff of another book.)

You see echoes of our stance throughout this book and we do not propose to belabor the point here. However, we know that some researchers and researchers-to-be find that the understanding about and support for first person voice by various academics and publishers range from dim-but-possible to obdurate-and-impossible. This can be maddening in its waste of time and energy, but it is to be understood as part of the age-old phenomenon and bumpy progress of innovation.

There are a variety of ways to face the resistance. That said, most qualitative researchers can achieve the freedom to select voice purposefully. The word purposefully is important. It is as blind to overwrite in first person as it is narrow to stick obsessively with third. Both serve their purpose, and it seems a question of function and balance. However, to us, when the writing is distant, when the researcher comes off as THE authority, when participants are labeled rather than described, when the 'I' is totally missing, when the writing reads in essence like the multitude of quantitative research publications that were once our 'mother's milk,' these are danger signs that must not be avoided.

Rhonda Weller Moore used first person to layer the following story based on the anecdote of life in the adult day care center. She captured her characterization of some of the players in what we found to be a unique and effective way:

Nancy
My name is Nancy and I work as the nurse at the adult day care center. Most of the staff wear street clothes to work, but I'm more comfortable with a lab coat and stethoscope around my neck. I want these people to make no mistake about who I am. Being around these people so much drives me crazy. I just want some peace and quiet around here. Now take the other day — we were just sitting having lunch and here comes Mim in her wheelchair. Now she KNOWS they're not supposed to come in here until we've finished our lunch, but here she came anyway. You know if you give them an inch, they'll take a mile. Well, I let her know in no uncertain terms that she had to go back in there. I mean, when it's OK for them to come back in here, we'll let them know, but not until. And, then what happens?

Well, here comes that nurse who's been hanging out around here, and she's pushing Katherine's chair. Oh, for God's sake! I just had to get out of there.

Mim

My name is Mim. I'm 50 years old, and up until the time I had my stroke, I worked full time. Now my arm and leg are paralyzed and I have to get around in this chair. This damned chair. I get so tired of it. I can't afford a motorized one, and my arm gets so tired from pushing this around. It helps if I can sit in the sunlight, but they don't like us in that room while they're having lunch. I mean, what would it hurt? They just don't want us around. They treat me like I'm crazy, like I don't have a mind like some of them who are here. That really makes me angry. Take the other day. I started to wheel my chair into the day room so I'd get in there before the crowd. When I got to the door, it was already ten past one. Their lunch is over at one fifteen. Well, when I got to the door, Nancy yells, 'Whoa!!! Where are you going? You NEED to get back in there!' I tell you, I felt like she was talking to an animal. Who does she think she is, and where does she get off talking to me like that? Oh, well, better not make waves. After all, I do need her help to get to the bathroom. Oh, there goes that new nurse with Katherine. What the heck? If Katherine can go in there, so can I.

Katherine
I'm Katherine.

Katherine's silence carries a world of meaning.

In her reflections about writing, Rhonda describes her lack of ease with writing in first person. She found it more difficult than Judy to talk 'for' her participants:

I was particularly uncomfortable with the layering, with regard to getting into the mind of the other person, owning the other person's thoughts, so to speak. It was fine when I was describing my own thoughts and reactions, because I could lay claim to them as my own, and I didn't really have to question or validate, because they are MY feelings and thoughts. When it came to constructing an incident from another person's perspective, there was a real felt need to not make that up. There seems to be a fine line between 'making it' (meaning) and 'making it up' when it comes to construction. To me 'making it' is the process of assembling the meaning or constructing the story from pieces of data collected, whereas making it up would include the notion of not necessarily being able to check. I think one of the essential elements in both layering and constructing meaning is that there are pieces of data in the field log which permit the process of allowing the reader to see from where the meaning has been drawn. That ability to trace meaning is generally lacking in situations where something is 'made up.' One of the differences here, in the process of layering, is being able to track meaning.

Rhonda was more at peace with her portrayals of Mim and Katherine than with that of Nancy. She felt her extensive observations of the two clients had given her 'the sense of being able to read their minds in this situation.' With Nancy, the nurse, it was a different matter. Rhonda observed her often, so that was not the issue. What concerned Rhonda was the fact that she did not care for what she had observed. She felt that Nancy's behavior was antithetical to good nursing. Thus, she worried that she may not have done justice to Nancy's story. She did continue to wrestle with the issue:

> It was really this, the interest in being fair regarding what I perceived as coming from her, that sent me back into the field for participant checking. I was very aware that the intensity of my feelings might have gotten in the way of portraying Nancy fairly. In retrospect, I do not feel that this was the case. Her behaviors, at least, the perception of her behaviors, was upheld by the members of my support group, my group facilitator, and dissertation committee members. Although I was not able to substantiate by sharing my perceptions with the staff, obviously because of the sensitivity of the issues, I do feel that my description of what was happening was accurate and fair to the best of my ability.

For both Judy and Rhonda, layering helped them see through broader lenses. For Rhonda, it provided ongoing research direction. It exemplified for her several themes that ran through her observations 'especially issues of control and depersonalization.' In the end, Rhonda was more positive about her efforts to do justice to the participants through the layered stories, but was still concerned that she had not given a fair accounting because she reacted so strongly to Nancy's treatment of clients:

> The shifting of viewpoints that occurred as a result of the process of layering was beneficial in helping me arrive at a combined meaning of the experience for myself and the others involved. The meaning is richer than would be gained by the perspective of one person alone. With Nancy, one could look at her simply as a person who has become detached and lacking in respect which might attract some empathy for her. The richness of the constructed meaning is demonstrated in the complicating addition of Mim's rationales for responding the way she did. For example, Mim couldn't afford a motorized chair and she felt better sitting in the sunny room, which adds a very human element to the story. This makes it very real by demonstrating the consequences of Nancy's behavior.

Rhonda raises important questions about how we, as researchers, come to understand the motivations and feelings of our participants as well as the possible rationale for many of their actions, especially those that may not seem so clear on the surface. Part of the purpose of layered stories is to present the messiness of the researchers' attempts to understand the lives of the participants more fully and to own up to the fact that speculation and uncertainty remain even after we have written our best possible final drafts. We constantly remind ourselves when writing that we want to construct artful versions of experience that offer a complex sense of the *lived* rather than the *reported*. Rhonda's reticence at creating or eliciting subjectively relevant accounts of a given event will make her all the more vigilant in her constructions. She respects the dignity, experiences, and motivations of her participants, and we suspect that she continues to struggle with the blurry line between 'giving voice' and 'distorting voice.' We face the same demons.

Layered stories, after all, are interpretive. Mindful of what we said earlier in the chapter — that form and function work together — the layered story exhibits a dynamic quality at many levels. Judy and Rhonda's layered stories highlight the dynamic between different people's points of view on a particular incident. Carolyn Arnason creates a different type of layering to illustrate the dynamic between spoken and internal speech. In the layered story that follows, different type fonts are used to represent the 'spoken' [PLEASE TAKE OUT THE ARTICLE BY MCDONALD SO THAT WE MIGHT BEGIN OUR DISCUSSION] and the 'internal' [*They look so glassy-eyed that I wonder if they have read the material*]. Lucy is the teacher in a graduate class on human development. The other names represent student voices. Lucy arrives and the talking in the room gradually quiets down. Lucy begins by taking attendance, and calling out students' names as she marks the attendance sheet. She starts the class discussion. THE SPOKEN COMMENTS COME FROM FIELDNOTES; *the internal are compilations and interpretations from interviews.*

Lucy: WHAT DO YOU THINK OF THE READING BY MACDONALD?

Helen: *I really don't understand this. I think it's too dense to have any real meaning. I read this reading for today, but now I can't think of any particular questions. What if I say the wrong thing?*

Carolyn: *It's about the childhood of an artist. There's the word libidinal and I'm wondering why that is important. I'm really amazed how psychoanalytic this class is.*

Lucy: *Why is the class silent? Haven't they read the assigned reading? Maybe they didn't understand. So many are without backgrounds in human development. Good, there's someone who has something to say.*

Dierdre: THE ARTICLE IS TALKING ABOUT CHILDREN, AND ALL CHILDREN CAN DO ART.

Lucy: YES, BUT THE IDEA IS NOT SO MUCH ALL CHILDREN CAN DO ART, BUT THEY CAN GET AT PRIMARY PROCESS. I THINK IT'S IMPORTANT THAT EVERYONE KNOW THE DIFFERENCES BETWEEN PRIMARY PROCESS AND SECONDARY PROCESS. WHAT'S THE DIFFERENCE BETWEEN THE TWO?

Mary: (Audible intake and exhalation of air — a deliberate sigh)

Joan: WELL, THERE'S THE PROCESS THAT ACCESSES LOGICAL AND COGNITIVE WAYS OF DOING ART.

Lucy: SO YOU'RE STARTING WITH SECONDARY PROCESS.

Kate: (Laughing nervously) I WASN'T GOING TO SAY ANYTHING, BUT THE ARTICLE DID MAKE ME THINK OF SOME THINGS IN MY CHILDHOOD. *I don't feel comfortable sharing this in class. It feels too personal.* ACTUALLY I'M CLEAR ON THE FIRST TWO IDEAS ABOUT HOW CHILDREN BECOME PRODIGIES IN ART, BUT THE THIRD IDEA IS CONFUSING.

Lucy: WHY DON'T YOU START GOING OVER THE FIRST TWO IDEAS.

Kate: *I didn't expect this! I'll read the ideas from the article. I don't feel confident enough to explain them in my own words. Difficult.* I'M NOT SURE.

Lucy: LET ME HELP ON THIS. IT'S REALLY SIMPLE. THE FIRST IDEA IS SOME CHILDREN ARE DRIVEN TO DO ART. THE SECOND IDEA IS A PARENT'S WISH TO BE AN ARTIST IS FULFILLED THROUGH THE CHILD.

Kate: LET ME JUST READ THROUGH THE THIRD ONE. I CAN'T QUITE EXPLAIN IT. (Kate reads the third idea)

Lucy: (smiling) YES, IT IS A BIT STRANGE.

Sue: *The language! I just don't believe that this had anything to do with art and becoming a child prodigy, but ... maybe I should think about my own childhood.*

Lucy:	*Why are they silent? The discussion needs direction, and I'm still not sure if they've read the article. I'll give them a more focused question.* WHAT ARE YOUR REACTIONS TO THE IDEA THAT CHILD PRODIGIES SEE MORE THINGS OR ARE MORE SENSITIVE TO LINES, COLORS, AND SHAPES?
Sue:	*Here's a question I can answer. I better take my chance while I can. Oops! Brenda is speaking already.*
Brenda:	*I hope my tape recorder doesn't give out.* THESE CHILDREN ARE AT THE SENSORIMOTOR LEVEL, AND IT MUST BE LIKE THINGS ARE AMPLIFIED.
Nellie:	IT MUST BE OVERWHELMING FOR THE CHILD TO BE SO SENSITIVE TO THE WORLD.
Heidi:	THE PARENTS OF A CHILD LIKE THIS WOULD BE LESS IMPORTANT BECAUSE OF THE CHILD' LOVE AFFAIR WITH THE THINGS AROUND THEM. IT'S LIKE (reaching to a crumpled up brown paper towel on the desk in front of her and picking it up) HAVING A LOVE AFFAIR WITH THIS TOWEL.
Helen:	A CHILD LIKE THIS MUST BE SUFFERING!
Lucy:	(Smiling) YES. *I better check my notes to make sure we're getting through the important points. I want to make sure the students understand the main ideas in the article.*
Sara:	I'VE BEEN THINKING ABOUT THE ARTICLE WHERE THE MUSICIAN'S MOTHER ALWAYS SEEMS TO BE OFF SOMEWHERE. BUT ONE NIGHT SHE COMES IN TO TELL HER SON ABOUT AN UPCOMING CONCERT.
Lucy:	(Enthusiastically) YES, IT'S VERY IMPORTANT FOR A CHILD TO BE RECOGNIZED EVEN IF IT'S JUST OCCASIONALLY.
Sara:	(Looks ready to say something. Lucy looks at her.) CERVANTES HAD TO FIND HIS OWN STORY. HE WENT TO BATTLE FOR 20 YEARS BEFORE HE BEGAN WRITING. (She suddenly looks at the class and gestures with her hand.) WHAT DO YOU THINK? (The class is silent.)
Lucy:	YES, CERVANTES NEEDED TIME TO FIND OUT WORDS WERE HIS LANGUAGE.

The inner life of teaching and learning, including the complex relationships between teacher and students and the classroom culture, has a buried layer of the unspoken that Carolyn attempts to portray in her story. Both teacher and students in this story acknowledge that the discussion isn't satisfying to them, yet their feelings remain unspoken. Just what teaching and what learning is going on here? What hierarchies are evident? What subject matter is actually being discussed, questioned, or challenged? The external and internal speech provide multiple facets for inquiry. Carolyn offers her readers a chance to penetrate various dimensions of the classroom through the organization of the spoken and unspoken experiences and what those suggest about the meanings that individuals may create from the experience. We are hoping that other researchers will push this form even further — possibly asking teachers and students to reflect in logs after class sessions, trying some method of written protocol during sessions, or creating other possibilities that might lead to the revelation of the buried life in classrooms. Carolyn considered another dimension of the layers that might be valuable in future work as well:

> I'd been thinking of interaction on an interpersonal level only, but interaction can also be affected or guided by something coming from outside the class. Perhaps Lucy and the students interact the way they do because of the expectations of their

shared context: a context where the teacher is the giver of knowledge, and the students are the receivers of this knowledge. I may be going out too far on the limb of speculation, but the essence for me is that Lucy and the students interact the way they do, not only because of the classroom dynamics, but also (and perhaps this is the strong influence) because of outside dynamics — the context or cultural expectations of an academic setting.

The search for narrative understanding of such things will go on. We believe that the development and refinement of forms that represent particular functions — like multivocality represented in layered stories — have particular promise in the future of qualitative work.

Illustrations can give only limited representations of the uses and types of layered stories that might enrich our reports of research. Ellen Margolin demonstrated another possibility in her study of a young mother, Katherine, who is torn between her desire to support her son who has anxiety attacks about going to school and her certain knowledge that it is best for him to be in school. Katherine's warring selves became the layers in Ellen's portrayal:

The 'nurturing' mother is represented in *italics*.
The 'responsible' mother is represented in **bold**.

I'm awake but I'll wait to open my eyes. The morning sounds infiltrate, but I try to push them back, to return to sleep, to not face what I know awaits me ... my son. **Maybe today will be different. I must be strong. If I am strong and resolute then he will draw from that and do what he must and he must go to school. All the children go to school though most might rather not because all mothers insist. I will insist.** *He must have had a bad time of it last night. When I went to bed it was already almost midnight and Alex was wide awake. Sunday nights are thick and heavy with anticipation. Don was with him trying to get him calm enough to sleep. Don has a way of distracting Alex from his anxiety. I went to sleep hearing their two voices singing along to Don's guitar and I smiled, but I knew that no melody could spare Alex his terror for long.* **The principal is being very patient and understanding. We must not insult her by not trying to follow her program. 'Just get him to school,' she said. 'We can take over from there but you have to get him here.' She's right. That is my responsibility and whatever it takes, I will get him there.** *Look at him sleeping, so peacefully. I wish I didn't have to wake him. I wish I could just give him some relief from this. I know he's not doing this on purpose. It may not be real, but his fear is real to him. His eyes startle open. 'Good morning, sweetheart. What do you want for breakfast?' Look at the color drain from his face. 'I feel sick, ma. I don't want any food.'* **Don't give in. Don't be manipulated like that psychiatrist warned. 'I'll just go and make something anyway. Why don't you get dressed and maybe you'll feel better enough to eat something before you go to school.'** *Leave quickly. Don't look at his face, so white and pasty. I hate to see those sweat beads forming on his forehead like a condemned person. What did I do wrong? How can I make him go when it makes him physically ill. If somebody saw him now they would see he is sick, not bad, but sick.*

(In the kitchen making breakfast) **Just don't cave. School hasn't killed anybody. The people there are nice enough and Alex is so smart. I can't allow him to ruin the rest of his life over this. I'll drag him if I have to. Maybe he'll hate me today, but he'll thank me someday. Back in this room I see Alex dawdling, half-dressed. 'Look Alex, I'm sorry you don't feel well but you will be fine. I don't care what you say or do, you are going to school today.'**

I think he's going to vomit. His lips are quivering and he is breathing fast and shallow. I hear his words: 'Ma, I'm sorry. I don't mean to put you through this. I wish I could just go, but I can't. I feel so sick like I'm drowning.' Where are they now. Where are all those experts like my mother and the psychiatrist and the principal. Where are they now with their great advice? If I keep on pushing him, I think he's going to crack and then who will be around to pick up the pieces. Not them. I don't know what to say.

'Come on Alex. Try to pull it together. Just let's get into the car. We'll drive to the school and sit until you're ready to go in. I know it's the best thing for you. Trust me, just try.' I hear his words again: 'I want to, ma, but I can't. Please I'm begging you. Don't make me.' I'm still a bit bigger than he is. I suppose I could drag him, head-lock him. But then what? I don't know what to do.

I want to do the right thing but what is the right thing?

I want to do the right thing but what is the right thing?

Layer on layer, then, adds to our knowledge of the multiple impulses that define action.

Elizabeth Merrick's layered story that follows is an interesting presentation because of the way it interweaves the voices of two people from their interviews. Marisol lives in a group home and attends an alternative high school. Rob is a counselor in that high school:

Marisol: Most of the girls in the group home, they disrespect the staff. They drink, they smoke, they do a lot of things I just don't do. And they look at me when I tell them I don't want to do it. They be like 'You a nerd' and stuff. I have fights over that. I be like 'I do what I want to do. If you can't respect me as a friend, that means doing what I wanna do, then go find another friend. Understand?'

Rob: She's a very straight kid in a sense. There's support for that here. I think a lot of kids in family group are like that. They really avoid drugs. Or they were involved and they changed that and don't want to go back to it. A lot of kids come in and feel this is a place where they can be different. You know they figure this is a good opportunity to change.

Marisol: I study and study cause I have a B+ average in this school and I'm gonna be 16 and graduating and going to college when I'm 17. So, I'm not a bad kid. I don't drink, I don't smoke, I don't do no types of drugs. I mean a lot of people get the idea that people in group home are bad, they're wild, they do bad things, that's why they're in there. But I'm in here because I wanna be. So, I'm not what people might think.

Rob: Marisol does very well in school. I mean she has some problems like getting up and getting here on time. And there are some subjects that are very frustrating to her — math and foreign language. They just drive her nuts. But she's a good writer. And she thinks. She takes advantage of things. During the summer she always does this sponsored arts program. She's very interested in singing and dancing. I mean, she talks about dancing but she also talks about being a social worker. She's always been consistent with that. She always says she wants to be a social worker. No matter what, she wants to be someone who helps other people.

Marisol: All my life I wanted to do something with my life, not just sit around and collect welfare. I mean I've seen people waiting for their check and after the initial excitement of getting their first check that's all they have to look forward to each month. But I'd like to earn a paycheck, to work for my money. I want to go to college and be a social worker. I want to work with children.

Elizabeth's juxtaposition strikes us as a strong example of how the words of two people can be shown to agree as well as allowing each person to contribute unique information.

Because the authors of the previous three examples chose to present in different fonts, boldness, or type size, this seems like a good place to spotlight that technique. The thoughtful use of these can serve a variety of purposes: Carolyn highlights the dynamic between spoken and inner speech; Ellen presents the dialogue of one person in two roles — the 'nurturing' and 'responsible' mother; Elizabeth weaves the voices of Marisol and Rob as they talk of similar events. On pp. 312–13 we used italics to put a personal spin on what we had just written more abstractly. On pages 351–2 Andrew Weitz talks to and argues with himself — with what he had written months earlier. Many of our colleagues use different fonts, boldness, or size of type to set off thematic statements from the discussion that supports each separate idea or perspective. Meloy (1993) uses upper case for her voice as she disagrees with parts of another author's work. First she quotes an excerpt from Warnock's text (1984). Then she interrupts the text at various points to comment. Here is an excerpt:

> . . . the naturalistic research Donald Graves and his colleagues Lucy McCormick Calkins and Susan Sowers [produces models that] despite their empirical basis do not count as scientific.

> WHAT DO YOU MEAN BY THAT? WHAT DOES IT COUNT AS? WILL YOU TELL ME?

> They contain a great deal of information, and many teachers have learned from this work . . .

> YES, THAT'S TWO GOOD THINGS, INFORMATION AND LEARNING. WHAT MORE DO YOU WANT? I HAVE SUCH A HARD TIME GETTING MY MASTERS STUDENTS TO GET ANYTHING FROM MOST RESEARCH ARTICLES; THIS MATERIAL BEING CITED WOULD PROBABLY BE USEFUL TO THEM AND IN A FORM THEY COULD COMPREHEND, MINUS JARGON, NUMBERS AND PROCESSES FOREIGN TO THEIR BEGINNING UNDERSTANDINGS. I CAN FEEL THE BUT COMING UP . . .

> But this naturalistic–observational work does not offer us any prospect of a deductive system; we might say instead that it presents us with a dramatistic scene.

WHY DOES THAT SOUND LIKE SUCH A PUT DOWN INSTEAD OF A RICH
OPPORTUNITY FOR A READER?

It offers us . . .

WHOA . . . MAYBE YOU, DEAR SIR, BUT DON'T INCLUDE ME IN THIS!

. . . not so much the prospect of control as the prospect of a more thorough
participation in the actuality of language learning with children . . .

YES! THAT'S EXACTLY MY POINT! IT IS ALMOST LEARNING BY DOING
OURSELVES IF THE DESCRIPTION IS RICH ENOUGH. IT IS VICARIOUS PAR-
TICIPATION IN EVENTS WE AREN'T ALL EXPERIENCING.

Teachers, however, seem to find the images of such research more useful than
research models.

BUT OF COURSE! IT'S IN A LANGUAGE THEY RECOGNIZE AND ABOUT
A PROCESS THEY ARE FAMILIAR WITH AND TRYING TO BETTER
UNDERSTAND.

To report this observation is by no means to sneer at research models;

SOMEHOW, I DIDN'T THINK THIS WAS YOUR POINT.

it is to suggest that the kind of knowledge that is most useful to performers
may differ from the kind of knowledge that is useful to inquirers. (p. 15)

Meloy continues:

After a second reading, I had had enough. Questions in the margins of my copy
included: Is he admitting that Graves, Calkins, and Sowers generate knowledge?
Is he arguing two forms of expression — art and science? Or, that the only 'real'
form is that for inquirers? Aren't Graves, Calkins, and Sowers inquirers? How
does he separate this out? Terms up the margin of my notes included: 'a mono-
theistic culture,' 'an ethnocentric emphasis,' 'an isolationist attitude.'

The use of upper case serves to illustrate Meloy's reaction to specific points as well
as questions generated from her reactions to the reading. We've discovered that
multiple font styles draw readers' attention to complex and multiple perspectives,
simplify the need for a ponderous explanation that often precedes the presentation
of multiple viewpoints or levels of abstraction, and emphasize particular points for
consideration. The use of different fonts, boldness, and size of type, indeed the use
of any layout techniques in general, can burnish and facilitate readers' interaction
with content.

As we read through example after example of narrative reporting to find those
included here, we were reminded of how many times we've read research writing bereft of passion, of commitment to the topic or of understanding the many
resources of form, rhetorical devices, and crafting that we research-writers have at
our disposal. We think this may be because the forms typically relied upon and
valued in educational discourse communities have influenced some researchers to
lose an interior relationship between self and study. Partly, it may be not knowing

the possibilities for shaping the research or the rhetorical resources that can serve as tools. But, as we are emphasizing in this book, we do possess ways to use structure and language to depict not only the content but the journey toward understanding. For example, MacLean's book, *Young Men and Fire* (1992), isn't a typical report that abstracts, introduces, reviews literature, describes methodology, highlights findings, and reaches conclusions and implications. It is a creative and potent weaving.

As writers of research, we might encourage you, our readers, as MacLean suggested, to part the grass by providing richly layered perspectives that entice participation in the multiple stories within the research story. Layers are one way through which we have created clearer images of setting; fine-tuned character in ways to highlight physical attributes, inferred capabilities or mental states; and recreated actions to demonstrate sequences of events. An additional layer might provide the researcher's commentary on the narrative reconstructions of the research story. The layered stories, then, are one way that you might consider to offer research data in more than a neat package of findings and to fashion reports that emphasize the complexity and individuality of your search toward understanding. In our opinion, it helps to remember that research is discovery, bringing together multicolored threads of meaning in endless patterns of momentary emphasis and compactness, and then entangling them into new webs of meaning — always elusive, shimmering, and fascinating. Actually, the whole of a story can never be told, no matter how much space or what devices are used to tell it. Insofar as any structuring or special positioning of layers contributes to a total narrative emphasis, they can be thought of as resources. The intricate questions of when and how to use these resources can't be answered. Writers must experiment with various forms and methods to determine for themselves the effects that are achieved through various configurations. Notice, for example, the quite different emphasis that is achieved through the narrative layers we've just introduced and narrative pastiche that is described in the following section.

Pastiche and Other Quiltings

One of Ruth's current research projects has taken her into a sophomore high school classroom where she spent the past year collecting data on how the students work in and feel about their writing response groups. Using fieldnotes from her observations, transcripts from interviews with students and their teacher, and excerpts from students' written artifacts, Ruth compiled portraits of the members in each group as part of her attempt to understand the complex interactions taking place there. The way these students felt about themselves and about each other as classmates, as writers, and as contributors to the group seemed related to both their opinions about the purposefulness of their group as well as the ways in which they individually contributed to the group's work together. In Figure 3.1, a partial portrait of one of the students, James, demonstrates the struggle to represent the complexities of the group's, teacher's, and researcher's understanding and experience:

Figure 3.1: *Perceptions of James*

ME, MYSELF DON'T LIKE TANISHA'S PIECE ABOUT 'GIRL'S OUT.' THEY'RE DOIN' THE BLACK IS BEAUTIFUL THING AS THEY GET READY TO GO OUT AND ACT **BAD**. TOO MUCH TALK AND NOT ENOUGH TO DESCRIBE. I DON'T UNDERSTAND WHAT SHE'S SAYIN' EXCEPT THAT HER GIRLS IS COOLER THAN ANYONE ELSE. (EXCERPT FROM JAMES'S RESPONSE JOURNAL, 10/20/94)

He's too cool to say much about my writing. He's hanging out with Sheridan and Willy. They don't give girls a nod. Too cool, yez, that's James. Won't put his opinions out front. He's thinks his writin' is better than the rest of us. (From interview with Tanisha about the group, 1/16/95)

Mrs. R.: James doesn't talk ever. 'James,' I say, 'you speak up and have your say.' He isn't shy particularly, just, well, detached. It's almost like he's too good for everybody and has other things swimming in his mind. (From interview with teacher, 1/18/95)

**james
'He'll be a famous writer one day.'
(From interview with Nadine about the group, 1/16/95)**

What I want to know is how Tyler didn't get his self killed by the brothers. We got Lonny, Jimmy and Sheridan — sound out his name long and slow like he likes to hear it — Say it with me now — S-H-E-R-I-D-A-N. ONE OF THEM GUYS COMES ALONG I'm leaving only my shadow for their pleasure. My grandma says, 'You James, my one grandbaby, I want you to grow up, be a man.' She don't know what she's askin. (Poem written by James on 12/13/94)

james's all mixed up and changin'. He's got no 'homey' — and don't seem likely to. It's like that in our suppose-to-be group. 'Where is you James? You with us, man.' We's talkin' and James, he's just dreamin' out there somewhere. Maybe his mind's on the womens. He's a damn good writer though. I loves his writin'. (From an interview with Noah, 11/21/94)

The neighborhood here is notorious for gang activity, violence, and drug trade. As I walked this morning from subway to school, I felt how much like any other place this is. Kitchen lights glow and the clink of dishes signals breakfast preparations. A dog barks. A darkened apartment — people still sleeping, I think. A bird nestled between cherry blossom twitters. Buds of tulips are beginning to break through the dark earth. A baby cries. No one on the streets yet — I imagine the kids I'll see in less than an hour are showering, fighting for the bathroom, looking in the mirror, putting on a second earring. Somewhere a mother is braiding a daughter's hair. (From Ruth's fieldnotes, 4/3/95)

Unfortunately, it isn't easy to refigure multiple perspectives simultaneously. Such versions may be frustrating for some readers. Ruth's attempt to portray James as a paradoxical, complex member of his group is an illustration of the experiments in textual practices that many researchers are undertaking to challenge more linear or simplistic versions of meaning that seem increasingly less than satisfying. To come to grips with multiple realities, Ruth used various sources of data and layout to capture 'James' as a text on the page. Hers is a most obvious type of 'pastiche;' separate pieces that the reader must stitch together from the separate parts into a more meaningful whole.

Various textual experiments that interweave or link data, descriptions, analysis, or multiple genre into diverse configurations, demonstrate how form affects meaning. We have chosen to label these hybrid texts 'pastiche.' The *American Heritage*

Dictionary (1983) defines pastiche as 'a dramatic, literary, or musical piece made up of selections from various works'. If this definition were to be taken literally, then all qualitative research writing might fall within its purview. After all, we do amalgamate various pieces of data, and we do use literary devices to emphasize certain qualities within the subject matter. But, there is more to it than that. Pastiche assumes that the pieces — the selections — that make up the whole communicate particular messages above and beyond the parts. So we are experimenting with juxtapositions, layered additions, multiple tellings, parody, mixed forms, and experiments with layout — to emphasize ambiguity and uncertainty. The *raison d'etre* of pastiche is to create texts, as Atkinson (1992) describes it, '. . . in which the authority and superiority of the author give way to a variety of reticence. The "meaning" and the "culture" are to be constructed *by* the reader, rather than being constructed *for* the reader by the implied narrator' (p. 44).

Like layered story, then, pastiche directs the readers' attention to multiple realities by combining various representations to emphasize the relation between form and meaning. We think one kind of pastiche uses layouts that break linear representation more overtly than does layered story. Other versions of pastiche rely on multiple forms in combination — vignettes, theoretical constructs, first-person accounts, layered stories, plays, poetry, autobiography, biographical data, allegories, diaries, parodies, songs, picture strips and their narratives, direct quotes, multivoice accounts, collage, and the researcher's own stories and musings — all important means through which pastiche may be composed. The forms selected may reflect various states of mind (interior monologue combined with dialogue); relate events (narrative); capture images, sounds, or rhythms (poem); or emphasize conversation (dramatic scenes). Each medium of telling makes reference to a different way of knowing or coming to know that adds to the fabric of total meaning.

Consider in the 'James' pastiche, for example, what the excerpt from James' journal offers in comparison with the perspective contributed by his poem and the statements made by his group members Tanisha, Noah, and Nadine. The constant slippage of definitive meaning from these multiple versions thwarts a singular meaning. Each piece, finally, depends on the others for comparison and elaboration. The portrayal of James through these many pieces is intended to evoke questions about, rather than represent, the relation between James' perception of himself and James as a referent for others. We think pastiche requires readers to begin their own interrogative work and pattern making. Oftentimes the pastiche invites the reader into paradoxical stances — seeing two viewpoints simultaneously within the limitations of the layout of a printed text. This paradoxical pull invites readers to experience each representation and then, when juxtaposed with another representation, pulls the reader out to analyze and reflect. Pastiche enables readers to distinguish the meaning of one perspective from another by providing a structural framework of comparison that involves the reader and certainly the writer in reflection on the qualities of various perspectives.

The use of pastiche emphasizes how arbitrary it is to rely on one perspective, one set of relationships, or one telling of the research story. Pastiche attempts to bridge rifts of perspective wherein each separate piece illustrates a meaning within it as well as the identifiable gaps in meaning across the pieces. For example, Tanisha's statement 'James is too cool to pay us any mind,' and James' statement at another point 'I remain detached to survive' both reveal something of what James' teacher, Mrs. R. recognizes when she states that 'James is so hard to pin down sometimes. I can't tell if he just isn't interested or if he has some load on his mind that keeps him from being with us.' The gaps become recognizable and signify a 'reading' of James through a network of meanings based on relational and referential meaning. In the illustration just presented, the meanings are horizontal, showing James across informants from Tanisha, Nadine, Noah, Mrs. R., Ruth, and James himself.

But pastiche can also show the vertical relations of James' impressions of himself. Figure 3.2 (p. 99) shows another piece of representation from Ruth's experiments that attempts to illustrate in more depth James' perspectives on himself.

It's possible, then, for pastiche to be arranged according to actual sequential relations but also organized in contiguous relations such as horizontal or vertical meaning. These relations form the basis for rendering complex meanings. Such narrative combinations present a feel of the complexities researchers study, communicate multiple realities, and draw readers into the experience while, at the same time, distancing them for the purpose of reflection. What is more, different rhetorical forms ask the reader to perform different tasks. Consider how the interview with James and James' poem call you as reader to experience James' conceptions of beauty differently. Here are other questions for consideration: What kind of text are you reading and what does it expect of you and you of it? Does the poem, for example, draw you to contemplate different ways of reading James than does the log entry written by him? How do you construct information about James from the story excerpt? Finally, as a reader, how do you come to terms with a difficult, abstruse, and resistant 'reality of James' as represented through pastiche?

Matisse's Chapelle du Rosaire in Vence seems a fitting metaphor for what it is we are laboring to say in this section. Construed and constructed during Matisse's final years, it looks, yes, almost conventional from the street. Once inside, it is an awe-inspiring surprise. The physical placement of the chapel, its dimensions, the floor planks, the simple wooden moveable seats, the open spaces, the stained-glass windows that catch the light and disperse it diagonally across the floor and seats, the brilliant colors and clear glass and white paint, the altar, the steps to the altar, the candlesticks, the cross, the priest's robes spread like a matador's cape on one wall, the carved doors, the grill work, the outside greenery, the immense silence — and surely many more facets not so easily noticed by a novice visitor — are all painstakingly crafted to create an integrated symphony of forms — an absolutely right place of serenity, simplicity, and reflection — a place that invites the visitor to enter rather than to stay apart from matters of religion. Matisse was both the master visionary and the creator of the pieces that comprise the whole in this amazing place.

As with the Matisse Chapel, pastiche produces a *text*ure — a weave of coexisting meanings. These *text*ures, then, create a thematic statement. The advantage of pastiche is that the multiple pieces actually open up spaces into a full *texture* — a range of meanings that can coexist because of the meaning that the form of

Figure 3.2: James on beauty

What I noticed first is that her teeth look too big for her body. Then I'm thinking that the nose ring looks too small for the broad bridge of her nose on a wide spread face — that's Nadine to me and it's really hard to say, but I'm thinking if I'm goin' learn from you (Nadine) I want to like the way she looks. I know that I'm too fixed on looks and I want my characters beau-ti-ful so why not in real life. Noah say, 'TOO unrealistic. You make 'em like you'd want to have 'em.' But I'm seein' the connection here between what advice I'm takin' from which members of the group and how physical counts for me. So, you're laughing inside now, I know and think, so how would we organize these groups? (James from interview with Ruth, 11/22/94)

Come to think of Delia waving her glistening/far across town like a slap of heat in the face/that brings boys to their knees and old men to fumble/at their testicles tryin' to remember what's for/what. (James' poem in progress, 10/26/94)

I made Jozetta a character who is black and glistening. I think Rashid should be beautiful even when I hope to make my reader hate him. That gives a reason why Jozetta wants him. I think physical beauty is important to the story so that I can make characters in other ways out of that. (From James' Process Log, 2/22/95)

RASHID LEFT HER BY PHONE ON THAT SAME DAY THAT SHE'D LATER REMEMBER WAS FULL OF RAIN. THE SKY DIDN'T STOP WEEPIN' THEN OR THE NEXT DAY. SHE'D TILT THAT CHIN SKYWARD UNTIL ANYONE WHO WAS LOOKIN' COULD SEE THE COLOR OF TOBACCO GLISTENIN' IN THE SMALL FOLDS OF SKIN THAT STRETCHED SMOOTH THE FURTHER SHE'D TURN HER NOSE TO HEAVEN. RASHID HAD ONCE THOUGHT HER NECK BEAUTIFUL. HIS FINGERS, FATTENED BY LONGING, COULDN'T GET ENOUGH OF THE TOUCH OF MOISTNESS THAT BEADED HER NECK. ON THE DAY SHE CHOSE TO LOOK SKYWARD TO FORGET RASHID, HER NECK, RIGHT BELOW HER PERFECT U-SHAPED EARLOBE, SHOWED A DEEPER COLOR, A CRESCENT SHAPED BRUISE WHERE RASHID'S TEETH BARED WHEN HE COULDN'T GET ENOUGH OF HER. (FROM JAMES' STORY, 'WHAT A WOMAN' — IN PROGRESS, 2/5/95)

My Mama tells me I need to easy up on my friends. 'Nobody's perfect,' she keeps saying, over and over until I feel the heat under my collar. I want friends who's glistenin' with beautiful right down to their toenails. (Interview with James, 1/10/95)

pastiche inscribes. The form is thus a field of play — lacking a 'center,' a singular meaning. Every piece of text harbors traces of other related texts. Julia Kristeva (1980), semiotician and psychoanalyst, named the blend of signs *intertextuality*. 'Any text is constructed as a mosaic of quotations; any text is the absorption and transformation of another' into a new articulation of meaning (p. 66). Thus, arrangements of *text* impinge so that each *text* acts upon another until a *texture* results. The effect is kinetic, giving a dynamic quality and a sense of immediacy as the separate pieces deliver new meaning, at times complementary and at others contradictory.

Variations of Pastiche

Pastiche defines fissures and discontinuities with some ease, works to produce intrusions into the unfolding of events, has the potential to constantly shift perspectives, or may carry a sinuous thread of narrative to weave events, characters, and interpretation together. One of the novels that we see working through pastiche is Leslie Marmon Silko's *Ceremony* (1977). The text mixes accounts of the character Tayo, living on the reservation in the years following World War II, with the myths and poetry of the Laguna Pueblo people. Silko makes time fluid, easily shuttling back and forth among at least four periods of Laguna Pueblo history. Silko braids a social criticism through the comparison of the predominant attitudes toward nature and nuclear arms with traditional Native American beliefs. *Ceremony* is a technical experiment as well as a powerful story. Other examples that might be instructive to any of us who are struggling to learn variations of this technique are Michael Dorris's *A Yellow Raft in Blue Water* (1987) which features three generations of narrators, and Momaday's *The Way to Rainy Mountain* (1969) which combines personal narrative, myth, and historical accounts to interweave various types of knowledge. Any of these texts might be worth examining for both practical ways of crafting pastiche and as a way of discerning the effect of pastiche on the construction of meaning. Additionally, we'd like to offer some variations of pastiche that our students have been experimenting with as well.

Version 1: Multiple forms

Sharon Shelton-Colangelo crafted several stories and poems from her log to open avenues of expression through which she might represent the experiences of Amanda, a third grader in the classroom where Sharon observed. The two examples we've included here highlight her interpretation of Amanda. Her juxtaposition of a vignette and a poem emphasizes the dialogue between Amanda's perspective as represented in the interior monologue and Sharon's perspective imaged through the poem about Amanda.

Amanda

Mmm. Popcorn! I am so hungry. It's almost
lunchtime, and I only had a bao, a Chinese
bun, for breakfast. I can smell that popcorn. I
want to eat it right now. But first we have to   Amanda 1992
make our names and glue popcorn on them.
Or make popcorn people. I know! I'll do both.   It feels like 1949
Ms. Thompson will be so happy when she sees   To me

I'm doing both. I wish my hair were blonde instead of straight and black. I'm glad my pencils are sharp. I'll draw my letters as carefully as I can. I am going very slowly on the sides of my A to make them touch each other at the top. A for Amanda. I don't want my lines to wobble. Ms. Thompson doesn't like wobbly lines.

Mimi is saying she's writing her name. I'll bet she doesn't draw a picture, too, though. I like Mimi's shoes. They look like grown-up's shoes. I wish I had clothes like Mimi, but my mother always says we wear the same clothes as long as we can. She always says, 'Three years new, three years old, three years patched.'

Ms. Thompson is stopping at our desk! She is dressed in a purple top and pink pants. Pink is my favorite color in the whole wide world. Ms. Thompson looks so pretty today. She's picking up my picture! What's happening, though? She's turning it over. Why is she turning it over? She's walking away. What is she saying? What does she mean, 'Start over. Too small?' Doesn't she see my neat lines? Doesn't she know I am going to draw a girl, too?

Don't cry. I mustn't cry. Good girls don't cry in class. Start over. Just start over. Remember to make my A bigger. Remember to make my lines straight. Remember to be quiet. Always remember to be quiet.

Watching you there,
Bright sparrow eyes
Your wings folded,
Cold,
No singing.

You pick at crumbs
Of learning
Flung unthinking,
Unseeing.
Your mind flitting
Through
Other people's stories,
Other people's songs.

I was once a fledgling,
Caged in silence,
Frozen by obligation,
Hungering for spring,
Longing to take wing,
Crying, dying to sing.

Sharon wrote her response to the poem:

> I was happy with the poem I wrote about Amanda, comparing her to a bird who could not yet sing or fly. I identified with Amanda and expressed great hope for her through my poem. I feel that it was coherent and had unity and clarity and the honest belief that Amanda shows her promise in such important ways (that are sometimes ignored) in the class.

For us, the poem captures a different essence than the interior monologue, but in combination — monologue set in dialogue with poem — the hopeful and the less-than-hopeful portraits of Amanda show something of the complexity of 'being' a child in this classroom that neither the story nor the poem alone could depict.

The form of knowledge produced from Sharon's pastiche is local, contingent, and ephemeral. It is tolerant of interpretation. As you experiment for yourself with pastiche, don't hesitate to risk unusual configurations and refigurings as long as you believe that what you achieve is an honorable telling. Whether or not pastiche is used, when and where it might be useful, how you employ it — all of these issues deserve your careful consideration.

Version 2: Co-researchers' viewpoints

Some of our students have been co-researching and experimenting with how to link multiple interpretations into one text. As Michele Bellavita suggested: 'I've often thought it would be interesting for two or three doctoral students to do a study together, but I've never really considered how that would work, especially the final product.' Ruth followed the progress of three doctoral researchers through their collaborations — Geana Harris, Ray Matthews, and Amanda Hahn — as they investigated the relationship between adolescents' television viewing and their self-sponsored reading as leisure time activities.

From the beginning, the co-researchers had different takes on the best ways to introduce their discussion of the influence of television on the youth with whom they had examined this issue. They decided that they would each write up an introduction as a departure point for a beginning discussion on how best to begin. Geana, for example, started with a quote from Thomas Pynchon's *Vineland* (1990) to emphasize Pynchon's notion that the 'boob tube' is part of 'rewiring' humans. Geana opens with the hymn sung by patients at the Institute for Tubal Detoxification:

> While you were sittin' there, starin' at 'The
> Brady Bunch,'
> Big fat computer jus'
> Had you for lunch, now Th'
> Tube —
> It's plugged right in, to you! (Pynchon, 1990, p. 337)

Part of Geana's strategy is to emphasize the contradictions of life that Pynchon emphasizes in the novel: people fantasize themselves into popular film; hum themes from game shows; spend their leisure hours watching 'classics' like Pee-Wee Herman movies. Geana begins with the idea that she was gleaning from the students: television is the narcotic, a constant rerun of life through which the world is reduced to an eternal present that confounds fact and fiction.

Ray takes another tactic to introduce his discussion. He begins with literature's powers — image, figurative language, structures — to complicate story rather than reduce it. He uses Italo Calvino's (1981) *if on a winter's night a traveler* to ground his readers in the event of 'reading' as an active, engaged and engaging process. 'Chapter I,' he starts, 'invites the reader into the narrative. Relax. Concentrate. Dispel every other thought. Let the world around you fade' (p. 3). Ray continues: 'The novel begins and propels a series of unfinished stories and segments that short circuit completion of any one story. Each story initiates a new narrative without leading to resolution. For all its frustrations, the novel closes with the fulfillment of the desire to complete the book and experience the experience. Television doesn't work to complicate meaning.'

Amanda begins with a quote from one of her interviews with Lettie, a 14-year-old who is the mother of 6-month-old Jeremy:

> Me, I like to watch them shows that has elements of truth. My favorites is 'Cops,' 'Unsolved Mysteries,' 'Prime Time,' 'Rescue 911' and other shows like that. It's like real stories of what's happenin' around us all the time. These is true to life and I like that 'cause we is livin' on these streets all the time. Television is trying to show what's happenin' out on the street — lettin' that into our livin' rooms and I think we needs to see that. That's a way for all the rich people to see what's really goin' on in their own town but on the other side of their streets. My baby needs to see this. I want him aware of what's out there. TV's the best way. Think of 'Hill Street Blues.' Now, they do real stories that happen in L.A. Me, I hopes Jeremy'll decide to be a cop. There's good models for him there. I reads 'People' and 'Seventeen.' I finds the stories are good — about real people. My mom buys those so they're around for me to read. Sometimes I'd like to be them in those magazines with their easy lives. I got it bad with Jeremy.

The incorporation of these three viewpoints could take many forms: juxtaposing, turn-taking, or weaving. By accommodating these three different ways of opening their study, Geana, Ray, and Amanda can 'spin out' more complex issues than any one of them could accomplish with their individual takes. Part of their next task is to figure how sequence and spatial possibilities might accentuate what they try to do with these three different views.

Version 3: Multiple stances and perspectives

We can't help but think of Wallace Stevens' cubist poem 'Thirteen Ways of Looking at a Blackbird' when we talk about pastiche because it is not only a poem about thirteen ways of looking at a blackbird but also a contemplation on what looking, knowing, and seeing mean. In each stanza as the speaker surveys the landscape, the 'eye' and the 'I' are intertwined and clearly not separable. The poem, then, is both a poem about seeing blackbirds in the natural landscape and how that 'seeing' is influenced by the landscape of the beholder's mind. If you haven't read Stevens' poem, it might be worthwhile to do so as a preface to this particular section on pastiche.

Point of view has a determining effect on the 'closeness' or 'distance' of the seeing. The emphasis by degree can be illustrated through various techniques of immediacy, authority, or even intimacy. Take, for example, Julia McKinney's way of introducing the big city school that was the site of her study. Julia deliberately chose pastiche to give her reader a sense of the 'flood of various perspectives that hit me on that first day.' She begins in the following way:

> 'Come up the hill and you'll just stumble onto it,' the principal assured me. When I got off the train and came above ground, I felt the cold air slap against my face. Snow and fog made the air so thick I couldn't get a sense of direction. With the

principal's words drumming through my head, I started up the slippery path of hillside behind several children who assured me this was the way to their school. Suddenly, the building loomed ahead as promised, and I inhaled the cold air sharply as I saw the light-filled windows gleaming toward us. The building was a rambling one, especially emphasized with the drifts of snow that piled against eaves, chimneys, and window ledges. As I approached the door, a man bundled in at least three layers of wool and rubber, turned with a smile and reached for the over-sized handle, sweeping the door open so that a wave of warm air bolted right into my face. 'Welcome to North Middle School,' he gestured for me to enter.

* * * *

Mr. Monroe, principal for nearly three decades, walks me to a set of rust colored double doors through which I hear the whines, shouts, and jibes of adolescents at play. The pungent air mixes raging hormones with the smell of the sour apple and grape gum. A sea of colors swarms before me as adolescents who don't notice us enter continue with their games of tag and basketball. In twos and threes, girls huddle in corners, telling their secrets. A sharp pain emits from my eyes, letting me know I'm trying to see too much at once. Sound bounces off the cinder block walls. Even painted in a robin egg blue, these walls show the signs of a building nearing a hundred years old. 'And yet,' Mr. Monroe is saying, 'we keep this gym open sixteen hours a day including weekends with volunteers. These kids need this place. It's a haven and the hub of their social life. It keeps them in school.'

* * * *

My hand glides over the wooden table top filled with runes. 'Shit Happns.' 'Dis A Teacher.' 'Tego' enclosed in a heart with 'Maria.' Mostly names — a way of recording their presence in this place. 'What you thinkin'?' the girl sitting next to me bends over to get a good look in my face. 'Don't believe,' she smiles at me, 'everything you read or hear in this class. We're not so scary as we look.' She throws her head back so that the sheen of her black hair reflects the fluorescent lights above. 'Me, I wanna' be a heart specialist. I'll save your life someday,' she laughs and pats the table top. 'I got to hang in this school and do everything right.' She wrinkles her nose as she says this. 'Next step is one of the top high schools for me if I can make the grades. I gotta do that. Single goal — to the top of my class.' So began my long conversations with Diana, a 13-year-old who seemed to have complete trust that her future was bright and that through hard work and careful critique she could attain her goals.

* * * *

In this flurry of 20 minutes, I began my one year residency as a researcher in this school. What I couldn't have predicted then was just how much Mrs. DeGraff's warning would be an apt one: Words won't ever pin down the experiences you'll have or the students you'll meet in this school. Think carefully before you let something stand as truth.

Spatially, distance or closeness may be controlled by the movement 'in' and 'out' of scenes. Notice how Julia moves from outside to inside in the three scenarios you've just read. She stands at some distance from the school as she comes 'above ground' in snow and fog thick enough to distort her sense of direction. Progressively, she moves inside the school, describing the physical facility but also the activity and people within. As a narrator, Julia is not 'removed' from the scene. She reports as 'objects of examination' what she sees and hears.

One advantage of the pastiche is that time and perspective can become manipulable and malleable. While it is true that Julia sequenced the events of her entry into the school in the order in which they occurred, there are other places in her reporting where her knowledge of prior events and situations resonate in a present moment. Again, Stevens' poem is instructive in providing a model for pastiche. Although the blackbird flies from the circle of visual perception in stanza IX, it returns or is still 'present' in stanza X as an object of contemplation and as a catalyst for reflection. When the blackbird is literally out of sight it is still hypothetically in the mind's eye, stressing that sight has little to do with seeing. So, like Stevens, we are puzzling with ways to represent in writing the 'looking' that suggests presences (as in the mind's eye) in absences. Used consciously, such a construction represents how one incident carries within it the presences or shadows of others. For example, Julia describes a particular moment when Tego, one eighth grader in her study, declared his decision to drop out of school. Embedded within this moment are resonances of the earlier scenes through which Julia introduced us to the school:

> When I get the news, the first thing I do is think how Tego needed a small glimmer of hope to keep going in school. One of Tego's motivations for dropping out of school was his adamant belief that school could not help him in the future. Tego's words echo through the darkening corridors as I leave the building through the east wing. 'I gotta' work,' he'd say over and over again. 'I gotta' live. School don't help with that.' 'Come up the hill,' Mr. Monroe's invitation echoes in my head. Yes, the gym might 'give some kids a place and keeps some of them in school,' as Mr. Monroe suggests, but I'm finding that here is Tego at thirteen years of age, thinking that money can buy him a bit of happiness. I see Diana wrinkle her nose as she says 'I gotta hang in this school and do everything right.' I want her trust in education to seep into his pores. Within a week of his long walk away from the school gates, Tego's found in a long alleyway beaten up, his face slashed by an Exact-o knife.

The alternation of the present moment with key phrases from the earlier scenarios creates particular emphases or stresses on meaning. In some ways this version of pastiche has a sense of what the poet Ezra Pound described as 'vorticism,' the simultaneous experience of something moving inward, describing the circumstances around Tego's dropping out of school, and darting outward, the larger events surrounding the culture of this school. It is helpful to think of the structuring of pastiche as a visual entity, and, again, Stevens' poem is a helpful example for demonstration. Mind, the poem emphasizes, creates bird through its phenomenological evidence of actual bird — feathers, flight, whistle, shadow. But, the mindscape is more — bird is a principle of life and movement. The blackbird's mark is everywhere, even as the moving shadow, in the traces it leaves behind, and in the recalled or imagined perceptions; that is, in the memory of movement or whistling, the innuendo of appearance. In much the same way Diana's sheen of hair and wrinkle of nose, the rusty doors, Tego's slashed face, the sea of color in the gym — all are phenomenological detail juxtaposed to highlight not only Tego's personal story but the story of the school. Pastiche can free us from conventional notions of time and from linear relationships between past and present by providing the opportunity for us to present a curvilinear flow of movement forward and backward through past, present, and future.

Version 4: Braiding

The mingling together in writing of various aspects of thinking — of perception and conscious thought, of description and analysis, of what is seen and what is imagined — is not easy. We refer to the process as 'braiding.' The word itself gives us a concrete way to think about how we might converge more than one level of thinking at a time. Together, as in most other versions of pastiche, the separate parts are dynamically related. In the following example, Ruth created an exaggerated braiding that is intended to demonstrate the dynamic between her description of the research process as it moves forward and her thinking about the process which slows down forward movement:

> I decided to write a piece of historical fiction as a deliberate way to test the processes involved in conducting historical research. I began by writing down all the ideas, images, and rhythms that I remembered from my trip to the Blue Grotto in Italy. From all this I could see figures rise, as Henry James suggested, in the carpet (A form of Improvisation no doubt, but not enough detail to really put me onto an accurate portrayal of the grotto. I just don't know enough). Questions emerged from these first thoughts, and, in the asking, direction was set for the first steps of my research (The fact is I needed a plan). I need sources of knowledge that I didn't have (should I draw upon local knowledge to give spontaneity and naturalness to my fancy? I could conduct interviews with several people who have visited. Maybe guide books could give me information. Obviously historical records will have the most detail but might control the tone. I do want to remain imaginative.) I'll have a writer visiting the Blue Grotto (Do I remember enough of the landscape both in and out of the grotto? What's the Italian word for rowboat and the men who row visitors there? tides? water currents? changes in sea level over the years?) where he, the writer, goes into a reverie on Tiberius (which Tiberius? What will I need to know about him as a ruler, a man, a lover? a man of orgies I remember. Is that documented?) and some vague remembrance of a private entrance that Tiberius used (Is there evidence of another entrance or is this the writer's imagination? Has sea level changed and the land entrance is under water? Maybe the character swims into it — A secret liaison? What will I need to know about the water temperature? seasons? What marine life?) This, after all, will be a life changing moment for the writer I've imagined (What will make it so? A little heroism?) I go to the library. I call friends. I pull out slides from my trip to the Grotto. I reread my journal. The place is of longitudes and latitudes, a set of speeds and slownesses between a wind and some fog (Where

can I get this information?) A cloud of locusts. Describe a full moon in the scene (What date? How to read the phases so far from home?) and then, I begin writing again. One sentence, maybe two. (I'm irritated because the writing can't go well without enough information to make the story believable.) The learning comes slowly as I write my way into the grotto, the sea currents, the private entrance. Now, to the writer's mind. (I read sections of Freud's *Civilization and Its Discontents* to remind myself of the manifestations of libidinal desire and review Lacan for the working principle for my writer's interior monologue — 'the unconscious is structured like a language.' How can I enact such language in my writer's inner thoughts?) I work one inch at a time. I think that is the way with learning.

Bird by bird as Anne Lamott reminded us. One bird can lead us to another, can lead us to air currents and habitats and food chains and natural selection, can lead us to flight and feathers and symmetry, can lead us to Icarus and labyrinths and to Wallace Stevens' 'Thirteen Ways of Looking at a Blackbird,' can lead us to — not birds, but theories about alternation of generations — that is, birds of birds.

David Guterson's (1995) 'Acknowledgments' for *Snow Falling on Cedars* suggests what a tangle or coil of learning must finally be represented in writing:

> I thank the many people who contributed to the writing of this book: Mike Hobbs at Harborview Hospital in Seattle, for his help with matters of forensic pathology; Phil McCrudden for taking me salmon fishing . . . Steve Shapiro for his insights about gill-netting; . . . Ann Radwick for assistance with local sources; Murray Guterson and Rob Crichton for their assistance regarding legal esoterica; Frank Kitamoto and Hisa Matsudaira for help in my research and interviews; the Bainbridge Historical Society for access to its archives and museum . . . Captain Alan Gill for his expertise regarding ships and shipping . . . Dudley Witney's fine book *The Lighthouse*, an architectural and pictorial history; Charles F. Chapman's *Piloting, Seamanship and Small Boat Handling* . . . Hazel Heckman's *Island in the Sound*, a psychologically and culturally accurate portrait of island life in Washington . . . Sallie Tisdale's *Stepping Westward*, with its brilliant and exacting descriptions of the Pacific Northwest woods . . . James L. Stokesbury's *A Short History of World War II*, Richard F. Newcomb's *Iwo Jima*, Rafael Steinberg's *Island Fighting* . . . Ronald Takaki's brilliant book, *Strangers from a Different Shore*, a history of Asian Americans . . . Seymour Wishram's *Anatomy of a Jury*, an exacting account of our criminal justice system; to Peter Irons' *Justice at War* for its insight into the internment years . . . Julia V. Nakamura's *The Japanese Tea Ceremony*, and Alan W. Watt's *The Way of Zen*. (p. ix)

We can be defeated and disoriented and overwhelmed by the vastness of the learning before us when we start writing up any research project. We can try to fit knowledge into neat boxes and discrete fragments — into charts and graphs and tables and units. It helps sometimes. Guterson, of course, uses narrative fiction, specifically historical fiction, as the ecological environment through which he learns about relations.

At times, the use of different voices and the interchange of forms is so subtle that the artistry slides past unless we stop and look. Here is a deceptively simple-seeming paragraph from Philip Taylor's work (1992) about drama and action research in a seventh grade social studies classroom:

> 'While we're doing this glitter,' Susan dictated to Madelene, 'Joyce steps into the time machine'. Susan was describing how she felt her group's film should begin. This film was going to recreate the journey back to Boston through the eyes of Joyce, a time-traveler. 'No, that would take too long,' Madelene insisted, 'the camera will pick up Joyce preparing.' The problem was, it seemed, would there be sufficient glitter, a prop used to suggest a flashback, to enable Joyce to set up for the next scene? Susan clearly thought there would be. (p. 263)

In this paragraph Philip braids his participants' voices with his own. Look at the information these few lines hold. We are privy to Susan and Madelene's process. We hear their verbal interactions. We learn what they are doing. We are witness to their negotiation–disagreement. Philip's narrative sets the job at hand into a broader context. Toward the end of the paragraph he moves from having been a tour guide to being an analyzer, all the while talking to his readers.

Pastiche makes us rethink boundaries regarding communication and response, recreating meaning, indirection and direction, nearness and distance, and author's stance. Controlled, deliberate pastiche enables the reader to explore possibilities and experience the tensions among them, causing deep involvement with the meaning. We are learning for ourselves the potential of pastiche by experimenting with variations of it in our work and hope you will find useful variations of your own.

Version 5: Electronic publishing

What, you might ask, is this piece doing in the pastiche section? While certainly not 'forms' of writing but more like a series of possibilities, we feel that electronic publishing deserves some consideration here. Its impact on what research writers might do and produce is bound to ripple out in ways that most of us do not even imagine at present.

There are of course a variety of electronic journals and ways in which the medium allows for collaborative writing across huge distances and with a great variety of known and unknown colleagues. It can be mind boggling and, not surprisingly, this phenomenon is viewed by some with great anticipation and by others with great caution. Our friend William Colangelo showed no such caution. His dissertation, a study titled, 'The Composer/Performer Paradigm in Giacinto Scelsi's Solo Works' (1996) was published electronically exclusively. Bill writes:

> The findings are presented in the form of a Web Page interactive computer presentation. To directly link recorded music examples, the score, analytical charts and graphs together with the text, a multi-media presentation was created using the Macintosh Computer and a writable CD-Rom. The presentation is in the form of a Web application, presented by the Web Browser Netscape and a set of 'helper applications' for sound listening, graphical viewing and video-viewing. Contained in the presentation are the full text of this study, the additional text of translations of articles by and about Scelsi, the musical recordings, graphical images of the scores, photos of the performers, and excerpts from the recorded interviews.

Different sections of text, pictures, and music are connected by means of hyperlinks, a generic term for the use of a string of text or picture as a button to open another file on a related subject. In Netscape, hyperlinks are indicated by a brighter color such as bright blue, or in the case of a picture, a border of bright blue. Viewers can also navigate between the component parts of a presentation by means of buttons (Forward, Back), by means of a pop-up menu above which is a record of titles of all the 'pages' the viewer has seen thus far, or by means of 'bookmarks' which permanently record a page of interest for the viewer. (Personal communication, June, 1996)

We are convinced that by this time you are makings links to the concept of pastiche. What may make this sort of electronic presentation slightly different is that it depends so heavily and directly on the 'reader' to create order and experience from the menu and, further, from what the menu can offer, a greater variety of information and media. However, it seems to us that the reader is no less involved in any of the versions of pastiche that we have offered so far. It takes an active, selective mind to enter a pastiche, whether it is printed in a book or presented on a computer screen. All of these forms remain essentially linear — even hypertext. That is, we go from one page or screen to another, even if these include multiforms such as score with music, voice-over with interview transcript, or poem with vignette.

In broad strokes, we see two major functions of electronic publishing: the dissemination of rapidly evolving information and the networking in particular kinds of writing efforts. For these, the speed at which they may be accomplished and published is a decided asset. However, in our opinion this does not do away with the need for conventional publication routes. Here the comments of Burbules and Bruce (1995) seem particularly appropriate:

> But when an essay's form is closely linked in design as well as in substance with the expression of a distinctive point of view; when it has an aesthetic quality that cannot be hurried or rushed into preparation for print; when an author's voice and style depend on saying things in just this way and no other, then the rapid turn-around and fungibility of electronic media do nothing to help, and might in practice hinder, the preservation of a form of writing and publishing that cannot be reduced to an information dissemination model. (p. 16)

(Whew! The authors of this book give a collective sigh of relief!)

The idea of electronic publishing is not new in this book or elsewhere. If it serves a need, use it. If it doesn't, use other forms and ways to communicate, or create your own. There seems to be plenty of room for qualitative research writers to benefit both from the possible information and dissemination links of electronic publishing, if they care to, as well as from conventional writing and publication. Other people may opt for one route only.

Finally in this section, it has taken us tremendous soul searching and some agony to present here an electronic solution that may well do away with the entire premise and need for this book. In the spirit of true intellectual forthrightness, however, we feel we must dare (see Figure 3.3). Of course, this cartoon holds equally as well for qualitative research writing. You wish. Or do you?

Figure 3.3: FIC PRO

Drawing by R. Chast; @ 1996 The New Yorker Magazine Inc.

Metaphor

'Why is a raven like a writing desk?'
    'Come, we shall have some fun now!' thought Alice. 'I'm glad
they've begun asking riddles — I believe I can guess that,' she added aloud.

'Do you mean that you think you can find out the answer to it?' said the March Hare.

'Exactly so,' said Alice.

'Then you should say what you mean,' the March Hare went on.

'I do,' Alice hastily replied; 'at least — at least I mean what I say — that's the same thing, you know.'

'Not the same thing a bit!' said the Hatter. 'Why, you might just as well say that "I see what I eat" is the same thing as "I eat what I see!"'

. . . and the party sat silent for a minute, while Alice thought over all she could remember about ravens and writing-desks, which wasn't much. (Carroll, 1990, p. 83)

The Mad Hatter has a point of course. He's teaching Alice something about the relationship between meaning and the structure of language. More particularly, the question posed to Alice about how the raven is like the writing desk calls for a comparison of 'thingness' which is how Heidegger (1971) labelled the concept that he believed was at the core of metaphoric thinking. Alice is called upon to make a metaphoric leap through which she can 'imagine' one thing in another or merge two seemingly different qualities into one. Alice is on the verge of metaphoric thinking as she catalogues what she remembers as the 'thingness' of both raven and writing-desk.

Metaphor:

The darkness is like wool prickling my arm.
Fate is a jagged-edge tooth that rips at faith.
The silence grows fat around us.
Crane your neck and you will see the moon.

Consider how the metaphoric structure in each of these statements differs. In the first, the use of 'like' reminds us that two things are being compared. The darkness isn't wool, it is only 'likened' to it in the quality of 'thingness' that the two share — that of 'prickling.' 'Fate,' however, is a 'jagged-edge tooth,' and both fate and tooth 'rip,' yet we are told that fate rips 'faith.' We are left to determine for ourselves what a tooth may rip because we are expected to imply that part of the comparison. In the third metaphor, however, we are expected to make the comparison that 'silence' can 'grow fat.' Properties of comparison exist only in our own potential to make the imaginative leap for ourselves. Next, 'crane' is a verb turned metaphor. The long neck of a bird gives meaning to a human action — to 'stretch the neck.' In this metaphor, the comparison is embedded in one word rather than among words.

Metaphor. The great closet organizer of comparison. All those shelves, bins, boxes, drawers, hangers, and nooks of meaning! Some well lit, neat, useful. Consider a metaphor like 'the black flower of my umbrella wilted under heavy rain' as a metaphor that is neat and well lit in its understandability if not usefulness. Some metaphors get murky and messy in their complexity: 'My breath forms a blossom of iris on the pane and outside's coldness shivers the petals to near quivering.' We all have metaphors that seem to come to us naturally. Some useful: 'Hello! Happy to see you. Think you're perfect for this situation.' Some annoying in the cliché we recognize in ourselves: 'What! You again? Thought I got rid of you long ago.' Some upsetting: 'No! I hate it. Must be someone else's.' Some provocative: 'If I could shine you up a bit I can make you it into a whole new statement of meaning.' Get our drift? Are we in synch? Cat got your tongue?

Figures of speech that help us see one thing in terms of another are ever present in our speech, thinking, doing and writing. What conclusions, what plans of action, what interpretations do metaphors have the power to suggest? We think it is worth spending some time to explain our understanding of the uses of metaphor in research writing. We also hope to challenge you to consider the uses of metaphor in your work. It seems fitting that we spotlight metaphors as they apply to qualitative research writing. In a way we're playing the role of Mad Hatter with our question: How is metaphor like an apple dropping into deep early snow?

Lakoff (1993) proposes the idea of metaphor as a cross-domain mapping in how we think and reason. Indeed, Lakoff states that '. . . the locus of metaphor is not in language at all, but in the way we conceptualize one mental domain in terms of another' (p. 203). In this sense, the language we use — the metaphoric expression — is but an indication of the more essential bedrock of how and what we understand.

In analyzing our metaphor of metaphor as a closet of meanings, for example, we find that it sends these messages:

1   We attempted to clarify something, metaphor, by comparing it to another something, closet, and our interactions with what is contained in that closet.
2   Our shaping of the metaphor meant that we knew something about closets. But in writing, we did not use our extensive knowledge about closets. We took for granted that one metaphor, as is, would resonate with other peoples' ways of thinking about closets.
3   We could have talked about metaphor in a number of other ways (road map, straightjacket, bridge) but we did not. Thus we organize meanings in some way and label that meaning through comparison to make it clear and accessible, although sometimes it remains fuzzy and hidden.
4   When we surface our meanings via comparative language we can increase our understanding of how we think and reason, change some meanings that we don't find compatible, and strengthen the meanings we do find compatible.

Because qualitative research writing rests both on how we make meaning and how we communicate our understandings it is essential to consider how metaphors may illuminate and illustrate meaning. Perhaps if we think of how we illuminate an idea or object by describing it, then metaphor can be understood as a way to provide *illustration* of that illumination through its comparative qualities. Metaphor is a tool that can move us away from predictable lines of seeing. Sharon Shelton-Colangelo, while conducting research in a 'whole language' classroom, began to understand the importance of metaphor in her work:

> In *Metaphors We Live By*, George Lakoff and Mark Johnson (1980) note that surfacing the metaphors we use can be a way of understanding a situation we might not fully grasp in other ways. 'Metaphor,' they write, 'is one of our most important tools for trying to comprehend partially what cannot be comprehended totally:

our feelings, aesthetic experiences, moral practices, and spiritual awareness. These endeavors of the imagination are not devoid of rationality: Since they employ metaphor, they employ an imaginative rationality'. (p. 193)

Metaphor offers a structure that aids us in establishing a relationship between something that we already know and something else that we are attempting to understand. Metaphors are particularly useful when attempting to explain abstract concepts such as 'class,' 'authority,' 'power relations,' or 'control.'

Notice, in what follows, how Sharon's examination of various classroom rules and configurations led her to connect the control, authority, and power structures through the metaphor of fake green grass mats:

> Next the children gather on little fake, green grass mats pushed together to form a sort of carpet.
> The rules for the meeting are posted. They clearly say you have to stay on your piece of grass.
> I notice that the students seem to be in the same position on the grass that they were in last week and maybe before. Tyrone is sitting in the back rear on his piece of grass, which is, I realize, just too small for his large body which spills over onto his neighbor's turf.
> She often calls on children whose hands aren't raised. One Chinese boy sitting in the middle of the group has a hard time answering her question. He falters, looks down at the grass.

The fake, green grass became for Sharon a binding metaphor. She explains:

> I feel that the fake, green grass upon which the children in Mrs. Thompson's classroom sit while they participate in what the teacher likes to call 'whole language' activities furnishes my case study with an important metaphor. Just as green grass is alive, growing and nourishing of all human life through its role in photosynthesis, real whole language learning involves growth, change and nourishment. By stark contrast, the 'grass' in this classroom, so bright and alluring, is fake, unchanging, un-growing, un-nourishing. Dead.

Of course this explanation might have been sufficient. However, Sharon's metaphor became a springboard from which she could explore the concrete details of how this classroom represented for her a harsh, bleak picture, one filled with unrealized constructive possibilities:

> Metaphor is a wonderful tool for reflection and for exploring meaning. My reference to fake green grass is a special way of describing what is going on in the classroom and contains within it the vision of other ways of doing things. When I note, for example, that Tyrone is uncomfortable, too big for the little square on which he is confined, I am raising the possibility of a classroom that is more expansive and freeing in which he might feel more comfortable and nourished. By making the fake, green grass a metaphor for student disaffection, I am also envisioning an alternative to that disaffection, envisioning another way of learning, a truly whole language class, one that involves growth and sustenance.

One function of imaginative comparison highlighted through Sharon's work is that metaphor can help us see what is *not* there, what is missing and then, as in

Sharon's case, what might be needed. Metaphor offers its creators and readers a free play with what Lakoff and Johnson (1980) term 'imaginative rationality,' an essential mindset, one that helps lift our research writing so that it does more than inform, so that it inspires our readers to create their own visions and their own solutions. Next, Sharon considers how metaphor may provide a unique experience for a reader:

> I am wondering what it is about metaphor that makes it such a potent way of sharing experience. Maybe its power lies in the invitation to participate that it offers another person. Maybe metaphor, like story, is a way of drawing another person in to the aesthetic event and thereby giving her ownership of it. I think metaphor also allows a full range of non-verbal ways of knowing to enter into an aesthetic event. Like poetry itself, metaphor creates space for the reader, giving her blanks to be imaginatively filled in. The reader gets to undergo an experience, to creatively bring in her own subjectivity, in a way other forms of expression that are less overtly metaphorical might not allow.

Sharon's research writing certainly echoes her comfort with taking creative risks in the service of communication. For some researchers this comfort is not quite the case. But we have noticed that people's discomfort is often allayed as they become more practiced, more experienced with various ways of presenting their understandings. This is particularly so in situations that are psychologically safe and supportive and peopled with others who are also finding their way.

We routinely return to our field logs, as we know other researchers do, in order to distill and reflect on embedded metaphors that we've used to describe the research experience and the data. Try it. Start with one section of a log. Mine the possibilities. Sometimes this work seems forced and not overly productive, but on occasion, when we least expect it, we find a metaphor or one comes to mind that accounts for a relationship we've been struggling to understand or write about. In the discussion that follows, several researchers describe their processes of thinking about and producing metaphors:

Carolyn Arnason shares some metaphors from her field log that she binned under 'My Experience as Research Instrument':

1 (p. 19) I'm foggy on this because I'm recovering from my debut
2 (entry to the field).
3 (p. 26) I can feel myself consciously pulling back on the reins of my
4 research horse that smells the scent of an informal interview (beginning
5 phase of observing).
6 (p. 38) This research instrument felt like giving into a Garfield nap
7 attack.
8 (p. 61) I didn't feel like leaving, because there seemed to be lots more to
9 see and hear. What was everyone talking about? Will just have to put the
10 computer into overdrive.
11 (p. 62) Here I am setting out to do another observation — no notebook, no
12 pen, no tape machine, no one with me, just me and my shadow. It's an
13 exciting kind of loneliness in the Star Trek sense of going where no one
14 had gone before . . . Feeling I'm chartering unknown territories. This

15 excitement, however, is strongly tinged with the feeling of going it
16 alone. But not in the John Wayne sense, or the Sinatra *I Did It My Way*
17 sense. I don't really know yet what I'm discovering, and it's not all my
18 way but their way — the people I'm observing.
19 (p. 62) . . . it was difficult to focus because I was used to trying to take in
20 as much as I could — a wide angle lens, the whole spectrum of colors.
21 But I kept reminding myself that tonight I wanted to stay true to my
22 focus and try a more focused view — to focus on a few selected colors.
23 (p. 74, Analytic Memo) I visualize my thoughts and feelings as circling —
24 circling around some emerging trends, feelings. At times I have
25 something in my view, a destination or place to land, and then back to
26 circling/observing.
27 (pp. 126–7) I feel I miss really understanding what is being alluded to,
28 which affects my log descriptions: as if I am looking in from the outside,

Carolyn writes:

This study of my metaphors helps me see my difficulties as a qualitative researcher. I can acknowledge my frustrations and concerns, and attempt to accept them as an integral part of my learning process. My feelings as a research instrument are not something to be denied or hidden from view. The beauty of metaphors is their gentle 'sneakiness.' I think I'm writing the participants' story in my weekly logs, and then in reading my data I realize I'm also writing my own story in relationship with the other people in my data. When I read over my rough notes for this memo, I was amazed how much I wrote about myself, as compared to what my metaphors told me about the people I studied. We are definitely in this together.

The subtleness of metaphors belies their power to speak to me. In reading my metaphors I am brought face to face with a gamut of feelings that I experienced while collecting data. It's as if these metaphors have already begun to analyze my observations and feelings: a transformation of my data. This is exciting because it shows me that the integration of my feelings into the data connects with being trustworthy as a researcher. Metaphors bring things out in the open. They bring me face to face with myself, and to ignore this interaction between myself and my data would jeopardize the integrity of my research striving.

Carolyn's is an important statement about how the study of our own metaphors can provide a mirror for self-reflection. It is after all, a study of *how* we say things and what that might mean. It can, at times, provide us with impetus for change. For example in Barbara Miller's study of a classroom for five and six year olds she analyzed her metaphors about her participants, decided that they were too one-sided and worked to recast them. This gave her a new direction for collecting data and for analyzing them, with far more attention to the cultural surround in the school and how that might have contributed to the classroom experience.

Sherry Davidson gives us a glimpse of herself as a flexible, determined, intelligent researcher through her metaphoric journey. Notice, as we saw with Barbara and Carolyn, how Sherry learns about herself through this exploration:

23 I liken my experience to 'swimming in uncharted waters.'
24 After deciding on a site location I plunged into the mysterious

25   waters, not knowing what to expect, but taking the risk.
26   Beginning with an attempt to gain entry in the field, I was a bit
27   disoriented in my initial immersion, but at times resorted to
28   treading water to contemplate my next move. Despite my
29   uncertainty of how to proceed, I always felt the support of
30   the lifeguard(s) — my professor and my support group — on shore who
31   were keeping watch, to prevent me from drowning. As I began
32   to record my observations, I often felt as if I was trying to keep
33   my head above water with the voluminous information that I was
34   recording. However, as time passed and several analytic memos
35   later, I began to feel comfortable in the water. I realized that
36   by going with the flow of the current, I was able to see emerging
37   patterns and engage in more even strokes in the process. When
38   the water became rough, I learned to get out for awhile, until I
39   was prepared to test the waters once again. In reflecting upon
40   the total experience, it is either sink or swim and I am
41   determined to swim.

This piece, as is, could very well be included in Sherry's final reflections on method.

The link between an examination of metaphor and analysis has been important to many researchers as Margot discovered with researchers in her qualitative class:

> At that time we were ready to lift to other levels of analysis from side comments, analytic memos and preliminary categories. The metaphor work was like a well oiled automatic doorway to more complex, overarching analysis. People just did it! And this happened in the process of studying our metaphors and writing about them. No starting lectures, no readings — these came later — no agonizing in support groups. I knew that we were into something far bigger, far more important than I had ever imagined. Now, I wonder why I was so surprised. Then, it was a revelation.

A testimony like this one shows that the metaphorical concepts we live with and think through in our everyday lives may structure the ways in which we orient ourselves in our research studies, giving a coherence that is embedded and not easily recognized until we go in search of it. Of course, this isn't to suggest that metaphorical orientation shouldn't be examined for biases that might skew our understanding. As John Locke warned, figurative language can deceive and mislead. We aren't tempted to be as cautious as John Locke, but he does remind us of how important it is to question our language about our own assumptions and beliefs.

We remain optimistic that metaphor has the potential to structure experience and interpretation in ways that are productive for moving the research forward and for communicating our understandings with our readers. Carolyn Arnason points out that as she examined her use of metaphor she began to realize the integrative forces undergirding her research study and her professional life:

> When I read my metaphors I liked some of what I had written! What a revelation that I can like my ideas, or the way I formed them into written language. In qualitative research I can develop myself intellectually and emotionally. There doesn't have to be a dichotomy between me as a person, me as a music therapist, or me

as a researcher. The more qualitative research I do and the more I learn about it, the more I can develop my professional role and the profession of music therapy.

What emerges, is, we suppose, obvious enough. Metaphor gives shape to the analysis and writing and our beliefs give impetus to the metaphors that we find, imagine, and create in the first place.

The various strategies for engaging in this metaphoric work are interesting. After studying her list of metaphors, Diane Austin sorted them into three major categories and then found that this way of binning created a poetic form. Here is one 'metaphor bin poem':

In the Darkness

trapped in a void
    a black hole
wearing a mask
    a lizard self
living in a glass cage
    getting high with sugar daddies
    lighting the fireworks
hitting bottom

This poem becomes an extended metaphor in its own right. The poem structures a conceptual system for Diane and her readers from which to understand her analysis process. Bruner (1986) says that metaphors are the 'crutches to help us get up the abstract mountain. Once up, we throw them away (even hide them) in favor of a formal, logically consistent theory' (p. 48). He goes on to suggest that the hypothesis making that occurs through metaphor 'comes precisely from the rich bed of metaphor from which it grows' (p. 53). Consider what you learn about Diane's conceptualizing through her particularly vivid poem on process.

Often metaphors serve as an anchor for how we organize our data. Gayle Newshan studied the experience of pain for people who were dying of AIDS. What follows are two ways in which she categorized her metaphors. First she wrote:

I. Patients' Metaphors

Pain is like
    someone poking you with needles
    electricity
    someone driving a spike in you
    Pacman, eating you up inside
I feel like a bulldog in sludge
I was treated like a dog

II. Gayle's Metaphors

An AIDS patient is a leper
Pain is
    a mystery
    the last embers of a bonfire
    the last chapter of a book
    the final exit of a highway

From these categories Gayle might write about pain from the patients' viewpoints and from hers. Both of these ways of presentation would rest on her analysis of the two groups of metaphors. What was of concern to the AIDS patients? How did their metaphors reveal their experience? How do the researchers' metaphors compare to the participants'? What, if anything, is missing? For example, Gayle's metaphor of 'AIDS patient as leper' may link to the patients' metaphor of 'patient as dog,' but it does more. The metaphors reveal insight on various levels of abstraction from the purely physical struggles to Gayle's and the patients' more philosophical viewpoints.

Gayle experimented with another way to shape the metaphors. These rely exclusively on the AIDS patients' perspective:

Pain as movement
> rolls around
> moves up and down
> jumps
> jolts
> goes back and forth
> comes and goes

Pain as friend
> always there
> tells you something is wrong

Pain as puzzle
> Don't have all the pieces
> comes in different shapes

Pain as war
> wounds
> battle for medications
> taking sides
> being treated like the enemy
> needs strategic planning

After completing this second version, Gayle wrote, 'I think this latter one — pain as war — is a metatheme. It seems to be an overarching theme in what the participant tells me.' Gayle finds the metaphor structuring important to the formation of themes and to what she will use to document those themes from her data. Further she sees 'pain as war' as a binding theme, or metatheme, that characterizes, much like a good book title, a great deal of the experiences that she has studied. This is one route by which Gayle's catalogues of metaphors have led her to some 'promise' of a metatheme, at least temporarily.

Perhaps she might combine some metaphors from her various versions to bolster the details with which she now intends to work. In reading through Gayle's metaphors, we were particularly taken with the 'pain as mystery' and with some of the metaphors that bring the paradox to the surface that people dying of AIDS often feel mistreated by the very people who are there to help. Of course, this calls for other studies that document the experiences, feelings, and opinions of people in the helping professions. Some of our colleagues are doing just such work as we are finishing this book.

Metaphors, it turns out, are helpful in fleshing out the characterization of the participants in our studies. Sometimes these metaphors are overdone — they puff and gasp and occasionally strangle themselves with a too conscious attempt to be insightful. We thought about one example where a researcher tried to make a case for a high school principal as Dracula but, beyond the idea that both 'drain' the energy from others, the metaphor just couldn't be played out in interesting or honest ways. We think, however, metaphor can, with some subtlety, enhance the portraits of participants. Sherry Davidson who studied Fran, an exercise instructor at a senior citizens' center, plays out a metaphoric rendition in this way:

> After another metaphor analysis of my field log, Fran continues to stand out as 'an entertainer.' I previously used this metaphor as a prominent theme; however, 'the entertainer' is clearly the meta-metaphor that captures Fran's humor, style, appearance and actions. In fact, Fran corroborates this orientation in her own words in the interview, indicating that everybody responds to entertainment. But Fran is not just any entertainer. In my perception of the total person, she's a combination of Cher in her appearance, Phyllis Diller in her frequent off-color humor, and Jane Fonda in her focus on exercise, movement and instruction.

Because it lends itself so well to the task, we will use Sherry's paragraph to highlight some other aspects of metaphor. The paragraph is replete with references to what Sherry must believe are common understandings. Thus, in order to grasp what she is trying to communicate with the entertainer metaphor, we, the readers, must be 'in on' who Cher, Phyllis Diller and Jane Fonda are, what characterizes their appearance, style, professional bents and what a combination of these might look like in terms of Fran. We must know also what aspects of those three people's lives — the political and personal, for example — are not meant to be included in the message Sherry is sending about 'the entertainer.' What is more, we must link our understandings of 'entertainer' to broader terms as they are seen in our culture. What does it mean to entertain? To be entertained? When are we *not* entertained?

Another example of the participant taking on a metaphoric life occurred because the participant's description was so vivid as to give Jane Martin, the researcher, a possible metaphor. Jane creates a theme from the actual words of Nancy, a woman in mid-life who has not married:

> Recovering from Marty . . . these feelings were so full of life, full of blood, like I had cut off a limb, a live limb. You could say it was something that was big and live and pulsating and real. That's how I saw it.

This theme was one of Jane's beginning attempts to present Nancy's viewpoint. Perhaps she will prune and shape it to emphasize the bit about 'I had cut off a limb'. Perhaps not. Jane went on to explain:

> Nancy used this metaphor to describe her feelings after she and Marty broke up. Marty was a man with whom she had a relationship when she was in her early 30s. It lasted for about four years. Nancy says that Marty was the only man that she ever really wanted to marry. She also expected that they would marry and describes him as the love of her life. Their breakup was extremely painful, which

her chosen metaphor vividly depicts. Nancy also defines certain years after their breakup as the period in which she mourned Marty.

In Jane's reflective memo, she recognizes how metaphor helps her get at the essence of her participant:

> I've realized that metaphors help me in framing my work and my feelings about my work. I also realize, particularly after this exercise of listing some of Nancy's metaphors, that using the participant's metaphors in the final write-up will be important in helping to convey the essence of each woman. Metaphors are so commonly used in our speech that I must not let them slip by my sight . . . Yes, another useful reason to read the original transcripts over and over.

The use of our own metaphors, then, assumes some cultural bridges with our readers. This is true also about how our participants use metaphor. At times, this takes on a different twist as their metaphors are analyzed. Here the researcher may not share the participants' cultural taken-for-granted knowledge. And so the task becomes to make oneself aware of it — to attempt to learn it through the participants' metaphors. The question about those metaphors remains the same: What do these metaphors tell us about the person who is communicating them? What cultural insights do they provide? What is the person saying with these metaphors? What is assumed as shared knowledge?

We have a hunch that 'The Entertainer' will be a title for a major section or chapter of Sherry's work, and that she may use subtitles having to do with humor, style, appearance and actions to present her reasoning to her readers. Perhaps she will create a pastiche.

Sometimes we find a metaphor that just tickles us. It seems just right. When Jane Martin read the following lines to our group of qualitative researchers there was a collective smile, a collective sigh:

I was Kidnapped by My Data

> The feeling of being 'kidnapped by the data' is somewhat difficult to express in words . . . Thus, the power and efficiency of the metaphor shows its colors again! Nevertheless, I'll try. To some degree this feeling refers to the sense that the data take on a life of their own, if we permit this to happen. How do we allow ourselves to be kidnapped? By keeping an open mind and not becoming tightly structured about agendas, biases, and expectations for the data, we allow the data to emerge more freely. So, by being kidnapped by my data, I was trying to let my data guide what I was seeing and shaping . . . letting the data have the upper hand in this analysis. Maybe this is about the difference between entering a study with ideas or hypotheses which you want to check versus entering by allowing the data to shape the questions. I believe that if I keep letting my data kidnap me along the way of analysis I will know that I am being more true to my data and may feel that I have captured the experiences of the women in my study in an authentic way.

Jane might include these thoughts in her written presentation to indicate how she educated herself to do the research, what she learned, and what she will apply in future research. She might include the piece to explain how she approached analysis. She might include it in her concluding reflections. However she decides, such a personal and meaningful metaphor-rich statement should not be relegated to the trash.

Since Jane's audience at the time of her sharing knew of our frustrating struggle to create a good title for this book, one as directly on target as *Circles Within Circles* (Ely *et al.*, 1991), they immediately suggested 'Kidnapped by the Data.' We loved it and played with it for a while before we decided that while it was a wonderful metaphor, it didn't stand for the entire book. By the time you hold this in your hands we sincerely hope that we've created a stunner. But it has been a dreadful struggle and a blow — especially for one of us who prides herself on making wonderful titles.

Most times the metaphors we write about come from our own words or the words of the people we've read. At times we create metaphors in our presentations, not from the people's exact words but from the essence of what they are saying as we understand it. Sherry, after all, created the entertainer metaphor. Sharon created the fake, green grass metaphor. These creations of essence often serve well as section titles or chapters in texts:

Chapter or Subtitle	Author
Don Quixote's Double	Michael Mulkay
A Bird Was in the Room	Gabriel Josipovici
Sailing in Smoke	Pablo Neruda
Mansions in the Air	Malcolm Cowley

Some metaphors make telling titles or parts of titles:

Title	Author
Ruth	Jane Hamilton
Mole People: Life in the Tunnels	Jennifer Toth
Bitter Milk	Madeleine Grumet
Playing in the Dark	Toni Morrison
Fear of Falling	Barbara Ehrenreich

We have chosen to describe Michele Bellavita's journey with metaphor as a final contribution to this section because she says things so well and because she adds other facets about metaphor that we find important:

Meditations on Metaphors and Metathemes

What a pleasure to meditate on metaphors and metathemes. I spend a lot of time thinking about metaphors in the course of my work, and I often feel like I spend my life with one foot in the literal and practical and the other foot in the metaphorical and sometimes the mythical. Metaphors are transformations. Metaphors can catapult even well-written, rich description from the realm of the particular and the time-limited into the realm of the timeless, the essential, the universal. Like myths. In fact, it seems to me that metaphors, metathemes, and myths are interrelated. I think that myths have grown out of the metaphors and metathemes that have the most resonance and power of meaning.

We narrate our lives, we create our personal metaphors, and through them our personal mythologies. And we also resonate more or less with eternal, universal mythological themes. Metaphors and metathemes together lead us in two directions at the same time. One path they lead us on goes straight to the essence of the self. The other path connects us to other individuals and to the larger human groups through culture, literature, and history (mythology).

I developed two, maybe three, metathemes for my participant after thinking about the metaphors I gleaned from the three interviews with him. My participant seemed to be involved in exploring several myths and struggling to create new metaphors, new meanings for himself: myths of masculinity; myths of fatherhood; mythologies of relationships. These are reflected in some of his mythological expressions:

'killing yourself to support the family'
'you sacrifice yourself for your child'
'I'm trying to break the mold'
(Spending time with his son rather than working) 'is no small potatoes'
(Initially envisioned parenthood) 'like a John Denver song' (i.e. sentimental, idealized)
(Fathering as) 'a test not only of your patience but your capacity to love'
Illness and death as equal to abandonment
The baby as his most satisfying creation (and possibly relationship): 'Something I made'; 'This thing that's giving back to you'; 'If you don't put in, you don't get out.'
(Relating to children): 'it's like punching a hole into another world'

The metathemes:
1) I am struggling to define for myself what it means to be a man and what it means to be a father.
2) Fatherhood has in many ways transformed me.
3) Becoming a father has caused me to reflect on my past and present relationships, my investment in them, and their effect on me.

What doesn't seem to come across here is how satisfying he finds his capacity to relate to his son and his son's responsiveness to him. His language is less metaphorical in those descriptions. However, themes about his relationship with his son could fall under the second and third metathemes. All of this could be subsumed under the first metatheme. A leitmotif throughout all the interviews is his struggle to find a way to balance his creative pursuits (painting) which conflict with his ability to support his family and his desire to spend time with his son which conflicts with how much time he invests in earning a living, and how to let go of the ghost of his father's definition of fatherhood (or his perception of it!)

A related theme is: Can I find a way of giving to my child without sacrificing myself (losing myself, and taken to the extreme, killing myself, like I believe my father did). Killing oneself to support the family can be viewed as a more general metaphor reflecting the fear that giving of the self can cause loss of the self. In one of the interviews Peter talks about how he had to learn that in order to get something out of a relationship a person must put something into it, invest himself in it.

But there is a more universal theme lurking around here: the tension between living for yourself and connectedness with others. The paradox is that you really can't have one without the other and each enriches the other. Yet, it's a real art balancing both, and there is always tension between meeting my own needs and responding to the needs of others; between enjoying a sense of connectedness with others and the need to revel in a sense of solitude and connectedness with myself; between the quest for self-expression and the need to have the expression of myself acknowledged by others.

I'm the gypsy who also wants to sit by the hearth and cultivate a garden. The gypsy who wants to put the books in storage and sell everything else and wander the face of the earth, who also wants to cook Christmas dinner for ten friends. A gypsy with the capacity for deep attachment and a profound need for solitude, who can love one man but has fantasies of loving every interesting man who crosses her path, even characters in books and artists long dead. A gypsy who has never desired to be a mother but who has nurtured many and who is forever touched by the poignancy of relationships between parents and children. Well, what can you say about a woman whose most profound personal metaphors come from dreams, especially dreams in which she's communing with animals — like wolves and tigers. But of course dreams are metaphors. The very best. In other cultures, they don't need psychoanalysts to understand this. They value their dreams. And they value their dream animals.

Drama

Drama brings into immediate focus the conversations, human responses, and actions that accompany or dramatize events. Unlike narrative which has the advantage of telling and showing the story, drama relies heavily on spoken language in its various registers — conversation, interior monologue, soliloquy — to reveal complexities of plot, action, character, motivation, and context. This is not to denigrate the contribution of nonverbal communication in drama — tone of voice, body language, silence, facial expressions, even *choice* of words and their timing, and — of course — stage settings — that helps to provide nuanced as well as broader meaning. Drama about research is often part of a larger document. In our experience such drama is more read than performed. One benefit of these conditions is that a reader can indeed see the copious stage directions (see pp. 126–9) as well as be situated in the textual framework of the research. Drama achieves a sense of immediacy difficult to replicate in other forms because the medium of dialogue isolates time into a 'present' moment. That sense of the present, however, is tinged with next or future moments which give dramatic form a unique power of presentation. As Langer (1953) has suggested:

> Drama, though it implies past action (the situation), moves not toward the present, as narrative does, but toward something beyond; it deals essentially with commitments and consequences. Persons, too, in drama are purely agents — whether consciously or blindly, makers of the future. (p. 307)

Drama integrates and orchestrates the elements of narrative, exposition, and description through language. It's difficult business to write monologues or dialogues that sound authentic as well as provide the stuff to help audience make meaning. A statement such as 'I haven't found a way to tell him' must carry within and around it reference to what is to be told, to whom, the possible consequences of the telling, and the motivations both for telling and for having to find a way to do so. Embedded in dialogue are references to exposition, dramatic irony, characterization, and setting. Dialogue must stand on its own but have foundations in all these other parts. Richardson (1994) believes that when 'the material to be displayed is intractable, unruly, multisited, and emotionally laden, drama is more likely to recapture the experience than standard writing' (p. 522). That's easier said than done. Dialogue is difficult to write.

To describe thoughts or feelings is one thing. Imagine how you might express *through dialogue* what goes on in the minds of two siblings who have just been informed their mother has been diagnosed with Alzheimer's. Or the conversation that you might create to replicate two kindergartners' impressions when they meet their teacher for the first time. Virginia Woolf (1967) offered a description of how the mind works when impressions come from all sides as 'an incessant shower of innumerable atoms, and as they fall, they shape themselves into the life of Monday or Tuesday' (p. 106). Now imagine again how such impressions might be revealed through conversation alone, a conversation, let's say, between a doctor who does not believe that his AIDS patient is really feeling pain and a patient who is hurting.

Drama is potent when employed well in research writing, and we're just beginning to understand its power and purposes in that arena. Take, for example, Lynn Haber's 'Playlet in Two Voices,' written out of her research in one kindergarten classroom. The following field log entries provide a context for her playlet:

On October 11th, Lynn wrote:
I decide to spend the next few minutes at the table where Walter has been playing with the dominoes. When I return to that table, Walter is sitting next to another boy, and they are both working on puzzles. Walter is telling the other boy, William, that he will be his friend and that William won't have to worry about not having any friends in the classroom. As Walter is saying this, William silently works on his puzzle. Sue, his teacher, comes over and separates the boys to different tables.

On November 8th, Lynn wrote:
At one point, she (Sue) tells Walter, who is sitting on a chair, that he didn't put his jacket away properly and that he should go back and fix it. Walter says, 'Oh yeah. That's right,' and rushes back to his cubby to pick up his jacket. As he starts to walk back to his chair, he says, 'May I' and Sue cuts him off and says, 'No, you may not get a mat. Now sit down quietly.' Walter has a pained expression on his face, and he looks as if he is about to cry. He sits down at a table and says, 'I want to lie down for my nap.'

And now, a piece of Lynn's 'Playlet in Two Voices — Kindergarten.' Please read it, keeping in mind how the dialogue has a multitude of other roles beyond simply hearing an exchange between Walter and his teacher.

A Playlet in Two Voices

Kindergarten (Walter's voice is inferred by the researcher, Lynn Haver)

Walter: It's nap time, and I'm so glad Miss Harris let me have a mat today. Last week I was so tired, and all I wanted to do was lie down and rest before snack time.

Teacher:	I'm going to put on a record that I know all of you will really like. It's from Peter Pan.
Walter:	My favorite Peter Pan song. I can fly! I love this song. I have to sit up to hear this. I want so much to sing along with this.
Teacher:	Close your eyes and listen carefully. Relax every part of your bodies.
Walter:	I want so much to sing along with this. I have to sit up.
Teacher:	Keep your bodies still. Relax your toes, and your feet, and your legs.
Walter:	I can fly! I can fly!
Teacher:	Keep still now.
Walter:	I'm Superman.
Teacher:	Your mouths shouldn't be moving.
Walter:	I have to take my sweater off. I'm so warm now.
Teacher:	Relax your stomachs and your arms.
Walter:	I'll just hold it in my lap and she won't care.
Teacher:	You should be wearing that.
Walter:	I wish I could really fly like Superman.
Teacher:	Keep your bodies still and lie down while you listen to the music.
Walter:	I can't sit still anymore. I want to fly out of this room.
Teacher:	Put it on now. You just got over being sick.
Walter:	Maybe I could turn my sweater into a great cape.
Teacher:	*Now*, Walter!

Perhaps you will read the playlet aloud, with another person so that each of you can take on the role of one of the characters. What did both the silent and oral readings contribute to your involvement in what may be happening in the classroom? Margot finds that even with a silent reading, she tends to 'speak and hear' the words. But, for us at least, Lynn's play works best as an oral text. You may differ. Here the essential issue is that a written play invites choice in the enactment.

Certainly the play is crafted. That is, Lynn created it, and as we read it we know this. While the teacher's lines are constructed from her observed verbal and nonverbal behaviors, Walter's lines are inferred almost entirely by Lynn from his nonverbal behaviors. Writing the lines in both cases was a job of selecting, juxtaposing, arranging and rearranging the information Lynn had collected in her fieldnotes and memos. The play is streamlined, pared down. It is precisely that sparse presentation, however, that allows us to feel its meanings. At times, brevity is both elegant and provocative — perhaps more inviting than if Lynn had gone on and on. We'll never know, of course. But we do know that, for us, the play works. For us, who have witnessed thousands of such 'rest time' events, the playlet is an intense emotional experience, heightened by the juxtaposition of the voices of the 'all knowing,' controlling teacher who seems to care less for Walter than for some other children, and of Walter, who is still struggling to find entrance and place in this classroom. Lynn wrote the following reflections on the playlet:

> I saw this particular piece of writing as more than an attempt to express classroom life from Walter's point of view. It was my attempt to understand how Walter thinks and to experience something of his struggle for a sense of power and voice in this environment. For me this kind of writing is not 'frills' in qualitative research. It seems to be an important and necessary part. 'Becoming the other' or using the

first-person 'I' helps me get beyond the limits of being in the 'researcher' mode. This kind of writing seems to be more honest in some ways than writing that aims to be 'objective.'

Lynn characterizes Walter as a living, thinking child. This required that Lynn take her reader into Walter's inner thoughts and develop what she imagined as the motivations for his particular actions. Lynn indicated that if she were to develop her playlet further, it would be important to work the teacher's motivations into the exchange. Various interviews she had conducted with the teacher would provide a useful source for understanding the teacher's action and reactions in this particular situation. What Lynn understands is the importance of representing as fully and fairly as possible the complexities of relationships among people.

Carole Di Tosti's dramas comprised entire chapters of her completed dissertation. At that time, we had never witnessed such extensive use of the drama mode in dissertations. Carole studied several people who were 'whistleblowers' on corruption in education. Gene Brown, the superintendent of schools in this play, went so far in real life as to wear a wire at meetings to record for authorities what was happening. Here is a piece of one of Carole's plays. As you read it, please keep in mind that while the schools are referred to by number, these numbers are fictitious.

Hidden Agendas and Educational Games

ACT I: Scene I
'There is No Black or Right'

The scene opens on a combination superintendent's office and conference area where school board members meet in executive session. This school district is one of many in a large metropolitan public education system. Along with a circular table in the center of the room, there are a desk and two tall filing cabinets off to the side. In another corner of the room there are two bookcases filled with books and bric-a-brac. The room has a look of clutter, organized disorder. Board members Steve Fava, Jimmy Jones and Pete Schaab are seated near each other around the table. Gene Brown, the superintendent, sits opposite them, by himself.

Each man has four pages of personnel sheets in front of him. The pages hold names of professional employees and regular staff employed in the district. The board members have been arguing with Brown about 'interim acting' principalships for which they want their people to be hired. The legal decision about appointments to these positions is solely the superintendent's.

The men have been at the process for some time; their voices are abrasive with the sound of frustration and annoyance. Gene Brown, who has been parrying with these men, has a cool reserve in his demeanor, but it becomes increasingly obvious that the situation is wearing him down. However, he will not stop the process because he wants to make sure that the investigator is getting every bit of the discussion on the hidden recorders scattered around the room.

Steve Fava:	So, who else would you put in there?
Gene Brown:	Well, right now, I'm thinking that one of my people from the junior high would do fine. Mary White.
Steve Fava:	(Rifles through the pages) I don't know her. She's not one of mine.

Jimmy Jones:	I don't know her either.
Pete Schaab:	Who is she?
Jones:	She's not from our community.
Brown:	(Gets up and goes to get some coffee at the table upstage center) Gentlemen, would anyone like more coffee? I'll make a fresh pot!
Fava:	(To Brown) Stop stalling, Gene. (Stands up) We don't know her. She's not one of ours. That means only one thing. (Pause) She's black!
Brown:	(Turns from his coffee making, looks directly across at Fava and the others . . . speaks in measured tones) Yes, she's black! (Slowly) And she's qualified.
Fava:	(Moves his chair back . . . Starts to pace throughout the exchange: shakes his head) No. No. This is no good. It won't do. I don't like what I'm hearing.
Jones:	(Jumps in) All of a sudden we're a ghetto district now? What is this, Gene? We're not Watts. We're not Harlem. We're not Detroit! (Punctuates each city by hitting the sheets with his hand)
	(Fava: returns to his seat, grateful for support)
Schaab:	(Calmly with soothing tones) Look Gene. We've discussed between ourselves this thing you got for blacks. Maybe because you came out of a black district and you got to know them a little. But things are very different in this district. This just won't work. Don't forget who you're dealing with.
Brown:	(Walks over to the table where the others are seated) The woman is qualified for the position.
Fava:	(Gets up and circles the table directing his comments to Gene) Hold it! Let's look at this. Do you realize what you're doing to us here? You're taking some people from 246, 210 and 106 and they're all black, and you're going to shift them to my community? My schools? (He slams his fist on the table in front of Gene) And in 106 you probably want the acting principal to be a black too. This is wrong. I got problems with this. (Sits down)
Jones:	Do you realize what an action like this is saying, Gene? People expect Fava to support them. They won't take too kindly to having these blacks in positions they wouldn't have gotten before.
Brown:	(Sits down) Now, just wait one minute here. What aren't people going to take too kindly? Remember we've got 17,000 blacks and hispanics in the entire district and 8,000 whites. That's practically two thirds minority and they're all housed together along with minority staff in the worst buildings, the most inadequately supplied programs in the district.
Schaab:	So what? The parents' associations that have power are gonna see your move for what it is and we're gonna have chaos. We'll be stayin' here for 1–2 o'clock in the morning having to hear every son of a bitch speak his three minute piece before God, man and us board members. The PAs heard about this. You know how they'll act!
Fava:	(Quietly gets up and paces) Bottom line, Gene. What are you trying to do here? It won't matter in the long run. And I'll tell you why. You see, these people you want in . . . yeah . . . they're not my friends. That's right. And they never will be. And here's where I'm different

	than you. I know this! You don't! You see, Mr. Brown, believe it or not, they aren't your friends, either. They never will be. And you can appoint these blacks to high positions and switch them to nicer buildings, but sooner or later, they'll walk over you like dirt under their feet. (Walks back to his seat, sits)
Brown:	(Quietly) You're wrong.
Fava:	Since when do we have to be in a position where we have to put on a show for the city and the country? Where is that a part of your job? You know damn well you probably have as many blacks in this district in jobs based on percentages as any other school in the city.
Brown:	(Looks down) In terms of this issue of minorities, we're the best in the city.
Fava:	(Loudly and triumphantly) There's my answer.
Jones:	(Gets back to business, feeling Brown's been made to lose face) So what happens now to Harris if Boyle doesn't go into 107?
Brown:	That's my problem. There isn't a certain opening, yet.
Jones:	So what you're saying is, we're not taking care of placing Boyle as an acting interim principal . . . tonight either?
Brown:	(Sounds strained) Look! An opening is being prepared.
Jones:	(Angry) You're stonewalling us!
Fava:	I'll tell you something. (Gets up. Stares angrily at Gene) I've heard enough. I don't want to see the lists . . . an opening is being prepared, you say? You bet it is, and Boyle is going to fill it! (There is silence. He looks at Jones and Schaab) I'm sorry . . . ah . . . I don't know about my colleagues, but . . .
Jones:	(Interrupts) I agree with ya. I agree with ya. I mean now it's getting political. (To Gene) You told us we were gonna be moving our people in. You let us think this. But I don't see it.
Fava:	Look! (Points finger at Gene) Qualified, unqualified? Bullshit! You heard my recommendation. No . . . (pauses, reconsiders, disgusted voice) Hey, do what you want.
Schaab:	OK. Why don't we finish these ratings. (Tries to smooth things over) We still have about a week before the administration gets our appointees. By then, this should all work out. (To Gene who stares back at Schaab) Right? (Gene looks down)
Jones & Fava:	It better! Yeah!
Schaab:	Let's do the ratings now. Who's the acting principal in 109? (The board members rifle through their sheets. They are synchronizing their lists making sure their friends and cronies get the highest rating, 1. It is obvious their people have the top priority. And in retaliation to Brown for not placing their friends in the acting principalships, they give the black candidates lower ratings and take them off the personnel lists for appointments)
Brown:	Soames.
Jones:	Give McCarthy a 1 and Soames a 4. In 124, give Soames a 4 and McCarthy a 1. (He looks at Fava to see if he understands how he is 'sticking it' to Brown)
Fava:	Jimmy (to Jones), give Brock a 1.
Jones:	I have Brock a 1 straight through.

Fava:	Great. Oh, also, Jimmy, give Gold a 1.
	(As they mark their sheets, Brown gets up from his chair loudly and goes to pour himself another cup of coffee. The others glance up, then continue, ignoring him. From the coffee area, Gene stares at them)
Schaab:	Give Peters a 1, OK? I've been playing fair with you guys. Now, you play me fair. Throw a couple my way. I have to keep my people happy too.
Jones:	You want Peters to get a 1?
Schaab:	Yeah.
Jones:	We can do that. He'll be up there for eventual appointment! (He looks at Gene Brown when he says this to give him the message which he is not sure is getting through)
Fava:	Give George Danders and Ben Washington 3s. (Looks pointedly at the others, then at Gene Brown)
Schaab:	3s? (Looks at Brown, then back to the others) OK, 3s. Marks the list. The others mark theirs.

Carole analyzed the characteristics and functions of her dramatic scene in this way:

> The play reflected the events, the major ones I selected as most telling about Gene's whistleblowing experiences. In addition, the play form gave me the opportunity to reveal the realities of the other individuals who helped the superintendent enact the drama that he went through. I shaped this play from my interviews, the taped manuscripts and the news reports. The stage directions help to give life to the people, foes and friends of the superintendent. I found the play form could best reveal the interplay between the disparate characters — the board members and the superintendent — and highlight their agendas in the clearest way. They were shown as individuals with separate consciences and feelings, with separate goals . . . all unique.
>
> If I had related the incidents in first person form from the superintendent's point of view, I feel I would not have gotten as distinct a portrayal of the way the board members felt. In other words, through the superintendent's eyes, these board members were doing wrong. Through their eyes, they were doing right. The essence of their attitude that they were doing right would never have come out as strongly if the play were written from the superintendent's point of view. Indeed, they stood for everything that he didn't like. From their perspective, they were doing a job that had to be done . . . If it involved patronage, so what?

Carole's play serves a variety of other purposes. The action helps us to consider its ironies and paradoxes without writing about them directly. Here are board members, supposedly people elected by their community to best serve its children, considering a whole set of issues but clearly not those about the optimum education of children. The children, who are never mentioned, seem to serve as pawns in another game in which the board members see themselves as the heroes and protectors of their friends and the community and the superintendent as the villain who must be neutralized. What shines through the dialogue are the not-so-hidden agendas; the political maneuvering, and the trading of favors. What we see, in addition, are the board member's and Superintendent's racial and cultural assumptions, feelings, and the hierarchies that are perpetuated in the educational enterprise.

When we read Carole's play, we were reminded that Dan Rose (1990) has long been an advocate for various types of ethnographic poetics. He suggested:

> ... the groundwork has been prepared to begin effecting reversals on received cultural practices and thought. Ethnographic poetics and fiction seek to move in the same direction. A reversal sets up a self-conscious counter-discourse and erodes the hegemonic position of the ideology of cultural purity and racist exclusion ... What is possible in this space of contact, crossing over, assimilation, appropriation, juxtaposition, and fusion has not been adequately explored, indeed, this space has no real name. What we know is that there are numerous ragged zones of contact between peoples who hold incommensurable values and beliefs, traditions, and philosophies. (pp. 43–4)

Of course, whether you, as readers, or other readers of Carole's play conclude that she presents an example of 'numerous ragged zones of contact' that involve paradoxes and ironies depends on your and their own stances. For some, we suppose, the play is quite ordinary and the action to be expected. For us, Carole made us uneasy about the confrontations of ideology, race, culture, and opportunism 'in which voices are raised that remain incommensurable; they do not map to one another, they do not share the same sensibilities. Indeed, they do not share the same historical moment' (Rose, 1990, p. 50).

Both Lynn's and Carole's dramas might have been used to support analytical themes, to introduce sections, or to move the stories forward in the telling. William Parker, himself a fine jazz musician, introduces his playlet in this way:

> This playlet is derived from a symposium in which a well known-young trumpeter talked about an experience with Miles Davis. To me the story symbolized the mentor style at the school where I did my study, and represented what most of the students would aspire to.

'The Mentor'

A short play about a historic meeting of a jazz master and one of his disciples. The master is ill and in need of support during a Parisian Jazz Festival. A recording session was also scheduled. The young trumpeter was drafted to play when he arrived on the scene. He was told nothing about money, but was put under a great deal of pressure to help. At the airport the disciple is greeted by a music critic who immediately attempts an interview.

Act One, Scene One

Critic: I've heard that you are going to be involved with the festival; tell me how this came about.

Disciple: I was hired to play with a big band of international musicians. I was flown to Nice and began rehearsals. After the second day, two trumpet players from Germany arrived, and I was told they were replacing me. I was paid in full and excused from rehearsals.

Critic: Why did you decide to come to Paris?

Disciple: Gerry Wild, the tuba player, told me I might be able to help the Master at the festival. He called Paris, and they told him I should come to the festival if possible. Right now I have to see what's what.

(The Disciple enters a limousine and rides off to Paris.)

Act One, Scene Two

(The Disciple has checked into the hotel and is greeted by the saxophonist in the Master's band who has access to the Master's suite. He escorts the Disciple to the room.)

Saxoph: Do you want to jam a little?

Disciple: Yeah, that would be nice. Let's play some of the Master's music.

(They jam about 15 minutes)

Saxoph: (Mimicking the Master's unique voice) I know you young dudes are always trying to out-blow me! But it's a long way to go before you can look back at me. (Big laughter from both musicians)

(Suddenly the Master appears as if from nowhere.)

Master: You cats sounded good!

(The two younger musicians look at each other with surprise.)

Master: Hey man, you sure sound like me!

Saxoph: Thanks man, I always wanted to do impressions!

Master: Not you, man. That was really sad, you trying to imitate my handicap! (Big laughter from everyone) I'm talking about Disciple here. Man you play my music better than me.

Disciple: No way man. I'm only imitating when I try to play you.

Master: So what? All I'm playing is Dizzy's music, you dig?

Disciple: No Master. You got your own thing. We all still look to Dizzy for inspiration, but you have inspired a whole generation of young trumpet players yourself.

Master: I like you. Let me show you this thing Yardbird did on 'Chasin' the Bird.' When you come tomorrow I'm going to give you a lot of solos. I understand you don't have an idea about being paid. I'll see that you get money for your time. Just hang with me and we'll go over the music and talk about life.

Disciple: I can't ask for any more than that.

For William, the play became the centerpiece around which to present his findings. The other authors of the plays we have shared so far all changed their data to another form, drama. They witnessed more of 'the real thing' than did William. That is, Lynn observed and interviewed, and while Carole was not privy at first hand to the meetings and court proceedings, she did listen to the actual 'undercover' audiotapes. William created his play solely from a lecture about an event. He takes us quite economically into a particular point of view of music mentorship and, while doing so, gives us one glimpse of a jazz great.

Kristan Ryan studied the experience of four poets in a writing workshop. Her playlet is another version of dramatic possibilities. We are quite taken with the idea that its characters are four poems talking to each other. For us, the play comes across with great impact when it is read aloud:

Poetry in Conversation

Scene: The play opens around a table in a kitchen in a one room studio about 20 feet by 20 feet. Four poems are sitting on a table around which four people are drinking beers. Papers litter the table and floor along with empty beer bottles. The poets are a man of about twenty-two wearing a baseball cap backwards, one man of about thirty-five, and two women, one also of about thirty-five and one about twenty-seven. The humans are saying nothing. The four poems do the talking.

Poem One: I belong to that one, over there, the older guy. You'd never know he was older. Everything in me stinks of his mother, the cat his girlfriend killed and God, will he ever stop filling in lines about blue pajamas at Bellevue? It gets so tiresome!

Poem Two: Well take a look at me, all this one does, yeah, this one, the younger one with the baseball cap on backwards, you know the young one, all he ever fills me with are his views on masturbation and that wretched girlfriend whose table he pissed on once when he was drunk. Look at me! Have you ever seen such writing? It's all he fills me with, Betty, Betty, Betty, Betty, Betty. I wish he'd get over it and on with some other babe!

Poem Three: You think you've got troubles! Personally, I think it's great to see them scribbling you into tortured bits, making you the old girlfriend who made him drink Red Dog beer until he tore down her shower curtain and pissed on her walls. Mine only writes about what she never had, some dream boy who'll give her the family she always wanted. She's pathetic the way she writes me, crying into her beer. Shit, she gets a new wrinkle every hour! I can't wait until she turns forty! I should be a real sight by then!

Poem Four: Wow, you three are pretty harsh. I get filled up with sweet lines about my girl's grandmother. I'm always filled up with pretty words, glamorous words, poetic words —

Poem One: Oh shut up! You suck! Yours isn't a real poet. She's too young to fill you with anything but pretty words. She stinks you know. At least I've been around the block.

Poem Two: Oh God, here he comes again. He's changing a line. Wow, I'm changing. Look, look, I'm becoming the story of his friend who — oh God, this is worse than I thought, I'm bleeding!

Poem Three: You got your wish, Poem Two, you're about death. Oh yeah, you're now his friend who shot himself in the head. You're right, you're bleeding everywhere. Shit, you're even staining me *and* Poem One *and* Poem Four.

Poem One: OH POEM FOUR, you're crying on us, oh stop crying. What? You think we're beautiful? Look, she said you were touching, Poem Two. You too, Poem Three.

Poem Four: (sobbing) You are beautiful, you're all beautiful.

Poem One: That's always the problem with you, Poem Four. You think everything is beautiful, even Poem Two masturbating in his bed to the evening news. I just want to go home, get some rest, you know? Just to stop chattering, chattering, chattering, chattering. He won't let me stop, just keeps adding more and more, goes on and on. I feel like that t-shirt he saw last week that said 'I'm talking and I can't shut up.'

Poem Four:	(still sobbing) You're all so beautiful!
Poem Three:	It's okay Poem Four. You shut your trap Poem One. When they stop changing us, it all stops. You get it? It all stops; the crumbling of paper, the tapping of keyboards, the beer spilling, the tearing down of curtains, the blue pajamas. The quiet will come back, like before.
Poem Four:	Like before?
Poem Three:	Yeah, like before when everything was black and cold and still. Before, like before we knew our lines.
Poem One:	(confused and thinking) I don't remember before.
Poem Two:	(arrogantly) There was no before. They can't fill us with before.
Poem Three:	Okay, maybe there is no before, but there is an after. I heard another poem talk about after. It was stuck in the trash, crumbled, old, yellow, not a line had been changed in months, it told me. Never would be. The line changer stopped, just stopped. That was done, cold, barely talking.
All the poems together:	(frightened, to the humans) Keep changing. Keep chattering. We are beautiful! We are!

The people gather up their poems and put them in their bags, getting ready to leave the studio apartment.

To us, Kristan's playlet is noteworthy for the insight it provides about each poet and more so for its smooth shift from comedic, sarcastic, near slapstick presentation to pathos and deep philosophical considerations, as Sartre would have said it, on 'being and nothingness.' Kristan brings her readers/listeners along on that journey in a seemingly effortless way so that we are left pondering the future of these poets, their poems, and our own. A play like hers allows her readers to take some sides, to work for dramatic impact, contrast, humor, movement. It allows those who read it to speak through the characters in ways that take more direct chances than we might in ordinary 'real' conversation.

Poetry

Please read this poem first. Then we'll work with it as we consider poetry:

Suddenly there was this Person-
on experiencing the birth of his son

We never expected three days of labor
The caesarian came as a relief by that time

And there you were — on the operating table
Awake and conscious
Behind a sheet like a curtain

And the doctor said —
'I'll tell you when it's coming out
You can get up and look.'

And the midwife came in — just to be with us

So she said — so she said —
So she pulled down the curtain

And I said, 'I can't —
I don't think I can watch this.'

I didn't — I couldn't
Imagine what it was like

I mean — I wasn't at all squeamish
About a natural birth

But a c-section —
I was a little —
I didn't know what was coming

So the midwife — so well —
She put it back up

So she said,
'When he's out, I'll tell you
You can look.'

So the doctor said — 'Here he co — omes.'

So I stood up
And I peeked over
And I saw him — I actually saw him
Coming out

It was just like a dream
I couldn't believe it

There was this **person**
Suddenly, there was this **person**
Suddenly —
He was just **there**

And the staff — they all started carrying on —
'It's a boy! It's a boy!'
All really excited

And it was just — it was just
Just a magical moment

I mean — he was there
He was there
I didn't know what to do

So the midwife — she said
'Well touch him — he's **yours**!'

And so I leaned over
And I put my finger
And I touched his hand

And he tipped his head back
And he looked right up at me

It was just — it was just

Wondrous!

And I'll never forget, I'll never forget
I'll never forget that moment
(Michele Bellavita)

Michele's study is titled 'Good Enough Fathers: Fathers of Toddlers Tell Their Stories.' We think Michele's poem brings the situation to us vividly. She tells a powerful story with a plot and characters that whisk us along on a journey that compels, demands, and persuades. She condenses the story into images that pack the data into one scene. It provides us with a window to the feelings of this father — to his emotions. It encapsulates the essence of an event that many of us may have lived in our own way at one time or another. And, for those of us who have only lived births as supporting players, it also commands the emotions and mind. It is a stunning poem for qualitative research communication and evokes the spirit of the 'poetic' that Langer (1953) describes in *Feeling and Form*:

> The poet's business is to create the appearance of 'experiences,' the semblance of events lived and felt, and to organize them so they constitute a purely and completely experienced reality, a piece of virtual life. (p. 212)

Well then, couldn't Michele have written this in story form, perhaps as a vignette, play, or profile? Of course. But the intensity and compression of poetry emphasizes the vividness of this moment. The whole complex happening of Michele's poem is represented in a few words, giving emphasis to the brief images that distinguish the moment. Again, Langer (1953) is helpful on this point:

> ... its [poetry's] distinguishing marks, which make it quite different from any actual segment of life, is that the events ... are simplified, and at the same time much more fully perceived and evaluated than the jumble of happenings in any person's actual history. (p. 212)

Poetry allows for maximum input — in and between the lines. Through Michele's poem our writing team saw the father's experience happening, smelled the smells, and heard the sounds. We certainly felt the awe, hesitation, and joy of this man. For us, the power of this poem was to affect in sensuous ways — to touch our bodies/minds. The only thing we missed in the poem was the presence of the mother's experience.

You may have assumed as you read Michele's poem that the lines stemmed from an interview. They did. The poem is an example of what Patai (1988) recommends in light of Tedlock's (1983) ideas on how to make spoken narratives more accessible by creating 'dramatic poetry' from them. That is, Michele presents the father's report practically in entirety as it was transcribed. However, she breaks the lines 'following the pauses and inflection in the speaker's speech in the form of free verse' (Patai, 1988, p. 149).

Michele worked in the spirit of what Laurel Richardson described in the

Handbook of Qualitative Research (1994) as the advantage of poetry in representing speaker's voices:

> Writing up interviews as poems honors the speaker's pauses, repetitions, alliterations, narrative strategies, rhythms, and so on. Poetry may actually better represent the speaker than the practice of quoting snippets of prose. (p. 522)

Please reread Michele's poem to examine the representation of the young father. What strikes you as particularly strong about his voice? Can you hear the rhythms of his voice? Do you hear the more halting moments of wonder? In rereading, we noticed the repetition as well:

> 'So she said — so she said'
> 'And it was just — it was just'
> 'I mean — he was there — he was there'

What to you are the functions of such repetitions? What do they bring out in you? What about the pauses, often signalled by '—'? What about the rhythm of the lines and the five words that are printed in bold? What about the fact that six of the nine final lines begin with 'And'? Most of these strategies didn't just happen, and the transcript did not contain the poem exactly as it was crafted. Creating it demanded that Michele select and edit in cycles. This included putting the poem away for a while, reading a version to her support group, to a larger group of qualitative researchers, and to the man who provided her with the story to begin with. Making this poem was hard work combined with the pleasure of knowing that it was as faithful as Michele could be to the actual words of her participant. This is becoming an increasingly important issue in the qualitative research community, and to us on the writing team in particular.

Often we enter more directly into the poem than did Michele. And for good reasons. One joyful thing about writing poetry is that, given the same data, different people create differing versions. Try it with a small group. Select an excerpt of your log that is meaningful to you. Ask each person to write a poem about it. In our experience, many of the resulting poems are similar in essence although their presentation is not. Different poems about the same data can help a researcher to rethink the data and to work on creating additional ways to highlight them.

Creating poems from in-depth interviews has been an extremely successful activity for many qualitative researchers. Diane Austin introduces her poem in the following way:

> This poem was written with quotes taken directly from my interview with a person who considered himself a recovering alcoholic. This interview was part of my research about an organization that aims to help people recover from the disease. My initial research question was 'What is going on here?' This changed to 'What keeps people coming back?'

Parallel Process
by Diane S. Austin

'No judgment' he says.
Yeah, I think — don't we all long for that.

'Somebody to understand' he says.
Yeah, I think — don't we all long for that.
'Watching people grow and recover.'
I *know* just what he means.
'Keep it simple, saved my life.'
and I think about my complicated life.
'I've got to tend my garden,' he says
and I think about the weeds in mine.

This poem, too, is an example of sparse shaping and dramatic representation. However, to us, its major contribution lies in the fact that Diane shows as much of herself, maybe more, as she does of the participant. In our experience this is quite rare in the poetry our colleagues have created. We have written already, and will again, about the dictum to share self in our writing about studying others. What we find and report about others is intimately meshed with our own ways of seeing-or-not-seeing our 'selves.' Because of this, we owe it to our readers to be up front about our feelings, our process, our puzzlements, our disasters, and our victories. Diane's poem makes both people come alive. What insights about herself does she share with you? What hunches do you have about her experiences and about the kind of person she is?

In Carolyn Arnason's poem, she shares a vision of herself as a writer of qualitative research. She introduces her poem to provide context:

Prelude to a Poem

One of my pastimes when riding subway trains in New York is to read the advertisements. One day I noticed, squeezed between two advertisements, a Poetry in Motion. They are short — sometimes funny, romantic or poignant, and they make my ride a bit less tedious. This is:

Poetry in Motion on Writing

Sitting at my desk,
Staring into my mind to find,
Flitting ideas like butterflies in a field of flowers.
Sounds of sirens wafting into the room,
Fog sitting over The City.
Maybe a cup of coffee would help,
Is this what Friday means for writers?
Suddenly I catch an idea,
Iridescent and shimmering I place it on the page,
I begin to write.

To us Carolyn's poem also provides an insight into herself. But it is different from Diane's. It is far more directly focused on the process of writing — and how she feels about starting to compose. How often have we sat before writing the pages of this book, waiting for the muse? And while the details of Carolyn's process are hers, not ours, she has caught perfectly the essence of our own halting starts. The poem would do well in a section about Carolyn's research methods.

Susan Goetz Haver's poem is about Jamal, a 6-year-old child who frequents the library where Susan is doing her fieldwork. Jamal has been overlooked almost consistently by the adults who work in the library. He has finally gotten his library card. As you read this poem, please consider the messages you receive from it and make some hunches about how this poem functioned in Susan's presentation of findings.

Jamal's Voice

I belong.

Here it is
plain as day
official
for anyone to see

My name
my place in the world
member in full
Do you want to see it?

Do you want me
to show it to you?
Do you want me
to pull up a chair
and tell you?

Now I am important
Now I can be
the biggest
the fastest
the best
Maybe then you will like me

Will you read to me?
Will you hold me in your lap
and tell me a story?

See here, I must belong somewhere.
it says so right on this card.
I'm a member . . .
if I only knew
of what.

While not one word of this poem was ever uttered by Jamal within Susan's hearing, these lines did characterize for her Jamal's experience as she documented life in the library. During this phase Susan was witness to Jamal's actions — particularly his body language — his attempted as well as actual interactions with others, and the ways the adults and other children talked with and about him. From this body of data, Susan crafted her poem. She used it to introduce the story of Jamal. His was one of several stories about children in the library. The poem can be thought of as a snapshot of Jamal that can be revisited and reexamined by the reader after having read the various other interpretations that Susan presents about him. In this way,

Susan is inviting her readers to see if the poem makes sense, if it is fair to the data that she shared.

Poems make useful and provocative introductions. But they can serve wherever the author decides is best; at the end of a presentation, or in its body. The decision about placement of any literary device is not haphazard. It is a careful reflective action that is meant to serve particular functions: to foreshadow, to encapsulate, to move the story forward, to provide a breathing space for thinking, to contradict, to share the researcher's emotions and/or process, to involve readers in their own analysis of the data. Our readers will add some other uses as they think of them.

Here is one of Susan's mood pieces. Where would you place it in research writing? Why? Can you see several possible places for it?

The Teacher

She lines up the children carefully
row by row, table after
table assigned, symmetrically arranged

and named — the groups, the subject,
the time of day all in order,
one to follow another precisely.

She speaks. The children strain to hear
the lesson, practice the numbers
and letters, the sequences thoroughly planned.
She must continue. Her words protect them all,
shield them from the wakening cry,
the roaring silence.

For the next two poems, think about where you would place them in the body of your research writing. What impact do they have on you? It may be, of course, that you'd never write or publish such a poem. Think of this as an exercise that may be of use to you when you make decisions about your own presentation.

Jane Martin's poem is about 'Nancy,' one of her participants, a woman in mid-life who has not married:

What More Could I Want?

I was a whiz at relationships in my 20's
Because I didn't care
When it came time for me to start caring, I got horrible and
I've only gotten worse
I was so dumb about relationships
So dumb about what I wanted
If only I had been afraid
       I should have been afraid and just got married
       But for some reason, I wasn't afraid
I thought there was more
I thought I should feel more
I had these romantic visions
I kept thinking . . . There's more, there's more

Like my father . . .
> I've always been afraid to make a mistake
> Not a great risk taker

God knows what I was looking for . . . What more could I want?
What more could I ask for in somebody —
> Somebody who's crazy about me
>> who's really smart
>> who's funny
>> like being my best friend or sister or brother

What more could I want?

Barbara Ball's poem is based on the following piece of her field log which includes her Observer Comments at its end:

Log: December 4
Observation 2
From 9:10 a.m.–11:45 a.m.

1   Sofia enters with her mother. Clara informs them at the door that chicken-
2   pox is going around. Four children
3   have it already. Sofia's mother says 'Sofia got it on the
4   first day of our vacation in Mexico. We were staying in a really cheap
5   place, with dirt floors. The doctor said "No sun, no swimming," so we
6   had to go to a hotel that was cleaner. But after a couple of days it was
7   over.' Gina: 'Sofia, do you want to make something very small in clay
8   for me?' Sofia looks shy, she partly hides behind her mother. She is
9   very blond, her hair is in braids and she looks pretty and neat. Gina
10 repeats the request that Sofia should make something for her.
11 Slowly Sofia takes a small lump of clay and smiles at me. She
12 squeezes it and tears off little pieces. They look like little eggs or
13 cookies and she collects them in a box, in front of her. Gina is moving
14 around in the classroom and comes back, looking for a tray. She picks
15 up Sarah's tray with her clay work with a big smile. 'I want to keep it!'
16 says Sarah as she leaves the table. Then Gina takes Sofia's
17 little 'eggs' or 'balls' out of the box 'to keep them.' Sofia says 'I made
18 them.' She looks distressed when Gina takes away her product. Gina says
19 'I want to keep them and show other teachers what you do.'
20 Observer Comment: In this sequence, Gina appears so unrelated to the
21 children. Somehow her moves disturb the children's rhythms. She
22 takes away Sofia's work without asking her. Another example of
23 the emphasis on products and demonstrating achievements, as opposed
24 to the process. Here, the emphasis on products really seems to be
25 detrimental.

Barbara's Poem: Gina: Something Very Small

Do you want to make something very small,
something very small for me?

Sofia hides behind her mother.

She takes a bit of clay
squeezes, tears and pounds the mud

rolls little pieces, that look
like precious eggs
and collects them in a box.

I want to keep them,
says the teacher
She takes Sofia's little eggs

I made them,
says Sofia
her voice vibrates

I want to keep them,
says the teacher. I want
to show the other teachers what you do.

Barbara's poem stays reasonably close to her descriptive log. It supports her emerging analytical theme about emphasis on product in this classroom.

When sections of one's field log are amalgamated into the written qualitative research piece, they can also be considered a rhetorical device. You will see more field log examples throughout this book. However, your decision about what to share from your log, and the purpose you wish it to support will need to be as carefully planned as the use of any other piece of your writing.

Plans, Outlines, and Tables of Content as Forms

We think that the time to plan what our writing might look like should come as early as possible. Wolcott (1990) urges that a plan be written even before the start of the study, when there are many 'holes and spaces.' We recommend writing a beginning plan even if it changes in the doing. It probably will. After all, that is one characteristic of qualitative research. A plan, an outline, and a table of contents are literary devices in themselves if they are shared as part of the research write-up.

Plotting of Plans

What follows is, in our opinion, an elegant example of planning. Priscilla Butler's Reflective Memo 4 was written long before she completed her study. In it she wrestles with her own contradictory insights, her confusions, and some tasks she hopes to accomplish as she gives structure to the writing. Watch what happens though, as she 'shapes at the point of utterance' (Britton, 1982):

Reflective Memo 4

In thinking about 'The Plan,' I inevitably come back to the problem about my problem statement. In order to describe what I'm trying to do in Wolcott's statement of purpose, I am torn between two different stories I want to tell. In some ways, though, maybe my ambivalence has more to do with me trying to keep these two separate than with their innate separateness.

My problem is that in my observations, I was trying to describe an ESL (English as a Second Language) classroom. In my interviews, however, I find that what the students talk about goes far beyond just the ESL classroom that I observed. In other words, I am using interviews not only as a means of participant checking and of establishing the students' own stories of the classroom; I am also using them as places to explore other topics.

What has come up in several of the interviews is the students' own past learning experiences in their own countries, as well as their reasons for studying English, and their involvement in English studies outside of the classroom. While all these topics certainly are relevant for understanding these students' views of the classroom, there is a part of me which is confused by the degree to which this study has gotten beyond that one specific classroom. In some ways, I feel that I'm muddling my problem, confusing other issues with the one I originally started with. In other ways, I feel that it would be impossible to describe the students' experiences of the classroom without knowing something else about them.

I guess part of the problem is that not so long ago I thought that what I wanted to know about was the teacher. Now that I've started interviewing the students, however, I find their stories far more interesting. What I wonder, then, is if I tell the stories of these students, how do I incorporate stories of the classroom and still make everything cohesive?

In some ways, I seem to be having trouble conceptualizing what I'm trying to do. For example, if I do really want to represent the students' stories — not just of their classroom experience but of their language learning experiences in general or anything else which comes up which may shed light on their learning — then how do I incorporate these stories which I envision to be first-person stories with my observations which are third person? Do I just move between voices in different chapters? Am I trying to do too much?

With these questions in mind, I think my statement of purpose might be something like:

The purpose of this study is to describe the experiences of a small group of students attending a first semester ESL class in a USA school.

OR

The purpose of this study is to describe an ESL classroom. I'm not sure how to put these together or even if these should be put together. Considering that I want them both, though, my outline is based on including everything.

You might ask what a reflective memo about planning has to do with presentational forms. There are several possible explanations. One is that a memo is itself a form — and it communicates Priscilla's meanings to us. Another is that it is used, in this book, to tell something about Priscilla's process. Hence, it becomes an internal monologue illustrating the thinking behind her writing. Judiciously chosen and placed in the body of the dissertation, the book, the article, or in the appendices (although we like it better in the body) this form can provide a window into what the researcher has experienced and considered. In terms of distance between reader and researcher, such memos can function to bring the two nearer to each other since there is so much open sharing and so little obfuscation. The memo is not prettied up. It is what it seems to be; a conversation with self — with the added twist that in choosing to share it and in selecting a particular place in the work for it, the conversation is made public. Very subtle. Very useful. We recommend it highly.

After doing some trial writing, many qualitative researchers find it helpful to focus specifically on the forms that their work might take. They report that this moves them ahead and helps them to create a more complex outline. Jill Schehr writes:

> Tentatively, I have, somewhat grandiosely, decided to produce on an epic scale. The cinematic techniques I have employed in the field reflect my wish to describe the social culture of the prison nursery I am studying. Broad descriptive writing, from an observer's view, is how I intend to present this wide-angle camera 'pan.' I have tried it, and it seems just the brush I need to paint the backdrop. Thus, what started out to be a distanced descriptive account now comes more to life with the use of these new writing techniques.
>
> As I became more familiar with my data, I also became more comfortable painting more 'close-up' vignettes. Thus, I painted backdrops and zoomed in on vignettes . . . to my surprise, what evolved seemed 'alive' and true to my experience. I became proud of my ability to lift the 'doctoralese' censorship that had often encumbered my writing. This writing was much more personal than even I had been used to . . . and why not? This participant–observer experience had touched me way down deep. However, I still have a nagging feeling that my hard work will not be taken seriously . . . I am afraid that perhaps it is too passionately painted.

In the following excerpt, Ken Aigen, professor of music therapy, shares his thinking about form. It is clear that Ken wants both to do justice to his participants and to move beyond the usual forms of discourse of his profession:

> Besides having a concern for the welfare of the study participants, my respect for them has led me to want to find a way for their voices to speak in whatever form my final report takes. How a music therapy group is experienced by the participants is not something that has been written about extensively, but it is something which is of ethical concern and professional interest. Yet this task is quite difficult in the group under discussion because these children have significant communication disorders. One way I have discovered to get around this difficulty is to employ narrative devices such as constructs, critical incidents, and themes.
>
> First, in order to differentiate my research efforts from clinical documentation, I thought that it would be interesting to present the therapy group as a social system, including, of course, the therapists. In this way, I would move to a level of description and analysis not typically aspired to by clinicians themselves. I also became interested in communicating the evolution of the repertoire of the group, because I saw the unfolding of group process in the themes underlying the various song activities. Currently, my orientation point has been manifest in the group setting. However, I am still not absolutely certain that this will be the central theme around which I organize my report of findings. In fact, it may turn out that the final focus will emerge *as* I put the findings into some form to be shared with others.

Carole Di Tosti, high school teacher and school administrator, is the person who did a study of a small number of 'Whistleblowers' on corruption in education. Here she is talking about one superintendent of schools. She calls him 'my superintendent.'

> During the interviews, reading through transcripts, viewing the commission reports, I found the experiences of my superintendent to be fascinating, mythic, compelling.

My superintendent feels very strongly about the failure of American public school education to overturn what he deems to be the murdering of children every day in our schools. He is an impassioned man. He has, as I discovered both in interviews and through other accounts, devoted his life to serving children. His experiences of thwarting corruption in his district testify to the magnitude of his desire to thwart a system that he now believes refuses to reform itself toward producing quality life and learning. Hampered, encouraged, stirred, and burdened with my insights, I considered: Here is drama; here is a life of impact. Do I use forms which capture this life to make it vivid, vibrant, real? Or do I do what my various teachers have 'taught me so well?' 'Just do it and get it over with?' I made my decision; I had to be *just* to my superintendent. I had to be just and ethical to myself. I was compelled by conscience, thank God, compelled by myself and my support group to select the forms, the genres of revelation. Thus, I wrote stories, poems, acts of a longer play. As I began, I became more involved in the understanding that not only must I strive for accuracy of content, the spirit and flavor of my superintendent's drama, I must be ever vigilant about how I unfolded those dramas. To him, his life and actions held great meaning. The genres I selected should also signify and relate this meaning; the fusion of form and content should be complete.

Actually, the shape of your plan, whether you plan to create a complete outline right off as a leap of faith or begin writing sections in the various forms you've proposed, whether it is bare bones or expanded, whether you concentrate on one piece or many, is not as important as writing about your plans as early as you are willing to in the process. How you do this will, of course, be based on your own preferences. However, we find it not at all a bad idea to work on planning those parts about which we have some, or more than some, uneasiness and fear. Writing, being what it is, helps us think, unlock, and often propose a solution that is sufficient at least to forge ahead.

Pondering the tentative outline

Following the writing of her Reflective Memo 4 (p. 141), which we shared in the previous section, Priscilla Butler created this tentative outline for her study of an ESL class:

I. The Classroom: A Day in the Life
* I would want my story to recreate the mood of the classroom. I would hope that my reader could imagine him or herself there.

II. Characteristics of the Classroom
* For each of these categories, I would like to paint one characteristic scene. These stories would provide a gateway into sketching a larger picture.
— The nature of talk
— In class and out of class
— relationships
— classroom activities
— small group
— large group

(I do see that some of these categories are interrelated. Since I have not categorized yet, I'm sure that these may change.)

III. John (the teacher)
* I see these sections composed of at least two major parts, the first being John's behavior in the classroom and the second being the verbalized perception of his behavior. I think I might write two stories: each of them characterizing these not entirely consonant images. These stories would help point out areas of dissonance and of concord between the two images.

IV. The Students' Stories
* I would like to tell a story for each of these students. Rather, I would like them to tell their own stories. These stories would center around a theme which seems to most represent their experiences — either in or outside of class, whichever seems more important to them. One thing that I would like to show with these stories is how individual each of these students is, how unique each of their experiences is.
 — Naomi
 — Boris
 — Marta
 — Kon
 — Kula

V. Thematic Analyses and Conclusions.

Examine Priscilla's Reflective Memo 4 again (p. 141) to consider how the outline may be a reflection of the insights Priscilla gains through her writing. Do you agree that the 'problems' of presentation that Priscilla mulled over in the memo are already on the way to being solved in the outline? Certainly Priscilla made a tremendous leap with this outline. In fact, it didn't change all that much in her final research report.

As a final tidbit about her reflective memo, this is what Priscilla wrote in reply to the questions 'what holes and spaces are there in your plan that you need to address, and, what data do you intend to winnow'?

RE: Holes and Spaces

Without having a clearer idea of how these sides I am interested in mesh together,
I think that it is very difficult to point out holes. I would like to save this for later.
The same holds true about dropping data. Right now I think that the majority of
my data are relevant. I am not yet at a point where I can let go of any of them.

Obviously Priscilla felt that she was not ready to answer her professor's questions. However, Harry Wolcott might have insisted that she consider which data to retain as well as those to discard. He is also prone to asking his students to estimate the number of pages they might allot to each section. All of these ways of considering the shaping of the report can be helpful in moving the conception forward.

Priscilla's tentative outline does not include an introduction to her research purposes, her plan for collecting data, for making sense of them, or how she will weave in other literature related to her topic. Probably she had considered these parts previously as she planned her research proposal. Here, she focuses deeply on how she might present her findings without much attention to meta-analysis and discussion. This is what served her best at that time, and so it worked. Michele Bellavita, on the other hand, provides a more inclusive outline:

Good Enough Fathers: Fathers of Toddlers Tell Their Stories

Outline

OVERVIEW OF STUDY:
(Begin with poem? Maybe 'Suddenly there was this person' or one that captures the feel, tone, essence of the study; the experience of fathering; the impact of fathering on these particular men.)

Discuss why, when, where, how the study came to be, evolved, developed; Explain what actually took place. Work on Researcher's Stance here? Include anecdote, story (?) if available and as needed that reflects the men's experience/my experience of study?

THE FATHERS:
Give broad description of the men and their children as a group, including similarities and differences, if that seems warranted or helpful. Is there something — quote, poem, anecdote, imagined/inferred roundtable discussion — that is evocative of the broad contrasts and similarities of their lives? If so, include.

THEIR STORIES: 'The child is Father to the Man' (Wordsworth, 1948)
Tell each man's story and/or find some method of letting him tell his story, including profiles, constructs/inferred soliloquy, stories structured around critical events (like his child's birth, the decision — or not — to have a child, an illness, whatever), including and/or depicting relevant themes that emerged for each man.
    Peter: How Not to Play My Father's Tapes
    Jose:
    Allan:
    Trevor:
    Roger:

LULLABY FOR FIVE VOICES:
Overarching themes across the five interviews (Why not be optimistic?) and/or
LULLABY IN COUNTERPOINT FOR FIVE VOICES:
Contrasting but interrelated themes across interviews

DISCUSSION/ANALYSIS, including RELEVANT LITERATURE

REFLECTIONS, including where I would go from here if I had a grant from the Ford Foundation.

Michele's outline highlights some vital benefits of doing such an exercise. She tells us her purpose straight off in the first paragraph. Next, her outline provides a map for the planned sequence of presentation. In this she warmed our hearts by indicating that she intends to weave in related literature as a conversation with her findings and not as an isolated, often meaningless chapter near the beginning of her report. Third, Michele plays with the possibilities of presentational forms — poem, anecdote, story, imaginary roundtable discussion, profiles, constructs, inferred soliloquy, themes, overarching themes, contrasting themes. The poem 'Suddenly there was this person' that Michele alludes to in the first line of her outline, began our previous section about poetry. We get some clues about where her voice will be heard and where she will present stories in the voices of her participants who are the fathers of toddlers. Last, Michele considers some questions she will need to resolve and shares her sense of humor through the writing — a delicious and therapeutic talent. And she did all this by presenting a one page table of contents. Not a bad forum for all those messages.

As we have suggested, outlines themselves may be our latest, best drafts. They are usually prone to speedy revisions (sigh) as we continue. Magdalen Radovich allows a window into her process of outlining by providing two drafts and some of her explanation about her process:

A. The Tentative Plan — Draft I

My original outline focused a lot on the organization and structure of the soup kitchen rather than on the stories and lives of the participants, i.e., the volunteers and the clients:

Working Statement of Purpose — To explore various facets of an urban soup kitchen, including its internal organization and the experience of its volunteers and clients.

I. St. Theodora's Church
   A) Setting
       1 — External
           a) neighborhood
           b) building
       2 — Internal
           a) rectory
           b) basement
               — uses
               — floor plan
               — furnishings
               — posters and other visuals
           c) mood

   B) Mission

   C) Programs
       1 — AIDS Outreach
       2 — Caring Community
       3 — Meals on Heels
       4 — Soup Kitchen

II. Soup Kitchen: Organization
   A) Operations
       1 — Funding
       2 — Numbers Served
       3 — Structure
           a) shifts
           b) jobs
               — food preparation
               — food distribution
               — clean up
           c) rules
               — tickets
               — second helpings

B) Leadership
    1 — Coordinator
    2 — Volunteer Leaders
    3 — Volunteer Group Leaders

C) Indicators of Authority
    1 — Physical Appearance
        a) clothing
        b) body language
    2 — Verbal
        a) delegation of responsibility
        b) conferral of authority
        c) direct verbal assertion of authority
        d) signs

III. Soup Kitchen: The Participants
A) The Volunteers
    1 — Who Volunteers?
        a) economic status
        b) gender
        c) race
        d) age
    2 — How Do They Get Involved?
        a) parish
        b) schools
        c) university
        d) Catholic High Schools
        e) hunger organizations
            — Street Projects
            — New York Cares
            — YWCAs and other youth groups
            — friends and volunteers
    3 — Why Do They Get Involved?
        a) attitudes towards the clients
        b) attitudes regarding their own missions
    4 — Bonding
        a) common life experience
        b) stories about the soup kitchen
        c) offers of help

B) 'Our Boys' (or) The Clients
    1 — Who Are the Clients?
        a) economic status
        b) gender
        c) race
        d) age
    2 — Why Do They Come to St. Theodora's Specifically?
        a) space
        b) no hassles
        c) stockpiling
        d) second-helpings

  C) **Relational Dynamics**
    1 — Client Relationships with Each Other
      a) friends
      b) caretakers
      c) loners
    2 — Relationships with the Volunteers
      a) narrative
      b) power struggles
      c) mutuality

Magdalen writes:

In a better planned revision of the above, I would probably restructure my original plan VERY ROUGHLY, to provide more of a context, i.e., a description of the broader issues of hunger and poverty in the United States, and to focus more on the participants.

  I would add the usual, a stance, a section on methods, review of literature, a section on findings or tentative conclusions and possible implications. Although I do not do it in the working plan that follows, I might restructure by theme rather than category of participants.

B. Working Plan — Draft II

Statement of Purpose — To explore the issues of self-empowerment and social justice in one urban community church.

I. **Stance of the Researcher**
   — My history with the hunger movement
   — My choice of qualitative method

II. **Methods of Data Collection**

III. **Overview of Literature**

IV. **Overview of the 'Hunger' Problem in the United States**
   — Numbers/statistics
   — Commonly-stated underlying causes
   — Myths
   — Organizations that help
   — Serving organizations vs. self-reliance movement

V. **St. Theodora's — 'A Caring Community'**
   — Overview of Community Outreach Programs
   — Commitment to the Hungry
   — Service vs. Training
   — Theme Developments

VI. **Faces of the Hungry**
   — The 'Who' behind the numbers
   — Interplay of race/gender/age/socio-economic status
   — Attitudes toward their own plight
   — Theme Developments

VII. **Implications and Findings**

What do you think about Magdalen's move from draft to draft? Does it make sense to you? We believe that a third outline may well be on its way, given the phrase in her introductory paragraph to Draft II: '. . . I might restructure by theme.' And so it goes.

Obviously, we are not saying that an outline should work to reduce and narrow the focus in ways that will work against bursts of insight or the release of energy that often accompanies us when we write away from the plans we've made for ourselves. Those moments of moving beyond the expected remain important in spite of the road maps we've set for ourselves. We should be stirred by our realizations of the 'sea of possibilities' that William James (1897) perceived could and should work against determinism (p. 150). We recommend thinking of these planning forms as grounding rather than constraining. The ends cannot always be in view beforehand or even during the writing. A capacity to tolerate the unexpected and unrealized can, in fact, be supported and nourished by a tentative outline.

Providing direction with a table of contents

One way of keeping the tentativeness in the plan and outline is to be playful with the form and content. The next example was created by Rosemarie Lewandowski. In contrast to Priscilla and Michele, who were thinking dissertation, Rosemarie was thinking about a possible monograph and she crafted a tentative outline into a possible Table of Contents. As you study Rosemarie's table, please consider the functions of the quotations that introduce each section. The quotations provided Rosemarie with another route through which she might clarify the more subtle layers of meaning that she hadn't worked with in her outline.

TABLE OF CONTENTS

I. EXPLORING @ *13 pages*

THE PROCESS OF THINKING THROUGH MY PURPOSE

'Real qualitative research does not know what the thesis is until the interviews are done and analyzed.' (Meloy, p. 317)

Wolcott — The Plan
including statement of purpose

The New Plan
revised statement of purpose

Field Log — on gaining entree

Analytic Memo
on writing the plan and Tesch

II. DISCOVERING @ *50 pages*

induction, n. 2. Logic. any form of reasoning in which the conclusion, though supported by the premises, does not follow from them necessarily.' (The Random House College Dictionary Revised Edition, p. 679)

A. INDUCTIVE CONCLUSIONS

Anecdote: Joey's Sunset
Joey draws during journal time.

Playlet: 'Why won't you write for me?'
Writing is used as punishment for Joey.

'Why don't you listen?'

'Daydream' Drafts 1–3

'The Program' Drafts 1–3

'Let's Play School'
Mrs. Cato as a first grader

B. PREMISES

Participant Observation #4
Joey breaks the class rules (shared with Mrs. Cato during the participant
check, minus several Observer Comments).
A diagram of Mrs. Cato's classroom.

Analytic Memo on the Interview

Article — On myself as researcher

Layered Story/ First Person Narratives: 'Joey Draws a Kite'
Joey
Mrs. Cato — Draft 1 (shared with Mrs. Cato)
Mrs. Cato: A Profile — Draft 2 (revised to emphasize her point of view
on Joey's kite drawing)

III. *DESCRIBING @ 15 pages*

METHODS: SORTING, FILING, CODING, PLANNING, MAPPING

*Creating categories, subcategories, and discovering their links brings a researcher into
intimate reacquaintance with the data. There is nothing like a line-by-line or phrase-
by-phrase lens to accomplish that end. (Ely et al., p. 145)*

Reflections on Analytic Methodology,
On Returning to the Field

Categories and Labels

A Tesch Map

Themes from the Log

Metaphor Bins

IV. *UNDERSTANDING @ 30 pages*

METHODS: ANALYSES AND INTERPRETATIONS (READING, TALKING, THINKING, WRITING)

*Crystallization provides us with a deepened, complex, thoroughly partial, understand-
ing of the topic. Paradoxically, we know more and doubt what we know. (Richardson,
p. 522)*

Analytic Memos on My Metaphors and Metathemes

On Trustworthiness

Reflections on Reading and Writing

A Conversation with Atkinson

An Organizing Scheme: Reflections and Projections out of Tappan and Brown

On *Judging the Quality of Case Study Reports*
  Connections with Bakhtin

Mrs. Cato's Ladder
  Analytic Memo on my Participant Check
  Reflections on a Metatheme

More Reflections on Writing — Drafts I and 2

It may be that education can only take place when we can be the friends of one anothers' minds. (Maxine Greene, in Witherell and Noddings, p. xi)

At the heart of what we are suggesting is a sense of agency, of power to use the forms that are available and to extend, mold, or break them in ways that make sense for the particular work in which you are engaged. Unlike her two colleagues who provided the previous examples, Rosemarie did prevail on herself to estimate page lengths for each section. So Rosemarie's estimate of 108 pages, now in large font and double-spaced, will boil down to about 60 publishable pages. A nice size for a monograph. Can this change? Certainly, and it probably will as sections are developed and pruned. However, this page estimate does provide a sense of parameter and purpose. Such planning is a useful strategy. In fact, estimating length does help a writer conceptualize what material can be included. It is also the strategy, in our experience, vehemently fought by many writers. 'I mean, how can you expect me even to guess at length when I don't know what I'm going to say yet?' True. And yet we all live with page limits, notwithstanding that one wouldn't know it from the heft of some dissertations. Articles, books, monographs, and, yes, even dissertations demand a consideration of length. More than that, these limits are often key criteria for acceptance by publishers. At this moment, Margot's chapter in a book about to be published by the same house that is overseeing the book you are holding now will have to be cut back by about three pages. That is a painful task. Finally, estimating length provides a frame by which to imagine proportions to guide the writing. This is important.

In the service of not asking everyone to reinvent the wheel, published Tables of Contents can often provide qualitative research writers with ideas about constructing theirs. There are surely many examples of such Tables of Contents that provide more than a brief hint of what is to come, that may in themselves be considered literary devices. We'll describe aspects of three.

Renata Tesch (1990) presents a conventional Table of Contents first. This is followed by what she labeled as a Schematic Table of Contents (see Figure 3.4). The Schematic Table of Contents was created by Tesch because she reasoned that the information explosion of our time is so vast that people cannot learn everything that interests them. So they might as well rest easy in the knowledge that they need to be selective. And, since everything is linked to everything else, a scheme about the

Figure 3.4:   *Schematic Table of Contents (from Tesch, 1990, p. ix)*

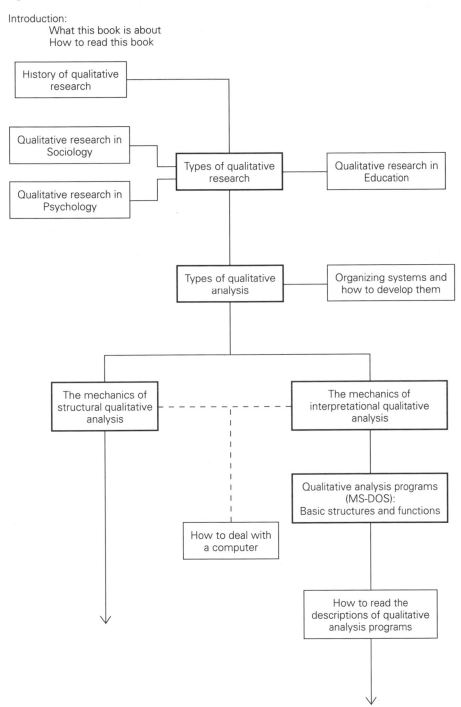

presentation of information should not be linear, but three-dimensional (Tesch, 1990, pp. 6–7). This sort of selective branching is harder to do in a book than, say, with a computer program, but Tesch makes her attempt. She invites her readers to select what they want to read and to leave out what they already know or do not wish to consider. Further, she urges her readers to create their own paths through the contents, and if that path is the usual one — from first to last page — so be it. Her invitation is to '... break out of the familiar mode' (p. 7).

In our own writing of this book and past ones, we have 'looped' from one chapter to others and have made many attempts to bind together and to expand on crucial understandings all through. Tesch's rationale has provided us with insights on what has been our tacit process up to now. Thus, while our Chapter 8 titled 'Qualitative Research Writing: What Makes It Worthwhile after All?' seems a logical piece near or at the end, there is really no good reason why you should not read it first or at any other juncture.

Kevin Dwyer (1982) in his *Moroccan Dialogues: Anthropology in Question* has been a provocative influence on us in writing this and other chapters. His thesis is that anthropologists must in their writing, share of and about themselves as they seek to share about the 'others' they study. This will be worked with in the pages to come (notice the forward loop please!). However, for now we speak of how this foundational belief shaped Dwyer's Table of Contents. Again, like Tesch, Dwyer presents a conventional table of contents first. Then, however, comes his stunning Detailed Contents. Here is its beginning:

Part I, and by far Dwyer's largest section of the Detailed Contents, is built around
those events of his fieldwork that became the foci for each interview — his major
data collection strategy. Next he explains:

> Once I had singled out an event, I prepared a number of questions for the Faqir
> [these questions are indicated in the text by bold face italic type and are collected
> in the Detailed Contents] other questions came to mind as our talk proceeded. All

dialogues were taped that summer and all the questions and answers we exchanged during them appear in their original order. (Dwyer, 1982, p. xxi)

What a useful coming attraction. Because we are so convinced that questions play an essential, often unexplored role in data collection, the Detailed Contents tell us right away that the book is worth our reading. Also, we are taken with the knowledge that Dwyer intends to present his dialogues for our consideration without the usual analysis that is peppered throughout so much of writing about qualitative research findings. Could it be that this man will share the interview data and leave it at that? Even his Detailed Contents of Part Two hint of the absence of categories, themes, profiles, and other literary devices:

On reading only the Detailed Contents as it was whisked past her nose by Sallie Motch, a colleague and doctoral student, Margot said:

I knew I had to purchase the book, notwithstanding its price tag. Not because Dwyer's scheme echoed mine — I do analyze and share my reflections about what I studied — but because I was convinced that Dwyer was saying something that would be important to me and to my work. Now I see that he did analyze in his way and for his purposes. Part Two tells me that Dwyer's analysis was of his process and what this has to say to his colleagues in anthropology. What is crystal clear to me, and most impressive is Dwyer's attempt to create a fit between his methodological assumptions — his philosophical framework — and the Detailed Contents. He is working to be true to what he believes.

There are many worthwhile and creative published Table of Contents spanning the history of writing. Lots of them may be hundreds of years old but new to us. We share one more piece. This is from Ana Castillo in her novel *So Far From God* (1993), an altogether charming, vivid and mysterious tale of two decades in the life of a Chicano family in New Mexico:

1. An Account of the First Astonishing
Occurrence in the Lives of a Woman
Named Sofia and Her Four Fated
Daughters; and the Equally Astonishing
Return of Her Wayward Husband

2. On Caridad's Holy Restoration and Her
Subsequent Clairvoyance: Both Phenomena
Questioned by the Doubting *Tomases* of
Tome

3. On the Subject of Dona Felicia's
Remedios, Which in and of Themselves
Are Worthless without Unwavering Faith;
and a Brief Sampling of Common Ailments
Along with Cures Which Have Earned
Our Curandera Respect and Devotion
Throughout War and Peace

4. Of the Further Telling of Our
Clairvoyant Caridad Who After Being
Afflicted with the Pangs of Love
Disappears and Upon Discovery Is
Henceforth Known as *La Armitana*

5. An Interlude: On Francisco el
Penitente's First Becoming a Santero and
Thereby Sealing His Fate

We have attempted to show that there is more than meets the usual eye to writing plans, outlines and tables of contents. Indeed, when we mine deeper than the obvious, these forms provide us with support in at least two ways: they are themselves forms of writing and can be utilized in research reports to move the story forward, and, they facilitate the what, when, and why of how we write.

Finishing the Hat

Finishing the hat,
How you have to finish the hat,
How you watch the rest of the world
From a window
While you finish the hat.

Studying the hat,
Entering the world of the hat,
Reaching through the world of the hat
Like a window,
Back to this one from that.
(Sondheim and Lapine, 1991, p. 66)

There is a scene in Stephen Sondheim's and James Lapine's 'Sunday in the Park with George' where the painter George Seurat is engaged, nay obsessed, with finishing the hat. Everything else pales for him — the pulls of the external world, relationships — as he labors to realize his internal vision, his sense of what must be done. Not only that, his painting consists of dots or points that do not make much sense up close. So he has to move back and forth, from near the canvas to further away. He knows what he wants. He knows that his creation means that he must break with conventional ways of seeing things, that he must re-vision for himself and others what many had always taken for granted:

And you sir! Your hat is black. So black to you perhaps. So red to me. (p. 36)

He must make his case. He knows he must give as delicate a scrutiny to getting the hat just right in painstaking pointillist detail as he must give to the larger forms. He knows everything must mesh.

You do receive our meaning.

Seurat was fortunate to have such a clear vision even though, we are quite convinced, it also got clearer in the doing. For qualitative research writers such internal vision is also paramount. It may suffice to say that where we stand about research, how we see our place in that endeavor, translates to how we write, and to the forms that we select in that writing. There is no escape.

If we see ourselves as the sole authors, the ones who really know what is happening, who feel that our readers need know little of the researcher or of the research process, we will write that way. There are plenty of past and present ethnographies, for example, in which the authors share little about themselves as creators of their work. Further, you will not find a researcher's stance or reflections braided into their texts. You will find that these authors speak *for* the people they studied, the 'others', in ways that allow little breadth for doubt or alternative possibilities, even when the participants are quoted. You will find a story told.

Look at some of the most popular qualitative research publications. You'll probably be as surprised as we were. A close scrutiny tells exactly where the authors stand. Not what they say about their stance, but what it is in actuality.

If we see ourselves as co-creators of our research, as people who believe that there are evanescent and various possibilities for creating meaning, we will write that way. There is a whole range of possibilities here. This moves from research writers who include scant opportunities for readers to see how they worked, what they felt, and how their participants helped to create the story; to writers whose stories are collaboratively created and whose roles in this are explicated; to writers who create a text that focuses almost entirely on the 'other,' writers who believe that it must be up to the reader to make meaning of the material with minimum input from the author and maximum input from the participants in the form of unedited, unnarrated material.

In our emphasis on 'we write what we are' we may have given the impression that all of us are consciously aware of 'what we are.' This is, of course, not so. In the rush of meeting other people's expectations and with what they take for granted, many researchers do not continue an ongoing search into surfacing their stance. Those of us in this group may well be unaware of the messages we are sending. But we are sending them nevertheless.

Lest we be misunderstood, we are speaking here to more experienced, highly acclaimed qualitative research writers perhaps more so than to beginners because acclaimed researchers serve as such potent role models. Nor is the process of translating our beliefs into text an easy one. It can be quite excruciating. Patti Lather (1994) provides a relevant example. She speaks of her deep commitment to fairly represent all voices of the players by creating a text that 'works at multiple meanings, a doubly coded text that is both accessible and fosters brooding' (p. 9) about the stories of women who are living with HIV/AIDS.

Lather describes how a variety of researchers have created their forms in line with their philosophies, and tentatively offers her major strategy in an early draft. In the chapters that center on particular topics discussed by her participants, each page is set up with the running interview on top. This is then demarcated by a line which is followed by the commentary of Lather and her co-researcher Chris Smithies. The commentary, in different font size, talks to what was said, what needs to be said, and at times includes some material such as letters and poems written by the participants in response to reading the manuscript. Lather and Smithies also include inter-chapters on angels to introduce and continue their working metaphor of the angel in the book. Lather writes:

> This text ... will not be written until I figure out how to not reduce this project to some network of themes, emergent or not, how to not inscribe some mechanism of identification and projection. Moving toward textual strategies which denounce the transcendental authority with which I, as author, am invested, I work toward a practice that erases itself at the same time as it produces itself. Such a practice makes space for returns, silences, interruptions, self criticism, and points to its own incapacity. Such a practice ignites in writing and reading what is beyond the words and the rationally accessible, gesturing toward a feminist practice of a double science (1994, p. 26)

What a glorious struggle. Surely one that can give heart to other people. And while Patti Lather may never be completely satisfied, she is pushing forward the possibilities for presenting research writing. Our struggle may differ from hers, our forms may vary, but it seems to us that the key to crafting research writing worth reading is the willingness to engage, puzzle, create and recreate the shapes of our writing so that they are increasingly congruent with our stance.

There have always been newcomers who challenge us to reconceive old forms. That doesn't make the old forms 'useless' or 'lifeless' but it does mean that we must be vigilant to how others shatter, bring long-repressed voices to bear on what we all struggle to do. Sometimes, without help, we cannot see or hear the multiple ways in which we think about writing the report into meaning. It may sound trite, but we are challenged daily by the multiplicity of meaning. We hope that, as qualitative researchers, we can stake a claim in defining the angles of repose that prospect many unimaginable diversities and passions — working to arouse feelings that strike confusion and cacophony rather than essentialism. But, we also recognize that this isn't easy and that the forms we have available to us may still contain elements that might exhaust rather than challenge the conditions that we strive to summon through the writing. We hope you'll plan for the complexity rather than try to obliterate it.

Chapter 4

Working in Analytic Modes

We debated for some time about where in our overall text to place chapters devoted specifically to the analysis and interpretation of data. It should be clear by now that we believe qualitative research is a deeply interpretive endeavor and that analytical processes are at work in every step of the crafting of the document. The forms of writing described in Chapter 3, even as they help move those processes forward, are also products of analysis and interpretation. There are times, however, when we work quite specifically at analysis, beginning with the moments when we first begin to reread and code our data. It is with these overtly analytical acts that this chapter is concerned.

Analytical and interpretive processes work in tandem in the construction of meaning. Wolcott (1994) claims that analysis carries with it connotations of acts that are 'cautious, controlled ... methodological,' whereas interpretation connotes the 'freewheeling ... unbounded, generative' (p. 23). We do not quarrel with the connotations Wolcott ascribes to these terms, but we would want to be a bit more specific about the way we see interpretation. As we are using the term in these pages, interpretation means drawing meanings from the analyzed data and attempting to see these in some larger context. Interpretations arise when patterns, themes, and issues are discerned in the data and when these findings are seen in relation to one another and against larger theoretical perspectives — our own newly emergent views or those to be found in 'the literature.' Toward the end of this chapter, then, we consider the analytic work that bridges into the specifically interpretive. Overall we give examples of how researchers have worked through a variety of analytic processes. In the next chapter we highlight interpretation.

Wolcott (1994) made distinctions between three aspects of qualitative writing that are so often separated in a finished document — description, analysis, and interpretation. For the sake of clarity, we choose to discuss each as a discrete activity, but we feel that we cannot emphasize too strongly that we consider all three as aspects of the basic analyzing/interpreting interplay of qualitative research writing and as way stations on a continuum along which our minds constantly travel back and forth.

In Ely, Anzul, Friedman, Garner, and Steinmetz (1991, Chapters 3 and 5), we presented some approaches to both beginning and final analysis. If you use that book and this together as a *vademecum* during the course of your research, you will know something of our approaches to analysis before you reach this chapter. Why, then, return to a consideration of analysis at this late point? What more is there to be said about the topic? In all honesty, we must admit that in the intervening years we have worked with these processes and thought deeply about them and we feel now that there is more we would like to say. Many approaches to analysis are set forth in the various texts on qualitative research, and it is not our purpose here to duplicate descriptions of these processes. Instead, our goal in this chapter is to expand the repertoire of possibilities and to detail how analysis weaves through the complete document as it is being structured.

The emergent and recursive nature of qualitative processes is dealt with in the second section. An important focus of this section is the actual coding and categorizing that carry the analysis forward. In the move from initial analysis during data collection through final analysis after leaving the field, certain findings will seem most salient, and others may have to be winnowed out for the sake of the writing at hand. There comes a time when we need to plot out, or to review an original plan for the document as a whole, and to consider how each section we intend to include can make an effective contribution. To highlight that step is our third purpose in this chapter. Fourth, most research reports contain a section in which analytical results are presented in a somewhat formal fashion. Most researchers write this section after completing descriptive and/or narrative writing, and many use it to 'pull together' the patterns and themes that they see. It can help at this stage in the writing to consider again some of the forms in which the results of analysis can be presented.

Researchers in the human service professions commonly make recommendations for both practice and additional research somewhere in the course of their discussion of findings or, perhaps more commonly, in a final wrap-up chapter at the end of the publication. This, too, is a piece of the overall analysis, one that usually involves a 'lift' in thinking — that is, a shift toward greater abstraction or generalization — and often a change of focus. It is at this point that the writing usually takes on a more interpretive tone, and the interpretive discussion in turn will lead into whatever recommendations for practice or exhortations to the world at large the researcher is now ready to make. We will discuss this aspect of the overall writing task toward the end of this chapter and return to it in the chapter that follows.

What We Are Doing When We Analyze

There is no way that as thinking beings we can *not* analyze. The same human minds that think and remember and relive and retell in narrative also work with a different and sometimes contrary motion to classify and abstract. We do it as we categorize, tally, label, and make sense of perceptions. Atkinson (1992) refers to the 'temporal quality' of human experience as it is presented in descriptive and narrative forms. When we analyze, we often stop the flow of the 'sequential presentation' (p. 13) and lift an element out from the whole to inspect it more closely. In analysis for qualitative research, we try to discern the smallest elements into which something can be reduced and still retain meaning if lifted out of immediate context, and then to discover relationships between those elements. By way of contrast, we can look at the crafting of a descriptive or narrative segment as an act of synthesis, a putting together of elements into a particular form for a particular end. These narratives are supported by ongoing analysis, however, whether or not the teller is aware of the mental processes that undergird story.

Drawing on the Random House *Dictionary of the English Language* (2nd edn, 1987), we find analysis defined as 'the separating of material into its constituent elements . . . studying the nature of something or of its essential features and their relations.' Constituent elements, of course, will vary from study to study, depending on the purpose of each study, the research questions, the data themselves, and, inevitably, the final shape of the document, the academic discipline within which it is written, and its intended audience. We like to call these constituent elements 'meaning units' (Ely, Anzul, Friedman, Garner, and Steinmetz, 1991, pp. 87–9) or 'thinking units' (pp. 143–4), since to us they are 'constituent' only because the researcher decides them to be. In addition, these terms emphasize that the elements may differ in length and conceptual density depending on what makes sense in the study. Practically, a meaning unit may be a sentence, a paragraph, even a sequence of paragraphs, but it might also be only a word or phrase if so brief a segment signals meaning to the researcher. What we say here about analyzing by focusing on elements holds for a great majority of studies, although perhaps not for those at the far ends of the qualitative spectrum. This might be the case on the one hand for linguistic analysts who have selected their constituent elements before their study proper, and on the other hand for phenomenologists who come at meaning making in such unique, personal ways that it makes no sense to describe meaning units (Tesch, 1990).

In actual practice, we read and reread a portion of data and provide labels — usually notes in the margins — that identify a meaning unit. This process is called coding. Tesch (1990, pp. 115–41) proposes beginning at the level of meaning units, listing these, and then sorting them into categories. We refer to the first broad categories as 'bins' into which the coded data can be given an initial rough sort. The next step would be to look for relationships among the categories and arrange them into some sort of organized form, an outline perhaps. We will describe how some researchers have implemented these analytic processes in the following section. Before we do so, however, we want to emphasize that these processes are not an end in themselves. They are done to enable the researcher to discern relationships, patterns, and themes that run through the categories. These are the basis for 'lifting' to a more abstract theme statement or other interpretive presentation.

Margot is fond of saying that 'all analysis is basically sorting and lifting.' The words sometimes take on the quality of a mantra. Deep into the analysis of data, Joan Zaleski wrote:

> Lift!
> Dig in, dig deeper.
> Bin, sort, chunk,
> Shape, winnow, layer, weave,
> Lift!
> Dig in, dig deeper.

Push into it, pull it apart,
Probe, and
Lift!

One would think we were in a gym class, not doing qualitative research! I've come to think of my experience as a sort of mental gym class, with Margot as a Jane Fonda leader standing before us urging us to 'burn' those muscles into shape. Speaking metaphorically, the exercises each week have been a form of mental gymnastics, leaving me out of breath, sweating with exhaustion, yet mental muscles ever trim and tighter for the work. I've learned it takes stamina to be a qualitative researcher. When I think of how flabby and shallow my insights were when I began my study, it scares me to think how close I was to being a 'blitzkrieg ethnographer.'

We recognize that there are many approaches to qualitative analysis, and that you are guided to some extent by the conventions within your own academic disciplines, by whatever texts you are reading, by your own previous experiences or those of colleagues. We think that it is more important for researchers to understand certain principles underlying qualitative analysis and to adapt approaches as the needs of their own data suggest rather than to attempt to follow any one approach too rigorously.

Tesch (1990) provides a thorough overview of her version of many types and schools of qualitative research, and then summarizes with a list of ten characteristics of qualitative analysis. She finds these ten common to all types of qualitative research except those at the extremes of either 'formal, partly quantitative types of research' on the one hand, or those so unstructured that 'the data analysis process cannot even be articulated' on the other (p. 95). We find the characteristics on this list to be so fundamental that we present them here for your consideration. Watch to see how they have been actualized in the pages that follow. (The numbered statements in italics are Tesch's, 1990, pp. 95–7. The comments that follow each are our own.)

1 *Analysis is not the last phase in the research process; it is concurrent with data collection or cyclic.* Analytic processes should be planned for and put in place as part of the design of the research project. The entire process of gaining entry often in itself provides useful data and is a suitable topic for observer comments and analytic memos.

2 *The analysis process is systematic and comprehensive, but not rigid.* The process itself emerges from the data and the purposes of the study. There are, as these pages and others indicate, many approaches to analysis. The point is not so much which you follow, as that you document carefully your reasons for your choices and that you are consistent in your use of it. The insights of colleagues can be very helpful in indicating where foci might be broadened or narrowed or where alternative approaches could be useful.

3 *Attending to data includes a reflective activity that results in a set of analytical notes that guide the process.* The members of this writing team can attest to the fact that this reflective activity is a never-ending activity, that cumulative experiences can inspire new insights months and sometimes years later.

4 *Data are 'segmented,' i.e., divided into relevant and meaningful 'units,' yet the connection to the whole is maintained.* By definition, qualitative research is holistic, and no analysis of data is meaningful except in its cultural context.

5 *The data segments are categorized according to an organizing system that is predominantly derived from the data themselves.* In whatever way we choose to do it, analysis consists of giving order to the details. We find that coding by topic is often a useful way to start. There are examples in the pages that follow.

6 *The main intellectual tool is comparison.* Maybe. We might part company with Tesch here because we tend to be more eclectic in the tools we bring to bear on analysis. However, sorting things by their likenesses and their differences is a basic human activity. Comparisons of all kinds and at all levels are evident throughout qualitative research reports.

7 *Categories for sorting segments are tentative and preliminary in the beginning; they remain flexible.* Flexible is probably the operative word. Categories are tentative because the analysis remains tentative. We call the original rough categories 'bins.' Sorting coded data into bins helps to bring some order to the mass of otherwise unmanageable data.

8 *Manipulating qualitative data during analysis is an eclectic activity; there is no one 'right' way.* Indeed, there are many right ways. Many researchers combine more than one approach to analysis in the course of a single report. We would prefer another word to 'manipulate' — perhaps weaving, forming, shaping, organizing.

9 *The procedures are neither 'scientific' nor 'mechanistic'; qualitative analysis is 'intellectual craftsmanship' (Mills, 1959).* The emphasis here is on 'craft.' In the next chapter we write about the concept of 'researcher as *bricoleur*,' or craftsperson. That idea is certainly applicable to this aspect of the research endeavor.

10 *The result of the analysis is some type of higher-level synthesis.* The purpose of this synthesis is to represent one version or combined versions of understanding. But the word 'higher' still bothers us even as we do not present you with a more suitable term.

Analysis Emergent and Ongoing

We are of the generation of researchers that learned our craft in part from Lofland and Lofland (1984), their visual image etched in our consciousness of side-by-side figures (p. 132) that depict alternative schedules for data analysis. One of these figures, a rectangle bisected by a straight vertical line, depicts model of research in which data collection is completed before data analysis is started. The other figure, a rectangle bisected diagonally by a curve, depicts an approach to research in which both activities are conducted concurrently, with the emphasis greater on collection at first and greater on analysis as the process continues. According to the Loflands, research proceeds most productively when 'analysis and data collection run concurrently for most of the time expended on the project, and the final stage of analysis, after data collection has ceased, becomes a period for bringing final order to previously developed ideas' (p. 131). Following their precepts, we ourselves learned to begin any research project by starting a search for categories in our earliest log entries and setting up our filing systems early on. Over the years, however, we have come to understand the Loflands' precept in a less linear fashion. We are not as concerned about the proportion of data collection to analysis as we are about reciprocity. The interweaving of data collection and analysis is highly transactional, each activity shedding new light on and enriching the other. The choice of foci for close observation in the field is very much part of the analytic process. So also are the choices of forms through which we communicate what we have understood. It is our experience that the writing process shapes and sharpens the analysis. We follow and teach Wolcott's (1990) advice that the researcher begin working with preliminary drafts of narrative while still in the field. New themes, patterns and metaphors emerge as various drafts of profiles, vignettes, layered stories, and other forms are written. Sometimes when we are convinced that we are done with collecting data, our analysis and the writing about it convinces us of the need to return to the field and collect more.

Coding and Categorizing

Among the many excellent texts that provide an introduction to qualitative analysis we find Wolcott's *Transforming Qualitative Data* a good place to start for a sense of the overall task at hand and Renata Tesch's (1990) *Qualitative Inquiry*, along with Coffey and Atkinson's (1996) *Making Sense of Qualitative Data*, helpful guides to the analytic process. These latter authors see coding as 'a common start-ing point for researchers' (p. 23). One of the ways Coffey and Atkinson describe coding is as 'assigning tags or labels to the data, based on our concepts. Essentially, what we are doing is condensing the bulk of our data sets into analyzable units' (p. 26).

> Mulling over the process of coding, sorting, filing, and organizing my data, I found that I was a moth circling the Wolcott and Tesch beacons, which sent some sliver of access out of the dark heaviness of my fieldnotes. The excess of my pages loomed overwhelmingly above my head. When the dust of my flitting back and forth had settled . . . I found a semblance of intellectual cohesiveness forming in the void of my inexperience with analysis.

So wrote Barbara Goddard as she approached the task of analyzing her data on storytellers. Her initial confusion, the intellectual 'flitting,' and some trepidation seem to be characteristic of the beginning stages of analysis for most of us. And why not? We are stepping off into an unknown. How many of us have had much prior experience in search of the 'smallest meaningful thinking unit'? And to com-pound the confusion, we are told that our codes and categories must 'emerge' from our data, our unique and very own data. So where is there a model we can follow? The process sounds somewhat mystical and, for some of us, mystifying.

Margaret remembers clearly her own first experience with emergent analysis. Ten years ago is a long time in the history of qualitative research. Those were the days before the current texts by Tesch, Wolcott, Atkinson had appeared in print to provide guidance. There were then few qualitative dissertations in her department, few models to follow, no support groups to look to for advice. For months she wrote out log notes after every session with the literature discussion groups she was teaching and studying. For months she pored over the transcripts of these discussions, carefully writing whatever notes seemed relevant and helpful in the margins, all the while wondering, with increasing panic, how she would ever be able to 'analyze her data,' wondering when something — anything — would 'emerge.' But finally she did glimpse an analysis — and another and another. Those marginal notes that were the basis of analysis could indeed be grouped into categories as the words and behaviors of the children fell into place as 'patterns of response.' The case studies of individual children detailed their ways of reading and discussing and revealed distinct response styles, and these styles could in turn be interpreted and discussed in the light of extant theory. In retrospect, Margaret realized that she had spent not only the two years of this project but also the years of some earlier work in the collection and analysis of qualitative data without always being able to name what she was doing. There is much more guidance available for beginning researchers now, less need for so much uncertainty. But her experience speaks very directly to the need to be faithful to and trust the processes from the very beginning.

At the start the analytical muscles are weak and the exercise is difficult. So wrote Anne Ellen Geller:

> But, I don't like analyzing.
>
> Well, that's not really quite true. I have found analyzing difficult.
>
> It is difficult for me to stay within my log and look at what is on the page, and hunch about what might be behind and beyond what is immediately apparent. When I push myself to do this I love this too. I love what I find, the surprise patterns, and the repetitions. I love that when I find one it leads me to another and a third. But, I hate that this important step in the cycle of qualitative research is so hard for me, when the other steps are so easy, and I think it is because to analyze I have to step outside of my observations, and yet I have to be inside of them at the same time. As the researcher I can no longer simply reel off whatever I notice, I must name what I see, even if only tentatively. I must be sure in a provisional way, I must make some decisions, choose some bins, and then after making those decisions I must steer my future observations accordingly.
>
> This has asked me to make commitments to my thinking. And making these kinds of commitments, truly believing that what I am thinking is valid, is difficult for me. I have not done as much of this as I should have.
>
> Ivy, from my support group, told me that she views learning new things like exercise. 'If it hurts at the beginning you are stretching new muscles.' She said that she usually pushes to do the things that hurt so that they become easy and eventually painless.
>
> Now, as I begin to push myself to stay within my thick logs long enough to identify and name what I see, I'm looking for ways to describe what the discipline that is unique to qualitative research looks like and feels like. It is different from any discipline I have known or tried out. It has a flexibility, I know that. It has a self reflective honesty I crave, and the responsibility I fear. I have recently begun to write my side notes on my logs in pen. I know that may sound silly, but it is me admitting to myself that what I saw as I observed does not stay still, it comes

to life as I continue to see within and across what I have recorded. I could deny as I was writing my field logs that I was creating what I saw as I watched, but I took no notes while in the field so as soon as I began writing, I began creating. And it is only now, as I push myself to analyze further, that I am beginning to take full responsibility for what it was that I noticed and why.

We all know that we must take the step, assume the responsibility, that Anne did. How, then, to begin? What follows provides several specific examples. For now, in our experiences, the following characteristics of the beginning process hold: we sit down with our earliest log entries or interview transcripts and begin to code them in whatever ways makes sense to us as a starting point. As we proceed, we will begin to note similarities and differences, to notice a variety of relationships and patterns within and among codes. In time we will make some kinds of more general or abstract groupings of them — perhaps structured into an outline or web or clusters — and also perhaps into thematic or other generalized statements.

Many researchers we know find it difficult to actually begin the coding of their log material, perhaps because, like Michele Bellavita, they are so caught up in the mood and emotions of their first observations or interviews that they find it difficult to step back to a more abstract level:

> When it comes to coding, I have trouble at the most basic level — the very beginning. It's hard for me to look at a transcript and come up with the simplest, most basic codes. (At least it was. It's better now, and I don't worry so much.) It's my chronic difficulty stripping things down to their most basic level, again. Maybe I also find this tedious as well. When I first look at a transcript, I'm struck and distracted by the participant's language, by his verbal style, by the tone, mood, shifts in emotion. I'm struck by powerful statements . . . and I'm flooded by ideas about them. I've learned finally that I have to let myself go through this process first. I can let myself be struck by all of this, note the statements, shifts, mood; write all my thoughts about them, hunches, etc. Then, once I have this out of my system for round one at least, I can go back with more patience and in a cooler frame of mind and do my basic codes and categories.

Jane Martin, who studied a small number of women who had not married, provides an example of rigorous coding right from the beginning of her data collection. Below is an excerpt from an analytic memo in which she outlined the procedures that she followed during her first attempt:

> Coding, sorting, filing, winnowing . . . Organizing the data. Feeling a bit overwhelmed by the volume of my data for my first participant — three interviews, each one and one-half hours taped, which transcribe into approximately sixty pages each, fieldnotes and analytic memos — I decided to read about coding, as Margot suggested, in Tesch, Wolcott, and *Circles*. This reading proved helpful . . . I found *Circles* and Tesch's eight steps for developing an organizing system the most helpful and each supported the other.
>
> So, I have these thick transcripts filled with rich information amidst some unessential description waiting for me to make some sense of it. Informed by my reading, I can continue more securely along my way through my data. My system of organizing/coding consists of reading through the transcripts and making initial

comments, noting impressions and possible categories. I have subsequently gone back over the transcripts to make further notations and to circle or write topic (category) titles. Of course, I have read through each transcript a few more times in the course of pulling out information for a poem, a layered story, etc. Text is underlined and line numbers are bracketed throughout the documents. Here are some of my preliminary codes:

Family [FAM]
Parents [PAR]
Early childhood [ECH]
Educational background [EDUC]
Work [WORK]
Friendships [FRND]
Relationship with family [RELFAM]
        mother [RELMO]
        father [RELFA]
        sister Lindy [RELSIS-L]
        sister Celeste [RELSIS-C]
Romantic relationships [RELROM]
Relationship with Victor [RELv]
        Jack [RELj]
        Marty [RELm]
        Don [RELd]
        Tom [RELt]
        Larry [RELl]
        Jeff [RELj]
        Alan [RELa]
Sex [SEX]
Physical appearance [PHYS]
Body issues [BODY]
Personal insights [PI]
Life expectations [LE]
Dating [DAT]
Leisure activities [LEIS]
Loneliness [LONLI]
Marriage [MARR]
Identification with father [IFA]
Money [MON]
Future goals [FUT]
Children — Having children [CHILD]

My plan is to go back to the first interview and try to code the entire document using these codes, adding new ones and making changes when necessary. Then I will do the same with the second and third interviews. (The third is not yet completely transcribed and was predominantly a participant-checking session, but it includes a lot of new, rich, important data.) I think that I will try Tesch's idea of comparing categories created from each different interview and then listing them side-by-side in columns for comparison. OK, Tesch. Perhaps when I see these categories listed before me I will be moved to draw lines between some. I'll try it!

Notice that not only is Jane beginning to code with her earliest interview, but she also makes reference to writing early on — 'pulling out information for a poem, layered story, etc.' Whether or not she uses these in her final document, Jane will have the benefit of the interaction of ongoing coding and continuous writing to help her distill the essence of her data.

When Tesch (1990) talks about developing an organizing scheme, she provides her emphatic rule:

> Note the topic, not the *content*! When you look at a piece of data, ask yourself, 'What is this *about*? Don't pay any attention yet to *what* is said, i.e., to the substance of the statement; you will deal with this at a later stage. (pp. 142–3)

For an example of coding by topic, look again at Jane Martin's list of codes. Notice that it is by topic (e.g., family) rather than by content (what was said about the family).

Another example of coding by topic is illustrated by Dora Tellier-Robinson, who studied the experiences of Portuguese-speaking parents of children with special needs. Her particular focus was their involvement in their children's education. Her first broad category — 'first awareness' — was about the experiences of the parents as they first noticed that their child was handicapped. As it happened, her participants all had children with severe physical or mental problems, and the parents spoke at length in most cases about the birth of the child. Dora then created a subcategory which she labeled 'birth of child.' This was the code used for the textual analysis of interview data. Dora did not label the content of these individual statements in this preliminary coding. It was not until all of the excerpts dealing with this topic were brought together that Dora began to work with content statements like 'At first I didn't realize that there was anything wrong,' or 'I tried to tell the doctor that my son was not developing normally, but he didn't listen to me.' This of course does not mean that Dora was not keenly aware of the content or that she did not reflect on it in analytic memos. However, Dora dealt with content only when she began an analysis category by category, sorted the quotations, and then developed thematic statements from the content of the interview data. Again, this highlights that the entire process of data collection, analysis, and interpretation is tightly interwoven. By now you must know how serious we are about this!

Most of the examples we have provided so far about analysis are taken from analytic memos and from our own remembered experiences. By way of contrast, and to provide an example of how a description of coding might appear in a published context, the following excerpts are taken from the section on 'Analysis of Data' in the chapter on method of *Conversations at Home* by Judith Evans (1994). This is a study of the language experiences of a deaf child in a family in which all others can hear. Her interest in this topic was kindled by the realization that research about deaf children has tended to focus on deficits; Judith wished to explore the child's communicative competence. Notice that Judith began to code with broad focus, looking at the 'general flow of activity within the family.' This resulted in more general categories at the beginning. Here Judith writes in traditional dissertation style:

Analysis of Data

Analysis began with the first fieldnotes and was carried out recursively in cycles of data collection and analysis. Observation fieldnotes and interview transcripts were examined initially to gain a sense of the general flow of activity within the family. Earlier comments laid the groundwork for later coding more directly related to the research questions. Videotapes were analyzed in terms of the language issues addressed in the research questions.

Observations

Observation fieldnotes were organized in paragraphs based on what made sense to me in the context of activity observed. For this reason, the unit of analysis was the paragraph. Initially, codes were established for their relevance to the interactions between participants, the conditions under which they occurred, the strategies used by the participants, and the consequences of the interactions (Strauss, 1990). Such code headings include direct interaction between Kristin and her hearing siblings, the creation of plays, the mother's function as an interpreter for Kristin during First Communion classes, and argument resolution among the children. Other subheadings continued to emerge as the study progressed. Later levels of analysis highlighted some links between the contextual information and what I was seeing in communication and conversations . . . (p. 58)

As categories and patterns emerged, they became the basis for later data collection decisions, as well as for the generation of notions. Data were also continuously examined for negative cases as a way of testing and refining generated speculations. In keeping with qualitative research practices, analyses also generated further research questions, which were modified as patterns and themes were discovered in the data. Findings are described in terms of both emerging trends and unique cases.

Emerging categories and subcategories were examined with respect to the regularities in interactions within the participants' lives. In looking for patterns of daily activities, I was able to recognize and better understand rare events and put them in perspective within the context of the whole body of data.

Judith's description of her analytical process provides us with at least two major characteristics to ponder: she returned to her data any number of times, each for a distinct purpose, and her analysis provided her with ongoing direction for further data collection as well as analysis. Next, Judith described how she narrowed the focus of her analysis to the features of language addressed in her research questions. She worked particularly on the following: How are conversations constructed between the deaf child and other family members? What structural features are incorporated into family conversations?

I next returned to the data for a different purpose — to focus on conversations. For instance, some categories pertained to the structural features of conversation, such as attention-getting devices, some related to the functions for which the participants used language, such as regulatory or instrumental purposes. Other categories described family views on deafness and Kristin's needs . . .

Identifying the interactive episodes enabled me to classify and organize my understanding of Kristin's communication experiences in relation to the types of activities and characteristics relating to the participants. It also guided my selection of activities for videotaping.

An example of this selection process came from my realization that play with her siblings and cousins occupied much of Kristin's time at home. I saw which games she participated in, with whom she played, and when she had access to a primary communication partner. The phrase *primary communication partner* has been selected to indicate a hearing family member who, either self-selected or chosen, serves as Kristin's interpreter and/or conversation partner during interactive episodes.

I returned to the fieldnotes and searched for the regularity with which play activities occurred. The process helped me recognize exceptions like the visit by a deaf classmate. This line of action also directed my selection of events to video tape as representative examples of Kristin's play experiences.

For an example of Judith's initial coding of fieldnotes, please see Figure 4.1. This was included as appendix material in Judith's dissertation. This coded log segment contains examples of elements upon which Judith had planned to focus. Clearly the episode related in this segment of log about Kristin, and involving the straying toddler, documents Kristin's communicative competence. It also provides a discrepant case; because Kristin was without a primary communication partner — and thus outside the communication pattern of others in the family — in this instance appeared to work to everyone's advantage since her attention was free to notice her baby brother wander off. This is one among the many examples in these pages that illustrate the importance of context in qualitative research to interpreting social interactions.

Judith used the same recursive approach for her analysis of interview transcripts that she had applied to the observational data. She had also videotaped various events in the life of the family, and with some of those the focus was narrowed for a microanalytic study of communication episodes. The choices that Judith made are described in these next excerpts (Evans, 1994, pp. 62–3):

Selection of Videotaped Segments
After I classified the interactive episodes by type of activity and participant characteristics, I tallied the categories to see which were representative of significant percentages of Kristin's communication experiences. I then selected three videotapes for full analysis. Each tape to be analyzed contained an example of one major activity type combined with one of the major group size classifications when Kristin had access to a primary communication partner . . . Because one of the purposes of the study was to highlight Kristin's competence as a communicator, only those situations in which she had a primary communication partner were used for close analysis. She had greatest access to language and the greatest degree of engagement in those situations . . .

Analysis of Videotaped Segments
First, the sample segments were examined for the features of the context of situations, defined by Halliday (1989) as the field, tenor, and mode of discourse. I did this by looking at the *field*, which relates to the activity or topic of the discourse as it is expressed in experiential language. I reviewed the *tenor* of the discourse, expressed in the interpersonal language, as it pertains to the roles and relationships between the participants. I studied the *mode* of discourse, concerned with the

channel and textural features of the text, to see the ways it was expressed in the textual components of the language.

Figure 4.1: Sample coded observation fieldnotes

Context for creative play
(1–2)

1 opening between two bushes at the edge of the lawn and
2 used it as an entrance to the fort.

analytic consideration re:
communication (3–6)

3 *OC:* (This is another incident in which Kristin is
4 participating in an activity with her sisters without
5 being included in the communicative interaction
6 accompanying their play.)

k — drifts at will
(7–10)

7   At one point when Kristin lost interest in their
8 project, she stood on a tree stump near them and began
9 doing the motions from the new cheer that Andrea had
10 showed me inside. Andrea and Rose tired of the fort,

others drift too
(10–14)

11 too, and began to go for a hike that led them into the
12 edge of the woods across the driveway near the garage.
13 By this time, Marypat and Nicholas were also among the
14 hikers.

children's independent
spirits (15–>)

15   While the girls were discussing their next move,
16 Nicholas took off by himself down the driveway toward
17 the road. It would be quite a long walk for a toddler,
18 but when he had gotten about a third of the way to the

k — communication strategy
observation (19)
k — takes initiative,
responsibility for younger
sib (19–21)
k — needs to communicate
(21–3)

19 road, Kristin saw him and got very upset. She dropped
20 her walking stick and ran down the driveway until she
21 had placed herself in Nicholas' path. She yelled at
22 him, 'No. No. No. Nicholas. Nicholas. Stop.' She
23 tried to stop him with both her hands. He threw

older children take
responsibility for
younger ones (24–32)

24 himself on the ground in a tantrum. Andrea saw this
25 and came to Kristin's aid. The two of them tried to
26 get him up and walk him back up to the house, each
27 taking one of his hands. He didn't want any part of
28 this either and threw himself on the ground again.
29 Finally, Andrea managed to pick up the struggling
30 toddler and carry him up the hill. The others followed
31 with Marypat yelling that he should not go down there
32 alone.

analytic consideration:
k — pattern (?) for
initiating communication
(33–45)

33 *OC:* (This was one time that not being engrossed in
34 conversation with her sisters had worked in everyone's
35 behalf. Kristin had spotted her toddler brother moving
36 toward potential danger, the road. She understood the
37 situation, the rules of the family and acted spontane-
38 ously to protect the baby brother from possibly harming
39 himself. She also initiated verbal communication,
40 vocalizing loudly enough to get her sisters' attention
41 to come to her aid. Her behavior in this situation was
42 similar to her action at the end of the basketball game
43 when she took it upon herself to alert her mother to
44 the possibility of not being able to retrieve her
45 coat.)

The conversations were then analyzed for the pragmatic dimensions of language: functions, structural features, and strategies. To do this, I used the conversational turn as my unit of analysis . . .

Next, the transcripts were analyzed for the *structural features* of conversations.

I examined the use of attention-getting devices and openings, topic initiations, maintenance and shifts, breakdowns and repairs, and closings (Ervin-Tripp, 1979; Levinson, 1987; Wells, 1981).

Third, the transcripts were examined for the *communication strategies* used by the participants to understand and be understood by each other. Communication skills also include the ability to fine tune to audience (Lund and Duchan, 1988) and convey the meaning of intent (Halliday, 1975).

For her microanalysis of language functions, Judith used ready-made schemes, since she found these suitable in light of what she wanted to find out about communication in this setting. This approach provides a contrast to the work of Belén Matiás who also began with preselected schemes for microanalysis but found that she needed to devise her own. Examples of presentations from the work of both of these researchers are included in a later section.

Consonant with much of what we have shared, Coffey and Atkinson (1996) remind us that there are many ways in which any given set of data can be categorized:

> ... codes are organizing principles that are not set in stone. They are our own creations, in that we identify and select them ourselves. They are tools to think with. They can be expanded, changed or scrapped altogether as our ideas develop through repeated interactions with the data. Starting to create categories is a way of beginning to read and think about the data in a systematic and organized way.
> (p. 32)

The authors illustrate this vision throughout their book with examples based on data provided by Odette Parry and Sara Delamont from their study of the culture of anthropologists (1994, pp. x, 33). Coffey and Atkinson made an initial coding of interview transcripts from this study by drawing selectively on the methods for 'open coding' (Strauss, 1987) to answer 'What makes a good Anthropology PhD?' and 'Why do people do Anthropology PhDs?' They applied the categories thus produced to another interview transcript with results so 'thin and flat' that they returned to the entire body of data to ask a different question of them: 'What is special and distinctive about anthropology?' In order to probe people's descriptions of these distinctive features, Coffey and Atkinson applied 'axial coding' (Strauss, 1987) to all of Parry and Delamont's data for a better understanding of the conditions, antecedents and consequences of these features (Coffey and Atkinson, 1996, pp. 50–1). We would add that the introduction of a fresh approach to analysis or a new question often demands a return to the field for new data.

Coffey and Atkinson (1996) devote subsequent chapters of their book to the presentation of alternative approaches to coding. These include narrative analysis as described by Cortazzi (1993), analysis for metaphor, and domain analysis as prescribed by Spradley (1980). Cultural domains as defined by Spradley (1980) are categories of meaning derived by the way the participants in a setting use language. Spradley posits that 'If you can record numerous samples of the way people talk you can use their *folk terms* to construct cultural domains' (p. 89). He provides examples from his own work: 'witnesses' as a term for a cultural domain — i.e., category — in a study of a grand jury; 'stages in shopping' as a domain in a grocery story; 'kinds of bartenders' as a domain in Brady's Bar in the study *The Cocktail Waitress*. Coffey and Atkinson provide an example of domain analysis using the anthropologists' term 'fieldwork' (1996, pp. 92–105).

We do not attempt to describe any of these approaches in detail. We think you will be better served by going to the sources to which we refer to study the various steps of analytic processes that interest you. We do emphasize, however, that although all of these analytic methods might differ in their specifics, they each employ a coding of data. In basic, or open, coding, the labels are derived from the topics introduced in the text. When analyzing for metaphors, some label about each metaphor becomes a code. In domain analysis, codes are developed from the 'folk terms' used by participants. In narrative analysis, coding based on a scheme for organizing structural elements in a narrative is used to tease out such elements. For example, Coffey and Atkinson (1996) applied the labels of 'orientation,' 'complication,' and 'turning point' drawn from a narrative told by a participant (p. 58). In some cases, then, the terms used in coding are formulated by the researcher based on topics in the log text; in other cases, they stem from the actual words of participants; in still others, the terms used for coding are derived from the vocabulary of an analytic system, but in all cases the thinking and labeling processes are the same.

The approaches to coding and categorizing that we have been presenting have presupposed that researchers start to do this important work concurrent with planning the study and starting fieldwork. We will say honestly that we have known researchers who have collected data and not analyzed them from the beginning. Wolcott (1990) has come to the rescue of those who have not followed these or any guide to ongoing analysis:

> If your data remain in essentially the same form in which you originally collected them — pages and pages of notes and interview protocols — I hope you don't advertise to your colleagues that you have 'writer's block.' Your blockage has occurred at a prior stage. If you have embarked on a descriptive broadside, you had better get back to some very basic sorting into some very basic categories, and then see if you can discern some very basic questions that could guide the development of your account. (p. 32)

Wolcott then proceeds to offer two pages' worth of very practical suggestions for reducing a bulky mass of unanalyzed data into some sort of order. We cite Wolcott here as an aid to readers who might be in such dire straits. However, we are of the mind that analysis must begin at the beginning. If it does not weave its way throughout there are a host of dangers to which we have alluded, not the least of which may be the need to scrap the study and start all over again. When analysis has not been ongoing, the end results tend to be less rich and insightful. They also tend to have big holes in what is needed to tell the story.

Jayashree Iyer commented in an analytic memo about the link between writing and analysis as she worked through the seventh month of her study of an Indian dance class:

I noticed that the write-ups of the observations I am doing now seemed much richer and also more colorful than the log I maintained last fall. Is it because I am more involved in analysis now and so have stayed with the log longer? There seems to be a difference in texture.

We do agree with Jayashree that devoting more time to rereading and re-analyzing the log can produce a difference in texture. We also think that when researchers are faithful to qualitative methods, alternative points of view and discrepant and negative findings can emerge which need to be explored in more detail. Foci for yet more detailed analysis present themselves through the transactions among analysis, time in the field, and the ongoing writing.

The Process in Action

One of the most fascinating — and sometimes frightening — aspects of qualitative research is its emergent nature. Nowhere is this more evident than during the interwoven processes of writing and recursive analysis. Qualitative analysis requires that the researcher go back again and again over the accumulated log material in a process that for many has a cyclical feel. Carolyn Arnason describes it as follows:

> The circular nature of recursive ruminating has really highlighted, for me, the different world of qualitative research. Other academic ventures have tended to be linear ... the directional flow seemed to be always pointing forward, with few backward glances. I found with the qualitative research process there always had to be backward glances, if not long, deep looks.
>
> As well, there always seemed to be this research voice, or hand, that continually reached out to grab me even if I was sick and tired of the relationship! I felt, at times, that I was literally running on the treadmill of those circular diagrams that were handed out in class on cycles of action research and the flow of naturalistic inquiry. My solace, however, was that the research voice would whisper, 'Give it time. Write it down. Try again. Don't assume. Seize your opportunities. Live with your feelings.' This voice helped to keep me company not only in the beginning of my qualitative research process, but also throughout. I wrote in one of my logs, 'I need time to digest, to pull back and think about what has been said. I need to sift through what is meaningful to me, what makes sense and what doesn't.'

This recursive analytical process, and the shift in analytical focus that is frequently a part of the process, is seen in the history of Barbara Miller's study of a K/1 classroom as recorded in her log notes and analytic memos. Barbara began her log by explaining that she, an experienced high school English teacher, had decided to study a primary classroom because she had become 'fascinated' reading about the acquisition of early language as described by Jerome Bruner in *Acts of Meaning* (1990). Her entree into nearby Hamilton Elementary School (a pseudonym, as are all the names in Barbara's study) was made surprisingly swift and easy by the hearty welcome of the principal:

> My explanation of my project seemed to have won her over because she began to write four names down on a piece of paper, speaking about each as she wrote. 'You should speak to Danielle Fowler first. She's a K/1 teacher, and she's got a really interesting approach to teaching. She's studied in Japan and she's centering her curriculum on Japan this year.' (*OC*: Although I had a million questions on how curriculum topics were determined, I didn't ask and just kept listening.)

Barbara was surprised also by the teacher's easy welcome — 'I frequently have observers' — and two days later Barbara returned for her first formal observation. Her first notes were devoted to detailed descriptions of the classroom, the teacher, her assistant Jenny, the student teacher Claudia, and the whole group activities that occupied the first hour of the morning. She ended that day's observation as the children were put into three groups, one to remain with Ms. Fowler, one to work with Jenny, and one to work with Claudia. She pondered:

> What are these children like under circumstances led by a teacher other than Ms. Fowler? How do they feel about me? I realized with some poignancy that after Walter took me on my guided tour first thing in the morning, where he exuberantly described his whole environment and the pride which he took in his work, I didn't hear his voice again except to admit before the entire class that he didn't remember what he had submitted for his homework. I felt strongly that I wished that I could express to each of them that I cared about them.

Barbara followed this log entry with an analytic note:

> I like rereading about Glaser's constant comparative model of research in Bogdan and Biklen (72–5). It seems to me that this could be a useful method in many instances of qualitative research, because the areas of study naturally emerge from the researcher's constant re-examination of her fieldnotes.

Her analytic mind was already at work in the questions she asked herself, and clearly Walter, at least, caught her sympathetic attention. Two weeks later Morris also became a center of her focus as she observed both his and an obstreperous Walter's participation in a small group session led by Jenny. Her notes for that morning conclude as follows:

> Jenny takes Walter by the shoulders, forces him into the last seat at the end of the horseshoe table, and tells him to 'be silent.' He immediately jumps up. Morris begins yelling, 'I don't want to do this.' (I made eye contact with Jenny to see if she wanted me to get help; she shook her head, no). I left at 9:50 am. (*OC*: I wonder if I will have an opportunity to see what happens to children like Morris and Walter over the long term in a situation like this. They are both dysfunctional at times in class, but not in exactly the same ways. Morris hasn't seemed to figure out yet how to act in a large group without getting negative attention from the teacher, nor has he mastered some small-group interactions (*cf.* the unsuccessful block area negotiation). But he seems clearly very bright: I watched as he learned

chess. He remembered and applied what Jacob taught him. And yet he is in the 'slow' math group. Why? Ability or behavior? Or both?

Meanwhile, Walter, who is very verbal and outgoing one-on-one, is largely disengaged in organized activities. He already sees that he makes more 'mistakes' (*cf.* the worksheet) than other children. Why isn't he being supported better? There are three adults working with twenty-three children, when everyone is there. And yet, Walter does not seem to be getting enough attention. Why else would he pay so much attention to me? Claudia tried to give him individual attention, but it was for something he wasn't 'good' at, reading, and he wasn't interested. Why doesn't Ms. Fowler seem to be paying more attention to Walter's and Morris' special needs? Perhaps she does, at other times. Perhaps I can ask her. In any event, Jenny does not seem competent to handle Walter and Morris together. They resist her only strategy, to control them directly.

As we continued to leaf through Barbara's log, it was interesting to note how the few children who captured Barbara's attention — among them Walter and Morris — were those who seemed to have trouble fitting in with Ms. Fowler's expectations. The next excerpt is from Barbara's notes a month into her work in the field.

My seat is directly opposite the entrance to the room. I notice that Morris is sitting on a stool in the doorway. I look at him and smile. He makes eye contact with me but doesn't smile. He does not get off his stool, though he slides it a little further into the doorway of the room. Jenny comes into the room. She has dyed her pixie-cut brown hair bright red. She places some papers in a drawer of a small cabinet near where I am sitting. Then she leaves the room. As she leaves, she pulls the stool on which Morris is seated further out into the hallway and disappears from sight, although Morris, on his stool, remains in view. (*OC*: I realize that he is not permitted to join the rest of the class at their meeting today. Why? Is he being worked with individually or just taken out of class as a disciplinary measure? When I arrived, Morris was alone in the corridor. I would observe to see whether Jenny would be working with Morris while Ms. Fowler worked with the rest of the class. If she weren't, is this even legal? I don't think so. I realize that although I don't know what prompted Morris' temporary (?) expulsion from class, I am very angry about it. Does the principal know about this practice? Do the parents?)

We have singled out Barbara's fieldnotes about Morris and Walter to trace how she develops a strand of analysis. This strand of analysis, of course, does not do justice to the scope of her overall analysis. A few weeks after she entered the field she created a list of categories from the data she had collected thus far. She recorded the following list in an analytic memo:

Structure of learning experiences
    Large teacher-led groups
    Small teacher-led groups
    One-on-one teacher led groups
Student-selected ('free') activities
Teacher roles and expectations
    Teacher control
    Student rewards

'Ability' grouping
Gender issues
Notable students

Barbara's experience illustrates quite vividly the importance of planning from the outset to enter the field with a broad focus and, therefore, with research questions that are sufficiently open. It will be remembered that her original interest was in early literacy. A month after the analytic work outlined above, however, she formally noted in her log her decision to narrow her focus to those students who particularly captured her attention:

> Over and over my log kept coming back to the marginalized student. Who was he (or she)? What had gotten him there? What behaviors — on his part, on the parts of the other students, of the teachers — kept him marginalized? What had to happen for him to have a successful academic experience? Was that likely to happen in this K/1 classroom? Why or why not? Where was I located in these questions, both as a participant observer and as a teacher.

Barbara continued this analytic memo by reflecting on qualitative methods, acknowledging that at first she had doubts about 'what, if anything, I would find by using a process that required that I not frame specific questions or hypotheses ahead of time . . .' By not framing hypotheses ahead of time, Barbara was freed to become aware of these marginalized students, free to follow up on her interest in them. These excerpts from her log illustrate how the processes of observing, writing, and analyzing were intertwined for Barbara. In reading her complete log — and of course hindsight helps here — the strand that has become her focus stands out clearly. What we have not emphasized, but what is also obvious, is the rigor with which Barbara coded and categorized her data. There are many hours of data analysis behind a statement like 'Over and over my log kept coming back to the marginalized student.' In a later section we will trace where the process of analyses led Barbara in the course of several months' work.

The ongoing analysis also brought about a shift in understanding for Christina Lee, who studied a Buddhist temple group:

> Now that I have more of an 'insider's view,' I realize that some of my observations were biased. My two main misperceptions center on the 'demystification' of the minister and the Church, and ways in which I might have been reading more into what he did than what was there. But by the same token, I know that I am still missing things that have a much deeper significance — for example, the meaning of chanting — than I can grasp at the moment.
>
> I reviewed all my logs and constructed more categories to help me 'regroup.' Here are some of the new categories:
> English/Japanese cultural differences
> Presence of older women
> Role of the Church in the community
> Church member effort to sustain the Church behind the scenes
> Meanings: exit, memorial service, chant, dharma lessons, beads,
>   meditation, transference, prayerful pose

Christina then added to this list two additional categories that arose out of her reflections on herself as researcher in this scene:

'Me' in the field
Evolution of relationship with the researched

These last categories seem particularly relevant and useful for Christina. They may very well develop into a section of 'reflections on method' that some researchers have come to believe are important to weave into the final portions of a report.

As she continued this reflective memo, Christina described new understandings that were leading her to expand or revise her original categories. Here are her new insights into the 'demystification' of the minister:

> When I first began observing, I generally saw much more 'mystery' in the Church than I now see. The minister, as a symbol of Buddhism, fascinated me. I saw a spiritual person, not attached to material comforts who did not engage much with his congregation. I wondered how he came to be the spiritual leader of the Church — was it through years of meditation and abstinence, was he enlightened? I was so impressed by his chanting voice — I wondered how many years of training it took to master this particular timbre of voice. I saw him as an oasis of calm and wisdom.
>
> Gradually, through conversations with members, my idealized view of the minister began to deconstruct and expand. His humanity emerged. He had entered the ministry directly after college at the age of 22, clearly not after years of meditation. It seemed more like a 'career choice' to me. This impression is, I feel, somehow supported by the advertisement to recruit people to become Buddhist ministers. Then again, this could be another incorrect impression.
>
> I learned that he also enjoyed playing the guitar — loudly — practicing the same chords over and over again. This bit of information helped to 'flesh out' my image of him still further. I associate playing the guitar with long-haired adolescents, and creative sorts who need to express themselves.
>
> I think that what I learned during my last observation and in the course of the interview really 'pulled the veil' off the minister. I began to appreciate his struggle to lead. As a church leader, he is besieged by the same kind of demands that confront most: the need to impose direction, to raise funds, to address conflicts among members. I began to see that he might not act in his daily life (disembodied, serene) the way he does up on the altar . . .
>
> One of the members was quite upset with a conversation he had with the minister. Bob commented that in fact he too has had moments of tension with the minister. This added new dimensions to my view of the minister — was he a control freak? Was he being misinterpreted as a harsh person? Suddenly I could see that the minister's interactions are not all as tranquil and profound as I thought. He brings himself as a human, with all of his personality, outside of the service, and that might upset others.

In this memo, we see Christina moving toward interpretation. This is evident in the way that her reflections on the observations and interviews that 'pulled the veil' off the minister, that led her to 'demystify' him and see his 'struggle to lead' have helped her lift to a different understanding of her data. From this perspective she considers him as a leader, apparently struggling at times with the demands of leadership.

This insight also indicates a body of literature — on leadership — against which she might discuss these data should she choose to do so in the light of a fuller analysis.

Later observations led Christina to expand her views — and to create new categories — regarding 'presence of older women' and 'Church members' effort to sustain the Church behind the scenes.' Here are excerpts from analytic memos about those categories:

> I saw that the hard work of its members helped to keep the temple afloat. This labor was especially evident to me in the last service, during the after service tea. Because it was Bodhi Day, there were special refreshments laid out. The women buzzed around the table, setting it up, urging people to take more. Afterwards, I noticed that the same women cleaned up. (I wanted to help them.)
>
> This, then is my shift. In the beginning, I think I saw the Church as primarily a spiritual enterprise, with nothing so base as 'money' or the 'need for membership' on its list of concerns. Over time, I began to realize all of the activity that occurred behind the serenity of the services was necessary to keep the Church going. I began to develop a sense of the relationships and the dramas that occurred 'behind the scenes.' Bob described Ruth, an older Japanese woman, as being the 'General' who kept things moving. To him occasionally she was a 'nag,' but she always 'meant well' and 'whenever you needed anything to be done, Ruth was the person to ask.'
>
> I think that these added dimensions — of humanity, interpersonal conflict, struggle — will serve to broaden the meanings of my categories. I still feel there is something profound and mysterious that I have not managed to capture regarding the relationship of the minister to his teachings and his own embodiment as a spiritual symbol. Similarly, I feel that the congregation has a special meaning. But what has stood out for me at this point is the humanity involved, which was not as obvious to me in the beginning . . .
>
> I am becoming more aware of the congregation as a grouping of diverse little communities. I am particularly intrigued by the older Japanese women, who often move together in a group and who seem to know each other quite well. During last week's after-service tea, I noticed that they all sat in one corner — at least 15 people — and talked and laughed together.

Toward the end of this series of analytic memos, Christina reflected that the ongoing recursive processes of participant observation, log writing, and analysis had helped her to reconsider her original research question: 'I think that the architecture of the question — the different meanings and how they were deconstructed and 'built up' — has been worked on in a way that enhances the meaning of my question.'

At the beginning of this section we quoted Michele Bellavita on her difficulties with initial coding. In the same memo, however, she continues with a description of the approach that she devised over time as she worked her way through this process:

> It was very interesting to go back and really code some of this data. I've learned about coding and about how I have to let myself incorporate my idiosyncratic way of understanding data with a more formal method of coding . . . At this point in

my learning to do qualitative analysis, my approach to creating an organizing scheme is this:

1 Allow myself to play around with the content initially, noting ideas.
2 Go back over the transcript and try to create basic topic names for chunks of data. These are open to revision and renaming.
3 List the topic names and group them meaningfully (binning). Note connections and interesting exceptions and topics that are left hanging alone. Think about them and what they might mean. Write down any new brainstorming.
4 Make documents containing the content of binned categories and write analytic memos about them. Add or change anything that is relevant. Don't forget to look at the brainstorming that occurred in step one and use what might be helpful.
5 If necessary at this point go back over transcript and play with it by looking at things that I might have missed like metaphors, analysis of specific words, the flip-flop technique, whatever will help me look at it in a fresh way.
6 If I haven't done anything yet, now would be a good time to try to write a little more creatively: a poem, vignette, etc. Hopefully I might feel like doing this even at the document making stage.

I didn't go about doing all of the above that systematically before. I can really see the need for doing a fair amount of analysis of one interview before going to the next and from one participant to another. Otherwise, it's easy to become completely overwhelmed with and lost within the thicket of codes, lists, bins, arrows, especially when trying to take hold of metathemes and ideas that emerge across participants. I imagine that sometimes it might be necessary to have somewhat different schemes for different participants. All the more reason to have a flexible approach to creating an organizing scheme, one that does not feel too tight to me.

We find it interesting that Michele was not ready to synthesize her approach to analysis until quite late in the process, unlike researchers like Jane Martin and Barbara Miller who set forth quite early and clearly on an analytic path. Regardless of the way in which analytical processes work themselves out, however, they almost always lead to a change in the way the researcher sees the original research problem or questions.

In the final paragraph above, Michele refers to the possibility of becoming 'completely overwhelmed with and lost within the thicket of codes, lists, bins . . . especially when I am trying to take hold of metathemes and ideas.' Michele's is not an uncommon state. It is easy for qualitative researchers to begin to feel as though they are drowning in the details of the data. Here are Sarie Teichmann's thoughts after compiling a two-page list of categories for her study of a group of people diagnosed with fibromyalgia:

Now where I do seem to be getting lost is in narrowing down this study. It's a difficult project because it is so all-encompassing, the meetings touch on every aspect of people's lives (especially the negative ones) and I just keep seeing more and more. And want to understand more and more. I've always been the kind of person who sees a lot, sees the 'Big Picture' and the things that make up the big picture, but I'm feeling a little overwhelmed (obsessed?) by this, seeing things I've skipped, seeing the imperfections, trying perhaps, to do too much.

Sarie speaks of wanting to 'narrow down,' of wanting to 'see the big picture.' One way of handling the sense of 'too much' of which she speaks is to see how the pieces can be arranged into an organized whole. That is the topic of the next section.

Plotting the Whole

Decisions about the central story that is to be told in a particular research narrative lead naturally into a plan for its whole. Toward the beginning of his monograph on *Writing Up Qualitative Research*, Harry Wolcott sets forth three rules for getting started: formulate a statement of purpose, develop a detailed table of contents, and determine the basic story you are going to tell (1990, pp. 16–18). We now look again to Wolcott's injunction that in the earliest stages of your study you compose 'The Plan . . . a detailed written outline or sequence' (p. 16). You may wish to turn back at this point to Chapter 3, to the section on 'Plans, Outlines, and Tables of Contents as Forms.' This contains several examples of overall plans, including plans-in-process, along with their authors' analytic memos and our comments on the process. It may be helpful for you to consider these again.

If you have conducted a study through initial data collection and analysis, if you have reflected over your data to the extent that their most salient features are becoming apparent to you, if you have determined whether some of these or all of these can be shaped into the story that must be told – if you have followed all of these steps but still have not constructed an overall outline then you must surely make an effort to write at least a tentative plan for the whole. Such an outline fore-casts how you may structure the presentation of findings in an organized fashion, shifting from one focus or analytic approach to another so that each element will in turn contribute to an organic whole. This is an aspect of the craftsmanship of the qualitative researcher, this fitting together of parts to produce a finished mosaic.

We will presuppose that you have already written some sort of a brief intro-duction to your study, explicated the methods applied, and indicated the broad theoretical framework within which you are working. If you are writing a disserta-tion, this material may take two or three chapters. If you are writing a book or article, these sections may be extremely brief and material about method may be moved to an appendix or reduced to a paragraph. We tend to feel that such removal or reduction of material on method is dangerous, but we note that it is often done. Whatever the case, our concern here is with the presentation of findings. You will want to plan some sort of arrangement that will accommodate sections that are more broadly descriptive, sections that are more formally analytical, and sections that are interpretive discussions against theory. We find that reading studies we like pro-vides us with ideas for our own presentations.

In *Amish Literacy*, Andrea Fishman (1988) introduces her study by describing her first meeting with the Amish family who years later would become gatekeepers for her study of literacy in their community.

> 'We've been invited to the Fishers next Saturday,' my husband told me one evening. 'All three of us. For the day.'

'What Fishers?' I asked absentmindedly, attending more to my two-year-old's dinner-table needs than my husband's dinner-table news.

'You know . . . the Amish couple I told you about. That's how they want to thank me.'

That's how it all began for me, as unobtrusively as that. (p. 1)

The study then progresses in a chronological fashion, following the development of friendship between the families, Fishman's gradual understanding of Amish ways and her plans for a doctoral study in this community. In Chapters 3 through 5, Fishman then gives detailed descriptions of the contexts of community, school, and Amish teachers' community. In Chapters 6 through 9, Fishman narrows the focus more specifically to describe the meanings of literacy in the Amish community. These four chapters also present discussions of Fishman's broad analytic topics, or categories, as shown in her Table of Contents, and they include her interpretations of what literacy events mean within the context of the community:

Chapter Six: Literacy Defined
> [A discussion of the meaning of literacy in this Amish community.]

Chapter Seven: Literacy as a Cultural Imperative
> [A discussion of ways in which literacy serves this culture's social needs.]

Chapter Eight: Literacy and Cultural Continuity
> [A discussion of the continuity of definition and functions of literacy across home, school, and community contexts.]

Chapter Nine: Literacy and Meaning
> [A discussion of this Amish context as an interpretive community and of meanings for its members as 'cued by texts but created collaboratively by people'] (p. 167).

In Chapters 10 and 11, Fishman shifts her attention away from the Amish setting and describes what this study has come to mean to her as a teacher and its implications for the broader educational community. Finally, Chapter 12 takes a recursive turn: 'Getting Here from There: A Look Back at the Ethnographic Process.' This reflection on method includes a discussion of the process Fishman went through in the creation of her categories for analysis, which in itself is germane to this chapter. Overall, the study moves in two directions — both chronologically through time and with a gradual narrowing of focus that then opens out again at the end to look at broader implications of her findings for education.

We have already described the analytic processes used in Judith Evans' study *Conversations at Home* (1994). Now let us look at her Table of Contents to gain an idea of her overall organizational scheme. You will see how she has used metaphors from photography as chapter titles. Through these metaphors she seems to comment subtly on the importance of visual images to a person without hearing. Reading through the listing, we noticed that each metaphor title signals changes in focus from wide to narrow.

I   Framing the Subject: The Introduction
II   Opening the Album: The Review of Literature

In Chapter IV, Judith offers 'A Gallery of Portraits' that describe the setting, Kristin, and the members of her family. This is followed by a thematic analysis drawn from observation and interviews. Judith hones in more specifically on Kristin's communication experiences in Chapter VI, 'Through a Wide-Angle Lens' (the range of experiences) and in Chapter VII, 'Through a Zoom Lens' (microanalysis of selected episodes). Each of these chapters closes with an interpretive discussion of the findings presented in it. In 'The Final Focus,' Judith presents a metathematic discussion of three 'overarching ideas' that run throughout the entire body of data with particular emphasis on their implications for educators and others concerned with the welfare of deaf children.

Judith Evans and Andrea Fishman, like many qualitative researchers, open their accounts with descriptions of the context and participants, and this makes sense because these sections draw the reader into the scene. Some writers, especially anthropologists, have discussed such opening sections as the author's way of establishing authority, or supporting the genuineness of his or her claim to credibility. If, as Clifford Geertz (1988) puts it, one of our tasks is 'to convince our readers that we have actually penetrated (or been penetrated by) another form of life, of having, one way or another truly "been there"' (pp. 4–5), it is also important that we give our readers a sense of having 'been there' too. Qualitative narratives, or other rhetorical forms included as part of qualitative studies, provide the virtual experience that is characteristic of literary constructs. We want to keep in mind the 'virtual,' or created aspects of these products, but also the experiential. The sense of lived-through experience that a literary form can provide will help heighten the more purely analytic sections that are to follow — will help hold in the reader's mind that these findings are a part of the real lives of real people.

Although a movement within the text from general observation with wide focus to more closely focused observation and analysis appears to be the most common, the opposite approach can also be followed. *Slim's Table* by Mitchell Duneier (1992) is a study of a group of urban black men who meet as regulars at 'Slim's table' in the Valois Cafeteria in Chicago. The Table of Contents for the study is outlined below. Here the focus widens from 'The Caring Community' of the friends around the table in Part One, to the larger community of the Valois Cafeteria in its neighborhood in Part Two, to a still broader focus, the place of black working men in the broader society, in Part Three. In Part Four, the author looks at the findings of his study in the light of extant literature on black males.

The first chapter of this book, entitled 'Slim and Bart,' opens with the spotlight upon just these two men:

> They both came of age at the height of segregation. Sixty-five, a lifelong Chicagoan, Slim is a black mechanic in a back-alley garage in the ghetto. Bart, white, and ten years older, is a retired file clerk who grew up in the rural South. Both are regular patrons of the Valois 'See Your Food' cafeteria. (Duneier, 1992, p. 3)

We found the opening paragraphs of this book almost cinematic in their effect. It is as if the camera first picks out Bart and follows him to the place where the researcher first became aware of him — as an habitué of the International House cafeteria at the University of Chicago, 'one of many odd human beings who become attached to a university community as students and continue the association for decades.' Bart disappeared from the I-House cafeteria scene, however, and when the researcher became aware of his absence he assumed he was either ill or dead, until one day two years later when, on his first visit to the Valois Cafeteria, he happened across Bart 'sitting by himself eating a bowl of radishes, amidst black men sipping coffee at the surrounding tables.' Bart explained that he had left the dormitory cafeteria because 'although he liked being around the students, prices there were high and the quality of food very poor. He had been eating at Valois for a year' (p. 4). When Duneier renewed his acquaintance with Bart and asked him about the Valois, Bart replied that 'I don't pay any attention to the place. I just eat my meal and go home.' It became clear, however, over the weeks and months that followed that in spite of his protests to the contrary, Bart 'seemed to be well aware of the other habitual patrons of the restaurant, including the group of black regulars that congregated at Slim's table' (p. 5).

    The spotlight now shifts to Slim and to the group of men who meet here daily at this cafeteria. The researcher provides a brief description of the individual men and the cafeteria with particular focus (augmented by extensive endnotes) on the complexities of identifying them by socio-economic status. The camera lens then widens slightly, and the scene takes on life as it zooms to a few, highly selective, exchanges between Bart and the men of Slim's table. What we would like to point out here is the great economy of language and detail with which the researcher tells his story. Duneier gives us no information about his research methods, and tells us less about himself in this study than we would like to know. We can only guess at the extensive log notes that must have accumulated over his 'weeks and months' in this setting. However, it is as though, having structured the outline of this study and the basic points he wished to make throughout the whole, he selected those few most telling incidents that would illustrate those points.

Looking back again at the Table of Contents, we see that the first topic category to be developed is 'the caring community' formed by Slim and his friends whose care extended beyond the boundaries of the close group of their table to the other regulars at the cafeteria with whom they became acquainted over time. Bart, aloof and 'odd,' was one of these, and 'he found himself inextricably drawn into the social life of Valois as the men began to greet him cordially . . .' The author singles out the descriptive details and conversational exchanges that reveal Bart's personality:

> 'How you feeling today, Bartie?' Harold once asked him.
> 'I feel with my hands,' was his response. (p. 6)

> Bart was an object of curiosity to many of the men. When he was out of earshot, they would often try to size him up. 'Bart's unusual,' Leroy, an electrician, once said. 'He's antisocial. He don't care about nobody. He comes in. He eats. Sometimes he just sits there and don't say nothin'.'
> Slim balanced his chin on his thumb and forefinger, trying not to look in the direction of the old man. 'He don't bother nobody.'
> After a brief silence Harold glanced at Bart and ended the sober appraisal. 'You ever notice sometimes he fidgets around when he's eating? He be looking to see if anything is on his tie.'
> The group of men broke out laughing. 'You notice that too?' Leroy chortled hysterically. 'Then he'll take his coat and look it over to make sure there's nothin' on it.' Bart's little quirks were amusing to the men, but they were also endearing. (p. 7)

> Bart once let it be known that during the fifty years of his working life he had never been late or missed a day of work. The only technical exception was on account of a famous crash of the Illinois Central Railroad. Having been aboard the train on his way to the office, he once described the devastation for the men — seats flew out of the train, people were hanging out of windows, others were lying on the aisles screaming. Bart somehow remained unscathed. Stepping over bodies, he picked his way out of the car and got to work a few minutes late. He seemed proud to let the men know that under the circumstances, and given his prior work record, the supervisor decided to mark him on time.
> 'Did you help anybody?' Harold asked.
> 'No. 'Cause I figured there was nothing I could do, and anyway I didn't want to be late for work.'
> 'Didn't it bother you to just leave like that?'
> 'Why should it bother me? Wasn't a damn thing I could do. I was on my way to work.' (pp. 7–8)

Notice Harold's questions — 'Did you help anyone? . . . Didn't it bother you to just leave like that?' — so typical of the caring attitude and sense of responsibility for others that the author documents as innate in Slim's associates. Notice in contrast Bart's brusque responses. It is against the backdrop of these incidents that Duneier tells the story of the growing relationship of Bart and Slim. The men of Slim's table were concerned that an old man was not safe walking through the neighborhood alone at night, and in time Hughes, one of the white 'regulars' who was a friend of Slim's, and later Slim himself took on the responsibility of giving Bart a ride home. The researcher reported that 'the only resentment' about the disappointments of his life that Bart ever displayed 'was toward blacks in the local community' (p. 4). But over time his attitude gradually shifted. At first he referred to Slim as 'my man' — his chauffeur from whom he accepted rides home in exchange for cigarettes. Later, however, Bart made an admission of friendship: 'he had a "friend" in the restaurant, that the friend was a black man, "but" — he emphasized — "he is very nice and he *is* a friend"' (p. 11).

Duneier places his discussion of Slim's relationship with Bart within the interpretive framework of literature on pseudo-relational ties within the black community:

> In the black belt, where traditional family forms are more disorganized than in mainstream society, people often develop substitute kinship ties, in which many of the functions served by families are taken up by other caring individuals. Thus a man such as Slim might take a liking for a senior citizen and do the kinds of things for him that in white society would more normally be done by a man's son, if at all. At Valois, the black counter ladies sometimes even referred to Bart as Slim's 'pappy' ('Where's your Pappy tonight?') indicating that in their minds Slim had developed a substitute kinship tie with Bart. (p. 10)

A relationship of friendship between Bart and the men of Slim's table persisted through Bart's occasional attacks of illness and ended with Bart's death alone in his studio apartment. Slim and one of the white regulars in his circle missed Bart and called the police who eventually broke into Bart's apartment, and notified his brother, from whom he had been estranged for years. Through a close focus on this relationship, Duneier explores the unique characteristics of the ethics of caring:

> . . . Slim often tells me he doesn't think it right that people neglect their elders. His attitude of caring exists within a framework of barriers to closeness set up by Bart, perhaps to protect himself from developing too much intimacy with a black man, or simply with any man.
>
> The standards by which Slim treats Bart are universal, applying equally to any elderly person, black or white, in or out of the ghetto. Inside this restaurant on the margins of the ghetto the black regulars have entered into an affirmative relationship with the wider society, orienting themselves to situations that make it possible for them to apply their high standards and adopting unique social forms, like the substitute kinship tie, beyond the fringes of the black districts. (p. 15)

It is with this understanding of the ethics of responsibility and caring that underlie the relationship of Slim and his friends that a reader leaves this first section of the book and moves to the larger focus that is the topic of the second section — the

Valois Cafeteria and its role as a meeting place in this neighborhood on the fringes of Chicago. (It is interesting to note, incidentally, that the researcher explains that although the persons in his study have almost all been given fictitious names, the cafeteria is too well known to disguise, as is the urban locale, — Chicago, which is widely known as the setting of many famous sociological studies of the experiences of black males.) We have already pointed out the gradual widening of focus with which the author structured his analytical categories. To us this has made for an extremely effective study, allowing us gradually to see beyond the confines of Slim's table to a larger and still a larger context, until finally we look in some detail at the way in which black males are routinely viewed not only by the popular media but by sociologists as well.

The careful arrangement of sections and the frugal but effective use of episodes or conversations to highlight the findings of the analysis indicate to us a high degree of selectivity on the part of this researcher. We are reminded of the words of Wolcott (1990): 'The trick is to discover essences and then to reveal those essences with sufficient context, yet not become mired trying to include everything that might possibly be described' (p. 35). We led into our discussion of planning the whole with Sarie Teichman's lament that she was 'trying, perhaps, to do too much.' An outline will help us to determine the essence of the story we wish to tell and thus find a way to organize the 'muchness.' Winnowing will help us to weed out what we may come to consider, sometimes with pangs, as non essentials.

Winnowing

Wolcott (1990) contends, and our own experience bears out, that:

> . . . the major problem we face in qualitative inquiry is not to get data, but to get rid of it! With writing comes the always painful task . . . of winnowing material to a manageable length, communicating only the essence. (p. 18)

The winnowing process helps us to edit; to decide what is excessive and/or unimportant to the study. Decisions about the basic story we are going to tell will have implications for the shape that the overall document will take, for what pieces of analysis need to be included and what are now irrelevant or excessive for the purpose at hand. These decisions may often send us back to reshape descriptive passages as well.

Winnowing is not only hard work — once we start we usually find, as Wolcott warns, that it is painful. As Judy Kwak said:

> When I read about winnowing data, I thought it would be an easy thing to do. I was wrong. I held on to the data with two hands and it wasn't until my support group gently pried my fingers open that I was able to let go.

When we labor over the analysis of our fieldnotes and interview transcripts they often evoke for us far more than we have been able to capture in mere words, but these words are all we have. They represent people and places that may have become deeply entwined in our lives. Cutting them out of a final document is somewhat analogous to an amputation. Often it is only the thought that these portions discarded now, can be used in another piece that helps us take the (metaphorical) knife in hand. Here is how Shelly Krapes felt about deciding what to drop and what to keep:

It is certainly true what they say about becoming attached to your data — am I the only one who thinks it is all absolutely fascinating? The data I collected through the course of this project are extensive. In raw form they span more than 100 pages. Coded, categorized, cut and pasted, they weigh in at about 100 pounds also ... Because of the richness of the data, it has always been a problem deciding what to include in writing for presentation and what to drop.

As she worked through the winnowing decisions, however, Shelly found herself becoming increasingly clear about what to retain and why:

I think that in general terms, deciding what to keep and what to drop is more a matter of keeping in sight one's original questions, and how the data relate to them. What are the principal messages that I wish to convey to the audience, relative to my research questions? What has been the purpose of the study all along?

For Shelly, a return to the original research questions helped her hone in on the 'principal messages' that she wished to emphasize. This holds true also, of course, if the original questions have changed shape or have been supplemented by others in the process. Lynn Haber found that focusing on 'specific areas of concentration' would make her overall presentation more effective because it would help her to come to a deeper understanding of the themes:

Perhaps the hardest part of trying to make meaning from my data was the challenge of deciding what was and was not worth keeping. Decisions have always been difficult for me, and throwing things away can often be painstaking. However, I did find it liberating to narrow my focus and select the data that seems most relevant to me. When I read the dissertations that Margot brought to class, I realized how much could be said and done with very specific areas of concentration. Narrowing the focus and winnowing out data seems crucial to the process of studying and understanding the themes.

Once the attention of the study is narrowed, the process of winnowing through the data becomes more focused and more assured. The following excerpt shows Elizabeth Merrick at work on her study of a teenage woman in a group home:

Re: DROPPING. Within those pieces however, I guess I did have to cull a bit. I chose to drop some parts of the interview where she was talking about one thing and then went off on a different subject. I culled that part which was digression at that point. I feel this didn't take away from her perspective, and helped to distill it more. I also chose to drop some things which struck me as not being particularly illuminating in terms of the themes and categories that developed. For example, Marisol began the interview talking about her experiences of family group and since my focus was more on her, I dropped this. I also dropped some grammatical things that didn't make sense, trying to make her meaning clear when it sometimes was confusing. That process was a bit hard, I felt so tied to keeping her words. Sometimes, it was difficult to let any go. The cost of dropping these things was losing the verbatim, actual words she spoke, quality. And yet I felt the gain of getting a clearer, more cogent, richly-conveyed picture was worth that *IF I COULD

DO THAT WITHOUT COMPROMISING ANY OF HER MEANING! That was the big cost benefit thing I had to struggle with. I felt I decided it the best I could at this time, perhaps hanging back a bit from being more creative and deviating from the verbatim. I feel this was a learning experience that will continue to change/ improve as I keep working.

All of us, also, have many times faced the same struggle in our very real wish to keep 'the actual words she spoke . . . the quality.' There certainly are researchers who do, in fact, report talk — particularly segments of interview transcripts — verbatim. Every pause, 'like,' 'uh,' and 'If you know what I mean' is faithfully repeated. It is our conviction that at times we can be more true to a person's meaning if we edit the passages — sometimes rather drastically — while leaving in enough of their pauses, colloquialisms and idiosyncrasies to give their flavor. We wrote in Chapter 2 (pp. 21–2) of Elizabeth Merrick's hovering on the brink of composing, not letting go of the literal words of her participants for fear that she would somehow lose them. Another excerpt, that of Marisol, (p. 75) shows how Elizabeth learned to emphasize meaning through winnowing. Lynn Haber describes the process of her attempts to achieve focus. Notice how the broad categories that were the result of her coding became her guides, so that the passages she selected for the final document were those that would support her ultimate themes:

> In an earlier analytic memo, I wrote that it would be important to use data that focus on specific interactions between Miss Harris and her students. I still feel that this focus would be an important way of understanding how students learn and respond to her language and instructions. After reading and coding the data several times over the semester, I have come up with broad categories that include teaching style, classroom rules and limitations, teacher's control strategies, and student conformity and resistance. I think it would be important to me to retain all of the data that relate to the way the teacher interacts with or involves herself with students in her classroom. Since I first began my observations of this kindergarten, I have felt that the class atmosphere and the students' perceptions of it have been shaped by the language Miss Harris uses to talk to (or about) her students. By taking a closer look at her language during teacher-student interactions, I may be able to gain more insight into the way she creates and implements specific structures in the classroom.

The broad categories that Lynn identified — teaching style, classroom rules and limitations, teacher's control strategies, and student conformity and resistance — are now to be looked at within the framework of the teacher's language during teacher-student interactions. Having identified her focus, Lynn then began to specify which episodes would be relevant and which not:

> If I had to drop or weed out certain data from my study, I would want to exclude anything that does not relate to Miss Harris's talks and interactions with the students in the class. At the beginning of the study, I spent some time focusing on student–student interactions at various centers during center time activities. Although these exchanges were interesting to me, I gradually became more focused on specific students' experiences with the teacher. One of the advantages of cutting out some of this earlier material would be that it would free me to look at questions

that relate to themes that emerged during the course of the study. While I might learn less about specific students' learning and cooperation strategies, I would be free to explore their perceptions of their teacher and the classroom environment. Perhaps it would be valuable and worthwhile for me to keep the data that describe the teacher coming in on or involving herself in student-student interactions. For example, I wrote about one situation in which the teacher reprimands Walter for telling another student that it is time to clean up. ('What makes you think you can talk like the teacher in this room?') I feel that it would be important for me to concentrate on these kinds of incidents to see what they can reveal to me about specific students' experiences in this classroom.

I also think it would be important to retain data that involve student initiated conversations with or about Miss Harris. One pattern that I noticed as I was reading over my data was that some students would ask for feedback about their work, and Miss Harris would respond with a particular instruction (i.e. 'Did you put your name on the paper?' or 'Let's see you clean up now if you're finished'). This seems to be the kind of language I need to question and analyze more closely. How and when is it being used? When does it seem to be a control strategy? How and what do students learn from it? How might Miss Harris's responses to students' requests for feedback contribute to the overall mood or atmosphere of the class? How do specific students respond to her responses? Are these responses verbal or nonverbal? These are just a few examples of the questions I continue to raise as I read and reread my data on teacher-student interactions.

I also feel that it would be important to keep all the data that focus on Miss Harris when she addresses large groups of students or the whole class. These particular descriptions are important to the study because they seem to reveal a lot about her perceptions of specific students. When Miss Harris talks to the entire class at once, she seems most likely to use specific kinds of control strategies (i.e., 'Karen is ready. She may get her drink. I wish I had zillion Karens'). I have written a lot on Miss Harris's use of positive and negative example making, and this often occurs when she is talking to the entire group.

In the passage above, we notice that Lynn decided to retain only the data that showed Miss Harris in direct interaction with the students. In a later memo, however, she reconsidered and decided that much could be learned from being able to compare student interactions with Miss Harris, with a substitute teacher, and with each other while no teacher was present:

I feel that it is worthwhile to keep that data I collected during the day that a substitute teacher took over Miss Harris's class. Although that particular log entry does not describe direct interactions between Miss Harris and her students, it does seem to provide insight about how students act during their teacher's absence. I was very glad I had the opportunity to see that class because it provided me with a frame of comparison and helped me identify patterns in Miss Harris's language and teaching style.

Through my readings and analysis of my log, I have realized that some of the most significant classroom incidents occur when Miss Harris walks away from students or leaves the room for a very brief period of time. It may be important to keep these descriptions in my study since they also seem to reveal a lot about specific students' experiences with and perceptions of the teacher.

Lynn's account of her analytic thinking illustrates work-in-progress at a fairly early stage. Often, however, a researcher may be well into 'writing up' before the final direction of the study is determined. Sometimes a great deal of writing has been done but seems very wide of the mark. This might be part of a useful process. Sometimes it is not until a draft has been written that problems are apparent. In our experience, however, it usually happens when the researcher has not begun shaping the study from the earliest stages on. However, it might also be because the person has not sought advice. For whatever reason, it may happen that an overall focus is not determined until rather late in the writing process. A narrowing of overall focus at that point may require winnowing on a large scale. Midway through the writing of her study of children's book events in a preschool setting, Marlene Barron (1995) became involved in this process.

The school that provided the context for Marlene's study was rich in books. Not only were there frequent story events, but children also read on their own or shared books with one another informally without teacher intervention. After a few months of videotaping in a number of sites in the school, she found that she had far too much data to shape into a document with a clear focus:

> I expected to collect lots of data. But I did not expect the flood. And as most people do in floods, I alternated between drowning and coming up for air. The amount of data, coupled with my personal need to be thorough led me to try to do too much. Having to choose which events to study in depth was extremely difficult. Which were most representative? And of what? I therefore reviewed and reviewed the tapes, and I analyzed and analyzed. Over time, I felt that my categories had indeed become saturated, and I was finally able to let go of some of those wonderfully rich events. (Barron, 1995, p. 232)

Marlene first wrote lengthy descriptions of all types of book events in this setting. The bulk was overwhelming, both for Marlene and for her readers — committee members and members of her support group — who agreed that she had enough for several studies. One problem with such a wealth of detail is that readers find it hard to keep in mind the most significant points. Marlene eventually decided to focus exclusively on book events in which there was no adult intervention — what she termed 'child-constituent' book events. By doing this, she solved another one of her difficulties. As school head, she had struggled during data collection to function as participant observer when she observed a teacher working in a way that she felt was inconsistent with the school's philosophy. The narrowing of focus alleviated this difficulty. As Marlene expressed it, when the work of the teachers was not an issue, the 'final focus on child-constituent book events enabled me to function more fully as researcher' (p. 232).

Marlene divided the relevant data into sections — based on earlier analytic categories — on children alone, children with a partner, and children in a group. Within these data there were fascinating glimpses of children not yet reading in the technical sense of the word who were yet making meaning from pictures-and-text and often sharing their insights with one another about the books, as well as about how books work. They were reading in other ways. One provocative finding was that the very aspects of classroom life that might seem to work against structure and order — the prevalence of books lying about on the floors and stairs, the conversations children had with each other over books when they 'should' have been doing something else — were often rich in intellectual activity. Some of these findings had not found their way into Marlene's earlier account. Narrowing down her focus, re-analyzing more deeply, and reflecting on the findings again during the resultant rewriting, were all processes that helped Marlene see and highlight in her final narrative some significant findings that were 'lost' in her original document.

Most of the examples we have considered so far have had to do basically with winnowing out categories of data, although Marlene's work involved the drastic pruning of narrative material as well. Once we have made decisions about our basic story, we need to take a hard look at the kinds of narrative material we have composed and decide how they serve the overall purpose. By the time Marsha Slater (1994) was ready to develop the thematic analysis section for her study of a high school math teacher working with 'writing-to-learn' in an ESL classroom, she had composed about a hundred pages of vignettes that illustrated different aspects of the work in which this teacher and her students were engaged over a five-year period. However, it became apparent to her, in reading through this substantial amount of material — interesting and illustrative as it was — that in the aggregate it was not conveying any strong message. As Marsha talked through this problem with her advisors, it became clear that the most salient feature of this long-term study was the story over time of writing-to-learn.

Next came a decision about whose story would be the central focus. Was it that of individual students? of classes? of the teacher? Again, in winnowing through the data, it became clear that the teacher's story was the most interesting for her to tell at this time. Marsha returned to her narratives, sorted them in a strict chronological order, then grouped them into time periods that were significant in the professional history of the teacher and the school. There were, for example, those years in which innovations were introduced in the school as a whole. It then became evident that each of the time periods had a character of its own, that in each the teacher modified her teaching strategies in certain important ways, that she gradually became aware of and then struggled with her own feelings about herself as a writer.

Finally, Marsha pruned her mass of narrative material until only vignettes were retained that illustrated most tellingly what Marsha interpreted as the essential character of these pivotal times and events. The result was a vivid picture of a teacher's development over time that had been obscured by the original mass of narrative. In a following chapter, Marsha went on to present her thematic analysis and some thoughts about educational innovations. This picture, in turn, supported and illustrated a thematic analysis of elements in the setting that seemed to help or hinder the teacher's growth and implementation of educational innovation.

Using Graphic Displays and Microanalytic Templates

'Think display.' So advises Wolcott, quoting a dictum of Miles and Huberman (in Wolcott, 1990, p. 63). In this section we indicate some ways in which we and other researchers have done this and to explain ways in which we think displays can add to the overall effect of many research reports. One of Wolcott's reasons for this advice is that even as winnowing out is necessary, so at times are strategies that will help us 'crowd more in.' Within a research paradigm that relies so heavily on words, displays can often reduce a great deal of data and make them more readily graspable and memorable. See our 'Contents — Version Two' at the front of this book. Does it do for you what we hoped? Displays also often bring quantitative aspects of data to the forefront in ways that make them more telling than narrative alone. And we think that figures sometimes say more than words. Look at p. iii of this book. We made this display a metaphoric symbol to tell you about our authorship without saying it in sentences. Figures, tables, and quantification thus supplement, extend, and enhance qualitative analysis.

In her study of the involvement of Portuguese-speaking parents of special needs children in their children's education, Dora Tellier-Robinson used a table with good effect to present data about the English fluency of the parents. This was an important component in her study, because one of the themes that ran through the interview transcripts of her parent participants was their opinion that lack of fluency in English often made dealings with educational officials more difficult. The tables were produced after Dora had already written portraits of ten families. She then turned her attention to a discussion of discrete topics suggested by her analytic categories. Based on one of these categories, Dora wrote another several pages to summarize the cultural experiences and language fluency of each parent. As she worked through these pages, Dora kept saying 'It sounds so repetitive. I've said it all before.' And indeed it was there, woven through the family portraits. Her support group concurred — 'Repetitive. Boring' — and suggested that these pages be transposed instead to a table. This solved the difficulty, and in a way that made the information much more accessible and easy to grasp for readers (Tellier-Robinson, 1996, p. 150). Dora's table is reproduced below:

Language Fluency of Participants

Name	Years in US	Interview Language Preference	English Fluency
Castelo	21	English	near native
Paiva	38	Portuguese	near native but accented
Xavier	2	Portuguese	fluent
Duarte	26	Portuguese	very fluent
Carvalho	27	Portuguese	moderate
Dias	21	Portuguese	minimal
Gomes	9	Portuguese	minimal
Davila	2	Portuguese	almost none
Tavares	27	English	near native

In the table, Dora summarized information about the length of stay in the United States and the English fluency of the participants previously dispersed through the individual portraits. The descriptive labels for English fluency were determined both from participants' reports and from Dora's own experience of talking in English with them. As readers, we also found it helpful to have this summary — in fact, we marked the page with a Post-it while reading the whole — to refer to when we read later sections about the participants' experiences with teachers and school officials.

Judith Evans (1994, 1996) had known from the time that she designed her proposal that she would carry out microanalyses of communication episodes as an integral part of her study of the communicative competence of a deaf child, Kristin, in an otherwise hearing family. Because of the type of microanalysis, Judith saw that the findings would best be presented in graphics and other displays. As is evident from the outline of her study provided by her Table of Contents (pp. 183–4), the chapter which includes these analytic segments is followed by one devoted to a description of the family's home environment and portraits of the family members, and a subsequent chapter devoted to a thematic analysis of interviews and conversations with family members. These chapters provided detailed data in narrative form about the setting and about Kristin as a communicator in the context of her family.

Seven-year-old Kristin is the fifth of eight children in a family that lives on a small farm outside of town. Her father, Peter, is a teacher; her mother, Barb, works part time and has returned to school. Kristin travels one hour each day on the bus to a state-supported school for the deaf. The school uses simultaneous communication, that is, manually coded English accompanied by speech. Communication at home is more haphazard — a combination of simultaneous communication, speech only, and nonverbal behavior, depending upon the situation and the ability of various family members to sign. The family is depicted as lively and self-sufficient, and traditional. Barb and Peter, state that 'We do the best we can' in the face of the many demands on them, and this was selected as a major theme for analysis:

> Barb and Peter Harris have developed their own system of organization in order to maintain their large family. Claims on their time have caused a division of labor to evolve in which each parent assumes primary responsibility for tasks he/she does best. Sometimes life becomes more chaotic than they would like, but they try to keep things balanced ... Barb feels the pressure of time even more acutely in relation to the attention she is able to give Kristin. She must squeeze in time to communicate with her in general, to find occasional moments to talk, to help her with her homework, or to read a story to her. (Evans, 1994, pp. 106–7)

The family division of labor resulted in Barb's becoming the most proficient in signing with Kristin, some of the older sisters acquiring a moderate proficiency, and Peter's acquiring little. Attitudes that support special attention being given to Kristin's communication needs 'when we see she needs it' are supported by the family themes that 'We have mixed feelings about Kristin's deafness and special need for attention' and the parents' theme that 'We want Kristin to be just one of the kids ... We don't want deafness to be the focus of the family ... We want

Kristin to mesh with the hearing world' (p. 105). Kristin, for her part, expressed a clear awareness of family roles, routines, and attitudes that appeared to reflect the themes of the parents:

> Kristin's understanding of life at home begins with her knowledge of her place in her family. This confidence emanates from her understanding of the makeup of her family constellation and her inclusion in family activities . . . Kristin's conduct indicates that she understands the family expectations for her behavior. She knows what is expected of her at home and at outside events such as church services and family parties. She also knows that older children look after the younger ones and how people are expected to treat one another . . .
>
> Activities include daily household routines and being held responsible for self-care and behavioral standards. She goes on shopping trips, is read to, attends special events such as family celebrations and activities at her siblings' schools. She also has traveled to see relatives, attended the circus, gone on field trips with her sisters' classes, and observed and cared for the farm animals. Indoor and outdoor play with both older and younger siblings is always available to her after school, on weekends, and on school vacations. (Evans, 1994, pp. 121–2)

It is within this background that the microanalytic analyses took place. In a review of her entire body of log data, Judith identified 144 interactive episodes. In 66 per cent of these episodes, Kristin was with a primary communication partner, and in 34 per cent without one. Judith presented these data verbally in the text of her Chapter VI and also in the figure reproduced here as Figure 4.2.

Judith tabulated the functions of language used in three videotaped segments that were used for close analysis. That table is represented in Figure 4.3. It is in a table such as this that the power of numbers becomes apparent. Notice the line labeled 'Imaginative' in the table. The numbers indicate that no imaginative use of language by Kristin was documented in any of these three segments. The results of this analytic procedure, together with the findings from other approaches to analysis used in the study, combine to indicate that Kristin's opportunities for inclusion in a broad range of language functions was more limited than that of her siblings. To us, the microanalysis adds an important dimension to the broader description.

These findings were set against the earlier thematic analysis that documented the insistence of all of the members of the family, including Kristin's seven siblings and Kristin herself, that 'she is just one of us,' and 'she is treated just like all the other children.' It would appear that precisely because signing with Kristin or making other accommodations for her special needs was not a high priority in the family, she was in fact not 'just like all the other children.' During a full third of the time in the episodes analyzed she had no communication partner. Judith also documented that, unable to hear what was going on out of her sight, Kristin missed much of the background talk that could have broadened her awareness of family interaction or exposed her to a broader variety of language use.

Even when Kristin did have a primary communication partner, the language that was signed to her was sometimes found to communicate only part of what was being spoken to the others in any given setting.

Judith documented this with a segment of transcript of a speech event centering

Figure 4.2: Distribution of interactive episodes by group size, with and without a primary communication partner (PCP) (N = 144)

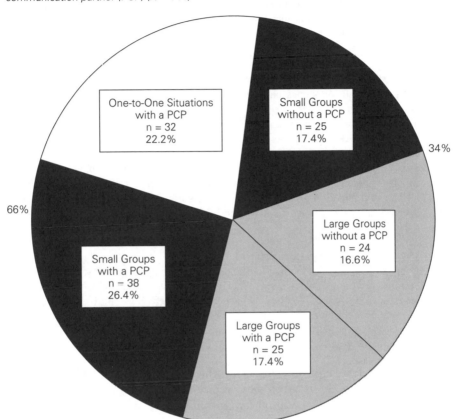

Figure 4.3: Frequency and percentage distribution of the functions for which Kristin uses language in the three closely analyzed language segments

Functions	Baking Cookies (N)	%	The Kitchen Show (N)	%	Dressing for Communion (N)	%
Instrumental	(2)	8.3	(0)	0.0	(1)	4.5
Regulatory	(3)	12.5	(7)	38.9	(3)	13.6
Interactional	(8)	33.3	(3)	16.7	(2)	9.1
Personal	(1)	4.1	(1)	5.6	(7)	31.8
Imaginative	(0)	0.0	(0)	0.0	(0)	0.0
Heuristic	(0)	0.0	(3)	6.7	(1)	4.5
Informative	(10)	41.7	(4)	22.2	(8)	36.4
Totals	(24)	99.9	(18)	100.1	(22)	99.9

% rounded to the nearest 0.1%

on Sister Margaret's talk to Kristin's First Communion class. The data that were presented as one of the appendices to Judith's dissertation are reproduced below. The parentheses in Sister Margaret's spoken message indicate where Kristin's mother started and ended her interpretation. Underlined words indicate where the mother tapped Kristin to get her attention.

> *Sister Margaret's Spoken Message*
> ... give out all the names and when you're in the church practicing for your different activities (Sister will let you. When we line up for church, when you go into church, we have to remember that we're in the presence of Jesus. God, our Father, who loves us very much, is filling you with His Spirit. And certainly we all know, again so many people have come and asked for your prayers. So if you can be praying, we certainly have a lot of things in our world to pray for, don't we? Let's remember all of those people who need our prayers. Let's pray for peace in the world and God give us peace. And let's ask God to be very close to us.) When Sister wrote the note that you're bringing home to your moms and dads today ...

> *Mother's signed interpreted message*
> [Tap's child's shoulder to regain visual attention.] I wonder what Kristin will do? Some special things? We will see. When you enter church, remember you are with Jesus, in God's house. You be quiet and good. [Taps child again.] You can pray for other people who need your prayers. Lots of sick people. Sad people need your prayers for them. [Taps child for attention.] Pray for peace in the world. Pray for God to be near us.

In a section at the end of the chapter in which these and other tables and figures were presented, Judith discussed the specifics of her findings in the light of other research about deaf children in otherwise hearing families. She returned to issues raised by her data in a broader way in the section in her final chapter entitled 'The Continuum of Kristin's Communication Experiences.' This section, part of which is reproduced below, recapitulates some of the discussion in her earlier chapters. It is a wide discussion, however, because in it Judith ties in to the highlights of the charts and displays. Such a synthesis, not uncommon in a dissertation or other formal document, summarizes findings and resultant issues as a lead into implications for professional practice.

> Kristin is one of eight children. The size of the group she was in, whom she was interacting with, and the role of the relationships in the situation all had an impact on her interactions with others. Patterns emerged from the overview of interactive episodes that suggested the concept of a communication continuum to describe Kristin's levels of engagement and access to language in use in her family.
>
> Exploring the notion of a communication continuum enabled me to see how Kristin's conversation experiences ranged from inclusion to exclusion. At one end of the continuum are the experiences in which she converses one-to-one or as a member of a small group with a primary communication partner. In these situations, ... she is an active, interactive participant with full access to signing partners and interpretation of the turns of others. She is an insider with full inclusion

in the group, one who participates as a competent conversation partner. At the other end of the continuum are episodes in which Kristin is a member of a large group without a primary communication partner. At large gatherings, she must fend for herself like her siblings do. The difference for her is that she must rely on her understanding of situations, her observation skills, and her lipreading ability to understand what is said around her. In these situations, she becomes a solitary observer with rare inclusion in direct communication. She can be isolated in the bosom of her family. Degrees of inclusion/exclusion along the continuum vary with group size and the presence or absence of a primary communication partner. The tenor of discourse expressed through interpersonal language is directly dependent on the partners she converses with as communication events fall along the continuum.

The size of Kristin's family and the policies and practices which they have established create the context for the continuum of her experiences. Those who are best at signing sign. They sign when they think she needs extra support rather than whenever she is present to be fully included. As a general practice, the family as a whole does not make accommodations to her communication needs. Rather, they require her to adjust to their expectations. She demonstrates her competency as a communicator as she varies the functions for which she uses language according to the features of discourse related to activities, participants, channel, the field, tenor, and mode.

Kristin's parents want her to be 'just one of the kids,' yet her access to family conversation and information is not equal to that of the other children, who can overhear even when they are not directly engaged with conversation partners. Also, as seen in the sample of interpreted text in Appendix G [the passage reproduced above], even with full access to family conversation through a primary communication partner, Kristin still receives incomplete language. The quality of the model is less than ideal, for it is neither complete English nor complete ASL. It is not equal to the spoken language model available to the hearing children in the family.

The point that we wish to make here is that an analysis of this kind, along with the numerical compilation, can provide unexpected and highly revealing findings. We have presented our belief in Chapter 3 that narrative is a 'primary act of the mind.' We also argue that numeric reasoning is a primary act of the mind, and as such it has an inescapable part in our work whether or not we choose to acknowledge it. The use of numbers often seems held in suspicion by some members of the qualitative community, perhaps because at times they feel like a beleaguered minority. While we are far from advocating that there be a specifically numerical component to every qualitative study, we also know that every qualitative study involves number, a compilation of some sort. We do urge that researchers consider whether a specific use of numerical representation would provide an element of enrichment to the whole. This might well require a graph or tabular display. Such a display can also often make certain points more effectively than words alone.

Like Judith, Belén Matías (1990) had also designed her study — the use of directives in a preschool setting — with a microanalytic component. She had selected the scheme she intended to use for this purpose, only to find — as qualitative researchers often may — that the schemes of other researchers were not adequate

Figure 4.4: Directives in entrance-transition to work: some descriptors (%)

| | | | | | Intent | | | | | Support | | | | |
| | | | | | | | | | | Ind. Needs | | | | |
	#	%	V	NV	Prox.	Inst.	Del.	Priv.	Pub.	Options	Soc-Emot.	Phys.	Curr.	Class Rule	Org. Routine
Phase I															
T→S	38	30.8	29.0	1.0	8.8	23.0	7.7	29.7	0.0	20.9	9.9	1.0	10.9	2.2	6.6
S→T	19	20.8	19.3	2.1	3.3	19.8	1.1	16.5	5.5	16.5	12.1	2.2	5.5	0.0	1.0
S→S	44	48.4	43.0	3.3	4.4	36.3	12.1	46.1	2.2	12.1	40.7	0.0	2.2	1.0	4.4
Total	101	100.0	91.3	8.6	16.5	79.1	20.9	92.3	7.7	49.5	62.7	3.2	18.6	3.2	12.0
Phase II															
T→S	32	52.4	46.9	3.1	6.5	41.0	11.5	24.6	27.9	16.4	14.8	0.0	3.3	31.1	3.3
S→T	23	37.7	34.3	6.2	8.2	37.7	0.0	27.9	9.8	19.7	32.8	3.3	1.6	0.0	0.0
S→S	6	9.8	7.8	1.6	0.0	9.8	0.0	9.8	0.0	1.6	4.9	3.3	0.0	1.6	0.0
Total	61	99.9	89.0	10.9	14.7	88.5	11.5	62.3	37.7	37.7	52.5	6.6	4.9	32.7	3.3

Key to Abbreviations

T = teacher
S = student
# = no. of directives
(per cent) % = % of directives
V = verbal directives
NV = nonverbal directives
Prox. = T. approach to provide directive
Inst. = sender expected instant response
Del. = sender expected delayed response

Priv. = directives expressed privately
Pub. = directives expressed publicly
Options = directives provided options
Support = Directives in Support of
Soc-Emot. = Social Emotional Needs
Phys. = Physical Needs
Curr. = Curricular Needs
Class Rule = inferred or public
Org. Routines = Organizational Routines

to the richness of her emergent analysis. Here is how Belén described her experience in the 'Method Considerations' section of her study:

> My secret wish before actual data collection was that a combination of the analytical scheme of Erickson-Mohatt and Ervis-Tripp would serve my study. I had done the best job I could of searching the literature and selecting the two systems for the beginning framework of analysis. At that time, these systems were congruent with both the kinds and functions of directives as well as the findings of my field trials. Right away I became aware that I was learning so much about the intricacies, the complexities of children's and teachers' directives and the richness by which they were being played out in the varied classroom contexts that I had to do different justice to my findings.
>
> I set out to make my own scheme. And what a scheme! I tried to capture the communicative flow of directives, their intent, effect, who communicated and who received each directive, and a slew of other descriptions. I tried to capture everything that was needed. The price? I labored with a huge analytical scheme in which the original two systems played minor parts. (Matías, 1990, p. 180)

Belén continues with an account of her intensive work in selecting which six videotapes to analyze from the 122 she had collected — talk about 'data overload' and the winnowing process! — and the equally demanding task of applying the scheme she had devised. We think it is a typically qualitative meta-reflection with which she concluded after all of this effort:

> . . . while I felt that the data from applying the system were extremely varied and descriptive, the microanalysis resulted also in my deeper understanding that much of the groundedness of what happened over the year would be lost if I had applied only that particular lens to the study. (p. 182)

The 'groundedness' of which Belén speaks provided a detailed context within which to examine the results of her microanalysis. She was surprised, however, by more than the need to devise her own microanalytic template. The study, titled *Getting Things Done*, was conducted in a private school in Puerto Rico that was founded by parents who were convinced that 'children needed to be nurtured from the very start to become more reflective, independent, and socially committed' (Matías, 1990, p.173). A Montessori approach was selected because that seemed most congruent with the founders' aims. However, when Belén compared the results of successive microanalyses over time in this classroom for 3-, 4-, or 5-year-olds, she discovered that the students were in some ways allowed less independence by Ani, their teacher, as the school year progressed. (A chart in which these analytic findings are displayed is reproduced here as Figure 4.4). Notice, for example, in this chart the highlighted portion of data for entrance-transition to work time. At the end of Phase I teacher directives gave children options 49.5 per cent of the time. At the end of Phase II, children were given options 37.7 per cent of the time. This indicated that by the end of the year the children were given fewer options than at the beginning and this very nicely highlights observational data Belén had presented in other ways. Contrast this with the marked rise in directives concerning

Class Rules: 3.2 per cent at the end of Phase 1 contrasted with 32.7 per cent at the end of Phase 2. The paragraphs below are excerpts from the portion of Belén's final discussion devoted to these findings:

> Ani seemed to be more willing to share power at the beginning of the school year. She supported the students' individual transition-to-work time; she communicated a complex set of rules that seemed to apply sensitively to different groups of children as well as the entire class; she welcomed the parents into the classroom; and she supported many of the students' needs in individual, child-centered ways. By her very actions she seemed to say that here was a place where everyone could contribute, develop, make decisions, and make mistakes. Further, here was a place where people's ideas were welcomed, their direction sought, and their learning styles respected.
>
> Over the course of the year these messages changed and by the end of the year the children seemed securely socialized into an understanding that the teacher makes the decisions, that school is where one obeys and follows and that there is little wiggle room for individual needs that do not match those of the larger group. All this happened in an atmosphere of great warmth. (Matías, 1990, pp. 172–3)

Because of the depth of the descriptive data she had gathered, Belén was able to discuss this finding, supported by the results of the microanalyses, as part of her understanding of the current school population and clientele, to demonstrate how the goals and practices had moved away from the original Montessori model, and to reflect on the ways in which the teacher negotiated her way through a mesh of conflicting pressures. The fact that Belén had not anticipated the shift toward greater control when she designed her study raises the issue of whether she would actually have perceived so gradual a shift if she had not had this finding from microanalysis to throw it into sharp relief.

A glance at the titles for the chapters in which findings were presented in *Getting Things Done* reveals where the microanalysis fits into the overall plan:

Chapter IV   The Setting: School and People
Chapter V   Directives in Classroom Life: The Broad View
Chapter VI   Microanalysis of Selected Segments of Videotape: The Focused View
Chapter VII   Social Rules for Getting Things Done
Chapter VIII Summary and Discussion

The themes of life in this classroom expressed as 'social rules' will be presented in a later section in the book. We would like to look now at the function of Belén's Chapter V, which includes vignettes of specific incidents in which directives were used to reveal life in this classroom. We are including one of these here to indicate the complexity of life that might go unnoticed in a busy setting except, perhaps, by one absorbed in ethnographic observation:

> José and Javi have been sitting next to each other and fighting. Javi has gone to the teacher twice to complain about this. He tells José that he is going to use the memory game and gets up to put his material away and to get the other. José reacts quickly and moves ahead of Javi and tells him, 'I am going to get it.' Javi says,

'Noooo,' whining. José knocks down Javi's work. Javi puts what is left on the floor and goes, crying, to tell Ani. Ani says, 'I told you to move away from him. If you had done that, the accident would not have happened. Now you have to go pick it up.' Javi goes back to the accident area crying and talking to himself.

Rafa and Adrian are discussing the accident. Rafa says, pointing at José, 'He knocked it down.' Javi, hearing this, says, 'I was going to use that.' José moves over, grabs the game and hides it behind his back. Javi begins to sob. Adrian tells Javi, 'You don't have to cry.' Javi, 'Yes, I have to cry.' Adrian says, 'Look, you tell him: Please let me use the memory game.' José answers, 'And I'll give it to you. You tell me, "Please, José, can you give me the memory? Ani says I was going to use it." You tell me and I will give it to you.' Javi is picking things up and tells José, 'You and I can play with it.' José nods and goes to set it on a rug. (Matías, 1994, p. 84).

It is vignettes such as this juxtaposed with the microanalysis that have the potential to be extra powerful. If Belén's readers had not already seen the quality of relationships children were able to build on their own, the finding that future schooling allowed them fewer interactions of this type would likely lose its immediacy and poignancy.

Devising effective displays is not always easy. There can be findings that are difficult to describe in any fashion, as Maryann discovered in her dissertation study (Downing, 1989). Her purpose was to explore the responses to non-fiction of eighth-grade readers, particularly through the lens of their ideas of author. As the study progressed, Maryann analyzed both written responses and transcripts of interviews with the student participants. It became apparent to her that each student had unique and strong responses to certain passages in the texts that all were reading, but each also ignored other passages. Along with the written discussion, Maryann wanted to illustrate the individual response patterns in a more vivid fashion. For each student, she selected the portions of the passage to which that particular student responded. After many versions at the drawing board, she created a display such as the one on the left in Figure 4.5. For the passage that is included there, she first highlighted the portions about which the students talked or appeared to reveal a strong response. Highlighting or shading would, of course, be reproducible in printed form, and it would serve when a separate copy of a passage was prepared for each student, but Maryann thought it was important to bring the response patterns all together to spotlight the uniqueness of each response to the same text and the extent to which each differed from the other. How was she going to put this together in an economical display? Transparent overlays would have been the ideal solution, but, again, this would not have been possible to reproduce adequately in photocopies. Maryann finally hit upon the idea of marking off the section of text for each student's version with a different style — a bold line for one, dashes for another, alternating dots and dashes for the third — and then reproducing one copy of the text in which these markings were laid one over the other to compare the responses of all three. The resultant figures that she used for her study are reproduced here on the right hand side of Figure 4.5. Maryann, however, still thinks back fondly to the unrealized glories of colored overlays.

Figure 4.5: Individual response patterns to the same text

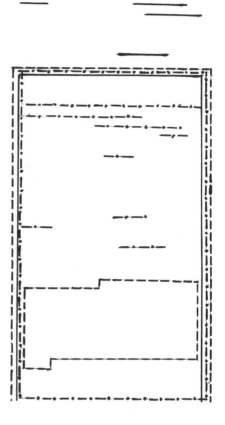

New England did not raise pepper or coffee or sugar or cotton or any other staple crop to sell the world. The greatest resource of New England was resourcefulness. Using the sea, New England versatility made the very menaces of the landscape into articles of commerce. "New England," went the common taunt, "produces nothing but granite and ice." The supreme proof of New England ingenuity was her ability to turn her rocky soils and heavy winters to profit.

Until almost the middle of the 19th century, ice from summer cooling had been a rare luxury. The ancient Romans had brought snow down from the mountains as a curiosity. But from the beginning of history, diet had been limited by the seasons. Generally speaking, fresh fruit and vegetables were available only when just ripe, meat only as it was slaughtered, milk only as it came fresh from the cow. A recipe for a syllabub about 1800 instructed the housewife: "Sweeten a quart of cyder with double refined sugar, grate nutmeg into it, then milk your cow into your liquor." Before the days of refrigeration, milk could be preserved only in the form of butter or cheese, and meat had to be dried or salted. Everything was spiced to lend variety or to conceal the staleness.

In the 18th century, ice cream was found in Paris, in London, or in the colonies only on aristocratic tables. Occasionally on the sideboards of a great English country house one might see a water cooler which used ice. An icehouse was part of the luxurious equipment of the palace of the royal governor's of Virginia at Williamsburg, in Washington's Mount Vernon, of Jefferson's Monticello, and of Monroe's Ash Lawn. Before the end of the 18th century, a few Philadelphia families had got together to maintain an icehouse, and at least one rich Cambridge estate had an icehouse of its own. But there had been almost no progress in the general use of refrigeration since that winter day in 1626 when Sir Francis Bacon caught a fatal chill while experimentally burying a chicken in the snow.

Randy's Version

Three Students' Versions

Randy's _____
Ted's _ . _ . _
Kevin's _ _ _ _ _

Bridging Toward Interpretation

One of the many tensions or paradoxes of qualitative research is that when we as researchers begin to move into specifically interpretive modes, we must take a step back from the immediacy of the field and of our data and see them again as 'the other.' Throughout the process of analysis we have been trying to present the meaning of our participants' experience in their own words and from their points of view. If we look back at the ten characteristics for analysis that Tesch suggested, we see that one of them, number six, focuses on the importance of comparison. We begin by comparing the content of one sentence or paragraph or event with another in our first interview or observation. In time, we compare the contents of one interview with another, actions we see in one situation in the field with those we see in another. The comparisons are internal to the data. We reach a point in our analysis where we must hold that internal vision of the field in tension against our own views. This process will have been inevitable in our thinking in any case — the automatic interpreting that everyone does as an element of all thinking, an attempt to make sense in terms of our own understanding of the world in transaction with that of our participants'. Usually researchers begin to move toward some specifically interpretive process in analytic memos, as they think through what kind of sense their accumulating data make to them. These tentative interpretations are often also tested against the interpretations of a support group or other colleagues. The sense-making activity — viewing the meanings of the participants against our own views — will also at some point need to be done against some specific theoretical frames. Thinking within theoretical frameworks and holding conversations with theory and with the findings of other research in 'the literature' is the subject of the following chapter. There we will describe how theory has been used in a variety of research writing. Antecedent to that process, however, we need to try to come to the essence of the meaning our findings have for us, to look at them from a variety of viewpoints, to try to establish our sense of the overall meaning. In other words, we begin to move toward work in interpretive modes. We will look at some ways to do that in this section, which is conceived of as a bridge to the following chapter on formal interpretation.

When we wrote about coding and categorizing, we were suggesting ways to think about and to break our data down into manageable chunks. We then considered how to arrange those chunks into an overall outline for a written report. Now, and it is in part a 'now' in time but even more a 'now' in emphasis and presentation, we look for ways to present the essence of the material that is in the categories. We need to tease out our meanings and discuss them with our readers. This is most commonly done by a search for important patterns, themes, and perhaps issues that seem to reach to the heart of those meanings. Thematic analysis is the topic of the next section.

Themes and Metathemes

An analysis for themes is one of the most frequently mentioned analytic approaches used by qualitative researchers. As Tesch (1987) phrases it, 'In dealing with their data, qualitative researchers "search" for themes, and they "find" themes, or they "extract," "recognize," or "identify" them. Most often, however, themes are said to "emerge" . . .' (p. 230). The search for themes and metathemes will thus be a major focus here. What with all of this emphasis on 'emerging,' the four of us on this writing team do need to sound a caution. We feel this kind of wording can be misinterpreted to mean that themes 'reside' in the data, and if we just look hard enough they will 'emerge' like Venus on the half shell. If themes 'reside' anywhere, they reside in our heads from our thinking about our data and creating links as we understand them. For Margot, for example, the most powerful of Michelangelo's works are his unfinished sculptures of slaves — caught in stone and straining to emerge. But it is Michelangelo who created this vision, this tension, and Margot who is reading her own meaning into it.

The fact that themes are so widely talked about in qualitative writing is perhaps part of the reason we find the topic a difficult one to discuss. There appears to be so much taken for granted, analysis for themes seems to be so much a given in qualitative writing, that the entire topic at times seems a bit like an unexamined assumption. Different qualitative researchers use the same term in somewhat different ways (Tesch, 1987), and certainly the ways in which themes are presented differ widely.

Let us return to the statement that 'all analysis is sorting and lifting' which we quoted in the section on coding and categorizing. Analysis for themes fits this description as well, because it involves a process of sorting through the fabric of the whole for our understanding of the threads or patterns that run throughout and lifting them out — as a seamstress lifts threads with a needle — to make a general statement about them. 'A theme can be defined as a statement of meaning that (1) runs through all or most of the pertinent data, or (2) one in the minority that carries heavy emotional or factual impact.' So we said in *Circles* (Ely *et al.*, 1991, p. 150), and we still find this definition serviceable. Tesch states that by 'themes' she means 'brief statements that describe the content of individual units of data text' (p. 231). Themes, then, are most commonly stated for particular categories of data. 'Metathemes,' on the other hand, are usually considered to be drawn from the entire body of data. Thus some researchers have referred to them as 'overarching themes.' To us, metathemes are major constructs that highlight overarching issues in a study which may be considered against extant literature and experience. They sometimes also have the 'meta' twist of reflecting back on the research process as well as on the findings. Because there are often countless themes embedded in any one body of data, it probably goes without too much saying that we will be concerned with statements of what are to us important meanings, essential to understanding what is perceived as the heart of the culture or experience being studied. Practically speaking, with themes as with categories, we may list many, go through processes of refining and combining them, and in the end select those that seem most salient, or most relevant to the story we have chosen to tell.

Throughout the literature, there are many descriptions and prescriptions for coding and categorizing, and we have worked at discussing what we consider to be the essential features of the process and some approaches to it. There is much less to be found, however, on analyzing for themes. For that reason, we reproduce here an excerpt from our previous book in which Margot described her process for thematic analysis:

> I am heavily influenced by the work of Bussis, Chittenden, Amarel, and Carini (1978) in how I develop themes. In brief outline, this is the process I apply:
>
> 1 Study and re-study the raw data to develop detailed, intimate knowledge.
> 2 Note initial impressions.

3   List tentative categories.

4   Refine categories by examining the results of steps 2 and 3 and returning to the entire database of step 1.

5   Group data under the still-tentative categories and revise categories if needed.

6   Select verbatim narrative to link the raw data to the categories.

7   Study results of step 6 and revise if needed.

8   Write theme statements for each participant from my best attempt to speak from her/his point of view by linking data in and across categories.

9   Integrate findings about each person.

10   Compare findings for all the persons for commonalities or patterns, differences, and unique happenings.

[At this point in time, Margot would add another step:

11   Repeat the entire procedure for each focus and/or question that is pertinent to the study.]

Quite frequently in qualitative work the categories that were created to organize data help the researcher to discover themes by highlighting some relation between them. This is certainly true in my case. For example, in the study, out of the many categories I established, were these three:

José's relationship to mother (Relm).
José's planning strategies (Pl).
José's financial goals (Fin).

After studying the supporting data for these categories, I wrote the following themes as if José were talking:

My mother supports me and helps me to clarify plans for the future.

I sometimes give up immediate positive experiences for what I feel I must do to establish later financial security.

These themes, among others, held strongly for the data about José.

Could I have established the themes without first building a set of categories? Some people might do that. But I feel most grounded in the data when I progress from category to theme. Could other researchers have discovered different categories and themes from the same data? Yes. And this would probably happen. The important process here is to be able to explain one's reasoning for whatever one created. On the other side of the picture, however, is the fact that I am often stunned by how similar the analytic categories and themes are when an entire group of people — a class — is given the same field log pages to analyze. That speaks to an aspect of the topic of trustworthiness, to be discussed later. (Ely *et al.*, 1991, pp. 150–1)

You will have noticed how in the above excerpt, Margot stresses that building categories is important to subsequent thematic analysis. A thematic analysis by its nature can only be developed over time. The attempt to identify and then find appropriate words for what we consider the essence, the theme, of our findings can be frustrating. Below is an account from an analytic memo written by Sarie Teichmann as she worked toward thematic analysis for her study of participants in a 12-Step Anorexic/Bulimic group. It reflects well a researcher's experience in trying to move beyond the bits and pieces of coding to a more holistic statement of the essence of the data.

> I've spent many hours there and many, many more with the logs and memos. Lots of thoughts, lots of ideas, and still lots more questions and not many answers.

Categories and Beyond Categories
Most of my categories from the first analytic memo still seem valid, though some have taken a back seat, at least for me. These include the **methods** (not as much talk of specifics), and the **physical ailments**. Even categories about **dysfunctional families** and **relationships** are moving back, and it is all the **feelings** that continue to move into the driver's seat — the **fears**, the **aloneness**. The category of **self hatred** I have expanded to **Sense of Self**.

After honing in on categories, I see many patterns, similarities, especially in the content of individual stories. But the categories don't seem enough. They provide some hints, hunches, but there is something larger going on. The closest I can come to it is to try to put myself in their shoes and make a broad statement:
MY LIFE IS ABOUT MY DISEASE. IT TOUCHES EVERYTHING. I CANNOT SEPARATE THIS DISEASE FROM ANY OTHER ASPECT OF MY LIFE. IT ALWAYS PULLS AT ME, REMINDING ME THAT I'M NOT WORTH MUCH EXCEPT WHEN I CAN CONTROL IT. IT IS OVER-POWERING. I'M IN A LOT OF PAIN.

The search for, or the recognition of, metaphors in the data can be a powerful heuristic in the identification and statement of themes. Please turn back now to the section on 'Metaphor' in Chapter 3, to the concluding excerpt, taken from the work of Michele Bellavita (pp. 121–3). Consider again what she has written about metaphors: 'Metaphors are transformations. Metaphors can catapult even well-written, rich descriptions from the realm of particular and time-limited into the realm of the timeless, the essential, the universal.' This is exactly what we are looking for when we make theme statements — a lift into the essential and, if not universal, at least more general.

Barbara Ball followed such a process — from the more particular to the more general — in analyzing her data from a preschool classroom. Below are two segments from her notes for her final analysis. These are based on two analytic categories. Notice that in each of the two main categories — Teacher's Instructions During Playtime, and Teacher's Moves Toward Control and Children's Answers — subcategories have been established and within the subcategories are the codes that Barbara used for the individual thinking units. Thus each step of the analytic process can be identified in retrospect in this final summation.

TEACHER'S INSTRUCTIONS DURING PLAYTIME
— CHILDREN'S CHOICES
        choice to join small group when teacher is present or
        to leave
— TEACHER'S INSTRUCTIONS (teacher is present all the time)

engaging child
instructing, providing structure/outline
directing children's activities
supervising and controlling if they do it right
goals and expectations
setting rules
settling conflicts
— CHILDREN'S RESPONSE TO INSTRUCTIONS
work within given structure successfully
do not follow the structure
choose to leave

Themes:	Clara: *I want to give a direction. Otherwise they just hang around and babble.*
	I believe it is important what I teach the children. They learn because of what I teach. My role is important.
	Child: *Sometimes the teachers show us how to do new things. We learn how to make paintings and we all work together.*
Metaphors:	*The frame, the scaffold*
Metatheme:	*The teacher has strong views about the importance of the structure she provides for children's learning.*

When we look closely at the progression from theme to metatheme in the above example we note that the themes are stated in the first person. They have a flavor of the speaker's own words, and may be based on them, but are constructed by the researcher to attempt to express the essence of their meanings as she perceives them. The metaphors that Barbara has identified in her data — the frame and the scaffold — have a thematic power, and in fact have been worked into the metathematic statements. Barbara has chosen to phrase the metatheme in third person, in contrast to her use of first person for the themes. This stylistic device has the effect of giving a greater degree of generality. However, we of this writing team can see room for further work here, because we believe that a statement such as 'The teacher has strong views about the importance of structure . . .' is no doubt a metatheme of the teacher but now may be ready for a further interpretive twist by the researcher. Notice in the next example that Barbara shows a similar progression of thinking from the more specific to the more general but creates a metatheme with larger implications than the previous one:

TEACHER'S CONTROL AND CHILDREN'S ANSWERS
— TEACHER'S CONTROL
choice and presentation of themes (plan)
setting of rules (you must . . . , don't . . .)
goals and expectations
questions
control of outcome/product/answers
— CHILDREN'S RESPONSES
no answer
answer within or outside the expected range
behavior that breaks the rules

— TEACHER'S REINFORCEMENT OF DISCIPLINE
    time-out
    lecture about rules
    using physical power to reinforce rules (pick up, carry away child)
— ATMOSPHERE
    tension/disruption
    confusion/chaos
    participation/attention

Themes	Clara: *When I teach the whole group I need to have a carefully prepared plan. Otherwise it just gets overwhelming. Having a plan helps me to feel in control during meetings. I want to have some authority over them.*
	Meetings require a lot of self-control from the children and I see who needs more attention and help with this. In a big group, discipline is important.
	Dustin: *I have to sit quiet with my legs folded and wait until the teacher asks a question.*
	Often I do not know the right answer.
Metaphors:	*The teacher as a general commanding her troop.*
	The teacher as judge, as expert, as trainer or tamer?
	The battle over control.
	The cage
Metatheme:	*In this room there is tension between imposed control and self control.*

In this example, it seems to us likely that the metaphors are Barbara's rather than the teacher's. The metathematic sentence again is in the third person and represents a shift to the researcher's point of view. Although this writing represents a draft of a final analysis, it has yet to be incorporated into a draft of a complete report. As Barbara decides exactly how she wishes to use her metathematic statements, the phrasing of them can be further shaped toward the ultimate interpretive purpose.

Each researcher must decide whether the final writing will benefit from the inclusion of individual themes for the various participants. We see the composing of such themes as a very useful analytic tool, perhaps even an essential one, for the researcher. What may be new is the fact that while teasing out themes is essential, the way we write about them is not set in stone. Thus, some researchers have found numerous ways to present and illustrate their themes, some that do not involve directly writing theme statements. We think of a powerful novel — *War and Peace* for example. Surely its themes are evident and yet Tolstoy did not write them out for us.

Whether and how thematic statements will be effective in the final document is a decision each researcher must make. Some research reports contain long lists of themes and/or analyses arranged under many themes. We become concerned when we are hit with such a multiplicity of themes, in part because the sheer number of them makes them difficult for a reader to keep track of, let alone remember. Another reason, and perhaps a more important one, is that when we see lengthy catalogs of themes, we begin to think about how they can be grouped into categories, about how they can be lifted to more inclusive, more meaningful statements. In other words, as readers we have a natural tendency to want to lift the level of thinking, and this is a task that we think the writer should have undertaken. Whether or not they are ultimately consolidated, whether they are finally presented in the form of theme statements at all, we do consider a thematic analysis to be a powerful aid in striving to see the essence of our data. At this point in her writing, Tina Brescia has identified the following themes for some of the ministers in the pastoral care group she was studying, and we think her notes are useful because in them she gives us a window into her thinking:

MEMO: THEMES
I have been thinking about some individual themes for the participants of the Pastoral Care group. As I read through my logs I discovered that certain themes began to stand out for me about certain people.

Anna
I am a good listener.
I don't always probe enough.
I don't want to be intrusive to others.
I speak my mind.
I help others to understand — I teach.
I am thoughtful of others.

Nora
I am quiet.
I am considerate of others.
I don't always give myself credit for what I do.
Others see me as warm and caring.

Stanley
I am uncomfortable with anger.
I identify strongly with other priests.

Brad
I make assumptions about other's feelings.
I feel uncomfortable with anger.
I identify strongly with patients at times.

John
I don't always understand what others are saying.

Rebecca
I am open and honest about my feelings.
I am willing to take risks to learn.

Arnold
I command attention from others.
I have clear ideas about how a chaplain should behave.

I didn't create any themes for Mona yet and I believe there are more themes for these participants as well. I am also trying to formulate metathemes for all of this.

This list is provisional. Tina is still working on it. She is starting to work on cross-case themes, however, and has formulated a number of these as social rules under the category 'Rules for the Chaplain':

> From RULES FOR THE CHAPLAIN:
> A good chaplain knows how to create a professional distance from the patients in order to minister.
> A good chaplain listens to the music behind the words of another.
> A good chaplain doesn't talk like a doctor. He uses the language of a pastor.
> A good chaplain allows people to talk about the cruelty of God.
> A good chaplain allows an open space for people to tell their stories in their own words.
> A good chaplain needs to be careful about putting interpretations onto the patient's words or situation.
> A good chaplain is a mirror who reflects what he hears.
> A good chaplain is able to be present with another person even if they are feeling angry, sad, fearful, or in pain.
> A good chaplain accepts and acknowledges another's feelings and doesn't try to change them.
> A good chaplain is one who ministers to others eliciting from them their spiritual resources to help them deal with the situation that they are in.
>
> The opening I used for these sentences (a good chaplain) sounds strange to my ears and yet that was the message I felt was coming through as these issues were discussed during the sessions I observed. I am open to another way to word this if anyone has ideas.
>
> FROM THE CHAPLAINS:
> Sometimes a pastor needs to take a break from the intensity of the emotion that we deal with.
> Sometimes I talk too much when I'm really feeling anxious. I need to watch out for this.
> Being a helper gives me power.

Finally, Tina started to work on metathemes. These are her overarching statements from the findings as a whole. Before listing these in her analytic memo, Tina wrote out her feelings about the process:

> METATHEMES:
> I really had to think a lot about metathemes for my study. It was not easy for me to lift from the data to find these metathemes. This process shows me how I really have to live with the data and look at them more deeply in order to find the meanings that are there for me but perhaps not so evident. I sat with my support group and we each tried to write up a few metathemes for ourselves. This is what I came up with to start.
>
> 1 There are many levels of relationship in a pastoral care visit.
> 2 Each pastor defines his or her own view of a caring visit.
> 3 Learning pastoral care can mean looking deeply at one's own views.
> 4 There is a strong desire here among pastoral care interns to 'Do good.'

Barbara Aventuro (1991), in her study of residents in a long-term healthcare institution, struggled at length with the formation and consolidation of themes. She had interviewed twelve participants, and, in her dedication to giving them a voice, decided to present a vignette about each followed by a list of personal themes. This undertaking proved almost unmanageable, and in the end, because the focus was on these people's perceptions of caring in this environment, she included in the final document only their themes about caring. Below are examples from two of the participants. The first, Jim, was an ambulatory resident but had lost much of his ability to speak due to a stroke. He spent much of his time working alone in the garden, and Barbara was determined to devote as much time as needed to interviews with him because she perceived that he had a great desire to communicate.

> *Jim's Themes about Caring*:
> I have always longed to be loved, but I've not found much love in my life.
> I have had problems with communication throughout my life. I've never talked to anyone the way I wanted to; now it is impossible.
> I'm neglected here. (Aventuro, 1991, p. 156)

In contrast, the themes of Gertrude, who was bedridden and a patient in the skilled nursing unit, expressed a very different personality and attitude toward life. This is one of the strengths of theme statements — they do throw such contrasts into sharp relief.

> *Gertrude's Themes about Caring*
> I use many resources for coping with the negatives in my life.
> I see and hear and then assess everything around me; my heart and mind are the antithesis of my paralyzed body.
> To me, caring means you belong to a family.
> I feel connected to the handicapped people around me. I reach out to them in every way I can. (p. 191)

After this presentation of the individual participants and their themes of caring, Barbara did a cross-case analysis of themes for a thematic discussion of her findings. Below is an example of one of these cross-case themes — a statement that could also be referred to as a metatheme — and the paragraphs from the discussion that pertain to it.

> Cross-case theme: 'I'd like to make it better for the people who come after me.'
> The participants in this study wanted to leave a legacy that would contribute to a better world. This finding is consistent with that of Bahr and Gress (1984), who wrote that individuals are motivated by a sense of social responsibility and concern for the well-being of others to better the human condition according to his or her value system and that this kind of concern is one of the ways in which older persons can transcend the physical self and find meaning in life.
> Although the participants in the interviews spent a great deal of time reminiscing, they spent an equal amount of time talking about the present and the future. They had deep-felt concerns about the world, and many did not see themselves as cut off from it. When I explained my reasons for the research, conducting the interviews, one of the points I made was that other healthcare professionals would

read such research. The study would be used in the future to help plan for care for the elderly. This was the single motive that seemed to impel most of the participants to become involved in the study. They knew the information they gave me would be used to help in the future. (p. 255)

Spradley (1980; Spradley and Mann, 1975) makes much use of the concept of cultural norms, patterns of behavior, or rules throughout his discussions of ethnographic analysis. Such cultural rules are most often implicit, part of the tacit knowledge of members of a culture about how they get along together. For example, in the Introduction to *The Cocktail Waitress* (Spradley and Mann, 1975), the authors make the following statement: 'The cultural rules and rituals of bar life reaffirm the definitions and status attached to masculinity and femininity' (p. 3). In the same vein, some of our colleagues have found a statement of social rules a productive way of bringing out cultural themes and/or metathemes. The following description of and rationale for social rules is taken from Belén Matías' (1990) study of the preschool setting to which we referred earlier:

The emphasis here on rules is spurred by their importance in social behavior. 'The method by which human beings manage their affairs, and create society, is by the invention and promulgation of rules in the following of which social behavior is generated' (Harre, 1974, p. 143). Thus, rules can be thought of as the accepted conventions that govern human interaction.

The view of social rules that undergirds the presentation to follow is that they are negotiated in context, they are understood by the participants in either tacit or overt ways (Berger and Luckman, 1966; Taylor and Cameron, 1987) and that they are sometimes recognized from the digressions to them that people make ... It goes without too much saying that the statements of social rules engendered by directives in the classroom that was studied are, in the final sense, the products of the researcher's inference. Great care was taken in cross checking data and in verifying with the teacher before the rules were considered reasonable. (pp. 140–1)

In the body of her work, Belén presented each rule separately followed by examples and a discussion. She also summarized the entire body of social rules as an Appendix, and presented them there in a table form that also indicated in which areas of the overall preschool setting each rule had been documented as being actualized. We are presenting here the first page of the Appendix in Figure 4.6 because we feel that this formulation helps us strengthen our point that we would like to see qualitative researchers provide more of the details and more examples of the 'bare bones' of their analytic processes in the final report.

Inspired by the example of Belén's work, Marlene Barron also found the concept of social rules a useful tool for analyzing book events in the preschool setting she studied. Here is an excerpt showing the social rules operative in one aspect of that setting:

About Book Events
Social Rule 15: I read pictures or words — whatever I want.
Social Rule 16: When I read to others, I show the pictures.
Social Rule 17: I don't have to put my book away. I can leave it on the floor.

Social Rule 18: Books are the only classroom materials I can use during transition
periods or nap time.

Social Rule 19: There's space for me when a teacher reads.

Figure 4.6: Appendix I: Social Rules-Belén Matías

		Classroom Event		
About Classroom Routines		Ent.-Tran.	Ind. Wk.	Circle
1 I learn to be responsible in this classroom:				
a. The classroom is not for running.		X	X	X
b. I put the materials back in place after I finish.		X	X	X
c. I clean up after myself.		X	X	X
2 At the beginning of individual work time I must work alone. Then after finishing I can work with others			X	
3 The teacher can change my entrance and transition-to-work routines.		X		
4 The teacher plans the activities we do during circle time. I must do as she plans.				X
5 We must bid for a turn, speak one at a time and listen to others quietly when the teacher presents material or gives instructions.				X

Notice that Marlene, like Belén, chose to formulate her sense of the children's understanding of these rules and express them in the first person as though the children were speaking.

We have already pointed out that when a researcher is ready to move from themes to metathemes, this process is often aided by the use of metaphor or of certain words or phrases that seem woven as a pattern throughout the data. Here is an example taken from Susan Goetz Haver's study of a library. The operative metaphor here is that of a turnstile. Notice how Susan now lifts the metaphor of the library patron's access to the library and the world it implies to a broader and more general level. The library turnstile becomes an access to full participation in a democratic society.

Metathemes
Susan Goetz Haver

1 Each person must go through a process of moving from outsider to insider in the library. The ways they go about that process are unique and individual. (Turnstile.)

2 The library provides a turnstile through which children may go to become 'inside' members of American society. They do this by learning to use the skills (e.g., listening, locating information) which unlock the ideas contained there.

These two are really nested versions of the same metatheme, that of passage from the margins to inclusion and membership at the center. Each child (and adult, although I saw less of that first-hand) went through a process that began with navigating the turnstile, but expanded into learning to find books, learning to listen and read, learning the rules of the library, and acquiring formal membership. The process was assisted by roadmaps and guides along the way; no one had to navigate it alone. In fact, if anyone looked lost, that was a signal for the librarians to move in and offer help.

Ms. Albert took that process further, looking into the future and anticipating what would be needed by the children in order to allow them full access to participation in a democratic culture. She worried that children do not have what they will need, and are in danger of being marginalized or excluded. Her role, therefore, was more than the immediate one of providing and helping to find books and information. She was a gatekeeper who could affect the country's future in a critical way, by giving the children what they could not, would not, or might not get from schools and families. She could help children become thinking, literate people who could listen, who could 'take notes' in college and therefore succeed, who knew how to use the books and reference materials that would lead them to empowering ideas. She is positioned at a point where she can affect the 'downward turn' of the country, possibly contribute to its reversal. (It's alarmingly easy to become carried away as I describe her role. There's something contagious about her language.) If democracy is about inclusion of the disenfranchised, the library seems to be a pivotal place where that can be achieved. Jamal's membership card is available to all, if they only reach out for it.

In the examples we have given thus far, researchers have stated themes and/ or metathemes in sentence form. A study may have been arranged so that data are presented in a straightforward narrative section or in any one or combination of such forms as are set forth in Chapter 3 of this volume. Thematic discussions may then follow at the end of each of these sections or chapters or may appear in a separate section or chapter. We have provided examples of this arrangement in the work of Judith Evans and Belén Matías. It is not unusual for a lift from theme to metatheme to occur near the end of the work, often in a final section or chapter, followed by the relevant discussion, as we exemplified in the work of Barbara Aventuro. Themes are also stated more implicitly in many studies, and may be woven throughout or referred to intermittently. For example, in *Women in Academe* by Nadya Aisenberg and Mona Harrington (1988), the authors describe a process of analysis that leads to the organization of 'recurrent patterns into larger clusters of related issues which form the basis for thematic chapters':

> At the end of the interview process, we were confronted with approximately 1,500 pages of transcription. We were determined to analyze it in its own terms, not to impose on it conceptions derived from the growing body of theory and observation concerning women's experience. Thus we went through a long process of naming — literally, in the margins of transcripts — the various kinds of episodes and comments in each interview, and then put together — again literally in piles of clippings — all recurrences of the same named experience. Then we organized the recurrent patterns into larger clusters of related issues which form basis for thematic chapters in which we interpret and explain the material in terms of our own analysis. That, after this deep immersion in the material, we found patterns corresponding in many instances to those proposed by other scholars increases our conviction that the experiences we document are widely shared. (p. ix)

The thematic chapters of which these authors speak are given quite brief titles: The Old Norms, Transformations, Rules of the Game, and so forth. Because of their brevity, some do not in themselves seem to us to carry the weight of thematic meaning. However, the theme is set very clearly early on in each of the chapters, although not always in the same way. For example, the first chapter, 'Norms,' opens with this sentence: 'Women are now laying claim to significant and satisfying work in the professions as a normal part of their lives and laying claim also to the authority, prestige, power, and salary that professional work commands.' The word 'now,' third in the sentence, implies that this was not always the case and that the norms are changing. In the third chapter, 'The Rules of the Game,' the theme is implied in an opening epigram, which is taken from *Alice in Wonderland*: 'She never knew whether it was her turn or not, the game was in such confusion.' In spite of the fact, then, that the themes are not treated uniformly throughout, in reading this book, we were never at a loss to identify them. Some members of this writing team (although not all) would probably have opted for more uniformity of presentation in their own writing. But we would all like to re-emphasize that there are many ways in which themes may be presented, some of them implicit, and that we favor greater diversity in qualitative research writing — and in academic writing in general. For further thoughts on this topic, please refer back to Chapter 3 in this book where Patti Lather eschews the direct presentation of themes and works in other ways to send her message of theme.

A few other thoughts on metaphor and themes. Throughout this book you will by now have read many passages in which the metaphor implies the theme. Please look again at Chapter 2, where Rosemarie Lewandowski describes her work with the metaphor of education as a ladder. Surely that expressed a powerful meta-theme statement for the teacher/participant. Such metaphors can be used in a variety of ways. For instance, some years ago Margaret and Margot worked together on an article that they titled 'Halls of Mirrors: The Introduction of the Reflective Mode' (Anzul and Ely, 1988). To us, the theme statement is in the title, and does not require a sentence stating that 'The introduction of the reflective mode into a classroom is like a hall of mirrors, in which . . .'

In the final discussion of his study of black males in a predominantly white college, Phillip Johnson (1995) chose not to employ metathematic statements. Nevertheless, this passage developed around a metaphor that emerged from his analysis of data and carries a powerful metathematic message:

> Inside the university where a positive sense of blackness was viewed as having no place, the men often felt that they were treated in ways that denied their humanity. The conditions under which the students tried to obtain a college degree were seen by them as warlike. Allen tried to form 'strategic' relationships with people who could help him make his way through school. He also tried to 'advance' the Black agenda and 'struggled' against the environment. Both Ron and Allen spoke of 'challenging' their professors and Ron felt that he was preparing for a 'war' with the 'enemy.' Elijah wondered how he made it through school because he and his friends had 'lost' so many Black classmates along the way. Ultimately Allen passed the baton to 'new soldiers' who had to carry on the fight. (pp. 269–70)

Tesch's tenth statement of the characteristics of qualitative analysis that we listed early in this chapter indicates that the results of the analysis be expressed by synthesis. Themes and metathemes provide examples of synthesis at work, composed as they are from the fruits of extensive coding and categorizing. They are far from the only example. All of the creative forms are synthesis as well. We mention this here to highlight the activity of synthesis, which takes many elements and combines them in new ways. We are not trying to press lifts in levels of thinking or abstraction for their own sake. It is part of our work as qualitative researchers to synthesize when we can, to make what lifts we can, to see our data against a larger whole.

Lifting and Extending Thinking

To lift levels of meaning, or, as we prefer, to deepen them, and to extend insights — these are all directional terms, and they are almost, although not entirely, synonyms for one another. They all imply looking beyond wherever we are now in our perspectives on our data for what more is to be seen and to be said. Lofland and Lofland (1984) point us in a direction also when they argue that one of the results of the qualitative process is that of the 'transcendent view.' When we think of trying to attain such a view, we imagine the researcher climbing a mountain. The higher one climbs, the more extensive the view, until at the very top it is possible to look in a great many directions. We've attained the vision to make those comparisons that lie at the heart of qualitative analysis. In addition, if we look, we see scenes set in a wider context. Even these contexts broaden, the viewer sees more of how what happens in the larger world impinges on the smaller world, or vice versa. The viewer also sees what elements are common to all that can be seen, or are specific to the view in one direction, or specific to only one person. Among the tasks of qualitative researchers are to lift the level of the interpretation, to set it in a wider context, and to see meanings from as many points of view as are relevant to the scene and the study.

Lifting levels of thinking or interpretation is a journey from the more specific to the more general. One route in which this is accomplished is by grouping codes into categories, then distilling meanings into the generalizations of thematic statements and then moving to the broader abstractions of metathemes. We have to ask the indulgence of you as our readers at this point. One of the difficulties in writing this book was deciding what to place where, because the processes of qualitative research are all so intertwined. For the purposes of these chapters, when we talk about levels of interpretation we are implying interpretation in the light of one or another theoretical framework. Theory is the topic of the next chapter, and there we also talk about levels of theory. We can only suggest that you read these two chapters in tandem, and see how each plays off the other.

Here we find it helpful to suggest Spradley's work on domain analysis as a bridge into our discussion of approaches to interpretation in the next chapter. In the following scheme we see a progression of statements from the most general to the most particular. The interpretive statements that he provides as examples are clearly taken from sociological theory. We list below Spradley's interpretive levels and follow each, as he does, with an example of a statement at that level of generality taken from *The Cocktail Waitress* (Spradley and Mann, 1975):

Level One: Universal Statements
Every society takes the biological differences between male and female to create a special kind of reality: feminine and masculine identities. (p. 145)

Level Two: Cross-Cultural Descriptive Statements
When anthropologists began studying small, non-Western societies they found that people participated in a single web of life . . . [W]hen we turn to complex societies such as our own, the number of cultural perspectives for any situation increases radically. (pp. 8–9)

Level Three: General Statements about a Society or Cultural Group
[The role of cocktail waitresses] in bars tends to be an extension of their role at home — serving the needs of men. (p. 145)

Level Four: General Statements about a Specific Cultural Scene
. . . Brady's Bar is a place where men can come to play out exaggerated masculine roles. (p. 131)

Level Five: Specific Statements about a Cultural Domain
One frequent way that men ask for a drink is not to ask for a drink at all . . . they ask instead for the waitress. (p. 132)

Level Six: Specific Incident Statement
She steps up to the table and asks, 'Are you ready to order now?' One of the males grabs her by the wrist and jerks her towards him. 'I already know what I want! I'll take you . . .' (p. 132)

In the light of our preceding discussion of themes and metathemes, the interpretive concepts from levels one through five could be expressed as thematic statements and, in fact, carry the weight of themes or metathemes whether or not overtly identified as such. In the mesh of actual research writing, statements such as those above, particularly at Spradley's first three levels, are usually interwoven with references to other theoretical work and discussed in the light of extant research. Readers are referred to the opening chapter of *The Cocktail Waitress*, 'Bars, Women, and Culture,' to see how Spradley and Mann (1975) have employed related literature in their introduction to the general concept that 'The cultural rules and rituals of bar life reaffirm the definitions and status attached to masculinity and femininity' (p. 3). A scheme such as Spradley's, organized by levels of generality, offers one way of structuring for oneself the results of analysis — the major categories, themes, metathemes, issues — so that they may be discussed in the light of one's interpretive frameworks.

We can trace how Spradley and Mann actually wove their analysis through the narrative:

It was sometimes stifling for Holly to be always taking orders from men, and, as she said, 'to always be the gracious listener to male proclamations about what life was really like, to always be looked at but never listened to.' But Holly learned to manage her conflicting feelings and one night, several months after she started work, she came to feel more a part of the Brady family. It started when she accidentally spilled a drink on the bouncer — he had playfully grabbed her wrists as she was cleaning up a table. He started chasing her; it was just after closing time. She ran to the kitchen to escape, but to no avail. He caught her and turned the faucet on her from the sink. Struggling to get free, Holly ran into the bar, her clothes dripping wet. The bartenders and regulars who usually stayed after closing were all there, and the whole place suddenly became a theater, and Holly felt like she was playing the leading role. The lights were up and the men at the bar added their shouts of encouragement to the bouncer, drowning out her screams of protest. 'Thatta boy, Larry. Go for it!' 'Hey, Larry, what were you doing in the kitchen?' 'C'mon. More. More.' It was as if she was running from all the men at the same time — trying to get away but trying to get caught. That's the way girls were supposed to be at Brady's. As the game ended and Holly went to the bar for a drink, she felt a simultaneous sense of victory and defeat. 'It was funny and I had to laugh. After that I loosened up a bit and found that working could be fun.' It was like she had passed through some initiation rite, and that was the beginning of a long list of similar escapades.

This passage is, throughout, a piece of Level Six writing, a very specific description, rich in detail, about an episode in Brady's Bar. The writers have lifted to a Level Five abstraction — a generalization about the specific setting — with the statement 'That's the way girls were supposed to be at Brady's' seemingly just dropped into the descriptive passage. The comparison of Holly's episode to an initiation rite in the final sentence provides a Level Two, cross-cultural reference. On the next page is another Level Two statement: 'Like others who live in complex societies . . . Holly had often experienced the transition from one social group to another.' These analytic statements provide the base for later interpretive discussion.

In order to lift levels of thinking, one must extend one's thinking as well. At the heart of qualitative work is understanding the meanings of others. We find, however, that it is easy for us and for our colleagues to become so involved with some actors in a setting that we become oblivious to the viewpoints of others. Barbara Miller presents a provocative example. Hers was the study of Mrs Fowler's kindergarten class. When we left Barbara, she had decided to focus on the marginalized students, Walter and Morris. She began to work further with this, to become aware of the metaphors that Mrs Fowler used when referring to her students, those who 'stood out,' those like Walter and Morris who did not. What was life like for those who did not stand out. At about this time, however, colleagues began to question Barbara's focus on the students who did not stand out to the exclusion of the other students. What was there in the wider school context, in Mrs Fowler's experiences, that would help account for what Barbara was observing? And how did Mrs Fowler herself look on what she was doing? These were questions that spurred Barbara to climb a little higher up the mountain of the transcendent view, to look at the same setting from a variety of perspectives, to take in more of the background landscape.

Similar experiences were documented by Barbara Ball and Rosemarie Lewandowski in analytic memos. We invite you to look back to their stories told in

Chapter 2. Notice how Rosemarie tries out her interpretations of life in Mrs Cato's classroom in vignette and layered story. Notice also how Mrs Cato's approval, her sense that Rosemarie had indeed captured the essence of the classroom and of herself as teacher, opened up the relationship to a freer conversation. Out of that session came Rosemarie's metatheme: 'Mrs. Cato sees first grade as a step on the ladder of education,' and the touching extended metaphoric vignette in which Mrs Cato extends a hand to help others up, but somehow does not see, or perhaps is not able to see that she is not reaching Joey.

As we seek to extend insight we may see ironies. Irony results from situations in which what happens is not what is intended, or in which the observer can see discontinuities in action of which the actors are unaware. If we are at the top of a mountain, we can see long stretches of road curving around it. We can see two cars coming from opposite directions that may well crash, although the drivers of the cars are unaware of each other's existence. If we are distanced as we look at the actions in a story, we often know things that people in the story do not know, are let in on thoughts and motives and experiences that seem to be innately ironic. Our qualitative narratives can highlight such ironies. See Carole Di Tosti's play in Chapter 3.

Readers who are interested in exploring the potential of irony in their writing are referred to the last chapter in Atkinson's (1990) *The Ethnographic Imagination*: 'Difference, Distance, and Irony.' Drawing on the work of R. H. Brown (1977), Atkinson sees the tension between the researcher as once-outsider-but-now-insider and the reader as outsider-in-need-of-enlightenment as one source of irony inherent in qualitative work:

> The authority of the text rests on the premise that a stranger has become intimate with the culture in question . . . The reader is constructed as 'outsider' . . . He or she may be expected to embrace naive prejudices and presuppositions. By contrast, the ethnographer can be taken to have transcended the shallow understandings of the outsider, in favor of more complex and hence more authentic versions of social reality. (1990, p. 163)

Atkinson explores how this tension heightens the effect of the findings in the work of a number of sociologists. In many of the accounts we have included in this book tension becomes explicit within consciousness of the researcher who contrasts his or her former naivete with the increased insights gained through the first weeks or months in the field. Sometimes ironies in the data are pointed out by the researcher. Other times they become apparent without such a road map, perhaps via the forms, the juxtapositions, the reporting.

There is irony in the picture of Mrs Cato on the ladder completely beyond the reach of Joey because we think that this does not have to be. There is irony for us in the story of Holly in Brady's Bar. As fellow working women, we want her to be relaxed and happy there. As feminists, we watch her find it necessary to abandon her womanly independence, her dislike of 'always taking orders from men . . . always being looked at but never listened to.' And there is surely irony in Phillip Johnson's metaphor of warfare in his synthesis of that aspect of the experience of his black male college students who came to the university for an education and found instead a battleground. We do not see ironies drawn out as fully as we would like in most qualitative research writing. Indeed often contradictions and ironies get short shrift. For researchers in the human service professions, a greater attention to the ironies in those contexts seems to us essential because of their power to highlight inconsistencies, disparate visions, and possible solutions.

The results of our work in analytic modes contain in themselves elements of interpretation and also give us the materials we need for extended, more specifically interpretive activities. These are discussed next. We see the thinking that composes themes and metathemes as the link to Chapter 5 that follows.

Chapter 5

Working in Interpretive Modes

In the social sciences there is only interpretation. (Norman K. Denzin, 1989, p. 500)

Writing theory is damnably hard. (Louise Wetherbee Phelps, 1988, p. xi)

Much attention has been devoted in the literature to the earlier stages of a research project — to negotiating entree, to relating with participants, to gathering 'thick description,' and to designing various approaches to data analysis; less attention has been devoted to the interpretive processes of qualitative research. When, however, James L. Peacock set out to explain what it is that anthropologists 'do' in his monograph *The Anthropological Lens* (1986), he highlighted the interpretive aspect:

> Ethnography is an interpretive endeavor, and the most treasured ethnographic interpretations provide not only substantive information but perspectives on that information. It is not the particular factual 'findings' of a gifted ethnographer . . . that are significant . . . What is significant is the vision of someone's (the native's) existence interpreted through the sensibilities of someone else (the ethnographer) in order to inform and enrich the understanding of a third party (the reader or listener). (pp. 99–100)

In this chapter we focus on how the writing reveals an interpretation as filtered through your own sensibilities and theoretical perspectives.

As interpreters we could be likened to filters through which we sift data in the process of making meaning. This is how Ori Caroleo described working in interpretive modes as he crafted the final chapters of his dissertation:

> I found the process of writing to be something like pouring the data/themes through a series of strainers, where each strainer has smaller holes. The result of this straining process is a more meaningful, rich-tasting presentation of the data.

We see filtering around us all the time. An interpreter may translate the words of one head of state for another. The United Nations is a vast network of interpretive systems — language to language and culture to culture. Persons in mediating positions, marriage counselors, for example, exert their expertise to help each participant understand the often unexpressed thoughts and feelings of the other. Mothers explain with pride what their toddlers 'really mean' by their babbling. Margaret recalls that when her two sons, now grown, were very young, the older would interpret the wishes of his 2-year-old brother and conclude the message with the sage observation that 'he knows more than he is saying.' So do we all.

Working in interpretive modes helps us shape meaning to express how we 'know more than we are saying.'

Elsewhere in this volume we will compare the researcher to a musician playing on the Stradivarius of self. Musicians interpret the music of another person — the composer — to an audience. Qualitative researchers are devoted to the task of communicating what they understand to be the meanings of the participants to an audience of readers. We have only to think about our experiences of concert halls or discos, jazz festivals or supper clubs, to realize how infinitely varied interpretations can be, how subtly different from one another. And while Bach is still Bach, Gershwin still Gershwin, in the hands of a gifted performer the essence of the original shines through together with the unique 'take' of the individual interpreter. That is why so many of us are avid fans of one particular interpreter of, let us say, a particular symphony.

Even so in research writing. 'Nothing speaks for itself,' Norman Denzin (1989) reminds us: 'Confronted with a mountain of impressions, documents, and field-notes, the qualitative researcher faces the difficult and challenging task of making sense of what has been learned through the art of interpretation' (p. 500). Denzin and Lincoln (1994) describe qualitative research as 'endlessly creative and interpretive' (p. 14) in their account of steps toward the construction of the finished document. For them, first there is the field text, consisting of fieldnotes and other documents that are already informal interpretations from the field. The writer next moves to a 'research text' comprised of 'notes and preliminary interpretations based on the field text.' We understand this to be the coded fieldnotes along with those notes and memos the researcher has written in the attempt to 'make sense of what is learned.' Certainly the point of working with the many rhetorical forms and the presentations of findings through such devices as thematic statements, tables, or displays is an attempt to give form to what the researcher perceives are important meanings. To the writer, such research texts may indeed seem to have been laboriously compiled 'bird by bird,' to borrow the words from Anne Lamott (1994) which we have quoted elsewhere (see p. 54).

We have focused in previous chapters on the elements and rhetorical devices that are used to compose research texts. The next step is to recreate 'a working interpretive document' — a draft that may be given mentors or colleagues for feedback. Lamott sheds light on this process as well. 'Writing a first draft is very much like watching a Polaroid develop. You can't — and, in fact, you are not supposed to — know exactly what the picture is going to look like until it has finished developing' (p. 39). With the working text in hand, the researcher can begin getting a sense of the whole — the overall story — that has been constructed. This working document, through the continuous process of revision may finally lead to a public text (Denzin and Lincoln, 1994, p. 15).

Although the entire process is broadly interpretive, there comes a time, usually in the drafting of the working text, when a researcher discusses how 'the literature in the field' and other sources of information led to understanding. Associated with the framing of the study through these contexts also includes an interpretive framework of theoretical perspectives as well as the inevitable personal theorizing

— stances, assumptions, opinions. The results may point toward developing new ways of understanding ideas or to an extension or modification of existing theory. The language of theory, in fact, often stands like parentheses at either end of academic research reports: a theoretical framework is proposed at the beginning and a theoretical discussion synthesizes findings and their significance at the end. An understanding of theory and the uses of 'theory talk' (Daniell, 1994) are important to qualitative research writing and thus are central to this chapter.

We invite you to become, along with us, more self-conscious about theory. The first and most basic reason is that we see the theoretical positions we hold, either deliberately or unconsciously, as shaping everything else that we do. In addition, 'theory talk' is a discourse we've become accustomed to in our academi and professional lives. We open this chapter with a discussion of what we mean by theory and look at how various approaches to theoretical generality or abstractness have been conceived. In the second section we consider the theoretical frameworks and the research questions that are derived from them and that are usually incorporated in some way into research writing. Of particular concern is that these sections be structured in a sufficiently open fashion to support the emergent design that is characteristic of qualitative research. In the third and fourth sections, in some ways the heart of this chapter, we describe how several researchers have woven interpretive discussions into their findings and into the implications for professional practice or social action that the findings imply.

We realize that the understanding and use of theory evolve throughout the course of a researcher's life. We hold that part of the writing task is making our stances and theoretical positions, both informal and formal, clear to readers. In the fifth section, 'Becoming Conscious of Theory,' we look at occasions and ways in which we and others have become more aware of theory and what this has meant in our academic and professional lives. We then consider, in the sixth section, how eventually we, and we think many of our colleagues, have found ourselves questioning or arguing against the theories we first received as students; those theories that are prevalent in our professional literature or in our workplaces, the latent and sometimes unrecognized theories that drive our actions. And finally, we will think about how theoretical lenses may change over time, both for individuals and throughout a given research community.

What We Mean by Theory (And Why It Is Useful to Think about It)

We hear many meanings of theory every day in our work:

'I have a theory about that.'

'My advisor told me it's not theoretical enough.'

'It's just a rehash of theories.'

'He's so theoretical — he's always floating around up in the air somewhere, never down to earth.'

'That's her pet theory.'

'What we need is ways to translate the theory into practice.'

There are also the many synonymous expressions . . .

'What's your conceptual framework?'

'Well, if you look at it from that perspective . . .'

'You really haven't developed your theoretical perspective adequately.'

'Your work is too thin conceptually.'

Many of us have heard phrases like these repeated often, and if you are like we were in graduate school, probably your response would be 'Huh?' The puzzled response reflects a lack of awareness of the intellectual processes behind the work as the authors of *Women's Ways of Knowing* point out:

> We do not think of the ordinary person as preoccupied with such difficult and profound questions as: What is truth? What is authority? To whom do I listen? What counts for me as evidence? How do I know what I know? Yet to ask ourselves these questions and to reflect on our answers is more than an intellectual exercise, for our basic assumptions about the nature of truth and reality and the origins of knowledge shape the way we see the world and ourselves as participants in it. They affect our definitions of ourselves, the way we interact with others, our public and private personae, our sense of control over life events, our views of teaching and learning, and our conceptions of morality. (Belenky *et al.*, 1986, p. 3)

To us, this passage highlights a reality of which we only gradually become aware: Our lives are guided by the countless concepts and assumptions, the theories-of-the-world, that we have developed, whether consciously or unconsciously, throughout our years. As part of this personal theory-making, we have also developed a mesh of beliefs and stances about important issues. That may be more or less well developed and conscious. Woven in with these more personal positions are the professional and academic theories that we have acquired, or at least verbalized, possibly at a more conscious level than those that guide our personal lives, because talking in terms of theory is what we've learned to do in our professional and academic lives. This complex of concepts, assumptions, biases, attitudes, stances, and formal theories provides the material for the interpretive frameworks through which we make sense of the world, carry out our personal, civic, and professional lives, and conduct research.

The word 'theory' embraces a broad spectrum of meanings. On the one hand, it is used popularly, and sometimes lightly, as a synonym for opinion: 'I have a theory about that' often prefaces an explanation of some everyday phenomenon or event. On the other hand, 'theory' is also used to mean a formal and carefully articulated system of thought designed to explain universal principles, as do the phrases 'Marxist theory' or 'Freudian theory.'

Theorizing considered in a broad sense is basic to the way people make sense of the world. The making and using of theories is seen by Frank Smith (1994) as the basis of human knowledge. Smith refers to growth in comprehension, from its earliest stages onward, as the development of 'theories of the world in the head.'

He views learning as the construction of increasingly complex sets of such schemata. We find this a refreshing reminder of the power we have to theorize. Theory has manifestations in everyday life — in the assumptions, biases, and stances that are part of all our activities. Wolcott (1992) observed that:

> ... most people do not think in terms of grand design or regard themselves as theory builders ... Personally, however, I am of the view that every human being is a profound theory builder, so long as that activity is defined to include the myriad 'little theories' necessary for each of us to negotiate our way through everyday life. (pp. 7–8)

Researchers often distinguish the popular use of the word 'theory' from its technical meaning. Flinders and Mills (1993) note that theory is used popularly to mean 'any general set of ideas that guide action. This usage encompasses beliefs ranging from one's personal philosophy and intuitive hunches to implicit assumptions, guesses, and suspicions about the everyday world in which we live' (p. xii).

The definitions for theory proposed by the *Random House Dictionary of the English Language* (1987) encompass both the popular and the technical meanings:

> [1] a coherent group of general propositions used as principles of explanation for a class of phenomena;
> [2] a proposed explanation whose status is still conjectural in contrast to well-established propositions that are regarded as reporting matters of fact;
> [3] the branch of a science or art that deals with its principles or methods as distinguished from its practice: music theory;
> [4] a particular conception or view of something to be done or the method of doing it;
> [5] Greek *theoria*, a viewing, contemplating.

The more popular uses of the term seem to us inherent to the fourth and fifth definitions: theory as 'a particular conception or view of something' or 'a viewing, contemplating.' The first definition is similar to those we find in the literature. Here, for example, is the definition provided by Flinders and Mills (1993): 'Theory can signify a set of formal propositions or axioms that explain how some part of the world operates. These theories are explicit, and often associated with an individual's name (e.g., Kohlberg's theory of moral development, Herzberg's motivation hygiene theory, or Festinger's theory of cognitive dissonance)' (p. xii). Elsewhere in the same volume, Mills (1993) presented a definition for theory that we find particularly compatible with the qualitative view: 'an analytical and interpretive framework that helps the researcher make sense of "what is going on" in the social setting being studied' (p. 103). All of these definitions contain more than a little of 'what is it for?' Elliot Eisner (1993) carries this line of thought a step further: 'Theory is supposed to make coherent what otherwise appears as disparate and disconnected individual events. Theory is the means through which we learn lessons that can apply to situations we have yet to encounter' (p. viii).

It is in the extension of the 'what is it for?' aspect of theory that differences become apparent between those in the qualitative community who are closer to the positivist tradition and those closer to the postmodern, constructivist, and interpretive positions. In telling how he came to his own stance on theory in the context of his research projects, the British educational researcher Stephen Ball (1991) distinguished between the approach to theory that 'stresses explanation and prediction' and the one that 'highlights understanding and insight' (p. 103). Both Ball and Thomas Schwandt (1993) see this debate over the nature and purpose of theory as actually a debate over the nature and purpose of the social sciences. Adherents of the first position are, according to Ball, exemplified by Martyn Hammersley who suggests that:

> ... there are four elements to theoretical development in ethnographic work.
>
> 1   the addition of new concepts and relations;
> 2   the clarification of concepts and relations;
> 3   the development of testing and measures;
> 4   hypothesis testing.
>
> Hammersley sees these as stages in a progressive hierarchy of worth with (4) as the ultimate goal. (Ball, 1991, p. 188)

Ball argues against this position. He questions 'whether social life can only be or can be best known in terms of "if . . . then," predictable relations. Is it really useful to reduce all social life to this form?' Ball himself prefers to work in the interpretive mode of 'understanding and insight,' reasoning that in his work 'complexity and interrelatedness rather than simplicity are the endpoints' (p. 189).

To us, the positions of Ball and Hammersley represent opposite points along a continuum. We see our own positions as coming closer to the one Ball has adopted for himself — that is, a definition of theory as a means to understanding and insight. Seen in this way, theorizing functions as 'a self-conscious replication of the processes of knowing and making sense which are common to all human actors' (Ball, 1991, p. 189). This approach, which also seems most consistent with the etymological root of the word theory as a 'viewing' or 'contemplating,' engenders a metaphor. Our theories provide us with sets of eyeglasses through which we look at the world. Just as with our physical eyeglasses, our implicit theories may bring into focus, sharpen, and angle for us our understanding of what might otherwise be a blurred stream of perception. It is thus that we are able to read a novel, to evaluate a situation, to transact with 'the field' and construct our fieldnotes, as we considered in Chapter 2. Our theories have probably been a powerful force for us in structuring our knowledge of our discipline or profession and may well have guided us in our choice of a focus for research. These same theoretical lenses can also sometimes hamper us, can cut off angles of vision, peripheral or otherwise. We can select sets of lenses that will help us to see up close or at a distance, different sets for different purposes.

Many contemporary qualitative researchers see the multiplicity of approaches to theory, and to other aspects of qualitative research that we have touched on throughout this book, as a distinguishing feature of the contemporary scene (e.g., Denzin and Lincoln, 1994; Richardson, 1994; Vidich and Lyman, 1994). In a survey of developments within the field of qualitative research throughout this century,

Denzin and Lincoln (1994) trace five 'moments' of historical time in the twentieth century. Each of these moments is identifiable by certain distinguishing intellectual trends. The moments have succeeded one another, as the underlying attitudes toward research, and thus toward the uses of theory in research, have shifted from positivist approaches to the postpositive to the postmodern. At this very writing, we have it on good faith that a 'sixth moment' is about to be described. Laurel Richardson (1994) observes that 'the core of postmodernism is the *doubt* that any method or theory, discourse or genre, tradition or novelty, has a universal and general claim as the "right" or the privileged form of authoritative knowledge' (p. 517, author's italics). One result for researchers working in a postmodern paradigm, as Vidich and Lyman (1994) point out, is that:

> ... the number of possible theoretical perspectives from which the world, or any part of it, may be viewed sociologically is conditioned only by the number of scientific worldviews ... At the time of this writing, a new outlook on epistemology has come to the fore. It disprivileges all received discourses and makes discourse itself a topic of the sociology of knowledge. (p. 25)

Atkinson (1992) has referred to a 'flux of contemporary ideas' that lead to 'a radical questioning of the certainty and authority of the scholarly text; a rejection of the search for 'truth' and reason as absolutes; a denial of the intellectual and moral distance between the academic and his or her human 'subjects'; a suspicion of the 'big' narratives of totalizing theory ...' (p. 38). From this postmodern perspective, theory itself, and academic texts in general, are now considered 'disprivileged' by many.

Denzin and Lincoln (1994) point out that 'each of the earlier historical moments is still operating in the present, either as legacy or as a set of practices that researchers still follow or argue against' (p. 11). Clearly this poses challenges for contemporary researchers. Harry Wolcott (1992) has advocated that each researcher adopt a posture along the continuum of possible qualitative perspectives. Where one falls along this continuum — from more traditional to more postmodern — needs explicit statement in any written reports.

In this time of shifting and emerging paradigms, certain writers have also suggested that researchers should feel free to combine features of the quantitative and qualitative paradigms or to adopt desired features from each at will. Denzin and Lincoln (1994) hold, and in their earlier writings Lincoln and Guba (1985; Guba, 1990) have argued forcibly, that there is a basic incompatibility between these research paradigms because of their conflicting philosophical positions or worldviews. That is our position as well. We believe that a researcher's clarification of his or her posture or postures within a research paradigm works to reveal epistemological assumptions. This does not necessarily preclude adopting a method or technique from another paradigm to provide an additional facet. In this book, we have already provided examples of some useful combinations of techniques such as the qualitative use of microanalytic techniques and displays of results, including statistical data, in table form. On the other hand, a researcher engaged in survey research may decide to include open-ended questions as an element of the survey and analyze the answers for themes. However, in this case and others that are similar, the researcher owes readers a sound rationale for such choices as well as a comparative discussion of the underlying assumptions of each technique and set of results. Without such, we have seen many combinations of techniques misused and misunderstood.

Each researcher also comes to the task within a specific academic discipline replete with its own theoretical traditions and interpretive approaches. A researcher must indeed work as a *bricoleur*, fashioning the interpretive framework that will best suit the needs of the study at hand. This means perhaps making selections from a vast storehouse of existing theory, perhaps devising a new theory of one's own, and relating theory to theory in a manner that best helps to interpret one's findings among the various perspectives that compose for us circles within circles of theory.

'Circles Within Circles' of Theory

Although researchers refer widely to 'levels' of theory, or levels of abstraction in theorizing, there is little uniformity in the ways these levels are designated. In the Introduction to their *Handbook of Qualitative Research* Denzin and Lincoln (1994), distinguish between theories as overarching philosophical paradigms and theories of somewhat more limited scope that provide interpretive perspectives within and among various disciplines or cultural systems (p. 2). We realize that the terms paradigm and theory are often used interchangeably. In this book, for the sake of clarity, we follow the usage that this distinction by Denzin and Lincoln suggests and adopt the term paradigm in its broader and more overarching sense. We speak of the qualitative paradigm in contrast to the quantitative or positivist paradigm because these paradigms rest squarely on clearly identifiable 'overarching philosophical systems denoting particular ontologies, epistemologies, and methodologies' (p. 2): ways of being, ways of knowing, ways of doing.

Within the qualitative paradigm, Denzin and Lincoln (1994) also refer to lesser but still overarching paradigms. For these authors, 'four major interpretive paradigms structure qualitative research: positivist and postpositivist, constructivist-interpretive, critical (Marxist, emancipatory), and feminist-poststructural' (p. 13). Working within the definitions of Denzin and Lincoln, these can also be considered 'paradigms' as they (and we) are using that term because each is a 'net that contains the researcher's epistemological, ontological, and methodological premises' (p. 13). A researcher may define herself, for example, as 'guided by feminist epistemology and methodology' (Rogers, 1993, p. 267). However, we also hear, and use, the term 'theory' to define systems of thought, as in 'Marxist theory' or 'feminist theory.' We think it is only fair to add that probably most people in society at large, as distinct from qualitative researchers, consider these theories as systems of thought unto themselves rather than as perspectives within the qualitative community. In other words, the distinctions made between paradigms within the qualitative community do not always appear to be in accord with usage we have read and heard in other contexts.

At the level below that of paradigms, Denzin and Lincoln use the term 'perspectives;' as in their statement that 'perspectives, in contrast [to paradigms], are less well developed systems, and can be more easily moved between' (1994, p. 2). It seems to us that here these authors are referring to what other authors refer to as 'theory,' or more precisely 'grand theory,' to designate the stratum next to paradigm. It is our own opinion that perhaps the essential difference between paradigms and the next level of theories or perspectives has more to do with how universal they are than with the extent to which they are 'well-developed.'

All in all, we have not found much uniformity of either definition or terminology in qualitative literature. Conceding that 'precise definitions of theory are hard to come by,' Flinders and Mills (1993, p. xii) also suggest that the terms 'formal explanatory propositions,' or 'concepts,' can be useful 'to accommodate researchers who are uncertain as to whether their hunches and ideas qualify as formal 'theory' (p. xiii). In addition, in our readings we have come across the apparently synonymous terms — 'theoretical constructs' and 'theoretical concepts' — that appear to be used in place of 'theory,' and we have thus at times used these terms in the same way ourselves.

In contrast to the metaphor for paradigm offered by Denzin and Lincoln as an 'overarching' system, the sociologist Robert Merton (1967) chose a different metaphor when he spoke of 'grand theory,' 'theory of the middle range,' and 'minor working hypotheses' (pp. 5–6): 'The paradigm is the foundation upon which the house of interpretations is built.' A grand theory consistent with a given paradigm might be seen as 'a new story' that can be 'built directly upon this foundation.' Merton goes on to say that

> . . . each new story that *can* be built upon the original foundation strengthens our confidence in its substantial quality . . . A paradigm worthy of great confidence will in due course support an interpretative structure of skyscraper dimensions, with each successive story testifying to the well-laid quality of the original foundation. (1967, p. 71)

One way of looking at the degrees of generality or abstractness of theoretical statements is suggested by Spradley's model for domain analysis which we introduced on p. 219 of the previous chapter. Spradley and other researchers speak in terms of 'levels' of theories; Merton speaks in terms of stories built upon a paradigmatic foundation. We are somewhat uncomfortable with these ways of viewing theory because we do not subscribe to the implicit valuing of the more general over the more specific. The theory is not more important than the ground. We do not advocate introduction of discussions of *levels* of theory into the research writing itself unless it appears to serve some essential purpose. We see this rather as a type of thinking that sometimes helps us to get our bearings on where we are in the world of academic theory talk. Such thinking can, in turn, help in the organization of a review of literature or similar piece of writing. One approach to such organization might be to discuss from the more general to the more specific theoretical level; another type of organization might be a historical development of theoretical thought in a particular field. We, the writing team, agree that a theoretical rationale or review of literature that appears to be little more than a hodgepodge based on the researcher's assorted readings doesn't inform the readers of theory's purpose in the research.

In our search for a less hierarchical image, we prefer to see clusters of theories as arranged in concentric circles rather than on levels — illustrating, explaining, synthesizing, hypothesizing, speculating — all are part of the circles. A different metaphor, still with overtones of concentric circles, and one we find very appealing, is offered by Annie G. Rogers (1993) in a study of 'Voice, Play, and the Practice of Ordinary Courage in Girls' and Women's Lives.' Here is how she introduces her theoretical framework:

> The particular practices of research I rely on throughout this article are drawn from an overlapping theoretical model much like Russian nesting dolls . . . At the broadest level, I am guided by feminist epistemology and methodology; then, nested in that framework is the voice-centered, relational approach to research developed by the Harvard Project on Women's Psychology and Girls' Development; nested in that approach is the subjective model of writing for social scientists outlined by the sociologist Susan Krieger (1991); and, finally, nested within that subjective model is the last 'doll,' the philosophical poetics of Gaston Bachelard (1958/1969). (Rogers, 1993, p. 267)

We do not know how Rogers worked. It seems to us, however, that perhaps only at the end of a project could a researcher be sure of the final shape the nesting and clustering would take — even though one begins with certain major theoretical guides. The assembling and arrangement of Rogers' cluster of nested theories illustrates well the eclectic and pragmatic nature of qualitative research characteristic of the 'researcher-as-*bricoleur* theorist' who 'works within competing and overlapping perspectives':

> The product of the *bricoleur*'s labor is a bricolage, a complex, dense, reflexive, collagelike creation that represents the researcher's images, understandings, and interpretations of the world or phenomenon under analysis. (Denzin and Lincoln, 1994, pp. 2–3)

The way theories are layered or nested is contingent on the context. For example, the transactional theory of literature falls within the general tradition of reader-response theory for those whose profession involves the teaching of literature. However, within the tradition of philosophy, the transactional theory of literature is one manifestation of transactional theory that was proposed as a way of knowing by John Dewey and Arthur F. Bentley. Certainly for many researchers within the human service professions, interpretive frameworks are very much a *bricolage* with the various components borrowed and adapted as fits the needs of a particular research project.

Designing an Open Interpretive Framework

Theory is usually addressed explicitly in the writing of a research document in both a 'theoretical rationale' or 'review of related literature,' and in a 'discussion of findings' that generally appears at or near the end of the report. This discussion may also include recommendations for professional practice or for social change. Researchers attempting to shape the written expression of theoretical perspectives work through different formulations of these sections for different publication purposes. We usually first learn to develop these elements in clearly marked sections in the highly structured thesis or dissertation format characteristic of most graduate schools. In less tradition-bound situations, as well as in some articles and books, theoretical elements may be less conspicuous, may be handled more briefly or more informally, or may be woven in a more organic way into the overall fabric of the discussion. This, of course, depends not only on the writer, but also on the publisher and the anticipated audience. (We know that some institutions are working against the rigid roadmap of the dissertation process. Stuff for another book!)

When our friend and colleague Judith Evans (1994, 1996) planned *Conversations at Home*, she structured the interpretive framework with a consistency among the constituent parts. The same basic assumptions about knowing and language learning undergird all of its theoretical elements. The qualitative concern for the meanings humans make of their experience in context is consistent with her focus on this child's language experiences within her family. Within this overarching paradigm, Judith chose as her theoretical frame Hallidays' social-semiotic perspective, with its broad concern for 'the relationship between language and social structure' (Evans, 1996, p. 325). She is currently producing a series of journal articles based on this research, the first already published and the second in press at the time of this writing. The rationale for her choice of a social-semiotic theoretical frame was expressed succinctly in the first of these articles:

> Recent work on hearing children's language development demonstrates that studies of language use in natural settings can offer insights about the impact of context and the nature of children's communicative experiences . . . This comprehensive view of language learning and language use seemed to be an appropriate perspective from which to look at a deaf or hard of hearing child's communicative competence in everyday situations. (1996, p. 325)

We are highlighting here the 'open' nature of the theoretical perspective that Judith used, one which allows the researcher to focus on what a child does — her competence. The assumption is that learners are actively engaged in constructing their own learning, their own meaning-making, their own communication within contexts of social relationships.

> Halliday (1975) describes language as 'a system of meanings in functional contexts' (p. 9). Halliday and others have used his frame to push the field in the direction of a functional view of language in use in naturally occurring social situations. (Evans, 1996, p. 325)

These excerpts are taken from an opening section of the article that is four paragraphs in length and that Judith titled 'Theoretical Background.' In that section, she also set forth briefly the three 'concepts' developed by Halliday — the 'field,' the 'tenor,' and the 'mode' of discourse — which she used as a basis for one part of her overall analysis of data and which we explored in some detail in the preceding chapter. The view of language within this theoretical construct is such, however, that in using it Judith gave herself room to analyze her data both within and outside the confines of these three concepts. A perspective that assumes active learning and is open to competence in whatever ways it may be expressed provides a far more open vantage point for observing 'what is going on' than would a theoretical frame more narrowly devised to look at specific skills and that, implicitly if not directly, is concerned with assessing deficits rather than exploring competence.

We said earlier that theoretical discussions often stand 'like parentheses' at the beginning and end of a study. You will have noticed also that we hold that this is not the only way in which theory can or should be presented. In his article 'Raising the teacher's voice and the ironic role of theory,' Joseph McDonald (1986) presented a narrative of the experiences over time of a group of high school teachers who met to talk, read, and in time write about their teaching. The theoretical perspective within which he worked is unfolded only gradually throughout the article, keeping pace with the understanding of the members of this group of which he was a part as the uses of theory became apparent to them. McDonald's own personal 'theory of theory' is implied in the paragraphs early in the article in which he critiques the split between theory and practice as it has developed historically in universities and professional schools in the United States. McDonald further commented in this early section that 'the group was later to use theory to illuminate the insufficiency of theory . . . But that is getting ahead of the story' (1986, p. 34). This foreshadowed his later theoretical discussion, which was told in the context of the teachers' discoveries. We are going to return again in more detail to McDonald's article later in this chapter, in the section 'Becoming Aware of Theory,' and you may want to jump ahead for more details on how the thinking of this group of teachers evolved. The point here is that theory, or a writer's personal interpretive view of whatever sort, does not have to always be set forth at the beginning. It can be, and sometimes is, woven throughout or developed in later sections of the work. Notice also that some writers may, as McDonald did, set their data within a historical perspective.

We read a lot about how theory is used, first to structure research and later to illumine the findings. Theory has also inspired researchers with ideas about how they chose not to conduct their research. We think that most researchers have a mental reservoir — and perhaps even a physical reservoir in the drawers of their filing cabinets — of studies that they find frustrating in one way or another. Sometimes the theoretical positions a researcher eschews are discussed in a review of related research, sometimes not. Neil Mercer (1991), in his account of a research project undertaken with colleagues in London primary schools, set forth both the theoretical perspectives that guided their work and those they rejected. The focus of the research was:

> . . . knowledge and how it was shared. Whatever else education is about, it is about knowledge. Every day in classrooms, knowledge gets constructed, presented, received, rejected, evaluated, understood and misunderstood. A careful examination of this process might well tell us something of psychological interest and practical value. (p. 42)

Here is how Mercer described in this article the overall stance that he and his colleagues adopted toward theory:

> One function of theories is to set agendas for research — to generate certain kinds of questions which the research will attempt to answer. Another function is to provide a 'universe of discourse' within which the discussion and explanation of research findings can take place . . . However, one aspect of the relationship between theory and research practice is, I think, relevant and interesting here. It is the influence of previous researchers whose ideas, while dealing with relevant aspects of the field of study and being accorded high status in the field of study, are nevertheless rejected as a basis for the theoretical framework. Sometimes the work of such researchers can be at least as significant an influence as more 'positive' sources, not least because it motivates: dissatisfaction may generate curiosity. An example may make this point clearer. It concerns our conception of the role of language in thinking and learning, and our model of the process of teaching and learning. We were familiar with the work of Piaget (e.g., 1971), and recognized its influence on both research into cognitive development and modern 'child-centered educational practice. However, we had become increasingly dissatisfied by the way that language was marginalized in the Piagetian model of cognitive development, and also by the way that the role of the teacher was represented as that of a provider of 'learning environments' rather than as an active participant or collaborator in the process whereby a child constructs knowledge. (p. 43)

When we read this passage, we felt a real sympathy for these researchers. We understood just what Mercer meant when he wrote that 'in a way that might seem ridiculous to an outsider, our discussion sometimes led us to get *angry* [author's emphasis] with Piaget and his followers . . .' (p. 43). Each one of us on this writing team has at times felt a similar anger or frustration with research that has seemed limiting — and also the concomitant exhilaration when coming upon a researcher or theorist whose work seems to 'fit' with our own inclinations.

We on this writing team tend to prefer that an initial review of literature in a research proposal be foundational and not too extensive, with the understanding that the researcher will return to that as well as different literature when data collection is well under way and particularly during the final writing in order to talk to the emergent findings. However, all four of us take it as absolutely bedrock that qualitative researchers have studied the literature deeply and carefully. Where we differ from some of our colleagues is in how much and what literature needs to be included during the design of the study and how it is used and placed in the final document. The idea here is that a review of literature can also be a tight constrictor. When formal theories or models are used to power the research, and this is often the case, it is essential that the researcher view this as a starting point, a series of questions against which the findings can be compared. The trick here is to compare where information fits, where it does not, and what is called for in reshaping a theoretical rationale or creating a new one. Too many researchers see the beginning theoretical frame as a structure into which they must shoehorn findings and somehow misplace those that do not make sense in that structure — a little like Cinderella's stepsisters trying to squeeze their feet into the glass slipper that doesn't fit. The reasons that researchers do this may be as glaring as the ways we have learned about theory and theorizing from our professors and mentors, the hidden and not-so-hidden messages about other people's theories as compared to our own, trends and vogues regarding particular theories at particular times, our understandings of the meaning and purpose of research, and our views of ourselves as makers of meaning.

An example. It is our experience that researchers in education and psychology often have done much reading about stage theories of development. One or another such theory, then, may be an integral part of the review of literature for a study. Thus, even if a researcher intends to go into the field with broad focus, previous writing has set the work up for a discussion of the findings within a theoretical frame that may turn out to be inappropriate if, in fact, the actual findings do not appear to have much relation to developmental stages or perhaps if they point to other directions as well. We remember one doctoral student who wanted to study a group of women at midlife. His review of literature was largely devoted to Erikson's theory of stages of development and feminist critiques of it. After he had collected data for only a short time he became concerned that this review of literature and the phrasing of the research questions were too specifically shaped, too leading: that they would limit rather than open up his vision. He felt that it was important to learn what about these women's chosen lifestyles would come to light with a less restrictive set of lenses. Because of this he next worked to open up to a wider range of questions and to the more complex data this engendered.

We don't know, of course, where you are in your research experience. If you are at the beginning of a project we encourage you to look very carefully at the theoretical frame you are developing and to be sure that it is broad enough to serve you rather than to hinder you. If you are writing your final draft, you may well need to revise your review of literature, along with other parts of the original proposal to fit the scope of your emergent findings. You may even need to do away altogether with a separate review of literature, break it out and move sections of it toward the end of your document to discuss them with your findings there. Many beginning researchers are appalled at this prospect, because they think that this means they have somehow done something 'wrong' along the way. 'Not to worry,' we hear ourselves encouraging them again and again. 'This is an important part of the qualitative process and indeed of the writing process in general.'

By now you know that we are particularly concerned when it appears that the theoretical assumptions with which a researcher has entered the field are considered carved in stone, not only in the review of literature but also in the research questions that are an integral part of the research plan. We find this a dangerous stance, although we think we understand its roots. We have struggled for many years with ourselves and with other researchers over how to rewrite theoretical rationales and rephrase research questions to support a more open approach to a study. Those of us in classrooms have long known that narrow questions will cut off and stifle critical and creative thinking. Narrow questions can, for researchers, just as surely lead to narrow findings. Questions can be narrow because they are not phrased felicitously. But they can also be narrow because, voiced or not, they already contain answers that stem too directly from a particular body of literature, a particular 'grand theory,' or from one's own personal theoretical constructs. Narrowly phrased research questions can lead to observations that are too closely focused in the beginning. This was Andy Weitz's experience as he prepared for his initial fieldwork:

> When I first wrote about going into the field I discussed some things I wanted to study: 'I think I will continue to study classroom language/interaction/teacher–student talk ...' In a handwritten note across the front of the log Margot wrote back, 'If you do go to study a classroom, please go without the stances of this paragraph — yet. After you're in you'll find things to study. Surprises are quite lovely at times — quite useful.' There was something clear in my mind. I had an agenda and Margot encouraged me to give it up.

Clearly Andrew was originally prepared to go into the field with a theory about what is important and fruitful to study in classrooms. His theories, whether formal or informal, seemed to have led him to think that the most important work in classrooms occurs during interactions of students with teachers. The lenses of such frames cut off peripheral events: students working with one another or on their own, students who drift off to a corner or out the door and seldom interact with anyone. Some of our favorite studies have been precisely those in which the researcher ended up focusing on classroom events outside of teacher interaction, as did Marlene Barron (1995) in her study of child-initiated book events which we discussed in the previous chapter (see pp. 192–3). The danger in entering the field with a very narrow focus is that the researcher may have closed off the possibility of being surprised by whatever else is there to be noticed. There are models for studying classroom talk, and researchers have gone in with such instruments and completed fruitful research projects using them. However, it is our position that even if researchers expect, hope, to arrive at a particular close focus, the study will be much richer if they are able to put such expectations aside for awhile. Many times, theoretical constructs such as Andrew Weitz's imply answers rather than questions.

Institutional pressures in the contexts within which much research is designed may well work to give a 'graven in stone' feel to the original research questions and the interview questions that follow from them. We think it is important to specify in the qualitative research proposal which is to be submitted to a dissertation committee or to a funding body that the research questions are provisional, and that a finer focus will emerge only as the study progresses. The researcher must then remember to return to the original proposal when deciding how it will fit into the final document and explain whether and how the questions have changed in process.

Likewise, in our experience a qualitative interview schedule should be a provisional outline of a limited number of questions from which it could be helpful to draw if the conversations with interview participants do not extend to the issues the researcher thinks it necessary to include. Several years ago we worked with a doctoral student in social work who was interested in the quality of life of members of a center for senior citizens in a large city. His review of literature was structured around a quality of life model, and the research questions were tightly focused on this phenomenon. When this researcher interviewed participants at the center his interview questions were phrased to address this topic specifically: 'What is your quality of life like at home?' 'Do you feel that participation in the activities at the center contributes to your quality of life?' These interview questions, presented wording drawn from the theoretical model. This turned out to be constricting and anti-qualitative research. We think that most if not all of the participants in this particular setting would not have introduced the phrase 'quality of life' naturally into their conversations. Instead, more open-ended questions such as those suggested below would have allowed for more interpretive interplay between the participants' experiences and the quality of life theory:

> Please describe for me a typical day.
> What is your life like at home?
> How do you feel about your life since you have been coming to the center?
> What works for you? What doesn't?
> When do you feel successful here? When not?

If the basic intent of qualitative research is to draw out the meanings that life in a particular setting has for its participants, we cannot really get at that by requesting that they discuss their experiences in what to them are unnatural theoretical terms and that, at worst, manipulate their responses. This researcher found that his interview data were so sparse and circumscribed that they provided little biographical ground in which to illuminate participants' remarks on the quality of their lives. In addition, the observation about the institutional setting was so skimpy that the people's daily lives could not be drawn clearly. In this instance, the researcher decided to return to the field. He conceived more broadly focused observations and conversational-style interviews that provided him with the information he needed to strengthen his study.

In the long run, even if a study is powered by a very tight, restrictive focus, it is often in the final writing that a broader, fairer perspective can be provided. That is, if a study documents only teacher–student verbal interaction, we would look to the kind of writing that asks some questions about that theoretical stance and provides other provocative, perhaps alternative ideas: writing that opens out, that argues with the frame. We do not mean here the cursory statements on ideas for future research that we suffer through in so many research reports. We mean a rich and artful tapestry.

Being Open to the Surprises

'Surprises can be quite lovely at times — quite useful.' It seems to us that this excitement of discovery should be one of the hallmarks of qualitative research, and it is much more likely to happen when we have left ourselves open to the unexpected. By one of those happy chances that occurs sometimes to researchers and writers, at about this point in the first draft of this chapter a new issue of *Qualitative Studies in Education* arrived in the mail. The lead article was an interview by Steinar Kvale with Jean Lave about her life's work as an anthropologist. In the course of this interview she told about her experiences studying apprenticeships in tailor shops in Liberia. Woven throughout this account are descriptions of her approaches to collecting and analyzing data, and of the ways in which her theoretical understanding of apprenticeship and of teaching evolved during the process. She also wrote about the power of surprise:

> You say to yourself when you start: 'I want to be surprised by what happens here. I don't want the questions that I have arrived with to be so narrow that I cannot see anything but the answers I expect. And I don't want to be so completely unfocused that nothing surprises me because I am not expecting anything.' You want to be somewhere in between so that what happens can lead you to be really shocked and surprised — you didn't expect things to be the way they are — and they really are different and you learn from that. If the enterprise of doing empirical work has any purpose to it, it ought to change your theory as much as your theory changes your empirical work. (Lave and Kvale, 1995, p. 223)

There are tensions throughout the whole of qualitative research — between being a participant and an observer, a professional and a 'stranger,' sympathetic yet detached, becoming deeply imbued with one culture in order to see it in the light of others. One of these tensions surely involves the attitude to which Lave refers above — to be both knowledgeable and capable of being surprised. As qualitative researchers we do not expect to enter the field like blank slates. Hopefully, in reality, we are scholars deeply read in our own and other fields. Yet at the same time we work to sustain an attitude of openness so that we can see much and be surprised. Belenky, Clinchy, Goldberger, and Tarule (1986) are models of this way of working as best described in *Women's Ways of Knowing*:

> We proceeded inductively, opening our ears to the voices and perspectives of women so that we might begin to hear the unheard and the unimagined. (p. 11)

Belenky and her colleagues were not working in exotic settings, the women they interviewed were often those they walked among every day. To us, their attitude is the result of a great respect for those whom they interviewed, a patience on their part to hold their interpretations in abeyance and to open their ears to catch what would otherwise never be heard from or imagined about the participants, some of whom had lived among them silent and inarticulate all their lives.

We cannot emphasize too much the importance for the researcher of writing analytical memos in order to be able to trace the growth of one's own theoretical understanding at some later time. Jean Lave spoke of keeping such a record in a daily journal:

> You always keep a record through time, because it turns out to be important to you; there is a sense in which it is the transformation of your own understanding . . . If you are lucky and work hard, three months later you will go back and laugh at your earlier interpretation. It should look very naive. (Lave and Kvale, 1981, p. 225)

This willingness to hold one's original expectations, questions, answers, under-standings, and interpretations in abeyance and enter the field asking 'What is happening here?' does not come easily. Jean Lave told this story of her first days in the field in Liberia:

> There is this dismaying story from when I first went to Liberia and I wanted to see apprenticeship happening, and I expected to see apprentices being taught by their masters how to make clothes. So I sat there a few days and it became clear, quite quickly, that the apprentices knew how to carry out many different aspects of tailoring, but I couldn't see anybody *teaching* them to do those things. I started asking masters if they would please teach their apprentices so that I could see how apprenticeship was done. And the masters, who were quite obliging, would get some little boy to sit there and they would say: 'Now here is how you sew a button, do you see it?' And the little boy would say: 'Yeah,' and sew the buttons on the trousers. But one day, one of the masters said to this little boy in a very loud voice (for my benefit): 'The fly always goes on the *front* of the trousers.' (p. 222)

Lave had originally gone to Liberia in order to work on 'the relations between apprenticeship and schooling and how people come to know and think' (p. 221). Clearly her search for occasions during which masters were giving lessons to apprentices was powered by her theories of how teaching and learning take place, which led her in turn to focus on overt teaching activities and direct instruction. Her original perspectives needed to be laid aside before she was able to look with a more open mind at what was going on:

> At that point, I said to myself: 'Okay I don't know anything about apprenticeship. I don't understand it at all. This has got to be the wrong question, and trying to get masters to show me how they teach cannot be what apprenticeship is about. That means I still have months of work to do, sitting here and looking for occasions on which I can come to understand better what is going on.' (p. 222)

Lave then backtracked and began to wander up and down the streets on which the tailor shops were located, asking permission to watch.

> What I did was pick one of the 20 tailor shops where there were several children of different ages — a couple were new, a couple had been there for a year or two, one or two had been there for several years. I figured that this was the social arrangement that ought to produce what I wanted to see. (p. 222)

It is her contention that it may take three or four months of living in a community before the researcher finds ways to ask questions. She also describes alternating months in the field with times of withdrawal to analyze notes and do further reading. A rhythm such as this is important to hypothesizing and theorizing. Regarding the need for initial visits to the field before the final formulation of research questions, she remarked that 'One of the reasons for doing field trips is that you are presented with how abstract are even the most concrete of your concepts and questions when you are at home in the library' (p. 221). We also believe that the concepts and questions are shaped by our lifetime of accumulated theoretical constructs.

Jean Lave describes the rhythm between work in the field and work with theory in this way: 'You keep doing your field research and you keep working on your theoretical understanding of the world — and hopefully, each of them makes the other better over time' (Lave and Kvale, 1995, p. 223). When describing her research project in Liberia, she told of alternating periods of time in the field with periods of reading and analysis:

> The first time I went to Liberia, I didn't know anything about it except for this manuscript ... I spent a few weeks, and I just tried to soak up a feeling for the place ... I went home and spent months reading about Liberia. Then I went back and spent six months. I went home again and analyzed that material for months and months, then went back again for three months. I repeated this twice more. And that was the way I did that field project. (p. 221)

Lave commented that 'if the enterprise of doing empirical work has any purpose to it, it ought to change your theory as much as your theory changes your empirical work' (p. 223) goes directly to what we consider the heart of qualitative research.

The rhythm between time in the field and time spent in analysis of data and careful reading of the literature seems to us to have prepared the way that led to unexpected findings for Leslie Rice (1995) in the course of her study of the experiences of recovering women alcoholics. She wrote of a surprise which, if it could not be called a happy one, was important and deeply useful to her. Here is her account of it:

> The data ... indicated that childhood was a difficult time for each of the participants and that each suffered different forms of abuse at the hands of adults. It was startling to me when I was gathering my data that three of the women spontaneously detailed episodes of molestations as they were telling me their stories. The fourth woman, Dana, talked about the severe violence she witnessed when her father beat her mother; as a result she wished her father dead when she was just a young girl. (p. 199)

This finding from the interview data was supported by an unanticipated and very emotional period of observation of a support group for recovering women alcoholics which some of her participants attended. When one of the women in the circle brought forth memories of childhood abuse in a flood of tears, the sharing went around from one to another, with the women present telling stories they had hitherto not revealed in their support group of traumatically abusive or dysfunctional families.

In her original review of the extensive literature on alcoholism, Leslie focused on historical shifts in theories regarding the causes of alcoholism: first that it was moral weakness, later a personality disorder, and then that it is a progressive disease. Much recent research has been conducted within a theoretical framework that sees alcoholism as a multifactorial disease, and Leslie indicated that 'Donovan's (1986) multifactorial etiological model' was used as a theoretical frame for her study. Leslie concluded this portion of her review, however, by commenting that:

> Even with the data that have been collected and, with several definitions which classify alcoholism as a disease, there are still those who believe that alcoholism is not a disease but a moral weakness (Fingarette, 1991; Peele, 1989). Some

authors believe that the disease concept and the moral concept co-exist in the minds of members of society and are transferred to alcoholics. (Rice, 1995, p. 14)

In the light of her findings, however, as Leslie was working on the writing of her final discussion, she returned to the literature and uncovered some pertinent articles that had been recently published. Some of these researchers argued that sexual abuse and violence are significant antecedents to alcoholism for women. Other researchers argued that childhood sexual abuse and/or violence may be responsible for creating a post-traumatic stress response in women with some of the symptoms being alcohol abuse. Those of us who were Leslie's colleagues recall her excitement at that time when she discovered the material presented below, new in the latest edition of the *DSM* (*Diagnostic and Statistical Manual of Mental Disorders* published by the American Psychiatric Association). The *DSMK-IV* (1994) lists post-traumatic stress disorder under anxiety disorders and classifies it as either acute or chronic or delayed:

> The essential feature is the development of characteristic symptoms following exposure to an extreme traumatic stressor involving direct personal experience of an event that involves actual or threatened death or serious injury . . .
>
> The following associated constellation of symptoms may occur and are more commonly seen in association with an interpersonal stressor (e.g., childhood sexual or physical abuse): impaired affect modulation; self-destructive and impulsive behavior; dissociative symptoms; somatic complaints; feelings of ineffectiveness, shame, despair or hopelessness; feeling permanently damaged; a loss of previously sustained beliefs; hostility; social withdrawal; feeling constantly threatened; impaired relationships with others; or a change from the individual's previous personality characteristics. There may be an increased risk of substance-related disorders. (DSMK-IV, 1994, pp. 424–5)

The formulation quoted above — in which possible links were recognized between childhood sexual abuse and/or violence and 'substance related disorders' in women — was seen by Leslie as a strong support to her own unexpected findings. Earlier editions of the *DSM* had defined 'alcoholism as secondary to an underlying personality problem or as a response to extreme psychological distress' (Rice, 1995, p. 11).

Leslie's purpose in her theoretical discussion was not to attribute childhood abuse as a 'cause' of alcoholism in women — that would be outside the scope of her study and not in accordance with its qualitative nature. From these data, however, and from other statements by her participants, Leslie became increasingly convinced that an important aspect of recovery for these women was not only abstention from alcohol and the support of AA (Alcoholics Anonymous), but also therapy that addressed the patterns of abuse that had marked their early lives. Additional therapies are not part of the AA or other model programs for recovering addicts, and a search in the literature on treatment of women alcoholics provided little reference to the need for therapies that would address childhood traumas.

Leslie's experience is an example of what we have stressed before. Reading that is both wide and deep is essential for the step that Morse (1994, p. 34) calls 'recontextualing' one's findings — discussing them in the light of extant theory. It is through this process that the researcher will be composing the recommendations for professional practice. Leslie expressed her concerns as a nurse working with addicted patients that treatment often did not address these underlying problems. Before she began her study there had been little in the literature to support such therapy. Her own work and the most recent literature seemed part of a trend toward looking more deeply at the holistic needs of recovering alcoholic women, and this was a cause to which she (and we, as readers of her work) became devoted. In her final discussion of the implications of her study for practice, Leslie strongly urged that nurses and other helping professionals consider the possible needs that alcoholics, especially women, might have for therapies beyond 'drying out' and attendance at AA:

> Throughout recovering, the participants appeared to experience constant new awareness of their feelings, and new memories, both good and bad, continued to surface. Trauma memories were clear for Martha, Dana, and Janet, but were hazy for Denise. Her memories might have been deeply imbedded and too painful to confront directly. According to most experts (Barrett and Trepper, 1991; Hurley, 1991; Root, 1989) sexual molestation and violence issues cannot be delved for directly but must be elicited in more indirect manners. Health care professionals who are treating recovering alcoholic women must be skilled and sensitive in helping women remember and face these traumas. They must be aware that facing these issues may put the alcoholic women at risk for relapse. Facing the pain of the issues may be more devastating than suffering the destruction of alcoholism. (1995, pp. 203–204)

Another possibility for the extension of theory was suggested by reading outside Leslie's original theoretical frame. While working with these data, Leslie and a colleague began to notice similarities between her participants and the 'silenced women' described by Belenky and her colleagues (1986). Leslie did not develop this concept at any length, but it did color one of the paragraphs in the section of the discussion from which we are quoting here:

> Traumas were not the only issues needing confrontation. The feelings of women about their roles in society need to be explored and women must learn to accept and affirm themselves. Perez (1994) said that in this culture most women are taught that they should be dependent and submissive and be 'nurturant, caring, soft, family-oriented, passive, supportive, good at cleaning house, sewing, cooking, etc. and this expectation is learned at an early age' (pp. 31–32). The cost of internalized gender-role behavior may be the abuse of substances that help to numb the 'pain of powerlessness and lack of freedom and choice' (Forth-Finegan, 1991). Women must be taught to be empowered by identifying choices and role models, and by being helped to define themselves. The shame of not achieving the image of the ideal woman must be faced; the ideal must be changed to include the image of the recovering alcoholic woman. (p. 205)

This paragraph was brief, and not central to Leslie's argument. We ourselves see it as worthy of fuller treatment in another piece of writing. We point to it here, however, to remind ourselves of the many possibilities for discussions around theory that may be implicit in a study.

Surprises can leap up at us from a scene unfolding before our eyes or can take us unaware in the words of our participants, as they did for Leslie Rice. They can emerge from our pondering the pages of a log or as the results of painstaking microanalysis, as we saw in the previous chapter was the case for Judith Evans. They can also arise from areas in the course of fieldwork that we had not originally anticipated. For example, Rita King (1996) planned to look at the experiences of students in a Basic Reading and Writing college class. To shape her study she used a theoretical rationale about this approach to basic English. Her intended research aim was substantially reshaped by experiences that led Rita not to study student writing in the depth she had originally planned, but to focus instead on the instructor's implementation of the program.

Because Rita's original review of literature had been devoted to the featured reading/writing program and the theoretical assumptions behind it, she was driven by the final shape of her report back to literature on a variety of topics — the literature on implementing change in educational settings; on the involvement of adjunct faculty; on inservicing and mentoring. In Rita's case this rethinking led her to place her findings in a broader interpretive framework that took into account more of the larger culture of a university than she had originally anticipated.

There are many safeguards built into the qualitative research process — our log itself, our analytic memos, the insights of others in our support groups (and it can be a great help in this regard when they are from disciplines other than our own), and of course the reading that we do during the periods when we withdraw from the field. Being true to the process itself will help us to examine our constantly evolving theoretical positions. In every study, the researcher reaches a point where decisions and a final plan must be made. Out of the many, and sometimes unexpected, possibilities the researcher must settle down to some final interpretations at this time and in this place for the piece of writing at hand.

Using Theory

Some beginning researchers we have known find the reconceptualization of a theoretical framework a difficult final step, perhaps because it signals a moving away from the immediacy of 'the field' and the stories of one's participants, and a return to the abstractions of 'the literature.' Also, structuring a theoretical discussion is hard work, and we know from our own experience how difficult it is to do justice to it toward the end of a long study. The work can loom as much more difficult if it becomes obvious that a restructuring of the theoretical rationale is in order or that the extant literature must be searched to see what, if anything, supports or conflicts with unanticipated findings. This step is an important one, however, because it is from within the research traditions of a discipline that a researcher speaks about the implications of the findings to professional colleagues.

To highlight the process of structuring an interpretive discussion, we are going to look at how a few writers have viewed their findings within specific theoretical frameworks. We have already considered how Judith Evans' review of literature and theoretical rationale provided a very solid frame within which to explore her findings about the communicative competence of a young deaf child in an otherwise hearing family. In her dissertation this review was divided into three main sections: the social dimensions of language; the communicative experiences of deaf children; and family systems. Judith decided to begin her presentation of findings (see pp. 169–72) with wide focus on the family context. Therefore the literature that was treated last in the review — that on family systems — was drawn on most heavily, although not exclusively, for the first and second chapters of her presentation. Judith concluded Chapter IV, 'Pictures at an Exhibition: A Gallery of Portraits,' with a discussion about family systems. Notice how she compares her findings with theoretical models drawn from the literature:

> Barb and Peter Harris maintain clearly defined, traditional parental roles which provide the leadership that Ackerman (1984) states is necessary for family identity and stability. As described by Land (1969) and Messer (1970), they have developed a system of management and division of labor. While both Barb and Peter have specialized functions, they demonstrate flexibility in sharing many of their responsibilities in order to maintain balance within the family (Ackerman, 1984). In addition to roles ascribed by age, gender, and position in the family, Barb serves as the family nurturer and Peter is the primary breadwinner. Barb is also Kristin's most frequent conversation partner and interpreter. Peter does the physical farm chores. They interchange child care, chauffeuring, and household work as circumstances require . . .
>
> As the only deaf member in the family, Kristin is dependent on others as willing partners for access and inclusion in family communication. Paraphrasing Ackerman (1984), her communication is at all times a function of the communication of other members. (Evans, 1994, pp. 99–100)

Aspects of family life are explored in greater detail in Chapter V, 'Darkroom Impressions: A Thematic Analysis.' Again Judith drew on literature pertaining to family systems:

> Family themes related to Kristin address the research question of the ways deafness affects the family. Correlating with the findings of Meadow (1980), Schlesinger and Meadow (1972), and Wood (1991) that deafness profoundly affects hearing families, Kristin's deafness has had a significant impact on the entire family constellation. Despite the Harris's efforts to deal uniformly with their children, the data indicate that the family's ambivalence about Kristin's deafness permeates their thinking and practices. Their ambivalence is expressed, on the one hand, by not wanting to feature Kristin's deafness while, on the other hand, realizing she does have special needs as a deaf child. They make a conscious effort not to let deafness be the primary focus of the family, nor Kristin's most significant characteristic. Such beliefs affect their decision making in terms of how Kristin's special needs are addressed in relation to the needs of others. (p. 137)

Judith then goes on to address ways in which deafness affects a family, thus turning to the literature on deafness treated in the second section of her review:

> As found in the work of Vash (1981), deafness can disrupt the emotional and functional balance in a family. The Harris's stated policy about Kristin's deafness may be an example of what Vash (1981) refers to as use of their inner resources to enable them to cope and neutralize their adverse reaction to deafness.
>
> Additionally, the parents' beliefs and practices have become the family party line as the other children adopt their parents' practices as their own. The children illustrate this in everything from the ways they include Kristin in their activities to following their parents' practices of signing when they think she needs extra support in communication. The children's behavior confirms the findings of Holman (1983) and Watslawick, Beavin and Jackson (1967) that parents' expectations and values are conveyed to children by the content and manner in which they are communicated. (pp. 138–9)

It should be pointed out that each of Judith's chapters in which findings are presented closes with a discussion specifically related to those findings. The discussions that end each of the two chapters are focused on Kristin's language use and competence. These discussions are structured largely within a very specific social-semiotic theory of language and are based on the findings set forth in the microanalyses we described in the previous chapter.

Metathemes or larger issues that are of concern to the profession or discipline of the researcher can often be better highlighted if not too many topics are crowded into one chapter. This practice served Judith well. Here is how she introduced her final discussion:

> The metathematic discussion of findings that follows is different from the discussions of findings presented in the previous chapters in that it looks at the outcomes as a whole and relates them to the research questions and theoretical bases of the study. Three over-arching ideas are presented below: the incongruities between home and school perspectives, the continuum of Kristin's communication experiences, and Kristin's strengths as a communicator under the contextual conditions that create her reality. (1994, p. 261)

Because her analysis-in-process yielded findings with implications beyond the initial scope of her original research design, Judith knew at this point that she needed to introduce differing theoretical models of the education of deaf children. It became evident to her that the staff members at Kristin's school had selected one model within which to design their instructional environment. Kristin's parents, on the other hand, functioned within a mesh of attitudes, beliefs, and longings for their child that, although not expressed by them in theoretical terms, fell within the scope of a theoretical construct that was not realized in the school. In addition to her discussion of this finding in the final chapter of her dissertation, Judith has developed it as the focus for her second article (in press) based on this study.

This is a study that has continued to engage the interest of all of us who supported Judith during the writing. There are poignant episodes in this writing, lively descriptions of family life and communication, and the immediacy of segments from interview transcripts and videotapes. We think it is important to recognize, however, that these are only part of this carefully designed report. Research writing in which the various components are artfully arranged, in which significant findings are highlighted, in which an argument is thoughtfully constructed, and in which theoretical considerations are faced and used has a power of its own. It is each of these elements working with the others that heightens the sense of 'story' for us, one that has taken on a life of its own and that plays in our minds against other stories of deaf people, such as that of a recently crowned Miss America or the mystery novel that tellingly portrays differing aspects of deaf culture, *For the Sake of Elena* by Elizabeth George.

In the article by Nancy Welch (1996), 'Revising a Writer's Identity,' the researcher followed the progress of a student, Sidney, and her growth as a writer throughout one semester's course. Welch does not tell us whether her study evolved because she recognized a 'fit' between her knowledge of relevant theory, her log notes and student writings. However, from her article, it would appear that Welch's reflections on the episodes involving Sidney and other students led her to consider them against a specific theoretical frame of 'learning-through-imitation' in a composition class. Welch commented that this model:

> . . . helps me to see how students and I in that composition and literature class were also in a process of identifying and re-identifying ourselves to and with others, reading and imitating the social models that surrounded us, trying to make a fit . . . (Welch, 1996, p. 42)

The primary source of data were the author's observations and Sidney's journal, in which she recorded her thoughts about her reading, her writing assignments, her relationship with her former instructor, Jim, and her present instructor Nancy. Welch begins with three short episodes, each one paragraph in length, each featuring a different student. In these anecdotes, each student reveals attitudes about writing in a classroom setting and each indicates what might be seen as an overly heightened awareness of audience — especially the teacher and her possible expectations as audience. In order to counter this trend, to move herself out of the center of students' considerations, Welch attempts to implement the idea of a 'third factor' as proposed by Michele Le Doeuff (1989). We see this similar to the 'third space' in which fresh ideas may unsettle the dualities of previous thinking:

> As a third factor in the student-to-teacher or student-to-student relationship, reading in the composition class can do more than encourage attachment between student and one particular model: it can work to disrupt limiting, dualistic attachments and set into motion a process of *re-modeling*, of addressing the restlessness we experience — or ought to experience — when we try to identify with, imitate, *be-just-like* another. (Welch, 1996, p. 43, italics in original)

In her subsequent discussion, Welch explores the psychological theories and theories of learning that support or challenge learning-as-imitation models. She then returns to Sidney and traces her development throughout the semester as she gradually moves away from her identification with Welch and with Jim, her previous composition instructor. As the course closes, Sidney is able to say to Welch that she has signed up for a different workshop for the following semester because 'Even though you and Jim have been really helpful, I need some other perspectives' (1996, p. 58).

Welch's study, along with others we are considering in these last three sections of this chapter, illustrates an extensive use of existing theory against which findings are viewed. The process of analyzing her data about the students' work and also of reflecting deeply on her own work in the light of a number of theoretical models illustrates the interplay also described by Jean Lave, and quoted earlier, of letting your 'empirical work . . . change your theory as much as your theory changes your empirical work' (Lave and Kvale, 1995, p. 223).

One of the problems in this notion of changing theory is that often it is difficult to describe it in written comments. Welch used endnotes as part of her article to continue the theoretical discussion beyond the arguments advanced in the body of the work. She also includes in an endnote reflections on the implications of Le Doeuff's theory for her teaching practice:

> Far from being an empty or easy term, this idea of the third factor tells me that when I ask students to meet together in a small group, I need to consider what else can be introduced to the group to complicate, enliven, and pluralize their discussions. It tells me that when I sit down to advise a student in my office, I need to consider what else can be introduced to help me and this student question my usual ways of giving 'advice.' It tells me that when I sit down to write an essay about Lacan or about Le Doeuff I need to imagine who else I can introduce to intervene in my identification with one theorist, one model, alone, draw me away from a strict focus that may also be a form of strict, unquestioning allegiance. (Welch, 1996, p. 60)

We would like to register our occasional frustration with style guides and publishers that discourage the use of footnotes and endnotes. This practice is particularly inhibiting to the treatment of theory. To us, notes permit a richness and flexibility of theoretical discussion that is not easy to achieve otherwise without interrupting the flow of the central line of thought. In a brief paragraph on 'content footnotes' the writers of the American Psychological Association *Publication Manual* (1994) state that such footnotes 'should not include complicated, irrelevant, or nonessential information.' The reasons given are that 'they are confusing to readers and expensive to include in printed material' (p. 163). Is it unfair of us to suspect that the expense of endnotes is more of a determining factor than we would like to think? We are certainly not in favor of irrelevance or complication, but such judgment calls are often in the eye of the reader, who, in any case, can choose to ignore them completely. As Laurel Richardson (1990) points out, these publishing practices in themselves impose a particular theory of method that may run counter to an author's intent:

> All the social sciences have prescribed writing formats — none of them neutral, all of them value constituting. How we are expected to write affects what we can write about. The referencing system in the social sciences discourages the use of footnotes, a place for secondary arguments, novel conjectures, and related ideas. Incorporated into the text, albeit in parentheses, are the publication dates for citations, as though this information counts the most. Knowledge is constituted as focused, problem (i.e., hypothesis) centered, linear, straightforward. (pp. 16–17)

As readers, we often particularly enjoy reading that is not too linear and straight-forward, that occasionally takes us along unexpected byways.

Welch's study urges the re-examination of received theory and suggests ways of introducing fresh theoretical constructs. In the following passage from an ana-lytical memo by Elizabeth Merrick, we see another researcher reaching toward new understandings and revising her former interpretations as she reflects on her findings:

> For the past several years, I have worked as a counselor at an urban adolescent health center where I counsel young women regarding birth control, pregnancy, abortion and parenthood. When I began, I held beliefs regarding adolescent child-bearing which, in retrospect, were largely unexamined. Like many people, I assumed that teenagers became pregnant either because they didn't know about or have access to birth control, or if they admitted a more conscious desire to have a child there must be something deficient or even pathological in their background; why else would people choose to have a child at that age, condemning themselves and their child to a life of poverty?
>
> These assumptions were challenged as they revealed their experiences and lives to me. The lack of fit between their perspectives and the 'ignorance' or 'deficit model' explanations of adolescent childbearing became apparent. While a few pregnant young women did reveal unmet needs that seemed to lead them to want a child, the picture was not what I had expected. The majority of those choosing to have children seemed quite reasonable in their assessment and their choice . . .
>
> I became interested in exploring alternative explanations for these young women's choice of childbearing. My interests and research in this area are in-formed and supported by theorists who assert that women may have alternative developmental experiences (Chodorow, 1978; Gilligan, 1982). I also assume that an individual's behavior is understandable and meaningful within its context. This perspective has been elaborated within a decision-making model (Asjen and Fishbein, 1990) in which individuals are seen as making what they perceive as the best choice for them although they may not always have complete or accurate information.

Elizabeth's consideration of new theoretical constructs within which to analyze her data indicate that she may be moving toward making new theory regarding teenage pregnancy. There have been suggestions of new theory in the other examples we have given in prior discussions in this book, although the major emphasis at those points was on the structuring of texts. We turn our attention now to the role of qualitative researcher as a maker of theory.

Making Theory, or Where Surprises May Lead

When we talk about 'making theory,' we want to be clear that, although we would not rule out the possibility, we really are not talking about 'grand theory' on the scale that it is occasionally produced. We find Howard Becker's (1986) discussion of 'normal scholarship' insightful in this regard. He points out that 'science and humanistic scholarship are cumulative enterprises' (p. 140) that develop over time and in the context of a scholarly tradition and community. He reminds us that Kuhn

(1962) used the term 'normal science' quoted in Becker (1986, pp. 140–1) to refer to this 'mutual interdependence,' and posited that scientific revolutions come about when 'large numbers of people, working together, develop a new way of formulating and investigating the problems they are interested in, a way which finds a home in the lasting institutions of scientific work.' Becker has noted a tendency for writers to use the term 'normal science' in a pejorative fashion, as though the goal to make such a contribution is too limited. He decries this attitude as unrealistic, and encourages his readers 'to pursue the goals of normal science: to do a piece of good work others can use, and thus increase knowledge and understanding' (Becker, 1986, p. 140).

The line between use of existing theory and new theory is hard to draw. Often it is a gradual process as a writer moves along a continuum from the established to the new. Bruce Kellerhouse's study of the bereavement experiences of HIV-negative gay men who have lost friends and/or lovers to AIDS seems to us significant for his rethinking of theory about bereavement and the grieving process as he saw these processes worked out in the lives of his participants. His new theoretical perspective evolved gradually, and painfully, out of the interplay between personal experience, theory in his field, and the data that gradually emerged from a succession of interviews and participant observations of support group sessions. Here, taken from the section on 'The Stance of the Researcher' in his study, is his story in his own words:

> During the 1990s, I had experienced the loss of several persons due to AIDS over the first decade of the epidemic. My relations to these persons ranged from distant acquaintances to close friends. At the time, I experienced many of the symptoms alluded to in prior research (Martin, 1988), chief among these a sense of being disconnected from others, although I was not able to see this state so clearly then. It struck me that connecting with other grieving people might help me break my isolation, and I began to investigate bereavement support or therapy groups for persons affected by AIDS losses. I found there were few and certainly none serving uninfected gay men exclusively.
>
> Remembering that each AIDS death affects at least one person, and probably more, I imagined that in the gay community there were significant numbers of men who had experienced one or more losses due to AIDS. I also felt intuitively and through a cursory examination of the statistics on HIV infection that a significant number of these men were probably HIV-negative and healthy. I devised for myself what I termed the 'survivor phenomenon' profile. The people I was thinking about were gay men over the age of 30 who were HIV-negative, had sustained multiple losses of loved ones due to AIDS, had survived the past ten years of the AIDS epidemic, and most likely would continue to survive if they did not engage in high risk sexual behaviors or succumb to other life-threatening diseases or catastrophes.
>
> At this point I decided to see if any research had been generated on my imagined population and made a search using such specific descriptors as 'bereavement,' 'HIV-negative,' 'AIDS,' and 'gay men.' Thus I discovered the work of John Martin (1988). His study of 745 gay men residing in New York City confirmed my hypothesis that there were large numbers of grieving gay men. He also

elaborated a very specific list of symptoms which he concluded were the result of experiencing multiple losses due to AIDS. He did not, however, control for HIV status and my curiosity about the 'survivor phenomenon' remained unanswered. I could find no studies which focused exclusively on healthy, HIV-negative gay men.

By the summer of 1992, I had become increasingly interested in the bereavement experiences of AIDS survivors. My curiosity had led me to participate in a ten-week AIDS grief support group and to enroll in a bereavement counseling course. It was through classroom study that I discovered the work of Kenneth Doka (1989) and his construct of disenfranchised grief. Reading his work, a hypothesis began to emerge: healthy, HIV-negative gay men experience difficulty resolving their grief for loved ones lost to AIDS because their losses are not fully recognized by most people and because they occur in multiples — few gay men have lost only one significant relationship due to AIDS. In continuing my inquiry into this phenomenon, I also found that in what little work did exist on this subject, the authors focused on symptomology. They spoke nothing of the daily lives of their subjects and left my earlier question largely unanswered. The stage was now set for my own work because an additional question remained unanswered: what must it be like to live day after day losing one's friends and partners?

As he continued with this section of his report, Bruce wrote movingly of his experiences while he located and interviewed members of a predominantly healthy gay men's bereavement support group. Of particular concern to him was coping with and working through his own emotional responses — depression, lethargy, a disgust for living — as he spent long hours poring over and analyzing the interview transcripts. In time, new theoretical insights began to emerge:

When I began my observations, I held certain beliefs about this specific bereavement experience which, in retrospect, were largely unexamined. Like much of the bereavement literature, I assumed that these men's lives were clouded with grief and sorrow, they felt pain and sadness, and they experienced their daily lives as hopeless and beyond their control. In the face of their losses, how could they experience anything else?

These assumptions were challenged as I continued to observe the group and to hear how its members struggled with the myriad of experiences and emotions they expressed about their lives. As their stories unfolded, their experiences revealed a larger picture than that painted by models of complicated grief reactions and my own dim impressions. Their worlds most certainly were filled with sadness and despair, but they also expressed humor and joy. Their experiences included moments of hopefulness and a willingness to consider a bright future, interspersed with feelings of hopelessness and loss.

In an analytic memo written at about the same time, Bruce returned again to his questioning of his own assumptions and the literature in his field:

Professionally, this work has blown the top off my understanding of bereavement and of the research process in general. It has led me to question all I have learned — forced me to open my mind and often made me feel like I was losing my foothold on my field. My rigid psychological conceptualization of bereavement has dissolved into a more fluid, open and multifaceted view which changes and shifts with each observation. I have had to find a new theoretical foothold, based on a continuum of experience extending from my own to that of others.

As of this writing, Bruce has written the formal statement of his theoretical understanding of the bereavement experiences of his participants for the final chapter of his report. Here are his latest thoughts expressed more informally in a memo to a member of this writing team:

> As I think back on all that is written about grief and bereavement, none of the authors or researchers has addressed the kind of multiple, continuous loss that uninfected gay men have experienced because of AIDS. Most literature addressed single, one-time loss — what we would diagnostically classify as simple bereavement. Some literature focused on one-time loss (deaths of children, etc.), and even less focused on multiple loss. When multiple loss was addressed, it usually focused on disasters, where the losses occurred over a short span of time. Other examples focused on the Holocaust — a tragic, traumatic occurrence like AIDS, which did, however, eventually end. AIDS has not ended, and there is little foreseeable hope for an end to AIDS in the lifetime of most adult gay men.

At this point in his memo — a turning point in his move away from the existing theory he has explored — Bruce reveals the doubts and reflections that led him toward a reconceptualization:

> I return to the question that has nagged me from the beginning. What must it be like to live day after day of one's life in the midst of a constant barrage of illness and death? There is no theory to explain this experience. Loss is not something for which uninfected gay men can create a 'location' in their lives. Loss is their lives. The everyday living of their lives entails loss. It is inescapable.
>
> The experiences of the men I interviewed and observed caused me to reject most tenets of a linear, stage-driven model of loss such as Bowlby's. Their experiences demonstrated that AIDS-related loss in uninfected gay men is a circular, continuous, multidimensional, multilayered, and multifaceted process. Traditional factors affecting grief such as the identity and role of the deceased, their age, the personality of the bereaved, etc., were just the tip of the iceberg. No unidimensional theory can explain the extraordinary coping mechanisms developed by these men. Their motto is, 'I'll get support wherever I can find it. I will survive by any means possible.' Certainly, sadness and despair were found in their experiences. But so were guts and glory. And that was the challenge of this research: to look beyond the obvious despair in these men's lives; to discover how they have survived.
>
> And now tears well up in my eyes as I am reminded of their courage. 'Courage' was not a stage of grieving in any literature I had read. These men have courage with their morning coffee. No literature suggested the transforming effects their losses would have on them. Yes, their losses seemed to have shut down parts of their lives, but the same losses also seemed to have opened new doors. The term 'pathological grief' as it is stated in the literature failed to recognize the inner resourcefulness and compassion of these men. And in the early stages of my research, so did I. To look solely at the distress the men faced and not to recognize the incredible strength and remarkable coping they demonstrated would have been a disservice to this research. The strength of these men is equally important to the data of multiple loss as are the emotional challenges.

This development of theory on Bruce's part would appear to be an apt illustration of Becker's (1986) description of normal scholarship. Bruce's presentation indicates a thorough knowledge of extant literature. He points out in what ways his participants are similar to or differ from those included in other studies. His argument for a cyclical and multifaceted model of bereavement experiences seems solidly grounded in his data. He does not suggest, nor would it be appropriate for him to do so, that his model applies to all persons who have suffered a loss through death or that it should replace extant linear stage models. It would seem likely to us, however, that his contribution could influence other researchers to revision ways in which they consider the bereavement process, and for therapists to reflect again on their practice. Surely a worthwhile contribution to the cumulative enterprise.

When Nancy Duggan (1992) wrote the proposal for her study, 'So Far So Good: The Experience of Male Ex-Offenders 2–5 years after Release from Incarceration,' she designed a theoretical framework 'derived from the literature in several disciplines' (p. 9). The overarching, or 'grand' theory was symbolic interactionism, which, Nancy argued, 'provides a theoretical framework within which to examine the interrelationships between society, the person, and social behavior' (p. 9). After pointing out that 'There is a large body of theory and research that comes from this tradition that stresses the reciprocal relationship between self and society . . .' Nancy indicated literature within her chosen interpretive frame that considered offenders and ex-offenders from this perspective. We quote a few paragraphs to illustrate her line of argument. Notice how she moves from symbolic interaction theory to the corollary that a person's self-image emerges from interactions, to the mechanism of role-taking, to the concept of role-exit, each theory 'nested' within the preceding:

> A basic premise of symbolic interactionism is that human behavior and personality are guided by the meanings that people assign to situations, events, and other people. It is people's interpretations of events, objects and situations that guide their personal and social behavior . . .
>
> In symbolic interaction theory, a person's self-image or self-concept emerges from interaction with others. According to Mead (1934), role-taking is the mechanism through which a person can put himself in another's position and identify with that person. Taking the role of the other depends on the ability to use symbols to communicate or transmit meaning. By learning the symbols commonly employed in the groups with which one associates, a person learns others' meanings and definitions of things and internalizes them. People are then able to assume others' roles and adopt others' perspectives. The views of others then become a platform for viewing the self as others do. Thus, the development of the self-concept emerges from the development of the ability to take roles . . .
>
> For symbolic interactionists, social roles are the behavioral expectations that adhere to a person in a given position. Roles are learned through social interaction and serve to organize behavior and perceptions with reference to others . . .
>
> A useful concept in thinking about the process an ex-offender may go through is that of role-exit as developed by Ebaugh (1984; 1988). In a series of qualitative studies, Ebaugh investigated the process of leaving roles that people conceptualize as being central to their self-identity. Although in much of her early work she

focused on nuns who left the convent, she expanded her studies to include a variety of ex-roles such as divorcees, ex-alcoholics, ex-prostitutes, retirees, widows, ex-police and ex-doctors. Ebaugh conceptualized role-exit as a disengagement from a central role in an individual's identity and the re-establishment of an identity in a new role that takes into account the ex-role. She described ex-roles as a sociological phenomenon in which self-definition and societal expectations are influenced and frequently determined by a previous identity . . .

Ebaugh conceptualized role exit as a process that occurs over time in stages from first doubts about an existing identity and the weighing of role alternatives to dealing with the voice left by the old role, and finally, the establishment of an ex-role identity . . .

Symbolic interactionism is a useful framework for studying the process of re-entry into society by ex-offenders because it focuses on the individual's perceptions of social role and social structure and encompasses the concept of role exit. (Duggan, 1992, pp. 11–13)

Unlike some of the other studies we have discussed in Chapter 4 and this one, Nancy's formal interpretive writing was confined to her final chapter. In a section devoted to 'Re-entry and Settling In,' she returned again to the literature on role-exit derived from symbolic interaction theory, which she had introduced in her second chapter, as in the following segment:

Support from co-workers was named as being crucial for those offenders who work in agencies that employ ex-offenders. It was particularly important during times of crisis when they could have regressed to maladaptive behaviors. Tyrone's temporary return to his old street behaviors after the death of his mother was understood and tolerated briefly by his co-workers, who also spent a lot of time talking with him. However, when he continued his negative patterns, he was generally confronted by them. As he said, 'They were there for me when I couldn't be there for myself.' Edward felt that support from co-workers and the administration was important in his career development, but crucial after he found out his HIV status. However, the four who work in agencies with others like themselves have not had to contend with managing their ex-offender status in conventional settings. They have managed their ex-role status (Ebaugh, 1988) by using it in their work and remaining within an ex-offender culture. (Duggan, 1992, p. 369)

In the course of her final analysis, however, Nancy found another theoretical model to use in the analysis of data concerned with the ex-offenders' decision to make changes in their lives:

What these participants describe is a process of self-initiated change that is consistent with a recently published stage model of change processes developed by Prochaska and DiClemente (1982, 1983, 1992). Because of the strong correspondences between these participants' self-reports of their process of change and the stages and processes of change outlined by Prochaska and DiClemente, their model will be used as a template to organize and discuss my findings in this area. (p. 350)

Nancy first described the model and then discussed her findings within the framework it provided, a process that we have seen used by other researchers whose work we have explored. When, however, she had completed her final analysis of data, she concluded that a different model would better serve for her discussion of one aspect of her findings: an unexpected, finding that jarred her because it did not fit in with her existing theories. It was hard for her to accept it or to theorize about it. As we look at it now, we see this finding as a step into new theory. Here is the passage as she presented it:

> One of the most surprising findings of the study is that five participants reported that prison was the single most important factor in their move away from a criminal lifestyle. None of them could conceptualize having changed their ways without having been incarcerated. With the exception of Sal and Brian, all stated a belief that they would eventually have self-destructed or been killed without the impact of a prison sentence. As adolescents, they described themselves as out of control and as not having been caught, which seemed to feed a sense of adolescent omnipotence. Only the experience of being caught penetrated that sense of omnipotence and made further change possible. However, while prison seemed to be a necessary condition for change for these particular men, it is clearly not a universal solution since many people go to prison without changing positively. (Duggan, 1992, pp. 348–9)

Nancy did not continue with any further formal discussion at this point. From our present perspective, we would like to have seen Nancy's unanticipated findings and their theoretical implications featured more prominently, nested within her theoretical discussion. She did, however, return to this particular issue again in her 'Reflections on Method,'

> One of the hardest parts of doing this study for me came after interviewing three participants in a row who said 'Jail saved my life.' In looking at the data, I was struck by the irony that I, who have spent much of my professional life trying to keep young people out of the correctional system, might have as a major finding of the study that prison was experienced as necessary and important to the change these men made in their lives. The fact that I was using a method that to me had such validity made matters worse. I couldn't tell myself that what I was hearing was an artifact of a statistical procedure or a badly devised questionnaire. When I went over the narratives and themes with the participants, I half expected them to say 'No, that's not what I meant at all,' but no one did. To me, this was a testimony of the power of the method which forced me to look at some basic assumptions I had been making about my own work. I cannot and do not support the current policy of the wholesale warehousing of minority male populations as a solution to crime and unemployment, but this study made me consider why, in the absence of societal and family structures that provide satisfying or consistent paths to adulthood, prison might provide an opportunity for growth as well as for oppression. Nonetheless, it is a tragic commentary that so many poor and minority male adolescents in this country find crime and prison part of their growing up. It is an expensive rite of passage. None of these men spent less than 5 years in prison. The most conservative estimates of the costs of incarceration that I have ever seen is $15,000 per inmate per year and most estimates are considerably higher. If even a portion of that money were used to aid the school systems in identifying children at risk for truancy and criminal involvement, for providing support and education to families with children at risk, or even for subsidizing the

employment of teenagers in poor neighborhoods or the salaries of ex-offenders coming out of prison, the impact on crime involvement, incarceration, and recidivism could be dramatic. (pp. 378–9)

One of the realities of any writing is that the author often comes to the final section or chapter rushed and exhausted. It has often seemed to us that the interpretive writing and the development of implications for practice do not receive the attention they deserve, may not be as well developed as the more narrative sections of the document that have been the subject of the earlier chapters of this book. We have already noted that the development of these topics has received far less attention in the literature than have those topics that are undertaken early in the course of the study — entry into the field, for example. The likely result is that all of us have less guidance for these final stages of the writing up of their report. However, just as Nancy does, we may find our way.

Aside from considerations of theory, we would like to make a point about the writing. Notice how Nancy's style changes in the previous segment from her reflections on method. It seems to us that it is freer, stronger, and more open. To us, this illustrates a value in bringing the personal into research writing — even to writing about theory.

Becoming Conscious of Theory

We have seen throughout this chapter that one of the characteristics of qualitative researchers is a certain sophistication with, and an ability to move about with some ease among, a variety of theoretical perspectives. Researchers usually construct and reconstruct the interpretive frameworks that most aptly express their positions throughout the course of a scholarly life. It is helpful for readers if the researcher explains his or her theoretical posture early in the work. Periodic immersions in 'the literature' and an understanding of the histories of one's personal positions as well as their opposites will help with this task and facilitate writing in which interpretations are more clear and well developed. Such writing will in turn support readers as they transact with the text and develop their own interpretations. In the following section we trace the paths we and others have followed in becoming aware of and learning to work with theory.

For a researcher first approaching the construction of an interpretive framework, the task can be daunting. We, on this writing team, consider our development very much a matter of individual hands-on trial and error as we read, think, and write, reread, rethink, and rewrite our way through first one research project or presentation and then another. We find looking back over the development of our theoretical perspectives a great help in this process. We also find it helpful and enlightening to read how others have experienced theory. And we have noticed that we are not alone in this regard. Rhonda C. Grego (1994), writing to fellow professors of composition, recommends the use of 'academic autobiographies' and suggests that these might 'enrich our thinking/rethinking of our research vocabularies and theories' (p. 227).

We invite you to step back into the past with us and to look at your own growth as a theorist in relation to some of the stories told here. (Does this have a rather Dickensian ring? Is there a 'ghost of theories past' to take us by the hand?) To become more self-conscious about theory and to see where the interpretive framework of our work fits in our own universe of academic and professional discourse is an aid to future writing. Perhaps we had not reflected consciously on the theoretical assumptions that supported our work and our lives until we embarked on a graduate program; perhaps we had always regarded our personal assumptions as the cornerstone of our understanding of 'reality.' Perhaps, our long processional experiences made us either ignorant about or disdainful of various theoretical perspectives within our profession because we prided ourselves on dealing with the 'down-to-earth' practical rather than the 'up-in-the-air' theoretical. By the time we were conducting formal research, however, we had acquired some very highly conscious understandings of at least some theories. We'd also acquired some metatheoretical knowledge, some theories about theory, because as beginning qualitative researchers we'd learned that we needed this insight to defend our choice of research paradigm and methods.

The journey through remembrance is often revitalizing, even salutary, and certainly disquieting. That is why we agree with Grego that it is important for professionals to write autobiographies. The four of us wrote 'theoretical autobiographies' as we were writing this chapter. We offer an excerpt from Ruth's to illustrate how past events speak to present concerns and bring a level of consciousness to one's current work. Noting autobiographical orientation points and correlatives helped Ruth recognize the contingencies and near artifices that constituted her 'lived experiences' with theory:

> The first conscious memory I have that theory had something to do with how I read or taught literary texts came through a joyous note from one young freshman at Yale, who had been a senior in a high school English class I taught. He wrote: 'Now I understand what you were doing all along. I am so grateful that you introduced me to this way of reading. It's all the rage here. I've enclosed a copy of Booth's *The Rhetoric of Fiction* . . . Love, Dan.' Although someone else had used theory upon me as I learned to interpret literature and I did so 'upon' students, Dan located me and put a name to a methodology of interpretation and a habit from which I read and taught literature — some blend of subjective and structural (New Criticism) combined. Or, so I thought. As with all things, nothing is quite so simple. Two weeks later Dan sent yet another note: 'When we began reading Lévi-Strauss, I realize you were teaching us this too. Sorry if I labelled you too quickly. I love it here as the world seems to be fitting together. Love, Dan.' Dan enclosed a copy of Lévi-Strauss's *Structural Anthropology*. Theorists guard against blindly accepting positions, but until Dan's notes I wasn't consciously aware that theoretical principles were driving forces behind both the ways in which I read texts (a 'schooled' experience to be sure) and the ways I taught others to read. From Dan, a freshman who had spent two years in high school literature classes that I taught and who was only six years younger than I, I located three conceptual crossings — subjective criticism, New Criticism, and ethnology-none of which have left me completely and which partially define me as a maverick

hybrid (a concept I learned from Homi Bhabha). Nearly 25 years ago now, my young friend helped me begin to see the critical coordinates of theory that I have learned to use consciously in my work.

Since then, I have spent long nights with Bakhtin who helped me realize that literature is dialogic among other things — of course, supporting again some of my proclivity for Lévi-Strauss, subjective criticism, and transactional theories. At least two of my recent studies on a dialogic pedagogy are the result of intimate conversations with Bakhtin: Vinz (1995) 'Toward An Understanding of the Blues and Beyond: An Essentialist Reading of Cultural Texts', and (1996) 'Horrorscapes: (In)Forming Adolescent Identity and Desire'. I am a stranger-bedfellow with Foucault although my studies with teachers, who are struggling at becoming themselves in the school culture, leads me to him in (1995) 'Opening Moves: Conversations on the First Year of Teaching'. In my concerns about the unvoiced complexities of interdisciplinary study, I have begun to court Deleuze because he gives language to the myriad 'folds' that might and must be considered pedagogically. The rhizomatics of thought help me begin to conceptualize what Interdisciplinarity might actually mean. Well, this is a beginning. I'm feeling the need to stop writing and head back to the overstuffed chair to read. Yes, I am a hybrid of many 'isms' that structure my tendencies of thought. These have become more conscious, more experimental over the years as I've learned that each is somehow implicated in how I pose questions — or even the ones I choose to raise — the types of questioning, the methodological vigilance with which I turn to read the text, and the way I understand, value, and examine spoken and implied discourses in all the work I do.

Joseph McDonald (1987) chronicled the growth in theoretical awareness of a group of high school teachers who began meeting periodically 'to discuss the work of teaching,' and over the course of three years progressed from meeting for 'gripe sessions,' to becoming a study group, to eventually seeking a voice and empowerment through professional writing. The members of the group moved from a general lack of knowledge about or concern for theory to an awareness of the role theory could play in giving them a voice with which to enter public debates on educational policy. He saw the role of theory as 'ironic' however: the group in time came 'to use theory to illuminate the insufficiency of theory' (McDonald, 1987, p. 34).

The teachers in this group over time felt a growing need to move beyond the enjoyment of the 'rich specificity' of the stories they told each other about events in their classrooms and to 'frame them with generalization' (p. 37) — in a word, to theorize. They set themselves an agenda of reading the several noted books on school reform that appeared during the 1980s. Reading these theorists enabled the teachers to claim the very tensions and uncertainties that made theory so untenable as they were accustomed to receive it: 'What if teachers, recognizing the uncertainty of their work, raised their voices instead of growing silent? And what if theorists recognized that intimate knowledge of this uncertainty was exactly what was missing from both their theories and the policies these theories provoke?' (p. 33). In time, the teachers in this group did, indeed, begin to raise their voices. As they found validation for their own conflicts, tension and uncertainties in the reading they were doing, they began to value the contributions they might make to policy debates. Thus another irony that, regardless of their previous attitudes toward the theoretical, the teachers' efforts helped them gain greater insight into their professional experiences and to share these in the light of theory. At the time of his writing, these teachers were beginning to move towards a theoretical framework for addressing social policy.

In McDonald's article, as a backdrop against which to trace the teachers' changes in thinking, he pointed to 'the long history of confidence among theorists that effective teaching can be empirically verified and thus becomes the basis for prescriptive school improvement' (1987, p. 26). As a result, teachers have historically been regarded as technicians whose role is to carry out the designs of researchers and academicians under the direction of curriculum supervisors. Teachers have, however, an 'intimate knowledge' of the struggles, the tensions, the 'uncertainty of teaching, its messy practicality, which theorists generally sidestep' (p. 48).

Schön's (1988) observations on the 'gap between the schools' prevailing conception of professional knowledge and the actual competencies required of practitioners in the field' are much like the attitudes reflected by the teachers in McDonald's group:

> The professional schools of the modern research university are premised on technical rationality. Their normative curriculum, first adopted in the early decades of the twentieth century as the professions sought to gain prestige by establishing their schools in universities, still embodies the idea that practical competence becomes professional when its instrumental problem solving is grounded in systematic, preferably scientific knowledge. So the normative professional curriculum presents first the relevant basic science, then the relevant applied science, and finally a practicum in which students are presumed to learn to apply research-based knowledge to the problems of everyday practice . . .
>
> But, in the throes of external attack and internal self-doubt, the university-based schools of the professions are becoming increasingly aware of troubles in certain foundational assumptions on which they have traditionally depended for their credibility and legitimacy. They have assumed that academic research yields useful professional knowledge and that the professional knowledge taught in the schools prepares students for the demands of real-world practice. Both assumptions are coming increasingly into question.
>
> In recent years, there has been a growing perception that researchers, who are supposed to feed the professional schools with useful knowledge, have less and less to say that practitioners find useful . . . At the same time, professional educators have voiced with increasing frequency their worries about the gap between the schools' prevailing conception of professional knowledge and the actual competencies required of practitioners in the field. (pp. 8–10)

A number of theorists (John Dewey, 1929; Philip Jackson, 1968; Arthur Bolster, 1983; and Donald Schön 1983) have delineated these tensions and conflicts in teaching as well as other professions. Perhaps these divides are fueled by the assumption that we can find definitive theory that provides definitive answers. However, as McDonald emphasized:

The problem with practice . . . (and thus with practitioners' knowledge) is that its most distinctive feature is uncertainty. No matter how smart practitioners may be, their 'judgment and belief regarding actions to be performed,' as Dewey puts it [1929, p. 6] 'can never attain more than a precarious probability.' Teachers in the United States, like others trained in Western habits of thought, come therefore to regard their own knowledge as inherently provisional — useful perhaps for getting one through a teaching day, but not particularly worth sharing with others, nor even worth articulating to oneself. Discovering uncertainty when certainty is the measure of knowledge can only produce demoralization, and perhaps paralysis of action as well. (1987, pp. 32–3)

It is probably safe to say that most of us came to our first comprehensive understanding of the major theories in our respective fields at some time during our graduate school days. Moving from the practical concerns and the often taken-for-granted 'common-sense' theories of the workplace to a world of abstract academic theorizing can be something of a culture shock. This was certainly the case for Anne DiPardo (1993) and for the teachers whom she interviewed about their experiences as graduate students in English education. We found her account compelling because in so many ways the experiences of DiPardo and her participant colleagues resonated with our own. Some of DiPardo's participants related how they had started graduate work with a fear that they would move away from their roots as teachers. They shared a seemingly common attitude that the academic concerns for theory and research are somehow outside of the real world: 'I don't want to be a different person when I finish this [doctoral] degree . . . I don't want to lose the heart, the compassion, the down-to-earth, the practical — you know, being real' (DiPardo, 1993, p. 197). The teachers reported that perhaps the biggest adjustment for them had been the discourse of the university classroom. 'Many . . . recalled being initially "frightened to death" by the language of graduate school . . . It was a different language — it was like learning a foreign language' (DiPardo, 1993, p. 201). However, once they got past 'the language barrier' in academic readings and discussion, they saw that their readings gave them 'some powerful new ways of conceptualizing the familiar life of classrooms':

Many of the teachers reported that new terminology gave them a way of rendering fully conscious beliefs that previously had been only vaguely articulated. Several recalled an acute sense of realization when, in a graduate-school discussion of Vygotskian theory, they were first introduced to the terms 'scaffolding' and 'zone of proximal development' . . . Similarly, two doctoral students recalled how a rhetorical theory course had given them new ways to reflect upon their own shifting uses of language. (DiPardo, 1993, p. 202)

Margaret recalled her own career as a graduate student. Until she started reading theory, she had not appreciated the vast number of theoretical positions in the field of language arts alone. There were deep differences in perspectives about learning and about the nature of reading that lay below the surface of disagreements in her own school district. Beneath the outwardly placid surface of classroom routines there were stirrings that sometimes boiled over into arguments among classroom teachers, reading specialists, and the director of curriculum, about the merits of different approaches to the teaching of reading — phonics; whole-word, language experience; literature based. Disagreements over methods were not talked about in terms of theoretical differences by most of the people involved, but Margaret had found new ways to make sense of what she saw going on. Her first readings gave her a vocabulary in which she could reflect on fresh ideas that were, however, compatible with her own hitherto inarticulate beliefs about teaching.

At the same time that DiPardo's participants reported a shift in their understanding of classroom life, they also found that their university experience had helped them to alter their understanding of the nature and uses of theory itself. They reported that they became aware of theory as emergent, socially constructed, negotiated. They had learned to use theory to ask 'what if?' but found that in school settings they were more often pressed to use it to answer 'what works?' (1993, p. 208).

> In the world beyond the university, worthwhile 'theory' and 'research' are often assumed to highlight effective strategies, sending teachers off like so many cognitive nomads to 'translate' these new understandings 'into practice' . . . Given the pressure to defend practices and expenditures, theory and research are typically regarded as ways to settle rather than unsettle. (DiPardo, 1993, p. 210)

Many of us, also, have realized that with sharpened awareness of our theoretical stances we have had to literally learn a new language to express the ideas with which we deal. And we might have found, as did Eliza Doolittle, that our new-found vocabulary separates us from our workplace colleagues as surely as Eliza's made her an outsider to Covent Garden. One of DiPardo's participants wrote of her conversation during a get-together with former school colleagues:

> They're saying 'you've moved beyond us.' And what I've wanted to say is, that's from your perspective. I don't feel I've moved anywhere beyond you. Certainly I want to move *among* you. (DiPardo, 1993, pp. 205–6)

DiPardo concluded that her graduate student-teachers wanted collaboration of a particular kind with both university and teaching colleagues — 'a collaboration that would allow them to forge links between theory and practice as they composed professional lives distributed across diverse terrain' (1993, p. 210). This desire, of course, also echoes an interactive, cooperative theory of learning and a theory of reflective practice.

It is this same desire to remain close to the lived experience of those whom we touch in the course of our professional lives that has led many members of the helping professions to find qualitative research most compatible. This in no way frees us from the responsibility of thinking deeply about theoretical issues, however. Quite the contrary. As qualitative researchers, it is important to achieve a certain sophistication and self-consciousness regarding theory. We must come to understand that theory is universal and inescapable. This is one of the fundamental tenets of our research paradigm. It is not just 'we' who have 'become' theoretical as graduate students and researchers. We always were, and 'they,' our fellow practitioners, always are. It is, rather, a matter of raising our implicit theoretical positions, or 'theories of the world in the head,' to a level of awareness and conscious reflection.

We assume that most of you, like us, have experienced the ironies of attitudes toward both theory and practice that appear to be part of the dailiness of life in all of the helping professions. A similar wish for collaborative work and the forging of links between theory and practice led our colleague Rita Kopf, a Director of Nursing in a large hospital, to consider re-entering a hospital as a staff nurse and using this experience as the focus of her dissertation research. Rita also found, in the literature and in her conversations with nurses, the same distrust of researchers and administrators that McDonald and DiPardo noted among their teacher particip- ants. Here is part of her story:

> In 1988, I assumed the position of Director of Nursing at a 240-bed hospital in a northeastern state. I quickly set about supplementing my clinical background with information necessary to organize, direct, and develop the nursing service. While I again experienced the joy of making a difference, I had to contend with waves of discontent and insecurity. I was, in some ways, out of my element. I missed the direct participation in practice. The angst was particularly violent during periods such as budget time. I spent long periods immersed in paper and projects related to the predictable but difficult realities of working in a complex, intractable hospital. (Aiken, 1990, p. 72)

> It was during periods of frenetic paper processing that I fantasized most vividly about returning to the world of nursing. In my fantasies, only the joyous, exhilar- ating aspects of the job were highlighted. There I would be — knowledgeable, caring, and expert — making a measurable difference by providing humanistic care during pain, fear, grief, joy. I wanted to return to this 'privileged place of nursing'. (Bennett and Wrubel, 1989)

The passages we have quoted here are from Rita's research proposal for 'Back to the Trenches: A Naturalistic Study of Re-entry as a Staff Nurse.' In addition to tracing the themes of this section — the growth in personal knowledge of theory set against the perceived gap between theory and practice in the professions — please also notice Rita's use of related literature. The above quotations, from the early pages of the 'Introduction', illustrates a trend we have noticed lately and encourage — a more organic and informal treatment of the literature. Rita introduced in the first paragraph a reference to literature on 'the hospital as an institution,' and in the second paragraph a reference to a theoretical perspective on the essence of the nursing profession.

In the following passage, Rita documented what is an essential part of the 'Methods' section of a qualitative study — an account of her initial entry into the field, in this case for a preliminary field study. In it, she returns again to the theme of the perception of a gap between the experiences of practitioners and researchers/ administrators:

> Staff nurses on one of the medical-surgical units known as 'hell unit' asked me what I was doing the weekend before when I followed the transportation aide around. I explained that . . . the shadowing experience is designed to increase [a

researcher's] understanding and grasp of a situation, to walk in another's shoes, so to speak, and try to see things from the other person's point of view. The nurses seemed fascinated, expressing their interest by turning their chairs and bodies to face me more directly, establishing and maintaining eye contact and giving no observable recognition to the housekeeper who began to clean the room. Nadine seemed most interested, saying 'Why don't you follow ME around then? I'd love to have you walk in MY shoes for a day. You should see what we have to put up with every day. I know that you are changing a lot of things around here and things ARE getting better, but you have to see what REALLY goes on to know what kinds of things have to be changed.' Terry, a nurse who works nights, invited me to follow her around suggesting that a view of nursing on the day shift would not tell the whole story. Laura nodded her head in agreement and supported the others to continue by comments such as: 'You're right,' and 'That's for sure.' I told the nurses that I would be honored to share their experience and thanked them for their offer.

In essence, the nurses' theme was 'Make your theory from our real lived experience.'

Conversations with Theory

There's always a hole in theories somewhere, if you look close enough. (Mark Twain, *Tom Sawyer Abroad*)

There is an element of wonder in the discovery of theory. We can become dazzled by the fresh insights it provides in those 'Eureka!' moments and by the power of its interpretations in situations that had previously seemed random or puzzling. It seems no surprise, then, that many of us may be fascinated by the vision of one or another theoretical stance. A particular theory or model may be seen as *the* one explanation rather than as one of several possible explanations that open a series of questions. It can also happen that the theoretical perspectives we first learn — and more particularly the mentors that open the door to these insights — may take on an aura of invincible certainty. Nancy Welch (1996) explored this danger in the study we have described in the previous section (see pp. 247–8). She drew upon the writings of Michele Le Doeuff (1989) and particularly Le Doeuff's metaphoric use of the relationship between the medieval philosopher Abelard and his adoring pupil Heloise:

In the Abelard/Heloise pairing, she [Le Doeuff] writes, Abelard attempts to represent himself and his philosophical system as complete, stable, and utterly independent, and he relies on Heloise's admiring gaze to maintain such a myth. (1989, p. 48)

It is Welch's contention that such a relationship is common in academic settings, and that it is, in fact, encouraged by an apprenticeship model of academic learning in which the student may move 'from semester to semester, from master to master' in an apprenticeship that never ends. Welch saw the student who was the focus of her study in such a relation to her instructors:

> ... apprenticing herself ... studying and imitating our ways of approaching academic projects, trying out discourses that are new and strange to her as if they were her own. (1996, p. 47)

It is easy to see how graduate students newly aware of the meaning and the power of theory can be drawn into an unquestioning adoption of theoretical positions that Le Doeuff and Welch see as a very present danger. Le Doeuff presents the concept of a 'third factor' as an antidote to this uncritical acceptance. The third factor places a system, 'a particular philosopher or teacher, in history, in interdependent relationships with others. It asks new questions, reveals unexamined assumptions, and works to deconstruct that myth of the complete and stable world' (1996, p. 48). The third factor can be whatever enters into the duality of all-knowing teacher and dutiful student to suggest alternative points of view.

> For Le Doeuff, the third factor can be found in interdisciplinary work, as the conventions, assumptions, and goals of one discipline reveal and revise that of another — as her work in feminist theory has turned her back toward revising the conventions, assumptions, and goals of philosophy. My reading of women writers works as a third factor too. As I read the autobiographical writings of Margaret Fuller, Simone de Beauvoir, and Adrienne Rich, all struggling with the models and influences of particular men ... my ideas about modeling in composition classes are disturbed. (Welch, 1996, p. 48)

Welch is careful to point out that not all reading becomes a third factor. In many classes, readings are 'carefully sequenced to lead students to preplanned conclusions ... are presented as a neat extension of the teacher and his or her model' (1996, p. 49). Reading may be a third factor, however, when it:

> ... highlights the limits of modeling, reveals our inability to see ourselves reflected entirely and unproblematically in a particular mirror, and produces, as a result, restlessness, examination, and revision. (Welch, 1996, p. 49)

We have likened the 'third factor' to Homi Bhabha's concept of the 'third space.' Both ideas suggest that there are places where multiple perspectives coexist. Margaret remembers well a graduate class that provided such a space in which the students were challenged to reconsider theories they had only recently acquired. The most memorable episode occurred around the stage theories of development which were so widely discussed at that time. Her own first encounter with stage theories had occurred during a course in developmental psychology a few years previously. Having a natural affinity for structure, she filled her notebook with columns marking off ages and stages for the intellectual, emotional, and moral development of children and adolescents. This new learning was reinforced by films and lectures in her school district on the theories of Piaget, Erikson, and Kohlberg. She still recalls several years later the waves of excitement that rippled through the graduate seminar as Margaret Donaldson's *Children's Minds* was introduced. This work questioned aspects of Piaget's developmental theory, and faculty and students passed it from one to another. Donaldson's book became for Margaret the first of many lessons in the questioning of received theory, and the entire experience was an object lesson in how theories — in this case, stage theories — can become socially constructed into 'fact' in professional practice.

Donaldson (1978) herself, in her 'Preface,' acknowledged the importance in her intellectual development of Piaget and the theory with which her own findings were to be at variance in certain respects:

> In the course of this book I argue that the evidence now compels us to reject certain features of Jean Piaget's theory of intellectual development. It may seem odd, then, if my first acknowledgement of indebtedness is to a man whose work I criticize. Yet the indebtedness is there and the acknowledgement is certainly due. Many years ago he was kind enough to welcome me to the Institut des Sciences de l'Education in Geneva; and much of my subsequent research was stimulated by the excitement of that first visit. If I must now reject some of his teaching, no lessening of respect for the man or for his vast contribution to knowledge is implied. No theory in science is final; and no one is more fully aware of this than Piaget himself. (p. 9)

We have often felt that this process of reconceptualizing received theory must have been a struggle for Donaldson because she was Piaget's protégé. Donaldson continued her 'Preface' with an acknowledgment of her work with other scholars and of collaborations with colleagues. These became for her third factors that contributed to the questioning of Piagetian theory.

When perspectives are in dialogue with one another, a 'third space' is created. For Margaret, her new conceptualization did not mean total abandonment of all stage theories; it was, in essence, something of a hybrid. There was a shift in the angle of her theoretical perspective, so that she became alert to instances, like those that Donaldson had documented, in which children's thinking did not fit the molds proposed by Piaget, Kohlberg, or other stage theorists.

We have spent profitable hours wandering through the endnotes to *Slim's Table* by Mitchell Duneier (1992) because they are filled with theoretical ideas related to his findings that we found fascinating. In some of these discursive notes, Duneier questions theory he 'received' during his days as a graduate student. Among them were discussions of the theories about social class that Duneier used throughout his work and theories of cultural differences between black and white people. In the previous chapter, we commented on the general arrangement of the analytical elements in *Slim's Table* that flow in an interpretive focus from smaller categories — at first two individual actors — outward to the setting of the study and then to neighborhood and society at large. Let us look now at the strong 'meta' twist in Part Four of the book. Chapter 9, 'The Stereotypes of Blacks in Sociology and Journalism,' consists of a meta-analysis of the sociological theories that inform the author's and other studies. In this chapter, Duneier makes the point that 'An educated public has long relied on sociology, as it has relied on no other academic discipline, to refine its conception of the black population.' He argues that the classics of the American sociological urban tradition that have focused on black urban males do 'transcend' some of the 'gross stereotypes' about blacks, but that nevertheless, 'as a body of work they confirm inaccurate stereotypes that happen also to be demeaning.' In part this has been done by authors who convey their 'essential goodness in relation to others, most commonly by simply advertising that his or her books present a less stereotyped view of blacks' (1992, p. 139). Duneier posits that often sociological researchers have studied 'young men who are members of the black lower class' because this focus produces data that are consonant with a particular theoretical framework:

> Part of the problem with these portraits lies in the theoretical framework which informs them. Since the 1920s, American sociologists — and especially the ethnographers among them — have been influenced by a view of human nature which largely derives from the philosophy of George Herbert Mead, especially as it was interpreted by Herbert Blumer, and as it found its fulfillment in the work of Howard S. Becker and Erving Goffman. This approach to the study of man — symbolic interactionism — views the self as created through the process of interaction itself and sees man as engaged in constant mechanisms of adjustment as he decides who he is based upon what others think of him.
>
> ... When fieldworkers enter settings convinced of the universal applicability of such perspectives, they are in constant danger of failing to allow for the possibility of an autonomous human being; they risk not perceiving a core self when it exists ...
>
> The problem is that black men can be found in a wide range of places, but the only public contexts from which sociological images of black men are derived are places where expressive styles would be most expected to manifest themselves and where sociologists see good opportunities to apply their theories of symbolic interactionism. (pp. 148–9)

Duneier's argument buttresses our own advocacy of a constant questioning of theory, and what is more, in how it is used. Throughout there are hints of his own growth in thinking:

> In discussing the urban ethnograhic tradition, I immediately recall how much more enlightened I felt after some of my own gross stereotypes about blacks were transcended through an encounter with these works ... Yet after my own years of attempting to build closely upon these inspiring [sociological] studies, I came to question whether the public influenced by such works has placed too much faith in them. (1992, p. 139)

Mitchell Duneier certainly provided fresh perspectives into the lives of his participants. We, who are educators rather than sociologists, are intrigued with his description of 'a caring community' among the men at Slim's table, with its overtones of an ethic of caring with which we are familiar through the writings of, among others, Nel Noddings (1984; Witherell and Noddings, 1991). We are interested in Duneier's theory of 'a core self,' and wonder as we read if and how it is addressed in the body of extant literature. We see in his work the conversations with theory that we ourselves try to maintain, the search for alternative interpretive angles of repose, for the 'third space' in which alternative theoretical constructs may be composed.

Changing Theoretical Lenses

We all feel that some of the best thinking on our early research, and on one another's work as well, has come after the work has been completed and published. Additional reading, advances in our field, the following up of new interests, sometimes above all the leisure for reflection, all suggest new ways of understanding and presenting our original findings, and of seeing other possibilities in the same data. Often an alternative analysis through the lens of a different theoretical framework is only possible after a lapse of time. This was certainly the case for Rachael Hungerford. When she designed her doctoral research, her purpose was to document children's responses to literature within a day-care setting and trace evidences of those responses in their play and other aspects of their life in that context. A major focus became the activities of one group of children who became caught up in the imaginary world portrayed in Star Wars videos and books:

> Josh rushed to the teacher, sobbing and holding out his arm, which had a red welt across it. Nora knelt down to examine his arm and asked him what had happened. 'We were playing Star Wars and Jack hit me during the fight.' The other four Star Wars players rushed up to defend themselves. 'You have to hit the enemies in a battle,' protested Jack, 'it's part of the game.' 'Yes,' agreed Kerrie, 'We have to beat Darth Vader and Josh was Darth Vader.' This was the third time that week that Nora had to stop the aggressive play that arose around the Star Wars stories. She took the group aside and talked to them about their play behavior. For a while they remembered — no hitting, no shoving. (Hungerford, 1993, p. 27)

The teachers in this class became increasingly concerned as the ongoing fantasy play of the Star Wars group became not only more physically violent but also excluded other members of the class. A fair amount of time and thought on the part of teachers and parent volunteers went into the planning and carrying out of instructional strategies to redirect the activities the adults considered undesirable. Rachael's study documents the class discussions during circle time about alternatives to punishing the 'bad guys' other than killing them; the children's imaginative extensions of the original stories into group writing activities rather than physical play; the attempts to draw in other members of the class by encouraging all to draw their favorite (or most hated) story characters; the restructuring part of the daily schedule to introduce new activities; the extension of the children's interest in Star Wars into a scientific study of space travel, complete with mock rockets for a trip to Mars set up in one corner of the room. Many opportunities were provided through group stories and dramatic play for the children to discuss aggressive feelings and behavior and find symbolic rather than physically violent ways of dealing with them.

For this study of children's responses to literature and, as it emerged in the course of the study, the efforts of adults to help them reflect on their responses and extend and redirect them, Rachael worked within a theoretical framework that included not only Louise Rosenblatt's (1978) transactional theory of the literary work but also the theories of L.S. Vygotsky (1962), Jerome Bruner (1983), and D.W. Winnicott (1971). These theories explore the relationships between a child's meaning-making activities, language, and play. In an article that is based on the aspect of her study summarized above, Rachael concluded that:

> [The teachers] expected and encouraged interaction with peers and adults as the means to negotiate meaning, and sharing and responding to literature played a major role in creating such meaning . . . Interactions with Star Wars books and the result-ant fantasy play provided long-term, multifaceted opportunities for the creation and exploration of meaning. (pp. 30, 40)

As Rachael continued her interpretation and discussion in this article of the value of the Star Wars reading and play in the lives of the children over the months, she saw the classroom activities as illustrations of the transactional nature of the reading process.

Rachael's more recent reading of multiple theoretical perspectives led her to look again at her data. In her original analysis, Rachael was interested in, among other themes, how power was negotiated between adults and children. For example Rachael read feminist literature after the completion of her original study, which led to a new examination of her data. In her words, 'The possibilities for gender construction and exploration have come out of further analysis of that data making use of feminist and critical educational theory' (Hungerford, 1994, pp. 2–3).

When we look at the passage quoted above from an article Rachael based on this study, we may notice that there were five boys in the Star Wars play group and only one girl, Kerrie. Kerrie was in a privileged position because the Star Wars videotape was at her house, purchased for her older brother, and she was the dispenser of largesse in the form of invitations to the other children to come over to view them. Rachael says that in the words of the theorists Henry Giroux and Peter McLaren (1992), Kerrie is looking for position and agency (power) in the day-care group. There are, of course, no meaningful opportunities for female roles in the Star Wars stories and being limited to taking on the role of Princess Leia does not give Kerrie sufficient scope for agency. Princess Leia does play a more active role than some of her fairy tale counterparts but, as Rachael states it, 'She is a supportive character and the story could proceed without her' (Hungerford, 1994, p. 11). Because of Kerrie's ownership of Star Wars knowledge, and of the videos and books from which that knowledge comes, she is able to exercise agency not only through her choice of whom to invite home to view the tapes but also in her assignment of parts and direction of action during the day-care games.

Over time, however, the other children in the 'clique' who have acquired a good deal of the Star Wars knowledge for themselves begin to grow restless under Kerrie's control, especially during the active fantasy play, and to demand more agency for themselves. First they approach the teacher to explain that it isn't fair that Kerrie is always 'the boss.' The teacher sends them to Kerrie to discuss the matter. Kerrie's reply is that she owns the books and knows the most. They dis-agree and enlist the teacher's support. Nora agrees with them and sets up a list of who can have a turn assigning roles when they play Star Wars. Kerrie is firmly told that the other children deserve a turn and that she must share. This episode becomes a decisive one for Rachael in her reinterpretation of these data. What would appear from certain theoretical perspectives to be a reasonable attempt by the teacher to establish fairness and order in the classroom now appeared as an imposition of traditional and unfair gender expectations upon Kerrie.

Kerrie, however, finds a way to counter this encroachment on her power. She does own the books and when forced to share her power over the physical fantasy play she takes her books to the book corner and invites the group to look at them with her there. Here she still decides who sits beside her, holds the books, and directs the talk. Because she does own the books, the teachers don't make her share this aspect of her power or the books, and she has retained some of the agency so important to her. However, the teachers are still not particularly comfortable with this setup and frequently suggest that this group look at other books or find other things to do. As Rachael continued with her re-analysis of data, following the interactions of Kerrie and the teachers and contrasting these with what was allowed or encouraged during the earlier play of the boys with the Star Wars game, it became increasingly clear that the staff of the day-care center 'strongly suggests that she do what is expected in the name of acceptable day-care behavior — take turns, share, and support' (Hungerford, 1994, p. 13).

It also emerged that differences in gender expectations were thrown into sharp relief when a new student, Alan, came to the day-care center.

> It has taken him some time to make friends and to find a place for himself . . . He made slight inroads into this group when he brought in his King Arthur story book to share with the class and sat with them to tell the stories. He also shared information about his visit to his grandparents in England where he saw a real castle. He manages to wrest complete control of the boys in this clique away from Kerrie when he brings in a large wooden castle, handmade by his grandfather and complete with whole sets of miniature knights, horses, and weapons. The boys are instantly captivated and surround him with questions and requests to play. Now it is Alan who assigns the roles, doles out the tiny figures, and directs the play. He keeps them focused on the actual King Arthur story . . . The girls in the core group are not invited by Alan or the other boys to join the castle play nor do the girls themselves ask to join. While they had all listened when Alan told the King Arthur stories, the versions he told had no female characters. There are no female figures among the miniatures either. While the girls have at least as much knowledge of the narrative as any of the boys except Alan, they have no access to either the story or the play. The girls stand and watch the play for a few minutes and then tell Nora [the teacher] what is going on. They don't ask Nora to make the boys let them play or complain about Alan being 'the boss.' They simply tell her that the boys won't play with them . . . Alan does not have to share his power. He is not told to share or to let everyone have a turn as Kerrie had been told. No suggestion is made by anyone that the girls might play the roles of knights. No one suggests to the group of boys that they should look at other books. The King Arthur play continues, without the girls, until Alan's mother takes the castle home again. (pp. 14–15)

Rachael's continued re-examination of her data in the light of fresh theoretical perspectives led her also to take another look at the reading material in this 'literature-rich' environment:

The literature texts made available are described generally as being those 'most pre-schoolers like' and they are representative of the accepted canon of children's literature. As might be expected the subject positions offered in these texts are generally those of passivity for females and activity for males, more and more variety of character possibilities for males than females and no expression or expectation of the possibility of crossing gender lines. Boys are revived but never rescued, girls support and help solve problems but are never the warriors or ultim-ate decision makers. Often they are not visible in the narratives being acted upon and seldom are they truly necessary. There were no stories that totally excluded males. (p. 20)

The contrast in the conclusions of these two articles is startling. By the criteria of the researcher, in the first study the setting was found to be 'child-centered' and 'literature rich.' Many episodes were documented that showed children involved in imaginative play resulting from transactions with literature. The fresh look at the data, however, indicated that:

> While this setting is considered ideal in its definition of being child centered and literature rich, it would appear that it is a bit more centered and more rich for some children than for others in both cultural and textual opportunities and expectations. (p. 21)

In this book, as in other writing and teaching, the members of this team have made much use of Becker's *Writing for Social Scientists* (1986). It was natural for us, then, to turn to it in the course of this writing. We have always enjoyed his style — relaxed, sometimes irreverent, occasionally a little flippant. Our attention was caught by what seemed a marked change in tone in the last chapter when he documents his own changing of theoretical lenses and use of 'the literature.' The story he tells illustrates his point that 'the bad side' of overreliance on traditional theory is that it can 'deform the argument you want to make, bend it out of shape in order to fit into the dominant approach' (p. 146):

> My work in deviance taught me this lesson the hard way. When I began studying marijuana use in 1951, the ideologically dominant question, the only question worth looking at, was 'Why do people do a weird thing like that?' and the ideo-logically preferred way of answering it was to find a psychological trait or social attribute which differentiated people who did from people who didn't. The under-lying premise was that 'normal' people, who did not possess the distinguishing casual stigma you hoped to discover, would not do anything so bizarre. I started from a different premise, that 'normal' people would do almost anything if the circumstances were right. That meant that you had to ask what situations and processes led people to change their minds about this activity and do what they formerly would not do . . .
>
> My eagerness to show that [the] literature (dominated by psychiatrists and criminologists) was wrong led me to ignore what my research was really about. I had blundered onto, and then proceeded to ignore, a much larger and more inter-esting question: how do people learn to define their own internal experiences? That question leads to the exploration of how people define all sorts of internal states, and not just drug experiences. How do people know when they are short of breath or have normal bowel movements or any of the other things doctors ask about in

taking a medical history? Those questions interest medical sociologists. How do people know when they are crazy? I think, looking back, that my study would have made a more profound contribution if I had oriented it to those questions. But the ideological hegemony of the established way of studying drugs beat me.

I don't know how people can tell when they are letting the literature deform their argument. It is the classic dilemma of being trapped in the categories of your time and place. What you can do is recognize the dominant ideology (as I did at the time with regard to drug use), look for its ideological component, and try to find a more neutral stance toward the problem . . . Use the literature, don't let it use you. (Becker, 1986, pp. 147–9)

We found it encouraging that Becker would look back over his research life with so critical an eye, would look for ways in which it could be revised. This recursive examination of our own work is a process in which we often find ourselves engaged. It seems to us as though he is being a little hard on himself, however, when he writes: about his original work, especially since what he learned 'use the literature, don't let it use you' is an invaluable piece of advice still needing attention today.

It seems to us that alternative perspectives reveal themselves gradually and over time. We have already indicated that we favor wide interdisciplinary reading as one 'third factor' that can ease and speed our progress out of the trap of our own categories. Collaborative work, in which members of a research team, each with her or his own theoretical vision, share their interpretations and, perhaps, attempt to forge a group interpretation, is another way to change theoretical lenses. We might better say to exchange theoretical lenses. A picture comes to mind of children seated around the cafeteria lunch table taking off their glasses and passing them around so that each could try on what it was like to see through the others' — an imperfect analogy, however, because another person's physical glasses will almost surely blur anyone else's vision. With our metaphorical glasses of new or expanded theory, however, we can see things hitherto unnoticed. In fact, in a certain sense we can now see from multiple angles of vision at once. If we want to switch metaphors, we are a little higher up the mountain of the trancendant view so more angles of vision have now become apparent from a new perspective.

When writing of their collaborative research work, Judith Davidson Wasser and Liora Bresler (1996) describe the same kind of exchange of theoretical perspectives over time. The team's focus was a qualitative study of an Arts in Education project, and plans for collaborative interpretation were, in fact, built into the makeup of the group (the collaborative aspects of this process are discussed in Chapter 6 of this volume). Here is what they said about the theoretical perspectives brought to their task:

An excellent example of the multiple voices/multiple lens dilemma we faced can be seen in the various ways members approached the issue of the purpose or focus of art education. For instance, Hertzog had a strong background in gifted education, a world in which careful attention is paid to individual children and their talents. When observing a class or reading the observations of others, she sought information on the ways teachers developed children's special and unique talents, and she worried when she found evidence of schools' failure to address children with unusual artistic talent. Lemons, with many years as an elementary music teacher, believed in public education, and arts education, as an opportunity for all children. She sought evidence that all children had equal access to participation and worried when she found schools lacking in their commitment to provide equal amounts and kinds of arts experiences to all children. In this sense, her concern with the potential of public education in the arts contradicted Hertzog's concern with the dilemma public schools face for providing special assistance to children with special talents. Similar to Hertzog's position, but nuanced in another way, was Bresler's position and, in some respect, that of Fertig. As a trained concert pianist, Bresler valued professional training, including the development of technique, the emphasis on excellence and hard work, and a concern with the traditions of an art form. Bresler's position, however, foregrounded the art discipline, whereas Hertzog's position, like Lemons's, emphasized the needs and development of the child . . . (p. 10)

Particularly noteworthy in their account of a collaborative project is the researchers' emphasis on developing an interpretive community, moving into what they came to call 'the interpretive zone . . . the place where multiple viewpoints are held in dynamic tension as a group seeks to make sense of fieldwork issues and meanings' (p. 6). This interpretive zone became a place in which it was safe to do a great deal of trading of lenses. As the authors of this article point out, in such a zone and over time the members adopted some of the perspectives of the others, and reached some group consensus as well.

If we step back from their research project described in this article, we see another change of theoretical lens for the same body of data on the part of two of the original researchers. In preparation for the article from which we have just quoted, Wasser and Bresler took the same body of data from which their group had prepared its report but now wrote about their collaborative efforts. The theoretical framework for those data was thus changed from one about the group's interpretive perspective to one about collaborative writing and research. Out of this, Wasser and Bresler evolved their theoretical construct of the 'interpretive zone.'

Egon Guba and Yvonna Lincoln provide for us what is certainly an effective collaboration of qualitative researchers. In an interview with Jo Michelle Beld (1994), they trace the course of their 'personal "paradigm shift" away from positivism and toward constructionism' (p. 100). The course of their intellectual journeying resonates strongly with us. Guba states that 'Paradigm shifts are like religious conversions' (Beld, 1994, p. 100). This is not surprising when one considers that these shifts involve changes in foundational assumptions about reality, roles, and method. Members of our writing team have followed the evolution in thinking of Lincoln and Guba and have been inspired by it. In fact, Lincoln's chapter on 'The Making of a Constructivist: A Remembrance of Transformations Past' (in Guba, 1990) spurred our chapter in *Circles* (Ely *et al.*, 1991) devoted to 'Metamorphoses,' where we traced the paradigmatic journeys taken by some of our students and colleagues as well as other published researchers.

Changing of interpretive perspectives is not always easy. There is often discomfiting relinquishment of the security of established philosophies. For some, the unknown brings a sense of challenge, for others it may bring a sense of disillusionment. Perhaps these are among the sadnesses and sorrows that are mentioned in this poem:

Anaximenes

Only Miletos of the cities that make
the modern world can boast a man
the like of Anaximenes.
Old, perhaps, our master and friend
showed us how the very stars
in their crown circle round the head
of our tired world, to disappear
behind the wild peaks at the
edge of the earth, now shining now dark.
And he taught us foremost of all comes air,
life's everything whose simple breath
we breathe and whose transparent arms
hold in place the moon and the sun.

Old in the service of philosophy
truth in full measure his, how
shall we believe him now, who tells
us knowledge brings sadness; wisdom, sorrow in its wake?
                    Peter Warshaw

For some of us who grew up cradled in the secure certainties of positivism, to relinquish those beliefs may have been like abandoning the 'fact' that the world had an edge. For example, to look anew at our classroom through the eyes of feminist theory may be unsettling to our former notions, as unsettling as it was to ancient philosophers to realize that, in spite of appearances to the contrary, the 'transparent arms' of the air do not 'hold in place the moon and the sun.' But all is not lost. We work to revision the possibilities that new theoretical perspectives can bring to our professional, cultural, and political worlds. Leaving behind the cradling arms of air has the productive effects of allowing us to explore yet again and further the wild peaks beyond what only *seems* the edge of the earth.

Chapter 6

Negotiating, Collaborating, Responding

Horatio: O day and night, but this is wondrous strange!
Hamlet: And therefore as a stranger give it welcome.
There are more things in heaven and earth, Horatio,
Than are dreamt of in your philosophy. (*Hamlet*, Act I, Scene 5)

This chapter title embodies our deep conviction that writing is best understood as a profoundly social act. Even in solitude, even if unaware, the writer carries on an inner dialogue with audiences as well as with past teachers and writers. To pursue the implications of this view, to be deliberate about cultivating a genuine exchange with others, can make the writing process the locus for an ongoing dialogue. This involves the writer in additional perspectives and cultural frameworks and beyond the personal domestication to see again what is strange. How does or how can social context help or hinder in shaping and revising that writing? Many of us have been taught — most particularly in English classes, as LeFevre (1987) suggests — that writing is a solitary act of an autonomous individual. Our experience, current theory, and the data we are examining point to the limitations and even counter-productivity of that view, and the potency of considering the social dimensions of writing.

Of course we sit alone to write much of the time. Of course no one can do it for us. LeFevre quotes from Dewey (1927) to make this point: 'Individuals still do the thinking, desiring, and purposing, but *what* they think of is the consequence of their behavior upon that of others and that of others upon themselves' (p. 24). LeFevre (1987) continues:

> What is unique about the individual inventor is his or her particular way of inter-acting with others and with socioculture — as Dewey puts it, 'a distinctive way of behaving in conjunction with and in connection with other distinctive ways of acting, not a self-enclosed way of acting, independent of everything else!' (p. 35)

If we recognize the reality of our interactions with others as a force in shaping our writing, we can cultivate these opportunities (LeFevre, 1987, p. 123) and exercise some choice in the midst of the human complexities that inevitably surface when people do sustained work together. In this chapter our focus is on the social inter-actions that help shape the writing; in Chapter 7 we focus on the writing tasks and the individual writer. Here we foreground the group exchanges that bring the writing to full growth. We do this because we believe that if the human sciences are to have a significant impact on people and situations, then those who do the research and writing that will make a difference for practice must educate themselves deeply toward that end.

We need to shape a collaboration that supports and develops the many, not just the few. How can we contrive to negotiate a preparation comparable to the initiation and immersion into their craft of anthropologists, actors, artists, dancers, and, we want to add, dentists? Having experienced a long course of state-of-the-art dental work at a college of dentistry, Maryann has had ample opportunity to observe the before and after conferences, the analysis of work, and the on-the-spot coaching by experienced faculty. This for a tooth; why less for the whole human being? We need to put together and sustain the elements of excellence and substantial preparation that in other times were, and too often still are, the province of a privileged elite. This may seem utopian, but we have seen the elements of such leavening come together with powerful effect in qualitative research. We think the social dimensions of writing are crucial in this effort: negotiating with close collaborators — peers, mentors, co-authors, and participants — and with what LeFevre (1987) calls 'social collectivities' — academic departments, editors and grant givers.

The qualitative researchers from whom many of our data are drawn did their writing in the context of a year-long immersion in a qualitative research course — a temporary community. To this database we fold in some accounts from the published experiences of teachers who sought to design and carry out a liberatory pedagogy — 'participatory, critical, values-oriented, multicultural, experiential' (Shor, 1987, p. 22). As we were shaping this chapter, however, we debated whether to discuss a classroom context for writing. Some of us felt we should not because this book does not center on the *teaching* of research writing. But Maryann persevered. In her view, the context was not tangential. She had observed the research writing group for a semester and was adamant that much of importance could be learned here by seasoned as well as by novice researchers. She was struck by the writers' sustained productivity and by the quality of their writing. Her interest was piqued to dig more deeply for what was going on. This chapter, then, explores the group experience because of our strong sense that the social context of writing can be a potent catalyst in the development of research writers.

In this chapter we first examine the variety of negotiations that can help researchers shape and revise toward writing of quality: the interactions with peers who help one another to move forward, with mentors who offer the wealth of their experience one to one, and finally with the range of those who weigh the final document for publication. Next we move to the intimate give and take of collaborative writing. Last of all, we look closely at a range of specific responses to writing that may facilitate giving and receiving useful suggestions.

Negotiating with the Support Group: Helping Each Other Along

To turn an ethnographic eye to the experience of recognized writers in any field is to discover the social dimensions of their writing lives. Charles Darwin and Mikhail Bakhtin both found the company of their peers indispensable. Stephen Jay Gould

(1985) asks: 'Where would Darwin have been in 1837 without Gould, Owen, and the active scientific life of London and Cambridge?' (p. 347). Darwin did not crystallize the doubts he had entertained into an evolutionist viewpoint until he was challenged in conversation with his colleagues back home in England:

> Darwin was exhilarated as he converted to evolution and prepared to reread his entire voyage in the new light. But he was also acutely embarrassed because he now realized that his failure to separate finches by islands, no particular problem in a creationist context, had been a serious and lamentable lapse . . . fortunately three of his shipmates . . . had recorded the islands of collection. (Gould, 1985, p. 357)

His friends' nudgings made the discovery a communal activity even though the giant step was Darwin's.

The experience of the Russian literary scholar Mikhail Bakhtin suggests what a centering place a writing group can be, especially if we find ourselves writing in a surround of conflict in many dimensions of life. Bakhtin's nine or so large books were shaped during the time he gathered with his circle of colleagues, even in the chaotic post-1917 years and the six years of his exile during the 1930s. From 1918 until his death in 1975, the 'Bakhtin circles' where he worked out his ideas over endless cups of strong tea were influential in developing Bakhtin's and others' lines of inquiry. So important were these meetings to him that for their sake he was ready to move to another city.

The camaraderie and intellectual stimulation of dialogue that both Bakhtin and Darwin enjoyed is enviable. These were experienced writers and thinkers; we are talking here to all qualitative researchers at whatever stage. The potential of such situations suggests that we consider creating something similar for ourselves. Here we want to examine the experience of participating in a collaborative group: the demands, process, and rewards many people have told us about.

Support groups probably are not for everyone. If your purpose is clear, your energy high, and your existing support system quite adequate, you may not need a formal support group. We know of some researchers who worked closely with a mentor/editor and preferred that kind of intense collaboration rather than group efforts. When support groups are introduced as part of the structure of a university course, some approach the experience with resigned skepticism as one more academic exercise. Beverley Shenkman, returning to school with a full-time job and a young child, was reserved and cautious: 'Could I siphon off more of my energies to this group, this class, my doctoral studies?' Larry Nelson wrote of his initial misgivings:

> Past experiences where group projects fell short because of ineptness or lack of commitment from particular individuals made it difficult for me to place complete trust in people whom I did not know in circumstances over which I had little or no control. The prospect of having my work critiqued by other students who knew as little as I did about qualitative research was not appealing.

Group work is not a magic bullet; Larry is familiar with what can go wrong. Immaculee Harushimana, recently from Africa, distinguished the role of the support group from that of discussion groups she had known. To her, the metaphor of support embodied care in that the other person be productive, while discussion implied combat:

> Maybe the terminology itself has a role to play in the way groups work. Unlike my negative experiences of anarchy and argument, in discussion groups I have found the support group vital to my research. For instance, at one meeting, a member told me, 'We need to read something from you next week.' To realize that the group was concerned about my work was very stimulating for me.

If you need what a support group can offer for your writing self, it is astounding how much time you can find. Still, as Larry's apprehensions suggest, a productive group will make demands for generosity and intellectual investment on each person in it. He continues:

> Surprisingly, the support group was not what I had expected. Constructive criticisms were aimed at problem solving, taking risks, clarifying issues, and exploring avenues of further creativity. Even commiserating with one another served constructive purposes, in assuaging our anxieties and vulnerabilities. The insights I received from my support group were helpful in directing me towards areas I had not fully considered. Consequently, during the semester, my attitude towards being involved in a group has changed from avoidance to the expectation of separation anxiety as the course terminates.

Larry touches on the deeper issue which perhaps underlies more circumstantial objections — the demand such a group makes for trust. Barbara Goddard found that she had to learn such trust through struggle and risk-taking:

> I am used to depending upon myself. Trusting others has not been a proven value or given in my life. People have always been divided into camps with all kinds of maneuverings that have kept me deliriously off balance. The little child's declaration of independence, 'Do it myself!' has always been a necessity for me as there was usually no one but me to do it. I learned this early. So collaboration is not something I naturally lean towards. It is hard for me to trust.

This call for trust enters into all the stages of a research process in which the researcher is the chief instrument. But for Laurie Holder, sharing her writing was the most threatening aspect of participation in a group, as her powerful analogy demonstrates:

> When I visited Hong Kong for the first time, I took my camera. I stopped at the concierge's desk for a map and directions, and he tagged a firm warning to the end of his instructions: 'Do not, under any circumstances, take any photos of the people in the part of town you are heading for. They are very superstitious there. They believe that each time you take a photograph of them, it takes away a part of their souls. It will make them very unhappy if you do so.' I feel a bit like that about writing. How you write, what you choose to write about, the words that you select to say something are very much a part of you. When I write something, I feel that although it does not take anything away, it exposes a bit of my soul.

Perhaps, then, support groups are not for those who fear too much letting their work be scrutinized — or then again they may be suited especially for them! Perhaps they are valuable to the extent that we are willing to embrace the growing pains of disclosure. Bruce Kellerhouse found the intimacy of the group costly, but in retrospect he viewed its give and take as intrinsic to the creative process:

> I often found the group work torturous. My experience of learning thus far had been 'Do it to me.' In our groups, we were required to do it to ourselves and others. It was laborious and tedious — and tremendously helpful. God, did I have to work! The experience was intimate, sometimes too much so. I had to reveal my soul — but how much? Not surprisingly, I enjoyed the 'paired sharing' experiences more, because it didn't seem so dangerous to be intimate with just one other person. In truth, some of the difficulty lay in my own reticence to participate in the creative process. Creativity is difficult; it's damn hard work — ask any artist. And that is what I became in this experience. An artist with a brush, who viewed an experience and tried to paint it as accurately as he could.

Fran Babiss describes in some detail how deeply social her writing process became as her group developed. She sees the group responses as increasingly implicated in each member's work:

> When Rashmini and Alberta performed the playlet written by Eileen, I felt a pride of ownership as if I had written the piece. And in some way I had, because I know that everything that I wrote this year (especially the later work) carried within it the feedback and comments of my support group and facilitator. My writing began to take shape when I wrote for the audience that would read it. Since I liked and respected the people for whom I wrote (including myself) my work is a product of their input. As the support group grew in intimacy, the feedback was more valuable and on target.

It may seem a happy accident, and perhaps sometimes it is, that a group gives the help writers need. When we collected the database about support groups, we analyzed and binned the data into major categories we labeled demonstrating, coaching, and internalizing. In this process we established the following themes about the experience of support group members:

1 They found in their groups DEMONSTRATIONS of affirmation, thought-provoking dialogue, and elegant strategies.
2 They gave and received COACHING as they attempted to adopt new approaches and strategies.
3 Over time they noticed themselves and each other INTERNALIZING fresh ways of thinking, working, and writing.

To explore these elements may heighten awareness of what to expect from a successful group and what we might do deliberately to foster one.

Demonstrations

To tout groups as a means of support and challenge is perhaps by now too obvious. Larry and many other researchers, however, mention the presence or absence of commitment to each other and of emotional support in their groups more than they detail specifics about the responses to their writing or ways they were helped with the craft of writing. Is that because so much of how to write is an accumulation of tacit knowledge garnered through watching how others work, through reading and through responding to each others' work? It does sound as if many people may need even more than explicit writing help. They need a place where genuine work is in progress, and where demonstrations abound of the marvelous complexities of writing.

What are the elements of creating such a place? How does the small short-term society that is a writing group evolve in a brief enough time and function well enough to meet its members' needs? The many pieces of writing and the comments we examined suggest concrete demonstrations of how to sustain productive work or an important dimension in the support group culture. In Margot's course for beginning qualitative researchers the sessions were structured to immerse them in an intense experience. Many of these people were not familiar with a class structure that involved them so intimately with a support group. Some indicated that they needed to rethink and to develop new ways of interacting. As Carole Di Tosti looks back, she acknowledges her need for the support of others more familiar with this research approach:

> It is very necessary to have encouraging, knowledgeable individuals who understand the depths of qualitative research. You are a goner if you have to deal with those who have a faint, arrogant comprehension of the paradigm.

Furthermore, in this context, groups had to be formed quickly without much opportunity for members to know each other well and on that basis to select compatible people. This situation was compensated for by a variety of demonstrations: the whole class functioned as a larger support group; smaller groups were formed on a fluid, ad hoc basis; other support groups came to visit — each experience offered conceptual underpinnings and examples of how a variety of writers worked. By 'demonstration' or 'modeling,' we mean the performance of complex behaviors by more experienced members of a group. Less experienced members can get an idea of the components of the behavior through watching or listening before doing it themselves, and can refine their understanding by further observation in the course of their own practice (Tharp and Gallimore, 1988). Often much more can be conveyed by a live demonstration than through words alone.

Full class sessions elicited demonstrations of people thinking aloud and responding to one another's writing. Zoraida Soliman-Cyr notes 'the climate generated made this support group noncompetitive and genuinely supportive.' Fran Babiss observes:

> How I came to respect my peers' opinions, intelligence, and motivation was part of the process of this year. I know that the modeling of Professor and the facilitators (sounds like a rock band) served to assist me in an unfolding sense of awe and appreciation of people's work, struggles, and products.

We understand Fran to be aware that the atmosphere of the class was no accident but was planned by the instructor and facilitators to be an ongoing demonstration of how people might respond to one another. Peter Elbow (1986) observes, 'None of us can function at our best unless we are *seen* as smart by ourselves and others' (p. xiv). How is this deliberately cultivated? Sondra Napell discusses how attitudes of mutual regard can be fostered in classrooms:

> As the quality of the teacher's questions improves, so too does the quality of students' questions; as the teacher demonstrates that he is listening and interested when others are speaking, so do students increase their attentiveness to each other; as teachers accede to, refer to, validate students' ideas — so then does student behavior begin to change. (quoted in Hawkins, 1976, p. 9)

During each semester of the qualitative course, an ongoing and successful support group, an offshoot of previous courses, presented a demonstration before the whole class who then analyzed and critiqued their interaction. It seems worthwhile to describe one of these groups in some detail because it represents how important the support group is in sustaining the writing. Rebecca Mlynarczyk, Jane Isenberg, Pat Juell, and Susan Babinski met every two weeks over a three year period. Two of the four, with dissertations completed, were in the process of writing books. As they explained to a class who had formed new support groups, each fall they set a calendar that committed them to certain dates. Only graduations and funerals might interrupt. They met on Fridays from 5 p.m. to 8:30 or 9 with coffee and soda on hand. Serious about being a working group, they saved their socializing for a late dinner afterwards. They planned so that they did not need to get up early the next day. They said that they 'gave one another the gift of time': if a person said she needed an hour and a half of time, she'd get it. Lots of writing happened early on Friday, fueled by the prospect of meeting in the evening.

The group described the kinds of help they gave one another. They demanded of each other: 'Read for . . .'; 'I need . . .' They took risks, they talked through their fears. They gave each other a variety of practical suggestions. For example, the group encouraged and prodded Susan, who had not talked to her dissertation committee for six months, until she re-established contact with them.

The four women demonstrated one of their group interactions for the class. Susan, the next destined to complete her dissertation, was doing an interview study of the experience of women who had served as nurses in Vietnam. She had shared a piece she'd written two weeks prior to this demonstration. Now she handed around copies and then read a bit aloud. Here are some snippets of her group's transactions:

> *Jane*: We love the fact that you took our suggestions about headings.
> *Rebecca*: What do you want us to listen for?
> *Susan*: Is it clear? Coherent? Does it belong here?
> *Jane*: Worry later on where it goes. For now keep writing.
> *Pat*: Are you talking about women in general there? Professionals? Nurses?
> *Rebecca*: I like the way you use the literature in your discussion; you're using it to 'talk with.' (Sounds of jubilation from Margot on the sidelines)

The people in the audience later referred to this as the 'perfect support group'; that demonstration led at least one other group to discuss its own ways of proceeding and to pick up the strategy of having an open time agenda for each member, based on need.

Susan Goetz Haver commented on another support group demonstration. Her words suggest that anyone who has not had this experience might seek out and sit in on such a group as a prelude to starting one:

> Hearing from people who were, or had been, working on their dissertations made the idea of dissertation research seem more real, and feel more possible. Just looking at Diane Duggan's binder made me run out to buy one (a small thing, perhaps, but it felt like an important first step). Watching the support group in action was worth hours of description. Listening to Priscilla's process, supplemented by reading the actual dissertation (yes, I know I was supposed to skim it, but it was mesmerizing!) brought a seemingly abstract process to life.

Demonstrations in the form of class reading and writing assignments helped members to build up their fund of knowledge and wisdom about research writing. This enhanced their roles in their groups. Iris Goldberg referred to the readings as 'the Circle of Intellect,' to be entered by pondering, probing, writing through obscurity and complexity to greater clarity and insight into the *why* and how of stories and other forms. Fran Babiss saw the readings as a necessary complement to the group interaction:

> While the support group spurred me on in my literary pursuits, the readings provided some of the how-to. The piles of handouts perched precariously throughout my apartment serve as useful resources when I get stuck with the writing or need to review a procedure. The readings were always helpful and interesting, although they paled in comparison to the human input. Yet either would have suffered without the other.

We think all support groups could benefit from some common reading to bring other voices, perspectives, and tools for thought into their conversation. Magdalen Radovich makes what to us seems a useful point; she viewed the authors she read as part of her community along with the facilitators and support group:

> I realized after talking to Mara and Judy and the members of my group that it is time to move beyond my resistance and confusion, that while exploring these issues is valuable, it can also serve as yet another block. So I set myself several tasks today. First I reread Wolcott; he provided the bridge, escorting me into the initial planning stages of my material. On the way over to the other side, I ran into several other helpful wayfarers: Corbin and Straus, Bogden and Biklen, and Ely and Company. The act of reading itself helped to locate me in a context conducive to reconnecting with my data.

The support group played an increasingly important part in each class session, so that by year's end, practically the entire time was spent in support group work. To offer the groups ongoing support, facilitators assigned themselves to work with one or two groups, spending more time with whichever group seemed to need their presence more. They attempted to actualize what Thom Hawkins (1976) says of writing teachers who adopt a facilitating role: '[Facilitators] do not tell students what they think they should know, but keep them company while they find out for themselves' (p. 8). Group facilitators in this context were the professor and other seasoned researchers: students from earlier courses; graduate students who were completing their doctoral research; and researchers in the field. The facilitators met for dinner once a week to reflect on what had happened in their group's session and to discover what might be learned for future sessions. They discussed issues of group dynamics, possible work with more and less productive students or with students who were struggling with particular problems. Each facilitator's view of the concepts and writing tasks were put on the table along with margaritas and tacos. Essentially, the facilitators were a support group themselves as they talked about what was happening, their stumbles as well as victories, their understandings about group process and individuals and their strategies. Their gathering helped them move to the support group session of the week that followed. Schön (1983) reminds us that even the seasoned practitioner's expertise is limited in the uncertainty and uniqueness of each fresh situation: 'The professional cannot legitimately claim to be expert, but only to be especially well prepared to reflect-in-action' (p. 345). The facilitators continued to learn as they experienced this work and looked back on it.

Facilitators took group members' writings home to respond to them in writing. This was deeply valued, as Karen Zielony explains:

> I was grateful to Carole for her very close readings. She obviously was committed to helping each one of us and, over time, came to know our stories almost as though they were her own.

Throughout the process, writing group members seemed to understand and appreciate how the facilitators were moving. Barbara Goddard recalled:

> New methods were threatening, especially when everyone in my group felt equally at sea. Sometimes we just ran around like chickens with their heads cut off. That made for lots of tension and frustration by the carload. Often one of us would see the light and lend some stability to the boat we were thrust into. Often Sarie Teichmann, our facilitator, was the stabilizer — lucky us.

Beyond 'outside' help to avert too much floundering, there was of course immense 'inside' demonstration potential in each support group. The members, though perhaps new to writing up qualitative research, brought formidable resources of experience from other contexts. Moreover those who entered fully into the course, making the time to do reading, writing, and research assignments with some thoroughness, were developing conceptual and writing expertise week by week. We heard numerous accounts of specific demonstrations by individuals that were seen as instructive and formative by their group. Beverley Shenkman learned from watching Joan Zaleski:

> We each cared about each other, and we worried if one person was more quiet one week. Ai-Ling didn't speak English very well. We would always try to give her a certain amount of time each session just to make sure we heard what was happening with her project and so that she would feel included. Joan particularly was very good at that. We did paralleling. Joan would say, 'Ai-Ling, what's happening?

Would you like to comment?' Then, recognizing what Joan was trying to accomplish, we would chime in.

In group meetings, members were asked to share their ongoing experience with a variety of writing forms. Beverley tells of suddenly assuming the role of comparative expert:

> We had to do a log analysis according to Tesch, and I did that. I took an excerpt from my log, and I went through it step by step. I had all kinds of lists and lines connecting things, and I gave everyone a copy. They were so impressed.
> Look what she's done.
> How did you understand what to do?
> What's this mean?
> Because nobody else had done it.

Molly Parrish compared her work in a constructive way with the writing she had the opportunity to hear, and moved to substantial revision:

> Listening to Iris's dramatic classical playlet, which beautifully represented her observations and her findings/feelings, pushed me to rewrite my own rather prosaic playlet. I became playful, stretched, risked, and wrote a little play that managed to intertwine what I saw of the students' learning interactions with their feelings and opinions about the dynamics of the class, in a setting which represented an actual part of the curriculum.

Dennis Parsons discovered that the effort he put into reading others' work taught him much about his own writing: 'Another factor in my change has to do with reading other logs. Seeing the way other group members write up their research gave me pause to reflect.' In such ways group members watched and learned from each other. We recognize, however, from years of witnessing teacher demonstrations in teacher-centered classrooms that demonstrations are necessary but not sufficient. Schön (1983) makes this point as he describes a situation in which a supervisor analyzed a case in conference with a third year resident in psychiatry. The demonstration was masterful. The resident reported, however, that while he valued the experienced therapist's knowing-in-practice, he also felt frustrated. Schön infers that this is because the supervisor did not draw in the intern sufficiently by explaining how and why he designed his strategies or what told him to shift from one to the next:

> [The supervisor] appears to be guided by a repertoire of story types, interpretive explanations, and psychodynamic patterns. He uses these but does not describe them ... His approach to instruction consists in demonstrating and advocating a kind of therapeutic reflection-in-action, but it is also an approach of mystery and mastery. (1983, pp. 125–6)

This was an impasse in which the supervisor did not model his thinking process out loud and the resident did not voice his concerns and needs. Often, but not always, a useful demonstration of qualitative writing needs to make public both mastery of the writer's craft and the thinking that underlies it. The art for the teacher is to energize group members to discuss among themselves until they see the point without the lecture. When Beverley's group saw her work and asked, 'How did you do it?' they were asking the needed question that moved Beverley from showing her work to sharing her process. Many of us have found essential this 'thinking-through' in a group situation that allows time and freedom to question. Moreover, as Richard Beach (1989) points out, modeling by the group of alternative strategies can encourage flexible notions of the task by supporting the idea that there is more than just one 'right' way.

Coaching

While Beach (1989) agrees that demonstrations are necessary, his research indicates that large-group demonstrations have little effect, at least for less experienced writers, unless individual conferences one-on-one with teachers or in a group of more experienced peers provide occasions to practice and receive coaching. By coaching, we mean guided practice, exactly the role Dewey has described:

> The student cannot be *taught* what he needs to know, but he can be *coached*. He has to see on his own behalf and in his own way the relationships between means and methods employed and results achieved. Nobody can see for him, and he can't see just by being 'told,' although the right kind of telling may guide his seeing and thus help him see what he needs to see. (Dewey in Archambault, 1974, p. 87)

Beginning researchers have told us that the opportunity for coaching by peers was one of the great benefits of their support groups. By sharing their writing in the smaller group they could take the time to pursue their questions, to clarify their expectations, to demonstrate and to coach each other as they wrestled with ideas and applications. William Parker wrote:

> The use of concepts new to me, such as metaphor, anecdotes, layered stories, playlets, and poetry as part of analytical writing of the report are clarified in the support group. The sharing of work and the discussions that follow teach me how to utilize the various genres. Once the concept has been clarified for me, either in the group or through personal remarks on assignments, I am able to utilize it.

Gradually he gets beyond, going through the motions to take possession of the conceptual instruments for himself and to handle them with increasing deftness, so that he can also coach others.

Support group members, by the very nature of the group and its tasks, receive a number of responses to their writing — usually the group total minus one. This supports Dewey's 'right kind of telling' because it provides contrasts as well as agreements that can help their understandings to crystallize. Fran Babiss describes how the process of practice and coaching worked for her:

> I got better at writing because I had to write so much. I wrote my logs for hours and hours, and practiced much like a piano player or gymnast. The more I did it, the better I got. However, this was not done in a vacuum — I received feedback on my work from multiple and various sources, so that I was able to mold my performance and improve it as well.

Fran indicates that her early approximations are refined by others' scrutiny and comments. She moves from the halting performance of the various kinds of writing to greater ease and fluency. Her facilitator and support group coach her from the sidelines. She understands that these ways of talking, thinking, and writing cannot be taught from outside the process. With the group's suggestions, she must mold the writing and herself as a writer as she proceeds.

Added to the complexity of any research writing process are the demands of the rigorous research that grounds it. It requires plenty of coaching to master the many understandings involved. Immaculee Harushimana had missed the first semester and had some catching up to do:

> Until I showed my work to the group, I had been interpreting previous to observing so I could base my interpretation on that. With their coaching little by little I learned to act as an observer. In my struggle to avoid judgments I started to better understand the function of fiction (layered stories, poems, and playlets) in an ethnographic study.

We are talking here about the need to build a personal repertoire of understandings and applications comparable to those that underlay the veteran therapist's elegant demonstration. Immaculee does not stop with seeing the forms as engaging. With the help of the group conversation she learns to use forms to see her data from multiple points of view and thus go beyond her judgmental tendencies.

Jane Martin, in her study of women who had never married, drew on the coaching of her colleagues as she practiced lifting from her data to a higher level of abstraction:

> What started with a theme about 'the right man at the wrong time,' evolved into a broader concept, something about 'wanting more from a relationship.' In discussing this theme continuum with my group we moved to 'I wanted more in a relationship than my parents had.' This is where a support group is really helpful ... for that brainstorming which seems imperative to take place, either within a group or with yourself.

Jane began with a simple, rather pat phrase drawn from an interview that gathered up the externals of her participant's predicament and attributed it to outside circumstances. It is a common-sense labeling that was less insightful and less generative to further thought than was worthy of the complexities of her data. With her group's input, Jane herself lifted to a level more inclusive of a sense of her participant as a person with desires and dignity, one that embraced more of the psychological understandings garnered from her conversation with the woman. With her group's coaching, Jane arrived at a theme that seems to us a richer, more promising analytical tool that could lead in a number of fruitful directions. Many people start out with very descriptive themes that need just such a lift. In the give and take of the group, they begin to glimpse the possibilities in their data. Another sort of lift was experienced by Jane and her group as they entered into the intellectual work involved in returning to the data. Together they persisted long enough for thought to ripen. In this example, demonstration and coaching seem intertwined, hardly distinguishable. One group member may watch quietly as others model a process and when he gets a sense of things, join in tentatively. Others coach him as they play with his contributions, and perhaps he, in turn, offers a demonstration of risk-taking or affirmation to someone else.

Sharing writing from the very beginning of the research helps the support group and other knowledgeable readers catch any glaring misunderstandings or misapplications or omissions early enough for a person to reconsider, perhaps to revise and to practice new ways, with the group's coaching. This is what happened to Der-lin Chao as she reconstructed her understanding of her role as observer. Her moment of insight was powerful and socially realized. She feels that her group saw what she could not at that time:

> I must say the support group is very hard to fool. My fieldnotes about a student interview contained no mention of feelings, no personal information. There were just lines of transcribed words. It did not make sense to the support group or to me. Not until then did I admit that trying to suppress my feelings did not help me in any way. I could tell from reading my later fieldnotes how different they were from the preceding ones. After this, I did not resist writing about feeling. I do not mean that it was easy. I had to practice again and again.

Magdalen Radovich, who wrote of her struggle with so much inner resistance, also appreciated that her group offered an external push:

> I spent a lot of time avoiding thinking about a research encounter that hit close to what is most important to me — my role as a single parent providing for my son. However, when my support group mates pushed me to write something, anything, about a section of my data on the spot in class one night, I found myself writing about this mother again.

Pat Gentile, too, avoided expressing her feelings. For her, she says, this resistance came from long educational and professional conditioning. She speaks of her group as a tool that aided her as she struggled to break through her 'settled tendency' to write in safe, distanced ways:

> Years and years of another kind of thinking, shaping, and modeling made this course difficult for me to adjust to. Add to this classroom writing experience my writing 'medical documentation' as a therapist and matters become worse. When I write about my patients' treatment I find I'm often thinking, 'Don't put your feelings down, don't write anything you can't prove, avoid being creative, remember this is a legal document!' Writing the log was similar to the observing and reporting I was used to as a clinician . . . But now I've been challenged to break my habit, to 'fly.'
>
> I heard myself say 'I'm not here for a creative writing course, I'm here to do research!' I persevered. I wrote and rewrote. I tried to 'loosen up.' I thought a lot about myself and what I wanted to accomplish as a novice qualitative researcher. My support group, I realized, became more and more a tool to break my habit. This kind of work, this kind of learning, this kind of being can't be done alone. Breaking my habit meant becoming more open, realizing it's okay to speak in another's voice, to use the 'I' statement. My group helped me to see the changes I needed to make, or more importantly, the different way I needed to look at this process.

The note here is not one of personal pain, but of effort to break out of a familiar deeply worn channel and lift, fly — perhaps to build a mental skyway? Pat is taking up forms left behind long ago — stories, poems, metaphors — and breaking out of a well-learned set of rules; she is the one doing the work. Notice her strategies — not only the willingness to do fresh revisions, but the effort to put on the mind of a qualitative researcher, to construct her personal rationale for the new ways of writing. Her mental effort is given added force and precision with her group's aid — the loan of their understandings and experience. Her words convey the view of coaching that Dewey and Vygotsky offer; the person does the learning but others can help in powerful ways. It is easier to construct a new set of assumptions and behaviors with the performance of others to glance at, with the sharp precision tool of agile minds nearby, and with their hands lightly on the learners to give the feel of how to proceed.

Another function of support groups was to help members balance between the poles of too much complacency and excessive self-criticism. Barbara Goddard's comments crystallize the stubborn self-doubt that plagues many experienced writers and suggests how much coaching helped her connect to her strengths:

> When I had to read this excerpt to my group, I did not volunteer. The others seemed to me to be much more sure of what they were doing so I went last. I felt that mine was much different from theirs in style. I was sure I hadn't done it 'right.' (How Catholic you are, my dear. Still trapped in right and wrong!) Nevertheless they seemed to like my piece and thought it was a good portrayal of Karen. I was surprised, as usual, that people liked my writing. Of course, I usually think they are just being nice, supportive.

Barbara's 'as usual,' 'usually,' 'still' and the self-berating tone of her asides suggest, as with Pat, the value of her group as a habit-breaking 'tool.' Gradually she is distancing herself from her often-played tape. She is not exceptional in this regard. Belenky, Clinchy, Goldberger and Tarule (1986) concluded:

> Because so many women are already consumed with self-doubt, doubts imposed from the outside seem at best redundant and at worst destructive, confirming the women's own sense of themselves as inadequate knowers. The doubting model, then, may be peculiarly inappropriate for women, although we are not convinced that it is appropriate for men either. (p. 228)

It seems to us that the supportive function of the group should not stop at what Barbara calls being nice and supportive. That demonstration of what Peter Elbow (1973) would call a 'believing model' is part of what needs to be practiced, with no small amount of coaching, to free the energy to do one's best work. Here is Margot's coaching comment to Maryann as she revises these very pages:

> There is substance here. Focus on that. Try not to go nutsy with all of our writing teams' 'outside' comments if you can make a good case for your decisions. I love it (sorry to be so positive!!)

We can't resist concluding this section with Joan Zaleski's vigorous gym class metaphor that speaks to the coaching she experienced as she shared her writing with her group. We look more closely at her group later in this chapter — they challenged her to the utmost:

> The exercises each week have been a form of mental gymnastics, leaving me out of breath, sweating with exhaustion, yet mental muscles ever trimmer and tighter for the work. I've learned it takes stamina to be a qualitative researcher. When I think of how flabby and shallow my insights were when I began my study, it scares me to think how close I was to being a 'blitzkrieg ethnographer.'

Internalizing

Many researchers mention that over time, and as members of support groups, they are increasingly prepared to actualize complex research writing strategies. The outcome that begins to surface by the end of a year is the developing sense that they are incorporating the kinds of questions and concerns that were demonstrated by others and that they had practiced with the coaching of their groups. When making suggestions, the facilitators would frequently add that they themselves had in the past been told the same thing and found it helpful. They in turn could risk being facilitators because they had made the conventions and procedures a part of their repertoire. Indeed, many facilitators report that seeing the process with new eyes by working with support groups has been a powerful educative experience. Internalization frequently takes time and may entail some misunderstanding or misapplication at first. We have seen that coaching focuses attention on what has succeeded and on what we still need to refine on the way to mastery as we gradually understand more of the subtleties. June Price and Carole Di Tosti observed this process in themselves:

> Many of my readers' questions I saw again and again in the margins were slowly becoming internalized, so that these same questions began to become my own in subsequent sessions of field observation. (June)

> Where I was not questioning myself enough, the group questioned me. Eventually, I began to comprehend the reflexive process and I was then able to better generate some of the concerns that I should have been dealing with at the beginning but didn't quite get the hang of until the group got underway. I found out in the revision and winnowing process of organizing data and then the writing up of the stories and the play, that I became self-correcting. I am not done with this process yet. (Carole)

It seemed that both June and Carole became more self-directed through their support group process. To profit from both demonstrations and coaching depends on what George Kelly (1963) calls permeability of constructs — the capacity of ourselves as old dogs to learn new tricks in a group of peers. It means seeing, listening, analyzing how it's done, and risking some clumsy efforts to incorporate what we judge to be worthwhile suggestions. Many researchers acknowledge that this learning involved stress, anxiety, even psychosomatic symptoms. A too defended, guarded stance makes learning difficult. Karen Zielony gives a good example as she shares how she was taken aback by the questions posed in response to her field log:

I would see all of those marginal comments and assume that I had the whole thing wrong and that there was no way to fix it. If she really thought my work was O.K., why all the questions? Very frustrating for a student like myself who had always had positive feedback. The mistake was to have seen the comments as determiners of a rather fixed evaluation. Perhaps because I was not used to working on an ongoing project, I was accustomed to end comments that suggested that I was where I was supposed to be, if not beyond.

Notice Karen's underlying assumption of 'one right way' and of 'if there are comments on my work, I must be wrong' — a starting point that soon went through a metamorphosis. In another key, we have heard from a fair number of 'successful students,' writing teachers, professors, and other professionals who saw themselves as excellent writers, and who had a serious struggle before they could allow themselves to be coached by others. Because they had some artful strategies, at first many avoided bringing writing to share and being open to hear people's responses. Some people spent time focusing on anyone else's writing but their own, some became defensive and angry. Most, if not all, quickly relaxed and entered into their group life with good spirits and better results.

Over a long time in a group that works well it is possible for members to get to know each others' work intimately and to recognize each others' styles and patterns. Margaret and Maryann worked from 1984 to 1990 in a support group named The Kitchen Group. This started as a group of three and ultimately grew to six long-time members. Maryann kept a log. In this series of quotes she records some of the coaching she had experienced and begun to internalize:

> Both Margaret and Judi found the parts readable and comprehensible, but could not follow where the whole thing was going.
>
> *Judi*: A little control on the rudder!
>
> *Margaret*: Move this up here; shorten this; you're writing too much.
>
> Make your headings parallel; distinguish this level from the one below it; conflate this very short section with that one.
>
> Margaret urged a return to the outline, a fresh view of the whole. Judi thinks she and I are both linear in the way we work and tend to get lost in the part we're working on. The reason Margaret can move around is that she keeps returning to her outline of the whole — can go from one piece to another. She suggested both a large general outline, and a sentence outline.
>
> *Margaret*: I suggest you make an outline with a sentence for each paragraph so the thought and the continuity are spelled out — and keeping in mind the dimensions — how many things can be grasped, how many points usefully made.

Notice the cordial tone of this exchange, the pointing to strengths. There is a succinct statement of the overarching problem, no minor diversions. This is accomplished by well-tailored suggestions that are at the same time powerful maxims for shaping pieces of writing. The options Margaret offers in her final comment reflect the gracefulness of her own writing as she imagines the reader and creates the rhythms and dynamics of her prose. Maryann hears and accepts while still seeing at the end that it is she who is in charge.

In The Kitchen Group, members often raised to awareness issues the writer had noticed peripherally. Many times their comments helped to hasten the process by suggesting solutions the writer had either wrestled with without resolution or avoided. As sessions progressed, they read over their own writing with something of each other in their heads. Margot speculates that groups foster a *degree* of revision that might not otherwise happen, and that this happens faster.

Maryann's log focuses on what we find are important linked criteria about group size and time that in this case allowed substantial work to take place:

> When another person wants to join the group, it causes some distress. We would like very much to work with the 'applicant' but we realize as we talk this over that adding one more person would surely work out to less time for each to present and discuss. The group feels there is a maximum that is workable to give this kind of attention to each writer. We agree that few committees give such an in-depth scrutiny or have such a picture of the whole work. I keep watching the mail for some great response from my committee members when the truth is it might not compare in value to the group responses.

Philosopher Michael Polanyi (1962) distinguishes *the articulate contents of science* from what he calls *the unspecifiable art of scientific research*. The latter can only be passed on by example — 'because you trust [the experienced person's] manner of doing things even when you cannot analyze and account in detail for its effectiveness' (p. 53). To the example of others — the demonstration — must be added a long course of hands-on experience under guidance — the coaching. The process is effortful. He describes the apprenticeship of doctors; we recognize similarities:

> Unless a doctor can recognize certain symptoms, e.g. the accentuation of the second sound of the pulmonary artery, there is no use in his reading the description of syndromes of which this symptom forms part. He must personally know that symptom and he can learn this only by being given cases for auscultation in which the symptom is authoritatively known to be present, side by side with other cases in which it is authoritatively known to be absent, until he has fully realized the difference between them. (p. 54)

We have listened to committed members of support groups in the early and later stages. We have heard them mouthing unfamiliar concepts with the awkward accents of a new language and then, when the knowledge has become personal, with a tone of authority. They tell us that doing and sharing the writing has ripened their understanding — the successful internalizing. To the extent that members of the group are committed to develop as researchers, everyone has progressively more to offer as the group evolves.

Glitches and Strategies

Besides observing support groups of qualitative researchers for over four months, we interviewed two people about their experience. Unlike most class members, these two were in the same group during the first semester and joined separate support groups in the spring term. Their accounts seem worth quoting at some length because the many positive comments we have reported thus far may obscure the reality of complexities and difficulties. Beverley Shenkman recalled from her vantage point:

> My first support group was a little nurturing klatch, week after week. Joan was particularly sensitive to the needs of each member. We were basically on our own, a mature group. I looked forward to it. We gave each other copies of our work the week before so we'd have time to read and comment. Each week we tried to focus on one person. Discussions were on target. I learned a lot from the group. They were responsive to the detail in my writing, to the power of what I was describing. That spurred me on to give more. I liked these women. I understand the value of a support group that clicks.

Beverley felt she got what she needed both emotionally and for her writing. She experienced that people were responsive to each other, with Joan Zaleski setting the tone. Since Beverley wrote and spoke about groups toward the end of the second small group experience, the first semester had receded a bit in memory to become more generalized, and is recalled in contrast to what followed. While Beverley remembered her first group with some nostalgia, she described herself as 'outsider' in her second support group. She felt inclined to pull back. Moreover she says that she was unavoidably late every week, which reinforced her sense of separateness:

> The second semester group was composed of strong individuals, intriguing. I felt like an outsider trying to break in, but I assumed this would pass with time. I experienced the group as competitive and aggressive and unlike the nourishing, supportive, and safe environment I had left behind last semester. It was a tough love group, not the right match for me. They almost never commented on my work, and I probably could have asked, but I didn't . . . I missed the point of what a layered story was. Meg, our facilitator, was the one who talked to me about it. In retrospect I don't think *anyone* got much help with their writing from the group. Lil, for instance, wrote in a very removed fashion. Rose had written something in first person, fascinating stuff. People told Lil, 'You wrote very well, but look at the effect it has on us. We don't want to find out much more, whereas with Rose we want to read every detail.' Lil fought them tooth and nail.

Beverley's account does suggest her awareness that this is her particular 'take' on her group. In the interview she went on to describe how the group wrestled with the ethical dimensions of qualitative research writing. Another member of their group wrote about the help she received from the group in recognizing and handling the problem of being co-opted by her participants. We can infer from these accounts that good things did happen. The issue is not whose version is 'right,' but how participation in the group helps people to produce writing they feel says it the way they want it.

Joan relates the experience of her first group quite differently than Beverley:

> In the first group I felt rather on the outside. I didn't get the help I needed from the group. What helped most were the written comments from Andi, our facilitator.

> There wasn't enough drawing each other out. We never established a rhythm, didn't bring in writing to be read ahead of time.

While Joan felt she had not found too much value in her first support group, she used the word 'breakthrough' about her second group:

> Dan, Ellen, and Pat had been together, but were happy to include me, and I felt comfortable with them. People were very sensitive to each other's needs; sometimes we would spend the whole time on one person's work. Ellen was particularly sensitive to the needs of group members. She wrote and said positive things, but she kept pushing me to loosen up my writing. I felt this helped me to blossom. One breakthrough came when Ellen found a piece of my writing that she thought had my voice. She pointed that out and urged me to continue in that vein . . .
>
> The group kept at me. One session I felt as if I'd been beaten up. Pat even came to me afterwards, apologetically, fearing they had been too hard on me. I was exhausted, but valued what had happened. I was angry, even devastated, but was able to step back and regain the real intent of my research, from which they saw I had been drawn away.

Even 'successful' groups have their struggles and certainly group members may see the benefits in different ways. Both second semester groups seemed more challenging than the first, but for different reasons.

Issues that show up in these interviews and that recurred frequently in talk and writing about the groups were quality of relationships, resistance, and lack of experience. Quality of relationships seems crucial if people are going to lay open their work to scrutiny. What if mutual commitment doesn't seem to happen? In Barbara Goddard's group, the facilitator attempted to intervene:

> Esther tried valiantly to get us on track, but the chemistry was just never right. I'm convinced people need to merge around shared interests, congenial personalities, something.

While Beverley felt she did not integrate herself in her second writing group, she recognizes the quality of their relationships:

> It soon became clear that they had been a group from last semester . . . They knew about each others' research, their obstacles, their strengths, their weaknesses. But more than that, they seemed to really know each other, like each other and be friends beyond the classroom setting.

Anne Lamott (1994) maintains that we do not need to be members of a group in which we feel diminished. Perhaps our own sturdiness and appetite for challenge and for other perspectives override our difficulties in those instances where we do stick it out in such a group. Beverley said she was intrigued by her second semester group even though she continued to feel like an outsider. Perhaps she gained more than she realized; her descriptions hint that this may have been so.

Rhonda Weller Moore's group faced difficulties directly. They approached problem behavior with what she reported was 'open, frank discussion in a most humanistic way.' For Tina Casoglos's long-term group, the observation of another group at work led them to make their next session an evaluation of how they were doing and whether to continue. This gave members a chance to reflect and encouraged them to suggest alternatives. Tina describes this:

> The ability to see how another support group works was very important. My group spent its next meeting discussing whether or not we should continue as we were. We have some problems: size, level of commitment, time constraints, and various levels of understanding, to name a few.

Resistance can sabotage group sessions; Rhonda writes about that:

> Procrastination occurred when people had not done the work; sidetracking detracted from the quality of the group's time. The facilitator was instrumental in bringing the group back to the topic at hand and in drawing out the ideas of the entire group.

In another group, two members created a strategy to deal with another person who monopolized the time with diversionary conversation. They agreed to insist firmly at the outset on an agenda, with time limits for each person. This worked for them. Shirley Matthews, who is a psychologist, came to the group she was facilitating as they struggled with their rather clearcut directions for the day's task. She identified what she witnessed as 'resistance and avoidance'. This offered them a language and some insight into what may have been going on. The group members were startled and mildly defensive, but Shirley did shake them loose. She shared this incident at the facilitators' dinner the same evening. Because it seemed valuable to highlight, during the next class session Margot pointed out to the entire class possible forms the 'R & A factor' might take. 'Don't spend the time asking, "Is this what she wants? Is this right? Focus on your writing."' After this, people in their groups often identified diversions as 'R & A' and called each other back.

In her facilitator role, Barbara Miller demonstrated ways of helping a stalled group to move forward. One time, for instance, rather than to suggest what members might do, she asked direct questions that called for an answer: 'Who's going to read?' 'What's your agenda for today?' Maryann's 'Maybe you might set an agenda' was a suggestion that had melted into the air like a ball thrown upward; Barbara tossed it to the group and members caught it. At another point she led the way back from a diversionary anecdote to the presenter's need: 'From your experience, what can you say to X?' Barbara's intuition was well founded: the narrator then spoke to the situation with the authority of her experience.

There will be times when group members lack the expertise they need. At times they can be quite off-base about the advice they give each other. A support group composed of writers for whom English is a relatively new language may be wonderfully comforting but less than adept at helping with matters of English usage. A group of neonates in qualitative research is likely to be ill-equipped to parry the thrusts of an unconverted positivist battling the notion of writing poems and layered stories, or of a strong voice fiercely opposing such an approach on ethical grounds. In fact it is a good principle to seek input from a variety of sources; we will elaborate on some of these in the next section.

Beyond the commitment, the modeling for one another, and the coaching, what finally explains the power of a support group when it works? Maryann likes Polanyi's use of the fine Latinate word, 'conviviality,' which manages to sound warm and lively and allows him to link images of pups in a litter and birds on a branch with the high reaches of intellectual exchange. Camaraderie is another way to say it, suggesting laughter, food, a shared goal that spawns its in-jokes, fondness, liking, ease in each other's company. Ruth suggests 'presence.' At its best, a support group offers presence — mental, social, emotional, and physical presence. Margot thinks of Annie Steinmetz, a member of the team that wrote in *Circles* (Ely *et al.*, 1991). The gifts of her hospitable presence — humorous and human-centered — helped create a climate where people wanted to work together. People maneuvered and, at times, fought to get into Annie's group. The team that wrote this book has come together at intervals over three years, long enough for loves, losses, births, endings and new beginnings, heavy responsibilities, struggles and victories, to swirl around and threaten to submerge one or the other of us. Yet friendship, mutual commitment to our common goal, the pleasure in each other's company, the challenge of the task, and the nudging of our publisher, have kept us coming together.

In her wise, witty book about writing, *Bird by Bird* (1994), Anne Lamott captures the growth of a group that met in one of her classes and continued to help each other go on writing:

> They've gone from being four tense, slightly conceited, lonely people who wanted to write to one of those weird little families we fashion out of whoever's around us. They're very tender with one another. (p. 159)

Lamott's book was recommended to us by that 'perfect support group' who found that she seemed to be describing them.

Negotiating with Mentors: Being Helped Along

In the dialogue that shapes our writing, we do well to explore the possibility for broadening the range of voices with whom we converse. Even if a person carries on a lively conversation-in-the-head about research writing experiences and directions, further challenge and exchange with others can extend that vision. As we have described, a successful support group can provide all sorts of peer resources. However, especially if a group remains bogged down or if the needs for expertise, support, or challenge are not being met, there are other ways to get help. In the event that the researcher is part of an effective support group, we still highly value one-to-one work with mentors as a special avenue of support. In the *Iliad*, Mentor appears as the trusted, sage, sometimes garrulous counselor of Odysseus. Athena, disguised as Mentor became the guardian and leader of Odysseus' son Telemachus. She pointed out his strengths and encouraged him to grow up and to take bold action. Homer tells us, 'she led the way, while Telemachus followed in her steps' (*Odyssey* Book II). She also flew off and left him to learn to rely on himself! For the researcher, mentors may be any one or a combination of committee members, friends, unexpected strangers, or consultants. At particular junctures mentors and support groups may be books, even though they don't talk back. A reader of *Circles* (Ely *et al.*, 1991) recently wrote this comment:

> Your book has served as my support group, and it has been an excellent one. You have provided the words which are essential to hear as one struggles and grasps for the meaning of the work and to formulate creative results. Whenever I start feeling lost and forlorn I draw upon your words.

What can be so special in live relationships, beside the possibility of invigorating attention and encouragement, is the up-close opportunity to witness the thinking process, the manner of questioning, the way of framing a problem, the careful focus of an experienced partner. Mathematician Reuben Hersh, who co-authored *The Mathematical Experience*, recalled the offer to supervise his dissertation by Professor Peter Lax at New York University:

> Lax's way of thinking about what he does is so clear, original and beautiful, and it is possible to get a glimpse into the inner processes of his mind while working with him. (John-Steiner, 1985, p. 201)

John-Steiner, who interviewed Hersh, adds that 'in establishing collaboration endeavors across generations, the mentor and the apprentice teach each other the value of interpretation and synthesis' (p. 201).

All of this is in the nature of exhortation to the writer and assumes that resources abound if only we will cultivate them. But the assumption needs scrutiny. For those beginning research, we need to ask whether graduate schools are places that initiate mentoring relationships, particularly for people who arrive with the constraints of little preparation in this type of work. The question is of vital importance. The answer of course varies. Mike Rose (1989) looks back to his experience in academia:

> My own initiators to the canon knew there was more to their work than their mastery of a tradition. What mattered most, I see now, were the relationships they established with me, the guidance they provided when I felt inadequate or threatened. This mentoring was part of my entry into that solemn library of Western thought — and even with such support, there were still times of confusion, anger, and fear. It is telling, I think, that once that rich social network slid away, once I was in graduate school in intense solitary encounter with that tradition, I abandoned it for other sources of nurturance and knowledge. (pp. 235–6)

Rose's experience suggests that mentoring needs to be institutionalized so that the opportunity is more widely available.

Committee Members

For many a qualitative researcher who is embarking on a dissertation, negotiation with committee members plays a crucial part in shaping the writing. At their best, committee members help ready the document to be accepted by the academic world. Judith Meloy (1994) corresponded with researchers who had completed their dissertations. They insisted on the importance of knowing the research predispositions of potential committee members and of winning their respect:

> I picked my graduate committee after I had begun my research and selected both data gathering and analytical techniques. I point-blank asked potential committee members about any biases they had concerning qualitative approaches. (p. 13)

> It is most important for the student to demonstrate scholarly competence in small ways over a long period of time; for example, by undertaking independent studies with prospective committee members that require readings, research and a written report — and then by attempting to get the research report published somewhere . . . When the time arrives to begin writing the thesis, the student may enjoy the unexpected freedom to act independently of close faculty supervision. This situation allows a student creativity in thesis preparation that otherwise might not be tolerated. (p. 15)

Phillida Salmon (1992) maintains that a view of PhD research that calls for researchers to 'evolve their own structure of meaning' asks not for training but for education that fosters intellectual independence rather than conformity. Her student Sheila comments on the value for her of their supervisory sessions:

> . . . as I begin to see new directions in which to move. It is essential to make clear that the new directions are of my own choosing and not suggestions from [her supervisor]. Never does she tell me to do this or not to do that. From her questioning and probing I am encouraged to explore and articulate my unexamined motives, my taken-for-granted assumptions about the research . . . I am enabled to reformulate my ideas and see new angles of approach. By this time I usually experience a renewed sense of excitement about the research. This undoubtedly results from the fact that I have chosen the next steps — they, therefore, have personal meaning and resonance for me. (Salmon, 1992, p. 27)

Accepting authorship of one's own project demands a mentoring relationship with the supervisor of the research that is based on sympathy, talent, trust, and mutual resonance through often trying times. Listen to Phillida as she comments on her own practice:

> The kind of supervision I try to practice can make for a bumpy ride. One major reason for this is that insisting on the value of prolonged reflection and the avoidance of cut-and-dried solutions imposes personal discomfort on student and supervisor alike, and puts a strain on their relationship. When the student's forward thinking seems to have failed or the project to have reached an impasse, I feel huge pressures to step in, to offer helpful advice about the directions which might be taken. This betrayal of respect for the work would, in the short term, allow us both to breathe a great sigh of relief. Refusing to take this line means prolonging a difficult and uncomfortable period from which we would both be glad to escape. (Salmon, 1992, p. 118)

Surely it is an art to challenge in the way Salmon describes and to communicate in the same breath the unwavering confidence that the person is up to the task, even up to original and daring work. Another of her student comments: '[She] has never let me go away feeling destroyed although I think we would both agree that I still have a very long way to go (p. 88).'

Salmon describes the interaction at the stage of crafting the final presentation:

> Few people adequately anticipate the sheer difficulty of writing up: of transforming into coherent and sequential form the whole complex, wayward and chaotic process . . . Since to me it is absolutely vital that the written thesis does justice to the research, I view myself as the repository, the guardian of the student's highest standards. I do therefore set out to be as scrupulously critical of the write-up as I can: its style, its content, its structure, its inner logic. This period of supervision is often very fraught. Writing is an extremely personal matter, and it is necessary to approach with tact and delicacy. Yet even so, to urge reformulations can produce anguish or hostility. Among my supervisees, however, no one has actually followed through their threats to abandon the work. The write-up has, through the student's commitment and courage, become fruitfully revised — and the relationship has survived. (pp. 119–29)

Notice Salmon's attentiveness, her awareness of her own angles of repose and her willingness to put these into action even if some cause in-process distress. Not a feat for the faint-hearted.

If the faculty who are research sponsors make challenges about qualitative research and its forms of writing, there are some ways to take these points of challenge substantively, not defensively, and to profit from them. What diverse points of view should I be learning to understand? Why are they asking that? What are they seeing that I should consider? Some people have written an imaginary dialogue with committee members to spell out what they would say to imagined challenges. Some have written analytic memos to faculty. These writings often help to clarify where they stand and how they see issues before they are face to face. Sometimes, of course, people are in for a huge but happy surprise, as Barbara Ball discovered:

> I walked in expecting real trouble about the memo I had sent ahead of time. It was no problem at all. My chair agreed with all my points. I could have kicked myself! Why did I worry so?

Even in this example though, we believe that writing helped.

Some people have previewed their stances with friends and asked their support groups to play devil's advocate, all in an effort to deepen their understanding so that the person of good will who disagrees with them has something to think about. These strategies have helped many people, including the four of us, to shape our writing for our intended audiences and purposes.

For many of us, the positive outcomes for our writing from meetings with committee members lie in the preparation before and the follow-up afterward, in energizing encouragement, in suggestions tailored to the work by an expert reader, even in the definitive halt to an ineffective direction. Salmon's student Jocelyn voices the characteristic of what we think of as mentoring that empowers: 'I realized that here I could negotiate' (Salmon, 1992, p. 96).

Friends and Strangers

The informal sort of mentoring that develops unexpectedly from a conversation or is offered out of friendship allows the writer yet another perspective for seeing her work. Irene Gilman and Andrea Mandel come to mind as Maryann thinks about 'critical friends.' Irene completed her doctoral work the year ahead of her. She and Maryann often talked about Irene's work when they met in the library. Irene, a writing teacher, had begun a quantitative study of high school students' responses to literature and art. She found the statistical analysis too crude a tool, and added case studies that became, to her, the more interesting and valuable part of her work. When Maryann asked her to read her method section, Irene did it with a fine-toothed comb — with enormous generosity, she gave more than she was asked. Irene was unsparing; Maryann's revision shaped the chapter into its final form in a dialogue with Irene's meticulous notes. Andrea came to the hotel room before a presentation Maryann was to give. 'Can I do anything?' She listened to the draft and raised a question that generated the final piece Maryann needed to complete and extend her thinking.

Another useful discipline for our writing is to check on how we communicate with others who do not share insider language. Walker Gibson (1979) speaks of the 'dumb reader,' the person who can not and will not read our minds, will not supply what's missing as those who know us too well sometimes do, but insists that our words carry the meaning we intend. This is a reader who is not satisfied with or conditioned to the jargon of the trade but wants to be addressed clearly, who is not content with fuzzy half explained ideas or stock phrases that substitute for thought. This reader does not want to demoralize or diminish. This reader wants to understand. Often such intelligent readers, though they may be unconsciously merciless to our prose, are the clear-eyed children who can detect the empresses' nakedness before she steps out into the parade. We are fortunate if we have a friend or two who will assume this role for us. Carole Di Tosti tells how she joined a group of fiction writers and benefited from their perspective as she tried new forms. A reading by someone from another discipline — another friendly eye — can bring additional lenses for viewing our work.

Consultants

As the consultant and/or editor has a different relationship than either chair or committee member with the qualitative research writer, so the writing negotiation can be different also. For example, some writers need a good editor whose task is to help them craft, no holds barred. Depending on the need of the person, the help can be at a level of fine detail hardly possible with a committee member or a support group, as well as at the level of overall organization or analysis. If the person needs work on writing narrative, or with the use of detail, or with analysis, the consultant may become teacher and coach who demonstrates and supports until the writer starts to internalize the ways of thinking about how to present the study with detail and meaningful interpretation. This kind of intense collaboration is strenuous and can be transforming. We know at least one person who says that her editor saved her a whole year. It is also expensive.

Maryann sat in on a session in which Margaret served as consultant-editor to Fay (a pseudonym), who was working on a study in an urban university. Margaret had prepared for the meeting by doing close reading and annotating of a narrative section describing Fay's entry into the research setting. In the following excerpt, Fay and Margaret go through the text together; Margaret alternately demonstrates and coaches; Fay's language is particularly interesting to us as she mirrors what she has learned.

M: This is an awkward sentence though the idea is fine — perhaps you want to rephrase ...

F: How about 'I felt more a part of'?

M: I like that. So let's take out the parentheses. Let's make two sentences. What I suggest is to make the sentences a little shorter, more direct, more punchy (reads on). How would you feel about saying 'stage fright'? That's the kind of anxiety. Now, why put this in (Fay chuckles) since the data make the point just by stating it? (Margaret reads on). If you add this here you shift the reader's attention to other issues that interrupt the flow of thought — the atmosphere is the point ... 'too familiar *but* not very inviting' — how about 'and?' Now, from the university as a whole to the department handbook is too big a jump. You need a physical description of the department.

Margaret, in a sense; lends Fay her ear and her rationale for the writing choices she suggests; at the same time she invites Fay to chime in and retain ownership of her work.

F: That's tedious.

M: I think you need only two paragraphs: the office; then a physical description of Jennifer, however vague or fictionalized or impressionistic. Young, chic, and schoolgirlish, or middle aged and sedate, or ... some sense of her persona.

Here Margaret translates the task into narrative elements and suggests how Fay can use the transition to capture the feeling of the experience, accomplishing more than one function at the same time. She also invokes the structures and conventions of the dissertation as the need for them arises. It is not a solo performance but a pas de deux with an experienced performer who supports her partner.

After the session, Maryann questioned Margaret and Fay about their collaboration.

Fay, what stopped you along the way and led to your working with Margaret as consultant/editor?

The narrative presentation that my proposal readers suggested at first made me freeze. When I read another book on my topic, it was so well written that I felt overwhelmed. I began to see that this was not my project alone; I was writing it for the members of my committee, and I experienced some resentful feelings about ownership. Most of all, I was stuck in a mire of details. Margaret got me to move from this plight into a larger framework.

How has this close working together affected your writing?

At this point I'm learning to avoid making judgments and *describe*. 'The teacher in the class I was observing is very well organized and a strict disciplinarian.' No! Instead I'll show her in action, go back into the scene, be careful of judging. By now I can tell when I'm setting up the reader for interpretation, and I describe instead. I'm still not sure just how much description I want — but it's a breakthrough. Once having told the story, now I begin to think of it at a higher level — it's like opening a closed door. I hesitated for months over structure; I was eased into it by Margaret. She could figure it out.

Margaret, can you comment on your role?

We keep talking about putting the pieces together. I have to read a text through two or three times to begin or I won't see the gaps. Often it's not until after a second reading that I get a sense of the work as a whole and whether it's structured well and what the possibilities are for analysis . . . Fay and I are doing narrative now. I'm always saying 'you can't say that' when I notice Fay using a judgmental adjective or rushing to interpret on the basis of too little data. She needs to show the setting to the readers. The process makes you highly aware when something belongs later, not now.

When it's analysis, we're talking about levels of abstraction. For instance, I was working with one doctoral student who was studying the experience of black women who were blue collar workers. When she was doing her thematic analysis I felt she didn't lift enough. I felt that the writing was heavy with narrative, light on analysis. I recommended she look at *Slim's Table* for levels of analysis, Spradley too. In the literature, the authors move to a broad frame about social attitudes in the U.S. This student's findings show that racial attitudes are an enormous element in the participants' experiences. You would have to talk about a racist society in addition to the participants' coping strategies. In doing her rewrite, this student analyzed her participants' metaphors and concluded that they highlighted 'war' and 'warfare' against racist attitudes. She seemed inspired by this concept and was really on a roll.

People are very tired by the time they get to thematic analysis, and they are likely to be working toward deadlines. Another pair of eyes may see things they have blurred; they may be unwilling to take a direction which would lift their level of thinking.

I always remind people that I give lots of advice but have no power. The committee members — and the researcher — have the power. I tell them, 'Try it and see if it will fly.'

Afterward Margaret talked of another role for a consultant. Some people become defensive, angry, and highly emotional about committee members. Most often it is possible in a one-to-one situation to deal with this, to help students rethink their attitude towards criticism and suggestions. If the writer can recognize that people with more experience are sharing it and offering advice, not judging or condemning, this is a start. Of course this has to be the case. The work with the consultant is practice in selecting and using suggestions and articulating ideas safely.

Regarding the articulating of implicit ideas, Margaret recalls a meeting with

Margot at the beginning of her own doctoral work. Margaret was struggling to explain what she wanted to do for a particular piece of writing. Margot listened and then suggested 'What you want to do is write a theoretical rationale for teaching fantasy.' The effect was galvanizing. Here was someone who could name her intellectual groping.

Margaret in turn played a similar role for Linda (a pseudonym), who came to her in some confusion. Her chapters were disorganized, with profiles, categories, topics, themes, subthemes all crowding and jostling each other. Margaret asked Linda to explain in her own words how she saw the overall organization of her work. As Linda talked, Margaret wrote. Recognizing that Linda's implications for practice were buried in what she was saying, Margaret set up three file folders, one for each of the implications. Linda now had a plan for her final chapter and could begin to sort and arrange the elements that properly belonged in her earlier chapters. She was able to move forward.

Negotiations Toward Publication

Voices Bleached Out in Academic Laundering?

Ruth: Laurel Richardson maintains that people would do better not to spend time and energy fighting the university on the issue of writing in more expressive and varied genres. Get the dissertation done, get through, and get on with writing in these ways afterwards.

Margot: Well Ruthie, you love to write and you can do different kinds of writing at the drop of a hat. But what about the fact that the vast majority of doctoral graduates never do research or writing again. Could it be that the writing they 'had to do' was so onerous that they literally turned off — as I did for years. To me, Laurel Richardson misses part of the point. The forms themselves *create* the right audience. If you believe in transactionalism, and you do a good job, you will get through to the reader. For instance, if you read this poem, let's say, you'll transact with it. Form is sometimes the message.

Ruth: Not if you know the audience won't engage at all. You make choices based on who'll read it.

Margaret: Laurel Richardson's little book about writing for different kinds of readers deals with shaping to your audience. She notes how some opt to write in academic style for one audience and to rewrite in a more accessible style for a wider audience.

Maryann: Depends too on what you can do or not do without losing your voice and finally being destructive to yourself.

Margot: We have to find ways to mediate with the nay-sayers — to make things possible. For our students, but more for the sake of scholarship.

Maryann: Someone has said that if you estimate roughly one-fourth of the people you reach will agree with you most of the time and one-fourth never, that leaves fifty percent in between, who are open to be convinced by the power of your evidence. Those are the audience to go for. Of course the percents are place-holders, but they make a steadying point against unrealistic expectations or paranoia.

'Finished' texts are negotiated with institutions in a context of competition for status, power, and sometimes though not always, dollars — and maybe we find ourselves negotiating with our social self as identified by audiences or colleagues. As a social act, writing has already been shaped through talk with others, the responses of early readers, and much revision. From the start the writer may also have carried on an inner dialogue with the 'powers-that-be' as imagined. But actual scrutiny by these others, and new demands, begin when authors hand over their writing to academic departments that assess for degrees, tenure, or promotion, to boards and superintendents, to journal editors or book publishers, to government or corporate grant givers, perhaps to a wider general audience. If they submit for publication, the negotiation process can go on in communication with editors and referees. Once the work is printed, they may write further in response to public critique by reviewers and readers and perhaps by audiences. Cy Knoblauch says that writing is 'never finished, only abandoned'; and George Eliot emphasizes: 'Never concluded, only negotiated.' Karen LeFevre (1987) puts succinctly our focus in this section:

> Invention is powerfully influenced by social collectives, such as institutions . . . and governments, which transmit expectations and prohibitions, encouraging certain ideas and discouraging others . . . It is in our interest to recognize the influence of social collectives on what and how we invent, attempting to make explicit their tacit rules so we can decide which to abide by or what the consequences may be if we do not. (pp. 2, 122–3)

Academic Departments

Once chairs and committees have signed off and a study is submitted, tacit and not so tacit demands surface in the quest for academic approval. Here we want to ponder some examples and how people have negotiated these. Writing is all about choices, choices far wider than the borders of blank page or screen. Choice of philosophical orientation, research method, topic, rhetorical forms are all facets of the perceived expectations of the academic institution that can help or hinder the development of the writing.

Carole Di Tosti's experience demonstrates the working through of one such decision and its aftermath. Carole struggled with her own past academic expectations as she tried to capture in her dissertation the story of a whistle-blowing school superintendent. She summoned up the courage to labor intensely as a writer and to risk challenging the resistance she anticipated from some of her professors at her orals:

> I had to be just to my superintendent. I was compelled by conscience to select the forms, the genres of revelation . . . stories, poems, acts of a longer play. The removed scholarly approach was not trustworthy to the life experience of the

superintendent. I was concerned about the technical writing fulfilling the expectations of the professors on my dissertation committee, who would perhaps not understand the forms I wanted to select to express the superintendent's and the others' multiple realities. As I agonized, the support group and the class and professor helped me overcome this difficulty.

She was further helped to prepare herself when she shared her work with other colleagues, who were still, as she put it, 'awash in scholarspeak':

They listened intrigued as I explained my excitement at the writing process I was developing of using various genres to reveal the multi-realities of my superintendent's experiences. They couldn't begin to grasp this. In noticing their reactions, reminiscent of my own at the outset of the semester, I realized how far I had progressed. I also realized that I must with patience and understanding help them to understand, if they are interested. This realization helped; I will have to defend this approach, I fear, with my other professors.

In anticipation of a skeptical response, Carole reached for other arms:

I feel that Lincoln and Guba give the most credible argument to pose to professors who have determined that case study reports should be done in only one surefire way. I intend to come armed with the article to fend them off from the work accomplished on my dissertation. I have to persistently, with patience and extreme forbearance, review and review and review the process and my reasons for my presentation with them.

Certainly Carole was realistic in her preparation to, as she said, 'mediate with possible naysayers.' Carole's experience points up the importance of educating oneself in order to counter misconceptions and suspicions about qualitative work and not to lose one's sense of direction. We have found that people of good will can be convinced of the worth of qualitative writing approaches by the excellence of the work.

The culminating hurdle in the dissertation process is usually called 'the defense' of the dissertation. Some of us like to call it a final discussion or a dissertation conversation. The metaphor of dialogue should be more apt than that of battle. Ideally speaking, the event might be considered an opportunity to talk with intelligent readers about something on which one has spent enough time to be considered an expert. Thus we ought not to have to be on the defensive. If, however, the academic representatives called as readers are antipathetic to qualitative research, perhaps a defensive stance is realistic. If so, Carole's anticipation and arming of herself is a fair model. The 'defense' metaphor resonates for Janet D'Arcangelo:

DEFENSE
STRATEGY
ARGUMENT
REFUTATION
These are words of violence.
                    Janet D'Arcangelo

On the other hand, we feel deeply that very often doctoral students are so ready to bow to the myth of 'doing it the way others want' that they miss many opportunities to do what they want. We firmly believe there are ways for most to get the support they need, that we are downplaying people's individual initiative, creativity and enthusiasm. For most, some place there are those who will understand and support them. Margot thinks we don't emphasize this sufficiently in higher education and thus she responds with some heat to Laurel Richardson's 'Do it their way and yours later. You'll learn. It will be fine' message. Instead, we might think about playing to extend the possible, about a proactive instead of a reactive stance, not pushy or overbearing, but convinced and hopeful. It has worked for a lot of people.

Journal Editors and Referees, Publishers, Grant Givers

How can we write in ways that support publication? Some people have created amazing ways to do this. To reach an audience in the heavily censored Soviet world, Mikhail Bakhtin couched his ideas in the acceptable ideological terms of the day; he even let his work appear under the names of his friends instead of his own.

John Hersey (in Agee and Evans, 1988) writes of how Agee, who empathized with the outcasts of this world, found a way to highlight their plight during his first job at Henry Luce's *Fortune*. Agee was assigned to do a story on sharecroppers in the deep South; he wrote to a close friend: 'Feel terrific personal responsibility toward story; considerable doubts of my ability to bring it off; considerable more of *Fortune's* ultimate willingness to use it' (p. xv). Despite his reservations about the feasibility of reconciling these demands, Agee took the risk. He immersed himself as far as possible in the sharecroppers' daily lives, living for some months with one of the families and shaping their story into a work of art along with Evans' poignant photographs. 'The job had in it a special challenge for Agee — to try to set truth free in what he saw as the headquarters of lying' (Hersey in Agee and Evans, 1988, p. xxvii).

His concern about publication was born out. When Agee and Evans returned to the *Fortune* office, its 'businessmen readers had been criticizing the liberal tone of many of the magazine's pieces and Luce had decided that *Fortune* must set a more fittingly Republican course.' The editors tried chopping up Agee's piece but gave it up as hopeless, and in the end, let him expand the piece into a book. Had Agee not been working for Luce, we would not have *Let Us Now Praise Famous Men*.

When Laurel Richardson turned her study into a trade book: *The New Other Woman: Contemporary Women in Affairs with Married Men* (1985), she determined to go out on the book circuit to get her book to audiences. She undertook an arduous preparation, working on clothing, appearance, interviewing techniques, and how to deal with the media. The most costly part of this intense process was coping with the norms and expectations of talk shows and the moral dilemmas she had to resolve. She speaks out of this experience:

> For sociologists, the naive notion that the media is simply a tool for them to pick
> up at will, hone, use, and put down should be abandoned. The media and sociology

are competing institutions. The task of the sociologist is the discovery and implementation of ways to *use* the media rather than being used by it. (1985, p. 294)

Of course, it is as possible to be so 'pure' that ideas wither as it is to lose
integrity and be co-opted by those who do not share the same values. The aim
should be to steer through these shoals. In brief, we think that the habits of mind
researcher-writers seek to cultivate in examining their data need to be applied also
to issues of audience and purpose. Writing contexts need to be carefully observed,
thoroughly analyzed, and reflected on in the light of our goals. Knee-jerk, simplistic
formulations of situations, constrained by our nuttiness and impatience miss the
mark. By and large, social organizations are not monoliths, as Agee discovered.
On the other hand, we may need to become very choosy, to avoid some journals
altogether, however prestigious, because of their message, ethical or political. What
writing is worthy is an intensely personal question.

Ruth found that an article she submitted to a major journal would only be
accepted if she reshaped data in more analytic and less narrative ways. She decided
to attempt such an approach. The revision forced her to see her data differently and
from the experience she learned some things she had not known before. However
in making this move she remained aware of limits beyond which she would not go.

Margot directs a research team studying Headstart programs. Although she
came to think that a significant direction would be to study and write about life in
the children's homes, the terms of the grant allowed only a focus on life in the
children's classrooms and schools. Margot says she went along with this because
she feels that the classroom focus is essential to document. However, at this very
moment Margot is setting out to do her original study in children's homes and
writing about this experience on her own, as an unfunded project.

Some of us get rude surprises even when we select carefully the publications
to which we submit our writing, even when our choices are based on philosophical
or political considerations or the fit of our work to what is usually accepted. Maryann,
Margot, and Marilyn Sobelman wrote an article about the experiences of student
teachers who studied the contexts of their field placements. These authors submitted the article to a journal that had recently solicited writing about just such work.
The three reviewers granted that this was a valuable topic and that the paper was
well-written and interesting. Two of them, however, had some doubts about qualitative research. This showed itself most clearly when one reviewer wrote: 'Yes,
but is it research?' Those doubts carried the day for the editor, who in her rejection
quoted that statement but none of the other reviewer comments having to do with
the strength and value of the article. Thus, at times, a mismatch between reviewers'
opinions, the real stance of the editor, and those of the writers creates unforeseeable
barriers. When that occurs we find it most useful to submit to other, possibly more
compatible, publications.

For some authors who want to be published, either real or perceived gender
prejudices can be a problem. However, here too, there are ways to learn the rules of
the game. Robert Boice (1985) who has studied factors that engender writing blocks
offers strategies for negotiating the situation and addresses both sides of the problem:

> [Women] are apparently discriminated against by male gatekeepers (Spender, 1981) who have low expectations for them . . . What can be done to help change these political conditions? . . . My colleagues and I are painstakingly examining the files of journals to see what factors in submitting papers correlate with success. We have an opportunity to go beyond the usual conjectures of how unfair and unreliable the publication process is. If, in fact, male reviewers do give female authors crueler comments and more rejections than they direct to male authors, the evidence can be used to demand changes. Reviewers might, in such an outcome, be subjected to more extensive education and supervision. Authors, similarly, who fail as writers because of naivete about stylistic and ritualistic niceties could be given feedback in those dimensions, and not in vague terms that do little to promote constructive change. (p. 214)

We think that in the celebration of at last readying a piece of writing for publication, it is worth taking a moment for a retrospective look and a savoring of the process that led to the finish line. The four of us have experienced and observed the intimate give and take with groups and mentors, the openness to listen and respond to the challenging voices in the wider world, and the growing confidence of writers to add their own voice to the conversation — the lively, unpredictable journey of negotiating writing. Unsettling it can be, but never dull. The possibilities are worth the risks.

Collaborating

> Try to conceive new and more expansive ways of experiencing and representing authorship. (Ede and Lunsford, 1990, p. 131)

This section looks at two aspects of collaboration, of multiple voices producing one text. At first we labeled writing produced by more than one researcher as 'coauthoring,' and text produced when a researcher writes with participants as 'collaborating.' It didn't take us long to see that we were folding in a not-so-subtle denial of coauthorship in the latter case. Hence both of our sections have the same label with a numerical designation only to identify order.

Coauthoring 1 — Researchers with Researchers

In the modern world, the Romantic idea of the writer as a solitary worker is countered with images of close collaboration. In the sciences and other professions collaboration is taken for granted; people in the humanities have been more resistant. More recently this situation is beginning to change. When Judith Entes (1994) looked at collaborative writing in journals, she found a dramatic increase of articles with joint authorship, particularly by women. Studies of collaboration like *Writing With* (1984) and *Single Text/Plural Authors* (Ede and Lunsford, 1990) are beginning to appear. We think it is important to invite reflection on collaborative writing for a host of reasons. Not least of these is the fact that such joining of forces multiplies the life times of experience and resources. We also want to offer some models for readers to consider and be tempted to emulate.

So many people devote a large piece of their lives to completing a dissertation and never follow it up. Frank Walters (1995) cites Maxine Hairston's 1986 report that 'at least two-thirds of college professors publish nothing after the dissertation' (p. 62). For some their wishful thinking about writing fails to take wing — a waste for them of valuable potential, a loss for their professions of fresh voices in the ongoing conversation. Perhaps their dissertation writing was so debilitating, so lifeless that they just don't want to write, see no benefit to writing. Margot could not get herself to read her own dissertation for ten years, wrote sufficiently in order to move through the ranks but with deliberate political strategy that did nothing to enhance her love of writing, and, finally, produced writing with joy and gusto only after she earned her full professorship. She is convinced now that such deadening effects should not, need not, be repeated by ongoing generations. She has found that one way to overcome is to join into collaborative writing efforts. If these are not a particular person's cup of tea then, at the least, to join a writing colleague group offers sharing, comradeship, and help.

What do we understand by coauthoring? This can fall at any place on a continuum of interaction, from the parceling out of chapters or tasks to be written separately and submitted to be edited, without any writing together, to the writing of a single text in which authors think so closely together that they sometimes finish each other's sentences. Lise Ede and Andrea Lunsford have collaborated on the latter end of this continuum and have written in a personal vein about 'conceiving, drafting, and revising a text together' (1983), as well as jointly producing a more formal study of coauthoring (1990). They found the joint effort made them more productive and efficient, although more pressured by the strict limits of time together. The process demanded 'flexibility and compromise.' Here they describe their contrasting styles:

> Lisa's basic approach to problems is broad and synthetic; she ordinarily begins by casting a very wide net. Andrea, on the other hand, approaches problems analytically, narrowing and drawing out implications, searching for closure almost at once ... As a result, one often felt we were circling endlessly, spinning our wheels, while the other alternatively felt we were roaring hell-bent toward our conclusion ... Coauthorship, as we have pointed out, makes the whole process of writing more difficult in some ways. (Perhaps our worst moment occurred one afternoon in Seattle when Lisa revised the mid section of our first project three times — requiring Andrea to change the following pages, which she was working on at the time, substantially every time.) (1990, pp. 154–5)

In the joining of authors, at best there is the possibility of new connections, intensity, sustaining presence and challenge. A writer interviewed by Ede and Lunsford (1983) commented on collaboration: 'I feel that I do a much better job than I would have done alone. I extend myself further and I think I have a clearer idea of what we are trying to do. It brings more out of me so I think it is more mine.' When we examined collaborative teams, we looked first at artists and published writers to situate ourselves in the context of other creative workers. We next moved to qualitative researchers writing together. Two themes stood out for us: the surprising potency of joining forces to shape a text — we have come to call it the 'dialogic of invention' — and second, the demanding, risk-taking character of ventures into the 'border areas,' so full of possibilities, differences, and unknowns both in oneself and in the other.

Dialogic as invention

'Dialogic' is a new-from-old coinage of Bakhtin's that we think offers a penetrating insight into the power of coauthoring. Bakhtin's (1981) conceptualization of *heteroglossia* is helpful in portraying how each person's vantage points, contradictions, and intersections of meaning exist as:

> Specific points of view of the world, forms for conceptualizing the world in words, specific world views, each characterized by its own objects, meanings, and values. As such they all may be juxtaposed to one another, mutually supplement one another and be interrelated dialogically. (pp. 291–2)

We use the term dialogic to refer not to the discourse *between* people but to serve, in Bakhtin's (1990) view, as a metaphor for the heterogeneity within the Self in the process of confronting and relating to multiple discourses of the 'I' and 'Other' within the historic/social world. From this perspective, listen to the artists. Glenn Zorpette (1994) interviewed pairs of visual artists who collaborated to create their works. 'Our best ideas are born from talking,' says artist Alexander Melamid of his collaboration with Vitaly Komar. 'Then the spark comes.' 'The real value of collaboration,' Zorpette finds, 'comes in the more conceptual stages of the artistic process: inspiration, criticism, and refinement of ideas.' Artists Andrew Ginzel and Kristin Jones reflect together on the dialectic of the process:

> 'You don't want too comfortable a situation. There's a capacity, in a collaborative situation, for some tension which can create an incredibly creative dynamic. You're never quite let off the hook. You can never regress into your own world, because someone else is listening. Sometimes at night, when we're working late, there's a subtle competitiveness at play. At the same time, there's a . . .'
> 'Momentum,' Kristin Jones supplies . . .
> 'It's easier to take risks, suggest something to Kristin that might be a little crazy, but to which I think there's some validity.'
> 'And I might say, that's absurd, but how about this. That's why it's impossible to say whose idea a project was. It becomes a fabric of conversation.'

The reflection of these two artists demonstrates the creative tension of their talk, each building from what the other has just said. Not-too-comfortable seems to be a fruitful condition for calling forth each other's best energies. Along with the intensity is a quality of playfulness once having limbered up, a pleasure in the activity, in performing well before each other, in being daring. Out of the flying threads as Kristin's metaphor implies, comes a fabric constructed from the warp and woof of each one's input.

These artists' description matches what Csikszentmihalyi (1990) has called 'flow,' states of optimal experience. These states involve meeting difficult challenges, using substantial skills, getting immediate and continuous feedback, and setting clear goals. The work time is so satisfying that it is possible to continue with great concentration. Seeing the work take shape arouses the desire to work some more and fans interests and ongoing creation.

Authors Joseph Conrad and Ford Madox Ford enjoyed a long collaboration, particularly intense between 1898–1909. Nicholas Delbanco (1982) drew from Ford's memoirs to describe the complementary relationship between the two. The collaboration was initiated by Conrad, who wrote of his 'particular devil' — uncertainty — which made writing painful for him. Conrad 'needed Ford's sheer energy and verve' says Delbanco. Ford wrote with ease, but he was not used to 'the continuing close scrutiny of language.' He writes; 'I, at least, learned the greater part of what I know of the technical side of writing during the process, and Conrad certainly wrote with greater ease after the book had been in progress some while' (p. 94).

In Delbanco's opinion, what they wrote privately was better than their work produced together. Yet he thinks that the coauthorship was instrumental to their later output. The enforced attention to form help Ford produce his best work. Conrad, on the other hand, might have quit without Ford's admiration and varied support. Sometimes Ford would literally stand behind Conrad and dictate a sentence to keep him moving towards their deadline despite the grip of his dark moods. Conrad's great creative decade followed right after their meeting. Twenty years later Conrad wrote of the novel *Romance*, on which they had collaborated. To us, he captures the shifting patterns of working together on a single project:

> First Part, yours; Second Part mainly yours, with a little by me on points of seamanship . . . ; Third Part, about 60 per cent mine with small touches by you; Fourth Part mine, with here and there an important sentence by you; Fifth Part practically all yours, including the famous sentence at which we both exclaimed: 'This is genius.' (Delbanco, 1982, p. 118)

Ford seemed to see the experience as a kind of apprenticeship. That he perceived Conrad as the better writer did not seem to matter. Each contributed vitally to the partnership. Burnett (1993) sees successful coauthoring as providing scaffolding that enables each person to contribute and develop maximally. Each supports the other by asking for clarification, contributing new ideas, modifications or elaborations of plans. Both direct each other to make necessary changes, and challenge each other's plans. Burnett has found that the most productive sessions occur 'when coauthors have thought about and prepared a preliminary plan before meeting together but are open to active exchange with their coauthor' (p. 131).

This sort of coauthoring seems closer to marriage than to the friendship relationship of support groups. It is different from allowing others, critical friends, to look at your brain children. It is more intimate and more risky — metaphorically naked, baring unformed thoughts, groping awkwardly to make connections, revealing gaps in knowledge. The process is anything but graceful. Difficulties can be greater in such close collaboration. The contributions and transformations can be greater as well.

Other coauthoring situations of brief duration offer their own opportunities. Maryann had the experience of sharing in the development and coauthoring of a report at a 1995 conference. Here, subgroups reflecting on various themes spent five days together, beginning with talk and then writing to further develop their ideas. They concluded with a written report. Later she wrote about the process:

> Our talking together was a method of composing. I experienced a level of affirmation that released energy and ideas. I felt sure and fluent, looking into 'the cloud of thought' and being able to distill it into words. Perhaps we should tape such composing sessions to capture the molten thoughts. People surprise themselves with the things they say and afterwards wish they could recapture those ideas.
>
> We found ourselves able to work long and intensely — we ignored breaks and distracting interruptions. Although the effort was so full-out that when we stopped we were quite tired, the work was immensely satisfying. When we returned and began another round of work, the group energy was re-charging. I found myself surprisingly reinvigorated mentally even though I was physically tired. Perhaps the short-term nature of this group and the solid five days of working together helped account for the momentum we established.
>
> I was aware in the beginning of John's reasoned resistance to going along with just anything, which made for some diversity of ideas instead of everyone's agreeing with everyone. I noticed that I felt unclutchy about my ideas, feeling they were given time and listened to. I was able to connect pieces of my experience to a theme dear to me — about how intention shapes experience — and to see how in this group discussion of 'power plays' in education, each of us who had been drawn to this topic pursued our own related themes and enriched the conversation.
>
> We began to use our ideas to theorize about what was going on in the group. We had grown open enough with each other to talk easily about Reba's power in the group, using her expertise to suggest we create in genres of drama and narrative to explore our topic, and now taking the powerful role of editor. As we dictated, the train of our sentences carried us along, someone offering the next word or phrase, someone else going on from there. Our last task was composing the introduction. By that point, it almost felt as if we were a single mind.

The *ad hoc* nature of this sort of group has its own kind of strength. It operates in a kind of 'honeymoon time' that has the charge of newness and freedom.

What stands out in people's accounts of coauthoring is the role of talk in each phase of the writing. James Britton calls talk 'the sea on which all else floats' (1982). In a writing group where people share their work there is a chance for dialogue about one's own piece. Here invention can take place and rhetorical and content ideas can be gathered for later writing. But the talk of coauthors gives even more scope for jointly building new ideas. Collaboration makes possible an abundance and fine-grainedness of talk in each phase of the writing that can add rigor to the thinking and clarity to the writing.

Andrea Lunsford and Lisa Ede (1983) write about discovering the power of talk in their composing process — and in this they echo the visual artists. When they met to write a draft together, they spent almost equal amounts of time on talking and writing, with more time given to talk in the earlier sessions and more given to writing in the last sessions. 'This talking seemed to be a necessary part of coauthoring

... it gave us the constant benefits of dialectic' (p. 153). To these authors, talking as well as writing was composing, because both processes gather and connect ideas:

> In some writing situations we were more likely to achieve a better understanding, generate potentially richer and fresher ideas, and develop a stronger overall argument than we might have done working alone ... Our own strong sense that two may create ideas that neither would have reached alone argues for the value of dialectic as invention. (pp. 155–6)

Researchers who have tried to tease out the ingredients of collaborative work (Burnett, 1993; Trimbur, 1989) are beginning to focus on the role of 'substantive conflict.' By this they mean learning to consider alternatives and to voice explicit disagreement about content and other rhetorical elements. Indeed, Burnett (1993) found that coauthors who agree with and expand on a piece of writing have been less effective than those who propose alternatives that imply disagreement or who explicitly disagree with ideas and ways of presenting them. Premature consensus can express mere acquiescence rather than agreement. To be fair, an immediate nod is often a necessary part of conversation, indicating the other has been heard and encouraging further exchange and completion of the task. Elaborating is productive when the idea is important and the elaboration is relevant. Still, Ede and Lunsford too (1990) found that the effective writers they studied tended to 'defer, and in some cases even actively resist, consensus in order to explore alternatives, and they valued explicit disagreement that helped them focus on potential problems' (p. 133). This is true also in a support group. However, in coauthoring it is not possible to go away and cut off dissent by asserting one's authorial privilege.

Affective and procedural conflicts can block progress, but struggling together over content and rhetorical concerns correlates with quality work. Elbow (1980) reflects on why this might be so:

> ... The organism 'constructs' what it sees or thinks according to models already there; the organism tends to throw away or distort material that does not fit this model. The surest way to get hold of what your present frame blinds you to is to try to adopt the opposite frame, that is, to reverse your model. A person who can live with contradiction and exploit it — who can use conflicting models — can simply see and think *more*. (p. 241)

Collaboration can help us see and live contradictions and 'see and think more.' Listen in on Ruth and Margot working on a 'twentieth' draft of Chapter 2, as they discuss their concerns with the ideas they are going to communicate and the illustrative data they will include. They talk to clarify distinctions, to describe choices they have made or are considering.

Margot: (looking ahead to Chapter 3) I think we need to put some chunks of raw data into the Forms chapter. If Elizabeth's is the only one we're putting in here, we can do this today.

Ruth: This works toward the point we're making, but it's long.

Margot: Could we cut it?

Notice how each contributes her particular concerns. Margot adds data and plans to write to it; Ruth trims for focus. More aspects get attended to than a single author might have room to notice. That way, much gets accomplished in even a brief exchange.

Margot: (back to Chapter 2) Then you chose the piece of the larger quote about crystallizing . . . Richardson is interesting about the notion of truth.

Margot confirms Ruth's choice, brings closure to prior indecisions and moves the writing plan forward.

Ruth: (going through her pages) I separated those from the analytic memos . . . reflective memos. I spent a few days trying to figure out what seemed a distinction. It may not work that way, but reflective and analytic seem different to me.

Margot: Maybe we should make a case here for that distinction — working on self, working on material.

Here Ruth has rearranged a chapter section. Previously, Margot had thought 'reflective' preferable to 'analytic.' Ruth has overridden and applied her distinction. Notice her tentativeness even though she has given much time to playing with this move. Margot is willing to entertain it and makes the further move to define the difference. You can see how this plays out in the final version, where the distinction is developed wholeheartedly, yet as but one way of viewing memos. Both authors are of one mind about memos' vital role.

Ruth: Here is the introduction to stance/theory/-isms — you'll see.
Margot: That's nice.

Ruth describes the piece she's added.

Ruth: In this part, Christine Lewis walks through three different perspectives: feminist, critical . . .
Margot: This is what's important — lenses . . .
Ruth: And here is the constructivist.

Ruth points out additions she's written in and their purpose. (As a team we often clarified our purposes and structuring through explaining our reasoning.) Margot emphasizes the point to be made.

Ruth: This is the heart of it, the layering of interpretation via different perspectives. It's useful under stance. The quote by Bhabha opens 'the third space.' It's really important.
Margot: Third space — a subtitle? . . .

Margot translates Ruth's concern into graphic emphasis so the reader will not miss the importance Ruth wants to convey.

Ruth: I separate theory from 'isms' — more internally based — informal ways that influence us — trying to figure out the difference. I used a dissertation piece.
Margot: (Shifts to the next section on plans and outlines which she has written) What I was doing here was writing about Priscilla's plan for writing. My thoughts were emerging. *I didn't know what to write, so I wrote, fighting to get in.*
Ruth: You're starting to activate the issues.

Margot describes her writing strategy. Ruth voices a rationale for it. Afterwards Margot comments on their writing together:

Margot: We used to know what each of us had written. We've written and rewritten so much that now we can hardly tell.

This dialogue suggests a stance for qualitative researchers who collaborate. Is it chauvinistic to call it feminist? Instead of a fight to be right, to have the upper hand, it is like Tevye's dialogue with himself: 'on the other hand' allows full voice to the other — what Elbow calls 'the believing game' — and the experience of thinking from a different starting point — a 'both-and' instead of an 'either-or' that gives access to the best of both worlds. Notice the almost ballet-like movements between Ruth and Margot as they shape their writing.

Border areas

To speak of writing collaboration among qualitative researchers, Wasser and Bresler (1996) coin the metaphor of 'the interpretive zone': 'the place where multiple viewpoints are held in dynamic tension as a group seeks to make sense of fieldwork issues and meanings' (p. 6). Wasser became 'ethnographer to the team' of five investigating an Arts in Education project. She took notes that tracked the ideas and concerns as they emerged from the discussions. In reviewing these, she began to focus on and write about the interpretive process itself. Viewing the group as an interpretive tool, interacting from different perspectives, the authors ask: 'At what point and in what manner is interpretation fixed? How does the "fixing" of an interpretation present the multiple voices that led to its final form?' (p. 8). They emphasize the importance of trust in dialogic inquiry to enable the participants:

> to tolerate ambiguity, sustained moments of misunderstanding, not sharing the same views, continuing the discussion even when it makes one uncomfortable, and not being forced into one position or another. (p. 11)

> Like most who have tried coauthoring, the authors attest to how arduous it can be: 'not everyone wants to make this their working space, nor would anyone want to be permanently located here.' (p. 13)

As they explore their metaphor of interpretive zones, Wasser and Bresler (1996) describe 'zones' as border areas: unsettled locations, areas of overlap, joint custody, or contestation where 'unexpected forces meet, new challenges arise, and solutions have to be devised with the materials at hand,' implying 'dynamic processes, exchange, transaction, transformation, and intensity' (p. 13). Are the inner demons abroad in such uneasy closely shared territory? Zorpette (1994) didn't find it so in his interviews with visual artists: 'Within most of these teams, there is no overweening visionary, egos are kept in check, and demons are mostly unknown' (p. 165). This sounds quite wonderful, and it can be. However, his 'most' and 'mostly' remind us that there are usually struggles in the normal course of close working relations. Ede and Lunsford (1983) acknowledge, 'We have by no means given a full accounting of the ups and downs, ins and outs, arguments and counter-arguments involved in working together' (p. 155). The writing team that produced this book held a five-day working session in the Adirondacks at the very beginning of our project. By the end of that time together, we were aware of our lack of voiced dissonance and our need to grow more open. Maryann wrote:

> The general harmony of our working sessions is deceptive. It occurs to me that it is rather like a sandwich — the achievement of accord at particular times is the top slice; genuine regard, friendship, and shared passion for a larger creation is the bottom layer in this group; but in between is a complex and mysterious spread that includes left-overs of unfinished conflicts from elsewhere — hopes, fears, rages, doubts, ambitions, longings — at times spilling out and oozing through, but mostly contained between the breads.

Since then we have learned much about surfacing and working through differences, but not everything. Even though Belenky, Clichy, Goldberger and Tarule (1990) are not writing about coauthoring in their study, we feel that they offer a provocative antithesis to consider. They found that most of the women they interviewed experienced their mentors' and peers' expressions of doubt about their work as debilitating rather than energizing. To them, a midwife model seemed more conducive to their thinking than a conflict model of aggressive challenge. We will return to this point later. Here we want to note Lunsford and Ede's (1990) caveats about encouraging collaborative writing, particularly in classroom settings. Even when a group is formed voluntarily by people with previous knowledge of each other's work and personalities, a host of issues are present and those involved are vulnerable:

> Issues of power and authority, of consensus and conflict, of gender, race and class raised questions about a pedagogy of collaboration that we could not ignore. And our growing awareness of and sensitivity to such issues made us particularly cautious in recommending any one kind of collaborative writing activity. (p. 13)

And then there is the authorial *et al.*, as in Smith *et al.*, which can become a sore point with the *et als.*, as well as the Smiths, and is worth addressing at the start of a project. Dual authorship makes it easier of course:

> *Andrea Lunsford* and *Lisa Ede*; who have been writing together for some fifteen years now, here follow their practice of alternating their names as one small way of resisting the academy's privileging of first authorship and as a way of acknowledging their deeply interconnected ways of thinking and writing. (1996, p. 167)

On their 1990 title page, the two have a printed strip that merges their names into one, breaking off at the edges so that neither appears first: DEANDREALUNSFORDLISAE. We too have attempted to express our collectivity and equal partnership on the title page of this book. All that said and despite deliberate efforts, there will probably be inequalities in some aspects of coauthoring — or in how those aspects are seen.

> Successful teams, like Tolstoy's happy families, may all seem alike, friendly and intimate, with partners easily accessible to each other, but the failures prove how

hard collaboration can be. The most typical obstacle is the inability to discuss and resolve conflict. (G. Jacobs in Ede and Lunsford, 1990, p. 65)

This would seem to be true of conflict on various levels. It might be useful for coauthors to follow one of their sessions by freewriting a reflection. What were my feelings in the course of the session about each person there? How were my contributions received? What was the impact of what others said? What is my overall sense of satisfaction or dissatisfaction with the experience? Susan Krieger (1991) applied such questions to good results when she found herself unable to analyze her data. We think her experiment is worth applying to a collaborative situation. Some of our feelings are fleeting, but some are likely to deepen existing channels and to interfere with or facilitate our willingness to contribute. We may discover that deeply held feelings can sabotage the coauthoring enterprise to a greater or lesser degree. Or we may throw light on our belief that there is a not-so-subtle hierarchy in the 'partnership' with one person still at the helm, even though the process has been described as collaborative. That's *fakerai* as we call it; pseudo-collegial ethnography.

In considering the results of their study of coauthors, Lunsford and Ede (1990) described such pitfalls as unevenness of commitment, unevenness in writing skills that had not been evident at the outset, and lack of organization. As coauthoring becomes more common, more is being written about the process. It becomes easier, too, to find coauthor writers and researchers who will share their experience and its residue of wisdom. We think that if you write, or perhaps especially if you could but do not, coauthoring is worth trying at least once.

Coauthoring 2 — Researchers with Participants

Beyond trying to go past our narrowness of vision through reflective writing, support group perspectives, participant checking of our writing, creating writing forms, and writing with fellow researchers, we want to reflect on the possibility of enlisting participants as coauthors. This does not mean that we romanticize our participants. They, like ourselves, will have limitations of bias and perhaps of false consciousness. But they see experience in ways we cannot. Honoring their voices allows us and others to see past the edges of our vision. Through the dialectic of this exchange our writing will be further shaped. In his 1993 *Culture and Imperialism*, Edward Said writes of authors from colonizing powers; qualitative researchers might take note:

In your narratives, histories, travel tales, and explorations, your consciousness was represented as the principal authority, an active point of energy that made sense ... of exotic geographies and peoples. Above all, your sense of power scarcely imagined that those 'natives' ... were ever going to be capable ... of saying anything that might perhaps contradict, challenge, or otherwise disrupt the prevailing discourse. (p. xxiv)

Many qualitative researchers go to people by way of interview to hear from them about their experience and to observe them in their everyday setting. When we write, it's often we who make the choices, who select from our data and do the shaping. Even when we share selected pieces of our writing with participants, our position gives us the upper hand. Often people are awed, surprised at being asked their opinion, deferential to our status and education. In many instances people are handed excerpts and asked to read them through in our presence. Perhaps they feel insecure in this unfamiliar situation, afraid of what we might say, pleased to be understood, rushed to a foregone conclusion. Although research authors report their own trepidation at sharing their writing with participants, the general response seems to be gratifying and largely uncritical. Ruth Linden (1993), who interviewed Holocaust survivors and their families, went beyond participant checking. She relates how she includes the voices of her participants in their responses to her writing, making these often dissenting views an integral part of the text:

> In the spirit of open dialogue, I have encouraged my key informants to respond to my writing. They have often contested my interpretations, including the 'facts' as I presented them. I have incorporated their comments and our disagreements into the text and/or revised my original statements as I have deemed appropriate.' (p. xv)

To take the further step of sharing the author role with participants is to change the rules in ways that can disconcert, even as in productive ways they shake up the researcher's thinking, theorizing, and writing. As for participants, suddenly they have access to some of the benefits of writing over speaking.

What are these? They too can acquire the advantages of time and distance to think about their words, to choose the right phrase, to qualify what they have said, to talk over ideas with trusted acquaintances, to follow their train of thought without the constraints of our presence. Perhaps many can get past their feelings of awe or awkwardness, beyond the unevenness of power, to share with us what they really think. Obviously such participants must have some ways to express their thoughts in writing and a willingness to give the time and effort. We will say more of this shortly. Right away coauthorship calls for a different relationship in which researchers and participants 'shift' to become colleagues. Particularly in working with teachers, student teachers, parents, and students, some researchers have begun to expand participant involvement strategies.

Three dimensional theory

Here we examine two collegial efforts, one between teachers and researchers, the other between a student and a teacher/researcher. Susan Florio-Ruane and other researchers from the University of Michigan had presented East Lansing public school teachers with documents that represented the fruit of two years of research in their classrooms (1991). The research team had shared data and analysis in the early stages with the teachers, and returned to the university to write up the final reports. After the teachers read these reports, however, and joined in a session meant for discussion, the researchers were faced with a room full of polite silence. Clearly their telling lacked resonance. What to do? The research team decided to invite the teachers to participate further, in a series of conversations about the research findings. Thus was created the *Written Literacy Forum* designed to address questions about this snag in communication. By doing this, the researchers placed themselves in the vulnerable position generally reserved for participants. Together they collaborated in ways that ultimately reinterpreted and transformed the major findings of the classroom research. Their joint efforts resulted not only in journal articles coauthored with the teachers but in other forms of presentation targeted to the specific audiences they hoped to reach.

A notable feature of this kind of coauthoring is the need to alter status differences. This demanded attention more insistently than the inevitable inequalities that appear even among so-called peers. With the teachers, a conversational model was chosen to facilitate smooth, frank exchange. This wasn't easy:

> In a social world that is unequal, you don't get a democratic or open conversation simply by saying that everybody's free to talk. (Florio-Ruane, 1991, p. 239)

One teacher's comment demonstrates the tendency to defer to the university folk:

> When you start talking about us handling the agenda, I can think of agenda items, but I think that you have the overall picture and I'm really not sure I want you to abdicate that responsibility. (p. 239)

The Michigan researchers persisted past slow beginnings and ended by sharing stories about the teaching of writing. This gave rise to complex and stimulating discussions. The university team as well as the teachers concluded that practitioners have a kind of knowledge of social and contextual dimensions that is particularly needed in stubborn or difficult cases and in creating the theory that applies to field situations. Florio-Ruane comments:

> To move toward [useful] theories, practitioners' knowledge and meaning systems must be tapped as part of the explanatory process . . . Erickson recommends the crafting of 'stories of teaching and learning' in which practitioners play key author roles. (p. 242)

> Because our initial formal accounts were biased toward the typical, they were unable to capture conflict, compromise, and change. In story and conversation we had access to a great many more of the tensions and contradictions in teachers' work. (p. 252)

The recognition that the teachers' voices were central to a vital portrayal of teachers' work (p. 253) was similar to what happened in Joseph McDonald's group, discussed in Chapter 5 (see pp. 258–9).

The goal of the particular collaboration described by Susan Florio-Ruane and set off by the *Written Literacy Forum* was to understand how to devise research and research writing that is of genuine use. This generally calls for bending the conventional ways of going about writing and finding new modes of presentation. The researchers discovered that participants contributed beyond the descriptive levels of the research in the meta-conversation about process and presentation. From their negotiations with the teachers came a metamorphosis of their earlier writing. The teachers taught the researchers that presentation matters in an applied field, not superficially, but essentially:

> In the process, we identified new audiences for our research and created new textual formats for reaching them. In altering such givens as author, audience, format, and purpose, we also transformed the content of our theoretical work. (Florio-Ruane, 1991, p. 244)

> The Forum teachers were particularly struck … by the contextual constraints to teaching writing that arise from outside the classroom. They saw in our notes and reports the possibility of powerful presentations about the multiple and conflicting forces that work on them as they teach children how to read and write. (p. 252)

Florio-Ruane's account strongly suggests the value of a plan from the beginning to involve participants more fully in the deliberative and expressive phases that create the final document. Some research writers see this as an ethical necessity and would never consider doing otherwise.

Strong enough to bend

The second example of collaboration with participants that we examine involves two people who produced an article. Veronica was the teacher and primary researcher; George was the student who returned to school in his mid 30s. The research project was to document the writing process of the adult student, George, from both his and his teacher's perspectives. In the process of this work, Veronica assisted George in writing an autobiographical piece; after that, they coauthored the article. Their story points to some of the complex and often difficult facets of such a writing partnership.

Unlike the teachers above, who initially deferred to the researchers, George struggled from the start for recognition as an equal. Veronica recalled in a conversation with Maryann (May 12, 1996):

> Working with George was complicated from day one. He came to the developmental class thinking of himself as a writer; he had written poetry and had had it published by the student literary journal. He asked me, 'What have you published?' He was frustrated by the class writing and my requests that he revise and write more. On reflection I realized that my demands discouraged him rather than helped. I apologized to him in private. As he saw it, Veronica had backed down. He said he found this the most amazing experience in his whole educational life. When the class later read Freire, he connected this incident with Freire, viewing the apology as problem posing as opposed to telling him what to do, which he saw as a kind of 'banking.' He praised me, saying now we were on the same level. It seemed he had to knock the icon down.
>
> When we had finished writing together, George said, 'We're partners now; we're equals.' I found that I had some feelings about that which I still need to explore further.

Perhaps Ruth Behar (1993), an anthropologist who collaborated with a Mexican street vendor on a life history, speaks to this yet unexplored issue of Veronica's:

> I learned a valuable lesson from my initial reaction . . . I was . . . forced to realize the extent to which the ethnographic relation is based on power, for indeed, I had felt uncomfortable when an 'informant' — particularly another, less-privileged woman — was assertive and aggressive, rather than complicitious and cooperative as informants 'should' be. (p. 6)

'How did you overcome the status differences between George and you?' Maryann asked Veronica:

> We never did. Our lives, our personal styles, our writing styles, our environment for writing were so different. My goals and his were different. We had disagreements from the beginning. I felt that I did all the bending. We would have an appointment to write and George would be distracted by life problems with family, finances, friends. There were times when he did no writing; we talked about these issues. I began to suspect passive resistance. Deborah Tannen in *That's Not What I Meant* sees this sort of behavior as a way of handling power differences.
>
> When we had completed our work, George said he wanted to do more coauthoring with me. I said that I did not, that I had a dissertation to complete, and that this collaboration had not been an easy thing. I told him that I felt I'd done all the bending. I pointed out that *I feel strong enough to bend.* I think he was shocked. He had never seen things from my point of view. Conflict is not the right word to describe what went on between us.

Indeed, in this kind of writing relationship, the researcher starts out holding by far the greatest amount of power. If she hopes for authentic exchange, she must expect that the participant will say things that might, in Said's words, 'contradict, challenge, or otherwise disrupt the prevailing discourse.' Veronica agreed that 'dialectic' was more accurate than 'conflict,' since she tried to take in George's perceptions without losing her own. We see in her actions a purposeful effort to bend conventions and expectations. In consequence George shared with her some of the generally buried experience that helped her understand more.

In the case of Veronica and George, both needed to learn how to work together in a new way. When Veronica said they never bridged the status differences, we do not understand her to mean that in an absolute sense. George was inexperienced at writing, despite his poetry, and inexperienced at coauthoring with someone who had been his teacher. Veronica, too, was inexperienced at this sort of relationship. Moreover, at moments she switched hats, continuing to function in a teacher role when she felt he required this. Both were bending the rules and were in the process of learning these things. There are advances here as they explore ways to make their writing genuinely collaborative:

> I taped our conversation. Sometimes what he said blew me away! I insisted he had to write. His arguments had insight but he must write in order to make an author's contribution, to represent himself on paper. George had serious doubts that he could write his autobiography, that he could even remember enough. Finally he wrote seventeen pages. When we were ready to mail the disk to the editor, he counted

the pages, wanting to know if the article was more representative of him than of me. Now he talks about writing a book.

Veronica described several outstanding insights she gained about writing. These centered on the importance of talk for helping George to compose, the strength of his feelings about revision — often negative — that had to be faced and, most important, issues about power that run through the story.

The Veronica-George story seems important because it surfaces a lot of the sticky stuff that people tend to gloss over when they talk about collaboration. Both examples of coauthoring highlight the idea that if we really write with our participants, we must be willing to go in new directions, to listen, to reshape our plans when that is called for, to bend without losing our own voices.

Responding

The four of us on this writing team often discuss how writing for particular readers guides our writing choices. If we know that some others will read our work with attention, we write to some set of expectations we have come to associate with them. Perhaps we dig deeper, trying to avoid saying obvious things, trying not to be reductive, sentimental, or grandiose. We have internalized some sense of how others will respond. A sort of writer's superego? When we actually share our work, the responses can surprise us. Real readers are perhaps more generous than we are to ourselves. Or perhaps they relate what we have said to a broader context. Perhaps our responders recognize a small spark and fan it to a larger flame, or name our groping and so propel the embryo to a fuller, more shaped existence. In the end, our writing is different because of such transactions.

Maryann remembers the suggestion of a committee member to combine two sections of a chapter into one. It made for so many new and interesting connections that she had not seen before the shift. Indeed, often the acknowledgments that preface a book are not politenesses; frequently they list people who have been, in effect, contributing authors. We marvel at the substantial role of others' responses in our writing process. LeFevre (1987) maintains:

> We will more fully comprehend the process of creating new ideas when we think of it as an act that is social even as it is individual, with the other always implicated in the inventions of the I. (p. 140)

Knoblauch and Brannon (1984) talk about the importance for writers of having 'access to the reactions of as many readers as possible: multiplying perspectives, introducing legitimate differences of opinion, and portraying the broadest possible range of effects that a given discourse can have on diverse readers ... a provocative range of responses' (p. 138). Anthony Conelli comments in his log:

> I feel that everything I write is tentative. I like writing situations in which I can write something, present it, receive some feedback (through a conversation), think about it, then re-rewrite it ... For me, writing is not presenting the finished product, but a work in progress. It is a way of putting what I am thinking in front of

me, separate from me, but connected to me. It is less 'I think this' and more 'I may be thinking something like this.' I am amazed by people who write and rewrite without sharing their work with others and talking about it. It is during that talking with others that I learn what I am thinking and what I want to say.

What strikes us is the improvisational quality of working in this unprotected manner. Anthony's successive approximations as he considers other perspectives, takes him from a rough view to a more nuanced and complex expression.

Zooming in: Dualistic, Relativistic, Reflective

In the section on support groups we looked with a broad focus at the sustaining and challenging potential of sharing writing with peers. Here we want to examine more closely the characteristics of helpful responses. Then we will offer some thoughts about developing the skills both to give and to receive responses in constructive ways.

As a point of departure, Chris Anson (1989) offers a helpful sorter. With Perry's (1970) study of Harvard students' intellectual development as a guide, Anson examined teachers' responses to beginning college writers; he found three general styles of response and called them dualistic, relativistic, and reflective. The *dualistic* response is dogmatic, implying that there is but one right way, concerned with the surface features and the conventions of formal discourse; meaning fades from view. The *relativistic* response, in contrast, imposes very little, expressing enjoyment or its lack, encouraging fluency through respectful questions, but providing no explicit options for revision. Meaning is central; careful planning, making rhetorical and linguistic choices, and thorough revision are left to the writer. Perhaps in reaction to a dualistic approach in our own education we tend towards the relativistic sort of response. Moreover, it does not demand the knowledge of the craft of writing assumed in giving a reflective response. Most doers of qualitative research are not teachers of writing; they may not be accustomed to such 'meta' conversation. The third approach, the *reflective* response, without 'taking over' the text, offers the writer some options. The text is central as the conveyor of events and ideas. The content is reflected on, but so is the way this is or might be transmitted through the text itself.

Which response style is helpful? It depends. If you are ready to submit your work, the *dualistic* responder's eye for detail may be just what you need. Masterful fine-tuning and picky proofreading may be in order. If you need to be informed about the conventions of dissertation or article writing, downright didacticism will save time, energy, and attention for other matters worth pondering:

- Important to be sure that what's in the Table of Contents reflects the headings here.
- You need to get your headings right for your committee.
- Is this source right?
- Put that piece in the methodology.
- This is an awkward sentence.
- Should all be in past tense?

The *relativistic* response, too, has a crucial place. Knoblauch and Brannon (1984) note that there is a stage when responses to the ideas and pleasure in the writing are called for, without dealing with how the writer is shaping the text. The need may be to think more deeply, to become intellectually more fluent and articulate before the moment for shaping has arrived. Even at later stages the writer may need assurance that a direction taken is worth pursuing, may need a gut reaction about sections that worked and others that did not. Some relativistic responses are as minimal as the written equivalent of a smile, a sigh, or a raised eyebrow. They signal that the reader is attentive and that the writing is having an effect:

- Wow! • Yes! • Hurray! • Oh?
- This is very powerful! • I want more. • Vital.
- Here my eyes glazed over. • Mmm . . .
- You are your own best problem solver.

A comment may suggest a train of thought; a question prompts further investigation. A word of praise encourages the writer to become aware of what worked; wit and skepticism, expressed in a word or phrase, can impel her to think again, to question an assumption, to revise. Responses to content express interest in pursuing the writer's meaning:

- Something's wrong here. What? (response to a description)
- Important question.
- What about student-to-student [questions]? (pointing to an omission)
- How is this [spontaneous child contribution in the midst of the teacher's plans and routines] encouraged? Received? (probing)
- Yes, or perhaps control? (offering alternative interpretations)

Tina Casoglos tells of her facilitator's after-class comment: 'You really seem to have a good handle on your data.' Diane did not elaborate; Tina did not ask her to say more. But she went away feeling so confirmed in what she was doing and what she understood about how to work with the data that the response marked a kind of turning point. 'I was shocked. I didn't know that!' Was this a dogmatic, one-right-way kind of response? Tina seems to have understood it as a celebration of what she had accomplished.

Frequently the writer who is on her way needs no particular writing advice, needs only the response that her writing is working for the reader and that she should keep going. If she is inhibited by being overly self-critical, we know that celebration and encouragement are sometimes more productive than suggestions; on the other hand, we are not talking about being patronizing. People want and deserve to be taken seriously. The point is that many writers can be trusted to make their own course corrections at particular points. But if a writer is floundering, the relativistic response may be too airy to be helpful. A relativistic response may also mean that the responders do not know how to respond in writerly ways, whether to their own work or to that of others. They can develop their skills by having reflective responses modeled and by practice in articulating their responses (Knoblauch and Brannon, 1984). Gradually most will internalize a widened range of rhetorical awarenesses and strategies. Our hope is that some insights from theory and research, and from our data about oral and written responses to qualitative writing, may help further and deepen such reflective conversation. In the next section we will discuss reflective responses at some length.

In the second session of Margot's course, students were asked to respond to each other's writing in the *reflective* way that had been demonstrated and coached in previous weeks: to describe, evaluate, and, if called for, offer strategies for revision. In the small groups, people read what they had written in response to Wolcott's question: 'Do you see yourself as a reader or a writer?' Responders were asked to describe how the piece worked for them, to point to specific parts that elicited a response, and to describe what it was in the writing that helped or hindered. At the end of this experience, individuals went to the board and put items on lists labeled 'Helped' and 'Hindered.' These items facilitators copied down so all would get the lists the following week.

The beauty of this opening task for the groups was the movement to looking at craft fueled by the power of the experience, but then distancing themselves to understand the way the words conveyed the experience. The close-to-the-bone personal writing assignment, with its call for self-discovery, generated powerful responses, but could have stopped there. However, the ensuing criteria drawn from each of the groups and the whole class sharing allowed for public communication of perceptive comments as well as questions about the items. This was an experiential lesson in how to respond; as a follow-up, students had their own just-completed work to examine in the light of the listed criteria. The experience also made clear that both responsibility and opportunity were involved in having some writing ready for the group.

Unpacking Reflective Responses

In thinking about this process of reflective response, we find Richard Beach's (1989) assessment model a useful unpacking of what is involved in Anson's 're- flective response.' He distinguishes three basic intellectual tasks involved in critiqu- ing and improving one's writing: describing, evaluating, and selecting appropriate revisions. Responders can model these for one another.

Describing what someone has written, naming the shape, is seen by Beach (1989) as a first step in taking control of one's writing. Some writers work by sheer intuition without the need to reflect, but most of us need more to produce consist- ently effective writing. We think of two situations in which this sort of description was evoked. Lil Brannon (Brannon, Knight and Neverow-Turk, 1982) taught her expository writing students to go paragraph by paragraph through a draft, at each paragraph writing a sentence in response to the question, 'What are you doing here?' (e.g., in this paragraph we explain what we mean by describing, we promise two examples of coaching and we offer the first one.) Some writers work by sheer intuition without the need to reflect, but most of us need more to produce consist- ently effective writing.

The second situation is a session at the Center for Collaborative Education in New York City, where educators gather to do a descriptive review of a student's writing. They listen to the whole piece read aloud. They then go through a second time with each person paraphrasing two or three sentences. Only after this, with a better sense of what the writer has said, do they begin to describe what they see. What is interesting in this process, as with our reading and rereading research transcripts, is how much more the readers begin to notice, beyond the facile labels we sometimes call on to describe writing. To hone describing skills takes time; in groups this means that some silent or oral reading is in order and that copies of written work are available for everyone so that they can reread. We also need some language for talking about the writing.

Describing what the writer has done seems like a way of helping both author and responder to develop the sense of form. Moreover, the energizing words that point to something a writer has already succeeded in doing allow him to savor his accomplishment. By articulating what he has done, the writer gains more control — what he has once done and named, he can do again. Recognizing for himself the form he has produced, he owns it in his repertoire of forms that are available for particular purposes. He can read others' attempts with a writer's eye, learn from them, and so fine-tune his work. He can push a good beginning a bit further. He can reflect on how he got this effect, what there was about his writing process that worked well in a given instance and bears repeating. Once we know what the part does and how it relates to the larger whole, we are in a position to evaluate what is or isn't working.

Here are some descriptive reflective comments culled from the margins of student writing. We picked them for their description, but they imply the pleasure in the writing that we saw in the relativistic responses as well. Some name what the writer has done; others describe the function the part plays in the larger whole.

'You did it, Julia! A layered story.'

'Your feelings seem to be giving you important clues about how people are treated here.'

'This anecdote — both the situation and your reaction — certainly captures the feeling tone of your site for me.'

'This anecdote gives an up-close view of a major theme in your setting, and your awareness of your own reaction adds to its power.'

'This piece really takes off — you shout, through language and character, the essence of what you've been studying.'

'A strong picture with just a hint at the end about what is to come.'

'A friendly, gentle feel to this "room."'

'This parallel construction joined the two narratives and really magnified such divergent perspectives.'

In these next examples evaluation is more explicitly stated. It is usually added to some description. In Beach's scheme, evaluation means detecting dissonance between the writer's goals and the actual text, those aspects that might frustrate the reader, or possible reasons for problems. Here are some responses that ask writers to compare their texts with their intentions:

'These strike me more as 3 "I-stories" than a layered story. Do you see the difference?'
'What I love about this is that you didn't overly simplify a difficult situation. Both
    characters remained whole people!'
'Don't break the narrative flow.'

We think Lil Brannon's general questions (Brannon *et al.*, 1982) are useful
prompts to help writers articulate their goals: What are you trying to say? What
have you promised your reader? What effect do you want to have on your reader?

The last batch of reflective examples describe and evaluate, and then go on to
make *explicit suggestions* for further writing and revision. Some research (Sommers,
1989; Rubin, 1983) indicates that writers develop the skill of a critical reading of
their own work before they learn the skills of revising it. Some may require one-
to-one coaching in carrying out the suggestions. In the following examples notice
the affirmative tone of the evaluations and the note of deference to the author in
offering possibilities to explore. Generally there are few imperatives and they are
coupled with some words of praise:

'Great metaphor here — develop it more.'
'This piece goes beyond escape from surveillance into many of your other themes.
    Might be a good overall piece to begin the presentation of your story.'
'A wonderful piece (though more an "I-story" than a layered story) using the train
    metaphor. Perhaps you could check it with participants to see if you are "on the
    right track." I have some concerns about how much of this comes from the stu-
    dents themselves.'
'This is very powerful. Are you only referring to learning through restraint? What about
    other themes?'
'Do try to fill in the picture and make it truer to the participant. This seems to me a
    particularly fertile area to develop.'
'Include the rationale for her divergent perspectives. This is important and poignant.'
'You're right. We didn't really understand this. Perhaps we didn't try enough, perhaps
    you could have been clearer by supporting it with more examples.'
'I think J's narration might also work as "stage directions" in a play or screen play —
    rather than a separate character — especially the last few pages. Just a thought.'
'Powerful capturing of ideas/feelings. Reflect on your insights in this story.'
'Try hard to expand this article and the last memos — especially these two pieces.'
'Some critically important analysis here, though sometimes your voice sounds vague
    and distant. I find that the more concrete you are in your examples, the more I can
    see what you're trying to say.'
'Nice use of theme. Later you can look at the instances together — possibly re-group,
    change words, lift.'

Schemes such as Beach's can be useful for someone unaccustomed to critiquing
writing and new to the group response process. Often writing support group members feel the need to make better use of group time, to focus and raise the level of
response, to incorporate certain helpful questions, to shape their directions. The
schemes can serve as models and tools.

Dene Thomas and Gordon Thomas (1989) recommend a scheme of Rogerian
reflection, particularly for oral interaction about writing. This means the repeating
or 'reflecting' of what the writer is saying. When applied in small groups or written

response this technique includes: 1. pointing to structure; 2. clarifying; 3. expanding; 4. recalling; 5. summarizing.

1   You indicated that you wanted to introduce Jay's profile with a poem. How do you think that poem would work for your reader?
2   You said the teacher was angry at Bob. Did I catch your meaning?
3   When you said that the AIDS ward was a grey place, what did you mean specifically?
4   At the beginning you said that these fathers learned a great deal about parenting. What incidents helped you to make this statement?
5   What to you is the essence of the experience of this homeless woman on the streets?

Most often such comments encourage the writer to go on talking and writing.

All this being said, we want to emphasize certain characteristics shared by these schemes on responding. They can 'force' new awareness, lead us to notice the responses we give and receive and to think about how these insights can be of use in writing. They provide a structure to practice and, if we choose, to continue. These characteristics may be more important to writing than following any one specific scheme.

We offer a final point about varieties of response because it represents our own voice on the matter. Onore (1989) emphasizes that after her study of teacher commentary and student growth in writing, she concluded that the form and content of comments are only part of the story. Incisive critical comments can be ineffective if they fail to take account of the receiver. For instance, the writer may be at a stage when he or she needs to explore new ideas. Until there is something to say, producing a better text is beside the point. Hints and implications can be picked up eagerly by some writers or totally missed or misread by others. So we come round full circle to writing as a social act.

Sometimes other people's responses to our writing can confuse or puzzle us. As the receivers of such responses we can perhaps learn to look more deeply for their intended message or at least learn to push for more direction: 'Please tell me what you mean when you say "__."' Sometimes we fear what the reply might bring. Then, of course, we have to decide whether to avoid feedback we may consider destructive. But if we are ambivalent about whether to hide or stick our necks out by asking for clarification, we might notice how our more assertive peers hang in until they get comments that address their issues and we might try on some of their strategies.

Finally, two further issues that emerge from our response data seem to us to need a bit of individual attention: being provocative and being tough. We culled a small cluster of what we thought of as 'provocative marginalia' from our data and felt they merited reflection. We have placed them in caps after the texts:

THE TEXT: This impact is noted in the conscious way it occurs. However, in group dynamics, the observer's impact has significant unconscious value as well. This may be barely discernible to the untrained clinician.

THE COMMENT: AHEM

THE TEXT: The first was when I was doing a participant check on a statement made while describing his days in the service, about being the 'Luckiest Sons of

Bitches in the World.' What sounded from a feminist frame to be a sexist inference about mothers, meant something quite different to him.

THE COMMENT: REALLY? NO KIDDING!

The explication of 'Pooh!' and its equivalents deserves a special place in a discussion of kinds of responses. The qualitative researcher must cultivate what R.H. Brown (1977) calls DI-STANCE, the dual stance of involvement and distance, capturing the acts, words, and perceptions of participants, while always bearing in mind that fullness of meaning is not able to be contained in words and appearances. A 'pooh' (or an Oh! Yes? Gee! Hey! Really? Watch it! — we could go on . . .) asks the writer to step away from the words and to listen harder. If we present situations at face value, without ironic awareness of complexities and tensions at work beneath the surface a 'pooh!' can call us on sluggishness of mind obtuseness naivete. Moreover, we need to remind ourselves that relationships of power, less power, and powerlessness may underlie what anyone chooses or manages to say; how we may speak in the common-sense or pious phrases we have received, not our own voice — maybe because we have no words or no voice in that area or in those circumstances. Maybe our unconscious biases have surfaced in our words. Maybe our voice is a tad pretentious or pedantic and we need a humorous nudge to jog us back to what's 'real.' In short, a 'pooh' is meant to provoke us to think more and better about what we are saying. It may be the sort of response we crave to push us to further insight and questioning, a more authentic level of understanding. Yet its usefulness depends a lot on the relationship. A pooh can lighten the load or make it heavier. But it must be understood as it is meant — offered, we hope, with affection, collegial, not sarcastic. It supposes a receiver who is able to be open to challenge. Which brings us to our final issue. There are times when toughness is tenderness.

Carolyn Hill (1990) describes a scene in a writing class of adult learners in which she is a team teacher. The group has revised a long memo. Teacher Kevin inquires:

How're you doing?
Fine. Not much to revise. We're just about done.

At which Kevin's deep voice resounds through the room:

Not by a long shot you aren't.

When is it good to 'zap'? Hill ponders the question. One meaning of 'zap' is to 'attack, defeat, or destroy with sudden speed or force' but another is 'to add a sudden infusion of energy'. Hill sees her usual approach as mid-wifing writers' ideas and efforts, not zapping. In her admiration for Kevin as a teacher she finds her theories about partnership and negotiation challenged. She starts to recognize, on the one hand, that at times her disagreement with a writer's way of proceeding comes across in indirect, perhaps confusing, ways and, on the other, that zapping requires the intuition to use the strategy with care and a sense of timing: She sees the limitations of both extremes — of a hard and authoritative response, which can squelch, and of a soft and understanding response which can leave the reader without motivation or guidance.

Our own thoughts are that while there is no formula or recipe, no ideal text of a perfect response, we would lean to responses that can energize further writing — tough, tender, or seasoned with both. We also want to say emphatically that a larger issue is at stake in the process than the writer's local problems. The writer needs to learn to trust her own intelligence and intentions, not to conform to someone else's responses but to understand them. Deborah Wooten's comment about her facilitator sums up what we are aiming for:

> Nancy [facilitator] was a guiding light. She never told me what to do but instead let me make the decisions. I had to free myself from the blinders that schools in my past had put on me and ask myself, 'What do *I* want to do?' That is what I did and I had a splendid time doing it.

We have tried here to focus a more specific lens on some words and concepts — negotiating, collaborating, responding — that are mightily taken for granted by most of us. Writing this chapter, teasing out some specific ways that negotiating, collaborating, responding can be nurtured, has been for this writing team a learning experience we hope to carry forward as we work with students and with other qualitative research writers. We have attempted to stretch past glibness and facile enthusiasm for the labels to detail *how* negotiating, collaborating, and responding can function as essential and necessary in the service of qualitative writing.

Chapter 7

Ripples on the Self/Ripples on Others

The page, which you cover slowly with the crabbed thread of your gut ... Annie Dillard (1989)

The deepened understanding of a Self deepens a text. Laurel Richardson (1994)

We are, it might be said, the Stradivariuses of our own performances as qualitative researchers. How do we fashion the Self to be a responsive and trustworthy instrument? This is, to say the least, a central issue. The instrument metaphor is widely used in qualitative research texts, and we trust that you understand it as person-centered, sensitive, and exquisitely human. Some, indeed, feel the metaphor is misleading because an instrument often evokes, for them, images of blunt, non-human tools — tools that can help, to be sure, but also tools that can give bloody thumbs and dents in the wall. Nevertheless, this team is of the opinion that the researcher-as-instrument metaphor is quite wonderful because it speaks to the researcher as a powerful, central, active force in shaping and creating. In this chapter, we look at writing as it helps us shape the instrument, the Self, of our research. The ripples of our writing on others is our second major concern and focuses on the orientation of the whole enterprise.

This chapter first considers people's reflections on how research writing reaches inward to tune the Self in the research process. We then pick up themes from our data about how people perceived particular writing tasks that changed them: how writing aided their development as observers; how through writing they recognized and worked through biases and blocks; and how writing about the Self as a figure in the research story affected their self-understanding as researchers. Third, we offer some accounts of people's growing awareness and cultivation of their writing selves that may help you consider how researchers tune themselves as instruments. Finally, we ponder the impact of qualitative research writing on others.

Writing Can Transform You

Recently Maryann viewed a TV documentary about the internship of novice doctors. One of the initial profound experiences they shared as a group was witnessing and then participating in an autopsy. One intern fled, at least temporarily; another stayed, weeping. Surely a potentially transforming experience. Poet Ted Hughes writes of having participated in another transforming experience, not so obviously shocking, yet of surprising power. This was an intensive five-day workshop, where the high school students lived, wrote, cooked, and ate with experienced writers who modeled, guided, and coached them. Afterwards he wrote:

> Far-reaching inner changes, creative revelations of our inner self, the only part of us with any value, are usually triggered in the smallest fraction of time. The operations of the inner life are more analogous to microbiology than to the building of a motorway. Inevitably our lives are shaped by our daily work, but what transforms our innermost self — when it is transformed — are those momentary confrontations, either with some experience that somehow opens internal connections between unexplored parts of ourselves, or with some person whose mere presence, the mere example of their living being, does the same, or with some few seconds of spontaneous vision that does the same. The analogy is with contracting an infection — the single touch of the virus is enough, only in this case what spreads through the cells is illumination, a new richness of life, a deeper grip on ourselves. (Hughes, 1981)

We might expect the mystery of the cadaver emptied of its throbbing life, and the obscenities of the invading knife to 'somehow open internal connections between unexplored parts of ourselves.' Hughes, however, speaks in such terms when describing an intensive writing workshop. The observation of the interns and the writing of the researchers are both situated in a group context that adds intensity to the experience. The presence of experienced practitioners and of other learners, a place with resources a lone individual could not command, seriousness of purpose, and engagement in a task that calls for rigorous self-discipline — all these conspire in both situations to overcome the dilutions of everyday life. But above all, something profound seems implicated about the central experiences.

One major theme that emerges when qualitative researchers talk about their experiences as writers is that the writing changed them — as writers, as researchers, as professionals, as people. We need to take a closer look. To see others, recognizably like us, embark successfully on a writing and research life can be heartening. To tease out some elements that catalyzed their growth can spur us on to apply at least some of them.

Beginnings and Catalysts

In looking back over their qualitative research initiation, our participants found that writing began to transform them early on:

> The experience of diving into qualitative research has been one of the most profound and moving experiences I have encountered in my academic career. Personally, my own bereavement experience was validated and recreated. Professionally the work blew the top off my understanding of bereavement and of the research process in general. I can see people, hear them, reflect on their experiences and my own, bring my guts and intellect to the table, and make my very best attempt to share my writing with others in a meaningful way. (Bruce Kellerhouse)

> My writing tended to be distanced, removed, and safe. I've been challenged by my group to break my habit. I'm told to 'lift,' and 'fly'; to create, feel, do whatever

it takes to tell the story. It was hard to let go. Was it difficult? Yes. Was it worth it? Absolutely. This kind of writing, this kind of learning, this kind of being can't be done alone. (Pat Gentile)

However, testimonials are often suspect, and the power of an experience is surely not conveyed by superlatives from a distance. You, our reader, we suppose, want a thoughtful conversation about doing and facilitating qualitative writing, not conversion stories. And yet . . . let's be provocative. Perhaps we need to start with the stories of surprising change and to plumb their depths, to enter the experience that seemed to catalyze the change, and to find there something of and for ourselves in the service of our writing.

Reflective approaches that bring the Self into the written report are sometimes considered ill-conceived incursions into therapy. How to draw the lines between one's right to privacy, the self-indulgence of hanging out one's intimate laundry, and the kind of self-scrutiny and self-disclosure demanded for trustworthy qualitative writing? This last, it must be emphasized, is what we are about here. We do not, however, subscribe to a common-sense, reductive notion of the task. Qualitative writing by its nature involves the Self too intimately to ignore the wounds, scars, and hard-won understandings that are to some degree part of our baggage. The conditions that allow people to make new beginnings in their writing are what we are after. We speak here of contexts where this happens. We hope these descriptions will be helpful to you in abstracting elements that you might apply in your own work. Beginning researchers are much like any students. They come in need of educational experiences that address the whole person. As bell hooks observes:

There are times when I walk into classrooms overflowing with students who feel terribly wounded in their psyches (many of them see therapists), yet I do not think they want therapy from me. They do want an education that is healing to the uninformed, unknowing spirit. They do want knowledge that is meaningful . . . addressing the connection between what they are learning and their overall life experiences. (1994, p. 19)

We appreciate the distinction hooks makes. The implications we can draw for those who teach qualitative research writing are daunting yet promising. First, they must model the process of bringing personal experience to qualitative research writing. This asks that they share something out of their own stories, and that they give the sharing focus and purpose:

Professors who expect students to share . . . narratives but who are themselves unwilling to share are exercising power in a manner that could be coercive . . . It is often productive if professors take the first risk, linking . . . narratives to academic discussions so as to show how experience can illuminate and enhance our understanding of academic material. (hooks, 1994, p. 21)

We have found that people are eager to follow. 'Focusing on experience allows them to claim a knowledge base from which they can speak' (hooks, 1994, p. 148). Writing about themselves, beginning researchers rummage in the ragbag of experience, and with amazement, pain, and delight pull out pieces they have not recognized as treasures, tacit understandings that were there all along. Listen to Marilyn Adler as she narrates her personal history with writing:

> I began writing for and to myself when I was in third grade, an only child and a latchkey kid. I wrote in my diary daily. Writing to myself was a way I could share the thoughts of my day with someone. For some reason, seeing my thoughts on paper made them clearer to me. Made me laugh at myself and get those bundles of emotion unwound into lines on the paper.
>
> When I was 12 and at school, my mother found and read my diary. I came home to find her angry, holding my green and gold diary in her hand, pages ripped out of it. She had read stories in it about her, about the affair she was having at the time. 'You can write about yourself, but not other people,' she screamed. I thought I could write about anything I wanted to.
>
> I continue to write for and to myself. Since that episode with my mom, my books are all in Pittman shorthand . . .

Marilyn taps into her vivid sense that her words have power. They can both comfort and enrage. Now she can harness the power in the research task. Researchers can ready themselves to go past the surfaces of the people and situations they study because, like Marilyn, they have remembered and acknowledged the value and complexity of their own lives. They may then be willing, as hooks found with her students, 'to surrender to the wonders of relearning and learning ways of knowing that go against the grain . . . We can teach in ways that transform consciousness' (1994, p. 44). She is convinced, and so are we, that where this linking of experience and research is actualized, writing can become a transforming action.

The Baggage We Bring

Researchers bring to their qualitative writing all that they are, and this includes what many refer to as their 'baggage.' Michael Agar (1980) observes in *The Professional Stranger* that ethnographers carry considerable inner baggage by way of growing up in a particular culture, developing personal idiosyncrasies, and going through a professional training that conveys a particular set of lenses. We have considered this inner baggage at some length in speaking earlier of the researcher's stance. In popular parlance, and in our data, however, 'baggage' has some negative connotations — one's 'hang-ups,' aversions, the residue of one's past unhappy experience — a legacy that burdens down and makes progress difficult. It seems that something else needs to be said. We feel strongly that the so-called baggage that emerges in people's writing about themselves is more than a negative impediment. It is also a unique life experience and strength. But we do not wish to minimize the understated courage with which we have seen people press on despite formidable burdens. Sometimes these include emotional and physical problems and heavy family and personal responsibilities. Some writers have found themselves preoccupied and their energy used up, even to the point of preventing their immersion in the research experience or confronting their data. We marvel at the many times people have shared the struggle with distressing realities and found that writing all along helped them wrest meaning not only from the experience of their participants but from their own. Many found common themes with their participants and useful metaphors that grew out of their situations. One of Van Manen's (1990) suggestions for researchers before they ask their participants to share their experience is to '. . . write a direct account of a personal experience as you lived through it' (p. 65). Read Barbara Ball's reflections on a personal turning point in her life, page 349 in this volume, that helped her to shift her own understandings, so that fifteen years later this transformed vision allowed her a broader perspective about learning and teaching. The baggage becomes useful.

Besides personal problems, and beneath the more obvious intellectual and professional incentives to pursue qualitative research, many people brought deeper issues in need of resolution that led them to or were triggered by a qualitative research experience. These could be hindrances, sometimes were, in fact, but writing about them frequently enriched the work. These disequilibriums that initially appear to be paralyzing can become liberating as they are worked through.

Disequilibrium, Carl Rogers (1959) maintains, is conducive to significant learning. We found some beginning researchers who arrived searching for themselves, at times in considerable pain; some with a lost joy in writing; others with restlessness about their academic and professional lives; some with a clear vision seeking a way to be realized. And all of that means change:

> The student in the regular university course, and particularly in the required course, is apt to view the course as an experience in which he expects to remain passive or resentful or both . . . When a regular university class does perceive the course as an experience they can use to resolve problems which *are* of concern to them, the sense of release, and the thrust of forward movement is astonishing. (Rogers, 1959, p. 158)

The sense of unease often seems impetus to change; it holds a charge of energy. Let us illustrate from our data. People's resources of experience, intelligence, and language are evident as they write about their concerns. Sung-Goo Hur recently arrived from Korea. In his first poem he reveals a sense of being an outsider that preoccupies him. As the semester begins he writes:

> I was a stranger.
> Still I am a stranger in this world.
> Wherever I went, I was not comfortable.
> I was always ready to start to some place.
> I didn't know where I was going to.

We marvel both at how writing opened the door to communication for this then quiet and seemingly withdrawn man, as well as his courage to share what must have been some intensely private thoughts and feelings. We doubt very much that we would have tackled the writing of a poem in Korean, all things having been equal. Some months later his next poem is about the bilingual teacher he is studying. It captures his fresh realization of human qualities more fundamental than cultural differences and sense of uprootedness. He faces and then sees past the stereotypes he has encountered and perhaps internalized. In what he says of the teacher we hear his self-understanding and what sounds like a renewed sense of purpose and direction:

> You have a flat nose
> You have small eyes
> You have yellow skin.
>
> You can't speak Korean like a Korean.
> You can't speak English like an American.
> Not Korean, nor American
> You have crystal eyes
> You have the loving heart for the world
>
> Your love will break the wall
> Your love will build the bridge between the islands

We dare say Sung-Goo brings new eyes — crystal eyes — to the classroom he has chosen to study.

Michele Bellavita experiences joy in finding her way back to a compatible kind of writing, even though she finds that the joy is at times outweighed by remnants of old, deeply ingrained attitudes:

> Doing qualitative research writing can sometimes make me feel whole, buoyant, like an artist who's found the right medium. It's like coming home. It suits my personal quirks. So why get so frenzied, frightened, and disheartened? Why hold myself back? It has to do with how I used to see myself before the 'homecoming.' Coming from a rather working class Italian-American family where none of the adults and only one male cousin except for myself went beyond high school, let alone a doctoral program, I never thought of myself as particularly intelligent. Maybe creative in a sloppy undisciplined way. Not wonderfully creative. And certainly not an intellectual. So it took time and struggles to feel comfortable with the fact that I am intelligent and capable of creative work. But something about writing a dissertation throws me right back into those insecurities.

Not surprisingly, insecurities about belonging reassert themselves with the challenge of a new intellectual step. Michele looks afresh at her feelings and the history that helps account for them. Writing allows her the distance to reduce the force of negatives and to connect with her strengths.

Others, like Diane Austin, brought a love of poetic writing that coexisted uneasily with the desire for professional credibility and the hope to get past the frustration of a writing block:

> I used to love to write — stories, plays, and poems. I think in a way the writing I did helped me survive an unhappy and difficult childhood. I would go into a world *I* created and I suppose you could say had some control over. During adolescence I wrote poetry, depressing and melodramatic stuff about the real pain I felt. I began Jungian analysis in my early twenties. For the next fifteen years, I wrote songs. They became a journal of my analysis and another form of therapy for me. Then about three years ago, I just stopped writing. I tried to force myself but something in me had died. So reluctantly I let go. I had to trust that I was meant to express myself in some other way. The following year I wrote an article

for a music therapy book. I was extremely anxious. Who was I to give my views? I needed the experts to back me up each step of the way so I quoted as often as possible. I wanted to be poetic and creative but I wanted more for my work to be taken seriously.

Both Michele and Diane are creative and self-reflective, and at the same time drawn to advanced academic work. They need to integrate these too-often disparate tendencies. They are receptive to embracing the ways of qualitative writing with its promise of channeling diverse strengths.

Ann Buhman Renninger wrestled with professional isolation. She chose a qualitative writing course in the midst of the experience of writing for an audience with little or no understanding of qualitative research. She looks back with wry wit at her 'prolonged immersion and onetime belief in the accuracy and objectivity of positivist research':

> It has been said that there is no one more zealous than the convert. I am a convert to naturalistic research. Having earned a bachelor's and a master's degree in psychology in the 70's, I knew my rats and my chickens and my statistics. I measured and manipulated human behavior as well, but what I measured and manipulated, I could only tell you if I went up into my attic and retrieved boxes of lab reports, which appropriately enough, are by now most likely covered with mouse droppings.

Ann regards the stories of students and teachers as central to her research. So for her it is enabling to be in contact with like-minded people and to have the opportunity to develop her writing and ponder the issue of audience. It sounds as if, for a variety of reasons, all of these researchers were ready to take risks and attempt new ways of writing.

Even when people are disposed to welcome change, it comes at a price. Scrutinizing the Self as researcher can be costly and is called for right from the start. Beyond writing that examines Self, the arduousness of the creative process which is so closely bound up with the Self supplies its own occasions for confrontation. Together with the external context of a vigorous writing community, these inner tasks entered on wholeheartedly can be a powerful force for change, and it is writing tasks that call for both self-scrutiny and creativity that we examine in the next section.

Tuning the Self

Things as they are/Are changed upon the blue guitar. Wallace Stevens (1937/1990)

It is intriguing, we think, to imagine the artist of the Self selecting from an array of tools the appropriate ones to tune the instrument of the Self in particular ways. Among the benefits of a formal qualitative research course are the intense writing experiences and the steady pressure and support to write in a variety of forms one might not otherwise choose to try. People told us that the writing tasks changed them. In the next sections we share a range of forms that they attempted — personal narrative and reading logs that give voice to the Self, descriptive writing in the field log that develops the Self as observer, observer comments, notes-on-notes and memos that uncover and work past stances of the Self that may limit and distort. We will examine the increasing tendency to write about the Self in interactions with others. We hold that this kind of writing constitutes important data in telling the research story. This sharpened awareness of the Self affects the data gathering and is thus useful to the researcher as well as to the readers. Last, we look at the creative process involved in qualitative research writing. Perhaps you will be moved to try these ways of writing and to see for yourself. If it is difficult to spur yourself on in your solitude, you might commission your support group to set the tasks!

Inviting in the Self

Annie Rogers (1992) tells us about her invocation of the 'I' and of how she invites her students to broaden their reflections to include not only the personal but the cultural context of their lives as women in their society:

> I invite my students into a powerful place of disruption — the margins of academic orthodoxy — through writing and theater exercises designed to reveal what is not spoken in the academy. I invite my students to write candidly in the first person, to place the voice of 'I' in the center of the page, and in this way, to enter academic discourse through the authority of their knowledge as women. (p. 250)

Rogers seeks to counter the loss of voice and of women's knowledge, which she finds a particular dilemma for women as they try to enter and to be heard within their disciplines and professions through adopting the dominant discourse. In the qualitative research class Maryann observed, specific writing tasks and interactions incorporated invitations to bring the Self into the research process, and through reading logs into conversation with the academy. People told us the personal experience assignment was for them a galvanizing one. The invitation had its source in Harry Wolcott's *Writing Up Qualitative Research* (1990), where he observes:

> People whose occupations require continual engagement with written words gravitate toward the extremes. They become preoccupied either with consuming words or producing them. How about you: essentially a reader, or essentially a writer? (p. 20)

Then he himself addresses his question, by sharing some of his life stories. His message is two-fold: bring into this reflection your own life, and, recognize you are the authority on your own experience. As Rogers emphasizes, the hurdle is the public and inward silencing of the 'I' in academic discourse. On this point Tina Brescia and Molly Parrish speak for many:

> I remember struggling as a master's student to say what I wanted to, but never trusting that my opinion was valuable. I wrote but the words didn't seem to be mine; I always had to back them up with quotes from other people's work. (Tina)

> I learned to speak tentatively, not directly, as did many women of my age. As I began to write for academic and job-related purposes I felt I needed to write in

more voiceless ways, in more 'scholarly' ways, even to the point of making my writing dense and difficult to understand. (Molly)

In reflecting on her writing history, Margot saw herself silenced by conventions. She says that for years she hid behind her natural bent for communicating in person and her voracious appetite for reading in order to avoid writing very much or very well in a university context that demanded conformities she saw as stultifying. When she realized that she had created these barriers herself, she allowed herself to write — albeit with great trepidation at first — and found ways to share her writing more widely.

The problem of silenced voices, however, is not that of women alone. It is the burden of many others who have been marginalized in our society. hooks (1994) points to the fear of classroom talking about race, gender, sexual orientation, and class. To let surface these too-often silenced aspects of the Self, a measure of trust is a prerequisite.

Moreover, for anyone schooled in academic writing, the task of characterizing oneself as reader or writer could be a perfunctory and prim chronological account that in fact holds the Self at bay. This was not the case in the group we observed; spurred by Wolcott's questions, people felt sufficiently comfortable to speak and write of their cultural identities. Maryann sat in with one small peer writing group as people shared pieces about themselves as readers and writers. Her version of what went on suggests that when someone broke the unspoken taboos against certain topics, others were freed to speak:

> In her response to Wolcott's question, Liz had broadened 'reader' and 'writer' to the Freirian sense of 'reading the world' and of 'writing the world' as a way of acting in the world to change it. She related that she had just that morning written a long letter protesting about institutional treatment of her as a minority person; she was elated by her sense of her words as a powerful tool for action.
>
> Zoraida identified with Liz's experience, saying that she felt that her identity had been overshadowed by what she called 'stereotypes of dumb Puerto Ricans.' She admitted that she resists this image by refusing to give in to the pressure she feels to do her research about minority people. Her hypothesis was that she is perhaps actually a threat in one corner of the institution because some people sense that she is more intelligent and talented than they. In her written story she also resists the reader-or-writer image of herself — 'I am a *speaker*, although in order to speak I write.'
>
> In her piece she dares another image, which she reads with the disclaimer that the group may think she is a bit crazy: 'I am a goddess.' Her cheeks are flaming still and her eyes bright with the unshed tears and the anger that accompanied her earlier story. She relates that she teaches yoga and meditation, lecturing to audiences in Latin America. Her life was interrupted by an auto accident that left her blind for some months. Again we hear that she resisted. This time she refused the role of victim. Instead she used the time to enter more deeply into herself and emerged with new self-understanding and direction for her life. Now she is at the point where she needs to find a research topic she cares about and can pursue with passion.

The effect of her words is electrifying and the group gathers in around Zoraida. She writes and speaks with authority.

Besides drawing out such voices, the sharing of personal accounts with a group is a way to foster and celebrate people's connection of their inner lives, passionate and active, with their academic projects. Such sharing can jog memory and counter selective recall. For people embarking on qualitative research, such oral readings are a memorable demonstration of the power of story.

Clearly, researchers need not do, cannot do, this personal writing in a vacuum. The qualitative researchers we studied were asked to look at their reading and writing lives, while simultaneously keeping reading logs. Both readings from related disciplines and presentation of student work offered help. People responded to such texts as Max Van Manen (1990) on 'Hermeneutic Phenomenological Writing', Herr and Anderson (1993) on oral history, Makler (1991) on personal narrative in learning history, Annie Rogers (1992) on subtexts of resistance to dominant discourse. Qualitative research writing was done in a context of inner conversations with authors. As Carl Rogers (1959) has observed, the Self is not the sole resource. Here were ideas to thicken the creative broth as well as models of good storying.

The readings were a further reassurance about the place of personal experience in qualitative research, writing the Self 'not in a narcissistic sense but in a deep collective sense' (Van Manen, 1990, p. 132). Van Manen emphasizes that narrative is writing that shares a fundamental feature with phenomenological human science: 'Both story and phenomenology move in the tension between particularity and universality' (p. 120). Herr and Anderson point to the neglect of biography and historical context in much qualitative research, and to the power of narratives that include these aspects to go beyond the Self to common dilemmas. Makler, who undertook a personal history project along with her students, reflects on the intersection of personal with academic when the informed imagination seeks to unearth intentions and motivations behind the events, actions, and decisions of historical events, what she calls the 'common dimensions of shared humanity' (1991, p. 46). The theoretical lenses provided by these writers justified a personal approach and uncovered a rationale for personal narrative as part of a research repertoire. People needed this kind of reassurance, but Jill Schehr still debated with herself:

> I became proud of my ability to lift the 'doctoralese' censorship that had often encumbered my writing. The writing was much more personal than even I had been used to ... However, I still have a nagging feeling that my hard work will not be taken seriously ... I am afraid that perhaps it is too passionately painted.

Even though the initial response to the experience of personal writing was generally positive, it was necessary for many people to step back and meet their own intellectual misgivings, the other internalized voices that issued warnings about academic respectability. They could counter and dispel their common-sense suspicions that this kind of writing is sentimental, touchy-feely stuff without justification in a research course. The readings situated personal writing in context. By writing about these readings in their journals, they could work to assimilate a theoretical framework for situating stories of Self.

Rosemarie Lewandowski and Barbara Ball both provide vivid examples of how they made theory their own by dialoguing with the authors in their reading logs, thus deepen their conversation with their own data:

Beginning with 'Reading Women's Autobiographies' by Helle (chapter 3), I thought about Bakhtin and the notion of writing as 'dialogic,' continuing an ongoing conversation with other texts. This continued into chapter 7 by Narayan, 'According to Their Feelings,' where I noted the writers' variety of sources for their research/analytic frame for looking at their data, and made a connection, thinking about what I might read for research about Joey and his drawing before writing. I found myself returning to some of the issues/questions I want to pursue in my dissertation, i.e. the connection between visual and verbal thinking.

Things began to gel, evolving from the poem, through the readings, to the connection with my interests for research. Later on, for chapter 10 by Tappan and Brown, 'Stories Told and Lessons Learned,' I responded by connecting this essay with the moral issue I saw in my data: Mrs. Cato's imposition of the district's 'writing process' program on Joey, vs. Bakhtin's emphasis on 'the search for one's own (authorial) voice.' (Rosemarie)

After all, I tell myself, the classroom is a lively and stimulating place, inviting, and open. Children play, choose, construct things, parents bring in materials, flowers and food, the teachers take their work seriously. I really believe both teachers when they tell me how they take their work home, how they think about how to approach a child. They do. I see how they have thought about and planned the 'interventions' they make. They care for the children, they worry.

A thought in Van Manen's article was helpful. He talks about 'hope' in teaching, about teacher expectations and anticipations, objectives, plans, and aims. 'As teachers we tend to close ourselves off from possibilities that lie outside the direct or indirect field of vision of the expectations' (p. 123). Isn't this what I experienced in the classroom? The best intentions, plans, and interventions, but a lack 'of play between teachers and children.' 'A language of hopeless hope'? (p. 122). (Barbara)

Madeline Grumet (in Eisner and Peshkin, 1990) provides another approach to helping people integrate theory and their personal experience. She relates that she asks her education students to write several autobiographical stories about teaching and learning and then to rewrite them using whatever theoretical language they find useful in the texts they are reading. In this way, as well as by what she calls her 'experience-distant' comments, she works with her students to help them elaborate and then lift their stories.

Another value of a log or reading journal is to invite the Self into conversation within the academy. Lowenstein, Chiseri-Straton, and Gannet (1994), who have studied the long history of journal writing, focus on the use of the reading log to develop the researcher through dialogue with the literature. They speak of 'Writing the Self into Community':

We want to re-envision the academic journal as a mediator through which students can engage in larger academic and social conversations both within and outside the academy. We will view the journal not only as a locus for the construction and transformation of the self as learner but also as a means to define, maintain, and transform the writer's connection with discursive and knowledge communities. (p. 142)

The authors relate the story of Joanna Field (1934), who kept a diary of her course work, and then a journal of reflections about that diary. She continued this dialogic journal for seven years:

> During her training in psychoanalytic methods, Field uses her journal to mediate between the authoritative voices of those whose work she is reading (Jung, Freud, Piaget, Descartes) and her own developing habits of thought ... For example, Field observes that her fear of feminine knowledge and experience, which she calls 'subjective intuition,' prompts her to overvalue 'male objectivity' and the language of authority encoded in much of her formal reading ... Ultimately, Field uses the journal both as a way of joining a new academic discipline and eventually as a vehicle for challenging and transforming this community as well. (p. 143)

This was 1934!

Cultivating the ubiquitous Self

The perception and sensibility of the researcher need cultivation. A wide variety of writing tasks help toward this, including the forms we discuss in Chapter 3 of this volume. Here we focus on the field log because we see it as such an ongoing work-out for 'shaping up' the instrument of the Self. It is hard to exaggerate the importance of description in the development of the researcher-writer, the faithful keeping of a field log from the earliest observations. Description and observer comments are part of the same log and they work in tandem. The role of observer comments is perhaps more self-evident, but as Karen Zielony understands:

> The more I recorded, the more I learned. Even though the 'OC's [observer comments] in my log reveal more explicitly my attitudes and hunches and tentative assumptions about what may have been happening, the descriptions of the class environment also make apparent, if implicitly, my ubiquitous presence and perspective as a researcher.

Karen seems to say that description captures her as researcher in the form of the perceptions and evaluations that underlie her representation of a particular classroom. To do this well calls for intense focus, disciplining the Self to listen and to observe until one gets beyond the obvious, beyond what Molly Parrish calls 'premature observations and conclusions,' to ask, 'Is that really what I'm seeing?' William Parker writes of this as a major change for him, a change that is new and in the beginning frightening. He sees that he is moving from thinking that he must keep himself 'out of the issue,' to understanding that the best he can do is to concentrate, document carefully and in detail, and acknowledge himself as an instrument. He writes: 'I am trying to overcome lack of confidence and lack of focus, both due to inexperience. Nevertheless the metamorphosis is in process.' Inevitably it is a metamorphosis of the Self in coming to see more, and to see more deeply. Judy Walenta describes what she learned:

Writing the logs has helped loosen me up. I wrote about what I saw the way I might tell it to a friend, only perhaps slightly more detailed. I am a master of shaggy dog stories. Through log writing, I learned that truth, or a representation of perceived reality, can be as entertaining as fiction. The more closely my writing reflects my actual thought process the better it is.

Judy captures both the expansive reach of this kind of writing and the constraints that give it rigor: the demand for frankness and precision, the effort to listen intently to grasp what one is thinking and to reach beyond conventional statements to the unique perception. Denzin observes that people are not taught description. What inexperienced writers, or those accustomed to write clinical summations, tend to do is 'thin description': sparse, superficial accounts that offer partial, summary renderings of situations, seen through the researcher's rather than the participants' eyes, without conveying the possible intentions and meanings behind the actions (Denzin, 1983). Ori, in observing an AIDS service center looked back at his initial fieldnotes:

I wrote 'My overall impressions and feelings of this first observation were over-whelming.' [Describe in detail; what is overwhelming? What does it look like? What does it really feel like? This tells me nothing.]

Ori's bracketed critical comments in which he talks to himself, show that he is beginning to grasp the idea of 'thick description.' The first step is really to look at and listen to what is going on: the visual aspects of the scene; the mood it evokes for the viewer; the language, signs of emotion, and actions of those studied and one's own emotions as participant-observer. First impressions have a particular vividness worth capturing. Ori described himself not as a reader or writer, but as a feeler. Yet initially he had written very little about his feelings. In a long memo about the experience of preparing his log, Ori tells how, after writing the entry above, he continued to think about his feelings. 'What's wrong with me? Why don't I feel?' When he awoke at three the next morning, he confronted the seven years of painful experience that lay behind his avoidance of feelings and his reluctance to write about this. His writing and his perspective changed after this. At last he began to fill in the missing detail:

It was Daniel, a man who worked for me, a man who is my friend, a man that I spent time with outside of work. A person I know well. I panicked. How could AIDS have done this to him in such a short time? Thoughts ran through my mind. When was the last time I saw him? What happened to his long shiny black hair? Yes, I knew the answer. I opened my arms to embrace him as he said, 'You didn't even recognize me.' I said, 'No, not at first, I didn't recognize you with your hair shaved off.' His sense of humor had not died with the rest of his body. He laughed a deep hollow laugh as he responded, 'You never were a good liar, you're full of crap. You didn't know who the hell I was. AIDS. Isn't it great — my hair fell out from the drugs, I lost forty pounds in four months. Oh, and my skin, isn't it a lovely shade of yellow — it really does limit the colors I can wear.' I tried not to let him know that I recognized all the things he just mentioned, but it didn't work. Again, I said, 'I only noticed that your hair was gone.' His wonderful sense of humor shined through as he said, 'Sure, and I didn't notice you put on about twenty pounds.' We both laughed. We talked for a few minutes before I turned to enter the kitchen.

In a final memo, Ori reflects back on how he moved from seeing Daniel as a victim — swallowed up by his own dread at the imagined possibility of this happening to himself — and recognizing and presenting a much more complex Daniel who is definitely not solely an AIDS sufferer:

> Am I too close, too involved with my chosen participants? I don't think so. Not only can I empathize with them; I also have a tremendous respect for their courage and determination. It took me time to learn to observe AND experience with less sinister feelings. I was observing too seriously and shielding myself from the possibility of playfulness and humor within the workplace. I didn't write about my interaction with Daniel until weeks later, because I simply did not want to 'describe in detail' what I saw. But if it wasn't for the 'detail' I would have remembered Daniel for what AIDS has done to him and not his sense of humor. Because I had to stop and think and recall, I was able to write about how we also laughed that day about how bad he looked. My advice is: write it, no matter what it feels like and write it in detail.

When Ori writes about his particular feelings, paradoxically his vision enlarges. We are struck by the connection that surfaces in our data between feeling and perception as researchers attempt to do justice to participants' experience. It seems that feeling guides perception. Listen to Carolyn Arnason's analysis of 'feelings' for the light it sheds on why this could be so:

> I know I have feelings, and as a therapist, listening to my feelings is crucial for the therapy process. But I never envisioned a time when my feelings could enter into the research process, and be necessary for analysis to happen. By feelings I mean a whole range of intuitions, hunches, questions, concerns, frustrations, elations, and analytic breakthroughs.

Carolyn's last sentence seems a fitting springboard for us to reiterate that we advocate writing about feelings and how these are addressed, specifically so that they serve to carry the research forward in increasingly constructive, sensitive and powerful ways. The human observer is no neutral camera that registers impressions with indifference. Feelings are partly mental, partly physical, and to listen to them is to get the first inkling of meaning. Looking and hearing are suffused with the tendency to make meaning. If the observer tries at first to describe profusely, to name things with the 'experience-close' word, this is a way to get past the abstract and summary. Because each researcher has unique experiences and stances, we see an infinity of variations in how this might be done.

Description pushes the reader to heightened perception. Like a replay of a game to sort out the details of what went on, in written descriptions we must fill in the gaps to make some sense. Because our remembered impressions are fragmentary and blurred, we may supplement them out of our conventional expectations about such events or out of a tendency to see what we want to see. We can't help doing this, but we can benefit from a replay to see more and to see it more precisely. We can raise questions about what we have written that lead us to see still more on the next replay. We can share the piece with someone else who may have more experience or a quicker eye. We can clarify the sequence and see where other inferences are possible from the same behaviors. With insistence on rich detail, we can notice where we have gaps in information and things we missed that were outside our focus. In short, we are asked to capture as far as possible the stuff of the experience for the participants, and for ourselves as participant observers, or interviewers, or studiers of documents.

What is the effect on us as researchers? The effort calls for us to develop a keener eye, a subtler ear, a more perceptive Self. Was it Henry James who said to novelists: 'Try to become someone on whom nothing is lost?' As researchers, we can work toward getting out of the rut of habitual perception of situations and of other people. Rhonda Weller Moore describes the experience of coming to know her participants:

> Ruth is a wonderful woman whose mixing of the past and present, and forgetfulness led me to categorize her as an 'Alzheimer's patient.' Spending the time I did with Ruth, the label faded out of significance. I was focused on seeing and knowing Ruth and her experiences, and my own experience was one of enlightenment.
>
> I would have to say that the ability to question my impressions, to ask myself where those impressions came from, and to persist despite them to see what really may be there has been the most instructive [part of the process]. It has released new energy, new creativity, new motivation in me, that I have needed to find.

Effective description asks more than strenuously putting aside reductive labels (learning disabled, low IQ, hyperactive, over sensitive, prejudiced, mentally ill, mildly retarded). There is a wonderful exercise that charges people in their support groups to underline each other's labels and help to substitute other descriptive phrases for them. Careful description demands cultivating an expanded observational focus as well as developing the language of careful observation. Teachers at one of New York City's alternative public schools engage in an ongoing process of developing this sort of ability. Maryann attended one of their sessions, described as a Prospect Descriptive Review of a Child (Carini, 1986) and found that the task indeed called for somewhat of a novelist's eye. She writes:

> This process involves the effort to get beyond the easy categories we sometimes employ to 'place' people. Judgmental comments are discouraged. When the teacher's report is shared with staff, rounds of description are undertaken to pull out as thorough a description as possible of observable behaviors. For some of the aspects of the child we were asked to observe, I realized that I lacked the language. I had never, for instance, put into words details of others' body language, their way of coming into a room and joining a group, the quality of their presence and bearing.

Likewise, Barbara Ball speaks of her effort to find the words to convey rhythms and intonations and to reproduce the word choices of participants. Such writing up of observations sharpens perceptions, as we do exercise our seeing and listening perhaps to an unaccustomed degree. The change this can effect in the researcher is spelled out by Max Van Manen (1990):

> (I can now see things I did not see before.) Although I may try to close my eyes, to ignore what I have seen, in some way my existence is now mediated by my knowledge . . . we are what we can 'see' (know, feel, understand). (pp. 130, 132)

Thick description is more than a literal recording of what is witnessed, is something other than amassing great amounts of detail. It is the ascertaining of multiple levels and kinds of meaning in a culture (Denzin, 1989). One guide in the face of the endless details that confront any observer is the questions we bring; the quality of these can be reductive or can be broad, yet focusing. 'What is going on here?' 'What is the experience like for these people?' are powerful starters. There are also a few guides to help with thick description — lists of points to look for. Some we find cumbersome and as exhausting as they are exhaustive. We prefer a few thinking tools that are succinct, generative, and easy to remember. Other people offer concise guidelines that fit our criteria:

- Kenneth Burke's (1969) dramatistic 'pentad': agent, agency, act, purpose, scene;
- Van Manen's (1990) experienced space, experienced time, experienced body, and human relations as we live them;
- Denzin's (1989) four constants in every situation: history, power, emotionality, knowledge.

The phrase, 'Thick description' has become a reductive label for some. Margot says she flinches when, in research plans, this phrase is used as a self-sufficient indicator without an explanation of what 'thick description' means in the study, how it is carried out, assessed and analyzed. In order to get to thick description, students of qualitative reseach in her course are encouraged, nay 'ordered,' not to take notes in the course of observation because Margot reasons that too much is missed in pulling away from the scene. Iris Goldberg, who followed this dictum, discovered the power of the log to recapture the nuances of experience. She moved from her terror that 'without a notebook in hand each ephemeral moment would evaporate,' and from desperately reconstructing to trusting her memory. Thus she could re-enter the experience through her log writing:

> I literally dredged the beginning sentences from wisps of memory jotted quickly on a pad. Then something began to change. I stopped being me, in front of the computer, placing word by word on the screen. Writing merged me with the experience. I saw and I wrote: Some of the children are already dressed in dance garb, pink leotards and tights or black . . . I catch a glimpse of what appears to be a nursery school set up: wooden play kitchen furniture. A few mothers seem to be changing children in this area . . . I think I see that 'angry mother.' *I seem to have her dressed in her angry face.*

For many of us, our obsession with note-taking has longstanding and firm roots. Members of this writing team have repeatedly watched students in the very first grades struggle to 'take notes,' to get everything down in order to pass the test before the fragments disappear forever into the atmosphere. No wonder this distancing device is so strong, as we continue schooling, no wonder we persist and are encouraged to persist in it. No wonder it is a shock and even a threat to many when — possibly in mid-life and while earning the highest academic degree one can earn — along comes a person who insists that we don't take notes, who emphasizes that this is a blind, overused, and de-personalizing mechanism, that people will recall what is important and forget what is not.

Asked to work from memory, as an exercise and an act of faith, writers keeping their logs schooled themselves to passionate discipline in face of the limitations of memory to preserve vivid sensory impressions and feelings before their particularity faded. Molly Parrish wrote in her log:

> I want to try to capture the story of tonight in N. I don't want to lose any of the impressions I have right now, just after being there. I've driven to N, and while having a bite to eat, I'm going to write what I recall, by hand. This is different from my method lately, which has been to look for a chunk of time at the computer.

Tina Brescia, too, learned that she must seize the earliest possible moment, and then a powerful momentum made recall seemingly effortless for her:

> In the beginning the task was to write from observation and memory. There was something very freeing about this exercise for me . . . When I completed an observation I would sit down and type for hours. The words seemed to flow out of my mind faster than my fingers could type. I had so much that I wanted to say and so many things I wanted to be sure that I captured on paper before my memories of them slipped away. It was as if I was sailing on the wind of each new observation. There was a force behind the writing that seemed to organize it and move it forward.

Barbara Ball decided that since writing her log 'from her head' was a process of inclusion/exclusion (we didn't tell her that this is the case also when one takes notes), she would include loose ends, fragments that might jog needed memory at a later time:

> The events that stand out seem to serve as organizing structures in my memory, like figures in relation to the ground. A lot of classroom activity, movement, comments, play — observations of a more fragmentary nature — sink into the background. They may be forgotten if they are not somewhere anchored in my log, if my log does not contain some of these loose ends.
>
> Atkinson addresses an important issue in writing the fieldnotes. Do we attempt to give a 'readerly' account at this level? Do I strive for vivid evocative scenes, potential vignettes and impose an unwarranted degree of analytic closure? Do I smooth the fragmentation and complexity of the life in the classroom to make my log more readable, more interesting? 'Understanding is always bought at the expense of fidelity to the phenomena' (p. 14). I think the question is to be aware of this reduction of the complexities of life and to work on accepting fragments and loose ends as part of the log. It is an important issue in teaching. What constitutes a good log? Although we are tempted to be attracted to it, it may not necessarily be the most vivid, dramatic or heroic story.

The call to recapture the experience of an observation or interview while memory is still vivid can pin down impressions that are like threads to find the way back to moments before one's story line took over. In studying her field log, Lori Wolf noticed a gap in her writing where she had been reluctant to describe what her participant Valerie was wearing. She also found a fragment that helped her reconstruct the scene. Like Barbara and Lori, if researchers put down as many fragments as occur, they might get valuable details past the limits of their particular stance. Agar warns: 'An interpretive framework cuts into the world like a jigsaw, leaving much of the wood behind' (1980, p. 49). The field log is what is recalled, not what happened. We must be easy about the fact we cannot 'get' everything — what we must ask after a time is, 'Is what I have here sufficient to convey to me the outstanding events as I witnessed and felt them?'

The logs, understood as researchers like these understood them, become a record of the evolution of qualitative researchers into sensitive and disciplined observers. Van Manen (1990) distinguishes between appearance and essence:

> Our 'common sense' pre-understandings, our suppositions, assumptions, and the existing body of scientific knowledge predispose us to interpret the nature of the phenomenon before we have even come to grips with the significance and the phenomenological questions. (p. 46)

He observes, too, that 'thick description' as used by anthropologist Malinowski means that besides presenting and organizing the research story, one must aim to convey the deeper meaning structure. Here of course he moves from description to interpretation in the formal sense, but, as these researchers came to understand through their writing, the field log is already an interpretation. Their efforts to be faithful to the participants' experience and not to crop it to fit into narrow frames can break open those frames. We hear in their voices more precise language and greater capacity for understanding those different from themselves, the ring of authority that comes from truly having been there; not colonizing but listening, learning to combine and relate a multiplicity of points of view without homogenizing them.

Bias, Blinding, or Enabling?

In Chapter 2, we explored the researcher's stance and in Chapter 5, the researcher's choice of theoretical lenses. Here we circle back to look more closely at how some writing tasks and strategies foster the awareness of stance that makes for more careful, faithful presentation. The distortions, blind spots, and limitations that are contribute to our various stances are what people usually mean by bias. In an article that deals with teacher expectations, Susan McLeod (1995) notes Bertrand Russell's incisive comments about the 'eyeglasses' of bias in researchers who study animal behavior:

> One may say broadly that all the animals that have been carefully observed have behaved so as to confirm the philosophy in which the observer believed before his observations began. Nay, more, they have all displayed the national characteristics

of the observer. Animals studied by Americans rush about frantically, with an incredible display of hustle and pep, and at last achieve the desired result by chance. Animals observed by Germans sit still and think, and at last evolve the solution out of their inner consciousness. (1927, pp. 29–30)

What kind of animal are you? An animal ready to reflect on such a question, though perhaps not easily? How articulate are you about your own stance at this moment of reading? How aware are you of reading the world through particular lenses that define what you see? What is your habitual take on the world? What do you see and fail to see because of it? Have you managed to discern your own national (read ethnic, social class, gender, decade, X) characteristics? Have you owned up to the ways your blessed — or scarred-by-experience — perspective or your current life situation colors what you see? On the level of theory, have you ventured our challenge to construct the story of your -isms? What Wolfgang Iser (1980) says of the act of reading seems as true of what we do as we seek to make sense of our observations: we fill in the gaps out of what we bring to the situation. More than this, we structure, select details, and emphasize different parts of the 'text' of reality depending on the themes and values with which we approach it (Downing, 1989).

While we may smile at Russell's caricature, we might ponder the metaphor of bias as contrasted with that of stance for the different angle it offers on the same field. Perhaps we can say that bias is the effect of our stance on what we construct or craft. Since the term appears quite often in our data, let us pause over what we mean when we speak of biases. Bias, the dictionary tells us, is literally 'a line cutting diagonally across the grain of fabric.' To the researcher-writer this might suggest not getting the lines of the story straight, slanting from what 'really happened' — a positivist notion. But if we worry this notion a bit, it is hardly that simple. Let's suppose that the fabric is a plain weave. The dressmaker knows that if he follows the straight horizontal and vertical lines of the material, the material will tear more easily; cut on the diagonal it will resist tearing. He understands the simple facts of the fabric, and recognizes the strengthening effect of pursuing the bias. Even fabric, however, can be more elaborately woven. What the observant researcher soon learns is that the simple warp and woof of a story is the mind's simplification of an intricate fabric. Bias, in one who knows the Self, can perhaps lend strength to the story as we cut against the obvious grain.

Here are some other dictionary meanings of bias a) a bent, a tendency b) an inclination of temperament or outlook, especially a personal and sometimes unreasoned judgment. In this book, we understand bias to encompass our preconceptions, assumptions, passionate inclinations, aversions, all the experience and learning we bring to a scene. Some of these go unrecognized and prevent us — by rendering us blunt and clumsy cutting shears — from doing justice to our material. Some of these are recognized and act as energizers, facilitators in shaping our material just so. We are a host of biases. Some are helpful, some not, especially if we are unaware. Anthropologist Michael Agar (1980) writes:

As you choose what to attend to and how to interpret it, mental doors slam shut on the alternatives . . . (p. 48) By bringing as many of [one's biases] to consciousness as possible, an ethnographer can try to deal with them as part of methodology and can acknowledge them when drawing conclusions during analysis. In this sense, ethnography is truly a personal discipline as well as a professional one. (p. 42)

While Agar urges that self-awareness be programmed into preparation for qualitative research, he does not pretend to know all the answers about how to correct for bias. Should ethnographers be psychoanalyzed, Agar wonders. He cites both those who call for this and others whose studies indicate that therapy seems to make no significant difference. Jennifer Hunt, who writes of *Psychoanalytic Aspects of Fieldwork* (1989), observes that 'it is difficult for analysts themselves to persist in the arduous task of self-analysis, even with formal courses in theory and method, years of experience with patients, and a personal training analysis . . . Researchers will inevitably make mistakes and be tempted to indulge in "wild analysis"' (pp. 83–4). She herself underwent analysis and found that talking through her reactions in research situations reduced anxiety so that she went on to develop good working relations with participants. Here we examine some writing tasks that also have proved valuable for raising awareness.

Some people recommend keeping a diary. Patricia Waugh (1989, p. 99) describes Virginia Woolf's reflective awareness of biases and her effort in her diary to deal with what she calls 'screens.' We understand her to mean the barriers that are an intimate part of the Self and block the view of some dimensions of reality. Woolf records (20 April, 1919) that the importance of the diary form is precisely its screen-breaking potential, its ability to record the 'loose, drifting material of life,' in a form 'loose knit and yet not slovenly, so elastic that it will embrace anything, solemn, slight or beautiful that comes into my mind' (L. Woolf, 1954, p. 23). Like the field log, the diary inevitably offers a revelation of the Self in what the writer selects to focus on and in the evaluations implied or stated. An entry in Woolf's diary for 1926 examines her own negative response to appearances, which she reads as her way of evading the essential. Watching two girls walking down a dusty road, she writes:

> My instinct at once throws up a screen, which condemns them: I think them in every way angular, awkward and self-assertive. But all this is a great mistake. The screens shut me out. Have no screens, for screens are made out of our own integument; and get at the thing itself, which has nothing whatever in common with a screen. The screen-making habit, though, is so universal that probably it preserves our sanity. If we had not this desire for shutting people off from our sympathies we might perhaps dissolve utterly; separateness would be impossible. But the screens are in excess; not the sympathy. (L. Woolf, 1954, p. 100)

Woolf does not wish to identify with the girls so she makes a screen (integument — our own skin, part of ourselves) drawn, we may suppose, from her upper socioeconomic group feelings of superiority and her expressed disdain for graceless bearing and vulgar forwardness. Her diary is the place where she confronts her defenses. She can put down the nuances of her thoughts and feelings and listen to herself. Fred Daniele arrived at something like a diary, where each day in the field he wrote about his mood and circumstances as he approached the hospital to make his observations.

Another help to further acquaintance with one's multiple stances is to maintain a detailed autobiography that includes writings about formative experiences, personal accomplishments, and biases, and to update and revise it periodically (Werner and Schoepfle, 1987, p. 314). Barbara Ball wrote a piece of her autobiography that probed her own classroom experience in the course of her study of a classroom:

> Initially I was not particularly interested in observing a classroom. The image of the school of my past appeared gray, boring and impersonal, a place where I was silent and invisible. At the end of high school, when I graduated as the best student, I felt with pain that I had mostly learned how to fulfill expectations, to stay within given outlines, and to comply — I had made myself as invisible as possible.
>
> Only recently I remembered an essay that I wrote 15 years ago while I was sitting in the library of the History Department at the University of Heidelberg and looking through curricula. Teaching was supposed to educate students to become critical, responsible and active members of society. But something was missing, it seemed, in this educational system. In spite of our extensive learning about constitutions, political ideologies, and human rights from the French revolution to the Nazi regime, I felt that learning still meant receiving and swallowing the information presented by the teacher. We learned about critical ideas and various viewpoints, but we were still conforming and passive. The problem was not the assigned readings or the quality of the material we looked at, but rather the way of teaching and learning. Teaching and learning seemed impersonal.
>
> I was surprised to re-discover this essay recently. So maybe I have not been so disinterested in teaching and learning as I thought.
>
> When talking about school, teaching and learning, I realize that I do have a stance. I wished learning meant to get to know each other, to be able to trust, to own feelings, and to be creative. I wished that in a classroom of 3–5 year olds the teacher would play with the children. Thus I am at times very critical of the teachers' interventions and I tend to emphasize those aspects of the classroom that are troublesome to me.

Notice how Barbara explores what the school experience was like for her — she does not give 'just the facts,' but probes her strong reactions of boredom, emotional pain, and powerlessness, and her anger and sadness as she revisits her past self. She tells us that she now recognizes the sources of her sympathies and criticisms.

Writing to discover our stance can inaugurate change from the threshold of our research. Kleinman and Copp (1983) advise:

> We must do the impossible and start before we begin. Before making that first phone call or visit, freewrite (see Elbow, 1981) . . . Ask yourself, What images do I hold of the people and place I am about to study and how do I feel about these images? . . . Do I have an ax to grind? Do I have a mission? Am I looking for a cause or a community? Do I expect this study to help me resolve personal problems? (pp. 57–8)

Magdalen Radovich, looking back at her earliest notes, sees in them the germ of her eventual insight into her prejudices and stereotypes:

I had even written out my concerns in a fairly coherent fashion in my pre-fieldnotes:
'I am interested in seeing how communities reach out to [their] afflicted members, how the help is received' (PRE-FIELD 5:10–13) . . .
'I am interested in seeing if and how [the Catholic Church] is actually serving the needy and desperate' (PRE-FIELD 5:20–23).

For a long while, I didn't give these ideas much conscious consideration after those initial scribblings.

Time in the field was needed. It is not easy to recognize biases.

To Kleinman and Copp's questions we want to add: Which of my biases is likely to help or hinder? As Jane Martin asserts, 'a bias that we are aware of, a passion deeply felt may be an entree into the experience we are studying.' This is what Bernstein (1983) calls an 'enabling,' not a 'blinding' bias. The difference between the two would seem to lie in the self-awareness. Jill Schehr does what we believe to be a splendid job in examining the complexities of her stance and their possible pluses and minuses in producing a credible report:

Apart from my professional experience, there are personal experiences which may often serve to distort my perceptions. I am a mother who is raising two children. In some ways, this humbling experience has made me more sensitive to the complexities of the job of mothering, and counteracts my tendency as a clinician to be unsympathetic to parents (especially when encountering abuse and neglect). But, as a mother, I have slowly developed a personal philosophy of parenting and constantly have to guard against its intrusion into my observing and writing about other mothers.

The majority of mothers in the nursery, and general prison population, are women of color. Poverty and deprivation are often the common melody running through their stories. I have been raised in a different cultural environment. I am now immersed in a social culture with rules and customs that are diverse and, at times, very new to me. It is a challenge for me to try to 'understand' in so foreign a culture, and yet there are many commonalities that we share as women and mothers. As a psychologist, I have to consider how these different cultural aspects influence what I observe . . . guarding against relying on theory for understanding. As a mother, I have to guard against judging the quality of other mothering which I may not understand as it stems from different cultural practice.

Finally, I am working with women who are behind bars. Some of the women speak openly about their crimes, while others profess their innocence. Although they have been judged and stripped of their freedom, they have been allowed to raise their babies for one year. As a mother, I have strong emotional reactions to each inmate mother who is forced to send her baby away. As a citizen, I have a response to antisocial behavior. As a woman, I am aware of the victimization some women, especially from minority groups, experience in their relationships and in their treatment by authority. It is my job to listen to their stories, remaining aware of how my biases may interfere with a new way of understanding and writing about what I observe and experience. I have confidence that my personal and professional philosophy of looking within and without at the same time will keep me 'on my feet.' It is in this area of transition between self and other that my stance as researcher continues to evolve.

Notice that it is in dialogue with the unfamiliar situation of a prison nursery that Jill comes to articulate some stances that might either blind her to aspects of the women's experiences or enable her to empathize with them. Once having sorted out her stances, she can deliberately choose more than one lens for her wider understanding.

To be available to situations as experienced by those who are living them, qualitative researchers are counseled to bracket preconceptions, prejudgments, beliefs and biases as observer comments. How shall we understand this bracketing? Certainly we are not saying that what is in brackets does not count, nor are we asserting that the description that stands outside is objective and what's inside is subjective and therefore discountable. Then what? Bracketing could be interpreted as a metaphor out of positivism but it comes from phenomenology. Van Manen (1990) tells us that Husserl borrowed the notion from mathematics, where one works out what is bracketed separately before including it in the whole. Bracketing asks us not to ignore or put out of our minds our responses to experience but to articulate them and deliberately distance ourselves to look at them. 'Maybe,' June Price notes, 'bracketing is a continuous, recursive self reflecting process. The judgments are still there, still strong, and still direct my focus. I put them literally to the side. I feel I can come to conclusions despite my judgments.' Andy Weitz recalls that he misunderstood at first:

> As I wrote my logs and attempted to be value free instead of value conscious I became more and more frustrated with my field work. My logs were richly detailed but lacking in narrative account OCs [observer comments]. I was torn about my method. I had read about the importance of the OCs, but others in my group seemed to be taken aback and even angered by the questions they got from responders at points where they had inserted themselves and their biases into the text so overtly. I felt it was safer to keep these out of my text. I tried to do so.
>
> Looking back on this effort what I find is a subversive creeping lack of trust-worthiness; an insidious disease popped up in my data. I used careless phrases like 'chaos' and 'accused' in places, rather than taking time out for an OC in which I could reflect on what I had seen. I sacrificed trustworthiness for delusive safety.
>
> I was observing a class in which things I didn't want to see, things that scarred me deeply when I was a student, were occurring as a matter of course and in the name of 'progressive education.' I was livid at various points. I was so clouded by anger, my emotions so tangled up in what I was seeing, that I was unable to effectively engage in various kinds of analysis (side comments disappeared from my log at about the seventh classroom visit).

Read closely, Andy's account suggests that, more than misunderstanding, he was reluctant at a particular time to confront his intense feelings. 'It was safer' not even to mention them. This was not because the support group was angry, but because, he says, he observed that others who wrote openly of their biases were 'taken aback and even angered' when their self-scrutinizing comments were probed. He was 'torn.' Perhaps he understood qualitative method better than he admitted at the time. Although he tried to banish the welter of emotions he mentions, he recognizes later that he had felt 'livid,' 'scarred,' 'clouded by anger.' These feelings operated subversively to infect his data. Their charge of violence blocked his thinking. The metaphoric language in which they are couched belies what he considered objective descriptions. Without OCs, he recognizes his biases only when he looks back. His backward look here, taking stock of his experience, demonstrates how writing brought him to a finally formidable grip on the crucial issue of trustworthiness and to a new self-awareness for subsequent returns to the field. We think it worthwhile to monitor our logs for such 'loaded words' and to ask ourselves, 'How do I know that?'

For a sample of a log, with description and observer comments alternating, we turn to a page of Barbara Ball's. We have italicized the observer comments:

> Thomas' mother tries to sit her son on a small chair at the art table, but he cries so heartbreakingly that she holds him on her lap. With his small hands he holds on to her neck. Florence and Moni stand at the table and watch. Moni just stands there with her eyes wide open, her glance fixated on Thomas and his mother. Florence goes over to him and strokes his back.
>
> *OC: It seems that both girls empathize with Thomas's pain. Moni looks as if she recognizes her own fears in Thomas. She was clinging to her father at the beginning of the school year. Florence reacts in a 'maternal' way, as Gina described her before with Manu and Annie.*
>
> Slowly Thomas' mother puts her son on one of the chairs. The girls have been drawing and she gives him a piece of paper. Thomas scribbles with a felt marker and Florence offers him a new color. Then another one. He takes the markers that she offers and produces a colorful scribble. As she puts the markers back, she searches for the fitting cap. Thomas becomes active, 'There are two greens.' He looks for the fitting cap. Florence and Thomas exchange markers. Now, Thomas' mother gets up. She says that she is going to leave. With a clear voice he says: 'I want a chocolate milk, and a chocolate chunk cookie and . . .'
>
> *OC: This is the first time that I hear him talk. I am also impressed how his expression changes from his motionless face to vivid engagement and participation. Suddenly his eyes seem to be alive, there is a gleam in his eyes. Before I often wondered whether he understood and felt what was going on around him.*
>
> His mother leaves while Florence and Thomas still interact lively. Gina comes to the table. 'Can you paint this for me?' (she points at the scribble). Thomas nods affirmingly and she asks him to get a glass of water, a brush and a plastic apron.
>
> *OC: I did not observe the following painting process, because something else in the classroom attracted my attention. When Gina intervened, I thought: 'Oh this is one of the examples where she zeroes in on the activity of the child and then tries to extend it to another area.' I can't help the irony in my comment. To me she disrupted the very wonderful interaction between Florence and Thomas, that seems to be so important for Thomas who is such a shy and withdrawn child. As sometimes before, I feel that her interventions are disturbing the children's rhythms.*

Barbara relates that she followed a return to the field with a return to a portion of her log that was rich and detailed in order to rework her categories. By now, aware of her biases, she works to compensate for them; she sees more than in her first round:

> I found that there were indeed important pieces that I had overlooked in my first coding, for example how the children run into the classroom in the morning and

choose some activity. That was really significant for me, particularly in the light of my struggle for fairness. I am glad that these descriptions are in my log, so I didn't just miss pieces in my observation and writing. While I was changing codes in the margin of my log, I was also thinking about practical issues. I will start my second round of coding with a clean copy, so that I am not too much influenced or confined by what I have done before.

We want to show two of Barbara's categories and their subcategories, drawn from her close re-examination of her observer comments, as examples of dimensions of researcher stance that emerge from OCs:

The emerging categories are not altogether different from what I wrote down before, but for me accents have shifted, and some connections are clearer.

The Reflecting Observer — Observer Comments (internal process)

researcher as instrument: trustworthiness
      personal life situation — research project
      life themes — research themes
      biases
      gut reactions (likes and dislikes)

interpretation:
      essence of situations
      metaphors and emerging themes
      critical voice

Barbara says she realized that her metaphors, in particular, revealed her biases. They carried the charge of her strong emotional reactions that seemed negative to her. (Her outline too led her to question whether she had included the whole picture.) What she learned prompted her deliberate efforts to be fair and balanced. She worked to pay more attention to the teachers' experience and to the positive aspects of the classroom as well as broader school contexts. Her questions and insights could well be posted on the cover of any researcher's field notebook:

Themes appear in the field that I recognize as themes in my life. Am I projecting? Am I fair? When do my inner feelings and reactions carry me away, carry me to narrow perceptions and far-reaching interpretations that are no longer substantiated by observations? It seems that meaningful and interesting themes emerge out of the tension between the field, the Other, and my personal reactions, my Self. *It seems that personal sensitivities can become assets, if balanced by rigorous questioning and method.* [our emphasis]

Magdalen Radovich, too, experienced the value of rereading her log once she had written her way through her resistance and layers of biases and of writing another round of notes about the same data from her evolved perspective:

Interestingly, my second set of notes on these log pages look a lot different than my first set. Not surprisingly my focus on my own issues blocked my seeing that there is more to my data than I thought, though how much and of what quality I don't know yet.

Rereading allows a kind of slow motion replay in which one's knee-jerk reactions and simplistic assumptions can be discerned in retrospect for what they are. Jane Martin calls these ways of self-scrutiny 'researcher check' — we look back on our earlier selves with, we hope, more experienced and wiser eyes. But we, like her, insist on respecting the tendencies of the Self:

> Personal agendas, unresolved conflicts do enter the process, but why is this necessarily a 'bad' thing? We come to our research with our own history. I believe we are all drawn to our work for 'personal' reasons and our work is probably the better for it. My biases seem to lead me in one direction or another, pointing at one category or another, and through my biases I learn.

Writing the Unheroic Self

> The governing instrument — which is also one of the centers of the subject — is individual, anti-authoritative human consciousness. (Agee and Evans, 1941/1988, p. ix)

Beyond the constant writing to hone the Self during the research process, we want to consider self-scrutiny and self-revelation as themes in the final presentation of our work. We think that Self as a theme demands thinking and writing that further develop the researcher. In a sense, facing one's preconceptions may seem a bit like throat clearing, or a task that needs to get done in private so the eye and ear of the researcher will give as fair a perception as possible of reality. The conventional tendency for researchers in the past has been to cover blemishes and unsightliness of performance and to touch up the face presented to the reader. We have found many such shields: third person narration, a noble persona, or amazing disappearing acts. Recently, however, there is more insistence that the writer make explicit to the reader his or her stance, pertinent history, and relevant strengths and limitations. We discuss this first. Next, we consider the researcher as a cultural Self, whose identifications shape experience and perspective. Finally, we focus on interactions between researchers and participants. Here then we present examples of each of these themes and some issues and challenges researchers face in their self-presentation to audiences. Perhaps it will broaden the range of our considerations about stance.

It has become fairly commonplace to acknowledge that the writing Self presented in a qualitative text is constructed. The researcher is frequently portrayed as an admirable figure with selected human limitations that are gradually overcome as our hero moves toward understanding. This portrayal is a neat abstraction. In fact, not many of us are so heroic. Much gets in the way of a steady upward arc of progress: power relations, personal cross-purposes, sponsors, budgets, school interests, academic politics, the traditions and disciplines from which the writer has been launched. It is tricky to explain motives, even one's own. We are more like what someone has called 'a playground of contradictions' than 'a conquering hero.' It is a good thing that we have some models that do not gloss over the complexities, some examples that can suggest where to start our public self-audit. Lionel Trilling, for example, notes James Agee's stance in *Let Us Now Praise Famous Men*, a study of tenant families:

> [Agee] writes of his people as if there were no human unregenerateness in them
> . . . What creates this falsification is guilt — the observer's guilt at his own relative
> freedom. Agee is perfectly conscious of this guilt and it is in order to take it into
> account that he gives us so many passages of autobiography and self-examination;
> he wants the reader to be aware of what is peculiar and distorting in the recording
> instrument, himself. (Quoted by Hersey in Agee and Evans, 1988, p. xxxii)

Agee portrays himself as distinctly less than heroic, consumed with hypersensitivity about offending the dignity of the families, awkward and bumbling and rendered almost stupid at moments, as an intruder on what he sees as tragic lives. Surely, he infers, the tenant farmers can feel a certain momentary superiority to this abashed, guilt-ridden man on their own turf where they cope with its harshness. His utter seriousness and sense of responsibility for intruding into others' lives lead him to condemn himself for a kind of voyeurism. His book was reviewed scathingly by a critic as 'the choicest recent example of how to write self-inspired, self-conscious, and self-indulgent prose' (as reported by Hersey in Agee and Evans, 1988, p. xxxi). In fact, his constant self-analysis makes him a character in the ongoing story.

In the story that follows, Agee and photographer Walker Evans have just decided they want photos of the inside of a locked-up country church. Agee runs up behind a young black couple they have been observing ahead of them on the road to inquire about the minister. He contrasts their natural dignity with its disintegration in the face of what they perceive as sudden pursuit by a white man:

> They were young, soberly buoyant of body and strong, the man not quite thin, the
> girl not quite plump, and I remembered their mild and sober faces, hers softly wide
> and sensitive to love and to pleasure, and his resourceful and intelligent and with-
> out guile, and their extreme dignity, which was as effortless, unvalued, and unde-
> fended in them as the assumption of superiority which suffuses a rich and social
> adolescent boy . . . At the sound of the twist of my shoe in the gravel, the young
> woman's whole body was jerked down tight as a fist into a crouch from which
> immediately, the rear foot skidding in the loose stone so that she nearly fell, like
> a kicked cow scrambling out of a creek, eyes crazy, chin stretched tight, she sprang
> forward into the first motions of a running not human but that of a suddenly
> terrified wild animal. In this same instant the young man froze, the emblems of
> sense in his wild face wide open toward me, his right hand stiff toward the girl
> who, after a few strides, her consciousness overtaking her reflex, shambled to a
> stop and stood, not straight but sick, as if hung from a hook in the spine of the will
> not to fall for weakness, while he hurried to her and put his hand on her flowered
> shoulder and, inclining his head forward and sidewise as if listening, spoke with
> her, and they lifted, and watched me while, shaking my head, and raising my hand
> palm outward, I came up to them (not trotting) and stopped a yard short of where
> they, closely, not touching now, stood, and said, still shaking my head (*No; no;
> oh, Jesus, no, no, no!*) and looking into their eyes; at the man, who was not know-
> ing what to do, and at the girl, whose eyes were lined with tears, and who was

> trying so hard to subdue the shaking in her breath, and whose heart I could feel, though not hear, blasting as if it were my whole body, and I trying in some fool way to keep it somehow relatively light, because I could not bear that they should receive from me any added reflection of the shattering of their grace and dignity, and of the nakedness and depth and meaning of their fear, and of my horror and pity and self-hatred; and so, smiling, and so distressed that I wanted only that they should be restored, and should know I was their friend, and that I might melt from existence: 'I'm *very sorry!* I'm *very* sorry if I scared you! I didn't mean to scare you at all. I wouldn't have done any such thing for anything.' (pp. 40–2)

As Agee explores his experience, that of a privileged outsider living for a short time in the home of poor sharecroppers, he describes his behavior toward them, including what he sees as inept responses that he regrets and tries to repair. Further, he tells the reader that he watches constantly for what people do not say to him, for the nuances of their looks and gestures, beyond conventional words and awkward silences. And he notices also his responses to these. Of course, such self-analysis is not always authentic. It is a construct subject to scrutiny and some skepticism; we have noted the critical response of Agee's reviewer. Even when we show conflicted, imperfect selves in our writing, we choose what we say in constructing a public version of ourselves. How much should the qualitative researcher reveal of the Self? How can we steer past indulgence that actually merits the kind of critic-scorn Agee received? For the researcher, notice that this piece gives the reader more than Agee as an individual. It is a portrayal of a representative Self, as Agee artfully induces reflection on the researcher's role and on the larger racial and socio-economic issues that frame the encounter. This further dimension situates his self-revelation within the stated purpose of the work.

As the comments of Agee's critic suggest, facing the limitations of the Self in private or in the company of trusted friends is one thing; revealing the Self for publication is another. Right now, with personal revelation becoming more common, both in taking oneself as the research subject and in sharing one's stance as a researcher, one does indeed become vulnerable. Lauren Slater, therapist and author of *Welcome to My Country* (1993), said in an interview on Public Radio (24 March 1996) that before her book was published she thought people would be receptive to the story of her struggle with borderline personality disorder. However, she felt that her public disclosure led to some frayed connections and some decrease of confidence. She decided, however, to continue to speak and to write, and not to shut herself off to the consequences of her self-disclosure, whether positive or negative. In the 'Preface', Slater spells out what she sees as the import of her story:

> There is no way, I believe, to do the work of therapy, which is, when all is said and done, the work of relationship, without finding your self in the patient and the patient's self in you. In this way ... the languages of our separate lives might come to share syllables, sentences, whole themes that bind us together '. . .' These, then, are not just stories of my patients; they are stories as well of myself '. . .' including the route I have traveled to cope with my own psychiatric difficulties. (1993, pp. xii–xiii)

In her final chapter, Slater relates that in order to plan for one of her patients, she is obliged to return, after seven years, to the hospital where from age 14 to 24 she spent stretches of several months on five occasions. She finds herself back in the conference room where at age 14 she met with her mother and a social worker for the last time. As she describes how outwardly she now participates in discussing a client's discharge plans, she notes the practitioner language that distances those around the table from the afflicted person: 'We — I — hang on to the jargon that at once describes suffering and hoists us above it' (1993, p. 189). Inwardly she confronts a surge of memories:

> While part of me sits in this conference room, part of me flies out to meet this girl [herself], to touch the sore spot, fondling it with my fingers. For I have learned how to soothe the hot spots, how to salve the soreness . . . I can do it so no one notices, can do it while I teach a class if I need to, or lead a seminar on psychodiagnosis. I can do it while I talk to you in the evenest of tones. 'Shhhh,' I whisper to the hurting part, hidden here. You can call her borderline — call me borderline — or multiple, or heaped with post-traumatic stress — but strip away the language and you find something simple. You find me, part healthy as a horse and part still suffering, as are we all. What sets me apart from Kayla or Linda or my other patients like Oscar, Marie, Moxi — what sets me apart from these 'sick' ones — is simply a learned ability to manage the blades of deep pain with a little bit of dexterity. Mental health doesn't mean making the pains go away. I don't believe they ever go away. I do believe that nearly every person sitting at this oval table now has the same warped impulses, the same scarlet id, as the wobbliest of borderlines, the most florid of psychotics. Only the muscles to hold things in check — to channel and funnel — are stronger. I have not healed so much as learned to sit still and wait while pain does its dancing work, trying not to panic or twist in ways that make the blades tear deeper, finally infecting the wounds. (Slater, 1993, pp. 191–192)

Brave. We wonder how we would behave in her situation. Slater dares to speak out of her experience, out of the 'enabling bias' that takes her past the often grotesque behaviors of her patients to reach the healthy human impulses that are there as well. Thus she speaks to other practitioners and to those touched in any way by mental illness.

Sometimes people misunderstand and feel that they must publicize every nook and cranny of themselves. We think this can be hurtful professionally and personally. Disclosure is always selective. Our research does not demand that we unloose every secret; we have a choice. For example, one researcher shared in her public writing that she is a lesbian. Another didn't. One person who is a recovering alcoholic said so; another didn't. For many, it is more difficult to disclose personal information that can be used to stigmatize in our society than it is to disclose information 'about the study.' We know, for example, how the disclosure of Senator Thomas Eagleton's past psychiatric treatment ended his bid for the presidency; we know also how gossip, jealousy, and ambition can feast on or distort such information. Harriet Malinowitz (1995), who helps to break new ground with her innovative courses and her published work about her experience as a lesbian teacher, nevertheless warns of the professional price:

> Lesbian and gay scholarly work still has dubious cachet on a resume — outside
> of a cadre of avant-garde institutions and departments it can, in fact, render a job
> applicant unemployable in many cases — and has only barely begun to be sug-
> gested as a category of proposal or submission for conferences, journals, or other
> professional publications in composition and rhetoric. (p. 8)

Of herself, Harriet relates:

> I have been involved with lesbian and gay activism, performance, and writing for
> more than fifteen years. Yet I am also a lesbian teacher who, until four years ago,
> hesitated to come out to my students en masse and to many of my colleagues . . .
> Besides the fear of concrete reprisals or even violence, I feared . . . the loss of the
> warm, open supportive relationships I liked to have with my students, even if it
> was shakily based on false premises. (pp. 8–9)

There is no solid line; the researcher must judge what things in the Self a
reader ought to know. If researchers are also the subject of the research, desiring
to share their experience, they need to be clear about their purpose in doing so.
'How did your own personal experience help you help others?' an interviewer
asked Lauren Slater. She responded that she felt it was not so much the experience
of illness as it was the experience of recovery. At a certain point in her illness she
grasped that she could find and cultivate her Self within; and so she recognized her
own potential for recovery. Because in the US one in ten people are estimated to
suffer from depression, it seemed eminently worthwhile for her to speak about her
work with patients and her understanding about the experience that was both hers
and others. The point for Slater is not to write for sensationalism but to convey
what she wanted to in her book: that one is most human and most heroic in facing
and transforming one's relation to adversity.

For readers of qualitative studies, an author's forthrightness helps to estimate
the trustworthiness of the account, to understand the experience and empathy of the
researcher, and, perhaps, to learn from the researcher's blind spots and blunders, as
well as enabling biases and successes, how to approach the Other with genuine
respect and sensitivity. We remember a scholar who spoke of 'functional bawdy'
in Shakespeare's plays; perhaps the criterion here is *'functional revelation.'*

Besides bearing purpose in mind, we need to envision our audience and shape
our writing and our self-reflection to communicate with them. Perhaps we feel that
some audiences are not ready to hear certain things. Moreover, perhaps we find that
defensiveness in facing the uncomprehending or hostile is not the optimum stance
for writing, does not always present the writer in helpful ways. Harriet Malinowitz
(1995) observed the power of audience in teaching two writing courses that centered
on lesbian and gay experience and issues. She then published her research about the
class and what happened to the students involved. In her book she asks a broader
question as she reflects on the relatively safe space of those classrooms:

> What is the relationship between the lifting of the usual taboos, a writer's sense
> of intellectual and creative freedom, a writer's sense of confidence, and the work
> that gets produced? How do these issues become further complicated for students
> of multiple Otherhood — for example, a Latina lesbian? (p. viii)

Malinowitz's students tell her that their writing changes in a context where they do not have to justify being who they are. They find they have been able to move into an intellectually substantial examination of lesbian and gay issues. They conclude further that the diversity of perspectives in their immediate audience — homosexual and interested heterosexual students — takes their thinking much further than if they were the lone voice in a context in which these issues were not a central con-cern. About one student, Malinowitz relates:

> Adrian, who just a semester earlier had only vague, humanistic arguments based on a general notion of 'fairness' to offer the anonymous homophobe . . . now has a sense of roots and causes, a social theory to *explain* homophobia — which is an indispensable prerequisite to fighting it. (1995, p. 184)

Malinowitz notes how, in a final paper, Adrian connects theory with his personal journey:

> In terms of sexuality and gender, heterosexuality serves this purpose of setting the standards that serve as guidelines for human actions. I've succumbed and fallen under it, and it is only through this kind of deconstruction of gender and sexuality that I've been able to recognize its very construction as human induced, not necessarily one that is 'natural' and inherent. (1995, p. 183)

The writing in Malinowitz's class began with the personal story and lifted to the cultural context of the Self. This latter is what we consider next.

The cultural Self

When researchers scrutinize themselves, they tend to discover a mix of cultural, social class, racial, gender and other group identifications, perhaps formerly taken for granted. Being Catholic or Jewish, Korean or Italian American, gay, female, a Freudian or a Deweyite, in fact, being a number of these at the same time involves a whole range of expectations and assumptions that can cloud the researcher's vision. This further self-definition, which may not be so easy in private, carries another kind of risk and criticism when shared with a diverse audience. The choice itself can change the researcher. Unforeseen consequences of public response can also provoke change.

Sallie Motch, who did a study of a black family, began to examine her responses as a white woman when she read an account of an exchange between black and white scholars. She quotes from Mary Childers' and bell hooks' 'A Conversation about Race and Class' (1990). There Childers observes:

> It would be instructive to *scrutinize* some of the heated and anguished exchanges between white women and women of color, not just for their content but also *for the way we align ourselves in the process of reading*. (p. 76, our emphasis)

Our italics point to yet another way to uncover biases, to notice our responses as we read. Childers continues:

> An instance is the publication in *Feminist Review* of the responses of various women of color to an article by two white theorists trying to correct what they

called the 'ethnocentrism' of their earlier work. I read that exchange with great confusion and a sense of being threatened because I admired the effort of the white women to challenge their own work and then was shocked by the seriousness of the inadequacies the respondents pointed out. But even as I learned from the respondents, I was aware that as a white woman I felt very defensive: 'How can we take any risks in expanding the way we think if we are jumped on in this way.' (p. 76)

Then Childers follows her own suggestion by probing further:

The 'we' in my mind is white women; I identify with their exposure more than with the intellectual vigor and just anger of the women of color. I have to *work* on myself to remember that the women of color are participating in critical debate in the same vigorous and vituperative way that white women do among themselves across lines of theoretical difference. My defensive identification with the vulnerability of the white women who are making an effort to change their thinking is something I think many white women feel but haven't worked through to the point where we can distinguish unfair and fair critiques, critiques that leave room for heated dialogue and critiques that turn a cold shoulder on solidarity. (p. 76)

An interesting irony in all this! To publish where they might be heard and responded to by women of color was the real risk. In doing so, there might be for the white theorists the possibility of being 'understood' at a level up to now hidden from themselves. Not comfortable, but it offers the potential for more radical insight than is effected in private confessions or in admissions shared with participants when the relationships are perceived as hierarchical. As peers, scholars of color can articulate for white researchers what they hear. There is room for shock on the hearing, because our 'cultural screens' hide a great deal both for black and white people. In response to Mary Childers' account, Sallie judges severely what she sees as her unheroic self:

These are my anxieties as well . . . I want to be true to these ideals and yet I feel self-indulgent, self-centered, trite, trivial, hopelessly trapped inside my own limitations, blindly racist and laughably ignorant.

Notice that Sallie followed Childers' practice of observing and writing about the feelings she has as she reads. Here we want to juxtapose an account by Jacqueline Jones Royster (1996) from the other side of what she calls 'cross-boundary discourse' as an example of a researcher's public exploration of her complex response. In her article, Royster shares her initial feelings and later reflections on receiving a patronizing compliment. She had made a presentation to an academic audience in which she rendered a scene in a novel. She spoke in the voices of the characters and glossed the scene so listeners might understand more deeply the historical setting and the belief systems of the characters. Royster writes of what happened next:

One very well-intentioned response to what I did that day was, 'How wonderful it was that you were willing to share with us your "authentic" voice!' I said, 'My "authentic" voice?' She said, 'Oh yes! I've never heard you talk like that, you know, so relaxed. I mean, you're usually great, but this was really great! You weren't so formal. You didn't have to speak in an appropriated academic language. You sounded "natural." It was nice to hear you be yourself.' I said, 'Oh, I see. Yes, I do have a range of voices, and I take quite a bit of pleasure actually in being able to use any of them at will.' Not understanding the point that I was trying to make gently, she said, 'But this time, it was really you. Thank you.'

The conversation continued, but I stopped paying attention . . . I claim all my voices as my own very much authentic voices, even when it's difficult for others to imagine a person like me having the capacity to do that. From moments of challenge like this one, I realize that we do not have a paradigm that really allows for what scholars in cultural and postcolonial studies have called hybrid people. (pp. 36–7)

We find the obtuseness of Royster's respondent breathtaking, even as it recalls incidents of our own. Behind our words can lie a host of culturally conditioned attitudes of which we are quite ignorant. At this juncture, this writing team feels that in all of the self-scrutiny that is called for, we must be careful not to beat ourselves over the head too unmercifully; not to use the self-scrutiny as a stopping point. Liberation of all sorts is a relatively recent phenomenon for many of us. It's important not to overdo on the guilt. hooks (1990) suggests we work with the contradictions we find in ourselves and 'almost celebrate their existence because they mean we are in a process of change and transformation' (p. 70).

In considering herself as a white researcher studying the experience of a black family, Sallie Motch places her reactions in the context of her history and education. Beyond personal issues, she recognizes wider concerns and important theoretical tasks for herself and the research community as a whole. She comments further in her reading log:

My anxiety is further heightened by Stanfield (1995) who argues that, 'as much as researchers concerned with meaning and realities as social and cultural constructions should continue the noble tasks of confessing their human biases up front, we need to be about the more complex task of creating paradigms grounded in the experiences of people of color that offer more adequate knowledge production about non-Europeans and that offer fascinating turns of the table in which those of European descent are viewed from the standpoint of the "usually studied." '

Sallie acknowledges the inadequacy of her Eurocentric education in dealing with non-European rooted experience; like Royster she arrives at the recognition for the need of new theoretical lenses. Royster speculates that beyond insensitivity, her 'admirer' appeared not to understand 'long-standing practices in African-based cultures of theorizing in narrative forms' (1996, p. 35). She heard the stories as simply stories and Royster as simply a performer. She could not see past her culture-bound expectations.

Elsa Barkley Brown writes about how her professional training in history created problems for her despite her deep regard for her people. In 'Mothers of Mind,' (1991), she relates that when she returned to study her own African-American community in Richmond, Virginia, she found that she brought with her Eurocentric categories and even stereotypical notions about other black people. To represent this community in ways they could recognize, Brown returned to where her education really began, with her mother's stories as an informal historian:

> She taught me the importance of preserving the historical record of the community as the people within it understood it and thus grounded me in a far different historiographical tradition than the one I encountered in my academic training. (p. 91)

Brown studied the washerwomen in her community. While previous scholars had acknowledged the women's economic contribution to black community institutions, her mother's stories about her own mother and their neighbors described another level of involvement. Brown writes:

> They collectively scrubbed, rinsed, starched, ironed and folded the mounds of laundry as they talked . . . I came to realize that those mornings spent scrubbing were also spent organizing . . . When these women moved into developing mutual benefit societies and their affiliates, it was with clear planning and organizational skills that they had developed over the washtub — it was a commitment to each other which had been born in mounds of suds . . . When they moved to organize a bank and a department store, and then to dream of beginning a factory, it was with the assurance and the skills that came from already having been entrepreneurs. (1991, pp. 83–4)

Brown further realized that when she and her mother discussed her work, her mother's resistance to her interpretations gave her theoretical concepts and frameworks that did not distort — about African-American family relationships, for instance, and about adaptions of African values in the context of oppression. As researchers recognize and begin to transcend their cultural limitations, the conversation across boundaries can work to clarify dimensions that were concealed by alien frameworks.

Finally, Joanne King Griffin's poem stands as an antidote to cultural arrogance, as she speaks eloquently about her insights after studying a group of newcomers to the USA:

Life in a New Place

'I think it's hard to speak in English'
     wrote Mao one day last fall
'to live by myself, I have so much the time'
'it is so hard when I decide by myself'
     writes Hannah, homesick and lonely, and too proud to ask for help
'living alone is too difficult';
'I am too much the alone'
     says Pearl trying to paint a way out of her depression
'people around me talk too much
— they make me angry'
     growls Yuri, wanting a friend, but unable to find one
'people who don't listen to what I say,
who think I not smart; they make me sad, and then angry too!'
     sputters Fumi, surprised at herself

The sing-song rhythms of their talk
>   their smiling faces, cheerful bows of welcome
>>   hide the depths of disorientation in this alien place
>   which is so familiar and comfortable to me.
But I am the alien here, not them
>   they understand each other, while I do not

Who is the stranger here in this familiar place?
I am the native speaker who cannot understand, although I am understood.

From her own experience, Joanne comes, ironically, to understand that in this group, in this culture, she is the newcomer.

The dance of interaction

The researcher belongs in the study not only as a consciousness that filters the experience but as an actor as well. The presence and behavior of researchers — as individuals with particular personalities and with cultural, socio-economic, age, and gender identifications — have ripples on the participants. Participants, likewise, bring their identifications and related experiences, their backdrop of family, work, and community concerns. Then there are specifics of setting that weigh in: the place, noisy or quiet, the colors, smells, interruptions, other people; level of comfort, weather, time of day, as all these impinge on mood and energy. The list is potentially endless. And the researcher will never know the half of them. More immediately, participants have motives and agendas that factor in to shape an interview or influence observed behavior. This in turn affects the writer. At its most immediate, the writer's hard look at Self in interaction with participants is a kind of action research that can lead to self-knowledge and change. In current publications there is plenty of evidence that this emphasis is gaining favor. We will touch on a few examples here to prime our own efforts.

Phillip Johnson (1995) studied five black male undergraduates at an urban university. In his dissertation, he relates his initial expectation that his participants would talk with him freely, comfortable in the thought that they shared mutual histories, and would give him what he needed without too much hesitancy. He looks back at the actual interactions and shares his discomfort in some of them and the effect on his research behavior. Here is a bit of what he writes:

> I had a more difficult time interviewing Allen in part because I *sensed* that he did not *trust* me. I always had the *feeling* that he *felt* I was not black enough. I noticed that I was more *cautious* with Allen than I was with the other participants. I found the *intensity* of his *feelings* related to race somewhat *intimidating*. It was not until our final meeting, which took place approximately one year later, that I *felt comfortable* enough to ask meaningful questions about Allen's family. By that time, Allen's attitudes toward race had changed and he was *more relaxed, flexible, and reflective*, and I felt *more confident* about the study. (our emphases) (p. 238)

Phillip began to sort out his multiple identifications; his success in the academic world, his university position, his socio-economic status, perhaps his reputation on campus seemed part of who he was in the eyes of Allen. Their shared race and gender did not override their differences. Both of them needed time to get past mutual discomforts, a process that has often been glossed over in reports of interviews. Two aspects of Phillip's analysis seem useful strategies. First, he compares his behaviors with the various people he interviewed and between the early interviews with each individual and the later ones. Second, as the words we have italicized indicate, he draws on the language of feeling, moving back and forth from his own feelings during the process to his inferences about Allen's.

Sociologist Susan Krieger (1983) did an even more fine-grained analysis of her interviews. She studied a midwestern lesbian social group. When after a full year she still found herself unable to work with the abundant data of her interview notes, she decided to write a personal account of her experience. She then proceeded more systematically by writing a step-by-step analysis of and reflections on each of her seventy-eight interviews. At this point she began to recall and write about her assumptions, expectations, and emotions. She first wrote a 'pre-interview self-assessment' of the anticipations, fears, emotions, and plans she had brought to the specific interview. Here is a sample:

> PRE-INTERVIEW 32: B. was one of my neighbors across the street who had been fairly open and friendly with me. I chose her to do one of the first interviews because she had been 'public' as a lesbian and I felt she would be knowledgeable about the community and straightforward with me. Yet I was nonetheless concerned that she might not speak personally enough with me. (p. 172)

Next she wrote an interview self-assessment in which she sought to capture her emotions, stance, and learnings as the meeting progressed:

> INTERVIEW 32: This surprised my expectations, because B. was, it seemed, candid with me and more personal than I'd expected. I did not feel forced to adopt her views or anything of the sort. I really felt for her as a person at the end of the interview, as I had not before. (p. 173)

Krieger's third step was a re-analysis of her interview notes. In doing this she found that the self-assessment notes gave her a fresh perspective and important new insights. Through her writing, it became clear to her that her desire for acceptance was intense and prominent during the interviews. Further, she discovered that for her as a lesbian the potential for a sexual relationship with the women she interviewed created a kind of tension, and this seemed true for many of her participants as well. Through this writing to explore her own role in the interviews, she came not only to personal but to sociological insight 'about the collective reality of participation in the community':

> As I began to review my notes, seeking concepts appropriate for categorizing and 'making sense,' I found that I was drawing on my understanding of myself with far greater facility than on anything else that came to hand. (p. 179)

She writes of her care not to project her own feelings on others even as she recognized expressions of like feelings in many of her participants:

I sought not simply to impose or apply my newly developed recognitions, but to expand those recognitions by constantly challenging my existing understandings ... confronting my self-understanding with what my interviewees seemed to be telling me that was different. (p. 181)

What is so interesting to us is that Krieger never mentions her personal writing in her published study, *The Mirror Dance* (1983). Two years later she made this personal writing public in an article, 'Beyond Subjectivity' (1985). It seems that her dance of interaction, a great part of which was surely with herself, allowed her to move past her alienation and her blocks to analysis.

Anthropologist Kevin Dwyer recognizes the interdependence of Self and Other in the moments of direct confrontation. In *Moroccan Dialogues* (1982), Dwyer questions the credibility of his discipline and provides transcripts of his conversations with the *Faqir*, a Moroccan villager, so that readers can follow the actual progress of their talks and seriously study his work. He tries to locate 'the deficiencies that prevent both a sound appreciation of the Other and a serious examination of the Self' (pp. xxi–xxii). He encourages researchers to:

Confront rather than disguise the vulnerability of the Self and its society in the encounter with the Other and ... seek forms of encounter which allow the Other's voice to be heard at the earliest possible moment, addressing and challenging the Self. (1982, p. xxii)

Dwyer writes of his concern not to colonize his informants; he wants to resist the pattern of hierarchy and domination that exists between groups. To this end, Dwyer insists on the importance of preserving the actual sequence of events and their recursive meaning. He does not play with the order by combining bits and pieces to come up with a 'definitive' meaning out of context. That is why the bulk of his book consists of the actual, unedited texts of all interviews. Adjacent to the transcripts, Dwyer provides commentary that focuses on his role, the Faqir's responses and initiatives, and the interaction between them, as well as on the larger context. Here are some samples:

I continued to be preoccupied by the kinds of questions I was asking the Faqir in the dialogues. They were certainly not flowing simply from an event but more, I thought, from my own personal, social, and cultural concerns: from my political beliefs; from an awareness, heightened by my encounter with the Faqir, of my Euro-American origins; from my partial knowledge of the academic literature on Morocco; from my previous experience in Morocco. Even questions that seemed purely descriptive were often called forth by other people's behavior that struck me as odd, that disappointed my own culturally based expectations (for example, the questions I was formulating about enjoyment at the Amouggar were motivated by the boredom I myself felt there). (pp. 95–6)

The Faqir's answers, too, posed similar problems ... not so much answering my questions as assessing them and commenting upon them, not merely satisfying my curiosity but reflecting upon his experience and forcing me, as he did this, to follow him in directions he thought important. (p. 96)

> Where then did the Faqir end and Kevin begin? Where, then, did the Self's influence on this shared experience end and the Other's begin? Had we not only seen the objective character of the event disintegrate and the purely personal nature of questions and answers dissolve, but had we also called into question the independence and integral nature of one another and, therefore, on however modest a level, the identity and direction of Self and Other, in their extended senses? Had Self and Other each become, in some uncertain, ill-defined manner, vulnerable to the Other? (pp. 215–16)

Dwyer reminds us that the effort at understanding is altogether as messy as we know it to be. In ordinary experience we are forever confronted with the ultimate unknowability of even the best loved Other as well as the mystery of Self. More, we do not know how we will show ourselves in the unpredictable interactions with the Other.

At the same time, Dwyer's readers are able to make some judgment about whether he practices what he preaches. Some have criticized him as ultimately keeping control through, for example, the questions he poses. He himself observes that his questions 'must, by the nature of language and human experience, be culturally and historically phrased' (1982, p. 271). In print he has kept the dialogue going in his search for real communication. Via his writing, Dwyer listens to himself: the sexist comments he makes in this situation that he would never make in the USA; his loss of temper that establishes him as a 'real man' when he thinks he has alienated the farmer's relative; his efforts to direct the line of talk and his host's steering elsewhere; the ebbs and flows as their relationship deepens; his having the last word in the final meeting, only to realize that his host has gone to sleep on him, nicely putting him in his place. Dwyer's dance of interaction is with himself as much as with his participant. And from this dance of interaction, he teases out his major message to his anthropological colleagues. The personal, cultural, and interactional dimensions that enter into what becomes 'the data' cannot be ignored. Researchers are invited to take up such dimensions as themes.

Langer's (1953) definition of art as 'the creation of forms symbolic of human feeling' (p. 40) seems worth noting here. Dwyer's intense concerns impel him to create forms to grapple with issues of Self and Other, and to allow the reader to question and thereby enter into an ongoing collaborative process.

Lad Tobin (1993) and Nancy Welch (1996) study their writing classes. Theirs are nitty-gritty scenarios that share the complexity and the ups and downs of actual teaching–learning experience in small groups, and individually in writing conferences outside of class. Here are some of Tobin's comments about his study and about the substantive issues he uncovers at the heart of fleeting encounters:

> I hope that by telling stories that go beyond the happy talk of collaboration, decentered authority, and writing communities to moments like the ones with Polly and Steve — moments when I felt frustrated, angry, unsettled, lost, or bored — I will invite readers to identify their own problems and frustrations. (17) 'What I am attempting to describe, identify, and analyze is the interactive, dialectic nature of context as it manifests itself in classroom writing relationships,' (5) . . . 'It's about power and authority, identification and resistance, negotiation and compromise.' (7)

Welch provides a strong case in point with a vignette in which she shares her bittersweet feelings when Sydney, a student, develops exactly in those ways Welch says she values and promotes. We have examined her stance at length in Chapter 5 of this volume. Her dance of interaction seems to be, in part, between her professional ideals and her needs as a person, with the former winning out. In the following paragraph, Welch concludes her examination of a semester-long interaction, in which she moved toward helping her student to be independent, with an ironic aside at the moment that Sydney makes a difficult independent decision:

> Sydney has decided against signing up for the fiction class I'll be teaching. 'I hope that's okay,' she says, and I nod, saying yes, yes, of course it is ... But still, strangely, and never minding my desire that Sydney seek other relationships and models for learning and writing, I feel at this moment as much disappointed as pleased. At this moment, though I never sat down with her and explained about Lacan and Tobin and Beauvoir and Le Doeuff, Sydney knows much more about the trap of transference than I. She says, 'Even though you and Jim have been really helpful, I need some other perspectives.' (1996, p. 58)

If we uncover and trace the interactions between ourselves and our participants, if we go beneath each other's easy surfaces, we get to the interesting issues; those heartening glimpses of possibilities for how to go about our research in ways that better match our passionately held convictions.

Letting Go

> We participate in some dimensions that we could not know if imagination were not aroused. (Maxine Greene, 1995)

As we conclude our look at writing tasks that promote self-scrutiny and cultivate the researcher as an instrument, we want to call attention to the power of the creative process in meeting the multiple demands of qualitative research writing. Throughout this book, we have emphasized creativity at every turn. When creativity is considered as somehow central to the entire project, the invitation to write and think creatively can help us to find and to use energies we hardly knew we had.

Jane Martin, having learned to 'let go' and to 'play,' her words for describing what she does when she creates, tells us she found herself ready for sustained work:

> Oh, writing. Like a cold swimming pool — once you're in, you feel wonderful. This is where I have come to with my own writing process. Once I have let go, I feel comforted by having my thoughts on paper, I feel challenged to write something that really works about the women in my study, I feel there's a mountain of writing ahead of me, and I feel encouraged and yes, exhilarated!

In seeing themselves as creators, researchers use words like 'breakthrough,' 'turning point,' and 'newfound confidence in my ability to shape stories.' Rhonda Weller Moore elaborates:

> One of the greatest aids to creativity was simply being given permission for it to happen. Perhaps too it has been the valuing of creating which has been so refreshing

and invigorating. My schooling has worked, against my natural tendencies, to create distrust of the first person creative I. This has undermined the 'I' that I am and/or can become. The process of learning to write and to interact with the substance of the writing has been like turning myself out, freeing myself, learning to trust myself and the process.

We have come to view creativity as lying at the core of every facet of research writing. At the outset of this book we addressed the potent, creative power of the writing process; we considered ways that the forms can be used to convey the complexities of actual experience, the choice of different lenses for multiple views of reality, and the ways in which interpretation weaves through the fragments of our observations to tap the essence of experience. We described the resources of negotiation, collaboration, and response that can conspire to deepen and complexify our writing. We offered diverse writing tasks that help us become increasingly perceptive and sensitive readers of experience.

The creative process involved in qualitative research writing seems to us both an act of finding and shaping and, more particularly, of engaging in a dialectical process. Philosopher Richard Hofstadter describes the process:

> The essence of dialectical thinking is to find in each case what are the oppositions, conflicts, contrasts, contradictions, the otherness, estrangement, alienation that are possible in the context and to find the notion that unites them by incorporating and using rather than destroying their tension. (quoted in John-Steiner, 1985, p. 137)

We put the pieces of our data together to make a whole, but this task, as we have demonstrated in many ways, is far from mechanical and additive. Through imagination and craft, the researcher tries to penetrate the dimensions of experience below surface appearances and to represent these in compelling words that make the essence come alive. What sort of imagination fuels such efforts? For qualitative researchers involved in the human sciences and human service professions, it is the ability to imagine how things are for others and how conditions might be improved, to identify the tension between the perception of reality and the vision, each needing to address and draw from the other. We think of a moment in the film *Nicholas and Alexandra* when the sheltered, ineffective Tsar is confronted by a friend who tells him, 'You are not an evil man, but you lack imagination.' The exercise of such imagination requires more than a little intellectual daring — 'letting go' is charged with a sort of acrobat's in-flight savvy. Jane Martin conveys the shifts in her writing through metaphors that contrast her ways of imagining her work:

> I used to seem to be neither reader nor writer, but gatherer. I read, obsessed, wrote, gathered all kinds of information, and struggled to feel ready enough to put myself to paper. This qualitative research writing has provoked me to 'play with my data' and to write without fear. What I have learned is that once I let go, a whole new and somewhat unexpected relationship is waiting for me. What have I learned about myself and the writing process? Writing is the interaction between myself and my research and only writing gives my data life. And through this dialectic-like process I will also be given new life — both my data and I will become . . . will change

as a result of our interaction. Like the metamorphosis of the caterpillar, something new will form as a product of researcher and researched.

Notice Jane's insistence that the 'new life' goes both ways; the researcher, too, is transformed. She expands on the conditions that she has found to favor this fruitful interaction:

> How do we allow our data to have its own life and permit ourselves to be kidnapped? By keeping an open mind and not becoming tightly structured about agendas, biases, and expectations for the data, we allow the data to emerge more freely. I was trying to let my data guide what I was seeing and shaping . . . letting the data have the upper hand in the analysis. I feel that I'm on track if I follow the pull of the data and allow my agendas to go by the wayside.

Her description sounds like Bruner's (1962) observation that one element of the creative process is the ability to surrender to the object. Jane makes it quite clear that this creative process is both self-driven and data driven. She selects and shapes, yet allows the data to continue to speak. In accepting what the data suggests to her and setting aside her preconceptions, she is changed and her vision evolves.

Vera John-Steiner (1985) interviewed people considered creative, experienced, and productive in the arts and sciences about their inner processes of thought. Initially the working title of her book was *The Leap*:

> I had hoped to penetrate those rapid moments of insight and discovery that have fascinated so many previous writers on creativity. As the work of analyzing the interviews proceeded, a different conception of sustained and productive work emerged: while some thought processes are indeed rapid and condensed, the transformation of those inner shorthands into artistically and intellectually convincing achievements requires craft, logic, mastery, and commitment. (pp. 7–8)

The moments of insight seem gratuitous and ephemeral. Someone has said, 'Insights are a dime a dozen'; it is making something of them that concerns us. Those who write about the creative process have much to say about the demands of creative life — bohemian it's not. John-Steiner brings new weight to the old saws, often discounted by many people, with her finding that a sustained intensity of mental life, passion for the work, and pleasure in the doing were givens in all the accounts of creativity she analyzed. To realize the commitment to serious work, writers on creativity describe a discipline that is not drudgery. That does not mean it is easy:

> In the course of creative endeavors, artists and scientists join fragments of knowledge into a new unity of understanding. This process is demanding; it calls upon all the inner resources of the individual — active memory, openness to experience, creative intensity, and emotional courage. It demands self-knowledge in the use of expansion of one's talents. (John-Steiner, 1985, p. 73)

The interaction between Self and field crystallized in the writing can tap the imagining, feeling selves of researchers. John-Steiner's words are a sturdy bridge to our final consideration.

Writing Can Touch Others

Nudge the world a little. (Denny Taylor and Catherine Dorsey-Gaines, 1988)

I write now simply as a witness. (Jonathan Kozol, 1995)

Those of us in the community of qualitative researchers find that inevitably our writing has impact on ourselves and others. These after-effects are often unforeseen and most times have more to do with the process than with the topic. Certainly the learning we come to through writing and the shaping of ourselves as professionals are valid purposes; perhaps they are the ones that most matter ultimately. Yet, given the investment of self and life that goes into writing, more mileage is possible if we expect more and value more our hard-won findings and insights, if we burn to communicate what we believe important.

Most of us who continue to write do so in order to make a difference. Some of our ripples are gentle, hardly noticeable, incremental perhaps. Occasionally they cause boats to rock mightily. Here are some voices that sample the range of expectations writers hold about the possible impact of their writing. June Price tells us she was surprised to find that sharing her work effected change where she least expected it. While she doesn't say so, it sounds to us as if the quality of her work touched her husband in such ways that he changed some of his previously intractable points of view:

> My husband, the psychologist, the statistician. My husband, earlier described in my poem: 'Things. Gears. Answers. Easy. His world's Louder. Surer. Neater.' My husband's reaction to my layered story was cool at best. The essence of his remarks was 'so what' . . . a chilling response to an analysis of findings.
> But, wait — what do I see? All of a sudden he has rewritten a piece submitted for publication. He wants me to comment. He's added some case study material to his analysis to increase 'understanding'. And the other night we were discussing the dilemma of a fellow student who had done a masterly quantitative piece of research for her dissertation, but was only interested in the qualitative data from her interviews — not addressed in her proposal. 'But of course it has the most meaning,' he says. I'm stunned. The Grand Inquisitor couldn't have had more success in the conversion of the Infidel. I congratulate myself; maybe my writing did have an effect; maybe I have something to say.

On the other end of the spectrum is Jonathan Kozol, who first expected massive change in response to his copious and well received publications, but ended up disillusioned. For over three decades he has been writing about inner-city neighborhoods with the conscious intent to bring about social and political change. His evolution is documented from the crusading idealism of *Death at an Early Age* (1967) to the 'angry pessimism and tentative, weary spirituality' of *Amazing Grace* (1995). As he explained to his *New York Times* interviewer (25 November 1995):

> I wrote the first book, and I thought people would say: 'Separate and unequal schools in the City of Boston? I didn't know that. Let's go out and fix it,' I thought then the problem was lack of knowledge. Now I think it's lack of will. Now I don't expect what I write to change things. I think I write now simply as a witness.

This is how it is. This is what we have done. This is what we have permitted.
(C1:, p. 1)

It is true that we can be simplistic, at once too dismal and too grandiose in our expectations about the impact of our writing. And then, timing may play a part. A case in point is James Agee's 1941 study of sharecroppers, which went out of print after having sold only 1025 copies. Reissued in 1960, five years after his death, it became a kind of bible for the people who participated in voter registration drives in the South. John Hersey writes that the book has retained its appeal because of the 'many surprises and dazzling beauty of the prose' (in Agee and Evans, 1988, p. xxxviii). We may be neither a Kozol nor an Agee and yet imagine ourselves sending our writing into the world, not only to fulfill a research requirement, not solely under threat to 'publish or perish', but hoping to make a difference.

In fact, what we are reading and hearing from novice and experienced research writers is that the vision of needed professional changes they evolved in the course of their writing has been shaped by the perspectives of qualitative research. Here we want to tease out further dimensions of the qualitative research writing experience — that of the influence of writing on the writer as a professional whose work touches others in near and wider circles. Thus we begin with ourselves, a *sine qua non* of substantial change that is often either overlooked or taken for granted. We have seen that through the process of writing all along the course of their research, qualitative researchers developed a heightened sensitivity to their language and what their words disclosed of their biases, assumptions, glib categorizations of people and situations. Having set aside labels — poor people, prisoners, AIDS victims, Altzheimer patient, autistic child — to pursue the understanding of real people and their life experience, qualitative researchers report that they have come to question facile classifications, simplistic phrases, and premature generalizations, their own and other people's. They have a sharpened awareness of how words matter and must be chosen thoughtfully, and begin to 'insist on a respectful consideration of the particulars' (Belenky *et al.*, 1986, p. 149).

Besides the heightened awareness of language, research writers find themselves scrutinizing their own professional activities, questioning how they might change — sometimes the job itself, sometimes how they work in it — by seeing new approaches and possibilities. For example, Larry Nelson, who worked with teams of teachers in his school district, realized the value of multiple voices from sharing his writing with his support group. As he described it, he identified his tendency to function as a somewhat rigid leader. He began to develop a more open style that welcomed the teachers' input. He said that he felt he could have changed jobs but that he found ample challenge to foster genuinely collaborative conversations right where he was.

After Denny Taylor had written her 1983 study of children from middle socio-economic strata families who became successfully literate, she changed the direction of her future work. She knew then that she wanted to look with equal care at similarly successful children of families in poverty. In *Growing Up Literate* (1988) Taylor and Dorsey-Gaines, dislodge some stereotypes with their findings about the rich and multiple literacies in these families who are by many measures so disadvantaged.

Ripples in Professional Lives

Some people wrote about how they brought the reflective process into their professional lives. The heart of the effort to change organizational culture, Rexford Brown asserts, lies in reflexive conversation. He writes of school reform:

> Good schools are symbolically rich places, where vivid and interesting conversations are taking place up and down the hierarchy . . . Anyone who hopes to excite and challenge young people without exciting and challenging their teachers hopes in vain. How an approach to cultivating thinking or problem solving will fare in any particular school or district is a function of the conversations going on (or not going on) around and within it. (1993, p. 234)

This conversation may seem quite local and limited. Iris Goldberg powerfully describes her work with one teacher. Her official job is to provide extra support for special education students in Emily's class. Because Iris has internalized ways of writing, she brings this experience to planning sessions with Emily. Together they design a writing process for the children with whom they work. In a field log excerpt included in her article, Iris describes their collaboration and the realization of their plan. We have further abbreviated her description:

> 'I'd like to get these kids back into their journals this week,' says Emily. 'Maybe they can start to look for some repeating themes in their writing. What do you think, Iris?' (OC: I'm linking the children's writing process and my research process. I am grappling with analysis and synthesis of my field data. This is the experience the kids will face when they review the entries in their logs.) 'Here's a possibility,' I think out loud. 'As they re-read, when they come to a sense of a theme or title for an entry they can write it on a stickum, collect and lay them out on their desk.' 'So then repetitions become obvious in a concrete way,' Emily continues. 'And maybe we can help some of the kids cluster ideas and generate a new theme that pulls the clusters together . . .'
> [During writing workshop] The children are sprawled around the room, some propped up on the window ledge . . . (OC: The room has a natural quietness about it. The children are immersed in the process. A few are sharing some entries with a fellow student but most seem to be hooked into their journals and the process of 'lifting.' There is a natural quality to the process, an inherent truthfulness.)

At the same time as we smiled, we saw in the scene of small folks poring over their data a fine image of the concentric ripples of the qualitative process: Iris writes, Iris and Emily collaborate, and the children sail off in their wake.

Ellen Krammer's work as supervisor of teachers offered her wider scope for introducing change. She communicated that she could no longer work as she had in the past. Her vision of writing as a professional changed after she herself had written qualitative research. In going to classrooms, she learned to put her pen aside. After the visits she wrote descriptive and collaborative, rather than judgmental accounts:

> I will carry what I have learned into future research and more importantly to my observation and interaction with each of the 25 people in the departments to which I associate. As supervisors we were trained to make minute by minute notes in classrooms. The smiles we missed, the puzzled looks, the ahas, the teacher's excitement and body language trying to connect to the kids, the joy or misery the teacher creates in the classroom. We sounded pompous when we sat down with our teachers in post-observations, positioned as unwelcome god or parent. Now when I sit down with teachers, we talk about what each of us saw, how the teacher felt the kids reacted, and what we could both change.

We find this a meaningful move, laden with a number of important philosophical stances.

Rita Kopf wrote about 'administrative ripples.' She found ways to continue to share her writing in what she called her 'reflexive conversation' with the hospital situation and to enlist staff members in the process in a substantial way. Moreover she was able to convince her supervisor of the value of time given to the process:

> Since I chose to conduct my field work in the setting where I am Director of Nursing, my written observations led to some unintended insights which then created a rippling effect on my administrative behavior. Once I discovered the transportation department and described it in my log, I found myself feeling a deep connection with the transportation aides. I have since outlined all the departments in the hospital and am slowly making my way to the ones I have never visited. Whenever possible I now go to the other person's department to meet or hold discussions. Among the bonuses: observing things and people I wouldn't have observed if I stayed in my office; breaking down artificial barriers of title and position.
>
> My writing has introduced me to a whole new way of exploring issues and problems and evaluating programs and services. For example: there are constant complaints — from physicians, unit secretaries, nurses, the laboratory, the admitting office, medical records — yet problems are never solved. It dawned on me that perhaps the problems were never really identified. I developed a model for problem exploration that included participant observation, coding, analysis, and writing. I then met with the person appointed to chair the task force, reviewed the model and asked for her feedback. The task force is using the model and from reports to date is busily 'uncovering the reality.' I am excited about the possibilities for deeper and richer understanding of issues and hope to continue refining the model. Interestingly, I anticipated resistance from my own boss who tends to like things done quickly and tied up in a neat bow — more like a knot, actually. However, I negotiated for the extra time, explained the purpose and the potential gain in terms of a real solution and he gave us his support.
>
> I have discovered, uncovered, and been hit in the face with so many irrational traditions and practices that I cannot begin to describe them. Suffice it to say that 'but we've always done it that way' is alive and well. Writing about and sharing the experience of the transportation aides and the nurses has uncovered numerous practices that are inefficient, outdated, or both. I have my list and will work on items one at a time.

One person at a time, one group, one institution. In this manner researchers find substantial ways in which enduring change can come about, with writing as the 'still point' that fosters thoughtful action.

Ripples to Wider Audiences

Schön (1983), in *The Reflective Practitioner*, articulates what he considers the larger civic role for professionals as he directs to them the urgent question of whose descriptions of reality are going to be a base for public policy:

> Professionals are . . . appropriately seen, I think, as participants in a larger societal conversation; when they play their parts well they help that conversation to become a reflective one. In the processes by which ideas of social problems and solutions come into good currency, descriptions of reality are socially constructed (p. 346) . . . The struggle to define the situation, and thereby to determine the direction of public policy is always both intellectual and political. (p. 348)

Author and social critic Jonathan Kozol, who has been in the fray for a long time, believes solutions lie in systemic change, however small the steps. Although we have heard his pessimism about change, he also acknowledges that he has had some influence, directly and indirectly, through his writing. For example, as described by an interviewer from a major organization whose members number millions:

> His fervent views have been solicited by congressional committees, United Nations groups, universities and children's advocacy organizations. (Baker, 1996, p. 20)

Clearly some people are listening to Kozol's descriptions of the separate and un-equal lives of poor Americans. In many other areas, too, we already have a host of qualitative studies that document and describe a multiplicity of situations that cry for public attention. For example, studies have focused on what AIDS looks like, the experience of care in public hospitals, what returning veterans feel about the support or lack of support they encounter, life in prisons, surviving on welfare. On school reform, Brown, who urges cultivating a literacy of thoughtfulness, says 'We know more than enough about the substance of this literacy to get started' (1993, p. 233). In this spirit, we see a need for researchers who will undertake the task of pooling the many single qualitative studies that already exist for the sake of their cumulative impact.

Looking back over the data we have considered just in this volume, we find, for instance, a wide spectrum of studies having to do with the phenomenon of AIDS. These might well constitute a beginning core of a corpus that would have implications for policy at the highest government levels as well as in the intimacy of nearer circles. Bruce Kellerhouse (1996) studied healthy gay men who lost many people from their circle; Fred Daniele is studying therapists and counselors who work with AIDS patients; Ori Caroleo is looking at the experience of people with AIDS who are in a therapeutic recreation program; Sallie Motch is studying a family in which two members are HIV positive. Gayle Newshan has documented the hospital experience of people dying from AIDS. These are no dry studies; they call for a creative gathering of others. We hasten to add the caution that such an amalg-amation calls for specific 'quality control' of studies so that it is possible to have some confidence that they have been carried out in light of the qualitative paradigm.

Sometimes reaching out to broader audiences brings up unexpected problems. bell hooks (1994) provides an example of how her very language put off one audi-ence and attracted another. She gives priority in her writing to reaching beyond the academic world:

> My decisions about writing style, about not using conventional academic formats, are political decisions motivated by the desire to be inclusive, to reach as many readers as possible in as many different locations. This decision has had con-sequences both positive and negative. Students at various academic institutions often complain that they cannot include my work on required reading lists for degree-oriented qualifying exams because their professors don't see it as scholarly enough. (p. 71)

At the same time, hooks relates that she has received responses from black men in prison who have read her work. They want to share with her that they are work-ing to unlearn sexism. She concludes that her priorities about how to reach wider audience are exactly on target, even though she loses some readers. What is seen as unscholarly by some, hooks (1990) relates, is the use of personal stories as the starting point for theorizing. Yet those very stories find and hold other readers. hooks is still in the vanguard that struggles for academic acceptance of writing that resituates scholars in the broader societal conversation.

As a way of communicating with wider audiences, both Anna Deveare Smith (1994) and Patti Lather and her coauthor Chris Smithies (1995) have experimented with novel forms. Deavere Smith has devised ingenious ways to use what she calls 'documentary theater' in order to reach diverse audiences. She writes to share her research with them and to encourage people to participate in the dialogue about race:

> I am first looking for the humanness inside the problems, or the crises. The spoken word is evidence of the humanness. Perhaps the solutions come somewhere further down the road. (1994, p. xxiv)

For the theater piece, *Twilight: Los Angeles, 1992* (1994), Deavere Smith inter-viewed people representing a cross section of contemporary society in the aftermath of the riots that followed the Rodney King decision. She then shaped their words into monologue pieces. Her writing includes reflections from Los Angeleños of diverse ethnic and socio-economic groups: e.g., Rodney King's aunt, a street gang leader, a US Senator, a philosopher. As the monologues proceed, she moves back and forth from the experiential to the reflective through her ordering of the variety of perspectives, from the victims of oppression to the artists, philosophers, and policymakers. Deavere Smith enlisted the help of four people of various races and in varying professions to act in the role of 'dramaturges', people who 'assist in the preparation of the text of the play and can offer an outside perspective.' In bringing these people in, she attempted to counter her own possible narrowness and insular-ity and to be fair to the situation. What they led her to see is that 'the relationships among people of color and *within* racial groups are getting more and more complicated' (p. xxi) 'They passionately attacked the black-and-white canvas that most of us in the room were inclined to perpetuate' (p. xxiii).

We have already written about Patti Lather's quest to create writing that powerfully conveys the experience of her participants to a wider audience. One look at *Troubling Angels: Women Living with HIV/AIDS* (1995) convinced us that she and Smithies have made stunning progress toward that aim.

The central thesis of this chapter has been that writing can affect the writer and the readers in personal and professional ways. The examples illustrate that many researchers experience a lift from writing in the kinds of ways and for the purposes discussed here. This lift seems more important than the products — an article, a book, a play. It is indeed a life force.

Chapter 8

Qualitative Research Writing:
What Makes It Worthwhile After All?

When we were in the initial stages of planning this book, we titled this, our last chapter, 'What Makes A Worthwhile Report?' We believed that we could, at least by the time we finished writing, name qualities that make research writing worthwhile and memorable. Wouldn't our final reiteration cap what we'd been saying all along? We envisioned providing a logical and understandable set of guiding statements about 'worthwhility,' interesting, straightforward and preferably short. Preferably splendid! We were wrong, of course. What got in the way of a seemingly simple task was the writing of this book. *Living by Words* convinced us of just how complex the whole subject of writing research is and how difficult it really is to bring to words the multiple, often serendipitous, and ever changing experiences that represent 'researching.'

The conceptions of what makes qualitative research writing worthwhile are constantly being illuminated as research writers continue to struggle with various ways to represent their understandings through writing. What is more, writing is a central part of the warp and woof of the entire research endeavor, from idea to publication, and can never be viewed without considering of its situatedness in the contexts of particular moments, places, agendas, or ideas. To be sure, all of us can learn to invoke particular writing strategies, but these do little in themselves to define worthwhile writing.

In the spirit of our trust in the idea of reshaping and refiguring, we present you with several different ways of coming at the topic. What follows are nine scenarios. Taken as a whole, they name what we think are the key considerations for judging qualitative research writing. For you, one, several, or all scenarios may strike a chord.

Scenario 1: What Is Worthwhile Qualitative Research Writing?

Read this book.

Scenario 2: What Is Worthwhile Qualitative Research Writing?

Ideas Building on Ideas: A Conversation Over Lunch

Margot: This is craziness! How am I ever going to find time to transcribe the audiotape if we record our conversation in this way?

Margaret: I listen to tapes while I cook, peel vegetables, clean up the kitchen.

Margot: Now *if* I cooked! Of course, I could do it between ordering Chinese food and receiving it.

Margaret: Or folding laundry.

Margot: Who folds laundry? I haven't folded laundry in years.

So tell me. You've all written and read qualitative research. What keeps you really glued to some of that writing?

(Group laughter — large silence)

Ruth: Why does your question feel like a teacher question? Yes, teacher, I have an answer. I like writing that . . .

Margaret: NOW we have a little drama. (laughter)

Margot: Yes but . . . questions are important. Nobody likes my question.

Margaret: But it did get our attention! Which we needed. It's called 'lifting the level of concern.'

(Laughter)

Ruth: We could begin to answer this by pulling out details from our earlier conversation. We talked about ways of approaching our audience — like not lecturing too much up front or describing why and how we reconceived the shape of this final chapter.

Maryann: It seems to me that we are crediting presentational forms for helping us make our points. We want to show that we are 'walking the walk' of our talk — that we are true to what we say in this book so that those scenarios will allow people to contemplate, to 'get it' in the best ways.

Margaret: I'm glued to *The Cocktail Waitress* because of the immediacy of life. Spradley and Mann take me in concrete ways into a life where I don't spend much time — below the surface that one sees.

Margot: I'm glued to work that touches a chord in me — that starts a chord resonating because I didn't know before how important it was. But it's infinitely much better if it's written in a way that allows me entry. It's a very hard job for me to stay with something that fascinates me when the writing is obtuse — when the writer comes off as so self-important, or when I'm hit over the head with the writer's own version of her brilliance.

Ruth: I get involved with qualitative writing when I'm led to believe that the writer cares. I don't mean when the writer says, 'You see, I care about this topic. I care passionately so notice that.' A writer who does care tends to share details, the intimacy of details, that show how carefully attention has been given, a writer who is attuned to seeing, sensing, feeling, breathing the experience.

Margaret: I like when the theoretical is woven throughout so that it leaves you thinking 'Oh yeah!'

Margot: Sometimes I don't like weaving in. That is, I'm glad that sometimes the writer trusts me enough to say 'Now here's the story and we'll talk about it later!' With everything said about his work, Oscar Lewis does that for me.

Margaret: There are so many ways to present and write about theory.

Ruth: The evocation — of the place and happenings — this is so important. What turns me off are writers who say so many times what they're about and then aren't about that at all. They preach openness and then silence people.

I feel manipulated when writers say too many times how fair they try to be, how good they try to be to people, and yet — the writer doth protest too much.

Margot: I feel turned off when I can't believe in what I'm reading — when there is too much left out when I feel a lack of depth or when writers are not up front about themselves.

Maryann: James Agee is a good antidote for that. He is so profound. You feel you are there as he reaches beyond all appearance to the uttermost humanity of himself, us, them. He watches with such attention to detail. It's exquisite. You are really there on that country road in the South as he comes up behind a black couple to ask how he can get inside a church and the woman crouches down to the grass in terror. He does so much in one single scene. Some people might write twenty. He does one and somehow makes himself a stand-in for any white, well-off, well-intentioned bumbling person who comes into their world.

Margot: He really crafts.

Ruth: How does crafting evoke what happens? I mean, what is behind the word crafting?

Margaret: I think there has to be a certain sensibility to begin with. A way of seeing. But that's not answering crafting.

Ruth: Oh but it is!

Maryann: Agee tried to understand. He uses detail to come to that — for himself and us.

Ruth: Yes. You see him slant — angle a way of seeing that you hadn't seen before.

Maryann: Seems so obvious but it's not. It's exhilarating to me. Angles of repose!

Ruth: AND surprise in the way of telling. Surprise because you wouldn't have thought of seeing things in this way.

Margot: As I hear you talk I think a piece of it is not so fathomable. A piece is about ways with words. A piece of it is LOTS of experience in writing toward what you want to write. I think Agee didn't just come out of the egg writing this way. There's something like a personal stamp!

Ruth: A personal signature. I like signature better than stamp. I always think of crafting in terms of the 'carpentry' metaphor. Maybe because of my family of carpenters, I think of the notion of sanding, sawing, mitering. It's that kind of very careful way that words shape ideas.

Margot: Love it! But some people talk of crafting as a formula. That's why we didn't use the word in our title. By the way, what *is* our title? (Laughter) (Nervous laughter?)

What seems dangerous to me especially in a university setting is that people find ONE WAY! And then all of a sudden everyone is writing theme statements with supporting vignettes or quotes. It's not that they shouldn't have themes. They must have themes — overt or covert. It's that certain ways to present themes get valued at the expense of others. We don't have to sell only one way.

Maryann: So are we saying that ways with words are essential but there are other things that make research writing worthwhile to us? Like showing enough of ourselves as researchers and writers; showing how our work flows from our research vision and lifting from detail to broaden ideas —

What else? We've scarcely begun.
Indeed! What else?

Scenario 3: What Is Worthwhile Qualitative Research Writing?

What Do You Think Is Worthwhile?

Scenario 4: What Is Worthwhile Qualitative Research Writing?

Some Guideposts

Writing that focuses on readers:

1 invites readers into the worlds of the people being studied, the researcher as well as the participant;
2 encourages readers to reflect on what is being described;
3 creates openings for readers to voice, to examine, and to reconstruct their own thinking;
4 invites readers to come to their own conclusions and to construct alternative explanations;
5 provokes constructive action.

Writing that focuses on the researcher(s):

6 describes the stance/thinking/doing/feeling of the researcher(s) in all phases of the research;
7 describes the researcher's analytical/conceptual leaps or integrations and the bases of these;
8 communicates that the research is based on questions rather than answers;
9 honors both feeling and thought;
10 presents an account of what worked and what didn't, leaves loose ends, and shows that the writer has taken some risks;
11 provokes constructive action.

Writing that focuses on the participants:

12 resonates with participants' viewpoints and experiences;
13 spotlights insights negotiated with participants;
14 provokes constructive action.

Writing that focuses on presentation:

15 shares the complexity and feel of what was studied rather than simplifies meaning;
16 highlights contexts and how contexts relate to making meaning;
17 honors both feeling and thought;
18 is more close than distant, more personal than impersonal;
19 uses various forms and rhetorical devices in order to offer multiple perspectives;
20 places the data of the study as central and employs existing literature to compare, contrast, or puzzle — to talk to and about the study's findings;

21 gives each level of analysis its due without lionizing either the most abstract/ theoretical or the most concrete/descriptive;
22 allows readers to follow the process of making grounded theory and to consider how this relates to other theories;
23 opens up worlds rather than closes them down, shares rather than 'proves;'
24 provokes constructive action.

Scenario 5: What Is Worthwhile Qualitative Research Writing?

Writing that considers more than the carp alone. A Chinese Master is remembered for giving the following advice: It is not enough to consider the carp alone; but to consider the reed against which he brushes each morning, the stone under which he hides and the ripple of the water as he searches for food. The carp is an entity which has the power to affect and be affected by the world. While the advice surely suggests that context is important, the concrete details — the reed, the stone, and the ripple — remind us how writing often leads the reader to imagine odd intersections of meaning, takes us down unusual corridors toward understanding, helps us hear faint and unexpected echoes and resonances, and brings us to imagine relationships anew or differently. Writing opens up lived worlds for reflection and transformation.

Scenario 6: What Is Worthwhile Qualitative Research Writing?

Splendid Quotes

Although I'm much more conscious of my position as the shaper/choreographer/ creator of the realities I present, I feel a need to keep checks on the respect I owe the participants. I want to tell their stories as I see them, without claiming ownership of things that are not mine. It is possible to negotiate those boundaries, but not to forget that they are there. (June Goetz Haver)

Among the qualities I seek in research, I would rather my work be regarded as *provocative* than as *persuasive*. (Harry Wolcott in Eisner and Peshkin, 1990, p. 126)

I know of the dangers of posing solutions and answers. I attempted to reveal the multiple realities of the superintendent and his experiences so the events and his life would speak the themes to the reader, or speak additional themes to the reader that I didn't pose. I would hope that the readers see much more than has been suggested by the themes I stated after each selection. (Carole Di Tosti)

The search for justification often carries us farther and farther from the heart of morality. (Nel Noddings, 1984, p. 105)

I am beginning to realize that seldom is there a comfortable time during research writing. There always seems to be a question that develops that needs to be answered. I have realized that it is that feeling of discomfort which seems to keep me moving toward new learning. It appears to be a part of moving on to the next step. I have compared it to the grain of sand in the oyster which causes irritation, but ultimately creates a thing of beauty. (Judy Walenta)

... I conclude that there is no prototype qualitative researchers must follow, no mold we must fit in, to ensure that we are bound for the right track. (Alan Peshkin, 1993, p. 28)

The history of photojournalism over the past 100 years is the history of photographers' learning to say more than simply, This Is What It Looked Like. There have been technical developments, of course, but these have mostly served photographers by giving them more freedom and more choices. The real transformation has gone on behind the camera. Increasingly, photographers have said, through their pictures, This Is How I Saw It. They're able to accomplish this because they see what others don't. But once they *have* seen it — and this is the magic of photography — the viewer gets to see it, too. The camera fixes the image, but beyond that, the photographer's point of view works to bring things into a new, sharper focus. And in this way, the reader has become a part of the history of photojournalism. Over the years, the reader, too, has learned to look a little harder. (Kathy Ryan, 1996, p. 52)

I know I cannot paint a flower. I cannot paint the sun on the desert on a bright summer morning but maybe in terms of paint color I can convey to you my experience of the flower or the experience that makes the flower of significance to me at that particular time. (Georgia O'Keefe, 1 November 1930)

I have absolutely no ego about revisions. (Erica Jong, *NY Times*, 9 September 1996, B3)

Qualitative work, as is true for social science in general, is then essentially ironic, since it aims to disclose and reveal, not merely to order and predict. (John Van Maanen, 1983, p. 256)

The principle, in any case, we must hold if we are to survive as writers, deluded or otherwise: even when all evidence is to the contrary, we are steadily improving; whatever we are working on at the present time is the best thing we have ever done, and the next book will be even better. (Joyce Carole Oates)

Agee struggled in *Let Us Now Praise Famous Men* to set up a counterpoint between stark verbal photographs and — as if to provide glasses to help the reader see the pictures more clearly — long passages of filtration through his deeply kind, generous, quirky, guilt-ridden, hypersensitive consciousness. (John Hersey, 1988, p. xxiv)

The aim is to urge the engagement across social and cultural edges, to break frames, disciplinary rules, received notions, and the convention of fieldwork with its repetitious intellectual labors. My purpose in reading the poetic of cultures in contact is the result of finding there a nonhierarchical approach to knowledge, a refreshing directness of experience between one segment of humanity and another. (Dan Rose, 1990, p. 46)

A chaque étape, jái un équilibre, une conclusion ... A la seance suivante, si je trouve qu'il y a une faiblesse dans son ensemble, je reconçois le tout.

Ainsi pendant trois ans, jávais du reconçevoir constamment mon oeuvre comme un metteur en scéne. Quand je travaille, c'est vraiment une sort de cinéma perpétual.

At each stage I create, an equilibrium, a conclusion . . . During the following session, if I find that there is a weakness in its unity I reconceive the whole thing.

So for three years, I have had to reconceive my work constantly like a film director. When I work, it is truly a sort of perpetual cinema (movie). (Henri Matisse, La Danse de Merion, 1931–33)

Textual conventions do not merely raise technical or methodological issues: They have *moral* consequences. (Paul Atkinson, 1992)

Rilke in his 'First Letter to a Young Poet' observes: 'Things are not all so comprehensible and expressible as one would mostly have us believe; most events are inexpressible, taking place in a realm which no word has ever entered, and more inexpressible than all else are works of art, mysterious existences . . .' The poet's task: to translate experience into language, which then becomes a kind of transformation — its own substance, focused and elevated; something somehow worthy of our toil, a monument larger than the craft that gets us there. (Joseph Stroud, 1989, p. 317)

Scenario 7: What Is Worthwhile Qualitative Research Writing?

Ties That Bind: On Major Metaphors in this Book (Add your own)

stance

> field

> > *crystal*

> > > angles of repose

> third space

hybridity

> > braiding

> > > network

> > dance

> > > > *lens*

> > > *weaving*

> > > > crafting

construction

> > tracking

> > > cross boundary

> > *Rashomon*

> > > > interpretive zone

> > > *potter's clay*

> > > > Living by Words

Scenario 8: What Is Worthwhile Qualitative Research Writing?

Leticia Monroe wrote the following poem when she was a senior in one of Ruth's writing classes. The class was working on a research project documenting the history of the neighborhood. Leticia reminds us how writing can somehow preserve and nurture and lead us to understand and love the world.

Monuments

It's like walking into a museum
where stone has been cracked open
to let the spirits walk on earth
again.

Imagine the mother, holding
the dying infant in her arms.
All that's left now:
Lettie Burns Martin
September 7, 1893 — September 12, 1894.
What did father say to mother? To
baby Lettie lying too still? Who dug the earth
away, preparer for the box of bone and flesh?

Ernesto Martinez, dead at forty-two.
He loved the random joy of dance
and drink and cards. I know it by his name.
Beside him dark-haired girls who listen
now to unheard beats. Ernesto
doesn't come again, he's trapped
in earth so heavy it takes love and memory
to break him free.

Stones grow here like flowers in a garden,
cropping up like weeds too fast, too soon
for those who stand upon the hill shaded
still by maple, birch, and ash.

I pity them the memories I can't sow
for them in life, in love, in constant
competition with the loss. Monuments
of stone so deep I dare not love for
fear of what is lost in love. This
country of monuments has a silent
solace of its own, retreats into the dark
of night, the spade to clink again
another day.

Scenario 9: What Is Worthwhile Qualitative Research Writing?

Coming Full Circle

'Our lives teach us who we are.' I have learned the hard way that when you permit anyone else's description of reality to supplant your own — and such descriptions have been raining down on me, from security advisors, governments, journalists, Archbishops, friends, enemies, mullahs — then you might as well be dead.

Obviously, a rigid, blinkered absolutist world view is the easiest to keep hold of, whereas the fluid, uncertain, metamorphic picture I've always carried about is rather more vulnerable. Yet I must cling with all my might to my own soul; must hold on to its mischievous, iconoclastic, out-of-step clown-instincts, no matter how great the storm. And if that plunges me into contradiction and paradox, so be it; I've lived in that messy ocean all my life. I've fished in it for my art . . . It is the sea by which I was born, and which I carry within me wherever I go. (Salman Rushdie, 1991)

References

AGAR, M.H. (1980) *The Professional Stranger: An Informal Introduction To Ethnography*, New York, Academic Press.

AGEE, J. and EVANS, W. (1941/1988) *Let Us Now Praise Famous Men,* Boston, Houghton Mifflin.

AISENBERG, N. and HARRINGTON, M. (1988) *Women in Academe: Outsiders in the Sacred Grove*, Amherst, University of Massachusetts Press.

ALLENDE, I. (1994) *Paula*, (translated edition 1995), New York, HarperCollins-Publishers.

American Heritage Dictionary (1983) New York, Dell Publishing.

AMERICAN PSYCHOLOGICAL ASSOCIATION (1994) *Publication Manual*, 9th ed., Washington, D.C.

ANSON, C.M. (1989) 'Response styles and ways of knowing', in ANSON, C. (ed.) *Writing and Response: Theory, Practice, and Research* (pp. 332–66), Urbana, IL, NCTE.

ANZUL, M. (1988) 'Exploring literature with children within a transactional framework', Doctoral Dissertation, *University Microfilms International*, Ann Arbor, MI, No. 8825209.

ANZUL, M. and ELY, M. (1988) 'Hall of mirrors: The introduction of the reflective mode', *Language Arts*, **65**, 7, pp. 675–87.

APPLEBOME, P. (1995) 'Listening to the South Bronx: Interview with Jonathan Kozol', *New York Times* (October 30) C 1, 1.

ARCHAMBAULT, R.D. (ed.) (1974) *John Dewey on Education: Selected Writings*, Chicago, University of Chicago Press.

ATKINSON, P. (1990) *The Ethnographic Imagination: Textual Constructions of Reality*, London, Routledge.

ATKINSON, P. (1992) *Understanding Ethnographic Texts*, Newbury Park, CA, Sage Publications.

AVENTURO, B. (1991) 'The meaning of care to geriatric persons living in a long-term care institution', Doctoral Dissertation, *University Microfilms International*, Ann Arbor, MI, No. 9134718.

BAKHTIN, M.M. (1981) *The Dialogic Imagination: Four Essays by M.M. Bakhtin*, Austin, University of Texas Press.

BAKHTIN, M.M. (1990) *Art and Answerability* (translated by LIAPUNOV, V. and BROSTROM, K.) Austin, TX, University of Texas Press.

BALL, S.J. (1991) 'Power, conflict, micropolitics, and all that!', in WALFORD, G. (ed.) *Doing Educational Research* (pp. 166–92), London, Routledge.

BARRON, F.M. (1995) 'Doing books in the social context of Montessori early childhood classrooms: Children "reading" without teachers'.' Doctoral Dissertation, *University Microfilms International*, Ann Arbor, MI, No. 9609384.

BATESON, M.C. (1994) *Peripheral Visions: Learning Along The Way*, New York, HarperCollins Publishers.

BEACH, R. (1989) 'Showing students how to agree: Demonstrating techniques for response in the writing conference', in ANSON, C. (ed.) *Writing and Response: Theory, Practice, and Research* (pp. 127–48), Urbana, IL, NCTE.

BECKER, H.S. (1986) *Writing for Social Scientists: How To Start and Finish Your Thesis, Book, or Article*, Chicago, University of Chicago Press.

BEHAR, R. (1993) *Translated Woman: Crossing the Border with Esperanzas Story*, Boston, Beacon Press.

BELD, J.M. (1994) 'Constructing a collaboration: A conversation with Egan G. Guba, and Yyonna, S. Lincoln', *Qualitative Studies in Education*, 7, 2, pp. 99–115.

BELENKY, M.F., CLINCHY, B.M., GOLDBERGER, N.R. and TARULE, J.M. (1986) *Women's Ways of Knowing: The Development of Self, Voice, and Mind*, New York, Basic Books, Inc.

BERNSTEIN, R. (1983) *Beyond Objectivism and Relativism: Science, Hermeneutics, and Praxis*, Philadelphia, University of Pennsylvania Press.

BHABHA, H. (1990) 'The third space: An interview with Homi Bhabha', in RUTHERFORD, J. (ed.) *Identity: Community, Culture, Difference* (pp. 207–21), London, Lawrence and Wishart.

BOGDAN, R.C. and BIKLEN, S.K. (1982) *Qualitative Research for Education: An Introduction To Theory and Methods*, Boston, Allyn and Bacon, Inc.

BOICE, R. (1985) 'Psychotherapies for writing blocks', in ROSE, M. (ed.) *When a Writer Can't Write: Studies in Writers' Block and Other Composing-Process Problems* (pp. 182–218), NY, Guilford Press.

BOLSTER, A. (1983) 'Toward a more effective model of research on teaching', *Harvard Educational Review*, 53, pp. 294–308.

BRANNON, L., KNIGHT, M., and NEVEROW-TURK, V. (1982) *Writers Writing*, Monclair, NJ, Boynton/Cook Publishers Inc.

BREUER, J. and FREUD, S. (1895) *Studies on Hysteria*, (translated by JAMES STRACHEY) London, Hogarth Press.

BRITTON, J. (1982) *Prospect and Retrospect: Selected Essays of James Britton*, 'Shaping at the point of utterance', in PRADL, G.W. (ed.) Montclair, NJ: Boynton/Cook (pp. 139–145).

BRODKEY, H. (1996) 'This wild darkness', *The New Yorker*, pp. 52–54 (5 February).

BROWN, E.B. (1991) 'Mothers of mind', in BELL-SCOTT, P. et al. (eds) *Double Stitch: Black Women Write About Mothers and Daughters* (pp. 74–93), NY, HarperCollins Publishers.

BROWN, R.G. (1993) *Schools of Thought: How the Politics of Literacy Shape Thinking in the Classroom*, San Francisco, Jossey-Bass.

BROWN, R.H. (1977) *A Poetics for Sociology: Toward a Logic of Discovery for the Human Sciences*, Chicago, University Press.

BRUNER, J. (1962) *On Knowing: Essays for the Left Hand*, NY, Atheneum.

BRUNER, J. (1983) *Child's Talk*, NY, W.W. Norton.

BRUNER, J. (1986) *Actual Minds, Possible Worlds*, Cambridge, MA, Harvard University Press.

BRUNER, J. (1990) *Acts of Meaning*, Cambridge, MA, Harvard University Press.

BRUNER, J. (1991) 'The narrative construction of reality', *Critical Inquiry*, **18**, pp. 1–21.

BURBULES, N.C. and BRUCE, B.C. (1995) *Educational Researcher*, **23**, 8, pp. 12–18 (Fall).

BURGESS, R. (ed.) (1984) *The Research Process in Educational Settings: Ten Case Studies*, London, The Falmer Press.

BURKE, K. (1969) *A Rhetoric of Motives*, Berkeley, CA, University of California Press.

BURNETT, R.E. (1993) 'Decision-making during the collaborative planning of co-authors', in PENROSE, A.M. and SITKO, B.M. (eds) *Hearing Ourselves Think: Cognitive Research in the College Writing Class* (pp. 125–46), New York, Oxford University Press.

BUTLER, P.A. (1995) 'Looking in and seeing out: A qualitative study of an adult ESL classroom', Doctoral Dissertation, *University Microfilms International*, Ann Arbor, MI, No. 9603277.

CALVINO, I. (1981) *If on a Winter's Night a Traveler*, (translated by William Wevean), New York, Harcourt Brace Jovanovich.

CARINI, P. (1986) *Center Documentary Processes: In Progress*, BENNINGTON, N. VT, Prospect Center for Education and Research.

CARROLL, L. (1990) *The Annotated Alice: Alice's Adventures in Wonderland*, Martin Gardner (ed.) NY, Random House.

CASTILLO, A. (1993) *So Far From God*, NY, Penguin Books, USA.

CHILDERS, M. and HOOKS, B. (1990) 'A conversation about race and class', in HIRSCH, M. and KELLER, E.F. (ed.) *Conflicts in Feminism* (pp. 60–81), NY, Routledge.

CLANDININ, D.J. and CONNOLLY, F.M. (1991) 'Narrative and story in practice and research', in SCHÖN, D. (ed.) *The Reflective Turn* (pp. 258–81), New York, Teachers College Press.

CLANDININ, D.J. and CONNELLY, F.M. (1994) 'Personal experience methods', in Denzin, N. and Lincoln, Y. (eds) *Handbook of Qualitative Research* (pp. 413–27), Newbury Park, CA, Sage.

CLARK, K. and HOLQUIST, M. (1984) *Mikhail Bakhtin*, Cambridge, MA, Belknap Press.

CLARK, S. and EDE, L. (1990) 'Collaboration, resistance, and the teaching of writing', in LUNSFORD, A., MOGLEN, H. and SLEVIN, J. (eds) *The Right to Literacy* (pp. 276–85), NY, MLA.

CLIFFORD, J. (1986) 'Introduction: Partial truths', in CLIFFORD, J. and MARCUS, G.E. (eds) *Writing Culture*, California, University of California Press.

CLIFFORD, J. and MARCUS, G.E. (eds) (1986) *Writing Culture: The Poetics and Politics of Ethnography*, Berkeley, University of California Press.

COFFEY, A. and ATKINSON, P. (1996) *Making Sense of Qualitative Data: Complementary Research Strategies*, Thousand Oaks, CA, Sage Publications.

COLANGELO, W. (1996) 'The composer/performer in Giacinto Scelsi's solo works', Dissertation on Web Browser Netscape, New York University.

CORTAZZI, M. (1993) *Narrative Analysis*, London, Falmer Press.

CRAPANZANO, V. (1992) *Hermes' Dilemma and Hamlet's Desire: On The Epistemology of Interpretation*, Cambridge, MA, Harvard University Press.

CSIKSZENTMIHALYI, M. (1990) *Flow: The Psychology of Optimal Experience*, NY, HarperCollins Publishers.

DAIKER, D.A. (1989) 'Learning to praise', in ANSON, C. (ed.) *Writing and Response: Theory, Practice, and Research* (pp. 103–13), Urbana, IL, NCTE.

DANIELL, B. (1994) 'Theory, theory talk, and composition', in CLIFFORD, J. and SCHILB, J. (eds) *Writing Theory and Critical Theory* (pp. 127–40), NY, Modern Language Association.

DELBANCO, N. (1982) *Group Portrait*, NY, William Morrow.

DENZIN, N. (1989) *Interpretive Interactionism*, Newbury Park, CA, Sage.

DENZIN, N.K. and LINCOLN, Y. (eds) (1994) *Handbook of Qualitative Research*, Newbury Park, CA, Sage.

DEWEY, J. (1927) *The Public and Its Problems*, Denver, Alan Swallow.

DEWEY, J. (1929) *The Quest for Certainty*, NY, Minton, Black.

DEWEY, J. and BENTLEY, A.F. (1949) *The Knower and the Known*, Boston, Beacon Press.

DILLARD, A. (1989) *The Writing Life*, NY, Harper & Row.

DIPARDO, A. (1993, December) 'When teachers become graduate students', *English Education*, **25**, 4, pp. 197–212.

DOERR, H. (1991) 'A Sleeve of Rain', in STERNBURG, J. (ed.) *The Writer on Her Work* (pp. 50–1), New York, William Norton.

DONALDSON, M. (1978) *Children's Minds*, Glasgow, William Collins Sons.

DORRIS, M. (1987) *A Yellow Raft in Blue Water*, NY, Henry Holt.

DOWNING, M. (1989) 'Adolescents respond to nonfiction: Transactions with authors', Doctoral Dissertation, *University Microfilms International*, Ann Arbor, MI, No. 9004278.

DUGGAN, N. (1992) 'So far so good: The experience of male ex-offenders 2–5 years after release from incarceration', Doctoral Dissertation, *University Microfilms International*, Ann Arbor, MI, No. 9317661.

DUNEIER, M. (1992) *Slim's Table: Race, Respectability, and Masculinity*, Chicago, University of Chicago Press.

DWYER, K. (1982) *Moroccan Dialogues: Anthropology in Question*, Baltimore, MD, The Johns Hopkins University Press.

ECO, U. (1979) *The Role of the Reader: Explorations in the Semiotics of Texts*, London, Hutchinson.

EDE, L. and LUNSFORD, A. (1983) 'Why Write . . . Together?', *Rhetoric Review*, **1**, 2 (January), pp. 150–7.

EDE, L. and LUNSFORD, A. (1990) *Single Texts/Plural Authors: Perspectives on Collaborative Writing*, Carbondale, S. Illinois University Press.

EISNER, E. and PESHKIN, A. (eds) (1990) *Qualitative Inquiry in Education: The Continuing Debate*, NY, Teachers College Press.

EISNER, E. (1993) 'Foreword', in FLINDERS, D.J. and MILLS, G.E. (eds) *Theory and Concepts in Qualitative Research*, New York, Teachers College Press.

ELBOW, P. (1973) *Writing Without Teachers*, New York, Oxford University Press.

ELBOW, P. (1986) *Embracing Contraries: Explorations in Learning and Teaching*, New York, Oxford University Press.

ELY, M., ANZUL, M., FRIEDMAN, T., GARNER, D. and STEINMETZ, A. (1991) *Doing Qualitative Research: Circles within Circles*, London, Falmer Press.

ENTES, J. (1994) 'The right to write a coauthored manuscript', in REAGAN, S.B., FOX, T. and BLEICH, D. (eds) *Writing With: New Directions in Collaborative Teaching, Learning and Research* (pp. 47–60), NY, SUNY.

EVANS, J. (1994) 'Conversations at home: A case study of the communication experiences of a young deaf child in a large hearing family', Doctoral Dissertation, *University Microfilms International*, Ann Arbor, MI, No. 9502452.

EVANS, J. (1996) 'Conversations at home: A case study of a young deaf child's communication experiences in a family in which all others can hear', *American Annals of the Deaf*, **140**, 4, pp. 324–32.

FETTERMAN, D. (1989) *Ethnography Step by Step*, Newbury Park, CA, Sage.

FIELD, J. (1934) *A Life of One's Own*, Los Angeles, J.P. Tarcher.

FISHMAN, A. (1988) *Amish Literacy: What and How It Means*, Portsmouth, NH, Heinemann.

FLINDERS, D.J. and MILLS, G.E. (eds) (1993) *Theory and Concepts of Qualitative Research: Perspectives from the Field*, New York, Teachers College Press.

FLORIO-RUANE, S. (1991) 'Conversation and narrative in collaborative research: An ethnography of the written literacy forum', in WITHERELL, C. and NODDINGS, N. (eds) *Stories Lives Tell: Narrative and Dialogue in Education* (pp. 234–56), New York, Teachers College Press.

FRANKEL, M. (1995) 'Journalism 101', *The New York Times Magazine*, p. 18 (22 January).

FREIRE, P. (1983) 'The importance of the act of reading', *Journal of Education*, pp. 5–11.

FREUD, S. (1893–1895) 'Case history: Fraulein E von R', in BREUR, J. and FREUD, S. (eds) *Studies in Hysteria* (translated by STRACHEY, J.), London, Hogarth Press.

FREUD, S. (1913) *The Interpretation of Dreams* (translated by BRILL, A.A.), New York, Macmillan.

GARCÍA MARQUEZ, G. (1984) *Interviews, Writers At Work: The Paris Interviews*, PLIMPTON, G. (ed.) Sixth Series, New York, The Viking Press. (p. 319).

GARNER, D.J. (1986) 'An ethnographic study of four five-year-old children's play styles', Doctoral Dissertation, *University Microfilms International*, Ann Arbor, MI, No. 8625624.

GEERTZ, C. (1988) *Works and Lives: The Anthropologist as Author*, Cambridge, Polity Press.

GIBSON, W. (1979) 'The writing teacher as dumb reader', *College Composition and Communication*, **30**, pp. 192–5.

GIROUX, H.A. and MCLAREN, P. (1992) 'Writing from the margins: Geographies of identity, pedagogy, and power', *Journal of Education* 174, 1, pp. 7–30.

GOULD, S.J. (1985) 'Darwin at sea — and the virtues of port', *The Flamingo's Smile: Reflections in Natural History* (pp. 347–59), New York, Norton.

GREENE, M. (1995) *Releasing the Imagination: Essays on Education, the Arts, and Social Change*, San Francisco, Jossey-Bass.

GREENE, M. (1991) 'Foreward', in WITHERELL, C. and NODDINGS, N. (eds) *Stories Lives Tell*, New York, Teachers College Press.

GREGO, R. (1994) 'Writing academic autobiographies: Finding a common language across the curriculum', in SULLIVAN, P. and QUALLEY, D. (eds) *Pedagogy in the Age of Politics: Writing and Reading (in) the Academy* (pp. 214–29), Urbana, IL, NCTE.

GRIFFIN, S. (1980) 'Thoughts on writing: A diary', in STEINBURG, J. (ed.) *The Writer On Her Work*, Volume I (pp. 119–20), New York, W.W. Norton.

GRUMET, M. (1990) 'On daffodils that come before the swallow dares', in EISNER, E.W. and PESHKIN, A. (eds) *Qualitative Inquiry in Education: The Continuing Debate* (pp. 101–20), New York, Teachers College Press.

GUBA, E.G. (ed.) (1990) *The Paradigm Dialog*, Newbury Park, CA, Sage.

GUBA, E.G. and LINCOLN, Y. (1989) *Fourth Generation Evaluation*, Newbury Park, CA, Sage.

GUTERSON, D. (1995) *Snow Falling on Cedars*, NY, Vintage Contemporaries.

HAMILTON, D. (1994) 'Traditions, preferences, and postures in applied qualitative research', in DENZIN, N.K. and LINCOLN, Y.S. (eds) *Handbook of Qualitative Research* (pp. 60–9), Newbury Park, CA, Sage.

HAMMERSLEY, M. and ATKINSON, P. (1983) *Ethnography: Principles and Practice*, London, Routledge.

HARDY, B. (1978) 'Narrative as a primary act of mind', in MEEK, M., WARLOW, A. and BARTON, G. (eds) *The Cool Web: The Patterns of Children's Reading* (pp. 12–23), New York, Atheneum.

HAWKINS, T. (1976) *Group Inquiry Techniques for Teaching Writing*, Urbana, IL, National Council of Teachers of English.

HEGI, U. (1994) *Stones from the River*, New York, Scribner.

HEIDEGGER, M. (1971) *Poetry, Language, Thought*, New York, Harper Colophon Books.

HERR, K. and ANDERSON, G.L. (1993) 'Oral history for student empowerment: Capturing students' inner voices', *Qualitative Studies in Education*, **6**, 3, pp. 185–96.

HILL, C.E. (1990) *Writing from the Margins: Power and Pedagogy for Teachers of Composition*, New York, Oxford University Press.

HOLLAND, K.E., HUNGERFORD, R.A. and ERNST, S.B. (1993) *Journeying: Children Responding to Literature*, Portsmouth, NH, Heinemann.

HOOKS, B. (1994) *Teaching to Transgress: Education as the Practice of Freedom*, New York, Routledge.

HOMER (1942) *The Iliad*, (translated by BUTLER, S.) Roslyn, NY, Black.

HOMER (1944) *The Odyssey*, (translated by BUTLER, S.) Roslyn, NY, Black.

HUGHES, T. (1981) 'Foreword', in FAIRFAX, J. and MOAT, J. *The Way to Write: A Stimulating Guide to the Craft of Creative Writing*, New York, St. Martin's Press.

HUNGERFORD, R. (1994) 'Gender, agency, and resistance: Pre-schoolers and popular text', Unpublished Paper.

HUNGERFORD, R.A. (1993) 'Star Wars and the world beyond', in HOLLAND, K.E., HUNGERFORD, R.A. and ERNST, S.B. (eds) *Journeying: Children Responding to Literature* (pp. 27–42), Portsmouth, NH, Heinemann.

HUNT, J.C. (1989) *Psychoanalytic Aspects of Fieldwork*, Newbury Park, CA, Sage.

ISER, W. (1980) *The Act of Reading*, Baltimore, Johns Hopkins University Press.

JACKSON, P. (1968) *Life in Classrooms*, NY, Holt, Rinehart and Winston.

JAMES, W. (1897) 'The dilemmas of determinism', *The Will to Believe and Other Essays*, New York, Holt, 1912. (Originally published 1897).

JOHNSON, P.D. (1995) 'Beyond the timberline: The stories of five black males at a predominately white university', Doctoral Dissertation, *University Microfilms International*, Ann Arbor, MI, No. 9622007.

JOHN-STEINER, V. (1985) *Notebooks of the Mind: Explorations of Thinking*, New York, Harper & Row.

KELLERHOUSE, B. (1996) 'A loss of heart: AIDS-related bereavement in HIV-negative gay men', Unpublished Doctoral Dissertation, New York University.

KELLY, G.A. (1963) *A Theory of Personality: The Psychology of Personal Constructs*, NY, Norton.

KIERKEGAARD, S. (1940) 'Stages of life's way', in BRETALL, R. (ed. and translated by) Kierkegaard (pp. 98–109), Princeton, NJ, Princeton University Press.

KING, R. (1996) 'Implementing a basic college integrated reading/writing course: Lessons in complexity', Unpublished Doctoral Dissertation, New York University.

KLEINMAN, S. and COPP, M.A. (1983) *Emotions and Fieldwork*, Newbury Park, CA, Sage.

KNOBLAUCH, C.H. and BRANNON, L. (1984) *Rhetorical Traditions and the Teaching of Writing*, Montclair, NJ, Boynton/Cook.

KOHUT, H. (1977) *The Restoration of the Self*, New York, International University Press.

KOZOL, J. (1967/1985) *Death at an Early Age: The Destruction of the Minds and Hearts of Negro Children in the Boston Public Schools*, New York, New American Library.

KOZOL, J. (1996, April) 'Reaching and speaking to older people', *AARP Bulletin*, **37**, 4, p. 20.

KOZOL, J. (1995) 'Listening to the South Bronx', *The New York Times*, Section C, (30 October), p. 1.

KOZOL, J. (1995) *Amazing Grace: Conscience of a Nation*, New York, Crown Publishers.

KRIEGER, S. (1983) *The Mirror Dance: Identity in a Woman's Community*, Philadelphia, Temple University Press.

KRIEGER, S. (1985) 'Beyond "subjectivity": The life of the self in social science', *Qualitative Sociology*, **8**, 4, pp. 309–24, reprinted (1991) as Chapter 5 in *Social Science and the Self*.

KREIGER, S. (1991) *Social Science and the Self: Personal Essays on an Art Form*, New Brunswick, NJ, Rutgers University Press.

KRISTEVA, J. (1980) *Desire in Language: A Semiotic Approach to Literature and Art* (translated by L.S. Rondiez, T. Goria, A. Jardin), NY, Columbia University Press.

KUHN, T.S. (1962) *The Structure of Scientific Revolutions* (2nd ed.), Chicago, University of Chicago Press.

LAKOFF, G. and JOHNSON, M. (1980) *Metaphors We Live By*, Chicago, University of Chicago Press.

LAKOFF, G. (1993) 'The contemporary theory of metaphor', in Ortony, A. (ed.) *Metaphor and Thought*, 2nd ed. (pp. 202–51), NY, Cambridge University Press.

LAMOTT, A. (1994) *Bird by Bird: Some Instructions on Writing and Life*, New York, Pantheon Books.

LANDAU, J. (1992) 'The experiences of seven nurses who relate with violence-prone psychiatric inpatients', Doctoral Dissertation, *University Microfilms International*, Ann Arbor, MI, No. 9317672.

LANGER, S. (1953) *Feeling and Form*, New York, Charles Scribner's Sons.

LANGNESS, L.L. and FRANK, G. (1981) *Lives: An Anthropological Approach to Biography*, Novato, CA, Chandler and Sharp.

LATHER, P. (1994) 'Feminist efforts toward a double science: Researching the lives of women with HIV/AIDS', Paper delivered at the 1994 AERA convention, San Francisco.

LATHER, P. and SMITHIES, C. (1995) *Troubling Angels: Women Living with HIV/AIDS*, Columbus, Ohio, Greyden Press.

LAVE, J. and KVALE, S. (1995) 'What is anthropological research? An interview with Jean Lave by Steinar Kvale', *Qualitative Studies in Education*, **8**, 3, pp. 218–29.

LE DOEUFF, M. (1989) *The Philosophical Imaginary* (translated by GORDON) CA, Stanford University Press.

LeFEVRE, K.B. (1987) *Invention as a Social Act,* Carbondale, IL, Southern Illinois University Press.

LEVI-STRAUSS, C. (1969) *Structural Anthropology*, (translated by JACOBSON, R. and SCHAFF, S.), New York, Basic Books.

LINCOLN, Y.S. (1990) 'The making of a constructivist: A remembrance of transformation past', in GUBA, E.G. (ed.) *The Paradigm Dialog* (pp. 67–87), Newbury Park, CA, Sage.

LINCOLN, Y. and GUBA, E. (1985) *Naturalistic Inquiry*, Beverley Hills, CA, Sage.

LINCOLN, Y. and GUBA, E. (1990) 'Judging the quality of case study reports', *International Journal of Qualitative Studies in Education*, 0951–8398/90.

LINDEN, R.R. (1993) *Making Stories, Making Selves: Feminist Reflections on the Holocaust*, Columbus, OH, Ohio State University Press.

LOFLAND, J. and LOFLAND, L.H. (1984) *Analyzing Social Settings: A Guide to Qualitative Observation and Analysis*, Belmont, CA, Wadsworth.

LOPEZ, B. (1987) 'Interview', in O'CONNELL, N. (ed.) *At The Fields' End: Interviews With 20 Pacific Northwest Writers* (pp. 15–16), Seattle, Madrona.

LOWENSTEIN, S.E., CHISERI-STRATON, E. and GANNET, C. (1994) 'Re-envisioning the journal: Writing the self into community', in SULLIVAN, P.A. and QUALLEY, D.J. (eds) *Pedagogy in the Age of Politics: Writing and Reading (in) the Academy* (pp. 139–52), Urbana, IL, NCTE.

MACLEAN, N. (1992) *Young Men and Fire*, New York, Norton.

MAKLER, A. (1991) 'Imagining history: "A good story and a well-formed argument"', in WITHERELL, C. and NODDINGS, N. (eds) *Stories Lives Tell: Narrative and Dialogue in Education* (pp. 29–47), NY, Teachers College Press.

MALINOWITZ, H. (1995) *Textual Orientation: Lesbian and Gay Students and the Making of Discourse Communities*, Portsmouth, NH, Boynton/Cook.

MATÍAS, B. (1990) 'Getting things done: A naturalistic study of the kinds and functions of directive language in a Puerto Rican early childhood classroom', Doctoral Dissertation, *University Microfilms International*, Ann Arbor, MI, No. 9102626.

MAUGHAM, S. (1995) 'Just do it', *New York Times Book Review*, March 5, Section VII, p. 19.

McCULLOUGH, D. (1992) quoting Delacroix in *The New York Times*, Section C, p. 1 (12 August).

McDONALD, J. (1986) 'Raising the teacher's voice and the ironic role of theory', *Harvard Educational Review*, **56**, 4, pp. 355–78 (1 November).

McLEOD, S. (1995) 'Pygmalion or Golem? Teacher affect and efficacy', *College Composition and Communication*, **46**, 3, pp. 369–86 (October).

MEAD, M. (1977) *Letters from the Field 1925–1975*, New York, Harper & Row.

MELOY, J. (1994) *Writing the Qualitative Dissertation: Understanding by Doing*, Hillsdale, NJ, Lawrence Erlbaum Association.

MELOY, J. (1993) 'Problems of writing as representation in qualitative inquiry', *Qualitative Studies in Education*, **6**, 4, pp. 315–30.

MERCER, N. (1991) 'Researching common knowledge: Studying the content and context of educational discourse', in WALFORD, G. (ed.) *Doing Educational Research* (pp. 41–58), London, Routledge.

Merriam-Webster's Collegiate Dictionary (1994) (tenth edition), New York, Merriam-Webster Inc.

MERRICK, E. (1995) 'Negotiating the currents: Childbearing experiences of six lower socio-economic status black adolescents', Doctoral Dissertation, *University Microfilms International*, Ann Arbor, MI, No. 9622011.

MERTON, R.K. (1957) *Social Theory and Social Structure*, Glencoe, IL, Free Press.

MERTON, R.K. (1967) *On Theoretical Sociology: Five Essays, Old and New*, New York, Free Press Paperback.

MOMADAY, N.S. (1969) *The Way to Rainy Mountain*, Albuquerque, University of New Mexico Press.

MORSE, J.M. (ed.) (1994) *Critical Issues in Qualitative Research Methods*, Newbury Park, CA, Sage.

NODDINGS, N. (1984) *Caring: A Feminine Approach to Ethics and Moral Education*, Berkeley, CA, University of California Press.

OATES, J.C. (ed.) (1983) *First Person Singular: Writers on Their Craft*, Princeton, NJ, Persea Books.

O'CONNOR, F. (1985) *Preface The Complete Stories*, Robert Giroux (ed.) New York, Farrar, Strauss, and Giroux, p. ix.

ONORE, C. (1989) 'The student, the teacher, and the text: Negotiating meanings through response and revision', in ANSON, C.M. (ed.) *Writing and Response: Theory, Practice, and Research* (pp. 232–48), Urbana, IL, NCTE.

PALEY, V.G. (1992) 'You can't say you can't play: Free choice, friendship, and fairness among young children'. Address delivered at the Eleventh International Human Science Research Conference, Rochester, MI, Oakland University.

PARRY, O., ATKINSON, P. and DELAMONT, S. (1994) 'Disciplinary identities and doctoral work', in BURGESS, R.G. (ed.) *Postgraduate Education and Training in the Social Sciences* (pp. 34–52), London, Jessica Kingsley.

PATAI, D. (1981) 'Constructing a self: A Brazilian life story', *Feminist Studies*, **14**, 1, pp. 143–66.

PEACOCK, J.L. (1986) *The Anthropological Lens: Harsh Light, Soft Focus*, New York, Cambridge University Press.

PERRY, W.G., Jr. (1970) *Forms of Intellectual and Ethical Development in the College Years: A Scheme*, NY, Holt, Rinehart, and Winston.

PESHKIN, A. (1993) 'Goodness of qualitative research', *Educational Researcher*, **22**, 2, pp. 23–9.

PHELPS, L.W. (1988) *Composition as a Human Science: Contributions to the Self Understanding of a Discipline*, New York, Oxford University Press.

POLANYI, M. (1962) *Personal Knowledge: Towards a Post-Critical Philosophy*, Chicago, University of Chicago Press.

POLKINGHORNE, J. (1996) 'So finally tuned a universe', *Commonweal*, pp. 11–18 (16 August).

PYNCHON, T. (1990) *Vineland*, Boston, Little Brown.

Random House *Dictionary of the English Language* (1987) (second edition, unabridged), New York, Random House.

REAGAN, S.B., FOX, T. and BLEICH, D. (eds) (1994) *Writing With: New Directions in Collaborative Teaching, Learning, and Research*, New York, SUNY.

REED, L. (1985) 'Emotional scenarios in the writing process: An examination of young writers' affective experiences', in ROSE, M. (ed.) *When a Writer Can't Write: Studies in Writer's Block and Other Composing Process Problems*, New York, Guildford Press.

RICE, L. (1995) 'The experiences of four recovering alcoholic women', Doctoral Dissertation, *University Microfilms International*, Ann Arbor, MI, No. 9603300.

RICHARDSON, L. (1985) *The New Other Woman: Contemporary Women in Affairs with Married Men*, New York, Free Press.

RICHARDSON, L. (1990) *Writing Strategies: Reaching Diverse Audiences*, Newbury Park, CA, Sage.

RICHARDSON, L. (1994) 'Writing: A method of inquiry', in DENZIN, N. and LINCOLN, Y. (eds) *Handbook of Qualitative Research* (pp. 516–29), Thousand Oaks, CA, Sage.

RIESSMAN, C.K. (1993) *Narrative Analysis*, Newbury Park, CA, Sage.

ROBBINS, T. (1987) *At The Fields' End: Interviews with 20 Pacific Northwest Writers* (p. 284), N. O'Connell (ed.), Seattle: Madrona.

ROGERS, A.G. (1992) Marguerite Sechehaye and Renee: A Feminist Reading of Two Accounts of a Treatment, *International Journal of Qualitative Studies,* 5, 3, July–Sept. 1992, pp. 245–51.

ROGERS, A.G. (1993) 'Voice, play, and a practice of ordinary courage in girls' and women's lives', *Harvard Educational Review,* **63**, 3, pp. 265–95.

ROGERS, C. (1959) 'Significant learning: In therapy and in education', *Educational Leadership,* **16**, pp. 232–42 (January).

ROSE, D. (1990) *Living the Ethnographic Life,* Newbury Park, CA, Sage.

ROSE, M. (1989) *Lives on the Boundary: A Moving Account of the Struggles and Achievements of America's Educational Underclass,* New York, Penguin.

ROSEN, H. (1986) 'The importance of story', *Language Arts,* **63**, 3, pp. 226–37.

ROSENBLATT, L.M. (1978) *The Reader, the Text, the Poem,* Carbondale, IL, Southern Illinois University Press.

ROYSTER, J.J. (1996) 'When the first voice you hear is not your own', *College Composition and Communication,* **47**, 1, pp. 29–40 (February).

RUBIN, D. (1983) 'Evaluating freshman writers: What do students really learn?', *College English,* **45**, pp. 373–9.

RUBIN, L. (1976) *Worlds of Pain: Life in the Working-class Family,* New York, Basic Books.

RUSHDIE, S. (1991) '1,000 days inside a metaphor', *The New York Times,* Section B, p. 8 (12 December).

RYAN, K. (1996) 'The subjective eye', *New York Times Magazine,* p. 52 (9 June).

SAID, E. (1993) *Culture and Imperialism,* New York, Vintage.

SALMON, P. (1992) *Achieving a PhD: Ten Students' Experiences,* Oakhill, Stoke-on-Trent, Staffordshire, Trentham Books.

SARTRE, J. (1977) *Life/Situations: Essays Written and Spoken,* New York, Pantheon Books.

SCHÖN, D.A. (1983) *The Reflective Practitioner: How Professionals Think in Action,* New York, Basic Books.

SCHÖN, D.A. (1988) *Educating the Reflective Practitioner,* San Francisco, Jossey-Bass Publishers.

SCHWANDT, T.A. (1993) 'Theory for the moral sciences: Crisis of identity and purpose', in FLINDERS, D.J. and MILLS, G.E. (eds) *Theory and Concepts of Qualitative Research* (pp. 5–23), New York, Teachers College Press.

SCHWANDT, T.A. (1994) 'Constructivist, interpretivist approaches to human inquiry', in DENZIN, N. and LINCOLN, Y. (eds) *Handbook of Qualitative Research* (pp. 118–37), Thousand Oaks, CA, Sage.

SHOR, I. (1987) *Freire for the Classroom: A Sourcebook for Liberatory Teaching,* Portsmouth, NH, Boynton/Cook.

SILKO, L. (1977) *Ceremony,* NY, Viking Press.

SLATER, L. (1993) *Welcome to My Country,* New York, Random House.

SLATER, M. (1994) 'Pia's Odyssey: The longitudinal study of a high school mathematics teacher's explorations with writing to learn with limited English proficient students (Hernandez, Pia)', Doctoral Dissertation, *University Micro-films International*, Ann Arbor, MI, No. 9502443.

SMITH, A.D. (1994) *Twilight; Los Angeles, 1992.*

SMITH, F. (1994) *Understanding Reading: A Psycho-linguistic Analysis of Reading and Learning to Read* (Fifth edition), Hillsdale, NJ, L. Erlbaum.

SOMMERS, N. (1989) 'The Writer's Memo', in ANSON, C.M. (ed.) *Writing and Response: Theory, Practice, and Research* (pp. 184–5), Urbana, IL, NCTE.

SONDHEIM, S. and LAPINE, J. (1991) *Sunday in the Park with George*, New York, Applause.

SPENDER, D. (1981) 'The gatekeepers: A feminist critique of academic publish-ing', in ROBERTS, V. (ed.) *Doing Feminist Research* (pp. 186–202), London, Routledge and Kegan Paul.

SPRADLEY, J.P. (1979) *The Ethnographic Interview*, New York, Harcourt Brace Jovanovich.

SPRADLEY, J.P. (1980) *Participant Observation*, New York, Holt, Rinehart and Winston.

SPRADLEY, J.P. and MANN, B.J. (1975) *The Cocktail Waitress: Woman's Work in a Man's World*, New York, Knopf.

STEGNER, W. (1971) *Angles of Repose*, New York, Penguin.

STEVENS, W. (1937/1990) *The Collected Poems of Wallace Stevens*, New York, Vintage.

STRAUSS, A. (1987) *Qualitative Analysis for Social Scientists*, New York, Cam-bridge University Press.

STRAUSS, A. and CORBIN, J. (1990) *Basics of Qualitative Research: Grounded Theory Procedures and Techniques*, Newbury Park, CA, Sage.

STROUD, J. (1989) 'Geodes, Han-Shan, the Tehachapis, Rexroth: Some fragments', in DOW, P. (ed.) *19 New American Poets of the Golden Gate* (pp. 317–21), New York, Harcourt, Brace, Jovanovich.

SULLIVAN, P.A. and QUALLEY, D.J. (1994) *Pedagogy in the Age of Politics: Writ-ing and Reading (in) the Academy*, Urbana, IL, NCTE.

TAYLOR, D. (1983) *Family Literacy*, Portsmouth, NH, Heinemann.

TAYLOR, D. and DORSEY-GAINES, C. (1988) *Growing Up Literate: Learning from Inner-City Families*, Portsmouth, NH, Heinemann.

TAYLOR, P. (1992) 'Our adventure of experiencing: Drama structure and action research in a seventh grade social studies classroom', Doctoral Dissertation, *University Microfilms International*, Ann Arbor, MI, No. 9237780.

TELLIER-ROBINSON, D. (1996) 'The experiences of Portuguese-speaking parents with special needs children: An ethnographic interview study', unpublished Doctoral Dissertation, New York University.

TESCH, R. (1987) 'Emerging themes: The researcher's experience', *Phenomenology and Pedagogy*, **5**, 3, pp. 230–241.

TESCH, R. (1990) *Qualitative Research: Analysis Types and Software Tools*, London, Falmer Press.

THARP, R.G. and GALLIMORE, R. (1988) *Rousing Minds to Life: Teaching, Learn-ing, and Schooling in Social Context*, Cambridge, Cambridge University Press.

THOMAS, D. and THOMAS, G. (1989) 'The use of Rogerian reflection in small-group writing conferences', in ANSON, C.M. (ed.) *Writing and Response: Theory, Practice, and Research* (pp. 114–26), Urbana, IL, NCTE.

TOBIN, L. (1993) *Writing Relationships: What Really Happens in the Composition Class*, Portsmouth, NH, Boynton/Cook/Heinemann.

TRIMBUR, J. (1989) 'Consensus and difference in collaborative learning', *College English*, **57**, 7, pp. 882–539 (October).

TYLER, S.A. (1987) *The Unspeakable: Discourse, Dialogue, and Rhetoric in the Postmodern World*, Madison, WI, University of Wisconsin Press.

VAN MAANEN, J. (ed.) (1983) *Qualitative Methodology*, Newbury Park, CA, Sage Publications.

VAN MAANEN, J. (1988) *Tales of the Field: On Writing Ethnography*, Chicago, IL, University of Chicago Press.

VAN MAANEN, J. (1990) *Researching Lived Experience: Human Science for an Action Sensitive Pedagogy*, London, The University of Western Ontario.

VIDICH, A.J. and LYMAN, S.M. (1994) 'Qualitative methods: Their history in sociology and anthropology', in DENZIN, N. and LINCOLN, Y. (eds) *Handbook of Qualitative Research* (pp. 23–59), Newbury Park, CA, Sage.

VINZ, R. (1995a) 'Opening moves: Conversations on the first year of teaching', *English Education*, **28**, 3, pp. 158–207.

VINZ, R. (1995b) 'Toward an understanding of the blues and beyond an essentialist reading of cultural texts', *Discourse: Studies in Cultural Policies in Education*, Carfax International, pp. 347–63.

VINZ, R. (1996) 'Horrorscapes: (In)Forming adolescent identity and desire', *Journal of Curriculum Theorizing*, **12**, 4.

VYGOTSKY, L.S. (1962) *Thought and Language*, Cambridge, MA, MIT Press.

WALFORD, G. (ed.) (1991) *Doing Educational Research*, London, Routledge.

WALTERS, F. (1995) 'Writing teachers' writing and the politics of dissent', *College English*, **57**, 7, pp. 882–939 (November).

WARNOCK, J. (1984) 'The writing process', in MORGAN, M.G. and LUNSFORD, R.F. (eds) *Research in Compostition and Rhetoric* (pp. 3–26), Westport, CT, Greenwood.

WASSER, J.D. and Bresler, L. (1996) 'Working in the interpretive zone; Conceptualizing collaboration in qualitative research terms', *Educational Researcher*, **25**, 5, pp. 5–15.

WAUGH, P. (1989) *Feminine Fictions: Revisiting the Postmodern*, New York, Routledge.

WEITZMAN, E. and MILES, M. (1995) *Computer Programs for Qualitative Data Analysis*, Newbury Park, CA, Sage.

WELCH, N. (1996) 'Revising a writer's identity: Reading and "remodeling" in a composition class', *College Composition and Communication*, **47**, 1, pp. 41–61.

WERNER, O. and SCHOEPFLE, G.M. (1987) *Systematic Fieldwork, Vol. 2: Ethnographic Analysis and Data Management*, Newbury Park, CA, Sage.

WINNICOTT, D.W. (1971) *Playing and Reality*, London, Tavistock Publications.

WITHERELL, C. and NODDINGS, N. (eds) (1991) *Stories Lives Tell: Narrative and Dialogue in Education*, New York, Teachers College Press.

WOLCOTT, H.F. (1990) 'On seeking-and-rejecting-validity in qualitative research', in EISNER, E. and PESHKIN, A. (eds) *Qualitative Inquiry in Education: The Continuing Debate* (pp. 121–52), New York: Teachers College Press.

WOLCOTT, H.F. (1990) *Writing Up Qualitative Research*, Newbury Park, CA, Sage Publications.

WOLCOTT, H.F. (1992) 'Posturing in qualitative inquiry', in LeCOMPTE, M.D., MILLROY, W.L. and PREISSLE, J. (eds) *The Handbook of Qualitative Research in Education* (pp. 3–52), New York, Academic Press.

WOLCOTT, H.F. (1994) *Transforming Qualitative Data: Description, Analysis, and Interpretation*, Thousand Oaks, CA, Sage.

WOOLF, L. (ed.) (1954) *A Writer's Diary, Being Extracts From the Diary of Virginia Woolf*, London, Hogarth Press.

WOOLF, V. (1967) The Common Reader. 1st Series. London: Hogarth Press, 1925. Selections reprinted in *Collected Essays*. Vol. 2. New York, Harcourt, Brace, & World.

ZELLER, N. (1987) 'A rhetoric for naturalistic inquiry', unpublished Doctoral Dissertation, Bloomington, IN, Indiana University.

Zorpette, G. (1994) 'Dynamic duos', *Art News*, pp. 164–9 (Summer).

Colleague Contributors

Marilyn Adler
Kenneth Aigen
Carolyn Arnason
Diane Austin
Barbara Aventuro
Susan Babinski
Fran Babiss
Barbara Ball
Marlene Barron
Michele Bellavita
Tina Brescia
Priscilla Butler
Ori Caroleo
Tina Casoglos
Der-lin Chao
William Colangelo
Anthony Conelli
Fred Daniele
Janet D'Arcangelo
Sherry Davidson
Laurie Dieffenbach
Carole Di Tosti
Nancy Duggan
Judith Evans
Anne Ellen Geller
Patricia Gentile
Barbara Goddard
Iris Goldberg
Joanne King Griffin
Lynn Becker Haber
Michelle Haddad
Amanda Hahn
Geana Harris
Immaculee Harushimana
Susan Goetz Haver
Laurie Holder

Sung-Goo Hur
Jane Isenberg
Jayashree Iyer
Phillip Johnson
Pat Juell
Bruce Kellerhouse
Rita King
Rita Kopf
Ellen Krammer
Shelley Krapes
Judy Kwak
Christina Lee
Rosemarie Lewandowski
Christine Lewis
Mark Lipton
Ellen Margolin
Jane Martin
Valerie Martin
Ray Matthews
Shirley Matthews
Belén Matías
Eileen McEvoy
Julia McKinney
Elizabeth Merrick
Tony Messina
Sam Milburn
Barbara Miller
Rebecca Mlynarczyk
Leticia Monroe
Rhonda Weller Moore
Sallie Motch
Lawrence Nelson
Gayle Newshan
Sandra Nixon
William Parker
Molly Parrish

Dennis Parsons
June Price
Magdalen Radovich
Ann Buhman Renninger
Leslie Rice
Kristan Ryan
Jill Schehr
Susan Schlechter
Sharon Shelton-Colangelo
Li Shen
Beverley Shenkman
Judith Singer
Marsha Slater

Sally Smith
Zoraida Soliman-Cyr
Philip Taylor
Sarie Teichman
Dora Tellier-Robinson
Celia Thomas
Judy Walenta
Andrew Weitz
Lori Berman Wolf
Deborah Wooten
Joan Zaleski
Ronna Ziegel
Karen Zielony

Name Index

Adler, Marilyn, 332
Agar, Michael, 34, 332, 346, 347–8
Agee, James, 304, 305, 355–6, 371, 379, 382
Aigen, Kenneth, 143
Aisenberg, Nadya, 216
Allende, Isabel, 13
Anderson, Gary, 338
Anson, Chris, 321
Applebome, Peter, 467
Arnason, Carolyn, 89–91, 93, 114–15, 116, 137, 175, 342
Atkinson, Paul, 2, 17, 60, 97, 161, 165, 173–4, 221, 229, 345, 383
Austin, Diane, 117, 136–7, 334–5
Aventuro, Barbara, 213–14

Babinski, Susan, 280
Babiss, Fran, 278, 279, 281, 284–5
Bakhtin, Mikhail, 275, 276, 304, 308, 339
Ball, Barbara, 16, 25–7, 140–1, 208–10, 220, 297, 333, 339, 343, 345, 349, 352–3
Ball, Stephen, 228
Barron, Marlene, 192–3, 214–15, 237
Bateson, Mary Catherine, 49, 63
Beach, Richard, 284, 323, 324, 325
Becker, Howard, 249–50, 253, 270–1
Behar, Ruth, 319
Beld, Jo Michelle, 272
Belenky, Mary Field, 3, 48, 226, 239, 243, 287, 314, 371
Bellavita, Michele, 8, 9, 10, 17, 102, 121–3, 133–6, 146–7, 167, 180–1, 208, 334–5
Bentley, Arthur, 5, 232
Bernstein, Richard, 350
Bhabha, Homi, 40, 264
Boice, Robert, 305

Bolster, Arthur, 259
Brannon, Lil, 320, 322, 323, 325
Brescia, Tina, 211–12, 336, 345
Bressler, Liora, 271, 272, 313
Britton, James, 141, 310
Brodkey, Harold, 13
Brown, Elsa Barkley, 361–2
Brown, Rexford, 372, 374
Brown, Richard, 221
Bruce, Bertram, 109
Bruner, Jerome, 70, 78, 117, 175, 267, 369
Burbules, Nicholas, 109
Burke, Kenneth, 344
Burnett, Rebecca, 309, 311
Butler, Priscilla, 50–1, 54, 141–3, 144–5

Calvino, Italo, 102
Carini, Patricia, 343
Caroleo, Ori, 223, 341–2, 374
Carroll, Lewis, 110–11
Casoglos, Tina, 292–3, 322
Castillo, Ana, 156–7
Chao, Der-lin, 286
Chast, Roz, 33
Childers, Mary, 359–60
Chiseri-Straton, Elizabeth, 339
Clandinin, Jean, 64
Clifford, James, 2
Clinchy, Blythe McVicker, 3, 239, 287, 314
Coffey, Amanda, 165, 173–4
Colangelo, William, 108
Conelli, Anthony, 320–1
Connelly, Michael, 64
Conrad, Joseph, 309
Corbin, J., 281
Copp, Martha, 349, 350
Cortazzi, M., 173
Crapanzano, Vincent, 18
Csikszentmihalyi, Mihaly, 308–9

Subject Index